The Government and Politics of China 1912-1949

The Government and Politics of China
1912-1949

CH'IEN TUAN-SHENG

BRIAR CLIFF COLLEGE
LIBRARY
SIOUX CITY, IOWA

Stanford University Press
Stanford, California

JQ
1502
.C46
1970

Stanford University Press
Stanford, California
Copyright 1950 by the President and Fellows of Harvard College
First published in 1950 by Harvard University Press
as *The Government and Politics of China*
Paperback edition first published in 1970 by Stanford University Press
Printed in the United States of America
SBN 8047-0701-4
LC 77-108026
Last figure below indicates year of this printing:
79 78 77 76 75 74 73 72 71 70

PREFACE

This book has several parts. Chapters II and III are brief reviews of the political ideas and institutions of ancient China. The four chapters that follow give a brief account of political and institutional development during the generation preceding the Kuomintang Government of 1928. Chapters VIII and IX describe the Kuomintang and the theory and practice of political tutelage as advocated by it. The body of the book deals with the organization and operation of the Kuomintang Government. The last chapters, Chapters XX to XXIV inclusive, are concerned more with politics. There are also an introductory and a concluding chapter.

It is regrettable that a book on the government of China cannot be attempted in the manner either of President Lowell's classic treatise, *The Government of England*, or of Esmein's equally famous *Eléments de droit constitutionnel*. Not only are their lucidity and erudition inimitable; the Chinese government as a subject is not susceptible of such treatment. President Lowell was writing about a government of great stability and could avail himself of an enormous amount of reliable and well-edited official records. The government of France was less stable, but the laws of France nevertheless were carried out with a fair degree of faithfulness, and the authority of the courts was on the whole not flouted by the government. Besides, there were a great number of constitutional and legal treatises from which Esmein could draw summaries and formulate criticisms. None of these factors operate in the case of contemporary China.

In the present book, my intention has been both to analyze the legal structure of the Kuomintang Government, which is in substance still maintained as this is written, and to describe the practical operation of that government. But neither of these two aims has been satisfactorily achieved. I can only hope that this book will fill a part of the vacuum which exists on the whole subject.

There is another obvious shortcoming. The next few years will witness the most fundamental and truly great transformation in a long period of change, begun about a century ago. But the Kuomintang Government is still

62645

in control of the greater portion of China. I cannot treat in any detail the way in which other parts of China are governed nor can I elaborate on what is in store for the future. This can be done only at a more opportune moment.

This book was inaugurated and has been completed in large part through the assistance of the International Secretariat of the Institute of Pacific Relations. In completing it, I have become deeply indebted to many friends. Professor Arthur N. Holcombe, to whom I owe my early training in political science, and Professor John M. Gaus, both of Harvard University, Professor Nathaniel Peffer of Columbia University, and Mr. William L. Holland, Secretary-General of the Institute of Pacific Relations, and his staff, especially Dr. Lawrence K. Rosinger, all read the manuscript and made invaluable suggestions and comments. Dr. Chen Han-seng of Johns Hopkins University and Professor Yang Lien-sheng and Dr. Robert A. Scalapino of Harvard University read parts of the manuscript. They all saved me from committing many errors of fact and deficiencies in exposition. Through the drafting and preparation of this manuscript for publication I have also been fortunate in having the constant advice and encouragement of Professor John K. Fairbank and Mrs. Wilma Fairbank, who, in addition to reading and improving the text at the several stages of writing, have always generously contributed the kind of help which can come only from competent and critical friends. To Miss Anne D'E. Pratt, my secretary throughout, I am grateful for loyal and painstaking collaboration.

The point of view is naturally mine and mine alone. None of the persons who have aided me are to be held responsible for it.

Ch'ien Tuan-sheng

September 1, 1948
Harvard University
Cambridge, Massachusetts

CONTENTS

MAP

CHARTS

INTRODUCTION

Dr. Ch'ien brings to his task a rare competence. For a quarter of a century, during which the revolution in China has brought great changes in the government of the country and profoundly affected its whole system of politics, he has been a teacher of political science and public law in the leading national universities at Nanking, Kunming, and Peking. During the war with Japan he was a member of the People's Political Council at Hankow and Chungking. He also served on special missions to the United States. Throughout the quarter-century he possessed excellent opportunities to observe the operation of the Chinese political system.

Dr. Ch'ien understands the American as well as the Chinese point of view in the study of political structures and processes. He obtained his bachelor's degree at the University of North Dakota and his doctor's degree in political science at Harvard. In 1948 he lectured at Harvard on the government and politics of China. He wrote the present volume at that time, mindful of the interests and needs of American students of Far Eastern affairs. He has also written extensively in his own language on modern government and politics. Having recognized years ago the need for a modern government in China, he writes about the Nationalist regime with realistic understanding. Recognizing also the need for practical efficiency and popular support, if a modern government is to endure long, his writing is critical as well as expository.

A satisfactory introduction to the study of the government and politics of a foreign country must include more than a description of its actual government and an account of its principal political parties. There must be a general view of the whole political scene and some explanation of the way in which political conditions have come to be what they are. This calls for an interpretation of the political ideas which influence the behavior of the people and their rulers, for a state is an organized body of people joined together for certain purposes and engaged in the pursuit of those purposes by acceptable means and methods. The activities of politicians and statesmen are limited by the opinion of the people as well as by the form of the government. Theorists may speculate concerning the priority of political ideas and institutions, but writers on actual government and contemporary politics must be more concerned with the relationships between ideas and institutions which come under their own observation. The author of the present volume falls in the latter category.

The designation of the Chinese Republic in the Charter of the United Nations as one of the five major powers in the postwar world opened a new era in Chinese political history. The traditional view had been that China formed the center of an independent world of its own in which its people sustained a political order without need of relations with, to say nothing of improvement by, the outer barbarians. The nineteenth century brought new contacts with other parts of the civilized world and taught the necessity of readjusting traditional political ideas to the strenuous conditions of modern times. The Manchu Dynasty failed to make the needed readjustment. This failure, added to other deficiencies, brought about its downfall. The first problem of the Chinese Revolutionists was to raise their country to a position of independence and equality among the nations. How well they succeeded in this undertaking is attested by the decision of the United Nations at the San Francisco Conference on International Organization to recognize Chinese equality with the principal powers of the West.

The overthrow of the Manchu Dynasty and the raising of the Chinese Republic to an equal position in the family of nations were only the beginning of the revolution which had been planned by Dr. Sun Yat-sen and his followers. Other objectives were to make a place for the people of China in the government of their country, not inferior to that of the people in the governments of the most advanced countries in the West, and to improve their means of living by introducing the benefits of Western science and technology. The instrument for the accomplishment of these purposes was to be the organized revolutionary party. Dr. Sun planned to use enough military force to put his revolutionary party, the Kuomintang, in power. But his main reliance for the eventual establishment of a democratic republic under a modern constitution, dedicated to the improvement of the people's livelihood, was not a military but a party dictatorship. The Kuomintang, he believed, could justify its monopoly of power by its services to the people during a period of tutelage, when they would be learning what would be required of them in order to operate a political system fit to be described as a veritable government of the people, by the people, and for the people.

The dictatorship of the Kuomintang was formally established in 1928 after the defeat of the Northern Militarists and the occupation of Peking by the Nationalist forces. The party leaders organized a Nationalist Government, which they called the National Government of China, and entered upon the period of party tutelage. The political structures which they designed and the political processes which they instituted were presented to the people of China as the necessary foundation of a new system of law and order. The dictatorship itself would be only temporary, the party leaders insisted, but the system of political education, which was to be a principal function of the dictatorship, would lead eventually to the promised land of constitutional government, dedicated to the improvement of the people's livelihood. Eighteen years later the Kuomintang offered the people of China a written constitution, but the new constitution, which was declared in effect at the end of the year 1947, could not be made to work. Hope of improvement in the people's livelihood under the tutelage of the Kuomintang vanished, and the Nationalist Government fell.

The choice of the Chinese Republic as one of the permanent members of the United Nations Security Council marked the formal achievement of the first of the three principal objectives of the Chinese Revolution. The other two objectives were not achieved under the dictatorship of the Kuomintang. The party leaders never succeeded in presenting a united front to the people of China. The party, divided against itself, was rejected by substantial numbers of revolutionists. It not only failed to prepare the people for a constitutional government, it could not even create a powerful monolithic state after the fashion of party dictatorships in the West. While the formal government of the country remained a monopoly of the Kuomintang, revolutionists who put their faith in other parties could not be altogether excluded from Chinese politics. The study of Chinese politics under the Nationalist dictatorship, therefore, is more than a study of the organization and activities of the provisional government which the Nationalists instituted. It is also a study of the relations between the Nationalists and the other political parties, which competed for the support of the people of China, and of the political ideas which gave these other parties vitality and strength.

Dr. Ch'ien's book deals with the government of China under the dictatorship of the Kuomintang. It was a period when the organization and management of the governing party were originally more important than the formal structure and processes of the National Government itself. Though toward the end of the Kuomintang regime the provisional constitution was ostensibly replaced by a definitive constitution, this operation came too late to change the essential nature of the regime. The character of the party, the purposes of its principal members, and the policies of the official leader determined the character of the political system. In theory the differences between the tutelage of the Kuomintang and an ordinary party dictatorship were important, but in fact they were obscure. Chinese politics under the Kuomintang meant something more than merely government by a dominant political party, but precisely how much more it was difficult for foreign observers to perceive. It is one of the services of Dr. Ch'ien's penetrating analysis of Chinese politics that he makes these differences intelligible and vital. He rightly distinguishes in his treatment of his subject between the government and the politics of China.

The importance of this distinction is well illustrated by the role of the Communists in Chinese politics under the government of the Kuomintang.

Communist emissaries from the Soviet Union gave invaluable aid when Dr. Sun's revolutionary party was reorganized at Canton in 1923–24. The structure and processes of the new Kuomintang were copied from those of the Russian Communist Party and the conduct of party affairs was a joint enterprise of Nationalists and Communists until internal dissensions split them apart in 1927. Thereafter the Communists were purged from the Nationalist Party and excluded from the government which the party established at Nanking. But they remained an ever-present alternative to the Kuomintang in the leadership of the revolution and an irrepressible threat to its monopoly of power. Eventually a Communist regime became the only possible alternative to the dictatorship of the Kuomintang.

Dr. Ch'ien's analysis of the Kuomintang political system makes clearer to Americans why the people of China at last accepted the alternative of Communist rule. He does not seek to justify the program of any political party, nor does he plead a particular cause. He is content to explain how the Kuomintang Government operated, to point out wherein it failed to give satisfaction, and to expose the nature of the political problem awaiting solution. The skill which he has brought to his task and the wealth of evidence with which he illustrates his points make his book a major contribution to an understanding of Chinese politics.

It might be supposed that the destruction of the power of the Kuomintang by the Communists would deprive a work on Chinese government under the Kuomintang of much of its usefulness to students of contemporary Chinese politics. The value of this excellent study to the future historian of the Chinese revolution may be readily conceded, but what, a hurried reader may ask, can be the use of such a study to the observer of current events, eager for a better understanding of the political ideas and institutions of the Communists now in power? The Kuomintang will presumably have no part in the prospective government of China. It will presumably be excluded from any share of power by the triumphant Communists even more completely than the Communists were formerly shut out from the government by the Kuomintang. The concept of a loyal opposition, coöperating openly and actively in the processes of government, has no place in the political theory of party dictatorship.

The answer to this question is conclusive. A knowledge of Chinese government under the Kuomintang not only facilitates an understanding of the regime in process of establishment by the Communists, but some acquaintance with the record of the Kuomintang rulers of China is indispensable for any intelligent comprehension of Chinese politics in the next stage of the revolution. That the nature of the Communist regime can be more easily understood by those who are familiar with that of the Kuomintang is obvious, since the origins of both regimes were intimately related. The Communists who helped to reorganize the Kuomintang at Canton fashioned it closely in the image of their own party. The purposes of the two organizations were by no means identical, but their forms and procedures possessed much in common.

Moreover, it is evident that the Nationalists' failings define the tasks of those in power in the next stage of the revolution. The Nationalists attained one of their principal objectives, to secure world-wide recognition of the rightful equality of China among the powers. But they accomplished little by their efforts to introduce the common people into the government of China and to improve the common people's livelihood. It may be claimed that their efforts were frustrated largely by causes beyond their control. They could not prevent the Japanese from destroying their authority in large parts of their country by force and violence. Not even the measures employed by the United States and other parties to the Nine Power Pacific Treaty were equal to that responsibility. Nor could the Chinese Nationalists escape the pernicious consequences of the World War. They suffered with the rest of the world from the belligerency of powers greater than themselves. But history is not interested in the excuses of a nation's rulers. Not good or bad intentions but actions and events supply the evidence on which it passes judgment. It is now the Communists who will be held responsible by the people of China for introducing the common people into the government of their country, and for improving their livelihood.

The character of the government of China, since the Chinese Republic has become one of the permanent members of the United Nations Security Council, is a matter of great importance to the rest of the world. The purposes of statesmen with a veto in the Security Council must be taken into account by the governments of the other powers, particularly by those also possessing permanent membership in the Security Council. The practical capacity of the Chinese Government to take intelligent action in the interest of China is one of the conditions of good order in the rest of the world. The actual working of the new system of collective security, from which so much has been hoped, must depend in part on the working of Chinese political institutions. The time has passed when Americans can be indifferent to the government and politics of China.

The recognition of China's equal position among the powers was evidence of a belief on the part of important Western statesmen that China was capable of making extraordinary contributions to the maintenance of international peace and security. It was clear, of course, in 1945 that China could not immediately make a great contribution to the purposes of the United Nations. Its government was not yet strong enough to maintain good order within its own boundaries and could not be expected at that time to contribute anything more substantial than good advice to the pacification of the rest of the world. But there seemed to be a solid basis for great expectations of future political strength. The record of the Nationalist Government, despite the discouraging obstacles raised by economic depression and foreign war, seemed to many Western observers to disclose enormous vitality in the revolutionary movement. With the restoration of peace in the world at large the eventual establishment of constitutional government according to Dr. Sun's plan, it may well have been supposed, would be no impossible task. China's new age seemed indeed to be just around the corner.

The consequences of the recent change from a Nationalist to a Communist dictatorship lie outside the range of this book. Strictly speaking, the new regime, which moved into the void left by the collapse of the Kuomintang in Continental China, was not a single party dictatorship, but a government by a coalition, in which the leading party could exert a commanding influence without an actual monopoly of power. Again, as at the time of the original Nationalist-Communist coalition, a period of violent struggle and military government was to be succeeded by a further period of domestic tranquillity under a provisional dictatorship, during which the Chinese people would be prepared for a final period of self-government under a permanent constitution, to be constructed with the aid of the best modern political science. Doubtless different opinions would prevail concerning the nature of the best modern political science, but the structure and processes of the temporary regime could not be greatly different from what had been originally designed at Canton in the time of the collaboration between Dr. Sun Yat-sen and the agents of the Comintern. The politics of China entered a new phase, but the new government of China should seem no strange innovation to those who understand the nature of the regime established by the Kuomintang.

Prudent men in power will develop their plans in the light of their predecessors' experience as well as under the impulse of their own visions. What lessons the leaders of the "New Democracy" can learn from Chinese political experience during the preceding stages of the revolution is ultimately the subject of Dr. Ch'ien's book. His distinction between the government and the politics of China under the Kuomintang is important in interpreting the meaning of this experience. It has importance for people everywhere who may be concerned with the influence of the new Chinese government in the modern world. Despite the collapse of the Kuomintang the politics of party dictatorship in China will remain a subject of major interest to students of the contemporary political order.

Arthur N. Holcombe
Eaton Professor of the Science of Government
Harvard University

February 1950

The Government and Politics of China

1912-1949

SIBERIA
U. S. S. R.
OUTER MONGOLIA
HEILUNGKIANG
KIRIN
CHAHAR
JEHOL
LIAONING (FENGTIEN)
SUIYUAN
NINGSIA
KANSU
CHINGHAI (KOKO NOR)
SIN-KIANG
TIBET
HOPEI (CHIHLI)
SHANSI
SHANTUNG
SHENSI
HONAN
KIANGSU
ANHWEI
HUPEI
SIKANG
SZECHWAN
KWEICHOW
HUNAN
KIANGSI
CHEKIANG
FUKIEN
YUNNAN
KWANGSI
KWANGTUNG
BURMA
FRENCH INDO-CHINA
SIAM
KOREA
JAPAN
FORMOSA (TAIWAN)
SEA OF JAPAN
YELLOW SEA
EAST CHINA SEA
SOUTH CHINA SEA
PHILIPPINE IS
CHINA
POLITICAL DIVISIONS, 1930
Adapted from GEORGE B. CRESSEY

I

CHUNG-KUO [1]

Chung-kuo, or the Central Land, commonly rendered in the West as the "Middle Kingdom" and known as China, is a cultural, social, and political community unique in history. It has been a continuous and developing community. Reverses in the fortunes of its people have from time to time occasioned contractions in territory, decreases in population, and shocks to its institutions. But, on the whole, its expansion has been fairly continuous.

Compared with other countries of the world, China is remarkable for its size and the compactness of its territory. Like the Soviet Union and the United States, China's is a truly continental mass, stretching far and wide and covering a variety of climatic zones. It has an area [2] as large as the United States with its territorial possessions and nearly half as large as that of the USSR. In population,[3] China tops all other nations of the world.

China's Neighbors

In her long history up to a century ago, China had been menaced only by the more martial races to the north. Both the sea on the east and the inaccessible mountains on the southwest had acted as safe barriers, and the peoples who dwelt south and west of her were usually weaker neighbors. But this virtual isolation which had long conditioned the Chinese people to a sense of security was suddenly broken by the expansion of Europe and the resultant colonizing lust of the West. Strong antagonists pressed on her by sea. Burma and Indo-China to her southwest and Korea to her northeast, weak communities all, served as the corridors of invasion. And, what was more ominous, the expanding empire of the Czars stretched so far to the east as to form almost a semicircle around China, extending from her northeastern corner right up to the westernmost point of her domain.

China stays where she has always been. But since the world around her has moved, her geographical position is in fact changed. The last World

War has drastically altered the relative strength of the powers around her. Security has not returned. Her long seacoast remains the possible springboard for hostile invaders. The extended boundary with the USSR remains. For China, the only significant changes that have occurred as a result of the World War are that she has now to deal with Korea, Burma, and eventually Indo-China, all former tributaries, in a realistic fashion calculated both to give her security and to win for her trust and respect. Meanwhile the partial overcoming of the mountain barrier has made India a new neighbor, from whom she has no fear of aggression but with whom she has to work out a positive policy for insuring the peace in that part of Asia.

Regions of China

Within her confines, China is divisible into several fairly well marked regions, created in part by topography and in part by the cumulative effects of human effort: the northeastern provinces, an area of fertile plains and mountains; the northern provinces, consisting largely of the plains of the Yellow River; the northwestern provinces, reaching as far as Sinkiang and Tibet; the southeastern provinces of the lower Yangtze, thickly populated and intensely cultivated; the central provinces of the middle Yangtze Valley, dissected by rivers and spotted with lakes; the southern provinces of narrow coastland and mountainous hinterland; the southwestern provinces, which have no easy access to the outside; and Sinkiang and Tibet.[4]

These regions are both significant and indefinite. There is no single criterion by which the divisions can be sustained. The ever-changing demography and the economic and political conditions in the areas call for constant redividing and regrouping. For instance, Jehol, Chahar, and Suiyuan, carved out of Inner Mongolia, were once considered to constitute a region of their own. But for the last fifteen years or so, Jehol has usually been considered a part of the northeastern provinces, and Chahar and Suiyuan are often considered the extension of the northern provinces of Hopei and Shansi, because they have attracted settlers from Hopei and Shansi. In the discussion of Chinese politics, it is therefore well to have in mind the peculiarities of different geographic regions, and yet to remember that history is constantly regrouping them.

Land Utilization[5]

Topography and climate have greatly limited the land available for agriculture. China has around 400,000 square miles of cultivated arable land, about 10 per cent of her total area. Compared with the figure for the United States (23 per cent), this is unsatisfactory, especially if one takes into consideration the size of her population and the predominance of agriculture in China. Considering relative populations, even the 8 per cent of cultivated land in the USSR is a better figure. Yet the dictates of topography leave little possibility for further reclamation. The high plateaus and mountain ranges and deserts set a practical limit.

The inundations of the rivers have, in fact, reduced the extent of the arable land. Exact figures are not available. But it would not be surprising if, over the centuries, something like 15 per cent of the total tilled acreage has been laid waste by floods. With effective flood control there should be an actual increase in tilled acreage. With irrigation, some lands hitherto considered not arable might also be reclaimed. But it is doubtful whether the total of China's cultivated land could ever reach a maximum of 500,000 square miles.

Nearly one-fifth of the total land is in forest and pasture. But Chinese forests are mostly of the noncommercial type and pastures seldom form part of the farms. Even if more acres of pasture land were made of what are now more or less barren hillsides, the substantial increase of national wealth would still have to wait until dairy farming became more common.

The climatic conditions have affected both cultivation and pasture. The warmer climate and the greater rainfall make the southern and central provinces of the lower and the middle Yangtze Valley and the basins of the southwest the richest granaries of China. The plains of the north and of the northeast are suitable areas for agriculture, but the winter being longer and precipitation being concentrated in the summer, only one crop can be raised. The northern and northeastern plains are thus much less productive than the plains and the basins washed by the Yangtze. The mountainous terrain in both the southwest and northwest, and the rigor of the latter's climate, make agriculture less suitable in those areas.[6]

Mineral Resources [7]

As for China's natural resources, less is known. In the past the Chinese were in the habit of considering their country both "broad in area and rich in resources." Then they were told that, as far as natural resources are concerned, China was but a poor country. Recently, as the result of more intensive study, greater hopes have been again entertained. There is thus confusion as regards the nature and extent of natural resources in China. The current estimate of the scientists and statisticians is that China has anywhere from one-quarter trillion to one trillion metric tons of coal reserve, mostly to be found in the north, and especially in Shansi and Shensi. In petroleum, China is said to be very poor, but there are indications that in Sinkiang and in the northwest, there may be considerable petroleum yet undetected. The iron reserves are small. Only about one and one-third billion metric tons have been estimated to be in existence, mostly to be found in the northeast. In ferro-alloys, China is rich in tungsten and adequate in manganese, but sadly lacking in other items. Tin and antimony are abundant, but in copper, aluminum, lead, and mercury China is again deficient. The precious metals are present at best in moderate quantities.

The location of China's mineral resources poses a serious problem for future industrialization. Only in the northeast are large amounts of coal and iron ores in proximity to each other. The coal deposits of the north are far separated from the nonferrous metals of the Yangtze region as well as from the iron ores of that region and of the northeast. Perhaps if hydroelectric power is developed in the southwest and the middle Yangtze Valley, some of these difficulties may be solved.

Expansion of the Chinese

The people who now dwell in China consist mainly of the Chinese (or the Han). The score of other races that are to be found mostly in Tibet, Sinkiang, and Mongolia and the "aborigines" of the south and southwest form no more than 4 per cent of the total population.

The twin processes of absorption and acculturation are the secret of the expansiveness of the Chinese people, and the expansion of the Chinese was of course the cause for the expansion of China. In the past, the twin processes operated beautifully together, because the Chinese were able to absorb the culture of the races with whom they came into contact; whether they were invading or being invaded, they were able to absorb them bodily. Because ultimately they and their neighbors were completely amalgamated, they almost imperceptibly modified their own culture. The more this process went on, the more mixed became the Chinese race.

It is for this reason that any hypothesis about the origin of the Chinese race must remain a hypothesis.[8] Until the races that first came into admixture with the Chinese can be determined, there is no possibility of determining who were the original Chinese. In fact, it is perhaps unimportant for our purpose to find out where the Chinese came from or what the original Chinese were like. It is sufficient to know that by the time the Chinese had become powerful enough to occupy a fixed area they were to be found thriving in what is now the region of Shansi, Shensi, and Honan provinces. There they were able first to settle down and establish some kind of stable society, offering resistance to the more martial tribes on their north, and gradually to expand to the east and south, either on their own initiative or when pressed by their northern neighbors. They had already reached this complicated mechanism of defense and expansion by the time they were able to pass on to their posterity legendary tales of their endeavors. These tales, as recorded in the *Book of History* may indeed be grossly exaggerated; but there is a good deal of elementary truth in the general picture presented by them.

In the earliest periods of their recorded history, the Chinese in the north of present-day China were already being pressed upon by the Hsiung-nu.[9] Both the *Book of History* and the *Book of Odes*[10] are full of the epics of barbarian incursion and heroic defense. Beginning from the first years of the fourth century B.C. and lasting for about three centuries, the Hsiung-nu and the Hsien-pei, both from the north, and also the Ch'iang from the west, all nomadic tribes, overran the territory of North China. Foreign kingdoms were established in rapid succession and there was great chaos. In the course of time these barbarians adopted, however, the Chinese way of life and were absorbed into the Chinese community. In the meantime, the Chinese were extending further to the south, covering the southern parts of what is now the lower and middle Yangtze Valley and also some parts of the southeast.

In the early years of the tenth century A.D. and during three centuries thereafter, another group of northern barbarians, the Khitan and the Ju-chen, invaded North China. They had a longer and firmer control of the territory. The Chinese dynasty of the Sung was pushed to the south of the Yangtze. The southern coastal areas received a new impetus for development. In the end, the invaders were again absorbed, so much so that when the Mongol conquest followed in the thirteenth century, the conquering horde encountered a huge mass of Chinese resistance, and not a Chinese, a Ju-chen, or a Khitan resistance separately.

The Mongol conquest which set up the Yuan Dynasty (1260–1368) was both more gigantic and more ephemeral than its predecessors. The Mongols overran the whole country. No Chinese dynasty was left to rule over even a diminished territory. The Mongols were more conscious of their identity than the earlier invaders. They rather resisted Chinese assimilation, and guarded themselves from that danger. But they proved themselves unequal to the task of foreign domination over the great multitude of Chinese. They were shortly overthrown and driven back to the steppes of Mongolia, shrunken in population and disheartened in spirit. The Chinese people lived on.

The Manchus (1644–1912) took their lesson from the Mongols. Like the Mongols, they succeeded in controlling the whole of the territory which had been under the intervening Ming Dynasty (1368–1644) a purely Chinese dynasty. Again, like the Mongols, they strove to preserve their identity. But, unlike them, they saw the wisdom of applying Chinese laws and traditions for the government and regulation of a community which was Chinese. The Manchus succeeded in being the foreign rulers of the Chinese with the longest uninterrupted span of life. Theirs was one of the great dynasties in Chinese history. But in the end their fate was no different from that of their ancestors, the Ju-chen. They were completely absorbed by the Chinese. The Manchus no longer exist either as an ethnic group or as a political community.

Both the Mongol and Manchu conquests served to press the Chinese further and further to the corners and areas where they had not been present, either in large numbers or in strength. The general effect of these later conquests was the same as that of the earlier invasions.

But the expansion of the Chinese was not solely occasioned by the pressures put on them by the martial races on the northern border. The Chinese themselves were also capable of both gradual and steady expansion and occasional heights of imperial grandeur. The Han Empire under Wu Ti (140–87 B.C.) was able both to check the Hsiung-nu on the north and to expand rapidly and extensively to the far south and the far west. It reached as far as the northern part of present-day Indo-China in the south and Central Asia in the west. Even with the waning of the Han power, the Chinese were able to retain their hold on their foreign conquests. The T'ang Empire under T'ai Tsung (627–649) was also a huge one.[11] It covered almost the whole of the modern area of China. It is true that parts of the southwest and of Sinkiang were then still outside; but, in compensation, Korea, parts of Indo-China, and some areas lying to the west of the present-day Sinkiang were included. During the Manchu Dynasty, which became really as Chinese an empire as the Han and T'ang Empires, there was also a marked extension of the domain.

Other Races of China [12]

The Chinese people is thus a mixed one. We need not speculate on the elements that might have entered into it before recorded history began. In recorded history alone the Chinese race has clearly had in it the admixture of the invading races from the north and the conquered aboriginal races of the south. If the Hsiung-nu, the Ch'iang, and the Mongols had only a minor role in that admixture, either because they did not firmly establish themselves on Chinese soil or because they had a policy of conscious preservation of their own identity, the Hsien-pei, the Khitan, and the Ju-chen, later reinforced by the Manchus, certainly had an enormous if not easily ascertainable effect on the Chinese as a people.

But this is not to say that the entire population of China today consists of the Chinese just described. There are within the borders of China still a number of races who are different from the Chinese. The Tibetans of Tibet and the Mongols who are scattered over a wide zone in the north and northwest have certainly kept their identity as distinct groups. In Sinkiang a multitude of races of the Turkish group, the largest of which are the Uigurs, the Kazakhs, and the Kalmucks also form distinct communities. In numbers, however, these groups are all very small. The Tibetans, the Mongols, and all the Turkish groups number only about one million, a million and a half, and three and one-half million, respectively, out of a total population of some 460,000,000 in all of China.

Whether the other minor groups which dwell rather closely with the Chinese and with few separate areas of their own should be considered non-Chinese is more debatable. Without reference to scientific ethnology, these minor groups may be said to be four in number. They are the Lo-lo and the Tai peoples of the extreme southwest, the Miao-yao group in various parts of southern China, and the aborigines of Formosa.[13]

The Lo-lo group and the aborigines in Formosa are generally considered Tibeto-Burman and Indonesian respectively. There is much dispute as to the origin of the Tai. There are students who believe that in early times the Tai were the aborigines living in the central part of present-day China. Whatever may be the truth of these assertions or assumptions, all four groups, except the Lo-lo of the Ta-liang Mountains in Szechwan, and the Tai along the Indo-China and Burmese borders, have much in common with the Chinese of the same locality. Most of them speak the Chinese dialect of the area. They differ from the Chinese only in some specific beliefs and customs. In other words, the blending has gone far enough to make them virtually component parts of the Chinese race. There is more marked difference between the Chinese of the extreme southwest and those from the mouth of the Yangtze than there is between the Chinese and the Lo-lo of the same locality. It is indeed questionable whether these four groups can be considered as separable from the Chinese. At any rate, their aggregate number is probably no larger than 12,000,000.

There are people who would even consider the Mohammedans in China as distinguishable from the Chinese proper. This distinction is unfounded. That the Turkish races of Sinkiang are Mohammedan in religion does not make the Mohammedans a distinct entity. The Chinese Mohammedans are as Chinese as the Turkish Mohammedans are Turkish. The large concentration of Chinese Mohammedans in the northwest in close proximity to the Turkish Mohammedans of Sinkiang does not thereby create a new ethnic group out of the Mohammedans of both racial groups.

Therefore, in surveying the problems of China, one's main concern is with the Chinese. The minor races present distinct problems of administration, it is true, but they do not seriously affect the course of Chinese history.

Language

Language generally follows ethnography. The Chinese language, including several dialects, is used by all Chinese. There is only one written Chinese language. Only the non-Chinese races of China have other languages.

Although there is only one written Chinese language there are a number of spoken dialects. Roughly, the dialect which is called *kuo-yü* ("national speech") is spoken by three-fourths of the Chinese. The *kuo-yü* is further divisible into the Northern *kuo-yü* and Southern *kuo-yü*, spoken by about equal numbers of people. But the difference between the two is not very marked. Generally speaking, a Northerner has little difficulty in understanding a man who speaks the Southern *kuo-yü*, and vice versa.

The other four dialects, those of southern Kiangsu and Chekiang, of Fukien, and of Kwangtung, and the Hakka dialect spoken in Kwangtung and Kwangsi are, however, very different from the *kuo-yü*. Fortunately, increasing numbers of the literate in the regions with the non-*kuo-yü* dialects are now able to speak *kuo-yü*.

The non-Chinese peoples have languages of their own: the Mongols speak Mongol; the Turkish races, Turkish; and the Tibeto-Burman races, the Tibeto-Burman languages. The Tai and the Miao-yao also have Tai and Miao-yao languages of their own. Finally, the aboriginal Formosans use an Indonesian language. The numbers who speak these non-Chinese languages are relatively small, and those of them who are now living in the midst of dominantly Chinese areas are also able to speak the Chinese dialects of the region.

Demography [14]

The growth of the population has been seriously circumscribed by the scarcity of arable land. Since agriculture is still the predominant occupation of the people, there is a heavy concentration of population in the areas where agriculture is suitable and profitable. The most thickly populated parts of China are the plains of the lower and middle Yangtze, the narrow coastal belts of the southeast, and the basins of the southwest. The plains of the northeast are equally suitable for agriculture, and during the last forty years have been rapidly absorbing large numbers of migrants from the northern provinces of Shantung and Hopei. Thus the provinces of Kiangsu and Chekiang of the lower Yangtze have about 900 and 500 inhabitants, respectively, per square mile, and Shantung and Honan on the lower Yellow River about 700 and 420, respectively. If the more mountainous or otherwise desolate parts of these four provinces are taken out of account, the density figure can be even further raised. In other words, these provinces, though predominantly agricultural, contain a much greater population per square mile than even the most thickly settled non-urban areas of Belgium, northern England, or the North Atlantic seaboard of the United States. In contrast, in the regions where agriculture is not suitable, the sparsity is equally remarkable. Tibet has only about 2 persons to a square mile, Sinkiang about 7, and Chinghai, formerly Chinese Kokonor, perhaps a little less than 7. Compared with the average of 124 per square mile for the whole country, this disparity is not only marked, but gives rise to all kinds of social, political and economic problems.

Only a small fraction of the population can be rightly considered urban. The large cities are situated in the areas which have dense rural populations. Urban centers like Shanghai and Hankow are the product of the confluence of commerce and of the rise of industries of the modern kind. The smaller cities, like the walled seats of the *hsien*, or districts, often having populations of 50,000 or less, can hardly be considered anything more than market towns of a rural community.

Occupational Structure

In occupation the Chinese people are predominantly agricultural, as is obvious. But beyond this obvious truth, any other attempt at appraisal is fraught with dangers and difficulties. Statistics are either lacking or unreliable. Estimates are usually influenced by preconceived ideas. If, in order to give a rough idea of the occupational structure of Chinese society, it is necessary to attempt some kind of estimate, the following figures might be ventured: public servants, including the teachers and the officers in the armed forces but not the common soldiery, 5 per cent; liberal professional personnel, including the modern trained nurses and the old-style doctors, 1 per cent; artisans, 2 per cent; old-style entrepreneurs, such as shopkeepers, and their employees,[15] 7 per cent; peddlers, 2 per cent; household laborers, including servants in homes and in offices, 2 per cent; common soldiers, 1 per cent; modern businessmen, 2 per cent; modern laborers, 3 per cent; and agricultural workers, 75 per cent.[16]

In this occupational distribution, two points are worthy of the most serious note. The first is the overwhelming proportion of the people rooted in the land, the second is the small number of people connected with either side of modern business, whether capital or labor. These two facts are intimately related to each other. Except for the 5 per cent engaged in both sides of modern business, the four-class social structure which has long existed in Chinese tradition is still very much in evidence. The scholar, the tiller of land, the artisan, and the merchant still embrace practically all the occupational groups given above.

Since the three-fourths of the population engaged in agriculture are the backbone of the nation and determine the course of its development, their inner structure merits further consideration.

How are these three-fourths of the Chinese population constituted? What percentage do the landlords occupy? What is the number of tenant farmers? These are questions as difficult to answer as the over-all occupation groupings of the whole population. The fact that from the richest landlord to the poorest farmhand there are no clear demarcations adds to the difficulty. Let us classify as landlords those owners of large estates who live on rents and have no participation in farming; as managing landlords those owners of land who supervise the farming of a part of their land and rent out the rest and whose income is more or less equally divided between rent and profit; as farmer-owners those owners of land who devote themselves to farming for a living; as tenants those who till land held in tenancy; and, finally, as farm-laborers, those who are hired to work on farm lands either by owners or by tenants. On this basis the intra-group distribution may be somewhat as follows: landlords, 3 per cent; managing landlords, 5 per cent; farmer-owners, 12 per cent; tenants, 45 per cent; and farm-laborers, 12 per cent.[17]

Poverty

If the figures given above coincide with the facts, they explain why the Chinese poeple are generally poor. Only the landlords, managing landlords, modern businessmen, and men in liberal professions and the higher cadres of public servants (one out of five public servants) can be considered relatively well to do. Only the farmer-owners, artisans, modern laborers, three-sevenths of the old-style entrepreneurs,[18] and the bulk of the men in public service (four out of five public servants) live in relative comfort. The rest are either making a bare subsistence or actually living below the subsistence line. The upper group occupies 12 per cent; the middle, 24 per cent; and the lower as much as 64 per cent!

It is inevitable that the tenants and the farm-laborers should be poor. Divide the total cultivated area by the 75 per cent of the population engaged in agriculture and take an average family of 5.4 members — then the average holding per family would be only 4.1 acres! But the tenant's holding will be considerably smaller than the average. He cannot but be poor.[19] So are the farm-laborers. Since the tenants and farm-laborers constitute the great bulk of the poor, any social reform has to be first aimed at improving the lot of the great masses of these tenants and farm-laborers.

Education[20]

Closely linked with the general poverty is the restricted opportunity for education and the prevalence of illiteracy. There was never an ecclesiastical monopoly of learning in China as there was in the West. But poverty has produced the same effect of reserving education to a few. When one's subsistence is in jeopardy one does not bother about education. In China today, as has always been the case in the past, the vast majority of the people remain illiterate. Modern education during the last generation has reduced the illiteracy percentage, but still about 70 to 75 per cent of the people are not able to read, to say nothing of writing.[21]

The important fact that poverty is the principal source of illiteracy must not be lost sight of. Western students of China are wont to attribute the overwhelming illiteracy to the intrinsic difficulties of learning the Chinese language. Whether the Chinese language is or is not difficult to learn, given the prevailing poverty as it has existed and still exists, illiteracy is inevitable.

The coincidence of wealth with education results in a striking fact. There has been and still is a premium on education. The small number of persons in the educated class are able to control both state and society. The educated class in recent times has been inseparable from government officialdom and landlords, and also from the leaders of business and the professions. The richer class may not have anything in common among themselves, but with education as the common denominator, they are able to share the power.

The fact that education has long been a key to power in China cannot be overemphasized. Compared with other avenues to power, such as lay through the clergy and the nobility in the West before the dawn of the democratic era, education is the least objectionable. Indeed, it is the most acceptable. Reliance on education as the qualification for high office doubtless made the political institutions of old China far more stable than those of the West. Nevertheless, so long as education is limited to the few, the Chinese state controlled by the educated is not likely to be truly democratic. China was an aristocracy of the literati before the Revolution of 1911 and the literati have in general remained conservative despite the Revolution.

The restriction of education to a few and the monopoly of power by the educated also serve to explain why the radicalism of the student class and the conservatism of the scholar in government go hand in hand.

Since the end of the Han (206 B.C.–A.D. 220), Chinese students have been known for their radicalism. With the establishment of the modern school system and the concentration of large numbers of students in the schools, especially the more mature ones in the universities, students have repeatedly acted as the spearhead of radicalism and patriotic movements. Because they generally come from the better families, they are allowed a certain degree of freedom by the government. But also, because they are young and not yet concerned with the maintenance of the status quo, they agitate for change.

But when the students reach the age of maturity and take up responsibilities of their own, they are usually assimilated by the ruling class and take up the defense of the regime. Thus it comes about that while the students have served as a force of mild reform, they have neither succeeded in radically changing their society, nor have they gone so far as to invite suppression by the regime of the day. They have thus remained at the top of things.

The student class will continue to enjoy a position of prominence as long as education remains narrowly limited. But if the students should become real social reformers and succeed in realizing reforms of a radical order, these reforms might conceivably remove them as a dominant group. Any real reform of Chinese society will have to include the extension of education to all people. This may indeed be the final test as to whether the student class really is worthy of leadership.

Family System and Conservatism [22]

A predominantly agricultural society, poor and illiterate, is bound to be conservative. The immobility of the bulk of the population and their attachment to land are sufficient explanations for conservatism. The Chinese family system further aggravates the tendency to adhere to tradition.

The idea which prevails in the West that the Chinese are still living in clans under a family patriarch who has more or less authoritative control over the clan is not only exaggerated but also erroneous. If in some parts of the country there are such clans and patriarchs, it is only because the families of some clans are so well off that they can afford to have some property retained as common property, undivided among the families. The acknowledged elder of the clan can then be authoritative because, to some extent, he controls the common property. But since it is rare to find a clan of which all the families are wealthy, real patriarchs are also rare. Those elders who have no property to control can hardly have any authority over the independent families. They may have it, if they happen to be high officials. But in such cases their authority comes not from their positions as elders but from their official positions. As a general practice, the regime of clans ruled by a patriarch has not existed in modern China.

The Chinese family of modern times is generally a small one. The official figures giving 5.4 persons as the average size of a family in China may well be believed. Properties are usually divided among the married sons who live as different families, even though, being poor and immobile, they usually live in the same place. If a Chinese family is somewhat larger than that of the West, it is because the parents usually live with the married sons. Herein lies a cause of conservatism. The very fact that the parents continue to live with them until their death naturally reinforces the strength of traditionalism in each generation.

The very close tie between the parents and the married sons and the absence of primogeniture have also created in China a sense of family solidarity unknown to the West. Out of consideration for the feeling of the father, not only do brothers pool their interests, but even nephews and cousins and relatives receive help. In official life, this leads to nepotism of the most naked kind. Until there is a more general prosperity as the result of far-reaching agricultural and industrial development, the scarcity of opportunities for employment outside the family farm is likely to help maintain this close tie of family relationship.

Absence of Religion and the Chinese Affinity for Acculturation[23]

Conservatism arising out of the agricultural nature of the society and the family system is, however, compensated for by the freedom of the Chinese to believe or not to believe. Whatever may be the explanation, the Chinese people are unreligious. No great religion like Zoroastrianism,[24] Christianity, or Mohammedanism has captivated the bulk of the Chinese population as has been the case with other peoples. Mohammedanism and Christianity have come nearest to such success. But there are only 5 and 1 per cent, respectively, of the Chinese who are Mohammedans and Christians. At its height, between the fourth and eighth centuries, Buddhism was much more in vogue than Mohammedanism or Christianity at any time. But the influence of Buddhism in China is more in the realm of thought and fine arts than in that of belief. Since the Chinese are unreligious, they may have superstitions, but rarely taboos.

Free thinking and freedom from taboos make the Chinese people easily acculturable. The barbarian races of the north left indelible effects on the Chinese. Sometimes it was the clothing, sometimes it was the food, sometimes a musical instrument, and at other times methods of war. These and countless numbers of other things the Chinese learned from the barbarian races. The Chinese are practical-minded. They take what they think is good. Little false sense of superiority enjoins them from appropriating those outlandish things which appeal to them.

Foreign religions have affected the Chinese in the same way. Beginning from the first century A.D., Buddhism[25] came into China in wave after wave. Mohammedanism began to invade China as early as the seventh century, almost as soon as it was founded. Christianity came in the sixteenth century.[26] Some opposition and persecution occurred, but they were largely caused by political or personal, rather than religious, prejudices. Ultimately all of these religions produced their effect on Chinese culture.

The influence of Buddhism was tremendous. The Buddhist monks and, in the Yuan Dynasty, the Lamaist monks often mixed actively in the politics of the day. At its height, during the T'ang Dynasty (618–907), the large-scale landholding of Buddhist monasteries and the celibacy of the monks and nuns even caused the disintegration of the system of large estates and the maintenance of large numbers of retainers by prominent families.[27]

But it was in the realm of philosophy, of literature, and of fine arts that Buddhism exerted the most profound changes on Chinese society. The T'ang and Sung thinkers were heavily influenced by the Buddhist emphasis on the knowing of "nature."[28] The development of phonology[29] was largely the outgrowth of the study of Buddhist sutras and the chanting of the same. Belles-lettres were enriched by the Buddhist vocabularies and the development of the ornate style. In music, in painting, and especially in sculpture and architecture, Buddhist influence was even more pronounced. It was as the bearer of Buddhist sutras and art that Chinese influence spread far and wide into Korea and Japan.

The influence of Christianity was at first limited to the introduction of science and some other special branches of art or of knowledge, such as geography, calendar-making and painting.[30] In these fields the Chinese, as they were wont to do, also gladly absorbed what was a useful addition to their culture. But converts to the Christian religion remain small in number. Despite intense activities on the part of the missionaries for well over a century, there are perhaps no more than five million Christians in China today.

Evolution of the Chinese State

From a loosely knit domain of tribal rulers, to a number of feudal kingdoms and thence to an empire which claimed to be universal — this was the growth of the Chinese state.

Tribalism lasted from the beginning of recorded times to the first years of the Chou Dynasty (*c.* 1122–256 B.C.). The eight hundred baronial lords, large and small, who were said to have responded to the call of Wu Wang of the Chou were not feudal barons. They were the chiefs of tribes then inhabiting what is now North China. These tribes differed in manners and in culture; but they had sufficient similarity of interest to have long acknowledged a primate, either because they were usually threatened by some common enemy from the north, more different from them than they were from each other, or because the strongest among them was always strong enough and crafty enough to demand that acknowledgment.

In the beginning of the Chou Dynasty, due largely to Wu Wang's overwhelming military prowess and to the wise statecraft of his brother, the Duke of Chou, the commonly acknowledged primate was in a position to enforce his will on his fellow chiefs and to install a feudal regime. Wu Wang divided his domain among his kinsmen, made them barons of various ranks (duke, marquis, count, viscount, and baron). But he wisely added the strongest of

CHRONOLOGICAL CHART OF MAIN PERIODS IN CHINESE HISTORY

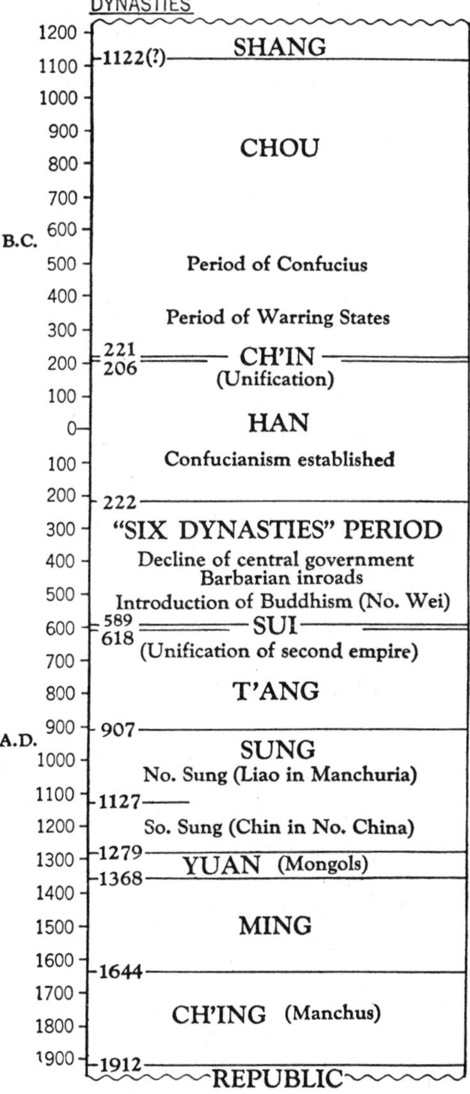

the old tribal chiefs to the list of his new barons, leaving them where they were. The land and military tenures which the barons owed to the ruler and the various ranks of fiefs owed to the barons were not dissimilar to what obtained in the feudalism of early Europe, and the system does not need elaboration here.[31]

As long as the royal house was strong enough to retain its distant control over the feudal lords, the authority of the king as the overlord of the kingdom was respected. But with the coming of the Spring and Autumn Period (722–481 B.C., so called because Confucius made a "spring and autumn record" of that period), that authority was weakened beyond repair, first by the onslaught of the northern barbarians and then by the dissensions within the royal household. The major barons began to parcel out regional hegemonies. The result was that in the ensuing period, the Period of the Warring States (403–221 B.C.), the seven strongest barons were able to contend for the hegemony of the whole domain of the Chou, with the King of Chou sinking even lower into oblivion than he was in the Spring and Autumn Period. The strongest of them all, the Count of Ch'in, in the person of Ch'in Shih Huang Ti (First Emperor of the Ch'in), finally emerged as the ruler of a unitary empire.

From the year 221 B.C., in the reign of Ch'in Shih Huang Ti (246–211 B.C.), to the last year (1912) of the Manchus, China remained a unitary empire which claimed universality, just as the Roman Empire did in the West. There were a few lapses, but they were infrequent and insignificant.

Efforts to restore feudalism failed. The overcentralization of both the Ch'in (221–207 B.C.) and the Wei (A.D. 220–264) was interpreted as weakness by their respective successors, the Han (206 B.C.–A.D. 220) and the Chin (265–420), who again resorted to the practice of the early Chou. Brothers and sons and cousins of the founding emperors of both the Han and the Chin were given feudal kingdoms with which to prop up the empire. But Ch'in Shih Huang Ti had done such a thorough job of unification that the new fiefs were unable to revive feudalism. Instead, they only created new strife in the form of pretensions, usurpations, and rebellions. The abortive attempts of the Han and the Chin to restore feudalism only ended in a firmer belief in the empire.

During twenty-odd centuries of monarchy, China was for most of the time effectively governed from the center. She never became a national state for she claimed to be a universal empire. The government that held China or a large part of it in its yoke could not, for evident reasons, acknowledge that a power equal in scope and dignity could exist on the same earth. If in times of civil war and invasion by the border races there actually coexisted a number of governments somewhat equal in strength, that was just an abnormal situation, to be reduced to normal by one of them finally exercising unified control over the rest.

Even the essentially foreign Mongols and Manchus also took that universality for granted. It was their ambition and aspiration to conquer the whole of China and become the masters of the universal empire, even when they were no more than expanding forces on the northern border of China. That they could remain independent states to claim equal existence with China was unthinkable even to them.

The idea of a national state is entirely Western and foreign to the Chinese tradition. When Western states first came into contact with the Ming and Ch'ing Empires, they were considered no more than border states which always ended in being vassals to China, however recalcitrant. It was therefore not until the Western states could by a show of force compel China to revise her concept of universality and to acknowledge the existence of political entities other than her own, that the concept of national states dawned on the Chinese.

That it took China longer than a century to transform herself into a national state is due not only to a tendency to hold on to the old universality, but also to the difficulty of developing a full national consciousness. During the long centuries of the universal empire, the Chinese had a political ideology and a system of political institutions which were both well fitted to sustain that empire. The Chinese clung to them even after China had repeatedly failed to resist the onslaught of the Western nations. They did not become fully conscious of their nation until the empire was overthrown and the thinking and the institutions which held it together were attacked by the more revolutionary elements of their own people.

II

THE POLITICAL THOUGHT OF OLD CHINA[1]

The history of Chinese political thought is undivorceable from the pattern in which the Chinese state took form. The gleanings one gets from the obscure historical records of the earliest times seem to warrant a picture of political rule mixed with theocracy. With political consciousness pointing toward a unified empire with an all-high emperor at the head, the religious element gradually lost its importance, and the Son of Heaven, as the only spokesman for Heaven, came to think and act for Heaven, practically nullifying Heaven as a kind of Supreme Being. Thereafter political thinking was absorbed in the maintenance of the all-mighty emperor and the all-inclusive empire.

The political thinking which guided the rulers and the ruled of China for about two thousand years, from about the time of Tung Chung-shu (179–104 B.C.), to the end of the nineteenth century, without serious breaks, was indisputably Confucian. But the founder of the Confucian school was merely one of the many thinkers that flourished in the Pre-Ch'in Era (551–221 B.C.),[2] and, like them, was a man buried deep in legends, a man of whose writings the authentic is difficult to separate from what is merely attributed to him.

Why is it then that while most of the other schools of that prolific era sank gradually into either oblivion or minor importance, Confucianism gained an unbroken ascendancy? Was it on account of the intrinsic merit of Confucianism as a system of thought, or was it merely because Confucianism had in it something the rulers of China could fall back on with great profit to themselves?

Early Schools

In his own day Confucius did not enjoy such prominence as was enjoyed by the most eminent of the Greek thinkers in their days. In the three centuries that preceded the burning of the books by Ch'in Shih Huang Ti, there were, according to the historian Ssu-ma T'an (died 110 B.C.), author of the *Historical Records*,[3] six great schools of thought, namely, the *Yin-yang* School (Negative-Positive School, or Astrologers), the *Ju* School (Accomplished Men or Philosophers, followers of Confucius), the Mo School (followers of Mo Ti), the School of Names (Logicians), the School of Law (Legalists), and the *Tao* School (followers of Lao-tzu).[4] It is impossible to say just how the various schools originally stood in relation to each other, either in the volume of their writings and recorded sayings or in the currency of their thought, because Philosophic or Confucian works were, in general, the sole survivors of the burning of the books. Nevertheless it is reasonably certain that none of them was either in a position to overshadow the rest or so insignificant as to command no attention from the rulers to whom all of them more or less catered. The frequent reference by one school to another seems to attest to that comparability of weight, influence, and popularity.

The *Yin-yang* School and the Logicians have left us very few writings, or very few of their writings survived the burning. Of the six schools they were least known to posterity. The fragments which have survived, or the scanty references their contemporaries made to them, do not justify us in attributing to them any well-formed theory of political action. We can only say that neither school abhorred politics and that many of their adherents were definitely interested in swaying the political order of the day to their own liking.[5]

It was, however, different with the other four schools, which have left us sufficient material to appraise their political views.

Of the Taoists, Lao-tzu (possibly contemporaneous with Confucius)[6] and Chuang Chou (365?–290? B.C.) were indisputably the greatest. The sum total of Lao-tzu's teaching is the denial of both the necessity and the wisdom of elaborate laws and institutions. His so-called *tao* (way) is nothing but the happy agreement of man with nature. Since to Lao-tzu nature is the original ordering of the things of the universe, his *tao* is inevitably negative. To observe the *tao* is implicitly to do nothing. Only when the *tao* is lost, one resorts to government and to such incitements to virtue as rites and music, with which man seeks to rule over an artificial community.

The negativism of Chuang Chou or Chuang-tzu[7] was, if anything, more all-absorbing than Lao-tzu's. With him a good government is also one which agrees with the nature of things, which in turn is ultimate simplicity. In his view it was the differentiation of the good from the bad, and the exalted from the mean, that led to a regime of artificial values and to government. There is indeed a persistent strain in all Chuang-tzu's thought that not to distinguish the good from the bad and therefore not to moralize is the very foundation of good living and the means of retaining the virtue of simplicity.

The School of Law was something of an antithesis to the Taoists. Its principal founders were often men of action as well as of words. Li Li (latter part of the fifth century B.C.) and Shang Yang (390?–338 B.C.),[8] two of the earliest code-makers, were respectively first ministers of Wei and Chin. Both succeeded in making the states they served strong and powerful. Both, and the latter especially, were relentless in trying to enforce on all members of the community a uniform body of rules which they considered to be a rationalization of the changed conditions of the time. Emphasizing the mutability of the conditions under which human society carries on its affairs, the Legalists had a tendency to favor the authority of the sovereign as against the crumbling elements of a disintegrating feudalism.

But, as a writer and a theorist, Han Fei (280?–233 B.C.)[9] was a greater Legalist than either Li Li or Shang Yang. His elaboration of a theory of rewards and punishments as a stimulant and deterrent to human action was unsurpassed. From this principal thesis he went on to emphasize the importance of the law's being made known and exact and also the importance of its just application without discrimination.

The Mo School had a great founder in Mo Ti (490?–403? B.C.),[10] who seems to have been followed by a group of faithful and militant disciples. He was known as the advocate of the doctrine of mutual love. But he was first of all a populist, in the sense that he emphasized the interest of the populace. To him a measure is good or bad according to whether it is or is not in the interest of the people in general. His great abhorrence of all war is based on the self-same doctrine, for according to him the interest both of the offender and the offended will be injured by a war. Also, because he cares so much for the interest of the people, he exhorts his fellow men to be simple in desires and frugal in consumption.

In politics Mo Ti would like to see the ablest men coöpted as the sovereign and the principal ministers, and to see the sovereign, thus coöpted, reflect unfailingly the will of the people, and, in turn, be listened to and obeyed by them. In Mo Ti's philosophy, there is then something approaching the democratic spirit.

That these five great schools of thought — the *Yin-yang*, the Logicians, the Taoists, the Legalists, and the Moists — existed side by side with the School of Philosophers is a fact to be always borne in mind if we are to understand and to give a proper appraisal to this last-mentioned school.

The Confucian School

Confucius (K'ung-fu-tzu) lived from 551 to 479 B.C. In order of time, he preceded all schools but one; for Lao-tzu is now generally acknowledged to have been his elder. But chronologically the most significant thing to remember is that the original founders of all six schools lived in extreme proximity to each other and none was able entirely to detach himself from the rest.

Confucius seems to have been a man able to take full advantage of that chronological proximity. He also made full use of his extensive travels. His prolific contacts with men of varying ages and in every settled community of what then was known as China enabled him to know the conditions and the ideas of a rapidly changing world as nobody else did. To put it slightly differently, he caught the spirit of the times. He lived and thought with it. He also tried to master it and was successful.

There are in Confucius' teaching the ingredients of almost all other teachings current in his time. The eight schools of Confucianism [11] said by Han Fei to have followed upon the death of the Master were at great variance with each other. They could no more be considered variants of one main theme than the original Six Schools themselves could. For example, the unworldliness of Yen Hui's school of Confucianism bears a resemblance to the naturalist teachings of Lao-tzu and Chuang-tzu. The kind of rite which Hsün-tzu (298–238 B.C.)[12] advocated as a means of enforcing uniform standards is akin to the laws of Han Fei who was in fact a Hsün-tzu disciple. The emphasis on the interest of the populace provides a link between Tzu Chang's school of Confucianism and the School of Mo. The mysteries about *yin-yang* and the Five Cycles attributed by Hsün-tzu to Tzu Ssu and Mencius (Meng-Tzu, 372–289 B.C.)[13] remind one of the *Yin-yang* School. Yet this divergence of views held among the disciples is no wonder, considering that Confucius himself, as a great teacher, might well have had, indeed did have, these views, one and all.[14]

Withal there is a definite strain of deep humanism that runs through Confucius and is shared by all his disciples. The central concept which is to be found both in the *Analects* [15] and in the sayings of all his disciples — at least not contradicted by them — and which is commonly acknowledged by the exponents and commentators of Confucianism, is that Man lives with and for other men. From this main theory there evolve Confucian ideas of Rites, of Virtue, of Names, and of the Five Relationships. Rites are little more than the norm by which to live an ordinary sociable and intelligent life; and those who do live such a life will also be practicing the greatest of Confucian virtues, *jen*, a term which to many Confucian scholars signifies the sum total of Confucian teaching. In fact there are Confucian dicta which amount to saying that virtue is the end and the rites are the means: together they make possible the ideal life. Names are the designations of status. Status, be it that of a political order or of a social relationship, must be clearly designated and adhered to, the aim being to prevent confusion. For instance, a person who is in fact a king must be known as such, and similarly one who is in fact his minister must also be known as a minister. Otherwise, honor will go astray and responsibility will be nowhere placed, and in the polity concerned, there will be only disorder. Thus, Confucius' stress on proper designations leads to the corollary doctrine of the Five Relationships, namely, the proper juxtaposition of king and minister, of father and son, of brother (older) and brother (younger), of husband and wife, and finally of friends.

The political theories of Confucius are but the application of his humanism to the affairs of the state. Orderly political life must come from orderly private lives. Since the latter are inseparable from notions of virtue and rites, political order, to be good and stable, must also proceed from those notions. That is to say, the people must be taught to be virtuous and to observe the rites. Confucius accepts reality, for refusal to do so would cause the ruler to lose contact with his people. It is true that he often invoked the legendary good rulers of old to exhort the men of his own day to live up to a higher level of rites and virtue. But in doing so he stubbornly refused to be budged from the position of a realist. There is in his whole teaching no suggestion of a negation of the present nor any advocacy of a revolution.

If the foregoing generalization about Confucius' teaching is accepted, there is nothing surprising in his latter-day followers' laying emphasis on monarchism and legitimacy and in general adopting a conservative social outlook. The refusal or failure of Confucius to be logical, to condemn explicitly and unequivocally those rulers who work against the interests of the people, made it possible for the post-Ch'in scholars to embrace Confucianism and monarchism with one embrace, and for the adherents of monarchy to proclaim themselves faithful Confucianists.

Tung Chung-shu: The Great Confucianist[16]

The man above all others to cast that adaptable and otherwise fluid Confucianism into its distinctive mold and endow it with a monarchical dogma was Tung Chung-shu, first minister to the great Han Emperor Wu Ti. In the short period that intervened between the end of the Period of the Warring States in 221 B.C. and the rise of the Han, the disintegrating feudal order of the old China had definitely given place to a firmly established new empire. Though Ch'in Shih Huang Ti failed to make his new order secure, and though rebellions persistently seeking to set back the clock occurred later, the Former Han Emperors (202 B.C.–A.D. 9) were great masters of consolidation; so much so that by the time of Wu Ti, the sovereign had become supreme and the empire secure, and almost any theorist with a positive nature and a perspicacious mind, determined to link the institutions of the day with a body of doctrine, would be in a position to inculcate into that body of doctrine a monarchical spirit. This Tung Chung-shu did not fail to do.

To be sure, Tung Chung-shu was a great Confucian scholar and was conversant with all the Confucian texts and commentaries that were then extant. He was especially a student of the Confucian *Spring and Autumn Annals*.[17] But his greatest contribution to Confucian thought was to interpret the *Annals* in such a way as to make Confucius an infallible prophet, an advocate of the doctrine of the Great Unified Empire,[18] and a believer in the theory that the Son of Heaven is the representative of Heaven in will and in virtues. Thus Confucianism and the divine right of kings became inseparable.

Tung Chung-shu's second contribution to Confucianism was to give to it form and substance, to infuse it with a definitive body of tenets. He did this by a happy, though necessarily opportunist, blending of the various kinds of philosophies of state then extant, which he thought were beneficial or otherwise conducive to the strengthening of the fast maturing regime of monarchy. In doing this he was greatly helped by the ferment of the preceding century, during which political thinking had by no means remained entirely inactive. There had been a free mingling of the original do-nothing-ism of Lao-tzu, of the *Lao-tzu* as a book of magic transformation (from earthly existence to unworldly existence), and finally of the teachings of the Legalists. This was most evident in the *Huai-nan-tzu*[19] of the Prince of Huai-nan (179?–122 B.C.). And in Chia I (200–168 B.C.) who preceded Tung Chung-shu, the idea of rites received a new affirmation. Yet both the Prince of Huai-nan and Chia I were accepted Confucianists. It was therefore not strange for Tung Chung-shu, the great Confucianist, to embrace many Pre-Ch'in schools as they then stood, and at the same time vehemently proclaim himself to be a faithful Confucianist, disdaining all the other schools. While stretching and distorting the old Confucian doctrines of virtue and rites to act as bulwarks of monarchy, Tung Chung-shu in fact freely grafted on to Confucianism the Taoist version of the *Book of Changes*,[20] the cyclic doctrines of the *Yin-yang* School, and the Legalists' insistence on meting out justice to both the high and the low. From then on, Confucianism was really nothing but a grand mixture of elements from many philosophies adapted to give dignity to and serve the needs of the monarchy.

The third thing Tung Chung-shu did was to make his own kind of scholarship the key to official position. He founded the system whereby the masters of the Confucian classics became the governors of centuries to come, thereby forever joining Confucianism to statecraft. The beginnings of the Chinese system of examination were laid in the time of Tung Chung-shu. From that time on only one ideal type, namely, the literati, were admitted to the ruling group, at first by recommendation, and later by formal examinations. Any man who entertained political ambitions must normally assume the mantle of a Confucian scholar. Thus Confucianism or Confucian scholarship was made, almost at one stroke, a dominant influence in the Chinese political world, though its free development as a school of thought must have suffered immeasurably by such an irretrievable entanglement in politics.

If Tung Chung-shu is accepted as the high apostle of the Confucian Gospel, the latter-day political theorists were all of them more or less faithful preachers of the Gospel, though necessarily with varying degrees of orthodoxy.

Further Enrichment of Confucianism

The four centuries after A.D. 222, known in Chinese history as the Six Dynasties Period (Wei, Chin, and the Southern and Northern Dynasties, 222–589), saw the vogue of so-called Pure Discourse and Mysticism. But in fact these were nothing but the further enrichment of Confucianism with Lao-tzu's and Chuang-tzu's naturalism, so interpreted as not to render them repulsive to the established order of Confucianism.

Later on, during the Southern and Northern Dynasties and the ensuing Sui (589–618) and T'ang (618–907) Dynasties, when Buddhists and Taoists vied with each other to court the favor of the emperors and when Buddhism and Confucianism were badly mixed up — or shall we say happily and skillfully blended together by the literati? — there was actually little new in political thinking that squarely departed from the path of accepted Confucianism.

As a matter of fact, Han Yü (768–824), perhaps the greatest Confucianist in the T'ang Dynasty, actually availed himself of Buddhist and Taoist speculations to enrich the Confucianist philosophy, at the same time denouncing both of them in order to proclaim the orthodoxy of Confucianism. It was Han Yü who, duly influenced by the Buddhists and Taoists before him, followed them in stressing the importance of mind and nature [21] as factors in ethics. It was he who sought to inject these same factors into statecraft, and insisted that the ruler must be upright in mind and sincere in thought. Yet it was the same Han Yü who enunciated the doctrine of the descent of the Line of *Tao* [22] and laid a new emphasis on "status," especially the relationship between the ruler and the subject. By thus holding the position of the ruler supreme and threatening to destroy the Buddhist worship which dared refuse allegiance to the temporal power, he was perhaps instrumental in compelling the Buddhists to accept the Confucian doctrine of state, thereby forever banishing Buddhism as a factor in Chinese political controversy.[23]

Confucianism Stereotyped

The Sung Dynasty (960–1279) was known for the emergence of the *li* school of Confucianism. *Li* and *tao* were in fact one and the same thing.

They were often linked together as *tao-li*, and it is quite proper to consider Han Yü as the precursor of the *li* school.

The *li* school was led in the Northern Sung Period by Chou Tun-i (1017–1073) and the Ch'eng brothers (Ch'eng Hao, 1033–1086, Ch'eng I, 1034–1108) and by Chu Hsi (1130–1200) and Lu Chiu-yüan (1139–1192) in the Southern Sung Period. During the Ming Dynasty (1368–1644) its leader was Wang Shou-jen (Wang Yang-ming, 1472–1528). While Lu Chiu-yüan and Wang Shou-jen emphasized more what is called "mind," the other Sung Confucianists stressed *li*. Both attributed justice and wisdom to Confucius and his precursors, idealizing the past and insisting on the immutability of the "ultimate truth,"[24] which according to Chu Hsi, perhaps the greatest of the whole school, must have resided with Emperors Yao and Shun and the other precursors of Confucius. Yet Chu Hsi was never explicit as to what that "ultimate truth" was.[25]

The so-called "*li* learning" (or Neo-Confucianism) has generally been acknowledged as the most important contribution to Confucianism in modern times. Yet aside from this school's speculation on cosmology and the rather unusual political experiments of Wang An-shih (1019–1086), there was actually very little in it that was new. We shall not pause to consider its cosmology, for it is beyond the scope of our inquiry. Wang An-shih[26] was, however, a most unusual adherent of the Confucian School. He was a Confucianist. He did not claim to be anything else. His detractors, Confucianists all, were unable to deny him that much. But though in theory and in practice he merely shuttled through the patterns respectively envisaged in the Rites of the Chou[27] and by Shang Yang,[28] he was at heart and in deed a revolutionist. His faith lay boldly on the side of the masses and his advocacy of their interest had none of the compromising ineffectiveness which characterized the attitude of the traditional Confucianists when they also happened to be speaking for the common people. The very fact that Wang An-shih failed miserably in all his agrarian experiments and was denounced by the good Confucianists of his own time and after only serves to demonstrate how immutable Confucianism as a body of political ideas had become!

During the Ch'ing Dynasty (1644–1912) the dominant school of Confucianism was known as the Classicists.[29] Because they were better glossarists of the Confucian classics than their predecessors in the Sung and Ming Dynasties, there were people who considered them also greater Confucianists. The truth was, however, the contrary. These Classicists closely confined their study and their speculations, if any, to safe subjects — safe in the sense of conforming to the accepted ethical and political standards of the time. Their political thinking seldom got out of the beaten path of the *li* school. This generalization embraces not only Tseng Kuo-fan (1811–1872),[30] but also K'ang Yu-wei (1858–1927)[31] who led the abortive Reform Movement in 1898 on behalf of Emperor Kuang Hsü against the Empress Dowager Tz'u-hsi.

The traditional inertia of Confucianism, prior to our own period, was only slightly marred by the few rebellious thinkers of the late Ming and early Ch'ing Period. In Huang Tsung-hsi (1610–1695) and especially in Ku Yen-wu (1613–1682),[32] the greatest of them all, there was more than perfunctory emphasis on Mencius' dictum of "People preponderant and Monarch secondary." There could actually be discerned an inclination, if not an open profession, to limit the authority of the government in favor of individual liberty. Had there not been an extremely vigorous reaction which set in following the firm establishment of the Manchu regime, something new and interesting might indeed have dawned in China.

Thus there is ample justification for concluding that as far as political thinking is concerned, from the early Han down to the last days of the Ch'ing Dynasty, there was on the whole both sterility and immutability. The Confucian ideology of absolute monarchy, to be tempered by mildness, or, to borrow a more technical term, by auto-limitation of power, ruled supreme; neither Buddhist religion from without nor the manifold interpretations of Confucian scholarship within were to weaken any essential part of the powerful dogma.

Traditionalism under Attack

The foundation of Confucian political thought, like the other aspects of Chinese civilization, did not suffer a rude shock until the impact of Western thought and institutions. The ideas of inviolable individual liberty, of popular sovereignty and of the rule of law over the ruler as well as over the ruled are all Western and did not gain adherents in China till the end of the nineteenth century, when the material aspects of Western civilization had already had half a century to make themselves unmistakably felt. There was an anti-Manchu ferment at that time, which made the Chinese nationalist movement of Sun Yat-sen easy for even the unsophisticated to comprehend. It was through the happy marriage of this movement to Western political ideas that the latter began to be discussed and appreciated.[33]

The one man who imposed acceptance of Western political ideas on a large number of Chinese intellectuals and revolutionaries was Sun Yat-sen. True, Kuo Sung-t'ao (1818–1891), the envoy to the Court of St. James's, had, as early as 1877, written appreciatively about the parliamentary institutions and local self-government in England. True, John Stuart Mill's *On Liberty* and Montesquieu's *Spirit of Laws* had already been rendered into Chinese as early as the 1880's by Yen Fu (1853–1921). But they were in those years seldom read and read only as literary pieces. It was not until Sun Yat-sen's revolutionary movement became a force, largely as the result first, of the Manchu blunders during the Boxer riots of 1900, and second, of Japan's victory as a constitutional state over Czarist Russia in 1904–1905, that Sun Yat-sen's teachings of Western political ideas began to have a wide hearing among intellectuals and those politically minded people who were sorely dissatisfied with the Manchus.

It is to the everlasting credit of Sun Yat-sen that, while other revolutionary leaders aimed mainly at the overthrow of the Manchu regime which was administratively corrupt and of foreign origin, he alone preached ideas of individual liberty and social equality and of popular and representative government, and insisted on the adoption of Western institutions, together with the overthrow of the monarchy.

With Sun Yat-sen's championship of the democratic ideas of the West, Chinese political thinking was set on a new course and began to follow the main currents of the West. Nationalism and democracy were first accepted. With the bolder elements of the intelligentsia, as with Sun Yat-sen himself, even socialism became an accepted tenet as time marched on.

It is of course not to be assumed that speaking for and being pledged to some doctrine necessarily means heartily believing in the doctrine, let alone fulfilling it. Democratic institutions are not to be realized out of nothing. The forces of traditional Confucianism are strongly entrenched. There are people in present-day China who go so far as to interpret Confucian thinking as democratic, thereby monarchizing democracy and silencing the Western accent of Sun Yat-senism. On whether this school remains in alliance with the actual political power, or that power continues to cultivate it, will depend the trend of Chinese political thinking for the next generation or two. The democrats and modernists of China fervently hope that the spirit of the times will make that sinister *mésalliance* either impossible or unprofitable. Then and not until then can Chinese political thinking be said to have definitely entered a new and more vigorous phase.

III

THE POLITICAL INSTITUTIONS OF OLD CHINA[1]

The Monarchy

Summarily stated, the monarchy, headed by the emperor with the title of *Huang-ti*, was, from the end of feudalism in the third century B.C. to the establishment of the Republic in 1912, the one institution of central importance. Changes in the social structure of the ruling class and in the framework of the central administration, as well as the personal aptitude of the emperor, greatly affected the actual exercise of the imperial power. But in theory the emperor reigned supreme. His power was limited neither by law nor by any other power. He had, especially if he were wise, to consider many a practical limit to that theoretically unlimited power. If he were wise, he usually surrounded himself with counselors who would spare no pains to fill his ears with constant exhortations about good government and against wanton exercise of power. Founders of dynasties, able leaders of men though they were, relied freely on the advice and services of their ministers, in contrast to the whimsical use of power by some of their degenerate successors. But the important thing is that the power of the emperor was in theory unlimited.

The theory of the unlimited power of the ruler, holding sway throughout the long centuries of the empire, had two significant results. The first was that it was difficult even for reflective men to imagine anything to the contrary. This deepened the sterility of Chinese political thinking. The second result was a corollary of the first. Men had to think of some palliatives to mitigate the evils of unlimited power, and the most apparent one was to humanize the imperial institution, to appeal to the emperor to make a humane and reasonable use of his power. Thus there came about the so-called "rule of man." There being no rule of law possible under the regime of unlimited power, men were driven to extol the rule of man. These two results were dependent on each other. The first called for the second and the second strengthened the first. It took the impact of the West to shatter the foundations of this age-old theory.

In practice the emperor was, however, not always able to exercise the imperial power personally. A little later we shall consider how the regularly instituted ministers of the emperor exercised for him a part or the whole of his power. Here we may mention the several categories of persons who at one time or another exercised that power either by trust or by usurpation.

The first category was the kinsmen of the empress or more usually those of the regent empress-mother. In the Han Dynasty, these kinsmen were in actual power longer than the emperors themselves. For the maternal families to grasp the imperial power was a firmly entrenched tradition, not to be shaken until the T'ang Dynasty.

The second type of holders of power was the eunuchs, whose rise to power was made possible when the emperors took on a deified character and excluded ministers from intimacy with them. When ambitious emperors found the firm grip of their maternal kinsmen intolerable, they usually called in the eunuchs for deliverance. The result was that an even more sinister group was helped into actual power. This situation prevailed toward the end of the Han Dynasty, and especially during the T'ang Dynasty.

The third category consisted of groups of powerful and interlinked families. The preponderant influence of family groups began during the Wei Dynasty, which succeeded the Han; it continued during the Chin, and was most marked during the Northern and Southern Dynasties. During these three or four centuries a number of powerful families were in control of huge estates and patronized large numbers of people who aspired to officialdom. Whether in policy-making or actual administration, their consent was absolutely necessary. They wielded the same kind of influence as that wielded by a political machine in an American state. And just as the boss sometimes becomes a governor, the heads of these families in some cases actually filled the position of first minister. The reigns of the Western Chin were in fact full of such cases.

The fourth important category consisted of military men. The men who wielded the sword could often monopolize the actual political power, making the emperor a mere figurehead. Toward the end of the Han Dynasty, prefectural commanders first made the imperial government a mere sham. From then on to the end of the Five Dynasties (907–960), militarists were often in actual control of power. Divided, they usually carried on internecine wars against each other. United, they seldom failed to usurp the imperial power and to found new dynasties.

The emperors of China paid dearly for the lessons of experience before they evolved a kind of personal absolutism to ward off the dangers arising from these four categories of virtual—and sometimes undisguised—usurpers of imperial power. Personal absolutism was first established in the Sung Dynasty and perfected during the following dynasties. Yet even during and after the Sung, power continued to slip out of the imperial hands and became the property of either kinsmen or eunuchs or militarists or a combination of them. And when power did reside in the imperial hands, it served more often to satisfy the whims and caprices of the individual who was emperor than to perform the duties expected of a good monarch by Confucian idealists. On that, history offered and continues to offer abundant evidence.

Principal Officers of State [2]

In a monarchy, the officials who are to bring to the attention of the monarch such affairs of state as are reported by the subordinate officials and who issue the monarch's orders to these officials in turn, are bound to be the central figures of state. They cannot fail to acquire for themselves whatever powers they can wring from the monarch.

The dawn of the Ch'in Dynasty [3] found the position of the Chancellor well established, all of the Warring States having resorted to the institution. As the title implies, the Chancellor was the first servant of the crown and as such he assisted the crown in the government of the empire and was superior to all officials. Occasionally, as in the Ch'in and also early in the Han, this position was split into left and right, with two incumbents. In that case one of them usually emerged as the sole holder of the honor. Next to the Chancellor there were also the Marshal, in charge of military affairs, but not necessarily in command of the military, and the Recorder, who originally served as secretary to the monarch. Since the monarch was often jealous of the Chancellor's exalted position, since the Marshal later in the Han Dynasty was frequently given additional titles and duties, and also since to the Recorder eventually accrued the functions of an assistant chancellor, the three of them were collectively named, in the first year of Han Ching Ti (156–141 B.C.), the Three Lords,[4] to serve as principal advisers to the crown.

Thus the first development was to expand the number of chief ministers from one to three. The second change occurred soon after. There had existed in China a number of private secretaries of the emperor called *Shang-shu* who acted as the liaison between the emperor and the chancellor. They grew in importance as the Three Lords became more remote from contact with the crown. Beginning from the time of Han Ming Ti (58–75), a Lord who was not concurrently a *Shang-shu* had really no say in the affairs of the state, and it was the *Shang-shu* who then became the principal officers of the state, though occasionally the position of the chancellor was revived to enable a usurper to ascend the throne with grace.

During the Chin Dynasty another group of private secretaries, called *Chung-shu,* who had originated under Han Wu Ti as mere eunuchs carrying messages between the crown and the dignitaries of state, succeeded to the functions of *Shang-shu*. They were men close to the monarch but without fame or political accomplishments, and far smaller in stature than either the Lords or the *Shang-shu* of former times.

Also during the Chin Dynasty, a third secretariat, the *Men-hsia sheng,*[5] had already come into existence and was on a par with the *Shang-shu* and the *Chung-shu*. If in the Chin, the *Chung-shu* were the principal important officers, in the Northern and Southern Dynasties, the Aides of the *Men-hsia sheng* were in the ascendant. The transfer of power first from the *Shang-shu* to the *Chung-shu* and then from the *Chung-shu* to the Aides bespoke the persistent effort of the monarch to entrust the powers of state to his intimates rather than to the great men of the day.

The third great change occurred in the Sui Dynasty, which though short in duration was a great dynasty nevertheless. The Sui emperors again entrusted the cares of state to three dignitaries, that is, the Chief of the *Shang-shu* Secretariat, the Collector of Opinions of the *Men-hsia* Secretariat, and the Chief of the *Nei-shih* Secretariat[6] who were the heads of the three central secretariats. There were again men of caliber and dignity in office. This was also the case at the beginning of the great T'ang Dynasty.

The fourth change was a reversion to the system of a single chief minister. In the T'ang Dynasty, in the time of T'ai Tsung (627–649), one or two ministers were again given the powers, though not the names, of the chancellor. This was done by authorizing the head of the *Shang-shu* Secretariat to carry also the titles of the heads of the other two secretariats, thereby giving him power over all the secretariats. Some of the *de facto* chancellors of this era were indeed the most capable ministers of any period in Chinese history. Unfortunately, in the latter half of the T'ang, there was again a tendency to split the responsibility of the principal ministers, first by giving literary secretaries (whose duty was to compose essays) and later private eunuch-secretaries (whose duty was to receive memorials) opportunities to meddle in the affairs of state, thereby creating much disorder and confusion.

But the greatest confusion existed during the Sung Dynasty when the emperor essayed to inaugurate a personal government by himself. The three secretariats existed then as before. There was also the Privy Council, in charge of military privy matters and three ministries of economics and finance. Sometimes the heads of one set of offices, sometimes the heads of another, and at still other times a combination of dignitaries served as principal advisers of the crown. There was no stability and no system, the emperor being always jealous of the supreme power. But towards the close of the dynasty when it was already threatened by the Mongols, power passed into the hands of treacherous men who assumed all kinds of titles and were as a matter of fact more powerful and exalted than even the chancellors of the Ch'in and the Han. Such was the fate ironically meted out to the weak sons of strong despots!

The system practiced by the Mongols during the Yuan Dynasty was a collective one. Of the three secretariats, eventually only the *Chung-shu* survived, the result being that that secretariat was able to have full charge of the matters of state. It was a collective system in that the head of the secretariat did not usually concentrate all the power in his own hands, but shared it with others of several grades.

The Ming and Manchu Dynasties employed what may be styled a secretarial system. During these two dynasties the administrative officials acquired more substantial power. But above them were the Grand Secretaries whose main function was to help the emperor in reading and considering the memorials and petitions of the subordinate officials, central and local, and in drafting instructions to these officials and edicts to the people. No doubt they should be considered the principal officers of state, but they only reflected the personal opinion of the ruler and were not in substantial control of policy matters.

Furthermore, during the eighteenth and nineteenth centuries, in the Ch'ing Dynasty, these Grand Secretaries were not even in hypothetical control, for the Military Plans Department (*Chün-chi-ch'u*, or Grand Council), originally only in charge of military matters, was also entrusted with civil matters. It was not until the latter part of the Manchu Dynasty that civilian Grand Secretaries again regained the power formerly belonging to them.

Thus it will be seen that it is quite consistent with the age-old tradition of China for the chief of state so to manipulate the machinery of political control that though the aim is to preserve the power in his own hands, the result is generally confusion, instability, and maladministration with but occasional realization of effective control by himself.

Central Administrative Departments

The departmental organization of central administration in China had a long history of steady development. At the time of the Ch'in there were Nine Ministers,[7] in charge respectively of (1) sacrifices and other ceremonies; (2) palaces; (3) security and garrisons; (4) the imperial stud; (5) justice; (6) affairs of barbarian peoples; (7) imperial relatives; (8) grain and other commodities; and (9) taxes on land, sea, and lake produce. Like the exalted title "Three Lords," the almost equally exalted title "Nine Ministers" lived long and died hard. It existed till the end of the last century, when the archaic names were abolished. But the individual titles suffered numerous changes, and the functions numerous fluctuations in the course of the centuries.

Alongside the Nine Ministers and intricately mixed with them, there began in the reign of Han Ch'eng Ti (32–7 B.C.), the practice of appointing five, and then six, *Shang-shu*, in charge of the departmental administrations. By the time of the Sui, the departments came to be known as *Pu*, or Boards, and began to be fixed at six. The six *Shang-shu* or ministers also became invariably the backbone of the Nine Ministers. In the Sui Dynasty the Six Boards or Ministries were Civil Office, Rites, War, Punishments, Revenue, and Public Works. This businesslike division of public functions was in force up to the end of the Manchu Dynasty. The changes in the titles as well as in the functions of the ministers were rather slight, though it should be added that a number of other ministers or officers in charge of the household affairs of the emperor continued to exist to supplement the substantive public administration of the Six Boards.

Civil Service [8]

The Chinese civil service is worthy of note both because it was an institution of long standing and minute regulation and because it was based on a system of public examination and recruitment.

There were three main developments in the Chinese civil service: the substitution of a strict written examination for recommendation by high and competent authorities, as the principal test of the fitness of the candidates; the quantitative elaboration and qualitative degeneration of the system of public examination; and the extension of the merit system from a few special posts to nearly all posts of the government.

The first Han emperors initiated the merit system of civil service. In their eagerness to strengthen the administration, both central and local, they called on the high-ranking local governors to recommend and send to the Court men of exemplary conduct and exceptional ability. These men were then interrogated by the emperor and if found satisfactory were given posts of importance. In the beginning the number of recommended persons was small, the posts given them were high, and the interrogation was free and discursive and in no sense involved a test or a sifting. In time, however, the number grew, the posts came to be varied, and some sort of substantive test became necessary. The system of graded recommendation in the Wei and Chin Dynasties [9] further hastened the institution of open and public examinations.

Generally speaking, beginning from the Sui and T'ang Dynasties, candidates for official posts had to pass an examination held publicly and at regular intervals. It is true that the earlier system of recommendation was allowed to exist side by side. But the small numbers of men thus recommended from time to time had also to submit to a formal examination before being qualified for appointment, thus losing the honored and privileged status accorded them prior to the Sui Dynasty.[10]

From the T'ang [11] and Sui Dynasties, therefore, a rigid examination took the place of a loose test which might consist of nothing more than an audience with the emperor. As time went on, this examination became more and more rigid until it became, in the time of the Ming and Ch'ing Dynasties, a stereotype. Also, as time went on, this examination covered more and more posts, until it embraced, also in the time of the Ming and Ch'ing Dynasties, practically all posts.

The growing rigidity of the Sui and T'ang and subsequent examinations deserves some special explanation, since it was in its later stages that the Chinese system of examination attracted, perhaps undeservedly, the attention of the West.

The subjects of the written examinations were at first sensible. Thus in the T'ang Dynasty, out of a total number of over fifty, the six principal categories of contestants were (1) the Versatile (*hsiu-ts'ai*), who was to compose essays to reveal his statesmanlike ability and knowledge; (2) the Classicist, who was examined primarily in his knowledge of the classics and secondarily in essays and other prose; (3) the Literary (*chin-shih*), primarily in belles-lettres (prose and poetry) and secondarily in classics and essay writing; (4) the Lawyer, primarily in law, and secondarily in essay writing; (5) the Philologist, primarily in philology; and (6) the Mathematician, primarily in mathematical and geographical treatises. These subjects nearly comprised the sum total of the learning and scholarship of the day and reflected the scope within which learning and scholarship were being put to practical application.

The degeneration was soon apparent. The Literary and Classical subjects were by far the most popular in the very beginning. By the time of the Sung, though other categories continued to exist, the Literary category had the lion's share of all candidates, and a *Chin-shih* always got appointed to an attractive post. From this undue emphasis on belles-lettres to the cursed "Eight-Legged Essay" [12] of the Ming and Ch'ing Dynasties, the step was but a short and easy one. The main course of the elaborately laid out examination became the classics, and the Eight-Legged Essay was the prescribed manner of serving it.

Not only in the matter of subjects treated in the examinations, but also in the manner of conducting these examinations, the rigidity grew to be absurd. Rules of examination must be justified on the ground of giving the candidates a fair and equal chance. But the strictness of the Ming and Ch'ing rules seemed to aim less at fairness and equality than at impressing the candidates and examining officials alike with the majesty of the examinations and especially the majesty of the emperor, by whose grace all examinations were bestowed on the populace.[13]

The spirit of the Sung and subsequent examinations was also amply reflected in the changing system of education.[14] Dating from the Han Dynasty, a National Academy had always been in existence. Whereas before the Sung the students of the Academy pursued diversified subjects of learning, not necessarily literary in nature, from the Sung period on, the Academy was either the retreat of successful candidates or the preparatory institute for those readying themselves for an examination higher up the ladder of imperial examinations. In either case the pursuit was literary. Moreover, from the Han to the Sung, local academies were few, but from the Sung on, colleges (*shu-yuan*) flourished everywhere, and to them flocked scholars preparing themselves intensively for literary examinations. It may be added that the local administrative authorities of the Yuan and later dynasties were also intimately linked with the examinations, having the conduct of preliminary or trial examinations as one of their principal functions.

The outcome of the whole system — of the kind of examinations and the kind of training sponsored or encouraged by the government — was the logical inseparability of Confucianism and public life. Scholarship had no meaning unless the possessor of it succeeded in the examinations, and there was no chance of passing the examinations unless the candidate was schooled in the Confucian classics. The upshot of this chain reaction was that in normal times public life became based on Confucianism and Confucianism became the key to political power. This was of course just what the emperor wanted.

But if the successful candidates were as a class mediocre and unimaginative, the examinations served at least to weed out those who were worse than mediocre.[15] During the long centuries there were occasional lapses when people were appointed to official posts outside of the examination system. The occasional bright finds discovered by this method were few in number, and the not-so-bright only proved that those who never went through the regular grind were even less worthy than the stereotypes. This was especially true toward the end of the Manchu Dynasty when large numbers of people filtered into political life not through examinations but through generous contributions to the state coffers.

For the inadequacy of the system of examination was in a way redeemed by another equally strict system of personnel management. The Board of Civil Office which began to be firmly established as early as the Sui Dynasty was a ministry in control of the appointment, dismissal, promotion, and discipline of the civil officials, while examinations remained throughout in the hands of the Board of Rites. Control over personnel was minutely regulated and, on the whole, effectively exercised. If the ministry often erred in paying too much attention to the letter rather than to the spirit of the regulations, nevertheless, it was exceedingly successful in resisting favoritism, the curse of all administrations which lack an established system of civil service.

It may then be said that though the civil service system failed to select always the best human talent, it was mainly successful in sending to the top the type of men best suited to prop up an ancient regime based on a monarchical interpretation of Confucianism.

The Censors [16]

The general modern notion of the censors has been that their function was censorial, to examine the conduct of officials and make an indictment of their illegal or other improper acts. This is correct, as far as the censorial institution of the Ming and the Ch'ing is concerned. But so simple a view is not conducive to an understanding of the system.

The ancient officials who were originally known as the "talking functionaries" or "officers of opinion" were in theory subdivided into two categories of "impeachers" and "remonstrators," one to impeach the servants of the crown for any misbehavior and the other to make remonstrance or suggest improvements concerning the acts of the Court. In origin, the two were distinct. In their heyday both functioned well. It was only during the last dynasties of the empire that the two were merged, the former absorbing the functions of the latter.

It will be recalled that one of the Three Lords of the earlier dynasties was the Recorder who served as secretary to the emperor. The Recorder's chief officer, the *Yü-shih chung-ch'eng*, assisted by a corps of lower officers [17] was responsible for forwarding to the throne the memorials of the ministers and principal officers of the state, and in so doing was in a position to scrutinize what the latter said and did. This was the beginning of the impeaching function and of the connection of the *Yü-shih* with impeachment. In the middle of the Han Dynasty (1 B.C.), this *Yü-shih chung-ch'eng* was removed from the Recorder's office, became the head of his own office, and had impeachment as his only function. As yet, however, his position was neither exalted nor his function considered important or well defined.

For about seven centuries the titles of the *Yü-shih chung-ch'eng* and his assistants underwent many changes and their functions also varied in importance. Not until the T'ang Dynasty did the position of the *Yü-shih* or Censors become exalted, when their chief was promoted to be *Yü-shih ta-fu*, their deputy-chief retained the title of *Yü-shih chung-ch'eng*, and the rank and file, now simply known as *Yü-shih*, were grouped in three colleges. Responding to the emperor's encouragement, the T'ang Censors were outspoken and unafraid, serving as the trusted ears and eyes of the emperor and acting against misconduct and maladministration on the part of the officials, high and low, central and local.

The system reached maturity at the beginning of the Ming, when an over-all Board of Censors was set up, at the head of which stood the two Censors-General, Left and Right, and two Deputy-Censors-General, also Left and Right. The number of the Censors was greatly increased. To bring about closer scrutiny of local administration, provincial administrators above a certain rank were also given titles of Censors-General and Deputy-Censors-General and were authorized to exercise the function of Censors in respect of their colleagues. In this way, the Court could enlarge the powers of officials in the provinces without incurring the risk of centrifugal revolts. In other words, during the Ming Dynasty the Censors were as much an instrument of effective monarchical control as they were a guarantee of clean and efficient administration. What was true of the Ming, was true also of the Ch'ing.

Unlike the impeaching function, the remonstrating function was of a more general and political nature. To be effective, remonstrance had to go hand in hand with proposing or suggesting. Thus, in the Ch'in and the Han it was the Three Lords who did the remonstrating. However, the *Chi-shih-chung* (meaning one who attends to the throne room business), who later came to be in charge of the remonstrating function par excellence, was, like the *Yü-shih chung-ch'eng*, already in existence in the Ch'in and Han Dynasties. Subsequently a number of middle-rank officials were also given the additional title of *Chi-shih-chung* and were authorized to express opinions contrary either to edicts of the emperor or to memorials of the high dignitaries.

After the T'ang[18] the *Chi-shih-chung* were less important. In the Ming and the Ch'ing they were incorporated into the new Censorate. Though in name they and the *Yü-shih*, or Censors, remained separate, they had the same duties. The function of both was principally, if not exclusively, impeachment. The Censors generally covered the provincial administrations; the *Chi-shih-chung* watched the central ministries. That both were still allowed to remonstrate and that occasionally some of them did remonstrate did not affect their principal occupation. In other words, by the Ming Dynasty, the *Chi-shih-chung* lost his traditional power of remonstrance and became a common censor in fact.

The merging of the two "talking" functions was not an accidental growth. It reflected the consummation of monarchical rule, and the much praised censorial institution can be viewed only in that light. Clearly, too much and too free remonstrating would impair the reputation for infallibility and consequently undermine the authority of the emperor. On the other hand, talking about or against his servants, the officials, high or low, did not call his wisdom into question. On the contrary, the emperor got a check on his officials and also a good name for being open-minded. Indeed, unenlightened and able rulers alike were always careful to maintain that convenient check and that good reputation. If Machiavelli had written *The Prince* with the experience of China as his background, he would not have failed to dwell on the good use of censors as an important princely art.

Law

Chinese law [19] in the past consisted of an extensive body of indefinite yet generally accepted ethical and political concepts and a voluminous body of minutely recorded rules and precedents. It may be convenient to speak of the former as law in its broad sense and of the latter as law in its narrow sense. Law in the broad sense can best be illustrated by laws such as the Six Laws of the T'ang (*T'ang liu-tien*), or the collected statutes of the Ming and the Ch'ing (*Ta-Ming hui-tien, Ta-Ch'ing hui-tien*). Law in the narrow sense can best be illustrated by the Codes, such as the famous T'ang Code and the equally famous Ming and Ch'ing Codes (*Ta-Ming lü-li, Ta-Ch'ing lü-li*).[20] But the two were never completely distinct from each other.

Chinese historical scholars like to give the Laws (*fa*, *hsien*, or *tien*) a very early beginning, coeval with the semilegendary Three Dynasties (2205(?)–256 B.C.). This is not to be wondered at, since the traditional Confucian scholars regarded every important aspect of Chinese culture as an integral part of the self-sufficient coördinated heritage handed down by the early rulers, developed by many sages, and perfected by Confucius, and Law was not to be an exception. Such Laws were therefore permeated with Confucian morals and ethics, and were quite different from laws in the Western sense.

It was about the time of the Sui and the T'ang that Chinese law began to be more or less divisible into Law and Code. It was true that, long before these dynasties, the terms *fa*, *hsien*, and *tien*, which we shall call Law, and the term *lü*, which together with *li* constituted what we shall call Code, were all in use. But before this time Chinese law consisted mainly of accepted moral and ethical precepts and only in a subsidiary way of enforceable legal rules; it was only after this time that the *tien* or Laws and the *lü* or Codes began to denote different bodies of legal concepts.

Beginning from the Sui and the T'ang, the Law and the Code had more or less different contents. In a very rough way, the Law, the broader Chinese law, may be considered as corresponding to the public law of the West, and the Code, the narrower Chinese law, as equivalent to Western private law.

The Law was concerned with the five relationships, the rites, and especially the position of the sovereign vis-à-vis the Supreme Being above him and his subjects under him. If we accept the premise that traditional Chinese government was based on these things, the law that covers them is certainly public in nature. It also follows that Law cannot be dissociated from Confucianism. In fact, the function of Law was to clothe Confucianism with a garment of authority.

The Code, as the codification of statutes and precedents, on the other hand, represents something more enforceable, more definite, and closer to law in the Western sense. Let us take the celebrated T'ang Code (A.D. 653) as an instance. It treats of family relationships, and the status and rights and duties of each family member; the various offenses against the sovereign or the public officials, or against the life and property of individuals; the various corresponding punishments, reprieve, and pardon, and what is known in the West as criminal procedure. The principal rules were the statutes (*lü*) which were either passed on from preceding dynasties or newly formulated by the reigning dynasty. But equally effective were the precedents (*li*), handed down from the past and not annulled by the present regime.

While in some ways the Code is comparable to Western law, there is this cardinal difference. Western law is a law of things as well as of persons, whereas the Chinese Code, from the early K'ai-huang Code of the Sui and the T'ang Codes down to the Ming and Ch'ing Codes, was almost exclusively concerned with the relation of man to man. As a consequence, the sanctions of law were almost all penal, and the conception of civil responsibility was undeveloped. This is why Western lawyers, though they might admire the procedural perfection of Chinese law, looked askance at its substantive rules.

In form, Chinese law is essentially customary. This applies not only to the broader law (the public law or the Laws), but also to the narrower law (the private law or the Codes). Being customary and not produced by a legislative process, Chinese law had two peculiarities. First, it was not fixed. It was being changed all the time, though perhaps imperceptibly. There was no legislation either in the modern sense or even in the sense that the law of pre-Revolutionary France was enacted by the consent of the *Parlement* of Paris. The Laws or *tien*, being concerned primarily with morals, rites, the imperial household, and the administration, changed with the will of the sovereign. There was no impediment to such change. The Codes (or *lü-li*) had also to reflect the changed social conditions of the times. They too could not remain stagnant. The second peculiarity of Chinese law was that, though undergoing slow changes all the time, it was largely traditional and continuous, and no matter what changes there were in the law, the continuity was never broken. This was also natural, since the foundations of the Chinese Empire have remained largely the same for the last two millennia.

In spirit, Chinese law, both in the form of Laws and in the form of Codes, was well adapted to sustain the social and political foundations of the monarchy. Its chief concern was to make the position of the emperor impregnable and the social order and administrative machinery that supported the monarchy unassailable. In other words, Chinese law implemented political thought. The assertion made in the preceding chapter, that Confucianism as it grew really absorbed the legalist philosophy, finds an additional proof in the spirit of Chinese law.

From the foregoing it follows that the aim of justice was less to protect individuals than to guarantee the social and political order, particularly the monarchy. The monarch was the fountainhead of justice. He made the laws and executed them. His servants in the administrative hierarchy might act as his deputies for the greater part of the execution of the law, but he was free to order retrials and change the verdicts rendered by his officials. The vesting of the judicial power in the hands of the monarch, both in theory and in practice, was again in full accord with the ethico-political nature of the Chinese Empire.

Local Administration

Like the central administration, local administration in monarchical China also had a great stability. There were a multitude of changes during the twenty-odd centuries of Chinese history, but they did not affect the essential features of the system.

Generally speaking, the local administration was guided by the following three principles. First, the country was divided into a number of regions and subregions in which central government functions and local government functions were kept separate. Second, local functions were reduced to a minimum compatible with keeping the peace of the realm and maintaining the cultural and moral standards of a Confucian state. Third, there was a persistent attempt to keep an effective, if not entirely firm, control over the local regions by the central government. These principles were sometimes found to be conflicting. It was the constant effort to harmonize them that caused the institutions of local government to be modified and readjusted from time to time.

The geographical divisions and subdivisions of the empire varied from dynasty to dynasty. The variation appeared to be more marked than it was in reality on account of the different names given from time to time to essentially the same areas. The areas of direct local administration generally consisted of three tiers—provinces, prefectures, and *hsien*.[21] In addition, there were often areas of supervisory administration, which might be either still larger areas superimposed over several units of the highest regular tier (like a grouping of two or three provinces), or intermediate areas between two tiers (like circuits which grouped together several prefectures). None of these more or less fluid areas of supervisory administration was a unit of local administration, properly speaking. They were set up to strengthen control by the central authorities and to discourage centrifugal tendencies, or to facilitate the discharge of certain special duties.

The contrast in the administrative divisions of the Ming and the Manchu Empires may serve as an illustration of this point. During most of the Ming Dynasty the country was divided into fifteen provinces, which were subdivided into nearly three hundred prefectures, which were again parceled into 1171 *hsien*. All were units of direct administration, and on the whole neither superimposed nor intermediate administrative areas were found necessary. The Manchus inherited and preserved this arrangement in general, but throughout their reign two provinces were usually grouped together and a trusted servant of the Court was appointed viceroy of the resulting unit to strengthen the hand of Peking. Toward the latter part of the dynasty the circuit was also interposed between the province and the prefecture, and a number of new and special functions were entrusted to the intendant of the circuit.

The various grades of local government below the provincial level defy general description. During the Ming and Ch'ing Dynasties the circuits, prefectures, and *hsien* each had a single responsible head, with varying numbers of assistants. The provincial government, on the other hand, was to some extent collegiate, in that beneath the governor there were commissioners in charge of civil, judicial, and educational matters (this last since the latter part of the Ming). These commissioners performed the several categories of supervisory and revenue, judicial, and educational and examination duties, respectively.

During the Ch'ing a governor was installed in each province, and in each pair or group of provinces a viceroy (or governor-general). Both exercised general control and supervision over the provincial commissioners and served as a check one against the other. They were given the titles of Right Censor-General and Right Deputy-Censor-General,[22] respectively, and were authorized to impeach not only the inferior local officials, but also each other and even the ministers of the central government. The principal purpose was to enable the Court, through the governors and the viceroys, to retain firm control over the provinces, and to provide an efficient administration of them. The devices used for this purpose varied in the earlier dynasties, but there were such devices in almost every period.

As to the aims of local government, generalization is equally difficult. The functions that were performed by the local officials varied naturally from place to place and from time to time. The personal factor, each official's concept of government and capacity for administration, also counted a great deal. This was especially true in the case of the *hsien* magistrate directing his administration from the walled town of the *hsien*. A little later we shall discuss those functions in the discharge of which the local officials merely acted as the agents of the central administration. Their functions of a more autonomous and purely local nature had one central aim; namely, to increase the people's good opinion of the Court and to inculcate in them a sense of awe and reverence for the emperor.

There were three categories of local functions: relief work, public construction, and what may be termed ritual and educational work. The most common forms of relief were the selling of grain at nominal prices, doling out rice or millet soup, distributing castoff clothes, and providing for temporary shelter, in case of famine or other calamities. Public construction took the form of building bridges, canals, and irrigation projects. But the last category, ritual and educational work, was the most varied in nature. Such work might involve establishing an academy for scholars or organizing literary competitions; promoting the worship of some being, natural or supernatural, or building a temple of worship or of commemoration; erecting an arch (*p'ai-lou*) or tablet to mark the worthy deeds of some meritorious official, martyred widow, or filial son; or setting up asylums for orphans, for the aged, or for chaste widows. The Confucian concept of rites and education was indeed broad and flexible enough to embrace all these moral and material deeds, which could easily be considered charitable or philanthropic in nature or as public works.

In carrying out all these three categories of activities, the local officials could go as far as their interest led them; they were limited only by the finances they were able to raise, either by free contribution or by local assessment or central government grants, and by the demands or tolerance of local public sentiment. There was no law to govern these activities. The only necessity was that they must do nothing to displease the Court. For instance, a local official obviously could not afford to promote the building of a temple to commemorate a great literary man who had written something against the imperial system, however accomplished or worthy the latter might be in the eyes of compatriots in his locality. Nor were there regulations as to which level of local government should undertake a particular function. The only consideration in a given case was that the authority who did anything must not incur the jealousy or disapproval of his superior, unless he was sure of approval from a still higher superior.

This indefiniteness or flexibility in the scope of local functions which local officials were free to commit or omit leads naturally to the question of local self-government. Was there local self-government in old China? The answer depends much on what is meant by self-government. If by self-government one means that groups of representative local people were usually allowed to perform a number of public functions, subject of course to the orders and interference of the officials, then there was local self-government. Since there was nothing inflexible about any of the three categories of local functions mentioned above, and since the local officials were free to take or not to take unto themselves any of these things, they were naturally also free to leave part or all of them to the local gentry. Furthermore, both the officials and the gentry were Confucian. Their attitudes towards things ritual and educational were in agreement. As to relief and construction works, there was also no necessary disagreement. When funds could be raised, both groups could do as much as lay within their power, and there was little reason for restricting the activities of the gentry.

But it is not to be suggested that the old China had local self-government in the sense that there were local self-governing bodies who enjoyed an authority with which the higher agents of the central government were not allowed to interfere. In the first place, the gentry who were active in local affairs owed their influence neither to election nor to formal appointment, but to a recognition, perhaps informal, of their local responsibility by the agents of the central government. In the second place, the gentry had to defer, in whatever they did, to the wishes of the officials above them in the same way that inferior local officials deferred to the wishes of superior local officials or of the central government. They had no domain of their own, protected by constitutional or customary rights against undue interference as has been the case with local self-governing bodies of the Anglo-Saxon world.

Thus, while there was a stable local administration marked by a growth, readjustment, and improvement similar to that of the central administration and of the civil service, local self-government was not among its merits.

Public Services

Throughout its twenty-odd centuries, the functions which the Chinese empire deemed essential to its existence and well-being could be conveniently grouped under four heads: defense, justice, economic affairs, and ritual and cultural affairs. The first two are common to all states. There is little difference in their general intent and content. It is in regard to the last two that the Chinese empire was different from the states of the West.[23]

a. *Defense.* As a function of the state, defense needs no elaboration. One country's defense system is differentiated from another's by the techniques of recruiting the armed and police forces and the form of military organization and administration. Until this century, a police force, as an instrument for keeping the peace against minor disorders, has been practically nonexistent in China. This was due to the close coöperation of the local authorities and the dominant elements of the countryside, such as the great families during the Wei and Chin Dynasties or the gentry during the Ming and Manchu Dynasties. Military forces to prevent rebellion or to repel invading hordes from the periphery of the empire were of course maintained. Methods of recruitment changed at different times, encompassing through the centuries almost every variety. The armies of retainers of the earlier days, the conscripted armies of the middle dynasties, and the standing armies of more recent times all had their day in China, not to mention the banner armies of the Manchu Dynasty consisting largely of Manchu and Mongol aristocrats.

The military organization varied with the organization of the local administration. Sometimes it formed a part of the local organization. Sometimes it was independent of it. In the latter case, the local military commander often served as a check against the civil authorities of the region.

b. *Justice.* Within the limits of the law, already described, the function of administering justice was consistently emphasized. One of the primary functions of all local officials, from the lowest to the highest, was to see that justice was done.[24] Though adjudication and common administration were not vested in separate hands, trials and the handing down of sentences had to follow a well-prescribed procedure, departure from which was not countenanced. Reviews by higher authorities were also adequately provided for, and the final review by the Board of Punishments was frequently made more careful by the participation of other ministers specially designated by the emperor.

c. *Economic affairs.* The field of economic administration was a broad one. The primary aim might be merely the raising of revenue to support the Court and the essential services of the state, but in order to raise sufficient revenue some amount of regulation of the economy was often found necessary. When the emperor or some of his leading ministers happened to be captivated by that aspect of the Confucian teaching which laid stress on making the people prosperous, as the best way to preserve the state, even bold economic experiments might be resorted to.

Among all economic matters, the question of land or public domain was of the first importance. All land was the property of the emperor. But this was so in theory only. In practice, land, at least the great part of it, was owned by individuals. Thus the administration of the proprietary rights of landownership, the making of deeds, and periodic survey measures constituted an onerous administrative burden. And when zealous reformers set their minds to equalizing landholding, the sphere of state activity was widened still further.

Land was important because it was always the most reliable source of revenue. In fact, during the Ming Dynasty the whole tax system was based on the land tax resulting in the so-called "single-whip system," [25] which meant that personal services and other contributions were all lumped in the land tax, thus greatly simplifying the tax system. The salt tax and taxes on metals, chiefly iron and copper, came next in importance most of the time.[26] All these taxes necessitated some degree of regulation of the commodities taxed, and at times the regulation even went as far as monopoly, for example the monopoly of salt or of iron. During certain dynasties a head tax also yielded a substantial portion of the revenue.

A levy of personal services was employed at various times from the early years of the empire down to the latter part of the Ming, when the single-whip system was adopted. It was especially complicated during the T'ang Dynasty. When there was such a levy, there was also the need of an elaborate administration. *Corvée* labor was used regularly on major public works.

Coinage was also a state function from the very beginning of the empire. At times the state also printed paper money, especially in the Sung, Yuan, and Ming periods.

Regulation of the grain supply was another function which was seldom neglected. It took the form of compulsory storing of grain at definite places and the setting up of a special administration to take charge of its transportation. Some of the famous canals in China, like the Grand Canal to Peking, were in fact built to facilitate such transportation.

The more conscientious emperors regarded relief of the distressed, especially the victims of flood, drought, famine, or war, all large-scale calamities, as an important function of the government.

And lastly, there were public works. Most of these works were local in nature. But there were national works as well, such as the digging of arterial canals, the construction and maintenance of post roads throughout the country, the building and periodic repair and enlargement of the Great Wall and the imperial palaces and tombs. Besides public construction, there were also maintained, especially during the later empires, elaborate silk, leather, paper, and other manufactories, all for the exclusive consumption of the emperor and his court. For all these works, construction or otherwise, there were offices of administration in charge both at the capital and, when necessary, in the country at large.

d. *Ritual and cultural affairs.* If in the field of economic administration the Chinese empire differed substantially from the states of the West, the empire was unique in its solicitous care for another group of functions, which, for want of a better term, we may call ritual and cultural. It is here that the Confucian touch is most apparent.

The Chinese state had always laid special stress on ritual. This was true before the Ch'in and the stress became more marked as time went on. There were all kinds of sacrificial rites to the supernatural and to the deceased; sacrifices to Heaven, Earth, the Sun, and the Moon; sacrifices to the legendary Founder of Agriculture; sacrifices to Confucius; and sacrifices to the imperial ancestors. Most of these sacrifices were performed with great care and pomp, and the administration of them was far from a sinecure.

But rituals did not stop with sacrifices. The ceremonies connected with the birth, marriage, and death of the emperor and his offspring and with his accession were also truly state functions. So, too, were the celebrations on certain great occasions such as the New Year or the emperor's birthday or the religious ceremonies in Buddhist or Taoist temples, fostered by emperors who believed in Buddhism or Taoism or who saw wisdom in supporting Buddhist or Taoist worship. One need only examine the inventory of the offices and bureaus of the central government to be convinced that all these rituals were administered with as much care and seriousness as were the revenue and the civil service.

Next to the ritual, the government of the Chinese empire also devoted much attention to the promotion and harnessing of Confucian learning and scholarship. We have noted the nature and quality of that learning and scholarship in the section above, on the Chinese civil service. Here we need only note further that elaborate administrative agencies for conducting the examinations were maintained both at the capital and throughout the country.

Several central offices, notably the *Hanlin*[27] Academy and the Historical Archives, also supervised functions of a literary nature. The literary or historical writing of the incumbents of these offices was often given an important recognition comparable to that given to work in the other branches of administration. In other words, such writings in China ranked as important functions of the state.

It may therefore be said that, by inquiring into the functions usually undertaken by the Chinese government, one can see the nature of the Confucian state which was China during the last two thousand years.

IV

THE IMPACT OF THE WEST AND THE FALL OF THE MONARCHY[1]

The universal empire, sustained for two millennia by a mellow harmony of political principles and institutions, had finally to yield to a new order of things, when Western ideas of nationalism and constitutionalism and Western institutions of election and representation descended on China in full force.

Western missionaries and traders were not primarily interested in importing into China their own political system. But coming at a time when Western nations had grown powerful as the result of industrial revolution and expanded trade and when the Manchu rulers of China had been weakened by corruption and misrule, they could not fail to shake the faith of the Chinese in their own institutions. They were backed by the full force of their governments, and those governments represented powerful states of the West. The Chinese were forced to question their continued allegiance to a monarch, and still more to the monarchy of the Manchus.

China had had many early contacts with the West and since the coming of the Jesuits in 1582 the contact has been continuous. But not until the Opium War in 1840–1842 did the West make its influence felt in China in a social and political way. The earlier Jesuits[2] who managed to maintain intimate relations with the Court were active in many ways but their contributions were mainly technical and scientific in nature. In astronomy, trigonometry, cartography, anatomy, and especially in calendar-making, the Chinese were their eager students, but not in matters political or social.

The failure of the Europeans to influence their hosts in ways other than technical and scientific was to be expected. The European nations in the seventeenth and eighteenth centuries were weak and poor by modern standards, and their colonizing programs were inhibited by conflicts among themselves. The Church of Rome was more or less on the defensive and the missionary work of the Protestant sects had not begun. In the face of the mighty empire of the East neither the church nor the states of the West could at first lay claim to superiority in social, political, or even military matters.

Imitation of Western Arms

The Opium War opened up a new phase of the West's relations with China. The defeat which the Chinese suffered at the hands of the British was a rude shock in itself. But there was more to come. The industrial revolution had begun in Europe, free trade was the order of the day, and Westerners had great confidence in that nineteenth-century model of Western civilization — a combination of Christian humanitarianism, political libertarianism, and economic laisser faire, all stampeded into immense activity by scientific inventions. The Manchu Empire, weakened by half a century of corrupt and ineffectual rule, and now disgraced by the results of the Opium War, could no longer resist the power and the wealth of the nations of the West.

Nevertheless, the reception of Western civilization was slow, reluctant, and intermittent. It was first the material aspects alone of Western civilization that were appreciated. Then came half-hearted reforms in education and administration along Western lines. Next there came some recognition of Western processes of thought. Very recently the emphasis on a higher standard of living for the masses has begun to stir up the national conscience of the Chinese people. But even now there are still powerful influences at work which would extol Chinese civilization, to the practical exclusion of that of the West.

The period that intervened between the Opium War of 1840–1842 and the Sino-Japanese War of 1894–1895 was one of admiration for and imitation of Western arms and manufactures. The efficacy of the British gunboat and other forms of Western arms was successfully demonstrated beyond doubt not only in encounters with the British in 1840–1842 and with the Franco-British forces in 1858–1860, but also in "Chinese" Gordon's effective aid to the Manchu supporters in their war against the Taiping Rebellion in 1863–1864.

The men who were most responsible for introducing Western arms and machinery were Tseng Kuo-fan, Tso Tsung-t'ang, and Li Hung-chang, especially the latter. They were all literati of the traditional type and believed in Confucian institutions as the cornerstone of the Chinese state. They accepted Western arms and machinery only to secure for China the benefit of equality of means in dealing with the West. Starting from 1865, when the Kiangnan Machine Works was set up in Shanghai, shipyards, fleets, military and naval academies, telegraphs, textiles, and mines were developed in various places along or near the coast. Students were sent to Europe and

America to learn navigation, the manufacture of arms, or some other useful technology. In all these efforts the idea that a commensurate modernization of social and political institutions might be a prerequisite to the successful operation of these more concrete undertakings never dawned on the minds of the leaders. They were simply practicing a prevalent motto of the time, namely, "Chinese learning for the fundamental structure and Western learning for practical services only."

In this business of sheer imitation, the Japanese were more successful. The Japanese won and the Chinese lost the Sino-Japanese War of 1894–1895. This new humiliation compelled the Chinese leaders to realize for the first time that something more than the mechanical superiority of the West might be needed.

Imitation of Western Institutions: The Reform Movement[3]

Consequently after the war of 1894–1895 there began a movement to modify the laws and institutions of ancient China, following the patterns of the West. The revolutionist Sun Yat-sen urged this,[4] men like K'ang Yu-wei and Chang Chih-tung who were fundamentally Confucianists tried to act on it. And when the Russo-Japanese War of 1904–1905 resulted in the victory of the Island Empire, even the Manchu Court saw the compelling necessity of political and educational reforms. Was it not, the Chinese asked themselves, because Japan had adopted a constitution and Russia had not that the former was victorious and the latter defeated?

The reform movement that ensued may further be subdivided into two periods: the first culminated in K'ang Yu-wei's brief ascendancy in the summer of 1898 and the second was characterized by the attempt of the Court to copy the constitutions and the laws of the West via Japan. K'ang Yu-wei was a Confucianist and believed in the supremacy of the monarch. In this he was not different from Tseng Kuo-fan, Tso Tsung-t'ang, or Li Hung-chang. As a Confucian scholar, he was perhaps greater than all of them. But whereas Tseng Kuo-fan and company were satisfied with the more superficial and the more concrete aspects of Westernization, K'ang Yu-wei and his friends welcomed the introduction of Western learning and Western administrative structure. They were indefatigable in establishing schools and publishing magazines. They believed in modernizing the governmental setup as a first step toward effective reform. Thus in the reforms of 1898, when K'ang Yu-wei and his followers succeeded in gaining a fleeting and partial control of the Court, many sinecure offices which corresponded to nothing in the West were abolished, the ordinances and regulations of the central military establishment were revised, and the system of examination was modernized to provide adequate tests for the modern knowledge of the candidates.

K'ang Yu-wei's failure was immediately attributable to the personal ambitions of the Empress Dowager Tz'ŭ-hsi, who was opposed to Emperor Kuang-hsü's partisanship for K'ang Yu-wei. But more fundamentally it was due to the anti-Western conservatism of the ruling class, who were not unmindful of their vested interest in the offices they held or hoped to hold and which had been abolished by K'ang Yu-wei.

The failure of the reforms of 1898 swept away the reformers. A temporary ban on all reforms set in. Even the humiliations resulting from the Allied occupation of Peking and the exile of the Court, following the uprising of the ignorant, fanatic, and anti-foreign Boxers of 1900,[5] did not quite turn the tide of reaction. An eminent historian of the period has concluded that the sum-total of the Manchu "new deal" from 1901 to 1905 was confined to the abolition of the old examination system, the opening of schools, and the dispatch of students abroad.[6]

The Japanese victory in the Russo-Japanese War of 1904–1905 gave the Manchu Court a new stimulus toward reform. Less conservative scholars also began to see something finer in Western society and institutions. More specifically they thought that the adoption of a constitution had given the Japanese advantages over absolutist Russia.

Thus began a second period of political and constitutional reforms. They were terminated by the Revolution of 1911, which expressed China's utter distrust in the constitutional pledges of the Manchus and ended their rule.

Summarily put, the reforms of 1905–1911 centered on the following political and constitutional developments:

1. *The dispatch of two commissions to study constitutional government abroad*, in 1905 and 1907. The first commission, composed of high dignitaries, visited Japan, the United States, and the countries of Europe. On their return they advised the adoption of constitutional government after the pattern of Japan as the only means of forestalling revolution. The second, made up of lesser dignitaries, visited only Japan, England, and Germany. Although they also advised constitutional government, their insistence on the Japanese and Prussian constitutions as the only ones suitable for China was even more emphatic.

2. *The organization in 1905 of a Constitutional Reference Bureau* to introduce Western laws and to prepare necessary drafts for future use. This was also an imitation of Japan's expedient when she was preparing to adopt a constitution.

3. *Reorganizations of the central administration* in 1906 and 1911 along the structural lines of the West. In substance, however, there was little change in the reorganization of 1906 and in the first reorganization of 1911. The

number and titles of ministries were changed, but the personnel and the power of the ministers remained the same. The Manchu nobility continued to be the dominant element and the ministers were not given full powers. At the second reorganization of 1911 which followed the last minute promulgation of constitutional articles, the change was more substantial, but it was too late to stay the hand of the revolutionists.

4. *The promulgation of the Constitutional Principles of 1908*[7] with the promise to realize full constitutional government by the end of 1916. A later promise fixed the date at the end of 1913. The Principles were promissory in nature and had no effect of law until they should be enacted. But, even if they had been law, they could have imposed very little limitation on the authority of the Court, since they were copied after the Japanese constitution and gave no substantive protection to the rights of the people.

After the Revolution of 1911 had broken loose, the Court promulgated the so-called Nineteen Articles of the Constitution.[8] These were more liberal and purported to establish a parliamentary form of government. As a result, Yuan Shih-k'ai was elected by the Legislative Council as the Premier, and a so-called responsible cabinet was set up. But in reality it became an instrument of Yuan Shih-k'ai to bargain with the revolutionary regime, and brought about the abdication of the Manchus.

5. *The promulgation of a series of electoral laws and the inauguration of Provincial Assemblies and the Central Legislative Council* in 1908–1911. The Provincial Assemblies were elected by a highly limited suffrage, the main qualifications for a voter being either education or property or his having held office under the empire. The powers of these Assemblies were also limited. The viceroys and the governors enjoyed the right to petition the central government to order their dissolution. Actually, there were about seventeen provinces where these Assemblies had been inaugurated at the time of the fall of the empire.

The Central Legislative Council[9] had its first meeting in October 1910. It was composed of two hundred members, of which half were elected by and from the members of the Provincial Assemblies, and the other half were appointed by the emperor from the peers, high dignitaries, distinguished literati, and rich taxpayers. This Council had partial powers of legislation and budget control, subject to the sanction of the throne. In the first year it was the practice of the government not to honor the statutes and the budget resolutions passed by the Council. After the Revolution had begun to show signs of eventual success, the Council became more assertive in a manner not unlike the behavior of the Russian Duma in 1916–1917, but it was already too late to give the Manchus the benefit of a genuine reform.

These reforms were characterized, as are almost all failing regimes of absolutism, by attempts to reform in theory while maintaining absolutism in fact. The Manchus had no sincere desire for any genuine constitutionalism. In no instance was the Court willing to impose any effective restraint on its own governing power. It clung so fixedly to its traditional prerogatives that even the reformist group of 1898, now under the leadership of Liang Ch'i-ch'ao, voiced bitter criticism. A reform political group, the Political Information Society, organized by Liang Ch'i-ch'ao in 1907, was vociferous in taking the Court to task for not giving up any part of its power, and for this it was suppressed in the following year.

In the reorganizations of the central administration, the Manchus continued to hold the controlling posts, with Chinese dignitaries only playing second fiddle. A host of loyal and subservient servants were kept in office, but the government was weak, poorly organized, and badly discredited. Loyalty and subservience alone could not function efficiently enough to do its bidding or to enable it to retain a grip on a situation which was fast getting out of hand.

Another aspect of the Manchu Court's attempt to retain its absolute power was its intentional imitation of the Prussian and Japanese political systems. Just as the Prussian king and the Japanese emperor were supreme, so the Manchu emperor under the Constitutional Principles of 1908 was also to remain supreme. Considering that the traditional powers of the Chinese emperor were altogether unlimited, any effective attempt at constitutional reform should certainly first have aimed at limiting his powers, however gradual the process of limitation might have to be. But there was not the slightest inclination towards effective limitation. As with the Prussians and the Japanese, there was the broadest possible interpretation of administrative power as superior to legislative power. Like them, there was to be no true regime of liberty. The constitutional guaranties of liberties could be easily swept away by legislation which could be in the form of ordinances.

There was also no subordination of military to civilian authorities. Previously, a clear distinction between these two authorities had never existed, but now, taking after the Prussian and the Japanese models, the administration and command of the armed forces were made directly responsible to the emperor. This imitation of Prussian and Japanese political systems not only characterized all the Manchu reforms but also left an indelible mark on all future constitutional developments in China.

It is not necessary to go into any detailed analysis of the Constitutional Principles of 1908. The various points just enumerated serve to show that even if the Principles had been duly enacted, the Manchu Empire would not have been any nearer to constitutionalism, as constitutionalism was then understood in English-speaking and Western European democracies.

For the promulgation of electoral laws and the actual holding of elections, some credit is due to the Manchus, no elections having ever been held in

China before. That the suffrage could not be made universal at once was understandable. But here again the Manchus could have done better if they had wanted to. There was no necessity to impose as high a property qualification as they did, thus preventing great numbers of even literate people from participating in the elections. Still another bad bequest from the Manchus was the two-class system of suffrage more or less like the Prussian which was again the result of the Manchus' blind imitation of things Prussian and Japanese. The local elections on the *hsien* level held in 1912, the first year of the Republic, were almost entirely according to the electoral laws prepared in the last years of the Manchu Dynasty and followed the two-class system. When one reflects that the subsequent elections of the last thirty-odd years show no improvement on the elections of 1908–1912, the conclusion is that the Republican regimes have done badly, not that the Manchu regime did wisely. If the latter had been wiser and more sincere in its professions of devotion to constitutionalism and popular rights, it could have made a much better beginning in electoral experiments.

The utter inability to appreciate the benefits that constitutionalism could give, and the fear of losing control colored all the reforms of this period. Though the reforms were intended to prop up the already tottering dynasty, they served in fact to redouble the revolutionary ardor of Sun Yat-sen and his party. The ineffective reforms even caused loss of faith in the Court on the part of the Chinese conservatives. For during this period, when the Court was instituting various reforms, there was a very active interplay of the revolutionary forces and the forces of reform in the country and abroad. The success or failure of the reforms depended on whether they were able to enlist the enthusiastic support of the reformers and remove the grounds for agitation by the revolutionists. When there was no enthusiasm for support, and ample grounds for agitation, the reforms were of course doomed to failure.

The Revolutionary Movement[10]

The revolutionary movement was under the leadership of Sun Yat-sen. It is somewhat difficult to state whether Sun Yat-sen in his earlier days was a political reformer, like most of his contemporaries, with progressive tendencies, or whether he was a thorough Westernist. He was a new type. His boyhood environment and his education were different from the literati of that time, who were or aspired to be officers of the state. He was not a Confucian, certainly not a Confucian of the traditional type, bent on blind allegiance to the monarch. The contacts he had early in his life with Westerners had also instilled in him a strong sense of national consciousness. Aware that the Manchus were alien rulers on the soil of China, he had as early as 1895 organized a society for the restoration of Chinese rule, the Hsing Chung Hui (Revive China Society). Though on a small scale, the first uprising against the regime had already taken place in the following year. But before 1898 it was difficult for him to enlist the sympathy of any large number of educated and respected people, by whom, of course, the regime was fully and unreservedly accepted, and to whom revolution and treason were identical and equally taboo. But the failure of the reformers in the coup d'état of 1898 caused some change in this respect and made Sun Yat-sen more acceptable to a growing number of people. The folly and subsequent disgrace of the Court in its dealings with the Boxers in 1900 further strengthened the revolutionary forces.

There began immediately a keen rivalry between the revolutionary and the reform movements. Both were now catering to the educated and respected classes at home and abroad. Those who abhorred violence and were more traditional sympathized with the reformers. Those who had lost hope in the Dynasty or were otherwise endowed with a sense of national consciousness were generally inclined to join with Sun Yat-sen. There was much confusion between the personnel of the two groups. There was even proselytizing of each other's adherents, especially of adherents overseas. On several occasions Liang Ch'i-ch'ao himself sought to merge his following with Sun Yat-sen, though the attempts all ended in failure.

By 1905, the year the Manchu Court dispatched its first commission to study constitutions abroad, Sun Yat-sen had considered it opportune to organize the T'ung Meng Hui, the Revolutionary League. It had its beginning in Brussels in 1905 when Sun Yat-sen was there to meet the Chinese students of revolutionary inclinations from the various countries of Europe. It had its formal inauguration in Tokyo in the same year when a program was adopted and various officers were appointed. The first point of the program was, of course, the restoration of China to the Chinese, and consequently the overthrow of the Manchu invaders. But from the very beginning Sun Yat-sen had included the establishment of the Republic and the equalizing of land holdings as parts of the program. All these points were in the oath which his comrades at Brussels had to swear. The program was, therefore, different from that of the reformers in kind rather than merely in degree.

From the organization of the T'ung Meng Hui one sees that Sun Yat-sen was now having a quite variegated following. No longer was it confined to those elements which usually made up the secret societies of old China. He had also as his followers the student class, some accomplished scholars of literary excellence, and a great many zealots of good birth who were able to secure for him wider contacts with the respectable and influential strata of Chinese society.[11]

When the revolutionists were thus organized, an intensive debate on the relative merits of constitutional reform versus revolution was carried on both in Japan and China. With Liang Ch'i-ch'ao then in Japan espousing the cause of reform, the debate was on a high level. If it was somewhat academic, it was nevertheless eagerly read by a great number of educated Chinese with progressive leanings as well as by the vast number of students at home and abroad. The influence the forums of both parties had on their readers was enormous. The half-heartedness of the Court toward the reformers weighted the scales heavily on the side of the revolutionists.

The frequent uprisings engineered by the revolutionists, almost annually, likewise enhanced the prestige of their party. The revolutionists were now doing their best to infiltrate the armed forces, especially the New Armies, which often had as officers cadets graduated from Japan. The increasing unreliability of the armies as an instrument of government, and the growing effectiveness of the revolutionists' arguments, often brought into greater relief by Manchu incompetence, were now producing a demoralizing effect on the otherwise loyal servants of the Court. Even the army began to consider the Manchu regime hopeless. Under these circumstances, only a spark was required to start the conflagration which would consume the 268-year-old Dynasty.

The Revolution of 1911 [12]

The Revolution of 1911 was both an accident and the logical outcome of the revolutionary travail of Sun Yat-sen and his party. In the sense that no one had foreseen that an uprising at Wuchang would result in the speedy overthrow of the Manchus, it was an accident. In the sense that the Manchu regime was fast crumbling and any uprising might prove to be the finishing stroke, it was the final act of consummation of the revolution.

The Revolution of 1911 started with a successful armed uprising on October 10 in Wuchang. In that year, the issue arising out of the nationalization of railways created a turmoil in Szechwan and Hupei Provinces. The rich merchants of these provinces had invested heavily in a railway. When the government successfully negotiated a railway loan with a consortium of British, American, German, and French bankers, it became necessary for the government to nationalize all Chinese railways and pledge them as security. The commercial lines were therefore to be surrendered to the government, and the interest of the private concerns in the lines to be given up. The unrest thus engendered was especially disquieting in Szechwan and Hupei, for the interested parties there were men of both wealth and influence. They clung to their rights; they held huge demonstrations against the government. But the government was in need of the loan and tried to coerce the populace which sided with the investors. The impasse was at once seized upon by the Revolutionaries as an excuse for action.

The Revolutionaries had suffered a heroic defeat earlier in 1911 near Canton. Their spirit was low. It was expedient for them to stage a new revolt. This they did on October 10 at Wuchang, the capital of Hupei Province, an area now severely affected by the agitation against the nationalization of railways. They had an initial success. The viceroy and the military commander fled and a brigade commander, Li Yuan-hung, a man who was neither a revolutionist nor a fanatic loyalist, was temporarily made head of the insurrectionary forces.

The capture of the provincial capital and the neighboring great city, Hankow, had its immediate effect in rousing to action the Revolutionaries who had been infiltrating into the armed forces elsewhere. By the end of the year almost every province south of the Yangtze and also a few northern provinces like Shensi and Shansi had revolted. The feeble loyalty of the Chinese governors of these provinces to the Court and the readiness of the followers and sympathizers of the reformist groups to join hands with the Revolutionaries contributed to the rapid spread of the anti-Manchu conflagration.

The Manchu Court was duly alarmed at the very beginning. When a couple of the New Army commanders telegraphed from Luanchow, some 150 kilometers east of Peking, demanding immediate and full-scale constitutional reform, there was for the Court no choice but to comply. By this time it had lost confidence in itself. It was willing to try an expedient which could give it some hope of prolonging its life. Thus, Yuan Shih-k'ai, an ex-viceroy who had created the New Army but who was *persona non grata* to the then regent, was reinstated and was forthwith elected premier by the Legislative Council in accordance with the newly promulgated Constitution of Nineteen Articles. He became thus the head of a new cabinet, composed almost exclusively of Chinese ministers loyal to him personally. More significant was of course his effective control of the New Army, on which hung the Court's only hope of defeating the widespread insurrection.

Unfortunately for the Manchus, Yuan Shih-k'ai's coming to power marked the virtual termination of the Dynasty. Yuan Shih-k'ai was ambitious enough, but loyalty to the Court was not consistent with his ambitions. From then on, the struggle was a duel between him and the Revolutionary forces. It was to be a race between the military moves and intimidations of the former and the political organization and maneuvering of the latter.

The rebel provinces were beginning to set up a central command as early as November. The military leaders of these provinces and certain other independent units had appointed delegates who met first in Shanghai and then in Hankow and who, on December 2, had agreed to an Organic Law of the Provisional Government of Twenty-one Articles. It was true that in the meantime Yuan Shih-k'ai had dealt some military blows in and around Hankow and the reverses were producing uneasiness among the Revolutionary leaders. But the fact remained that the separate units were continuing their over-all organization. It was also true that they had many quarrels on the choice of a Generalissimo of the Revolutionary forces. Nevertheless, they were able to make Li Yuan-hung and Huang Hsing Generalissimo and Deputy-Generalissimo respectively without causing dissension in their ranks. In other words, Yuan Shih-k'ai's military efforts alone were not enough to deter his opponents from effecting their political and military organization, thus paving the way for the establishment of a new government.

The Chinese Republic

The new government of the Republic of China was duly established on January 1, 1912 at Nanking when Sun Yat-sen, elected two days previously by the assembled delegates of the provinces acting as the Provisional Legislative Assembly,[13] was inaugurated as the Provisional President of the Republic. From then on, until the day of the merging of the new and old governments the problems Sun Yat-sen had to face were first, how to lure Yuan Shih-k'ai into the Republican fold without damaging the fundamental principles of a republic, and second, how to secure the enactment of a provisional constitution to meet both the clamor of the legislative leaders and the requirements of the immediate situation. The two problems were in fact closely related.

Yuan Shih-k'ai's sole ambition was to be the ruler of China. To him it mattered little whether the form of government was republican or not. In maneuvering for his ultimate goal, he had several advantages over his adversary. He could, with the consummate skill of a puppet player, use the Manchu Court to do his bidding. He was also sure of the loyal support of the divisions of the New Army, his own creation, which were still in effective control of most of the northern provinces. Thus if it suited him to arrange for peace, he could tell the Court that abdication was the best guarantee of its future safety. If, on the other hand, it suited him to go on with the war, he could threaten the Revolutionary regime with further bloodshed to be ordered by the Court. He was now wholly aware, and the Revolutionary leaders were no less aware, that the country as a whole preferred peace and unification to any particular leadership. He was in a position to persuade the Court to abdicate in his favor. Therefore, if Nanking agreed to make him President of the Republic, the country could be united, without further fighting, whereas a united China under Sun Yat-sen's leadership would have to be conditioned on Yuan Shih-k'ai's defeat or willingness to step aside.

Astutely, Yuan Shih-k'ai bargained and maneuvered, using the various means at his disposal. At times he cited the refusal of the Court to abdicate, and at other times the demonstrations of his military henchmen against locating the united government at Nanking. Sun Yat-sen knew his weakness and he had to give in. On the abdication of the Manchu Court, on February 12, 1912, he resigned, and Yuan Shih-k'ai was elected Provisional President by the Legislative Assembly on the 14th to succeed him. Regarding the seat of government, the Legislative Assembly later agreed to allow Yuan Shih-k'ai to be inaugurated in Peking, and finally on April 5, formally resolved to have the Republican Government transferred there.

However, Sun Yat-sen before yielding the reins of power to Yuan Shih-k'ai did have a new Provisional Constitution[14] enacted. There were two main differences between this Constitution and the Organic Law of the Provisional Government. There was in the Constitution a bill of rights to satisfy those members of the Legislative Assembly who thought that a republican constitution without a bill of rights was an anachronism. The other difference was the change from a presidential form to a cabinet form of government. Sun Yat-sen was the head of a presidential government under the Organic Law, but President Yuan Shih-k'ai under the constitution just adopted was to have a cabinet responsible to the Legislative Assembly, of which the Revolutionaries naturally formed a majority. This cabinet was to serve as a check to Yuan Shih-k'ai's personal ambitions. At least some of the principal followers of Sun Yat-sen hoped that it would serve as an effective check.

With this compromise which entirely satisfied neither side, Sun Yat-sen relinquished his presidency on April 1, 1912, and the Peking Government of Yuan Shih-k'ai became the government of the united republic. Thus ended the Manchu Dynasty and began the Republican regime at Peking.

V

THE TRIALS AND FAILURES OF THE EARLY REPUBLIC[1]

China became a republic on the first day of 1912 when Sun Yat-sen was inaugurated Provisional President. When Yuan Shih-k'ai assumed the Provisional Presidency on March 10 of the same year and the Nanking Government was moved to Peking in the following month, the whole country came under the Republican regime. In form, this regime lasted until 1928 when the Nanking Government of the Kuomintang, the party of Sun Yat-sen, obtained control of the length and breadth of the country. In substance, the republic was a farce, almost throughout the period. Events of this period demonstrated that a republic cannot be achieved merely by enacting republican constitutions and laws. Something more fundamental is needed.

A brief narrative of the period will suffice to bring into bold relief the political meaning of the kaleidoscopic changes that abound in the period.

Yuan Shih-k'ai and the Great Betrayal

The Manchus abdicated on February 12, 1912. The next day Sun Yat-sen tendered to the Legislative Assembly his resignation as Provisional President, and on the 15th Yuan Shih-k'ai was duly elected to succeed him. On March 10 Yuan Shih-k'ai took the oath and assumed the duties of office at Peking. Thus was established the Republican Government of Peking.

Upon his assumption of office, Yuan Shih-k'ai proposed as head of the Cabinet T'ang Shao-yi in accordance with the newly-promulgated Provisional Constitution. The new Premier was an old colleague and friend of the President, and he was also close to the Revolutionaries in his political sympathies. In fact, he later joined their party. He came down to Nanking and sent to the Legislative Assembly the names of the Cabinet Ministers for its consent. In accordance with the constitution, the policies of the Cabinet received the prescribed vote of confidence of the Assembly. The beginnings of the new government seemed indeed auspicious, and there was great hope that a ministry responsible to the assembly might prove to be a workable instrument uniting the Revolutionaries of Sun Yat-sen and the older elements of the North in a common effort to achieve both progress and stability. So, Sun Yat-sen deemed it opportune to relieve himself of the office of chief executive on April 1.

The elements that backed Yuan Shih-k'ai were generally composed of the mandarins of the ancient regime, the reformists of former days,[2] and his own henchmen, both civilian and military. The fact that he was the creator of the New Army naturally made the New Army commanders rally around him. In other words, his following had a predominantly military character. This was a situation with which the presumably responsible ministry of T'ang Shao-yi was confronted. From its very inception Yuan Shih-k'ai quarreled with the Cabinet over appointments and policies. In three months' time Yuan Shih-k'ai had so fully demonstrated his arbitrariness that T'ang Shao-yi quit in disgust. The subsequent cabinets were largely made up either of bureaucrats or of personal followers of Yuan Shih-k'ai. The majority of the Legislative Assembly was not, in 1912, ready to have a showdown with Yuan Shih-k'ai on the issue of confidence. Subsequent cabinets were also given votes of confidence, though always grudgingly.

There was a general election of the houses of parliament forthcoming, and the Revolutionaries entertained the hope that with their new victory they might be better able to force the hand of Yuan Shih-k'ai. They were successful in the winter of 1912–1913 in the election. Now reorganized as the Kuomintang, the Revolutionaries controlled the majority in both houses of parliament and their parliamentary leader, Sung Chiao-jen, was prepared to head a Kuomintang cabinet. He was on his way to the capital when he was assassinated at the railway station at Shanghai on March 10, 1913. The shock produced was instantaneous. It was intensified still more when on April 26 the military and civil governors of Kiangsu who had been instructed as a matter of routine by Yuan Shih-k'ai to probe into the case, audaciously made public their findings, implicating the Premier and the President himself in the murder, and when on the same day Yuan Shih-k'ai announced the successful conclusion of a loan with a consortium of foreign bankers.

These events made a parting of the ways inevitable. The foreign loan which naturally strengthened Yuan Shih-k'ai's regime was negotiated without the consent of the new Parliament which had begun its session on April 8, 1913. Yuan Shih-k'ai was also in various other ways overriding Parliament, acting without consultation and contrary to the constitutional provisions. The Kuomintang had hoped to check him by the emergence of a Kuomintang Cabinet, but now he had assassinated the one leader who was destined to head that cabinet. An armed resistance became the only choice for the Kuomintang.

The leaders of the Kuomintang had not been united in their attitude toward Yuan Shih-k'ai prior to the assassination. Some, like Sun Yat-sen himself, preferred to devote themselves to the advancement of the welfare of the people by way of education and industrial development, and were willing to let Yuan Shih-k'ai have a free hand with the government. Some, like Sung Chiao-jen, were earnest in leading the country on the road to a parliamentary democracy. The assassination, however, united them all in condemnation of Yuan Shih-k'ai and in the resolve to have him removed at once. A few of the southern provinces still under the control of the Kuomintang governors revolted in July 1913, but by this time Yuan Shih-k'ai had already garrisoned strategic points of the South with his own troops and he had no difficulty in quashing the rebellion in quick order. In so doing he was perhaps aided by that general anxiety for peace which prevailed among the Chinese populace as well as the foreign powers, the former not yet thoroughly disillusioned with Yuan Shih-k'ai and the latter generally standing for the apparent strong man. For the Kuomintang, the Revolution of 1913 was altogether a sad event.

Yuan Shih-k'ai now proceeded to have himself elected as the President of the Republic by the Parliament on October 6, 1913. At that time, the majority of Kuomintang members still remained in the Parliament. Only those who had actually participated in the insurrection had left. There were some difficulties in the path of Yuan Shih-k'ai's election which he removed by ordering a mob of thugs and soldiers, in the guise of the citizenry, to lay siege to the parliament building, pending the successful conclusion of the election. Having thus secured the definitive Presidency, nominally in accordance with the Constitutional Laws, Yuan Shih-k'ai dissolved the Kuomintang and unseated its members in the Parliament on November 4, 1913.

Just prior to their expulsion, the Kuomintang members had, in a temporary coöperation with the Progressives, drafted a constitution, the famous Temple-of-Heaven Draft of 1913.[3] When the Parliament lost its power to function as a result of the large-scale expulsions, governors of the provinces petitioned Yuan Shih-k'ai to dissolve the Parliament and to convene a new assembly for the consideration of the constitution, they having been, of course, duly instructed of his desires. With this Yuan Shih-k'ai naturally complied readily. For him the Kuomintang itself, the Parliament which it controlled, and the constitution which it wanted to impose on China were all at an end.

In lieu of a hostile parliament Yuan Shih-k'ai ordered provincial authorities to appoint delegates for the discussion of matters of state and formed these delegates into a constitutional convention. This new convention dutifully enacted a new Provisional Constitution which he promulgated on

May 1, 1914.[4] It was known as "Yuan Shih-k'ai's Constitution." Its provisions were, of course, to his taste and from now on he could rule supreme, unchecked by any law.

A more astute dictator than Yuan Shih-k'ai might have preferred to dominate the country according to the constitution of his own making, without ever assuming a monarchical title. Perhaps Yuan Shih-k'ai was not such a dictator, perhaps no dictator can be consistently astute. At any rate, he chose to be stupid. He wanted to be an emperor, in name as well as in fact.

Shortly after the promulgation of his constitution, discussions concerning the fitness of China to remain a republic began in earnest. Finally, in August 1915, the Society to Plan for Stability (*Ch'ou-an hui*) was formally launched and started with fanfare the movement to reconvert China into a monarchy. Its leaders were some of Yuan Shih-k'ai's most trusted servants and none could any longer be blind to his intentions. Events now progressed with an *opéra-bouffe* rapidity. By December of the same year, the nation, through the people's representatives elected according to the Law of October 8, 1915, had unanimously voted to establish a Chinese Empire and to make Yuan Shih-k'ai Emperor. While all this was beginning, the Japanese made their notorious Twenty-One Demands on China, and Yuan Shih-k'ai in the main acceded to them in May 1915. The complicity of Japan in Yuan Shih-k'ai's move was evident.

The monarchical schemes of Yuan Shih-k'ai united the Revolutionaries who had formed the Kuomintang and the reformers who had organized the Progressive Party under Liang Ch'i-ch'ao against him. On December 25, 1915, the Province of Yunnan declared its severance from the Peking regime. Antimonarchical expeditions under the joint control of the Progressives and the Kuomintang generals were immediately organized. The slogan of the campaign was "Protection of the Republic." The movement spread like wildfire; other provinces in the South soon made similar declarations. In the face of widespread defection, Yuan Shih-k'ai had to annul, on March 22, 1916, all his monarchical decrees, and decreed instead the continuance of the Republic. The long-prepared coronation ceremonies which had not yet taken place were, of course, to be canceled. Shamelessly, he acted as if he had never betrayed the Republic and continued to perform the functions of president. The seceding provinces which had organized a military government of their own in Kwangtung refused, however, to accept such a ridiculous arrangement. They redoubled their opposition to Yuan Shih-k'ai. His death on June 6, 1916 finally removed the obstacle to a real unification of the country.

TUAN CH'I-JUI AND HIS RIVALS

The removal of Yuan Shih-k'ai paved the way for the succession of Vice-President Li Yuan-hung as President of the Republic. The discarded Provisional Constitution of 1912 was revived. The dissolved Parliament was reconvened and at once resumed its work on the constitution. It will be recalled that when the Parliament ceased to function in November 1913 the Draft Constitution had only been reported upon by the Constitutional Commission and the Parliament as a whole had had no opportunity to consider it. The Parliament, sitting as a constitutional assembly, now began to deliberate on its provisions.

In 1916 and in 1917 the Parliament was sharply divided between two groups, one the partisans of the former Kuomintang, and the other those of the Progressive Party, as they were known in 1913. The controversy over some of the issues was bitter. The Executive Branch at that time was also divided, with Li Yuan-hung, the President, and Tuan Ch'i-jui, the Premier, at odds. There were two main issues which divided these two groups. One was the constitution to be adopted and the other was the question of joining the Allied Powers to declare war against Germany, an act which would affect the fortunes of the different parties in different ways. In time the controversy became extremely bitter, and in May Li Yuan-hung dismissed from the premiership Tuan Ch'i-jui, to whom the majority of the Parliament was opposed.

But Tuan Ch'i-jui was not an ordinary premier. He was, after the death of Yuan Shih-k'ai, one of two leaders of the Northern militarists, the products of the New Army already referred to. As soon as he was dismissed, he openly incited the Northern militarists who followed him to denounce the President as well as the Parliament. They sabotaged the government of Li Yuan-hung and refused to take orders from it. There was a virtual breakdown of the government. In desperation Li Yuan-hung called on Chang Hsün, the most vociferous of the militarists but now a follower of Tuan Ch'i-jui, to intercede. Chang Hsün accepted the invitation. While his troops were proceeding to Peking, he advised the dissolution of the Parliament. When this was done on June 12, 1917, Chang Hsün himself entered the capital. On July 1, he effected the restoration of the Manchu Dynasty with a coup d'état.

Chang Hsün was by no means strong militarily. As soon as the Manchus were restored, Tuan Ch'i-jui who had been on apparently good terms with Chang Hsün a month earlier, picked up the Republican banner. Enjoying the loyal support of a considerable number of forces in and around Peking, he was able to make a quick finish of Chang Hsün's resurrected dynasty. On July 14 he triumphantly reëntered Peking to resume the premiership to which he had been reappointed by Li Yuan-hung in the early days of July. Though Tuan Ch'i-jui owed his premiership to Li Yuan-hung's appointment, the latter was not allowed to continue as President. Feng Kuo-chang, who had been elected Vice-President when Li Yuan-hung assumed the presidency in 1916, succeeded instead.

Feng Kuo-chang and Tuan Ch'i-jui were, next to Yuan Shih-k'ai, the leaders of the former New Army, and as such had long been rivals. The friction between the two began almost as soon as they were brought together in the close relationship of president and premier. Thus began among the Northern militarists an internecine warfare which was to ravage China for years to come. In the beginning it was Tuan Ch'i-jui's faction which got the upper hand. Toward the end of the year 1917, the faction of Ts'ao K'un and Wu P'ei-fu, which was closely related to Feng Kuo-chang, came into the ascendant, and Tuan Ch'i-jui was forced to resign. Then with the aid of Chang Tso-lin, the militarist of Mukden, Tuan Ch'i-jui compelled Feng Kuo-chang to reinstate him as Premier, in May 1918. The friction ended only when the tenure of both was terminated by the election of a new President, Hsü Shih-ch'ang, on October 10, 1918.

When the Peking Government of Feng Kuo-chang and Tuan Ch'i-jui reëstablished the Republican Government in 1917, it did not reconvene the old Parliament and was silent as to whether the Constitution of 1912 was in force or not. A new Legislative Assembly, modeled after the one preceding the old Parliament, was assembled, and it was ordered to draw up a new Organic Law of Parliament and also electoral laws of the members of the two Houses in lieu of the laws of 1912 under which the Parliament of 1912 was constituted. The suffrage was now further limited.

A new Parliament of fewer members elected under the new laws met in August 1918. It was known as the Anfu Parliament, after the so-called Anfu group of politicians, henchmen of Tuan Ch'i-jui, who had manipulated the elections and obtained an effective control of the body. It was this Parliament which elected Hsü Shih-ch'ang as President on the expiration of Feng Kuo-chang's term on October 10, 1918, a term which had included the incumbency of both Yuan Shih-k'ai and Li Yuan-hung.[5] In this way, the Peking regime tried to convince the country that it was being scrupulously constitutional.

To keep up the appearance of constitutionalism, the Anfu Parliament in its year of existence in 1918–1919 also dallied with constitution-making. It appointed, like the old Parliament, a Constitutional Commission, and the commission in turn resolved to abandon the Draft Constitution of the old Parliament and adopted a new Draft on August 12, 1919.[6] There was in essence little difference between the two drafts. It was only the Chinese weakness for emphasizing legitimacy that made the Anfu Parliament eager to have a constitution attributable to it alone and to no one else.

Meanwhile a separate government was maintained at Canton, at times under the control of Sun Yat-sen and at other times under that of military leaders of the South who were not his followers. For a time the Canton Government, maintaining that legitimacy demanded the restoration of both the old Constitution of 1912 and the old Parliament of 1913, insisted on such restorations as conditions for discontinuing its separate regime. But there was also a faction there, the Kwangsi military faction, which was more eager to come to terms with the Northern Government than to support Sun Yat-sen in his intransigent attitude toward the restoration. In other words, internecine strife, which was disorganizing the provinces under the control of Northern militarists, was also the order of the day for the South. In disgust and as a protest, Sun Yat-sen resigned as Generalissimo of the Military Government and left Canton in May 1918.

There was a protracted period of peace negotiations between the North and the South from the spring to the fall of 1919. They ended fruitlessly, for the North and South could not bring themselves to agreement on the disputed question of the old Parliament, on the disposal of troops, and on some other issues. The Southern regime went on, and the country remained divided.

In the North, the struggle between the factions of Tuan Ch'i-jui and of Ts'ao K'un and Wu P'ei-fu came to a head by July 1920. Though Tuan Ch'i-jui was no longer the premier, his men had been enjoying political and military advantages, thanks to the financial and military aid given them by Japan in the name of common belligerency against Germany.[7] That domination was becoming increasingly intolerable to the other military factions. With the passive support of the faction of Chang Tso-lin, who had been growing in strength during the past years and who had earlier sided with Tuan Ch'i-jui and was destined to do so again, Ts'ao K'un and Wu P'ei-fu were able to deal a mortal blow to Tuan Ch'i-jui's followers. This marked the end of the Tuan Ch'i-jui faction as a decisive factor in the civil wars of China. Tuan Ch'i-jui himself reappeared later, but he reappeared only as the pawn of other military forces, and suffered accordingly.

With the defeat of the Tuan Ch'i-jui faction, Hsü Shih-ch'ang sought to placate the winning cliques by the dissolution of the Anfu group and on October 30 he invalidated the revised laws of 1918 and revived the original laws of 1912, regarding the composition and election of the Houses of Parliament. On the same day, he also ordered a new general election according to the original laws. But before it had time to be completed, before barely eleven provinces had held elections, the defeat of Chang Tso-lin by Ts'ao K'un and Wu P'ei-fu resulted in the expulsion of Hsü Shih-ch'ang himself. After the defeat of the Tuan Ch'i-jui faction in July 1920, Hsü Shih-ch'ang had held the reins of government very much like a circus rider standing astride two galloping horses. He had to hold together the two rival factions of Chang Tso-lin and of Ts'ao K'un and Wu P'ei-fu and balance them well. As the two maneuvered for control of the provinces, the balance was in constant danger of disruption. Finally, in April and May 1922, the break occurred. Chang Tso-lin was defeated, and Hsü Shih-ch'ang was also expelled for his partisanship toward a cabinet which had often done the bidding of Chang Tso-lin and had incurred the hatred of Wu P'ei-fu.

The exit of Hsü Shih-ch'ang paved the way for the second restoration of Li Yuan-hung and with him also the restoration of the old Constitution of 1912 and the old Parliament of 1913.

During the period of Li Yuan-hung's second presidency (June 1922–June 1923), the faction of Ts'ao K'un and Wu P'ei-fu maneuvered to have Ts'ao K'un made president under the new constitution to be completed by the restored Parliament. The maneuvers might not have succeeded if all the previous Kuomintang members had rejoined the Parliament at this second restoration. Instead, the irreconcilables stayed away and continued to oppose the Peking Government. The Parliament adopted the constitution [8] in a hurry in October 1923, and forthwith elected Ts'ao K'un President under the new provisions.

The Ts'ao K'un regime lasted for about a year. There was no unification between the South and the North, for by this time Sun Yat-sen had gone back to Canton and was building up a new regime of a revolutionary nature. Compromise was out of the question. Neither was there consolidation in the North, for the remnants of the Tuan Ch'i-jui faction were still dangerous, Chang Tso-lin was gaining and the influence of Feng Yü-hsiang and his allies as a separate force was beginning to make itself felt. There was not even the semblance of a government. The cabinets were being formed and dissolved almost continuously, and Wu P'ei-fu himself was at odds with the men around Ts'ao K'un.

In September 1924, Ts'ao K'un ordered an expedition against Chang Tso-lin that proved to be his own undoing, for all his enemies and rivals seized the opportunity to make war on him. Feng Yü-hsiang turned against him, marched on Peking, and made him a captive.

Prior to this the military government of Sun Yat-sen at Canton had entered into talks with all the three enemies of Ts'ao K'un and Wu P'ei-fu. It was almost like a holy war against Ts'ao K'un. With his downfall, it appeared natural that Sun Yat-sen should coöperate with the other three factions to set up a new government in Peking. Here the difference in interests as well as in ideology interfered with the possibility of coöperation. Sun Yat-sen wanted to carry out the revolutionary program recently adopted by the reorganized Kuomintang, whereas Tuan Ch'i-jui and Chang Tso-lin were only interested in jockeying for the control of Peking. The result was the personal victory of Tuan Ch'i-jui, who now installed himself in November 1924 as the Provisional Chief Executive without regard to any constitution. Chang Tso-lin was favorable to him. Feng Yü-hsiang was becoming more closely linked with the Kuomintang and consequently was rather hostile.

Tuan Ch'i-jui, considering himself unbound by any constitution, proceeded to convene one conference after another, claiming that he had in mind a new constitution and also a new parliament to be of popular approval. By December 12, 1925, a Constitutional Drafting Commission, the members of which were hand-picked by him, had completed a draft [9] differing little in substance from the Ts'ao K'un Constitution of 1923.

The Government of Tuan Ch'i-jui was perhaps weaker than any previous Peking regime. The Kuomintang Government in Canton was rapidly increasing in strength. Chang Tso-lin, nominally the supporter of the regime, was constantly interfering with it and threatening it. The armies of Feng Yü-hsiang, though once defeated by Chang Tso-lin, were still enough to constitute a menace. When, in the face of the threat from the Kuomintang, Chang Tso-lin and the remnants of the Wu P'ei-fu faction united to resist the common foe, there was no further use for the much-discredited Tuan Ch'i-jui. Tuan Ch'i-jui left Peking in April 1926 and the government of the so-called Provisional Chief Executive was at an end.

For almost a year the Peking Government was under one cabinet or another, acting for a presidency which remained vacant. This confusion and sham lasted until Chang Tso-lin, the real ruler, himself assumed in June 1927 the generalissimoship of the so-called Military Government.

His end was to come soon, for the sweeping victories of the Kuomintang Government compelled him to retreat to Mukden on June 3, 1928, only to be assassinated on the South Manchurian Railway by the Japanese the next day. This ended the Peking Government forever.[10]

Lessons of the Peking Regime

Some generalizations on a number of political and constitutional problems of significance may be drawn from the story of the vicissitudes of the Peking Government related above.

1. *Constitutionalism*

Like revolutionary France, the Chinese Republic had many constitutions and draft constitutions, some provisional and others definitive. Not counting the Constitutional Principles of 1908 and the Constitution of Nineteen Articles of 1911 of the Manchus, there were five such constitutions or draft constitutions: (1) the Provisional Constitution of March 12, 1912; (2) Yuan Shih-k'ai's Provisional Constitution of May 1, 1914; (3) the Draft Constitution of the Anfu Parliament of August 12, 1919; (4) the Ts'ao K'un Constitution of October 10, 1923, and (5) the Draft Constitution of Tuan Ch'i-jui's regime of December 12, 1926. All were government-sponsored. There were many more drafted by private persons or semipublic bodies.[11]

Of the five instruments, the Constitution of 1923 was perhaps the best drafted and the Provisional Constitution of 1912 the most respected. In 1912 the Republic was new, the hopes for the future were high, and the revolutionary spirit was not yet ebbing. The Provisional Constitution, representing the spirit of the times, was a symbol of a change and a promise of modernization. It was due to this quality that it was resurrected time and again and was always held in some measure of affection by those who were genuinely republican.

The Constitution of 1923 had a long and a checkered history. Its first draft made in seclusion by the Constitutional Commission of the old Parliament at the Temple of Heaven in Peking was not contaminated by the evil influence of Yuan Shih-k'ai. It was on the whole a carefully conceived instrument, impracticable for China at that time perhaps, but certainly no more so than any other constitution attempted by China before or since. The draft received careful consideration by the old Parliament and was the subject of many heated debates in 1916–1917 at Peking and also by the same Parliament in 1918–1920 at Canton.[12] It was finally enacted by the same Parliament in Peking in 1923. Because of the fact that the Parliament of 1912 was perhaps more representative of the people, at least of the politically articulate, the constitution which had undergone thorough deliberations by it could not fail to attract more favorable attention from the public than the ones which were made by less representative bodies.

But neither of these two constitutions, to say nothing of the others, was able to bring China any nearer to real constitutionalism. The Constitution of 1923 was utterly discredited, for it resulted in the election of Ts'ao K'un as President. The Constitution of 1912 was too often honored in the breach and too often suspended.

The experience of constitution-making during the entire period of the Peking regime had therefore meant nothing to the people of China. As far as the common people were concerned, it had not provided for them political stability nor improved their material well-being. It had only enabled the politically unscrupulous to take advantage of the constitutions to promote their selfish and personal interests, almost invariably to the detriment of the national interest.

2. *Parties and Elections*[13]

The early years of the Republic also saw a rich crop of parties and political groups, which yield a constructive lesson for the future.

There were before the Revolution of 1911 two main political groups, approaching the character of political parties. One was, of course, the T'ung Meng Hui of Sun Yat-sen, which operated underground. The other was the Hsien Yu Hui (Friends of the Constitution), composed of the more enlightened literati and mandarins with a mentality not dissimilar to that of the reformist followers of Liang Ch'i-ch'ao. The latter was operating openly in the Imperial Legislative Council in 1910 and 1911. There was no formal organization of the reformists at the moment, but their views were not unrepresented. The Hsien Yu Hui often expressed their views.

The Revolution made new organizations necessary. New groups emerged. Some were made up of the elements of one or the other of the two pre-Revolution groups; some were hybrid offshoots, and others were totally new. As the general election for the Parliament of 1913 approached, the T'ung Meng Hui, directed by Sung Chiao-jen and adhered to by a number of sympathetic groups, was reorganized as the Kuomintang. When the Parliament was convened in April 1912, the groups outside the Kuomintang were amalgamated to form the Chinputang (Progressive Party) with Liang Ch'i-ch'ao as its moving spirit.

Neither the Kuomintang nor the Chinputang was well organized and disciplined. Though they maintained branch organizations in the provincial capitals and other important centers, the relationship between the central and the local organizations was loose and haphazard. Discipline was so inadequate that the parliamentary members not infrequently belonged to two or more parties at the same time. Party programs were not clearly distinct one from the other.

In their attitude toward Yuan Shih-k'ai, both during and after the armed resistance of 1913, the Kuomintang had the better understanding of his character, and consistently sought to check Yuan Shih-k'ai's personal ambitions by means of a parliamentary majority and a responsible ministry. The Chinputang, following popular inertia and disposed to avoid violence, gave him full support. After the murder of Sung Chiao-jen, the Kuomintang was again right in its determination to remove Yuan Shih-k'ai by an armed uprising, but the Chinputang continued to support Yuan Shih-k'ai in the name of peace and stability. The Chinputang was not disappointed in Yuan Shih-k'ai until he put an end to the Parliament in the winter of 1913–1914, and was not completely disillusioned until his monarchical designs became apparent. Then it was too late for the Chinputang to do anything but resort to armed resistance, a device which it had condemned in 1913.

After the restoration of the old Parliament in 1916, party activities were again in order. The members of the former Chinputang organized themselves into two undistinguishable groups. For there was so little distinction between the two that to the outsider they were both collectively known as the Research Clique (*Yen-chiu hsi*). This clique supported Tuan Ch'i-jui both under Li Yuan-hung's presidency in 1916–1917 and under Feng Kuo-chang's presidency in 1917–1918. In fact, its leaders, and especially Liang Ch'i-ch'ao, actively participated in Tuan Ch'i-jui's cabinets until they were supplanted by Tuan Ch'i-jui's henchmen, the Anfu group.

The members of the former Kuomintang also formed parliamentary parties, and there were three or four groups so organized. But whereas the Chinputang groups were united, these Kuomintang groups were substantially divided among themselves. The extreme left remained loyal to Sun Yat-sen, but the extreme right, the Political Study Group (*Cheng-hsüeh hui*), was quite willing to compromise with the Research Clique. On the whole, the Kuomintang groups were opposed to Tuan Ch'i-jui, the degree of their opposition varying with the degree of their adherence to the Chinese Revolutionary Party which Sun Yat-sen had organized in Tokyo after the failure of the anti-Yuan Shih-k'ai campaign in 1913.

When the old Parliament was having sessions at Canton in 1918–1920, the Research Clique abstained and only the Kuomintang groups attended. But the inter-group dissensions were more pronounced than in the years at Peking. The Political Study Group was always intriguing with the militarists of the North. Altogether, the activities of the parties, if these groups could be called parties, were disappointing.

With the exception of the Kuomintang of 1912, its predecessor, the T'ụng Meng Hui and its successor, the Chinese Revolutionary Party, all the parties and political groups of this period were rather the children than the parents of elections and their resultant assemblies. They never organized the elections, they only followed. They were composed of members of the assemblies who united not to realize any program of national interest, but to bargain for personal advantage with men of power. In earlier days, these men of power were Yuan Shih-k'ai and Tuan Ch'i-jui, who controlled the central government, but in later days they could be any militarist, whether in the central government or the provinces. This entanglement of politicians with worthless militarists makes Chinese history of this period extremely painful reading. A few parliamentary members of old Kuomintang extraction were, to their credit, free from such entanglements. This accounts for their ability to hold posts of honor, if not of power, in the Kuomintang regime of later days.

That one who witnessed the behavior of these parties in their electoral, parliamentary, and other roles should develop a contempt for them is understandable enough. Sun Yat-sen's contempt for them went so far as to include the elections and the parliaments which were inseparable from the parties.

3. *Presidential versus Cabinet Form of Government*

In the early years of the Republic it was a moot question whether presidential or cabinet government would be better for China. Some favored the former, claiming that it was better suited to China; others favored the latter in their anxiety to guard against the personal dictatorship of an ambitious and unscrupulous man. There were repeated experiments with both. Sun Yat-sen's government at Nanking was admittedly presidential. Then the Kuomintang tried to impose a responsible cabinet on Yuan Shih-k'ai. But Yuan Shih-k'ai had no patience with any cabinet which even claimed to derive its authority from the Parliament. He bolted and resorted to personal government long before the promulgation of the Constitution of May 1, 1914 which made him the undisputed ruler in theory as well as in fact.

When Li Yuan-hung and Feng Kuo-chang were presidents, Tuan Ch'i-jui's cabinets enjoyed the powers of a responsible cabinet. The president was weaker than the premier both in personality and in military following. Tuan Ch'i-jui was in no danger of being interfered with effectively by the President, but his inability to recognize the limitations of the executive power, added to the disrupted state of the legislature and the incompetence of the individual legislators, also rendered impossible the normal workings of a responsible cabinet. From Tuan Ch'i-jui's own point of view the cabinet system must have seemed unsuitable for China, for when he had a chance to be a dictator he readily chose dictatorship rather than any other system. That was why he styled himself Chief Provisional Executive in 1924.

The alternation of the presidential and the cabinet systems and the failures of both resulted in a readiness to experiment during the first years of the new regime following the reorganization of the Kuomintang in 1923, with a third alternative — the collegiate executive which was also subsequently discarded. The important thing to remember is that the American presidential system, the British cabinet system, and the Swiss collegiate system all require for their successful operation the existence of a powerful assembly representing the people and strong enough to compel the executive to stay within the constitutional limits allowed him. Since there had never existed such an assembly in China, hope for the success of any of the three systems of the executive was vain.

4. *Legitimacy*

The decade and a half of the early Republican regime witnessed many an issue of legitimacy. In many controversies of a constitutional and political nature the question of legitimacy was brought up, and figured prominently or even predominantly. When Li Yuan-hung succeeded after Yuan Shih-k'ai's death, there was this controversy; under which constitution, the one of 1912 or that of 1914, was he succeeding? After Chang Hsün's fiasco of the Manchu restoration in 1917, Feng Kuo-chang stepped into the presidency but there arose, first, the issue of reviving the Constitution of 1912 and second, the issue of restoring the old Parliament previously dissolved on Chang Hsün's demand. Feng Kuo-chang was elected vice-president by the old Parliament under the old Constitution. If the Constitution were not revived and Parliament not restored, by what right could Feng Kuo-chang claim to be the president? That was exactly the stand taken by the Canton regime, which was set up in 1917 and which in fact styled itself the "Constitution-Protecting Government." The peace negotiations of 1919 between the North and South failed, partly because the two sides could not agree on the question of reinstating the Constitution and the Parliament.

When the old Parliament was again restored in Peking in 1922 there was new controversy as to whether the new members who had substituted for the old members absent from the sessions when that Parliament met in Canton, in 1918–1920, were to continue or the old members, disqualified by the Parliament in Canton for their absence, were to be seated. This controversy in turn arose from the controversy over the legitimacy of the Canton sessions of that Parliament. It was decided by the members who met in 1922 at Peking that those sessions were illegal and therefore the new substitute members could not be members of the Parliament in 1922.

These are only a few instances in which the question of legitimacy or illegitimacy was argued at great length and with vehemence. There are many more, some of which involved the legitimacy of particular leaders to be at the head of the separatist regime in Canton.

It may seem strange that legitimacy should became an issue, in a period of chaos and civil wars when the observance of law was not a marked virtue among politicians. But let us not forget that China in her long past had seen in connection with imperial successions many legitimist wrangles, compared with which the Papal Successions in the Middle Ages appeared quite simple. The wrangles might be unreal, but they nevertheless absorbed the interest of the literati-official class. It is conceivable that the question of legitimacy may loom up again in connection with a disputed choice of laws or men, in party or in government.

5. *The Farewell to Monarchy*

Although Republican China had experienced so many dictatorships, often military in nature, there was one hopeful conclusion to be drawn. That is, monarchy had left China for good.

In the first years of the Republic, none but the most sanguine could be confident enough to assert that monarchy would never return. There were many who, disappointed by the inefficiency of republicanism, even longed for the reappearance of monarchy with all the age-old traditions. But the manner in which Yuan Shih-k'ai, the old servant of the Manchu Court and new President of the Republic, created his new dynasty bred a revulsion and a resentment against all monarchies. As if this did not constitute a sufficiently strong innoculation against monarchism, Chang Hsün's ridiculous restoration of the Manchu Court added greatly to that immunity from monarchism. It is difficult now to contemplate the Chinese people accepting anyone's monarchy, still less wanting it. In this Yuan Shih-k'ai and Chang Hsün without knowing it themselves had really performed a service for the Chinese people.

6. *Warlordism* [14]

Constitution or no constitution, parliament or no parliament, presidential supremacy or cabinet supremacy, the core of Chinese politics lay with the men of military backing, usually themselves military men. These military men, often in control of the provincial administrations, sometimes even of the central government, were known to the Westerners as warlords, for they were constantly warring with one another.

The real founder of warlordism was Yuan Shih-k'ai. In the years around 1900 he was responsible for the training and organization of a number of New Army divisions for the Manchu Government. While there had been personal armies in the previous generations, for instance, the armies of Tseng Kuo-fan and the Huai Valley armies of Li Hung-chang, the leaders of those armies never desired to make use of them to advance their personal fortunes. But Yuan Shih-k'ai did otherwise. Year in and year out he continued to keep his hold on the commanders of the New Army divisions and these in turn emulated his example in keeping their hold on the inferior commanders.

This quality of personal loyalty of the New Army was to poison Chinese politics for years to come. Even before assuming the presidency, Yuan Shih-k'ai had made ample use of his military following to achieve his political ends. When he wanted the presidency he inspired his army followers to declare openly that only Yuan Shih-k'ai could unite the country without bloodshed, meaning of course that they would support the Manchu Court to suppress the Revolution unless Yuan Shih-k'ai was made president. When he wanted to have the government maintained at Peking, he again inspired them to threaten that if Yuan Shih-k'ai's government were to be at Nanking there would be disturbances and no peace in the North. Yuan Shih-k'ai continued to play the army game during his incumbency of the presidency which was in fact not terminated until after the same game was turned against him.

Yuan Shih-k'ai's death in 1916 caused the Northern militarists[15] to disintegrate between the Tuan Ch'i-jui and Feng Kuo-chang factions. Because Tuan Ch'i-jui and Feng Kuo-chang came respectively from Anhwei and Chihli Provinces, the two factions were also known as the Anhwei and Chihli Factions. When Feng Kuo-chang was himself eclipsed, Ts'ao K'un and, later, Wu P'ei-fu emerged as the leaders of the Chihli Faction. By the beginning of 1918 Chang Tso-lin of Mukden had already gained enough strength to count fully as the leader of a military faction of comparable importance. He was not a member of Yuan Shih-k'ai's old military gang, but his faction based on the northeastern provinces was also considered a Northern militarist group.

From the year of Yuan Shih-k'ai's death in 1916 to the year of Chang Tso-lin's end in 1928, the multitudinous alliances, counteralliances, struggles, and open wars among these factions ravaged China, year in and year out, almost without interruption. No fixed principles and no unchanging loyalties marked the factions. An ally of yesterday could be an enemy of today and the enemy of today could again turn to be a comrade of tomorrow. A faction could petition somebody to be the president today, but the next day it might denounce him and drive him out of office. Constitutions and policies suffered the same unstable support and whimsical denunciation. The only interest of each faction was to maintain itself in power, preferably at the seat of government, or, if that were not possible, at least in certain provinces.

Nor was the South immune from militarism and militaristic factions. In the southwestern provinces of Yunnan, Szechwan, and Kweichow there grew up in the same years a number of militarists who were neither Northern in lineage nor Kuomintang at heart, but who often allied themselves with whatever separatist regime there was at Canton or near by. The militarists of Kwangtung (of which Canton is the capital) and Kwangsi Provinces were of similar nature. Every time Sun Yat-sen attempted to set up a revolutionary regime at Canton, in addition to waging a war on those of the North, he was compelled to deal with the militarists of the South. The more he dealt with them, the less free became his hands. In the years from 1922 to 1924, in his eagerness to get rid of some of the Southern militarists allied with the Northern factions of Ts'ao K'un and Wu P'ei-fu, he even allowed himself to have an understanding with the Chang Tso-lin and Tuan Ch'i-jui factions. His purpose was of course to eliminate the militarists hostile to him but his means left an indelible effect on his successors. An undue reliance on military power and a tendency to prefer military support to loyalty to his political testament were destined to characterize the regime of his own followers.

7. *Federalism*

China in its monarchical days had always been a universal empire. It was an accepted institution; no alternative was ever conceived, still less tried. Intermittently the empire might be badly disrupted, but that was an abnormal situation. Normally the emperor reigned supreme throughout the empire not checked by any device of decentralization.

With the coming of a Western form of state, the comparative merits of a unitary versus a federal state also came to be discussed by the Chinese. The idea that a large country like China might do well to adopt the federal structure received attention in both the revolutionist and reformist publications in the first decade of the century. As early as 1911, when the Revolution was still in progress, the Provisional Assembly of Shantung had expressed its preference for federation. At the zenith of Yuan Shih-k'ai's autocratic reign in 1914–1915, some publicists again advocated federalism. They hoped that an increase in provincial powers might serve as a check to the despotism of the central government. For similar reasons, the Kuomintang members of Parliament in 1916–1917 were also inclined to stress local autonomy at the expense of the central government, which was, at that time, in the hands of Tuan Ch'i-jui and was therefore not to be entrusted with too much power.

In the years between 1919 and 1922 the movement for federalism gained some momentum. The civil wars not only between the Northern and the Southern regimes but among the military factions almost everywhere were creating a general pessimism as regards national reconstruction. Thinking people were led to ask themselves this question: If the country as a whole could not be saved by one stroke within a short space of time, would it not be more advisable to concentrate their efforts for the time being on the saving of their own provinces? When the peace negotiations between the North and the South were going on in 1919, the demand for some sort of local autonomy became fairly general. A gathering of eight civic bodies in Shanghai in 1921 which called itself the Conference on the State of the Nation even went so far as to draft a model federal constitution and urged both the central and the provincial governments to go federalist accordingly.

Unfortunately, this demand for an institutional change was readily utilized by the militarists of the provinces who were more interested in their own personal power than in real provincial autonomy. They advocated or accepted federalism for their provinces, not to give the people provincial self-government but to assure themselves of something like a permanent control, free from the interference of the central government. This was so in Hunan where the provincial military governor made full use of the Provincial Constitution of January 1, 1922 to make himself virtually independent of both the Peking and Canton regimes. That apparently democratic constitution was voted on by the people and was supposed to have been in force from 1922 to 1924. But certainly the people of Hunan never had any real self-government in those years. The Province of Chekiang also had a democratic constitution prepared in 1921, and its military governor also pledged to abide by it wholeheartedly. But he too never relinquished any part of his control and the constitution was not even nominally enforced. A number of other provinces also went in for constitution-making, but the result was the same. In no province was autonomous government brought nearer to the people.[16]

The Ts'ao K'un Constitution of 1923 was federalist in nature. But by that time the movement for federalism had already evaporated. No thinking man would still be naive enough to contend that federalism could be protection against the despotism of the central government or the civil wars among the militarists. Something else was needed to effect the eradication of both. Federalism might be a good thing for China but it would not work until despotism and militarism were first gone. No wonder the Manifesto of the rejuvenated Kuomintang of 1924 declared against federalism. Thereafter for a long time there was no further consideration of it.

However, the problem of an equitable division of governmental powers between the central and the provincial governments still remains. In China the tendency for a strong central government to absorb all powers and for recalcitrant provincial governors to be de facto autonomists has always been pronounced. A stable regime in order to remain stable has to devise means of distributing powers equitably between the two tiers of government. The failure of the federalist movement in the early 1920's only meant that it could not solve the pressing problems of despotism, militarism, and lawlessness and disorder in general. It did not mean that it might not be a good means to effect the desirable distribution of powers.

8. *The Incidence of Foreign Support*

In the pre-Kuomintang years of the Republic the giving or withholding of support by the foreign powers had a telling effect on the regime and the various factions. Those which enjoyed such support were better able to survive than those which did not.

As a matter of record, the foreign powers had a tendency to emphasize what they considered stable government to the exclusion of any other criteria of good government such as liberalism, progressivism, civilian supremacy, or decency in general.

Up to almost the last days of Yuan Shih-k'ai's regime the foreign powers were with him. He was considered the man capable of providing a stable government and therefore also of protecting foreign interests. Even the outrageous murder of Sung Chiao-jen directed by Yuan Shih-k'ai himself did not deter the foreign powers from continuing to pin their hopes on him. In the uprising of the Kuomintang in 1913 against Yuan Shih-k'ai the powers were almost outspokenly hostile to the Kuomintang. In a similar way the foreign powers subsequently supported Tuan Ch'i-jui, Ts'ao K'un and Wu P'ei-fu, Tuan Ch'i-jui again, and finally Chang Tso-lin, in succession. Theirs were all militarist regimes. In supporting them, the foreign powers were giving recognition to none other than the strongest military power at the time.

Even in the South the powers also favored whatever military factions they considered capable of sustained existence. For instance, in the years of bitter strife between Sun Yat-sen and Ch'en Ch'iung-ming, the British from Hong Kong almost plainly sided with the latter. In Sun Yat-sen's last years the Powers showed a marked willingness to thwart his success.[17] When the Northern Expedition was only beginning and was not assured of rapid and sweeping victories, there was little sympathy for it on the part of the foreign powers. It was not until the Kuomintang had succeeded in establishing a new central government at Nanking that the Powers finally ceased their backing of the Northern militarist factions.

The pattern of foreign support, the discrimination in favor of the strongest elements in the existing regime, never contributed towards either the stability or the progress of the Chinese nation. It did not make for progress because the elements in the existing regime by virtue of their predominantly military support have always tended to be despotic and reactionary. Foreign support did not produce stability because the strongest elements usually became so despotic and reactionary that they invariably brought upon themselves first the dissaffection of other groups and, when thus weakened, the general upheaval of the country.

In supporting the strongest, regardless of his vices or virtues, the foreign powers often found themselves in the position of backing a wrong horse. For the foreign powers themselves this was unprofitable. It neither increased their prestige nor advanced their interests. But for the Chinese it had a far more grievous effect. It tended to prolong the life of a decadent regime and retard the emergence of a new one. The foreign powers might of course claim the doctrine of international recognition as the basis for their action, but in most instances they went considerably beyond the duties required by that doctrine.

. . . . .

Such then were the experiences which the Chinese people had to go through under the regime of Peking.[18] The regime was never for a moment satisfactory. It was for most of its years unbearable. No wonder that when a genuinely revolutionary movement led by the reorganized Kuomintang of Canton made headway in the South, the more liberal and forward-looking elements all over the country, especially the intelligentsia of the great centers like Peking and Shanghai who had no vested interests in the regime of the militarists, should all turn their hopes to Canton. Many of them left in fact for Canton to join the movement, and a new chapter in China's political evolution began.

VI

THE RISE OF THE KUOMINTANG TO SUPREME POWER [1]

In historical perspective the Kuomintang [2] must ultimately be judged by its success or failure in creating a modern nation out of an old China rather than by its success or failure in overthrowing the Manchu Empire. The Manchu Empire was so obviously insolvent in the last decade of its existence that in the face of the onslaught of the West it could not have lasted much longer in any event. A great party with a mission to perform could hardly congratulate itself on being the effective instrument of its destruction. The valid claim to success must lie in the ability so to modernize the nation that the evil traditions of the empire could no longer persist, and a stable modern society could find an opportunity to establish itself. Merely to destroy the forms of the old empire was not enough.

It is with this perspective in mind that we now turn, in this and the following chapters, to view the organization and doctrines of the Kuomintang and to review its vicissitudes, its successes and setbacks, its lapses into the things of the past, as well as its valiant fights for modernism. We shall first give an account of its slow rise to power.

The T'ung Meng Hui

Since Chinese politics are represented by individual personalities, political history becomes, more than in the West, a record of personal relationships among leaders. The Kuomintang is no exception. From its very inception its history has largely been an interplay of the personalities of its leaders.

The early leaders of the Revolutionary movement out of which the Kuomintang eventually evolved were Sun Yat-sen and Huang Hsing. They were respectively the organizers of the Hsing Chung Hui and the Hua Hsing Hui, the two most important secret revolutionist societies before the inauguration of the T'ung Meng Hui [3] in 1905. There were many revolts against the

Mnchus at the turn of the century; for most of these the Hsing Chung Hui and the Hua Hsing Hui were responsible. In the eyes of the Court the two men were equally obnoxious.

After the organization of the T'ung Meng Hui in 1905, Sun Yat-sen became the acknowledged leader of all revolutionists with Huang Hsing pledging full-hearted support. The difference in their antecedents did have, however, a profound effect on the future of the organization. Sun Yat-sen came from a peasant family, devoid of contact with the literati-official class. His early education was unorthodox. It was Western and medical. Huang Hsing belonged to the respectable society from which came the literati and the officials. His relatives and early acquaintances were naturally men of the same class. He was, like Sun Yat-sen, convinced that the Manchus were thoroughly bad and must go, and his youthful rebellious spirit was urging him on to accept no more monarchy. But beyond their common hatred of the Manchus and the monarchy, they had few ideas in common.

Sun Yat-sen knew more of the West. As early as 1905 he was already advocating the so-called Three Principles of the People. He wanted the Principles of a People's Nation, of People's Power, and of People's Livelihood, or in more easily understandable terms, nationalism, democracy, and socialism. He openly preached that political and social revolutions should both take place simultaneously.[4] Huang Hsing was a man with an extremely good heart. He of course supported his chief loyally. But to say that he embraced Sun Yat-sen's Three People's Principles would overlook the fact that Huang Hsing understood very little of the social and economic currents of the West. He was principally a man of action.

There was unanimity in all sections of the T'ung Meng Hui as far as the speedy overthrow of the Manchus was concerned. Once this common aim was realized, differences of the leaders began to come to the surface. These differences were multiplied by the influx of hordes of opportunists and men of power. As the Revolution of 1911 progressed and the dynasty appeared doomed, people of vastly different antecedents climbed onto the band wagon of the Revolutionaries. It was not unusual for reformers and members of the Political Information Society, who were now convinced of the inevitability of republicanism, to change sides. A number of mandarins who saw no more use in remaining loyal to the Court and traditional scholars who considered themselves adaptable to progressive ideas, also sought to join the winning side. The number of erstwhile civil and military governors who continued to hold high office in the Revolutionary regime was legion. The influx of the multitude of self-seeking opportunists made a common policy definitely more difficult to agree upon.

Sun Yat-sen retired from the presidency at the end of March 1912. For a time he ceased to be politically active. According to the explanation he made years later, he was at that time extremely disgusted with the manner in which his followers approached the problems of the time. He protested that he would have preferred his party to adhere unswervingly to his Three Principles, and also to the Three-Stage Procedure of military unification, political tutelage, and constitutional government, which he had first advocated early in 1905.[5] Whether this was foresight or a mere hindsight, the fact remained that Sun Yat-sen was inactive in 1912 when the organization of the Kuomintang, of which he was made titular head, took place. He appeared sincerely to hope that Yuan Shih-k'ai would make judicious use of his powers as President of the Republic.

Huang Hsing was also largely inactive. He had goodheartedly, though somewhat naively, disbanded the forces under his command, thinking that his own example might be emulated by the other military leaders of the country. Like the scholars of the past he believed in the force of exemplary conduct.

The Parliamentary Kuomintang

Unlike Sun Yat-sen and Huang Hsing, Sung Chiao-jen was anxious to introduce into China and impose on Yuan Shih-k'ai the cabinet system of government, using the Kuomintang for the accomplishment of the purpose. Sung Chiao-jen was not a self-seeking man. He was enthusiastic, idealistic, and full of brilliance. He genuinely believed that a responsible party ministry with himself at the head of it was the only hopeful means of preventing Yuan Shih-k'ai from going astray, and of putting China on the path of a stable and progressive government. He wanted sincerely to work to that end with Yuan Shih-k'ai. He little realized that this coöperative sentiment was not reciprocated, and that he was to die at the hands of the man with whom he had contemplated collaboration.

The first step towards realizing his dreams of responsible government was to effect a reorganization of the party of which, next to Sun Yat-sen and Huang Hsing, Sung Chiao-jen was perhaps the most generally accepted leader.

By May 1912 the legislative assembly had moved from Nanking to Peking and there was a marked division in its membership of 120, between the members of the T'ung Meng Hui and those of the Republican Party, a new organization pledged to support Yuan Shih-k'ai. Outside of the Assembly, party reorientation was also taking place. In order to control the majority of the Parliament soon to be elected, Sung Chiao-jen effected, in August, the organization of the Kuomintang, with the old T'ung Meng Hui as its core, but with an amalgamation of a number of newly risen minor parties included. The election of 1912–1913 was a huge success for the Kuomintang and for Sung Chiao-jen personally. He was ready to head a new party cabinet to wrestle with Yuan Shih-k'ai who had caused the fall of the T'ang Shao-yi cabinet, a cabinet of the T'ung Meng Hui, by unconstitutional means the year before. But the prospective premier was assassinated before the convening of the new parliament by the order of Yuan Shih-k'ai.

The Parliament was opened in April 1913. In May, Yuan Shih-k'ai also announced the successful negotiation of an international loan, without previous consultation with the Assembly. The murder of Sung Chiao-jen and the successful negotiation of a loan which everybody knew would be spent for the consolidation of Yuan Shih-k'ai's power at once galvanized the Kuomintang leaders into action. Those members of the Kuomintang who were originally Revolutionaries now saw clearly that there was no further hope in Yuan Shih-k'ai. The Revolution of 1911 was not finished. The overthrow of the Manchus was not sufficient; Yuan Shih-k'ai and his group must also be overthrown. Thus took place the Revolution of 1913 in the summer of that year.

The Revolution failed, but there was to be no more reconciliation between the Kuomintang and Yuan Shih-k'ai. In the election of Yuan Shih-k'ai as President by the Parliament, the milder members of the Kuomintang participated, but even they would not vote for the man. So, when Yuan Shih-k'ai ordered the Kuomintang dissolved and declared it outlawed early in November 1913, there was no other choice for the Kuomintang members but to go underground or become renegades.

The Chinese Revolutionary Party

The underground organization was known as the Chinese Revolutionary Party.[6] Its leader was naturally Sun Yat-sen. He required an oath of loyalty and fingerprints from every member. Both the Three Principles of the People and Three Stages of Government above referred to were emphasized. Further, the members were to be divided into three categories: one, the founding members, who joined the party before the start of the forthcoming revolution, and who were to enjoy a privileged status under the new regime; two, the active members who joined the party before the establishment of the new government and who were to enjoy the rights both of election and of officeholding; and three, ordinary members, who joined after the establishment of the new government and who were to enjoy only the rights of suffrage.

At this time Huang Hsing, Sun Yat-sen's erstwhile lieutenant, somehow wavered in declaring his adherence to the new setup. One theory for this parting of the ways was that Huang Hsing objected to the stratification of the membership, and also to the fingerprinting. Instead of Huang Hsing,

Ch'en Ch'i-mei, a Revolutionary military governor of Shanghai in 1911, now became Sun Yat-sen's chief lieutenant.

Not a small number of the T'ung Meng Hui's original following stood aloof from the new organization. The mild, the respectable, and especially the intelligentsia had always been apathetic towards secret societies. Now that there was no longer the common cause against the Manchus, they had great difficulty in persuading themselves to join one. Some of them organized instead the so-called European Affairs Research Society, ostensibly a study group to discuss the issues arising out of the European war, but in fact an organization not unlike a political party. This also tended to weaken the Chinese Revolutionary Party.

As a link between the old T'ung Meng Hui and the reorganized Kuomintang of later years, the Chinese Revolutionary Party served a purpose. It carried on the revolutionary traditions, especially that uncompromising spirit of earlier days. But there was little actual accomplishment. There were one or two unsuccessful armed uprisings and that was almost all. The most significant act of a promising nature during the intervening years was the anti-Yuan Shih-k'ai campaign, and many actively participated in it. But the Chinese Revolutionary Party was not in a position of leadership. The initiative rested more with individuals who had formerly led the Chinputang, notably Liang Ch'i-ch'ao. The failure of Sun Yat-sen and his followers to play the leading role in that immensely popular movement cost his party the opportunity to focus the attention of the nation on its revolutionary program.

The Splinter Groups

During the 1916–1917 sessions of the Parliament at Peking and the 1918–1920 sessions at Canton there were naturally many party or group alignments among the members, and the old Kuomintang elements also naturally had groupings among themselves. In 1916–1917, the Kuomintang elements were grouped from right to left as follows: Political Study Society, Good Friends Society, Political Club, and Friends of the People Society.[7] All these names meant little of course. But it should be noted that the rightist Political Study group was somewhat inclined to bargain and collaborate with the Northern militarist factions, whereas the Friends of the People group was composed mainly of faithful followers of Sun Yat-sen who had been members of the Chinese Revolutionary Party, and also of a few members of the old Chinputang, who were now bitterly opposed to Tuan Ch'i-jui and the Research Clique.[8]

During the 1918–1920 session of the Parliament, the same groups were in existence, though the Political Club had been absorbed by the Good Friends group and was no longer in separate existence. It is to be remembered that the separatist regime at Canton in these years was insisting on the restoration of the old Constitution and old Parliament and had styled itself the Constitution Protection Government. Sun Yat-sen was there at the head of the movement. But this time the Political Study group was intimately allied with the Southern militarists, and also maintaining contacts with the Northern militarists. The tactics of the Political Study people were causing Sun Yat-sen endless and even intolerable difficulties.

Sun Yat-sen's Canton Regime

There is necessity for recapitulating the events of Canton at this period in some detail because they were instrumental in completing the disillusionment of Sun Yat-sen with the older leaders and the politician elements of his old following and thus preparing him psychologically to consider an entirely different set of political concepts and tactics.

In the fall of 1917 immediately after Feng Kuo-chang's assumption of the presidency at Peking, the Kuomintang groups of the Parliament had begun a special session at Canton, promulgated the Organic Law for the organization of the military government, and elected Sun Yat-sen Generalissimo. Sun Yat-sen expected the Parliament to be able to have a quorum for a normal session by June 1918, but before that was done the Political Study group, with the help of the Good Friends group, was arranging for peace and reunion with the Peking government. They did not want the Parliament to be in normal session. Instead, they sabotaged Sun Yat-sen, abolished the generalissimoship and set up instead a Directorate of Seven in May 1918. Sun Yat-sen was relegated to a mere directorship while an ex-viceroy of the Manchu days, the head of the Kwangsi militarist faction, in close alliance with the Political Study group, was elected Chairman of the Directorate. Sun Yat-sen never attended the Directorate meetings in person, and in August 1919 he sent in his formal resignation.

By September 1918 the Parliament did begin its normal session and did resume deliberations on the unfinished constitution, but on account of the anxiety of the Political Study group to reunite with the North, its sittings were sabotaged by that group, and often had to be suspended. In short, the activities of the Political group with the aid of the Good Friends, both of whom had formerly been Sun Yat-sen's followers, created in Sun Yat-sen an irreconcilable contempt for his old style followers, for party or group politics in Parliament, and even for Parliament itself as an institution.

The fate suffered by Sun Yat-sen at the hands of the Kwangsi militarist faction from 1917 to 1919 created in him also a new resolution, a determination to establish a firm revolutionary base at Canton. It devolved on him to clear all military obstacles at all cost. In doing so he was often compelled to enter into terms of alliance with other military factions, if they happened to be also enemies of his own enemies. If one sympathized with this determination of his, one may also take a charitable view of these alliances. Nevertheless, these military alliances, as has been pointed out above, had undesirable complications for Sun Yat-sen and a bad effect on the character of his successors.

The Kwangsi military faction was, fortunately for Sun Yat-sen, weakened by internal war. The Political Study group was also weakened by the defection of the Good Friends who were rather anxious for the enactment of a constitution and none too happy at the spectacle of the Parliament being made a complete tool of the Kwangsi faction. In October 1920, Ch'en Ch'iung-ming, the leader of the Kwangtung armies and a follower of Sun Yat-sen, had succeeded in entering Canton after expelling the Kwangsi militarists. This marked the end of the ascendancy of both the Political Study group and the Kwangsi faction—at least, for the time being.

Sun Yat-sen returned to Canton in December 1920 and resumed directorship of the military government. In the ensuing months Sun Yat-sen wanted to reorganize the military government and have the Parliament elect a new President of the Republic, thus to deny completely the validity of the Peking regime. But Ch'en Ch'iung-ming advised caution, for he was inclined to the idea of a federated regime of autonomous provinces, a movement which was at its height at the beginning of 1921.

Sun Yat-sen had himself elected President by the Rump Parliament at Canton and assumed the presidency on May 5, 1921. In doing so, he was in effect saying that a new regime had been decided upon and would have no further traffic with the Northern Government. After the successful attempt in June and July to gain control of Kwangsi by the Kwangtung armies under Ch'en Ch'iung-ming, Sun Yat-sen was determined to organize a northern expedition against the militarists of the North. To this Ch'en Ch'iung-ming was opposed. He was still doing lip-service to Sun Yat-sen but he did not offer his armies for the expedition.

The conflict between the two came into the open in the following year. By March 1922 Sun Yat-sen had already entered Hunan by way of Kwangsi, but he had to return to Canton to effect the dismissal of Ch'en Ch'iung-ming as Commander-in-chief of the Kwangtung Armies. He then again went northward. The expedition was having successes in Kiangsi when Sun Yat-sen, who had returned to Canton again to keep a watch on Ch'en Ch'iung-ming, was surrounded by the latter's troops. At the failure of his own troops to reach Canton to reinforce him, he was compelled to flee to Shanghai on August 9, 1922.

It is to be remembered that in June, in Peking, Hsü Shih-ch'ang had fallen and Li Yuan-hung had again been restored. Ch'en Ch'iung-ming was closely linked with the Ts'ao K'un–Wu P'ei-fu faction, which effected this change in the North. Both Ch'en Ch'iung-ming and the ascendant faction in the North were saying that since the old Constitution and the old Parliament were to be restored, there was no longer any constitutional controversy and, therefore, both Hsü Shih-ch'ang and Sun Yat-sen should step out of their respective presidencies.

The expulsion of Sun Yat-sen by Ch'en Ch'iung-ming made the former more than ever resolved to regain and consolidate the base of Canton. He considered any means justified which would contribute to the achievement of this aim. Early in 1922 Chang Tso-lin and Sun Yat-sen had already exchanged emissaries to discuss common action against common enemies. From September on, Sun Yat-sen made further arrangements with both Chang Tso-lin and the remnants of the Tuan Ch'i-jui faction, which had now become aspirants for the control of Fukien.

Fukien fell into the hands of the followers of Sun Yat-sen and Tuan Ch'i-jui by the end of October 1922. Simultaneously the Kwangsi armies, doing the bidding of Sun Yat-sen, were also marching down on Canton. In January 1923, Ch'en Ch'iung-ming was compelled to quit Canton, though he was still to retain control of the area east of Canton. In the following month, after the departure of the military governor appointed by the Peking Government, Sun Yat-sen triumphantly returned to Canton which was thenceforward to remain the base of his party.

On March 2, 1923 Sun Yat-sen assumed the title of Generalissimo and the General Headquarters was installed. By now, he had gained a new conviction of the necessity of revolution and also a new confidence in the success of that revolution. His party was in the process of a radical reorganization and the base was also to be speedily consolidated.

Sun Yat-sen's Reorganization of the Kuomintang

The reorganization of the Kuomintang owed its beginnings to the spreading influence of the Soviet Revolution, and the rise into prominence of the student class.

The intelligentsia in China had always enjoyed a position of preëminence, both social and political. It was the active participation in the T'ung Meng Hui of the Chinese students studying in Japan and in Europe that gave the Revolutionary movement a leadership and an impetus. During the last years of World War I, the students of China were much impressed by Woodrow Wilson's ideas of democracy and of international justice. Over the issue of Japan's hegemony in Shantung the students of Peking had struck against the government on May 4, 1919. The students all over the country followed suit. The movement soon acquired profound political and cultural implications. The new intelligentsia of China were ready for radical changes and were groping for them.

From 1911, the year of Revolution, to 1919, Sun Yat-sen had not been interesting himself in a student following. He now saw a new light. He began to receive student leaders. His utterances also began to evidence his new interest. This renewed partnership with the student body was to give Sun Yat-sen's party a new vitality unknown in the preceding years.

The success of the Soviet Revolution was also to awaken the Chinese to the possibility of an all-absorbing revolution, social as well as political, in any country whose institutions were so outworn as to make social changes inevitable. The Russians themselves did not neglect to stimulate the awakening. To the young intellectuals who had little interest in proprietary rights, communism was hardly an evil sufficient to weigh against the apostles of anti-imperialism. To many, communism had even a positive attraction.

When the Soviet emissaries came to China with the purpose of seeking the collaboration of the Chinese, they came into hospitable terrain where the body of the people were well disposed toward them. They came also with a free gift, for on July 25, 1919 the Moscow government had announced to the Chinese people the unilateral renunciation of the imperialistic rights which Czarist Russia in common with other powers had exacted from China. The first emissary was a man by the name of Yurin, a representative of the Soviet Far Eastern Republic. Yurin came to Peking in 1920. He failed to contact governmental circles, but the time he spent with the Peking intelligentsia was not without ultimate rich harvests. The Chinese Communist Party had been organized in 1921 and it is not inconceivable that their contact with him had increased their faith in communism and also their knowledge of revolutionary strategy. In August 1922 Adolph Joffe came to Peking. Not only was he warmly received by the intelligentsia, but he also succeeded in securing intimate contact with Sun Yat-sen in Shanghai. As the result of Joffe's activities, two events of great significance took place. The first was the declaration of adherence to the Kuomintang by the leaders of the Chinese Communist Party, and the second was the issuance of a ringing party manifesto by the Kuomintang.

The Chinese Communist Party[9] had been organized in July 1921. For some time it remained undecided on the question of joining the Kuomintang which had the support of Soviet Russia. After its leader, Li Ta-chao, a professor of the Peking University, joined the Kuomintang as an individual in August 1922, the party soon (in June 1923) gave approval to all its members to do so.

The Kuomintang Manifesto of 1923 ushered in the process of reorganization which was completed a year later. The Chinese Revolutionary Party had died out in 1918. On October 10, 1919 a new name, Chung-kuo Kuomintang, the Chinese Nationalist Party, had been formally adopted, but the party remained inactive. Sun Yat-sen was either in exile in Shanghai reading and writing, or conducting bitter fights with his enemies and rivals at Canton. He paid scant attention to the activities of the party. But with the issuance of the Manifesto of January 1, 1923 the party again came into the open. From now on it was to be ceaselessly active the whole country over.

The Manifesto reasserts the Three Principles and redefines them somewhat in the light of the Russian Revolution. This was especially true with regard to the Principles of Nationalism and Democracy. For the first time there was mention of the racial minorities in China and a denunciation of representative democracy. However, on the Third Principle, the Principle of the People's Livelihood, the connotations remained vaguely socialistic, and far from communistic.

That Sun Yat-sen was only friendly to communism because of his eagerness to inject the Soviet revolutionary spirit into his own party and was not himself converted to communism was made even more plain by the Sun Yat-sen–Joffe joint agreement of policy on January 26, 1923. The declaration says: "Dr. Sun Yat-sen holds that the Communist order or even the Soviet system cannot actually be introduced into China, because there do not exist here the conditions for the successful establishment of either Communism or Sovietism. This view is entirely shared by Mr. Joffe, who is further of the opinion that China's paramount and most pressing problem is to achieve national unification and attain full independence, and regarding this task he assured Dr. Sun Yat-sen that China has the warmest sympathy of the Russian people and can count on the support of Russia."[10]

Sun Yat-sen was now preparing in earnest to recast his party. He had had innumerable conferences with his lieutenants, informing the believers and convincing the unbelievers of the necessity for the party to follow the pattern of the Russian Communist Party in reorganization and in tactics. A preparatory committee for reorganization was instituted by him. On January 20, 1924 the first Party Congress was held at Canton with members of the Chinese Communist Party participating. The Congress enacted a party statute, set up an organization, both central and local, and adopted and issued a manifesto which looked forward to close coöperation with Soviet Russia.

The Russian impact was most manifest in the fields of party organization and tactics, of military training and organization, and of revolutionary strategy in regard to foreign relations. The party organization was now closely modeled after the Russian Communist Party with the Organization Department playing a dominant role in the organization and control of the membership. A new military academy for cadets was set up at Whampoa in May 1924, with Chiang Kai-shek, who had been in Moscow in the summer of 1923 to study the organization of the Red Army, at its head, and with Liao

Chung-k'ai, another man who had had intimate dealings with the Russians, as the party commissar. A group of Russian advisers, led by Michael Borodin and Galens[11] who had arrived in October 1923, were instrumental in effecting both the reorganization of the party and the establishment of the academy.

The Death of Sun Yat-sen and the Second Party Congress

From the reorganization of January 1924, to the establishment of the Kuomintang government at Nanking in April 1927, the attention of the party leaders was mainly focused on the consolidation of the forces in Kwangtung and Kwangsi and subsequent organization of the Northern Expedition. But it was also a period of internal conflict in the party and constant strife with the communists, neither of which was permanently solved by the Second Party Congress of January 1926.

The end of the year 1924 saw the fall of Ts'ao K'un as the president of the Peking government, and the ascendency of Tuan Ch'i-jui as the provisional chief executive. Sun Yat-sen had gone north to confer with the latter and had hoped that a regime to his liking could evolve by agreement. He failed to achieve his purpose, and died in Peking in March 1925.

Upon his death his principal followers at Canton set up a formally "Nationalist Government," or "Kuomin Government,"[12] a term in accordance with Sun Yat-sen's *Fundamentals of National Reconstruction*. This was to serve notice that, although the leader of the party was dead, the party was nevertheless fully determined to carry out his program faithfully and without compromise with forces outside the party. This new government, a committee of sixteen members chosen by the Central Executive Committee of the party with Wang Ching-wei as chairman, served as the model of government to the very end of the Kuomintang tutelage in 1948.

But the establishment of the Nationalist Government was not a sign of unity. The conservatives who had not liked the participation of the communists, and the radicals who had espoused and were still for communist participation, were soon to come to blows. Sun Yat-sen, by his unique position and prestige as the President of the Party, had been able to bridge over many internal differences. But he was no more.

The first sign of dissension was the assassination in August 1925 of Liao Chung-k'ai, an able and trusted follower of Sun Yat-sen, known for his outspoken radicalism. In November of the same year a group of rightist leaders assembled in the Western Hills of Peking[13] and, considering themselves to constitute a session of the Central Executive Committee of the Party, passed a resolution expelling the communists and denouncing the left-wing leaders of their own party. This Western Hills movement of the rightists as well as the new political and military problems facing the Nationalist regime made necessary the convening of the Second National Congress of the Kuomintang.

The Second Congress of the Kuomintang was held in Canton from January 1 to January 20, 1926. It paid homage to Sun Yat-sen and reaffirmed its faith in his bequeathed teachings. The central theme of the Manifesto it issued was "to arouse the masses and to associate ourselves with all the nations of the world who treat us as equals in a common struggle" in order to achieve the revolutionary objectives, as prescribed by Sun Yat-sen's will. The "masses" were of course no other than the peasants and the workers, in addition to the intelligentsia. The foremost nation which accorded the Chinese "equal treatment" was of course none other than Soviet Russia. Elaboration of that theme could not mean other than the redoubling of the policies of the First Congress. The Russian alliance was to be strengthened. Continuing collaboration with the Chinese communists was taken for granted and more communists were in fact elected to the Central Executive and Supervisory Committees, though, for reasons both of pride and perhaps of avoiding unnecessary controversies, the Congress passed no formal resolution touching on the question of communist participation. The Western Hills movement was of course denounced and the leaders were expelled from the party. In short the Second Congress provided anew a green light for the Nationalist Revolutionary movement to proceed.

The Northern Expedition and the Final Triumph

By the middle of 1926, the Nationalist base in the South had been consolidated and a Northern Expedition was ready to start. In October 1924 the Merchant Volunteers Corps of Canton, which had been in close relations of a treacherous nature with Ch'en Ch'iung-ming and made threatening demands on the government, was disbanded by the young cadets of the Whampoa Academy. In February of the following year Ch'en Ch'iung-ming's forces suffered a defeat in the areas east of Canton. The threat from that quarter was thus removed. The remnants were completely wiped out in October.

The Kwangsi troops under a couple of old-fashioned generals who had been helpful to Sun Yat-sen in expelling Ch'en Ch'iung-ming from Canton in the winter of 1922–1923, had also been a thorn to the Nationalist regime. They too were driven off in February 1925. In the years 1924–1925, by a series of successful military moves Kwangsi was also cleared of troublesome military elements and was brought completely under the control of the new regime at Canton.

Thus it may be said that by the end of 1925, or within a half-year of the founding of the Nationalist regime, the base in Kwangtung and Kwangsi provinces was well consolidated. The regime was ready for its next move, the Northern Expedition.

The Northern Expedition made its start in July 1926. To Chiang Kai-shek, who had contributed much to the consolidation of the base in the two previous years, naturally fell the duties both of organizing and commanding the Expedition. There was some dispute as to the wisdom of such a move, considering the rather inferior military position of the South as compared with that of its enemies and also the internal dissension that was increasing rather than subsiding. The advocates of a Northern Expedition, of whom Chiang Kai-shek was a leader, argued that a political vacuum already existed around the Yangtze and in the North, and consequently the resistance of the Northern militarists would be weak. They also argued that a successful Northern Expedition would divert the party leaders and even the communists from factional strife. They, therefore, maintained that the Northern Expedition should have everything to gain and nothing to lose.

There was indeed a vacuum to be filled. The rapidity of the success of the Expedition surprised even the most sanguine. Within three months of its start, the Nationalist forces had gained control of the important city of Hankow and its neighborhood. By March 1927 the lower Yangtze provinces and the Nanking-Shanghai area had also fallen into the hands of the Nationalist Revolutionary armies.

In January 1927 the Nationalist Government was moved from Canton to the Wuhan cities. A series of demonstrations to recover the concessions of the foreign powers in the mid-Yangtze cities were staged successfully. Chiang Kai-shek and his supporters became disaffected by the radicalism of the Wuhan government, meaning its collaboration with the communists, and they set up their own Nationalist Government at Nanking in April 1927. These two governments were later merged and the subsequent government at Nanking evolved as the common government.

While this split and reunification were in process, the Northern Expedition continued. The choice of the Northern warlords was between destruction and submission. The last ones to make that choice were Chang Tso-lin and Chang Hsüeh-liang, father and son, the heads of the Northeastern military faction. The former fled from Peking in June 1928 and was mysteriously done away with by the Japanese. The latter on the last day of 1928 hoisted the Kuomintang colors in his citadel at Mukden, thus signifying his submission to the Nanking regime. That was the final consummation of the Northern Expedition. A reunited China thus reappeared for the first time since Chang Hsün's restoration of the Manchus in 1917.

VII

CHIANG KAI-SHEK'S RISE TO POWER WITHIN THE KUOMINTANG

The Kuomintang which was to be the ruler of China after 1927 was not characterized by either unity or peace. Frequent schisms among its political leaders and costly wars among its military chieftains were to disrupt the party for years on end. The disruption was terminated only by the outbreak of the War of Resistance in the summer of 1937.

I. Political Rivalries

Right versus Left

At the time of the Reorganization a leftist and rightist tendency among the leaders of the party had already been discernible. The principal issue which divided them was the question of collaboration with the communists. It was due solely to the magnetic and forceful leadership of Sun Yat-sen that they stayed united for some time.

With the establishment of the Nationalist Government in July 1925, following the death of Sun Yat-sen and the assumption of the Chairmanship of the Government by Wang Ching-wei, an impetuous man who espoused collaboration with the communists, the Right became sorely disaffected.

The assassination in August 1925 of Liao Chung-k'ai, mentioned above, was the beginning of a dissension between the Right and the Left. Although the real culprits could not be found, Hu Han-min, a leader of conservative tendencies and a rival of Wang Ching-wei, was yet obliged to leave for Moscow, and suspicions and rivalries from now on infested the high councils of the party. The open denunciation of the Leftists by the Western Hills group led to the expulsion of that group by the party at its second Congress.

Shortly after the Second Party Congress, there occurred at Canton on March 20, 1926, the affair of the naval vessel *Chung-shan*. Chiang Kai-shek had suddenly arrested the captain of the boat and then relieved a number of communists from posts of importance in the Canton administration. Though he refused to give any explanation other than a necessity to maintain the harmony of the party, his action was plainly the culmination of factional strife within the party. It caused murmurs, suspicions, and unrest in Canton, and subsequently Wang Ching-wei, then Chairman of the Nationalist Government, who had not been previously advised of the affair, left his post and went abroad.

While Chiang Kai-shek's headquarters were at Nanchang in Kiangsi, the friction between the Nationalists and the Communists had come to a head. Chiang Kai-shek was determined to hold the communists in check by fair means or foul. This meant a struggle with Wang Ching-wei. When Wang Ching-wei, who had been away from China, rejoined the Nationalist Government in Wuhan in March 1927 and advocated continuous collaboration with the Communist Party, Chiang Kai-shek took action. On the basis of a resolution passed by those members of the Central Executive Committee of the party who followed his anti-communist lead, he set up a rival Nationalist Government at Nanking, and declared that the Wuhan regime was Communist-controlled and therefore non-Nationalist. A very severe purge of the Communists from the Kuomintang ranks and large-scale murder and persecutions took place in the lower Yangtze Valley. A little later in 1927, however, the Wuhan government also conducted a purge, and reunion of the Wuhan and Nanking governments became a possibility.

Temporary Reunion of the Party

Strangely enough, the Western Hills group, the rightist wing of the party which had been denounced by the Second Congress and had no voice either in the party councils or in the Nationalist Government, now undertook to act as intermediary between Nanking and Wuhan, generally taken to represent the center and left wings of the party respectively. The result was a tripartite reunion of the party in September 1927. A Special Committee was organized, composed of an equal number of representatives of the three wings. It was to take the place both of the Central Executive Committee elected by the Congress of the Western Hills group and also of the Central Executive Committee elected by the Second Congress of the Kuomintang at Canton, in which the groups of both Wang Ching-wei and Chiang Kai-shek had a share. The National Government reorganized by the Special Committee was of course also held responsible to it.

The Special Regime thus established did not last long. Chiang Kai-shek had been ousted and had gone to Japan as a result of the Nanking generals' anxiety to seek a reunion with Wuhan. But he had not relaxed his control of the army or of the Organization Department of the party. His followers in Nanking never ceased to denounce the Western Hills leadership of the Nationalist Government.

By November 1927, the position of the Western Hills group in the government had become untenable. Chiang Kai-shek and Wang Ching-wei made concerted efforts to effect their ousting. If the scheme had gone well, it would have meant a joint leadership of Wang Ching-wei and Chiang Kai-shek, but strange things again happened. There was a communist uprising on December 11, 1927, in Canton, and a number of Wang Ching-wei's followers were implicated. Wang Ching-wei never attended the sessions of the revived Central Executive Committee. Chiang Kai-shek was given effective control of the party and the Nanking government in February 1928, by virtue of his reinstatement as Chairman of the resurrected Military Commission and Commander-in-Chief of the Armies.

The Triumvirate of Hu Han-min, Wang Ching-wei, and Chiang Kai-shek [1]

An old disciple of Sun and also a leader of prominence in the Kuomintang was Hu Han-min, who was a scholar in the accepted literary tradition and had been active in the T'ung Meng Hui days. Hu Han-min had deputized for Sun Yat-sen as Generalissimo of the Canton Military Government when the latter went to Peking in November 1924. He left Canton on the occasion of Liao Chung-k'ai's assassination. He came back into politics to join with Chiang Kai-shek at the inception of the Nanking government, in April 1927. He also followed Chiang into the wilderness in June of that year. He was invited by Chiang Kai-shek and the right wing of the party to rejoin the government after Peking had fallen into the hands of the Nationalists in 1928. He counseled immediate adoption of a Five-Power system of government. When that was done in October 1928, Chiang Kai-shek became President [2] of the National Government and Hu Han-min himself the head of its legislative branch. Thus Hu Han-min and Chiang Kai-shek entered into a partnership in control of both the party and the government which was to last over three years.

The personal rivalry between Wang Ching-wei and Hu Han-min, both of Kwangtung, both old followers of Sun Yat-sen and both ambitious, had always been keen, since the early days of the T'ung Meng Hui. The difference in their temperaments, Wang Ching-wei being impetuous, demagogic, opportunistic, and Hu Han-min stubborn, pedagogic, but sincere, further widened the chasm. During the preceding four or five years the two had seldom stayed together at the seat of Kuomintang power. When the one was prominent and in control of the situation, the other usually stayed put, though no break had yet taken place, and the two had been equally devoted to the promotion of Kuomintang interests.

The different courses they took in the months immediately preceding the reunification of the two Nationalist governments of Wuhan and Nanking, Wang Ching-wei espousing the cause of Wuhan and favoring continued participation of the communists, and Hu Han-min upholding the communist-suppressing Nanking government, tended to make the two men the leaders of the left and right wings of the Kuomintang.

Chiang Kai-shek was a latecomer and in the few years he was at Canton he did not have much interest in things other than military. When the open break with the communists came in the spring of 1927, Chiang Kai-shek and Hu Han-min were together. But whereas, from now on, Hu Han-min showed a decided leaning toward working as well as thinking with the Western Hills group, Chiang Kai-shek's position remained fluid for a time. After the Canton uprising of December 1927, when the Wang Ching-wei group was bitterly denounced by the right-wingers as communist, Chiang Kai-shek kept his own counsel and appeared more often as the mediator between the two extreme wings than the ally of either.

The Chiang Kai-shek–Hu Han-min leadership of the new Five-Power Government of October 1928 marked the beginning of a period of tripartite factional strife within the Kuomintang. Chiang Kai-shek was never to give up his position of real power. But for the immediate future it still remained necessary for him to govern the party and the country with the help of either Hu Han-min or Wang Ching-wei. A combination of both of them in opposition was still too strong for him.

The Chiang Kai-shek–Hu Han-min Combination

After Chiang Kai-shek and Hu Han-min had come together, in October 1928, Wang Ching-wei and his group went further to the left. They accused the Nanking regime of having betrayed Sun Yat-sen's Principles and demanded both democracy and a radical program of socialist changes. They demanded further reorganization of the party to purge it of the reactionaries and unfaithfuls in order that the spirit of the 1924 reorganization might again prevail. They were thus known as Reorganizationists. They were able to find some following among the intelligentsia, who were disaffected with Nanking's undemocratic tendencies, not knowing that Wang Ching-wei himself was no democrat. The group was subjected to much calumny and denunciation. At the Third Congress of the Kuomintang held in Nanking in March 1929, some of the leaders were expelled from the party. That only drove them to seek any means to overthrow Chiang Kai-shek.

Wang Ching-wei had been in alliance with a minor militarist, T'ang

Sheng-chih, who revolted against Nanking in the winter of 1929–1930. When that fizzled, Wang Ching-wei coalesced with Feng Yü-hsiang and Yen Hsi-shan in 1930. In July, Wang Ching-wei called a so-called Expanded Session of the Kuomintang's Central Executive Committee at Peiping. Both a Central Party headquarters and a National Government were set up, with Wang Ching-wei and Yen Hsi-shan as their respective heads. Like the government at Nanking, it was a government in the period of Kuomintang tutelage. Therefore, if his party organization could claim to be the legitimate one, the government created by it could also be legitimate. Unfortunately for the secessionists, this grand coalition was attacked from the rear, by Chang Hsüeh-liang from Mukden, and by October 1930 the revolt had failed and both Wang Ching-wei and Yen Hsi-shan had to flee.

Ironically enough, Wang Ching-wei's movement was to drive a wedge between Chiang Kai-shek and Hu Han-min. Wang Ching-wei had insisted on having a provisional constitution as an instrument of government for the period of tutelage. He was, of course, catering to a group of non-Kuomintang intelligentsia, to whom a fundamental law which would be binding on the Kuomintang as well as on the people was considered a necessity. During the brief life of Wang Ching-wei's regime in the North, a Draft Provisional Constitution [3] was completed and even received some publicity.

While the campaign against the rebels was still going on, Chiang Kai-shek suddenly proposed to the party that the time had arrived to give the people a provisional constitution. He had not consulted Hu Han-min before making this rather unexplainable departure from the position he had taken in common with Hu Han-min at the time of the adoption of the Five-Power system of government in October 1928; at that time it had been agreed by both Chiang Kai-shek and Hu Han-min that for the period of tutelage the whole body of Sun Yat-sen's teachings formed the law of the land, and no provisional constitution was necessary. Hu Han-min was now taken by surprise. Being a man of stubborn convictions, he objected to the proposal, and did so uncompromisingly. Chiang Kai-shek was, however, equally determined to have the provisional constitution, and on March 1, 1931 had Hu Han-min taken into protective custody, meanwhile protesting that it was not an arrest, but was meant as a means of "conserving" the revolutionary reputation of Hu Han-min. At a later occasion Hu Han-min was allowed to leave Nanking again as a free person. But the wound was never healed, and the two never again saw eye-to-eye.

The Anti-Chiang Kai-shek Combination

The alienation of both Wang Ching-wei and Hu Han-min was followed by the gathering of anti-Chiang Kai-shek elements at Canton. On May 27,

1931, when Nanking was preparing to convene the National Convention to vote for the Provisional Constitution prepared by the Central Executive Committee of the party, an extraordinary session of members of the same committee met at Canton. Nanking was denounced. Both a party and a government headquarters were set up, each naturally claiming to be the legitimate repository of power. Hu Han-min was still detained at Nanking, but his friends and followers took an active part in setting up the rival regime. Wang Ching-wei's group also joined.

Unstable alliance of incompatible rivals that it was, it did prove to be somewhat too strong for Chiang Kai-shek. When Japan began its easy conquest of the northeastern provinces on September 18, 1931, and the country at large was eager for a united resistance to the foreign foe, it was not difficult for Canton to demand a high price for the union. Hu Han-min was given freedom. That was not enough. The leaders of Canton refused to come to Nanking for the united party meetings until after military control of the Nanking-Shanghai area was in their hands. Chiang Kai-shek again had to quit and in his place Lin Sen was elected President of the National Government and an adherent of Canton was made interim President of the Executive Yuan, later to be succeeded by Sun Fo. All this was done in December 1931.

The over-all situation at that time was such that Chiang Kai-shek, who was in control both of the armed forces and the financial interests of the country, had become indispensable to any unified government. A combination of the groups of both Hu Han-min and Wang Ching-wei might be strong enough to oppose him, but fell far short of the strength necessary for a stable regime of their own. The Nanking regime of December 1931 and January 1932 was not even the full strength of that combination. It was a patched-up coalition of minor leaders; neither Wang Ching-wei nor Hu Han-min, who had a common interest in the ousting of Chiang Kai-shek, were in the regime.

The Chiang Kai-shek–Wang Ching-wei Combination

If a weak regime had little chance to overcome the sabotage of the military and financial supporters of Chiang Kai-shek, it had still less chance to tackle the problems created by the war in Shanghai against the Japanese. In the early months of 1932, profiting by the sad experiences of governing without the aid of either Hu Han-min or Wang Ching-wei, Chiang Kai-shek now staged a comeback with Wang Ching-wei, aided by the accelerating paralysis of Sun Fo's administration. Wang Ching-wei took unto himself the important post of the presidency of the Executive Yuan. For Chiang Kai-shek the Military Commission was resurrected, and its chairmanship was created for him. Lin Sen was allowed to continue as the President of the National Government, now of little real power, as prescribed by the law of December 30, 1931. Thus began for nearly four years a partnership of Chiang Kai-shek and Wang Ching-wei.

The new partnership was a comfortable one for neither. Chiang Kai-shek was not comfortable because Wang Ching-wei was the head of the Executive Yuan, at least nominally in charge of administration. Wang Ching-wei was also uncomfortable, for the Chairman of the Military Commission had the control of the armed forces and when the anti-communist campaign was on in earnest, from 1933 on, the Commander-in-Chief was also in effective control of the provinces infested by the communists. That both were leading members of the party's Central Executive Committee meant also that there were in the party councils many mutual checks. On the whole, the man with the military forces behind him could naturally stay at the top as far as real influence was concerned.

When, at the Fifth Congress of the Kuomintang in November 1935, Wang Ching-wei was shot and lay sick, Chiang Kai-shek became in name as well as in fact the President of the Executive Yuan, a position which he had held before the end of 1931. There was, however, no open break between the two at this time. Later, Wang Ching-wei went abroad for a cure and returned before the start of the Sino-Japanese War in 1937 to accept the position of Deputy-Leader of the party. Ostensibly the collaboration of Chiang Kai-shek and Wang Ching-wei was also resumed. But the latter was soon to flee the country again and ultimately to set up a puppet government at Nanking to collaborate with the Japanese. His personal ambitions thus finally resulted in his complete ruin.

Hu Han-min, as has been said above, never again worked with Chiang Kai-shek after his detention by the latter in 1931. He died at Canton in May 1936. For about two years there had been a kind of autonomous regime in Canton. A Political Council for the Southwest, composed of those members of the National Government Council and the Central Executive Committee of the Kuomintang who enjoyed influence and had interest in the provinces of Kwangtung and Kwangsi, acted independently of Nanking. The relations between Hu Han-min and this Southwestern Council were close. In fact Hu Han-min could be considered the leader of the autonomous movement. Following Hu Han-min's death, the militarists who were backing the Council staged a revolt against Chiang Kai-shek. When that failed and the latter extended his military influence to Canton, the Council was dissolved and the semi-independence of the regime also vanished.

II. Military Rivalries

Side by side with the schisms within the party, there were incessant military defections which often took the form of large-scale civil wars.

The Four Army Groups

At the end of the Northern Expedition, almost the whole body of Chinese armies had been incorporated into the Nationalist Revolutionary Army, with Chiang Kai-shek as Commander-in-Chief and with Chiang Kai-shek, Feng Yü-hsiang, Yen Hsi-shan, and Li Tsung-jen, respectively, as commanders of the four Army Groups. There were a number of military commanders in the Southwest who had not yet been brought under close control, but none of them had great influence.

Outside the four Army Groups, the only group that was in a position to affect the course of events was the one commanded by Chang Hsüeh-liang, son of the Mukden war lord, Chang Tso-lin. Due to the opposition of Japan to the Nationalists' carrying the campaign into the northeastern provinces which she considered her sphere of influence, the Nationalist forces were precluded from the possibility of making a clean finish of Chang Hsüeh-liang. That Chang Hsüeh-liang declared for the Nationalist Government towards the end of 1928 was in a way fortunate for China, for she could thus postpone the dangerous decision as to when to have a showdown with the Japanese.

It was plain that if the four Army Groups could be closely knit together, bad units weeded out, and the total number greatly reduced, Nationalist China could have a new life, free from military domination and also from the civil wars that had so horribly sapped the strength of the Chinese nation in the years of the warlords. These needed steps the four great commanders, joined by General Li Chi-shen, had solemnly pledged themselves to carry out. There was solemnity in their pledge for they made it at Peking in front of the then resting place of Sun Yat-sen's remains after they had all made their triumphal entry into the northern capital. They agreed to call a conference forthwith to discuss and to effect the reorganization and disbandment of the armies.

As soon as the conference was called at Nanking in the beginning of 1929, dissension began to appear. Of the four Army Groups Chiang Kai-shek's was the strongest. The units officered by the graduates of the Whampoa Academy were in it. Naturally this First Army Group considered itself to be the backbone of the Nationalist Revolutionary Army and to have contributed most to the success of the Northern Expedition.

The Second Army Group, under the command of Feng Yü-hsiang, was also a huge one. At the time of his coup d'état against Ts'ao K'un, the President of the Peking Government, in October 1924, Feng Yü-hsiang had created the Kuo-min chün or Nationalist Army (the name of course to denote affinity with the Kuomintang) out of the forces he had himself commanded and two other large forces, commanded and to some extent officered by men who were either veteran members of the T'ung Meng Hui or sympathetic to the Kuomintang. The Kuo-min chün had three armies and Feng Yü-hsiang was commander-in-chief and concurrently commander of the First Army in it. In numbers it was a massive thing, and in quality Feng Yü-hsiang's men were no mean fighters. In contrast to the usual undisciplined and demoralized troops of the Northern military factions, they lived puritanically and fought doggedly. These virtues of his troops enabled Feng Yü-hsiang to keep himself from sinking as most of the Northern militarists did, and to shift his men to the popular cause of the Nationalist Revolution. In throwing in his lot with the Revolutionary Army, he indeed greatly facilitated the success of the Northern Expedition. It was therefore natural that he tended to resent any treatment that savored of discrimination.

Yen Hsi-shan's Third Army Group was somewhat smaller in size. It grew out of the nucleus of his purely provincial forces. Yen Hsi-shan had been in control of Shansi Province since the very beginning of the Republic. He had managed his fortunes well all through these years. He was originally also a T'ung Meng Hui member. After Feng Yü-hsiang had brought the Kuo-min chün into the fold of the Nationalist Revolutionary Army of the South, it was easy to persuade Yen Hsi-shan to do likewise, in the beginning of 1927. He also expanded his forces greatly. With Feng Yü-hsiang, he had a full share in making Chang Tso-lin's military position untenable inside the Great Wall. In other words, his contribution to the success of the Northern Expedition, especially in the northwestern provinces, was also not to be forgotten, and he also had valid claims at the Army Reorganization and Disbandment Conference.

The Fourth Army Corps of Li Tsung-jen had gained a commensurate position at the close of the Northern Expedition. Li Tsung-jen had long been with the troops of Kwangsi Province. By 1924 he had risen to such prominence that Sun Yat-sen saw fit to entrust to him the pacification of the province. From that time on, Li Tsung-jen played a prominent part in the military affairs of the Canton regime and the forces under his command also fought valiantly from the very beginning of the Northern Expedition. The Fourth Army Group which he eventually led as his military horizon widened was a collection of the units originally under his command and the other units of the southern provinces. If the term "northern" could be at all properly applied to the Second and Third Groups, to apply it to the Fourth was out of place. In other words, even more than the Second and the Third, the

Fourth Army Group prided itself on being a Revolutionary Army and so claimed equality of treatment.

At the Army Reorganization and Disbandment Conference, all agreed that the army had to be greatly reduced in number and improved in quality. The questions were where should the axe fall and where should preferred treatment as to pay and equipment go? It was natural for Chiang Kai-shek to have greater trust in the units commanded by graduates of the Whampoa Academy, for he understandably believed those graduates to be more deeply attached to the cause of Revolution than the other officers. Those units should therefore be kept and improved upon. But the heads of the other Groups maintained that military achievements during the Expedition should not be ignored, and in case of failure to agree on criteria satisfactory to all, pro rata reduction should be resorted to. The conference thus dragged on, without good results. Instead it engendered suspicion and eventually conflicts among the former comrades of a common cause.

Revolt of the Kwangsi Faction

The first conflict, in March and April of 1929, ended in the elimination of Li Tsung-jen and his friends as a military and political power of national importance. In the course of the Northern Expedition, the armies of the Fourth Group had spread far and wide. In the spring of 1929 they were still in firm possesison of the Wuhan area and the two provinces of Kwangtung and Kwangsi. But the intervening province of Hunan was not in their hands. In case of an assault against them, their position was vulnerable. So the more outspoken but less shrewd elements, in the name of the Wuhan Political Council, which they controlled and which had authority over the regions near by, ordered the dismissal of the governor of Hunan Province, alleging as an excuse his failure to suppress the communists in that province. Clashes occurred at once.

For a moment it looked doubtful that Nanking could win easily. However, the high Kwangsi leaders of the Fourth Army Group, including Li Tsung-jen himself, were hesitant to stage an open break. In fact, Li Tsung-jen was hoping for some amicable settlement, not based on the one-sided reduction of the Fourth Army Group. Another of their leaders, Li Chi-shen, even offered to mediate. But in the meantime Nanking had successfully exerted pressures of both a brutal and a velvet-glove kind, on commanders of the Group not strictly of Kwangsi origin, and they had agreed not to support the Kwangsi leaders. Nanking also detained Li Chi-shen. The open break came and the battles were soon fought. But pitched against Nanking were only the Kwangsi armies, and not the whole of the old Fourth Army Group. Nanking won easily. The Kwangsi forces were from now on to be confined to the province of Kwangsi, not to come out again until the war against Japan necessitated their service.

Revolt of T'ang Sheng-chih

The second revolt was that of T'ang Sheng-chih, who declared in October 1929 for Wang Ching-wei, then opposed to Nanking. T'ang Sheng-chih was the military chieftain of Hunan who had declared his allegiance to the Nationalist regime at the very beginning of the Northern Expedition. He was ambitious and was disaffected at not having received a position of influence which he thought he deserved. He was, however, speedily defeated, and by January 1930 his own troops had left him to take orders from Nanking, a pattern which was followed in almost all the civil wars of this period.

Revolt of Feng Yü-hsiang and Yen Hsi-shan

The difficulties that Feng Yü-hsiang at first alone and then in company with Yen Hsi-shan raised for Nanking were far more serious. In May 1929, shortly after the defeat of the Kwangsi generals, Feng Yü-hsiang had sensed danger in the areas controlled by his followers. There were troop dispositions which seemed to be threatening them. Feng Yü-hsiang had his troops in Shantung withdrawn to Honan, hoping to make a stand there. He was not destined, however, to make an all-out armed resistance, for some of his principal lieutenants had had secret understandings with Nanking, and their going-over left no choice for him except to give up the command entirely.

By May 1930, Yen Hsi-shan had also reached a decision to resist and had rejected the alternative of completely submitting himself to Nanking. He and Feng Yü-hsiang were able to work together, with the Kwangsi leaders voicing their general support. In fact, earlier in February, Kwangsi had urged Yen Hsi-shan and Feng Yü-hsiang to assume the titles of Commander-in-Chief and Deputy Commander-in-Chief of the armed forces of China, and in April they did take up the titles with Li Tsung-jen also becoming a Deputy Commander-in-Chief. There was fierce fighting around the railways of Central and North China. The war soon took on a political meaning when Wang Ching-wei arrived in Peiping and party and government headquarters were established there, as noted above. The revolting forces were to some extent the losers, but it was doubtful whether Nanking could take Peiping entirely on its own strength. Thanks to the march of Chang Hsüeh-liang, the Peiping regime collapsed by itself in October 1930, and another war was won.

Feng Yü-hsiang had more trouble in store for Nanking. He was never quite defeated on the battleground. The generals who deserted him and took orders from Nanking were also never too loyal to Chiang Kai-shek personally. It may be that they were different from Chiang Kai-shek's own followers; it may be also that they were differently treated. Anyhow Feng Yü-hsiang was able to retain some influence on many of his former commanders. In May 1933, as the result of the Japanese advance toward the Great Wall in the Jehol and Chahar areas, Feng Yü-hsiang set up a General Headquarters of Federated Kuomin Japan-Resisting Armies at Kalgan with himself as the commander-in-chief. This move of Feng Yü-hsiang's was very embarrassing to Nanking. Resistance was popular in the North. To order a punitive campaign against Feng Yü-hsiang would risk the popularity of the government still further. Furthermore, the deployment of troops to conduct the campaign against Feng Yü-hsiang was also physically difficult, for that part of China was already checkered with Japanese and pro-Japanese units, through which the Nanking troops could not easily move.

Feng Yü-hsiang was later persuaded to leave Kalgan and for some time he lived the life of a hermit on the sacred mountain of Taishan. But it was much later that he made up with Chiang Kai-shek. In November 1935, as a gesture of sacred union against the Japanese, both Feng Yü-hsiang and Yen Hsi-shan, together with all the civilian leaders of the party, especially Hu Han-min, were urged to attend the Fifth Kuomintang Congress at Nanking. Feng Yü-hsiang and Yen Hsi-shan did attend and they were made deputy-chairmen of the Military Commission. Thus ended a long feud between them and Chiang Kai-shek, a feud to be renewed in Feng Yü-hsiang's case in the postwar years.

Revolt in Fukien

Toward the end of 1933 another civil war broke out between Nanking and the forces which had played a distinguished role both in the Northern Expedition and in the earlier campaigns of Nanking against its opponents. A number of Kwangtung armies including the famous Nineteenth Route Army, which fought the Japanese in Shanghai in 1932, were suspected by and consequently disaffected with the government. Led by Li Chi-shen and Ch'en Ming-shu and joined by a number of civilian Kuomintang radicals, they set up a People's Government in Fukien in November 1933. Their slogans were resistance to the Japanese and democracy for the Chinese. They had hoped that a popular movement could thus be started and other disaffected military leaders would rise throughout the country. But the hands of Nanking were firm. No such movement and no such uprising materialized. Isolated, they were speedily defeated by January 1934.

Revolt of Kwangtung and Kwangsi

The fall of this People's Government of the Southern military commanders was, however, not the end of the troubles from that quarter. The year 1936 witnessed another abortive move from Kwangtung and Kwangsi provinces. When the Kwangsi generals suffered defeat in 1929 in the middle Yangtze, they were not annihilated. They remained in Kwangsi. In the meantime, the governor of Kwangtung, General Ch'en Chi-t'ang, had enormously expanded his armies. Both the Kwangsi and the Kwangtung generals were supporting the Southwest Executive Office and the Southwest Political Council, theoretically branches of the Central Executive Committee of the Party and of the Government Council respectively. Nanking's attempts to subjugate them only increased their resistance and insubordination.

In the summer of 1936 Ch'en Chi-t'ang and Li Tsung-jen assumed the titles of Commander-in-Chief and Deputy Commander-in-Chief of the Federated Japan-Resisting Patriots' Armies and moved forces northward, claiming that they wanted to contact the Japanese. The embarrassment for Nanking was extreme. To tolerate the move meant the loss of control of the situation; to fight it would seriously affect the Central Government positions in other areas.

The impasse was removed without a bloody fight only by a happy combination of skillful placating of the one and the desired defection in the ranks of the other. Some of Ch'en Chi-t'ang's generals were amiably persuaded to desert their chief with the promise of attractive placement. Ch'en Chi-t'ang was thus destroyed from beneath. To placate Li Tsung-jen, whose subordinates were more loyal than Ch'en Chi-t'ang's and were not to be easily shuffled around, a new National Defense Committee was ordered set up with the military leaders of the two provinces included, to symbolize Nanking's determination to resist the Japanese. Under the circumstances, there was scarcely any other choice for Li Tsung-jen than to accept the compromise and to wait for further developments. The abortive move of 1936 in the South thus netted for the Central Government the control of Kwangtung Province.

The Sian Incident

While units of the former Second, Third, and Fourth Army Groups, and even units of the First, were making recurrent trouble for Chiang Kai-shek, the Northeastern troops of Chang Hsüeh-liang served him rather faithfully. Chang Hsüeh-liang had been given high military commands with appropriate titles, second only to Chiang Kai-shek himself. A skillful splitting up of the Northeastern troops had led the Nanking authorities to believe that the Northeasterners were safe and reliable enough.

It was, however, a fact that many of the Northeastern commanders were homesick, and they desired a more determined policy of resisting the Japanese aggressors. Of that sentiment Chang Hsüeh-liang was aware. Communists had infiltrated into his headquarters, and he, an impressionable young man, had been favorably impressed with their ideas of a united front against the Japanese. So, in December 1936, Chang Hsüeh-liang, who was then in Sian ostensibly to effect the encirclement of the communist forces, executed something extraordinarily dramatic. In collaboration with the governor of the province, a commander who had once been a subordinate of Feng Yü-hsiang, he detained Chiang Kai-shek.

The detention naturally created a great stir throughout the country and even abroad. The government at Nanking was in a quandary. To order a military campaign against Chang Hsüeh-liang and his associates might endanger the life of Chiang Kai-shek, the head of the armed forces of China. To resort to peaceful settlement in order to secure the release of Chiang Kai-shek, the government might have to agree to something like a united front against the Japanese. The government was of course solicitous about the safety of its military leader; so also was the populace in general. The people were for a war against the Japanese; and the government could not profess otherwise. There was then very little avowed difference between the government and the people as to the wise step to take.

But this difference did exist: while the people had by this time come to the realization that to resist a common foreign foe was of urgent necessity and to continue with the civil war was a pure dissipation of national strength, the government's and Chiang Kai-shek's policy for the past years had always been "to suppress the internal foe in order to prepare for resistance against the foreign enemy." To agree to the united front, a condition upon which Chang Hsüeh-liang insisted and for which the communist emissaries, who were working for a peaceful solution of the incident, naturally stood, would mean the reversal of the policy towards the realization of which the government had in the past years directed its principal attention.

However, Chiang Kai-shek, the detainee himself, seemed to have discerned the expediency of agreeing to a united front against Japan. On December 25, 1936, Chiang Kai-shek was released. Immediately he flew back to Nanking, accompanied by his captor, Chang Hsüeh-liang, who was to submit himself to the disciplinary measures the government might see fit to impose on him. He was sentenced to ten years of imprisonment, was pardoned almost as soon, but has remained in protective custody ever since, a fact which has caused repercussions in the northeastern provinces in the postwar years, not altogether to the advantage of Nanking.

. . . . .

The peaceful solution of the two uprisings of 1936 constituted an augury for the war that China was to wage against Japan in the next year. During the decade preceding the war, almost all the military leaders of China had had encounters with Chiang Kai-shek, but by 1937 they and Chiang Kai-shek had all agreed to unite against Japan. In other words, by 1937, a united front against a foreign enemy had at last united the military leaders who, in the absence of a common ideal, had never before achieved unity. In this sense, Japan's aggression proved to be a blessing in disguise.

It is worth reflecting that if an equally worthy ideal could have prevented the military leaders from sapping the strength of the country by civil wars, or, still better, if it had also been able to prevent the schisms in the party, the country might have trodden the path of peace and progress in the very first years of the Nationalist regime. If so, it was a misfortune for Nationalist China that no such worthy ideal made itself comprehensible or acceptable to the leaders in general. A future generation which can force the acceptance of a high ideal on the leaders of military or political power will be able to enjoy peace and progress free from schisms, civil wars, and disunity.

VIII

THE KUOMINTANG: ITS DOCTRINE, ORGANIZATION, AND LEADERSHIP [1]

Up to the time of his death in 1925, the Kuomintang was Sun Yat-sen's party. He dominated it; indeed, he personified it. Upon his death, he was canonized. Though no dead leader, however sacred he may be held, ever dominates an organization, a study of the canonized leader's process of thinking and the environment in which that process matured is essential to a thorough understanding of the party's evolution, both in organization and in doctrines.

As early as 1905, Sun Yat-sen had already voiced objections to confining the attentions of the T'ung Meng Hui to a sort of anti-Manchu nationalism. The Court of the Manchus was corrupt and impotent. The Manchu administrators throughout the country were ignorant and malfeasant and generally held in contempt. One could always stir up the bitter memories of the Chinese against the Manchus for their massacres and brutalities during the time when their conquering hordes had held the country. It was therefore most profitable for the revolutionists to decry the Manchus. In fact, the majority of Sun Yat-sen's followers understood the revolutionary movement to be one against the Manchus. They gave little thought to the programs that should follow the successful ousting of the Manchus.

Sun Yat-sen was different from the body of his followers. His mental horizon reached far beyond theirs. The benefits of democracy with which he had come into contact during his extensive travels in the Western world had impressed him. The views of the socialists and possibly of Henry George had intrigued him. Still in his thirties, Sun Yat-sen was impressionable, idealistic, ambitious, and sanguine. He desired to have an old crumbling China transformed into a new nation of prosperity and justice almost by one stroke, a stroke not to take more than two or three decades in time.

Of the Three People's Principles which Sun Yat-sen advocated in 1905, Nationalism was the most easily understandable. China was to free itself from the yoke of the Manchus. As for the Second Principle, there was as yet nothing to show that Sun Yat-sen wanted for China anything other than a republican, democratic, and constitutional form of government, an institution which was then held by the progressives of the West to be the perfection of human wisdom. Sun Yat-sen was very vague about his Third Principle. He was impressed by the strikes and other labor troubles in the industrialized nations of the West. The rise of anarchist and socialist parties to him seemed to have made social revolution inevitable. He wanted to forestall social revolution by preventing in China the evils which had followed in the wake of the industrial revolutions in the West. He was vague on this point because he did not go beyond the expression of a pious wish.

As has been narrated in a previous chapter, the revolution against the Manchus consisted of a series of armed uprisings. The revolutionists were not doctrinaires. Arguments and propaganda centered almost exclusively on the necessity of overthrowing the Manchus. The revolutionists' theories concerning democracy or social justice remained obscure. Sun Yat-sen said little about theories in the years of frequent uprisings and growing successes. This was so, even during the years 1912 and 1913. It was not until the Revolution of 1913 had failed and Sun Yat-sen had taken refuge in Japan that he began to attribute the failure of the Revolution to the failure of his followers to pay equal attention to his other two Principles of Democracy and Livelihood.

It was true that in the 1914 Statute of the Chinese Revolutionary Party the party's aim was to be the realization of the Principles of People's Power and People's Livelihood. But there was no elaboration of either. A renewed emphasis on the three procedural stages, Military Government, Political Tutelage, and Constitutional Government, only served to indicate that the immediate concern of the party was the capture of power. The ultimate scheme of things remained to be more carefully defined.

Sun Yat-sen's overwhelming desire to regain the power which he had magnanimously yielded to Yuan Shih-k'ai and which had subsequently been greatly abused by Yuan Shih-k'ai and the other militarists of the North had become almost an obsession. Both his love of country and his pride in himself demanded that power be wrested from the Northern militarists. But for years he was not able to do so. On the contrary, he was even edged out of the Canton Government in 1918 by the militarists of the South. China was at that time a most sorry spectacle, badly divided at home, and contemptuously treated by other nations. If the morale of the nation was low, Sun Yat-sen's was by no means high.

It was in the years 1918 to 1920, when he had no hope of returning to Canton to regain his position of command in the Canton Directorate, that Sun Yat-sen elaborated on his theory, "knowing is more difficult than doing." This was known as *The Theory of Psychological Reconstruction*. He also wrote a plan for the industrial development of China, which was known as *The Industrial Plan* or *Material Reconstruction* (the English translation was published as *The International Development of China*). These two treatises dealt little with any of the Three Principles. The first was principally a complaint against, even a condemnation of, his comrades' failure to follow always his line of thought as well as his line of action. The second reflected Sun Yat-sen's eagerness to lift China out of poverty and archaic economic conditions and also his eagerness for international help. In these two books there was little that was indicative of the content which he later gave to the Three Principles.

It is certain that before 1919 or 1920 Sun Yat-sen was a combination of a revolutionary and Western democrat. As a revolutionary he was impatient, he could not tolerate any regime which seemed to him to be bad. As a democrat, he wanted to see China become a democracy. It was the inter-play of his revolutionary temperament and his democratic inclinations that sometimes made for a conflict within his personality. To understand him, one must keep both in mind. One must not, because of his emphasis on party tutelage which is indistinguishable from party dictatorship, deny to Sun Yat-sen genuine democratic inclinations. Sun Yat-sen understood democracy and up to 1919 never lost sight of it.

But beginning from 1919 the revolutionary aspect of his personality dominated his whole being, more than ever before. He was more eager than ever to wipe out the old regime and to install his party in power. He gladly embraced whomever and whatever could be of service to him in this regard. With some reluctance he deviated from his old stand. But deviate he did. One need only scan the differences between the Manifesto of the party issued on January 1, 1923 and that of its First Congress a year later to see his reluctance and also his shifting of ground.

Sun Yat-sen's Reorganized Ideas

Of the circumstances which led to the reorganization of the Kuomintang in 1924, some account has been given in a previous chapter. The principal influence in that reorganization came from Moscow. But the Soviet influence could not have brought itself to bear upon Sun Yat-sen had it not been synchronized with the rise of the student movement which was antagonistic to the imperialism of the Powers and the traditionalism of the Chinese state at one and the same time. The Chinese Communist Party was also beginning and after its second congress in July 1922 it was affiliated with the Comintern. Sun Yat-sen had much in common with the intelligentsia. He too hated the Powers; both Japan and Britain had been supporting the Northern Government to the disadvantage of his own cause. He was also eager for the support of the one power which was not tied up with the Peking regime.

There were preliminary conferences between Sun Yat-sen and the Soviets. It was Adolph Joffe who finally effected an understanding with him. On January 26, 1923 Sun Yat-sen and Joffe issued a joint statement[2] which cleared away the obstacles to Sun Yat-sen's orientation towards Moscow. The Soviet advisers arrived in October 1923 and Sun Yat-sen unhesitatingly reorganized the party in the following January. On January 1, 1923, Sun Yat-sen was still groping for ways and means of reinvigorating his party, and he was still dubious about the Soviets; a year later he had cast the die and accepted the aid of Moscow.

Sun Yat-sen's principal aim was to give a new vitality to his party in order that his revolution might soon succeed. He understood why the Russian Communist Party had succeeded, and he admired the organization and techniques of that party. If his own party could come to possess the energies and capacities of the Russian party, all else was of secondary importance. He did not like communism, and still less the dialectics of Marxism. But he was not worried by the inroad of such things in his party. He needed an ally to advise him on the improvement of party organization and tactics. He was eager to furnish himself with a strong and reliable military backing, a thing sorely needed for the establishment of a base. On this, he also needed Russian advice. To achieve his over-all purpose, in short, he needed Soviet aid. In order to get that aid, he was naturally willing to be allied with the Soviet, and if his allies should insist on his collaborating with the Chinese communists and on his enlisting the support of labor and the peasantry as conditions of aid, he would not mind. That is why the so-called Three Policies, "Russian Alliance," "Admission of the Communists," and "Emphasis on the Agrarian and Labor Policy," though not formally enunciated by either the First or Second Party Congresses, were clearly discernible in the spirit of the Manifesto of the First Congress, dated January 30, 1924.

On the other hand, the Three People's Principles as stated in this Manifesto had undergone great changes as the result of Sun Yat-sen's new orientation. If one sets the year 1921 as the line of demarcation and compares the party's and his own enunciations before and after, one cannot fail to be impressed by the new elements in both the content and the spirit of the Three Principles. In the Kuomintang Manifesto of January 1, 1923, a new chord had already been struck. By the early months of 1924, as evidenced both by the Manifesto of the First Congress and by Sun Yat-sen's lectures on *San Min Chu I*, the change was complete.

Sun Yat-sen's Three Principles of the People are the Principles of *Min-tsu*, *Min-ch'üan*, and *Min-sheng*, or, respectively, People's Nationhood, People's Power, and People's Livelihood. The first two can certainly be rendered as

"Nationalism" and "Democracy," for they are not different from them. The Principle of the People's Livelihood is neither socialism nor communism, and to translate it as "Socialism" would be out of place. It is better to let either *Min-sheng* or People's Livelihood stand.

1. *Nationalism*. The nationalist concept of Sun Yat-sen went through three successive phases. The first phase was simple. The Manchus who had ruled over China were considered an alien race denying self-government to the Chinese. Chinese nationalism demanded the liquidation of that group. When the Manchus were gone, the Chinese Republic of 1912 was regarded as a political community in which the five races, the Chinese, the Manchus, the Mongols, the Mohammedans, and the Tibetans, formed one inseparable unit. Nobody cared to subject that vague and confused conception to historical and ethnological analysis. Sun Yat-sen himself was no exception. For years he said almost nothing about his first Principle. In the 1914 statute of his newly christened Chinese Revolutionary Party, it was formally provided that the aims of the party were to fulfill the Principles of People's Power and People's Livelihood. At that time Sun Yat-sen must have felt that his first Principle had been fully realized.

A new interpretation of nationalism began with Sun Yat-sen's own disillusionment with the Powers and with the rise of the student movement and his contact with Soviet ideas. By 1924 the Principle had acquired new meaning and new substance. Nationalism is anti-imperialistic in its external aspect, and embraces self-determination of the racial minorities within the borders of China. It can be realized only by a nationalist revolution against imperialist control and also against the Chinese elements which have conspired with or tolerated the imperialists. Further, the Chinese were also to help other oppressed nations, especially those in the East, to shake off their foreign yokes. It is therefore also to be a world revolution of the oppressed nations. In this, Sun Yat-sen's nationalism differed little, if any, from the Soviet tenets at the time.

But in two aspects Sun Yat-sen was uniquely Chinese. First, he was in favor of self-determination for the minorities in China, or, in the words of the Manifesto, the "several nationalities" of China were to enjoy the rights of self-determination and finally to federate themselves into a Chinese republic. Yet at the same time he also said that national assimilation does not run counter to the Principle of Nationalism. Here he seemed to be saying that if the Chinese had succeeded in assimilating other races, the latter need not seek self-determination. Second, Sun Yat-sen continued to cherish the Confucianist idea of a "Great Commonwealth" which would comprise all mankind and would naturally obliterate all national and racial demarcations.

2. *Democracy*. Sun Yat-sen's second Principle also experienced historical changes and graftings. With one exception, there was nothing to show that

Sun Yat-sen's earlier concept of the Principle was anything other than the kind of democracy which prevailed in the contemporary West. The exception was that Sun Yat-sen did from very early times advocate a period of tutelage. His party was to enjoy exclusive political power during the period, and the veteran members were even to enjoy political privileges during their lifetime. But this was not to be a thing of permanence; it did not really cut into the principle of democracy.

With the coming of the Soviet anti-parliamentarian doctrine, coupled with the revulsion which the failures of the Chinese Parliament had created in him, he began to be harshly critical of the representative democracies of the West, considering them to be both anti-nationalist and anti-Min-sheng. Anti-nationalist because the Western democracies allowed only self-rule for the dominant race, leaving other nations or races subjected and oppressed. Anti-Min-sheng because the capitalists of the Western democracies denied livelihood to the less fortunate classes.

According to Sun Yat-sen, therefore, a tenable Principle of People's Power, or real democracy, must be in full conformity with the other two Principles. He proposed that the people should exercise directly the four powers of election, recall, initiative, and referendum. With these four powers directly exercised by the people, there would be no danger of the people ever losing their power over government. Then he went on to put what he terms "powers and functions" in juxtaposition. While the people should have the full enjoyment of powers, the functions should nevertheless be vested in the unfettered hands of the government equally fully. There were to be five functions, namely, executive, legislative, judicial, control, and examination. With gusto he argued for the separation of the functions of control and examination from the three older powers defined by Montesquieu.

Thus Sun Yat-sen advocated a government capable of the full exercise of five functions or, as he calls it, "an all-function government." At the same time he cast aspersions on the idea of natural rights. In subsequent years this has given rise to a school of interpretation which has done yeoman service to justify the disregard, if not suppression, of popular freedoms, and the emergence of an irresponsible and dictatorial, if not also totalitarian, government. A more sensible interpretation of Sun Yat-sen's second Principle would have emphasized the more positive aspect of his concept of the People's Political Powers, rather than either his criticism of representative democracy or his partisanship for a strong government. In the whole scheme of his second Principle, strong government certainly occupies only an auxiliary place, whereas the enjoyment of full political powers by the people was his main concern.

3. *Min-sheng*. The Livelihood Principle is not so susceptible to fair and intelligent interpretation. That Principle presents both a theory and a num-

ber of proposals. Sun Yat-sen was opposed to Karl Marx's materialist interpretation of history. He had no sympathy for the class struggle of Marx. Nor did he accept the Marxian theory of surplus value. He did not quite say that he would oppose his own interpretation of history to the materialism of Marx, but if any of his followers should, as some now do, pit Min-sheng-ism against materialism, or the Min-sheng interpretation of history against the materialist interpretation of history, they certainly cannot be accused of fabrication. Indeed, in his acceptance of an obscure American author's "social interpretation of history"[3] Sun Yat-sen accepted the idea that "livelihood is the central force in social progress, and that social progress is the central force in history; hence the struggle for a living and not material forces determines history."[4] Thinking along this social line, Sun Yat-sen, though recognizing the existence of classes, also repudiated class struggle, and favored conciliation among classes.

As for more concrete proposals, Sun Yat-sen advocated the equalization of land tenure, and the regulation of capital. To achieve the former, he proposed that the unearned increment of land value should accrue to the state. To achieve the latter, he proposed state ownership of principal industries and enterprises. While lack of precision characterizes the latter proposal, a lack of comprehensiveness marks the former. Finally his famous answer to the question, "What is the Principle of Livelihood?"—"It is communism and it is socialism," confounds his readers still further.

In justice to Sun Yat-sen it must be said that his economic thinking was progressive and that he was genuinely interested in the welfare of the little man. But he never formulated a well-thought-out economic theory or a well-planned economic program.

It is then not unfair to observe that the chief innovation in the revised Three Principles of 1924 was the harnessing of anti-imperialist sentiment, which was then popular with the more forwarding-looking elements of the country, to give the party a new battle cry and to accelerate the downfall of its enemies. The other aspects of the Principles were of no urgent import at the moment and they were still vague and obscure.[5]

Ideological Sterility after Sun's Death

Thus, the principal objective of the Kuomintang Reorganization of 1923–1924 was to equip the party with a new vigor, with effective revolutionary techniques of organization and agitation, and with a strong and reliable military support behind the whole movement. Such changes as there were in the interpretation of the Three Principles were only incidental to that objective. Accordingly the significance of the split with the communists in 1927 and then of the break with the Soviet Union depends on the question to what extent these ruptures tended to undermine the vigor of the Kuomintang, both in its use of revolutionary techniques, and in the military support behind them. On the surface, the fact that the Northern Expedition succeeded and the whole country was brought under the Kuomintang seemed to prove that there was no deterioration. One thing was certainly sure, that the Kuomintang lost little of the technique of organization and agitation which they had acquired in the days of collaboration.

But the purge of the communists, not to mention the murder of large numbers of the educated youth who formed such a small fraction of the total Chinese population, certainly also purged the Kuomintang of a group of more militant workers. The exit of the militant elements from the party tended to encourage the incoming of the more conservative and even reactionary elements of Chinese society. Though the revolutionary vigor persisted for a short while after the split, it could not be maintained for long. The Kuomintang became after 1929 not only conservative but also complacent. It was not until 1945, when it was brought face to face with the vigorous program of social and economic reforms of the militant communists, that the Kuomintang again bestirred itself to adopt an equally radical program, at the Sixth Congress in May of that year.[6] But it then found itself lacking in men of vigor and ambition to carry through such a program. In this sense, it is plain that the party was adversely affected by the split with the communists in 1927.

If the split with an outside party adversely affected its vigor, the schisms within prevented the Kuomintang from evolving carefully and logically a body of doctrines which could fit the conditions of China and, at the same time, implement the Three Principles of its founder. One may be for or against deifying a political leader and making his writings sacrosanct, but if deification is to take place one must interpret the writings of the deified in such a way as to give them a consistency and a living quality and yet at the same time not do violence to the original text. Unfortunately, the schisms and later the segmentation which have afflicted the party have also precluded the presentation of sharply distinguished interpretations of Sun Yat-sen's writings, but produced only second-rate and commonplace textual glossaries. The more radical theoreticians were sensitive to accusations of communist leanings; the more conservative were apprehensive of being called reactionaries. All were afraid of being criticized and condemned as unfaithful to the teachings of Sun Yat-sen. The total effect was that few cared or dared to venture beyond textual interpretations.

It is conceivable that if there had been neither schisms nor segmentation and the party had been more united, a different kind of interpretation might have resulted and a democratic political edifice and a program of expansive and egalitarian economic reforms might have been developed from his Second and Third Principles respectively. As it was, the Three Principles remained vague, incoherent, and at points inconsistent with each other and with the actualities, in spite of Sun Yat-sen's nobleness of heart, devotion to the national welfare, and, in general, enlightenment in regard to the future of the country. In this sense the evil effect of the schisms and the segmentation within the party has been profound.

Kuomintang Membership

The organizational setup of the Kuomintang has remained, on the whole, unchanged since the Reorganization of 1924.

Membership in the Kuomintang, as in the more highly organized parties of other countries, requires formal enrollment. It is difficult to ascertain the size of the total membership of the party at any one time because there has been only infrequent general registration, and no process of continuous registration. If, therefore, the authorities of the party claim that there are about eight and a half million members, that number may be quite off the mark. Also, in the years immediately after the Reorganization, the party considered the Nationalist Revolutionary Army, both officers and men, to be automatically members of the party. If that practice were continued, there would be even greater difficulty in ascertaining the exact enrollment of the party, since the size of the armed forces is not easily ascertainable.

In general it may be said that aside from the army factor, the size of the party has not varied greatly during the last two decades. Expulsions have been numerous, but they do not constitute a significant percentage in terms of the total membership. Older members have died, but younger ones who have joined, especially if we include the members of the San Min Chu I Youth Corps, have perhaps more than made up the loss. Not counting the armed forces, the total membership of the Kuomintang has probably remained somewhere between two and four million during the last two decades.

As to the make-up of the membership, the one single important category has been the college and middle-school students who, after leaving school, were employed as party workers, civil servants, or in such white-collar jobs as teaching and editing and the like. It is unfortunate for the party that during the past four or five years fewer and fewer students in the schools or new graduates have been joining. Few people who might be considered capitalists in the Western sense have joined the party. Small shopkeepers and factory workers, including such special categories as the postal and railway employees, usually became members of the party after it had been able to expand its organization to their several unions.

The usual procedure for recruiting members from the merchant and labor groups is this: first the party organizes a union or captures it if one has

STRUCTURE OF THE KUOMINTANG, 1948

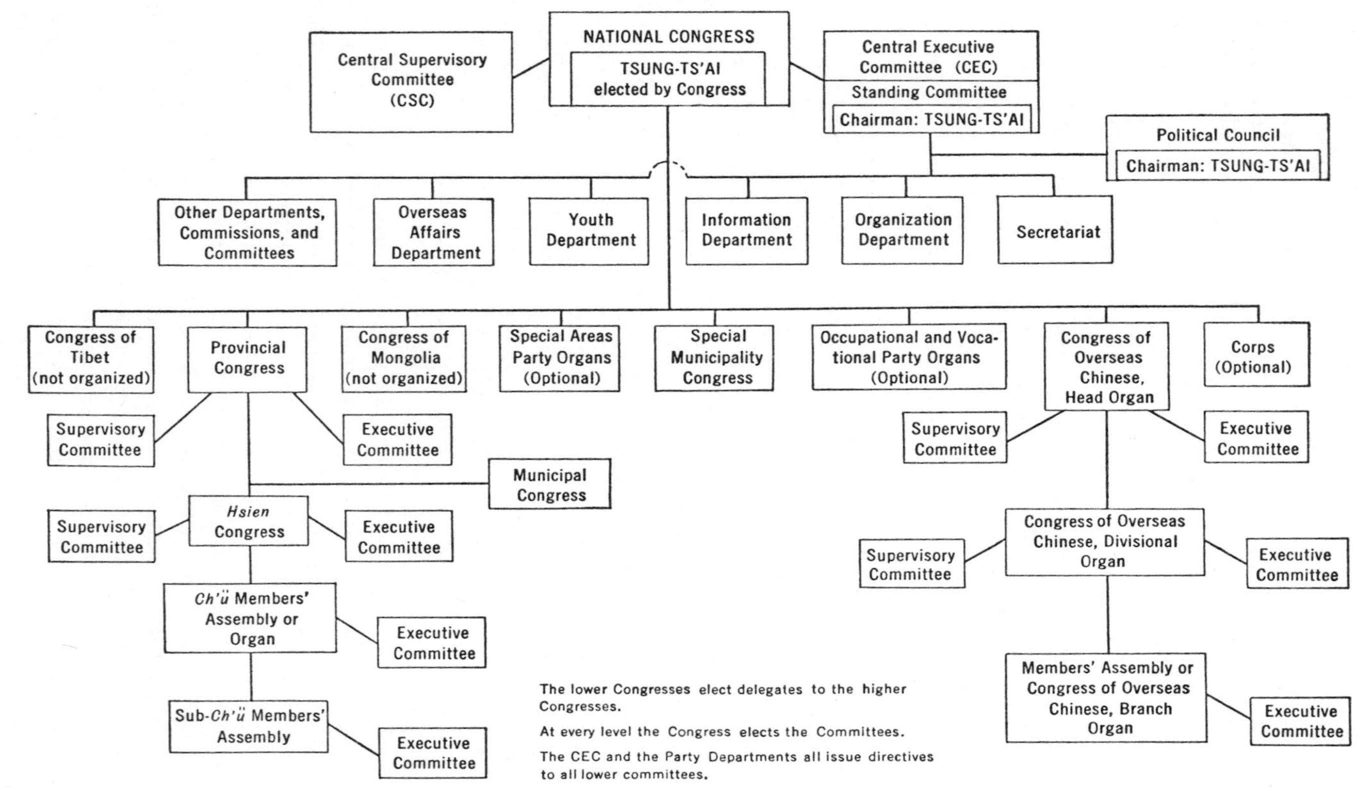

The lower Congresses elect delegates to the higher Congresses.

At every level the Congress elects the Committees.

The CEC and the Party Departments all issue directives to all lower committees.

already been in existence, then a part or all of the members of the union are ordered or persuaded to join the party. The same technique is used to enroll the party's peasant members, the only difference being that the party has founded a very small number of farmers' unions and that consequently very few peasants have been brought into the fold.

In other words, again not counting army people, among the component elements of the party in terms of the traditional four-class or four-profession division of the Chinese people (scholars, farmers, merchants, and artisans), the scholar element is still the dominant one. The future trend of the party seems to depend very much on that of the scholar class. If the scholar element that controls the party continues to maintain the outlook that their *raison d'être* is to become officials or to hold political jobs, the party is bound to remain stagnant.[7] And if the domination of the scholar group is ephemeral with militarists or army-minded people in actual control, something even worse can naturally be expected.

Congresses and Executive Committees

Like the Russian Communist Party, the structure of the Kuomintang forms a pyramid. In conformity with China's geographical divisions of governmental structure, the Kuomintang has, from the lowest to the highest, four tiers of authority. At the bottom there is the *Ch'ü* Organization; above, corresponding with the *hsien*, there stands the *Hsien* Organization; higher still is the Provincial Organization; at the top of the pyramid stands the Central Organization. Each level of organization maintains an executive and a supervisory committee, elected in the case of the *ch'ü* by party members directly, but in the higher levels by congresses of party delegates, elected in turn by the congresses on a lower level. To illustrate: the party congress of a certain province elects the provincial executive committee and supervisory committee which constitute the provincial organization; the delegates to that provincial congress are in turn elected by the *hsien* congresses of the province.

The *Ch'ü* Organization is the lowest functioning unit. There are, however, below it the *ch'ü* branches. The members of each are supposed to meet often and to discuss matters of interest to the party and perform duties pertaining to them as the élite of the general population.

Then there are some special organizations somewhat distorting the rigorous lines of the pyramid. Members who have no fixed residence, principally the railway employees and the seamen, form themselves into special organizations which are placed under the direct control of the Central Organization. The organization of the Kuomintang members overseas is also irregular and held close to the central body. But the most extraordinary is the party organization in the armed forces — the army, naval, and air units, all have their own party organizations. They form a separate pyramid, and are placed directly in the Central Organization.

According to the Statute of the Party, the National Congress, and, after its adjournment, the Central Executive Committee, is the highest organ of party power. The Central Supervisory Committee has only the power of discipline and financial control. All this was modeled after the Russian Communist Party as the latter stood in 1924.

In theory and also in appearance, the Congress has always remained supreme. Whether the Central Executive Committee can still be considered the highest organ depends on its position vis-à-vis the Party Leader, a post which has existed since 1938 and which will be discussed presently. But, in reality, both the Congress and the Central Executive Committee have long become ratification conventions or sounding boards. Neither enjoys the reality of power.

The Congress has always been a large-sized body. In the First Congress there were 150 delegates, and by the Sixth Congress, held in 1945, the number had grown to about 600. If the delegates are elected, the election is usually controlled by the party machine. If they are appointed, as has often been the case, they are under its absolute control. In either case, they cannot be expected either to want or be able to oppose the high leadership of the party. They may talk and at times even voice their grievances, but in the end they always accept what is handed to them.

The size of the Central Executive Committee has also grown rapidly. It grew from one of 24, with 17 reserve members, elected by the First Congress in 1924, to one of 222, with 90 reserve members, elected by the Sixth Congress in 1945. The last elected Central Executive Committee, which is still functioning, is almost as unwieldy as the Congress itself, for, whenever it meets, the Central Supervisory Committee of 104, with 44 reserve members, is also in attendance and in full participation, as is customary with such meetings of the party.

Furthermore, the statutory requirement that the Party Congress should be convened once every two years (originally every year) and the Central Executive Committee every half year, has never been faithfully met. In the course of twenty-four years since the Reorganization of the Party, there have been only six Congresses. The plenary sessions of the Central Executive Committee are more numerous, but they too are held at very irregular intervals.[8] The convening of the Congress is decided by the Central Executive Committee (often its Standing Committee), and that of the Central Executive Committee by its Standing Committee. The Standing Committee has complete control, and may decide whether or not to have a Congress or a plenary session of the Central Executive Committee, and if so, when.

The Central Executive Committee has abdicated in favor of the Standing Committee. For practical purposes, the Standing Committee of the Central Executive Committee controls the party. This was certainly the case before the creation of the post of the Party Leader in 1938.

The Standing Committee used to meet on a fixed day of the week to transact whatever business the party needed to transact. Though, unlike the Congress and the Central Executive Committee, it was never given full powers, its authority was practically unlimited. It could even modify the resolutions passed by the Congress or the Central Executive Committee in a plenary session. Whereas the larger bodies could only resolve, the Standing Committee can also make appointments and issue orders. The advantages it had over them are obvious.

However, as the size of the Standing Committee grew, it also lost its effectiveness as an organ. Originally there were only eight members, but in 1945 the number grew to fifty. As it became a miniature of the Central Executive Committee, it acquired the same impotence as the latter.

The Party Leader

In addition to this pyramid of congresses and executive and supervisory committees, the party has also had a Leader since 1938. During his lifetime, Sun Yat-sen had always considered himself head of the party. He was Tsung-li, meaning General Manager, or President. There was, of course, nothing extraordinary in this, for the party, be it the Hsing Chung Hui, the T'ung Meng Hui, the Chinese Revolutionary Party, or the Kuomintang, was his organization. When the party was reorganized in 1924, he again assumed the title of Tsung-li. After his death the Second Congress of the Kuomintang in 1926 decided to retain in the Party Statute the provisions concerning this office with the declaration that to do him honor and reverence, Sun Yat-sen, the "Founder of the Kuomintang" should always remain President of the Party, though the presidential functions were to devolve on the Central Executive Committee. Under this arrangement it was naturally difficult for anybody to aspire to be the sole leader of the party; to do so would run counter to that spirit of reverence.

Moreover, there was only one man who wielded enough actual power to assume the high post of command, Chiang Kai-shek. But the senior leaders of the party were loath to see a man younger both in age and in party affiliation rise to inherit the position of Sun Yat-sen who had often lectured to them like an elder of the family. The question of restoring the post of leader thus remained moot for many years. Even as late as 1935, at the Fifth Congress, the Kwangtung and Kwangsi group of delegates, who generally considered Hu Han-min the senior leader of the party, threatened to bolt the sessions if the followers of Chiang Kai-shek dared to press for the restoration of the post. By 1938, however, the situation had greatly changed. There was a war going on. The whole country, even more than the whole party, was disposed to favor increasing the power and prestige of their commander-in-chief. Hu Han-min was dead. And in the face of the war, Wang Ching-wei could hardly interpose objection to the enhancement of the commander's position in the party. The Extraordinary Party Congress amended the Statute of the Party, established the office of Tsung-ts'ai, and elected Chiang Kai-shek to the post.

Tsung-ts'ai, meaning General Director, or Leader, is to be distinguished from Tsung-li, forever reserved for Sun Yat-sen. The Congress, in order to be meticulously correct towards Sun Yat-sen as Tsung-li, even went so far as to differentiate between the powers of the two posts: while the Tsung-li possesses the powers of high command, the Tsung-ts'ai merely exercises in the Tsung-li's absence the powers reserved for the latter. In other words, the party could say that it is the Tsung-li alone who has the powers of command. Of course, these were pure literary niceties for which the Chinese have a great weakness. The new Leader, namely, the Tsung-ts'ai, was henceforth to be the head of the party in name as well as in fact.

Chiang Kai-shek was elected Leader by the Congress in 1938.[9] There is no provision in the Party Statute regarding the term of office. Presumably, the Leader continues in office until the Congress either abolishes the office or elects a new incumbent. At the following Party Congress, the Sixth, held in Chungking in May 1945, there was a difference of opinion as to whether Chiang Kai-shek should or should not seek a new mandate, or, more correctly, a confirmation. When Chiang Kai-shek tendered his resignation, the Congress at once unanimously resolved that he should continue as the Leader.

The restoration of a supreme head also posed the question of the party's repository of power. The theory that the supreme power was vested in the National Congress, and, after its adjournment, in the Central Executive Committee, was made no longer tenable. The Leader possesses an absolute veto over the decisions of the Central Executive Committee, and a suspensive veto over those of the Congress itself. If he disagrees with any decision of the Congress, he can ask them to reconsider. Then, he also presides over the meetings of the Standing Committee and there he controls all decisions made in the name of the party. As Leader of the Party, Chiang Kai-shek was given in 1938, according to the Statute of the Party, full powers, which he still enjoys.

Chiang Kai-shek is a man of strong will, fortified by an unusual amount of shrewdness and tenacity. Yet he is totally devoid of that quality of progressivism which saved Sun Yat-sen from prizing power for power's sake. A conservative by instinct, Chiang Kai-shek has no feeling of the spirit of the times. His lack of intimate contact with people of enlightenment, not to say common people, further deprives him of an opportunity to grow. The Actonian axiom, power corrupts and absolute power corrupts absolutely, is illustrated with devastating effect in his relationship with other men. In his anxiety to cling to power, more and more he mistrusts people who criticize him or even dare to differ with him. The men who work with him have to be first and last loyal to him personally. In the end he became the leader of a party of servile men but not a party of men and ideas, which were once the glory of the Reorganized Kuomintang.[10]

Democratic Centralism

Like the Russian Communist Party, the organizational principle of the Kuomintang has always been in theory what is known as "democratic centralism." An orthodox interpretation of the term is that members have the rights of discussion, but when decisions have been made, they are to be obeyed by the dissenting members as well.

But the term came to be applied not so much to the making and carrying out of a party decision as to the mode of election of the party authorities and the power these elected authorities were to enjoy.[11] According to the principle, the authorities were to be democratically elected by the membership, either directly by the party members themselves, or indirectly through intervening congresses, and, once elected, they were to have the powers of command and the right to be obeyed. Thus, the high authorities, in former years the Central Executive Committee or its Standing Committee, and since 1938 the Leader of the Party, have had the powers of direction and discipline over both the lower organization and the members; but since both the Committee and the Leader are elected, they can claim that they derive their supreme authority from the will of the members of the party.

In practice, however, "democratic centralism" can be democratic only when, in the process of organizing and electing, the members enjoy the right of forming minority groups, both to criticize the incumbents and to nominate candidates in opposition to the organization candidates. But that has not been the case. In the past the Provincial Executive Committees have more often been appointed by the Central Executive Committee than elected by the Provincial Congresses. The dominant group of the Central Executive Committee have therefore always been able to control the delegates to the National Congress and this in turn enabled them to perpetuate their own group in power. The established practice has thus become that whoever controls the Central Organization controls the party. There has been plenty of centralism but little democracy.

It is here that the hierarchy of party organization enters into the picture of party politics and strife. The dominant group may control all the organizations of the civilian party members. But the army organizations have always remained in the hands of a group of army politicians. The delegates sent by these latter organizations to the National Party Congress are naturally also from the army. They form a compact group. They obey the Leader who has been concurrently their supreme commander, but they need not submit themselves to or take orders from any civilian group, however powerful it may be. Within the hierarchy of army organizations, too, there is concentration of power to the exclusion of democracy. But in the party as a whole there cannot be monopoly of power either by a dominant civilian group or the army group. Whatever centralism there is is lodged in the hands of the Leader. Except in his case, neither part of the organizational principle of "democratic centralism" can be said to be in full operation.

Party Administration

Again like the Russian Communist Party, the organization of the Kuomintang does not end with the congresses and the executive and supervisory committees. At each tier there are a party secretary (always euphoniously titled) and a host of departments and commissions, appointed by the executive committee and responsible to it for their several administrations. The secretary occupies an important post, but not as important as that occupied by his opposite number in Russia. The number and the organization of these departments and commissions have varied greatly from time to time.

Of all departments, the Organization Department, having charge of the organization of the party branches below it, is naturally the most powerful. It picks delegates to the congress. It makes and unmakes the executive committees on the lower levels. It controls the membership, and consequently their votes. Its control is helped by the party secret service, innocuously called the Bureau of Investigation and Statistics, which keeps an eye on the thoughts and activities of the people outside as well as inside the party. It is correct to say that whoever controls the Organization Department controls the party. In fact, ever since the days of the split with the communists in 1927, a single group of persons has been in more or less full control of the Central Organization Department, all attempts to dislodge them having had no success. From the point of view of this group it is indeed a misfortune that they have not been able to control the organization of the party in the armies as well.

In addition, there have usually been departments for publicity and training, and also special units to cater to the special cadres of party members. These organizations are ordinarily more elaborate in the Central Party Headquarters and less so in the provincial or *hsien* party headquarters. They are often large establishments comparable in size and importance to the ministries of the Central Government or the administrative departments and bureaus of the Provincial and *Hsien* Governments.

Except in the years immediately following the Reorganization, the Publicity Department has propagandized very little, as the term is understood in countries like Soviet Russia. Its activities were generally of a negative and repressive nature. During the war years the attention of the department was devoted to preventing news and information, critical or otherwise unfavorable to the party and government, from reaching the public both at home and abroad. But little work of a positive nature such as the exposition of the party doctrine or the popularization of the party program was performed. If there was any indoctrination at all, it was largely confined to the glorification of the Party Leader. That preventive instinct has not ceased to work even since the termination of the war.

To the Training Department (or Commission) was originally assigned the ambitious task of equipping the party workers with the techniques of organization and the people with the art of self-government. With wars going on and with democracy temporarily shelved or completely forgotten, the latter phase was entirely neglected. Even for the first, the training corps soon outshone the Training Department. Of the training corps of various grades the most famous was the Central Training Corps, to which batches of party, government, and army officials were ordered to report for a short period (usually two weeks) of intensive indoctrination. Yet the total effect left on the trainees was negligible. Little enthusiasm for the party could be whipped up. If there was any enthusiasm at all, it was channeled toward the Party Leader who incidentally also acted as the Chief of the Corps. All this was perhaps inevitable, since for years the Kuomintang has had little party program other than the personal policies of its Leader.

In theory the functions of the party departments are strictly party in nature. But during the days of tutelage of the Kuomintang, the government and the party never had a clear line of demarcation, either in function or in personnel. The result was, of course, constant interference in the affairs of the government and the actual exercise of governing powers over the people in general by these party departments.

The assumption of governing authority by party departments and the bureaucratic manner in which these departments are organized and in which the officials function have tended to bureaucratize the party institutions. Had the party been careful not to go over into the fields of ordinary administration and satisfied itself with merely giving directives to the Central Government which it had set up, it might have been able to preserve a spirit of vigilance and a vision of the future. It might have avoided creating so many bureaus and consequently converting so many party members into party bureaucrats who depend on the party for a living. A bureaucracy that has few functions to perform but is dependent on the office for a living always demoralizes the body politic which it serves. It is a calamity for the Kuomintang that it should have tolerated or even encouraged, perhaps unwittingly, the rise of one of the most idle and spineless bureaucracies China has yet had.

The Youth Corps

The Kuomintang in the years from 1939 to 1947 also maintained a more or less autonomous youth organization, the San Min Chu I Youth Corps. In the years around 1930 discussions and proposals to form a separate youth organization were both numerous and enthusiastic. It was, however, not until the time of the Extraordinary Congress in March 1938 that the Youth Corps finally came into being.

By 1938, the war had begun and the Chinese communists had joined hands with the Kuomintang government in the common national effort. Chiang Kai-shek was himself dissatisfied with the low morale and even corruption of vast numbers of the party members in the face of both a brutal aggressor without and a formidable competitor within. He had hoped that a new organization of younger and more energetic men, thoroughly indoctrinated with his own *Weltanschauung*, and uncontaminated by the decadent spirit of the parental body, could in time build up a new Kuomintang. Acting on his proposal, the congress resolved to set up the Youth Corps, which was to have a separate organization of its own, but the Leader of the Party as its Chief.

During the decade that the Youth Corps maintained its autonomous existence, it had an organization similar to that of the party in its essential features. There were national, provincial, and *hsien* corps. The lower sent delegates to the congress of the higher and the executive body of the higher controlled that of the lower. Thus, the National Congress of the Corps was composed of delegates elected by the congresses of the provincial branch corps. The National Congress of the Corps elects the members both of the Executive Body and the Supervisory Body which, though slightly different in name, had exactly the same functions as the Central Executive and Supervisory Committees of the party. Under the Executive Body there were also a secretary and various departments in charge of organization, training, and other matters. Again, at the lowest level, the local corps organizations maintained departments similar to those of the party.

Had the Youth Corps consisted solely of youths, this organization would have been considered overelaborate. But it was not an organization of young people alone. The membership may have been largely young men and women, but the people in charge of the organizations, both central and local, were more often than not influential leaders of the party.

At its inception, the Leader of the Party charged a group of key men, drawn from various segments of the party, and a few university presidents and other men prominent in the educational world, with the task of organizing the corps. While the educational leaders remained in the corps as highly decorative figures, the party leaders of the different segments worked hard to tighten their control. During the last years of the separate existence of the corps, the Army Group, with the help of some of the men in education, ultimately gained something like complete control of it. The internal strife that characterized the life of the party under the leader also characterized the life of the corps under its chief.

The similarity in organization and the identity in the leadership made the corps in many ways a duplicate of the party. The corps had the same shortcomings and committed the same mistakes. The mission expected of it by its creator was not fulfilled. Young students were enlisted as members of the Youth Corps, but whatever vision or vigor the student members might have, they were not able to create for the corps something new and different from the party, something which might ultimately lead the Kuomintang to a "new deal." In fact, when the corps demonstrated its inability to dissociate itself from the lamentable ways of the party, youngsters of a rebellious and idealistic turn of mind turned away from the corps. The more they did so, the more the corps reverted to the party pattern.

The Youth Corps did, however, develop a keen rivalry with the party. Though both organizations were absolutely loyal to their respective leaders, identical in the person of Chiang Kai-shek, they were undermining each other's authority. Chiang Kai-shek was compelled to order an amalgamation of the two. For a while the corps resisted the amalgamation, but when it finally agreed in September of 1947, it exacted high prices for abolishing its own organization. Its executives and supervisors were automatically taken in as members of the party's Central Executive and Supervisory Committees. Its leaders were also able to have a large share of the departmental portfolios, though they failed to make inroads into the all-important Organization Department.

The amalgamation leaves the status of the San Min Chu I Youth Corps ambiguous. There is now again a Department of Youth in the party and presumably it will take care of the indoctrination of students and attempt to organize youth movements in support of the Kuomintang. But a resolution of the Sixth Congress of the party in May 1945 had ordered the administration of student affairs to be transferred to the Ministry of Education. How the Ministry of the Government and the Department of the Party will divide between themselves the encouragement or supervision, or, if necessary, the prohibition, of political activities by the youth remains to be seen. Perhaps confusion, including both overlapping and duplication rather than clear demarcation, should be expected.

The episode of the autonomous San Min Chu I Youth Corps betrayed one cardinal weakness of the Kuomintang. Its activities are too personal in nature. It is absorbed primarily in building up and then maintaining in power one person or group of persons. It is only incidentally interested in policies and movements as such. Had the party determined to adopt a more forward-looking social and economic program, the Youth Corps it established in 1938 would certainly have been a vanguard for both the propagation of the gospel and the carrying out of a new deal. Quarrels and struggles inside the corps there were bound to be, but the bone of contention would have been the matter rather than the men, the adoption of a certain policy rather than the control of the organization by certain individuals or groups.

Segmentation within the Party

Long before the appearance and disappearance of the Youth Corps, segmentation of the Kuomintang had been in the making. In an earlier chapter we have seen the various groupings competing with Chiang Kai-shek for control of the party. When Chiang Kai-shek became its undisputed leader, the process of segmentation continued.

The explanation for the existence of groups is to be sought in the nature of Chiang Kai-shek's leadership. He demands loyalty to his person. Having no conviction regarding any fixed policy and entertaining few fixed policies for any length of time, Chiang Kai-shek has naturally a tendency to consider his personal views of the moment to be best calculated to promote the interests of the nation and incidentally to be the most correct interpretation of Sun Yat-sen's ideas. He has deep faith in himself as the guardian angel of both the party and the nation. The convenient indentification of his personal views with those of the party and the people and of his personal interest with the interest of the party and the nation also caused him to confuse individuals' personal loyalties with their party and national loyalties. As long as a man or a group of men remain loyal to him and do his bidding, he will extend his protection. Two groups of his loyal followers may differ from each other in ideas and policies, but it does not follow that therefore one of the groups must also have differences with him. Groups with irreconcilable ideas and policies either entertain no difference with his own views, ideas, and policies, or, if they do, they can relegate the differences to the background in order to give him unqualified support.

To illustrate: in the years immediately before the war in 1937, the groups which loyally supported Chiang Kai-shek did have differences in their attitudes toward the Japanese. Some favored a Fabian policy, nay, a policy of appeasement. Some were anxious to pick up the gauntlet of resistance. But since Chiang Kai-shek was the all-wise as well as the all-powerful leader and therefore must be combining the spirit of resistance and the unerring intuitions of a tactician, neither of the opposing groups could find objections to the views he entertained. Thus it was possible for both to support Chiang Kai-shek, though in the meantime they struggled against each other for an increased ascendancy in the councils of both the party and the government.

The Kuomintang groups which support Chiang Kai-shek have been numerous and shifting. The groupings are not strictly organized. They are illegal, for on the proposal of Chiang Kai-shek the Extraordinary Congress in March 1938 ordered all sectarian organizations to dissolve. That prohibition still stands. Therefore, though one hears often that so-and-so belongs to this group, and so-and-so is opposed to that group, it is not always easy to prove or to disprove the correctness of such an assertion.

In general, it may be said that among the supporters of Chiang Kai-shek there are three main groups. Small groupings also exist, but their influence is largely derived from the peculiar personal position of their leaders. They have no large followings and no ramifications. They usually ally themselves with one of the three. They have no chance to compete with any of the three for control of power either in the party or in the government.

Of the three, the most powerful is the Organization Group.[12] Tracing its beginnings back to 1926, it has had an almost continuous hold on the Organization Department of the party. Having control of the party organization, it has been able to assume the pivotal position in both the party and the government, and thus enormously to expand its influence and increase its strength like an octopus.

The group is led by men who when still young fought the communists at the time of the split, understood the techniques of the Russian Revolution, and are prone to give a high evaluation, sometimes too high, to those techniques. But having fought the communists, they have acquired deep anti-communist and anti-Soviet convictions and prejudices. They have none of the literati tradition at all, though they take great pains to glorify the old in China. Some of them may make a great ballyhoo about Confucianism, but they do so only to echo some of Sun Yat-sen's dicta. They may be still feigning to be especially devoted to Min-sheng-ism. But their anti-communist obsession and their inability to draw really decent men of ability and honesty into their ranks has tended to make of the group machine-politicians solely intent on grabbing power, but without any idea of promoting the national interest.

Second, there is the Army Group. It consists almost wholly of the graduates of the Whampoa Military Academy. Its leaders have always adopted politics as their profession rather than active military command. The armies, certainly those units of which the Whampoa graduates have sole or even partial control, are the strongholds of the group. During the last years of the separate existence of the Youth Corps, their influence there was also predominant. They are now competing with the first group for hegemony in the Central Organization of the party.

The Army Group, though it has been carrying on an incessant struggle against the leadership and methods of the Organization Group, and has oftentimes been outspokenly critical, has very much the same outlook and tendencies in regard to the aims of the party and the ways in which the party should fulfill those aims. The members are strongly anti-communist and anti-Soviet. They also consider themselves revolutionaries and are not averse to using extralegal or even rather violent methods to achieve their purposes. They are opposed to the modern business and capitalist interests. In recent years they have directed some of their most violent tirades against what is known as bureaucratic capitalism, meaning officials accumulating fortunes by making use of their influence and position, though high army leaders themselves are not free from the selfsame practices.

Both the Organization and the Army Groups, or at least their younger leaders who have not yet acquired vested proprietary interests, are radical in their ideals for the economic rejuvenation of the nation.[13] Both groups are extremely nationalistic in regard to encroachments on China's rights from without and intolerant of the demands of the minor nationalities within the borders of China. Regrettably, both have a low and unfavorable view of the Western democracies and are likely to stress Sun Yat-sen's second Principle, that of People's Power, interpreted as they understand it or like to have it understood, namely, an all-powerful government checked by none.

The third group, generally known as the Political Study Group, is not a party group, strictly speaking, though their leaders have been made members of the party's Central Committees. They had no chance to compete for the control of the party's machine with either of the two groups described above. Instead, they interested themselves in increasing their hold on the provincial administration and also on the larger financial and business concerns of the country, whether private or government. In other words, if the Kuomintang Government and the Kuomintang are considered as different entities, this third group does not enter into the segmentation of the party. But if they are considered inseparable entities, this group is certainly next in importance to the other two.

The Political Study Group is quite distinguishable from the other two. Being led by men of greater maturity both in age and experience than the leaders of the other two groups, it tends to be opportunistic or practical. To those who loathe dogmas, it seems to be practical. To those who are allergic to plasticity, it seems to be opportunistic. Whether one likes the group or not, its motto is to ameliorate rather than to reform. It entertains no visions. It eschews violence. Since many of the leaders of this group are themselves men of wide financial and business interests, their views about the necessity of economic readjustment are naturally mild. Likewise, they are less nationalistic and somewhat more tolerant of the democratic spirit of the West.

All groups, including minor ones, covet the control of the commanding posts in government and in business as well as of the party machine. Since the Political Study Group has no hold on the party organization, the competition is between the two other main groups. In general, the Army Group controls the party organizations in the army and the Organization Group controls the civilian organizations of the party hierarchy. The civilian organizations being more numerous, the Organization Group can control a majority or something approaching a majority of the Party Congress, and through it a majority of the Central Executive Committee. That in fact has been the case during the more recent congresses. But the Army Group in alliance with the others who are opposed to the Organization Group is sometimes able to put up a stiff front against the dominant group. If an impasse is occasioned by some such rivalry, the Leader usually comes in to effect a kind of compromise, thus making himself indispensable to all.

The existence of two parallel secret services is the result of the existence of several groups in keen rivalry to each other, but all owing allegiance to one supreme leader. The Organization Group controls the party secret service. The Army Group has an army secret service ready to do its bidding. The two rival services may come into conflict. But pluralism has its rewards for the leader who can get reports on what he considers disloyal elements and at the same time use the service of one group to check on the activities of the other.[14]

Outside of the party hierarchy the three groups have had different strongholds. The armed forces are of course the Army Group's exclusive sphere of influence. The party departments on various levels are similarly identified with the Organization Group. The latter group has also succeeded in controlling the schools, the civic bodies, the trade unions, and several very special branches of the civil service. The third group has several provincial administrations, and some banking and business concerns under their control. Lately all three have been racing for a share in local government, both on the provincial and on the lower levels. The growing interest of the Organization Group in banking and industrial enterprises and the interest of the Army Group in making some inroads into university circles seem to have been creating a confusion of the erstwhile distinguishable spheres of influence.

In a country with a more established order, such groupings as have just been described would perhaps be more naturally divisible into a radical and a conservative party, or if the Kuomintang had to remain as the sole party, into two wings. But the Kuomintang has a Leader who leads all groups and is not averse to seeing the party rent into groups so long as they are unquestionably and intimately loyal to him. There is an advantage in having these groups. Since the leaders of one group cannot exact loyalty from those of another, the leaders of all groups must take orders from him. A groupless Kuomintang is bound to develop one or more leaders who, though under the Leader, are yet above others. The position and influence of such men might acquire threatening proportions. It is true that Chiang Kai-shek did order the dissolution of all sectarian organizations or cliques in the party, in 1938; and, in a resolution on organizational principles of the party, passed by the joint session of the Central Executive Committees of the party and the corps, in September 1947, the sectarian organizations were again repeatedly derided and prohibited. But it would be fantastic to presume that he is unaware of the existence of the groups which, though lacking in emblems and official headquarters, are yet operating entities.

It is then clear that the Leader of the Kuomintang is not only the head of its organization, but actually holds it together. Or, to state it in another way, the Leader has allowed the party to be segmented so that he alone supplies the link between its several segments. It is in this all-important feature, rather than in its doctrine, or in its organization, or even in the social basis of its membership, that one can discover a key to the understanding of the Kuomintang.

IX

THE KUOMINTANG TUTELAGE

Since the Nationalist Revolutionary Army ended its northern campaigns and the Five-Yuan Government was instituted in October 1928, China has been under the tutelage of the Kuomintang. The organization of a new government in April–June 1948, according to the Constitution adopted on December 25, 1946, formally terminated the period of tutelage. But in reality there is little difference between the "constitutional government" of 1948 and the tutelage regime of 1928–1948. The theories and institutions of the tutelage still constitute a key to the understanding of the forms and structures of the Chinese government of today, as they did to the government of the last two decades.

The Principle of Tutelage

As guiding principles for the period of tutelage, the Kuomintang has Sun Yat-sen's *Fundamentals of National Reconstruction for the Nationalist Government. The Fundamentals* bears the date April 12, 1924. It was written by Sun Yat-sen after the Reorganization of the Kuomintang, at the time of the completion of his lectures on the San Min Chu I. Sun Yat-sen was then full of confidence and hopes for an early consummation of the military campaigns against the opponents of the Revolution, to be soon followed by the Period of Tutelage. In anticipation, he worked out in more or less exact terms the steps which the tutelary party was to take up.[1]

The principal aim of the Tutelage Period was to enable the party, which considered itself to be the elite of the Chinese nation, "to instruct the people in the pursuit of constructive work of a revolutionary nature." The work is to be based on the *hsien*. To quote Article Eight of the *Fundamentals*:

> During the period of political tutelage the Government shall appoint trained men, who have passed the civil service examinations, to assist the people in the several *hsien* in preparing for local self-government. When a census of any *hsien* shall

have been taken, the land therein surveyed, an efficient police force organized, roads built throughout the *hsien*, the people trained in the exercise of their political rights and accustomed to the performance of civic duties according to the principles of the Revolution, and when officers shall have been elected to serve as *hsien* magistrates and councilors, then the *hsien* shall be deemed fit for full self-government.

The self-governing *hsien* is not only to be politically an advanced kind of democracy, but also economically, to embark on an ambitious program of social legislation and socialist enterprises. As soon as the *hsien* has initiated self-government, it sends an elected representative to participate in the affairs of the Central Government. When all the *hsien* of a province have acquired self-government, that province enters the constitutional stage, and its governor is also to be popularly elected. As soon as some one province has reached this stage, the country as a whole will be in the "Initial State of Constitutionalism." When a majority of the provinces reach the Constitutional Stage, there is to be a National Assembly which will enact and promulgate a constitution. The promulgation of the constitution will mark the consummation of constitutionalism.

Although the *Fundamentals* of Twenty-five Articles is at times precise or even minute, it gives no clear definition of the transition from one period to another. It is especially difficult to define clearly the beginning of the Constitutional Stage, for at the inception of the "Initial Stage of Constitutionalism" most of the provinces and certainly the Central Government would still be in the hands of the tutelary party. In this sense, the Periods of Tutelage and Constitutionalism overlap. When the majority of the provinces have entered into the Constitutional Stage and constitutionalism for the country as a whole has been consummated by the National Assembly's promulgation of a constitution, a minority of the provinces would still, for a while at least, be under some kind of tutelage. Here, too, the two Periods of Tutelage and Constitutionalism would overlap. In fact the Kuomintang has not followed nor been able to follow the *Fundamentals* exactly. Not a single *hsien* has ever reached the stage of development necessary for the fulfillment of Article Eight. Even if the party had been able to make some start in the development of the *hsien* and tried to follow the course of the *Fundamentals*, it would still have encountered difficulties of interpretation.

The Kuomintang through the Standing Committee of the Central Executive Committee passed the Essentials of Tutelage[2] of six articles on October 3, 1928. Although it claimed to be acting in accordance with Sun Yat-sen's *San Min Chu I* and the *Fundamentals of National Reconstruction*, the chief point was to proclaim that the party, through its Congress or the Central Executive Committee, was to exercise the sovereign power of the nation during the Period of Tutelage. It was a disappointing document, for it said too

TUTELAGE GOVERNMENT UNDER THE KUOMINTANG

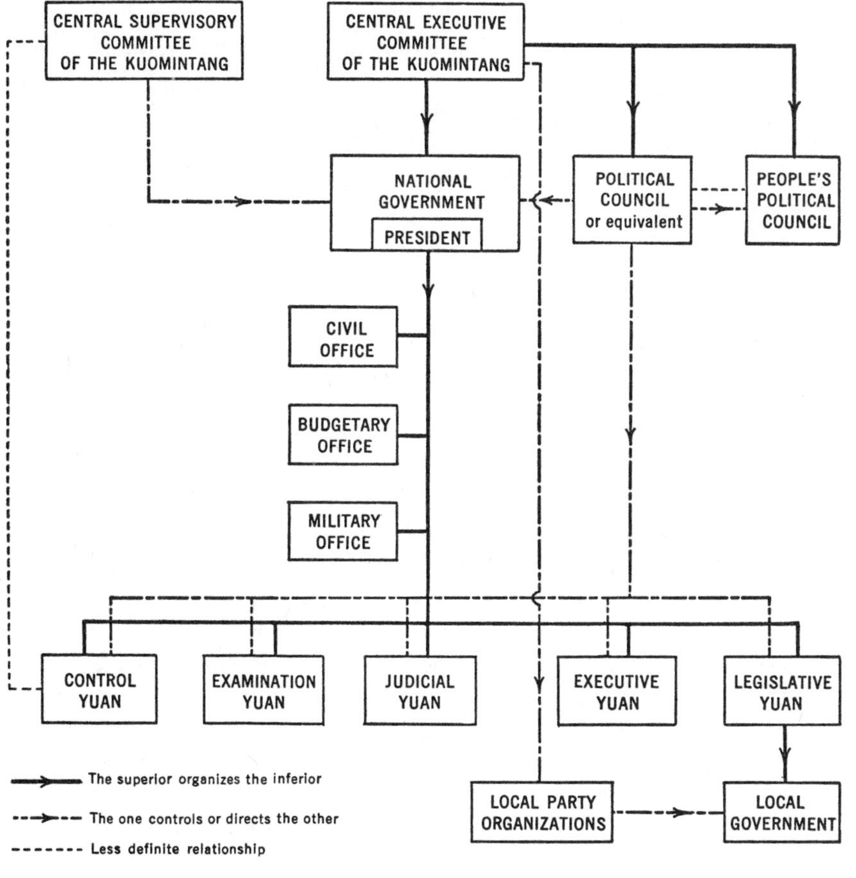

little. Then, in June 1929, a plenary session of the Central Executive Committee passed a long and extended document entitled "The Policy Plans of the Nationalist Government during the Period of Tutelage." It, too, was disappointing, for in spite of its length and minuteness—it had over a hundred items—there was really no program by means of which the *hsien* could be made to acquire the essentials of self-government. It was clear that Sun Yat-sen had prescribed high aims for Tutelage which his party, on account of its increasing complacency, was not able to fulfill or appreciate.

Instead, on October 8, 1928, a new Organic Law of the National Government providing for a Five-Yuan structure was promulgated. A powerful president of the National Government and under him five elaborately constituted Yuan came into existence, although according to the *Fundamentals* there would be no Five-Yuan structure until the country had reached the Initial Stage of Constitutionalism.

The Kuomintang continued to pay lip-service to the ultimate objectives of constitutional government, but, aside from the over-minute but rather meaningless program of June 1929, it was now more interested in governing for governing's sake than in considering the Tutelage Period a means toward the full exercise of sovereign power by the people themselves. During the ensuing years, no political training was given to the masses, who had no realization that they were, in Sun Yat-sen's mind, masters of the country. Also, no proportionate voice in the government was permitted to the few who did have a realization and capacity. Persons who were not members of the Kuomintang were regarded with hostility. Party members became rather the victims of "centralism" than the activitists of a "democratic" organization.

To be sure, party members could become powerful. But they became so only by submitting themselves implicitly to the party leaders and adjusting themselves to the party machine. They readily lost any interest in seeing the masses democratically conditioned and enfranchised. Some members who insisted at the very beginning of the Tutelage Period on the adoption of effective measures to enable the masses to acquire an increasing capacity for the exercise of the powers of government, such measures to be carried out by believers in democracy, ran the risk of being condemned as deviationists and were sometimes subjected to disciplinary action by the party.

Thus for years the party continued to govern with an increasingly firm hand, forgetting altogether that its governing was to be only a temporary phase in Sun Yat-sen's scheme of things. When first Fascist Italy and then Nazi Germany apparently were having successes of a dazzling nature, not a few of the Kuomintang gladly invoked those successes to further hypnotize themselves into believing in totalitarian party dictatorship as the New Order.

During the early years of Tutelage there did arise a controversy as to the necessity of a constitution for the Period of Tutelage. But that did not perceptibly alter the course of events. Once such a constitution was adopted, the Kuomintang went on governing without the slightest change of either heart or manner.

If power corrupts, dictatorial power corrupts by whetting the dictator's appetite for further dictatorial power. All party tutelage runs the risk of becoming a perpetuated dictatorship unless the party speedily and demonstrably identifies itself with the whole nation, thus obliterating the division of the dictators and those dictated to. Sun Yat-sen may have calculated on that speedy and demonstrable identification. If so, the Kuomintang has certainly done little to justify that calculation.

The Tutelage Constitution of 1931 [3]

The constitutional controversy began at the termination of the Northern Expedition in 1928. Some elements of the party as well as outsiders demanded a provisional constitution for the Period of Tutelage. It was largely on the insistence of Hu Han-min that the party in October 1928 resolved to embark on the Period of Tutelage by adopting the Essentials of Tutelage, without any mention of a constitution. But Chiang Kai-shek had perhaps little conviction either way. So when the separatist regime of Yen Hsi-shan and Wang Ching-wei adopted in 1930 a draft provisional constitution, he too demanded one for his own regime. That was the origin of the Provisional Constitution of June 1, 1931.

Chiang Kai-shek first proposed a provisional constitution in October 1930. Acting on the proposal, the Central Executive Committee in November decided to call a national constitutional convention in May of 1931. Subsequently, the Standing Committee of the Central Executive Committee appointed a drafting committee of eleven which worked from March 9 to April 22, 1931. After six meetings the committee completed a draft, which was accepted in rapid order first by the Standing Committee and then by the Central Executive and Supervisory Committees in joint session and was ready for reference to the National Convention meeting on May 5.

The National Convention was composed of 520 delegates, elected by the qualified voters of the provinces and municipalities grouped into (1) farmers' unions, (2) workers' unions, (3) merchants' guilds and industrialists' associations, (4) education organizations, universities, and professional associations, and (5) the Kuomintang. The voters' lists were crudely prepared. Not only was the last category the party itself, the other four categories were naturally also party-controlled. Furthermore, party members, who were members of the organizations of the first four categories, enjoyed a plural vote. The convention was a party convention, pure and simple.

As was to be expected, the draft of the party was accepted by the convention speedily and with little dissent. In four sessions the convention finished the three readings. There were only modifications of wording and insertions of platitudes. The significant change was concerned with the interpretation of the constitution. While the party draft provided that interpretation rest with an interpretation committee, the convention resolved that it should rest with the Central Executive Committee of the party. In other words, the convention out-partied the party in its eagerness to maintain the supremacy of the party.

The new constitution was promulgated on June 1, 1931, and was known as the "Provisional Constitution of the Republic of China for the Period of Tutelage." It had eighty-nine articles divided into eight chapters, namely: I. General Principles; II. Bill of Rights; III. Essentials of Tutelage; IV. National Economy; V. Education; VI. Central and Local Powers; VII. The Organization of Government; VIII. Appendix.

The most important chapter was of course the one providing for the organization of the government. But the most remarkable thing was the absence of any provision for an amending process. Since it could not be amended, and since the Central Executive Committee of the party enjoyed the power of interpretation, the government in subsequent years often drastically departed from the constitution, both in letter and in spirit, without any danger of being adjudged unconstitutional. In fact, the Organic Law of the National Government of December 30, 1931 was, as will be noted below, in open contravention of Chapter VII of the constitution, for the constitutional powers of the president of the National Government were very much reduced by the Organic Law. But who could hold legally responsible the party organs which passed that law? The provisions concerned with the freedoms of the people were also more often honored in the breach than in the observance. But if the party either condoned or initiated the breach, who would have the power to bring the culpable officials of the government or party to account?

A constitution operates only when there is effective sanction behind it. In a democratic country, the political sanction usually comes from the general body of the population, either reflected through a representative assembly or through other forms of public opinion. The legal sanction usually comes from the fact that the courts, in exercising their judicial power, are backed by the articulate body politic. In a country with a party dictatorship, the sanction has to come from the party itself. Unless the party is willing to limit its own powers, to have some kind of auto-limitation, there is really no sense in having a constitution. The Kuomintang, when promulgating the Tutelage Constitution of 1931, perhaps little realized these implications. If it had, either it would not have had the Constitution at all or it would have thought it out carefully and accepted only those limitations within which it was willing to live.

The Provisional Constitution for the Period of Tutelage was thus ordained only to be ignored. The ordaining might not have been too solemn, but the ignoring was complete. It is difficult to imagine that history could have taken a different course, for better or for worse, if the Constitution had not been in existence. The existence of the Constitution made no difference to the nature and quality of the Kuomintang tutelage. The Kuomintang continued to govern and to govern alone.

The Political Council [4]

a. *Evolution.* The form of Kuomintang dictatorship was meant to be a replica of the communist dictatorship in the Soviet Union. In the summer of 1924, in Canton, the policy of alliance with Russia was in full swing and Michael Borodin was functioning actively as the high adviser to the party. Sun Yat-sen, as head of the party, appointed a Political Council. Next to Sun Yat-sen himself, it was all-powerful, under the Central Executive Committee. In fact, on July 14, 1924, three days after its appointment, the Central Executive Committee passed a resolution instructing it to hold itself responsible to the Central Executive Committee for party matters, and to the President of the Party and Generalissimo of the Military Government, that is, Sun Yat-sen, for political and diplomatic affairs.

After the death of Sun Yat-sen, and the Second Party Congress of 1926, the Political Council became strictly a committee of the Central Executive Committee. For a while it remained small. When the Nationalist Government formally came into being in July 1925, the relation between the Political Council and that government was the same as that between the Polit Bureau of the Russian Communist Party and the Government of the Soviet Union.

It is conceivable that had this Political Council remained small and compact, composed of only the top leaders of the party, it might have given rise to a different and perhaps better kind of party dictatorship. It would inevitably have developed into some sort of oligarchy. But it might also have forestalled the government of one leader and the lack of deliberation arising from the unwieldiness of the council and the confusion of party and government directives. But the Political Council was enlarged and its effectiveness diminished in reverse ratio to its size.

Those members of the Central Executive Committee who were not members of the Political Council were often jealous of the council. By the summer of 1926 the Central Executive Committee ordered that a "Political Conference," a joint meeting of the Standing Committee and the Political Council, both of course committees of the Central Executive Committee, should take the place of the separate committees during the period of the Northern Expedition. The membership of the Political Conference was twenty-one at the outset and it grew steadily. From then on, though the Political Council persisted under various names, it was never to regain the compactness it once possessed.

To be brief, from 1926 up to 1937 when the Japanese War began, the Political Council had several changes of name. Generally speaking, when it was small and its members were chosen exclusively from the Central Executive Committee, it was usually called "Political Council." When, on the other hand, it was somewhat larger and its membership included persons from outside the Central Executive Committee, it was called "Political Conference." Whether it was called "Council" or "Conference," it never could remain small for any length of time. For example, after the Fifth Party Congress toward the end of 1935 when the name was again changed from "Political Conference" to "Political Council" and the membership was limited to twenty-five, it soon threw open its doors to admit a large number of so-called "attending members."[5] The point is that, since 1926, the Political Council has always been large and unwieldy.

When the war started, in the summer of 1937, the unwieldiness of the Political Council made it a poor instrument of counsel. A change was imperative. Earlier, the Committee on National Defense, a subcommittee of the Political Council, had been set up largely to circumvent the incapacities of the main body. Immediately after the outbreak of the war, the Standing Committee of the Central Executive Committee installed a Supreme National Defense Council to take the place of the Political Council. In fact, this Supreme Council was really a reorganized and reduced Political Council.

In January 1939, there was a further reorganization. The name was changed. The new council had as its chairman the Leader of the Party, and as its ex officio members the members of the Standing Committees of the Central Executive and Supervisory Committees, the presidents and vice-presidents of the Five Yuan, and the members of the Military Commission. In addition, the chairman could propose a number of members for appointment by the Standing Committee of the Central Executive Committee. Out of this large membership the chairman was authorized to designate eleven to be members of its standing committee.

The creation of a standing committee was to facilitate business; the inclusion of so many in the council was to humor the bigger names in the party's roster. But when the standing committee met, the chairman, whether by force of habit or out of the instinct to secure a following, always invited great numbers of people to attend. The chairman had of course nothing to lose, because his experience in such meetings must have convinced him that his authority could not suffer any deterioration because of the presence of a larger number of officials of the party and the government.

In April 1947, on the reorganization of the National Government to include the representatives of two minor parties and others, the Supreme National Defense Council was discontinued, and the Political Council was restored. It now consists of from nineteen to twenty-five members, appointed by the Central Executive Committee on nomination by the Leader, with members of the Standing Committee of the Central Executive Committee and Central Supervisory Committee and a number of high government officials who happen to be members of the party as ex officio members. Its function is to give directives to the Kuomintang members of the government and not the government itself. But this distinction is immaterial. The Kuomintang's position in the government being dominant, controlling the Kuomintang members is tantamount to controlling the government itself. In other words, the Political Council remains up to this day an organ of Kuomintang tutelage.

b. *Membership and Chairman.* The members of the Political Council have all been appointed by the Central Executive Committee itself, its Standing Committee, or the Leader. Usually the leading members of the Standing Committees of the Central Executive and Supervisory Committees have been included in the Political Council, if not all of them. There has been and still is an intimate interlocking of the leadership charged with party and government affairs. It follows that if the party leaders should be devoid of vision and vitality, the political leaders cannot be expected to have these qualities.

As a matter of theory, large membership in a deliberative body gives a democratic tenor to that organ. But in the case of the Political Council, numbers seemed to have contributed rather to the disappearance of responsibility than to the emergence of a democratic spirit. This is because the members participating in its deliberations cannot claim to have equal authority, as the elected representatives of an assembly usually do.

The members of the Political Council are of several categories. Some are there because they are veterans of the party or men who have served the government for a long time. Some were formerly high military leaders now relieved of active command. Some are high officials of government. Still others are the younger and the more partisan elements of the several party groups. Those who belonged to the Organization Group have formed a specially close coterie in the committee. The veterans and the officials usually take an inactive part. The partisans of the groups are active, but they have little weight of their own. They merely reflect the views of their leaders. A body so constituted has neither the advantages of intimate consultation among a small number of responsible leaders free from maneuvers and bickerings, nor the advantages of a truly democratic assembly [illegible]voking popular sentiment to arrive at decisions. Instead, it plays into the hands of the dominant group.

The invariably large membership of the Political Council led to the emergence first of a presidium, then of a head. During the first six-odd years of its existence, from 1924 to the end of 1931, its coöpted chairman was never very powerful. He was not much more than a presiding officer. From the end of 1931 to the end of 1935, a powerful presidium — first of three, then expanded to nine — was imposed on the council. From the end of 1935 to its reorganization as the Supreme National Defense Council in January 1939, a powerful chairman with a deputy-chairman took the place of the presidium. Since 1939, the Leader of the Party has acted as the sole chairman, hence also the head of the council. Thus, the unwieldiness of the council has resulted in the concentration of power in the hands of one man.

c. *Powers and Functions.* The powers of the Political Council are both supreme and extensive. Formerly it decided on (1) the principles of legislation; (2) the policies of the government; (3) military matters of importance; (4) fiscal policies; (5) the appointment of high officials; and(6) whatever else is referred to it by the Central Executive Committee of the party. The 1947 reorganization brought no diminution. It still has power to discuss and resolve on (1) measures for the carrying out of the programs and policies of the party; (2) the handling of important problems; (3) reports rendered by Yuan presidents and ministers who are members of the party; (4) nomination of party members to be candidates for high posts, both appointive and elective; and (5) other matters referred to it by the Central Executive Committee or proposed by the members themselves.

The ensemble of these items would seem to enable the Political Council to combine the powers of both the British Parliament and the American Congress. It has the power of passing on appointments enjoyed by the American Senate but denied to the British Parliament, and it has also the power of discussing and passing on the general policies of the executive enjoyed by the British Parliament but denied to the American Congress. Indeed, it has more. As we shall see later, it really monopolizes legislation to an extent unknown in both Great Britain and the United States. In the latter, the President in practice shares the legislative initiative with Congress. In the former, Parliament can in general only deliberate and pass on the measures brought before it by the Cabinet. But the Political Council initiates and elaborates legislative proposals on matters both important and unimportant.

In years past, the parallel existence of the Five Yuan and the indeterminate nature of the relation between the Yuan on the one hand and the National Government Council, on the other, have further enabled the Political Council to be the indispensable authority of government. The four Yuan other than the Legislative all proposed legislation. They sent their proposals directly to the Legislative Yuan; the Executive Yuan had no authority to interfere. In matters of appointment, all five Yuan possessed an equal authority in respect to their own personnel. Unless the National Government was able to exercise an over-all review, there was no other organ in the government to do so. But the National Government Council was often the asylum of venerable but powerless figures. The powerful figures chose instead the Political Council as the agency through which to exercise a general control over legislation, appointments, and administrative matters.

d. *Procedure and Actual Operation.* The procedure of the Political Council resembles that of a legislative assembly. It used to meet on a fixed day of the week; it still meets once a week or every few weeks. It is divided into a number of committees.[6] For most of the time there have been only four important committees, charged with matters of law, finance, economics, and education. The committee on law was naturally the most important of all, for law covers almost everything outside of the budget and the economic and educational policies.

A proposal before the Political Council may be initiated by a member or brought to it by the Central Executive Committee or its Standing Committee, or by Kuomintang members of the government (before 1948 by the National Government or the Yuan). Unless urgency is involved and the council desires discussion or decision at once, the proposal is always referred to one of its committees. When a committee sits to consider the proposal, the party or government department concerned with the subject matter is usually requested to send representatives to meet with the committee. The kindred committee of the Legislative Yuan is also asked to delegate representatives.[7] In a way, the committees of the Political Council act as the coördinators of all party and government authorities interested in the same matter. In this sense, in the days of the National Government the Political Council used to fill a gap in its structure. The position it thus acquired actually made the National Government more dependent on the party than ever.

As the volume of business transacted by the Political Council is enormous, the recommendations of its committees are usually accepted by the council without much discussion. As far as routine business is concerned, it is rather the committees than the council that enjoy the high powers of government. But, in the case of very important matters of policy, usually the chairman of the Political Council has the power of decision, and in matters of urgency he has long had that right.

In the same way that the chairman of the Political Council can impose his will on the Political Council, the chairman of the committees also have considerable power over them. They can control, by superior prestige or by outmaneuvering, the decisions to be reached by the committees. The fact that the Political Council is composed of members of unequal influence, as stated earlier, enables the powerful members to play the kind of role which prevents the Political Council from developing into a healthy deliberative body. Thus it may be said of the work of the Political Council: what the leaders decide, the ordinary members abide by. The latters' domain is that of the routine business of the government. Outside the routine, their voices can be employed only to support the Leader or to engage in factional politics, attacking the leaders of one faction on behalf of the leaders of another.

e. *Reflections*. The Political Council was originally intended to give general direction and supervision to the government. In that sense it was to be no different from the Polit Bureau at Moscow. But if the council were really to limit its attention to matters of importance, there must be in the government some centralized authorities charged with legislation and administration. Because of the virtual absence of such authorities in or under the National Government, the Political Council, besides acting as the organ of supervision and direction, descended to actual legislation and sometimes to administration as well.

When the Political Council descended to actual legislation, it itself became a government. When it attended to details of legislation and administration, it became an overburdened government. No government can be entirely efficient if it does not know how to discriminate between the important and the unimportant, reserving the former to the principal organ and delegating the latter to the subordinate organs. The Political Council was in this sense a poor government, for it permitted itself to delve into too many unnecessary details.

There is an explanation. The large number of rather small men who took part in the deliberations of the council, either as members or as attending members, must do something to justify their presence there. Unable or afraid to touch on the more important, they chose to be vocal and meddlesome in rather small matters. In the end, power became more and more concentrated in the hands of the chairman of the council, the Leader of the Party.

It is a misfortune for the Kuomintang that the Political Council has become neither a healthy deliberative body of many voices nor a small directorate. If it had become the former, there would have been at least some beginnings of a democratic process in the high councils of the party. If it had become the latter, the government it was meant to supervise and direct need not have been paralyzed by minute interference from the party.

It is to be borne in mind that during the whole period of the Kuomintang tutelage the Political Council, in spite of the frequent reorganizations and changes of name, has been an organ of great stability. Its constitution and its position in regard to the government have remained more or less constant. Therefore, if something either good or efficient, or, still better, both good and efficient, had evolved, it could not but have produced a salutary effect on the party on the one hand and provided the country with better government on the other. As it is, the experience of the Political Council has served no other purpose than merely to enable the high leaders, and ultimately the Leader of the Party, to control the National Government. It was established as a means of tutelage, but it has not been itself a training ground for anything better or nobler.

The Kuomintang now professes to have discontinued the party dictatorship. Theoretically a constitutional government came into being in May 1948. In the meantime, some minor parties, by invitation of the Kuomintang, are already having a share in the higher councils of the government. The Political Council, powerful though it still is, can no longer give directives to the government councils. It can only direct and supervise the Kuomintang members in such councils. But as a matter of fact, the Political Council's power over the government remains undiminished since the Kuomintang members are in fact still in complete control of the government councils. While it would be idle to speculate on the future of the Political Council, it is reasonable to assume that so long as the Kuomintang retains virtual control of the government, so long will the Political Council remain at the apex of power. It is therefore so much the more lamentable that the council has not had a healthier development.

Planning and Planning Machinery

From 1940 to 1948 two other party agencies which had to do with the guidance and supervision of the government were in existence. They were the Central Planning Board and the Party and Government Work Appraisal Commission. Theoretically subordinated to the Supreme National Defense Council, they nevertheless acted quite independently of it, for the Leader of the Party was the head of all three and subordination of one to the other was unnecessary.

In 1940 the Soviet system of planning became suddenly popular with some leaders of the Kuomintang and in the lull of the war Chiang Kai-shek, the Leader of the Party and the Chairman of the Supreme National Defense Council, ordered the institution of the so-called triple-linked system of administration. Briefly put, the Central Planning Board was to plan, the government and party departments were to execute, and the Party and Government Work Appraisal Commission was to appraise whether the plan had been duly executed. The Supreme National Defense Council was to serve as the link and organ of over-all supervision. This was evidently the Kuomintang's understanding of the Soviet system of planning, or at least a modified or even an improved version of that system.

a. *The Central Planning Board* was established in 1940. Its Chairmanship, also styled Tsung-ts'ai, was held concurrently by the Chairman of the Supreme National Defense Council. It had a secretary-general (with two deputies) who was the operating head of the organization. There were to be two councils. The first was the Council of Review, to be composed of a small number of members chosen by the chairman, who was also to preside over its meeting. It was never appointed. The second was the Planning Council consisting of a large number of members, drawn from various party and government departments and universities and professions. They were the planners, and were presided over by the secretary-general.

The members of the Planning Council were to plan for all conceivable work to be undertaken by the government, military, economic, as well as administrative. But results were meager. The so-called "annual policy plan" submitted to the Party Councils and the People's Political Council seldom held anything more than platitudes or aspirations of the most general nature.

The blame for having produced no plans was, however, not the Planning Board's entirely. In order to make sensible and practicable plans, full economic data were needed. So was the coöperation of the party and government departments. Neither was available or forthcoming. There was also signally lacking a belief that anything approaching a Soviet plan could or would be worked out in China at that time. The war was going on. The government was ineffective in the extreme. Morale was low. None but the politically naive would venture to do anything sweeping, for that would only result in frustration and in censure.

The Central Planning Board died a natural death in 1948 when the new constitutional government came into existence.

b. *The Party and Government Work Appraisal Commission* [8] came into existence late in 1940. It had a chairman, two deputy-chairmen, and eleven members. Of the eleven members, eight were ex officio, namely, the presidents of the Five Yuan and the secretaries-general of the Central Executive Committee, Central Supervisory Committee, and the Supreme National Defense Council. It had a secretary-general of its own. For the discharge of its function, it was divided into two sections, one on party work, and the other on government work. Chiang Kai-shek himself took the chairmanship of the commission, and the two deputy-chairmen each took charge of a section.

The function of the commission was to determine the extent to which the plans of the Planning Board had been carried out, and also to find out the state of the finances and personnel involved in the carrying out of the said plans. All party and government agencies and all their works, not of a routine nature, were within the purview of the commission.

For years the commission sent out a large number of its agents to do the appraising, both in the capital and in the provinces. While these agents were quite meddlesome, they could of course contribute nothing to the successful operation of the triple-linked system of administration. Since there was little planning, there could not be much execution, and still less the need for appraisal.

The Party and Government Work Appraisal Commission also came to an end in 1948.

The establishment of the Central Planning Board and the Party and Government Work Appraisal Commission was utterly meaningless, and did not further the work of tutelage. Nevertheless, the board and the commission were the organs of the tutelage, and during their existence, they did much further to complicate the government machinery of the Kuomintang.

Party Interference in Government

While in theory the Political Council of the Central Executive Committee of the Kuomintang serves as the only vehicle by which the party maintains its supremacy over the government, the practice has been quite otherwise. Both the central and the local departments of the party have often interfered directly with the central and local administrative authorities of the government. The personnel in party and government administrations, certainly the more responsible ones, are not always clearly separable. A responsible official in the government is often a party functionary, and vice versa.

Party officials who are not also government officials have a tendency to be jealous of the latter and derive some sadistic enjoyment from interfering in their affairs. This is especially true in the provinces and the *hsien*. If the local government happens to be in the hands of a local militarist who is a party member only by courtesy, the struggle between the government and the party in that locality can be quite intense. The same is also true if the government and the party organizations of corresponding nature or of the same locality happen to fall into the hands of rival groups of the party. The Leader of the Party does not need, however, to be overconcerned with such a state of things, for in case of an impasse the contending parties almost invariably appeal to him for final arbitration. The position and prestige of the Leader is not affected by the intense rivalry of his followers or even by the paralysis of the administration caused by such rivalry.

Besides the uncalled-for interference in central and local administrations by central and local party officials, party dictatorship also takes the form of filling government posts with party members. In the first years following the establishment of the Nationalist regime, the meaning of one-party government was debated at length. While the theory prevailed that one-party government means only that the doctrines and the policies of that one party should prevail and not be subjected to frustration, the practice has always been to fill all government posts, certainly the more important ones, with members of the party.

This practice can be sensible if enough members of proven faith and ability to man the posts are available. If such men are not available in large numbers, the more sensible move would have been to fill only the posts of pivotal importance with party men, abandoning the other posts to nonpartisan functionaries. Instead of so doing, the Kuomintang in the years immediately following its accession to power, either bestowed membership on de facto high officials who were not members of the party or tolerated the opportunists seeking membership in the party.

The result was that in the first years of Kuomintang government almost all functionaries high and low were nominally all Kuomintang men. What was true in the civil branches of the government was also true in the military services. Manifestly, such a practice was not conducive to an effective government by one party, since the government would naturally be neither efficient nor yet quite of one party, if by party one means a body of men sharing one definite political faith. In this sense the Kuomintang government from the very beginning was not much of a one-party government.

It was not until after the Japanese had started their Manchurian ventures in 1931 that Chiang Kai-shek, who had already attained leadership of the party, began to enlist support of men engaged in education and industry. When a number of these men did come to join the government they joined as independents, neither seeking membership in the Kuomintang nor compelled to join. However, most, if not all, of these men did join the party during the war years by command of Chiang Kai-shek, the Leader. It is not ascertainable whether his motive for ordering the nonparty high officials of the government to join the party was due to his desire to strengthen his party by their advent or to convey to the outside world an impression that there were in the party people of maturity, honesty, and reputation.

These new members, granted that they were able and good, have never been to this day active in the councils of the party, and they are decorative figures pure and simple. In this sense their relation to the Kuomintang government is not unlike that of the old-time provincial governors or military commanders, who when allowed to continue in their posts were given membership in the party in the first years of the Kuomintang government.

If it is true that the manning of government posts by nominal Kuomintang members is not real Kuomintang government, the manning of certain services by certain special groups of the party does constitute something like group government. For instance, since the army is consistently manned by the graduates of the Whampoa Academy, it is to that extent more a Whampoa army than a party army. Since the budgetary and personnel divisions in the various departments of government, both central and local, are usually filled with men of the Organization Group of the party, they are to that extent Organization divisions. So, though the government as a whole is in reality not much of a party government, many parts of that government are indeed group or factional governments. The segmentation of the party leads also to segmentation of the government. Here the attitude that a party government cannot be better or worse than the party which runs the government becomes a truism.

On examining and analyzing the Kuomintang government, one gets the impression that it has been not so much a government by the Kuomintang as a government by a group of men who have called themselves "Kuomintang" and who have all revolved around the Leader of the Kuomintang in the person of Chiang Kai-shek. The Kuomintang government of the last twenty years has never been noted either for the cohesiveness of its members beyond what the Leader has been able to provide, or for strict adherence to a party program. What has been known as the one-party government of the Kuomintang is in truth more a one-man government of its Leader. This is of course in complete harmony with the dominance of personal elements from which no Chinese government has up to this moment been entirely disentangled.

X

THE NATIONAL GOVERNMENT AND ITS PRESIDENT[1]

The National Government[2] of the Republic of China was originally set up at Canton on July 1, 1925. In his *Fundamentals of National Reconstruction for the Nationalist Government*, Sun Yat-sen prescribed that there should be a Nationalist government to lead the country through the military and tutelage stages to a full constitutional government. At the time of Sun Yat-sen's death in March 1925, his government at Canton was only the "General Headquarters" of the Generalissimo. It had to be reorganized and to assume formally the name of "Nationalist Government" because the Yunnan militarist, T'ang Chi-yao, who had been elected Vice-Generalissimo when Sun Yat-sen himself was elected Generalissimo by the Rump Parliament but had declined to serve, was claiming the right to succeed to the position of Generalissimo. In reorganizing, the Kuomintang naturally rendered invalid that undesirable militarist's claim to the succession.

Born of necessity, the Nationalist Government was subject to frequent changes of organization and personnel, whenever circumstances changed. As the Northern Expedition of the Kuomintang progressed, and the government was moved from Canton to Wuhan and thence to Nanking, there were changes both in the Organic Law and in its personnel. When, as the result of unification, the Five Yuan were installed in October 1928, changes of a more radical nature took place. The beginning of the Japanese occupation of the Northeastern Provinces in 1931 was the occasion for further changes which involved the stepping-down of Chiang Kai-shek as the powerful President of the Government and the succession of Lin Sen as a president of a different type. The war in 1937 brought about a total eclipse of the National Government as a functioning body and the concentration of power in the hands of Chiang Kai-shek in his multiple capacities as both party and military leader. The death of Lin Sen and the succession of Chiang Kai-shek in the fall of 1943 again restored the presidency, and with it the National Government, to their former position of power and importance. Finally, when representatives of two minor parties and non-party men were admitted into the government in April 1947, there was a further change.

The inauguration of a new government in May 1948, in accordance with the Constitution of December 25, 1946, brought the Nationalist regime to an end. The President of the Republic has taken the place of the National Government and its President. But the change is more formal than real in nature. The man in power remains the same. His chief lieutenants remain the same. The practice of government also has not changed. For an understanding of the present-day government of China a knowledge of the structure and procedure of the National Government has not diminished in importance.

The Organic Law [3]

The Organic Law of the National Government regulated both the organization and the functions of that government. With each change of the organization or of the functions, there was a revision of the existing law or an enactment of a new law. In the Provisional Constitution of June 1, 1931, which was supposed to have governed the country up to May 1948, the chapter on National Government of course stands as the most important part. The constitution was never amended, but one did not need to be meticulous about its provisions, for, constitution or no constitution, it was always the Organic Law which regulated the National Government. Or, to be more correct, it was the Organic Law as amended from time to time by the party resolutions.[4]

The last Organic Law was passed by the Central Executive Committee in its first plenary session in December 1931. The Fourth Party Congress, a united assembly of both the Nanking and the Canton organizations, had just been held. As their price for returning to the fold, the separatist Canton organization of the party demanded the substitution of a responsible cabinet for the presidential system under which Chiang Kai-shek had governed the country for some years. It was under this pressure that the new Organic Law was enacted. In form, the Organic Law of December 30, 1931 never underwent radical changes. The first change was the amendment of September 15, 1943, when the president was again given high powers. The second was the amendment of April 17, 1947, which enhanced the position of the council of the National Government in order to make membership attractive to the non-Kuomintang claimants to power. Otherwise, the 1931 Organic Law in its original form prevailed.

The Five-Yuan Government

The term "National Government" had both a broader and a narrower sense. In its broader sense it denoted the ensemble of the Central Government of the Tutelage; in its narrow sense, only the council and the president of the National Government. The Five Yuan and all other government agencies were parts of the National Government only in its former sense. While this chapter will be confined to a treatment of the council and President of the National Government, it is yet necessary to survey the position of the Five Yuan vis-à-vis the council and the President of the National Government. Without such a general consideration, the importance or unimportance of the council and the president cannot be appreciated.

The Five-Yuan system[5] is derived from Sun Yat-sen's so-called Five-Power Constitution. Sun Yat-sen had distinguished function from power or governing from political powers. According to him, the people should exercise the four political powers of election and recall, of initiative and referendum, and the government the five governing powers of administration, legislation, adjudication, examination, and control. He thought that these two sets of powers were clearly different from each other in nature, and therefore should be completely separated. In his anxiety for the most complete separation possible, he wished the government to be all-powerful, unhampered in its exercise of the five governing powers.

The five-power theory is obviously an elaboration of the traditional theory of three powers. Examination was separated by Sun Yat-sen from administration because he seems to have been greatly fascinated by the examination system of ancient China. For a similar reason control was separated from legislation. While Western political scientists from Montesquieu down advocated the separation of powers as a guarantee of political freedom, Sun Yat-sen deplored checks and balances, and thought that the five organs in possession of the powers should work in unison. But he failed to define how the president holding an office which he envisaged as one of importance could resist the temptation to interfere with some or even to dominate all of them. Nor did he offer any fruitful suggestions as to effective means by which the people could exercise their political powers to check a too-powerful government which became despotic.

The saving factor in Sun Yat-sen's apparently defective theorizing is that he did not contemplate the setting up of the Five Yuan until some provinces had fully reached the state of self-government and the country entered the Initial Stage of Constitutionalism. Furthermore, the final constitution, according to him, was to be drafted after weighing the actual experience of the five-power system. It therefore implied that, logically speaking, if the experience were to be unfavorable, the final constitution need not literally or even closely follow his views.

The premature adoption of the Five-Yuan system of government in October 1928 was not conducive to the realization of Sun Yat-sen's ideal, and to that extent was a misfortune for the Kuomintang. When the Five Yuan began, not a single constituted body of men existed who could claim to have a popular basis and thus be able either to support or to control the Yuan, when necessary. The Yuan were weak and impotent from the beginning. They had to rely either on the National Government or on the party. For lack of popular support, they were prevented from functioning properly as the great organs of the state.

It is unfortunate that the Five Yuan have generally been weak. But if they were strong would they be able to function properly? Suppose the party had not interfered and the National Government had been inactive. Presumably one or more of the Yuan would then have assumed real power, and the most powerful one might even have become oblivious of the existence and functions of the weaker ones. Who would supply a wholesome check and prevent them from running amuck? In the absence of a powerful public opinion or a popular body elected by the people, there was no prospect for the Five Yuan to function as powerful yet healthy organs of government. Inevitably they would be either pitiably weak, or irresponsibly strong.

The early adoption of the Five-Yuan system was largely the work of Hu Han-min. In 1928 when Wang Ching-wei was at odds with the Nanking regime, Hu Han-min's participation was eagerly solicited by Chiang Kai-shek. While still at Paris Hu Han-min proposed [6] the immediate adoption of the Five-Yuan system. But in justice to Hu Han-min it must be said that though the premature adoption of the Five Yuan disregarded the time schedule of Sun Yat-sen, he had a very serious purpose. He was apprehensive of the reëmergence of China's old scourge, the dictatorship of one person. He was for a collegiate form of organization for the top levels of government.

According to Hu Han-min's original proposal, all the Five Yuan were to be strictly collegiate; the Legislative Yuan to have from forty-nine to ninety-nine members, the Executive Yuan from nineteen to twenty-five, and the other three Yuan, from five to nine members each. The members of the Five Yuan together were to constitute the National Government, the five chairmen of the Five Yuan were to constitute a standing committee of the government; and one of these five was to be designated as the chairman of the National Government. The five members of the standing committee were to be automatically members of the Executive and Legislative Yuan. Further, to facilitate the close coöperation of these two Yuan, the ministers of the Executive Yuan were to be ex officio members of the corresponding

ORGANIZATION OF THE NATIONAL GOVERNMENT, APRIL, 1947

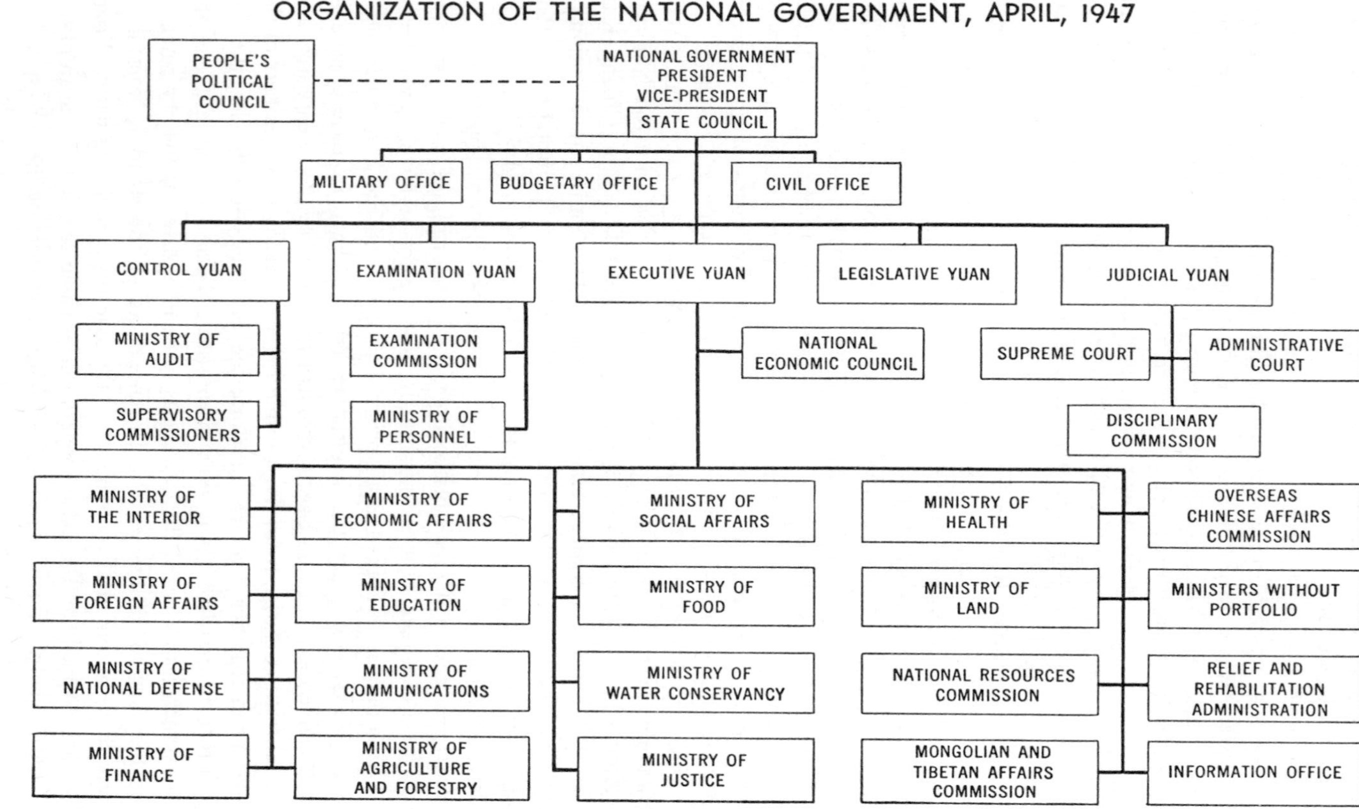

committees of the Legislative Yuan and, with the exception of the Minister of Finance, might serve as the chairmen of these committees.

Hu Han-min's proposal in fact envisaged a quintuple government. The all-powerful directorate of five would control not only the Five Yuan separately, but also the Executive and Legislative Yuan as well as the over-all setup, the National Government, collectively. If the selection of the directorate of five was well calculated, so that none could dominate the others, the emergence of a personal dictatorship could, in his opinion, be precluded. The proposal, considered in the light of Hu Han-min's crusading fervor against a possible personal dictatorship, was well considered. But he was soon outwitted and outmaneuvered. When the proposal was discussed by the party leaders in Nanking in September of 1928, it went through drastic revision.

The Organic Law of the National Government of October 8, 1928 set up a strong and relatively powerful National Government and relatively weak Yuan. Both the president and the council of the National Government were, according to the Law, functioning authorities. The presidents and vice-presidents of the Five Yuan were all members of the council, which then consisted of fifteen members in all, not counting the president of the National Government. It was at once evident that whoever controlled the council would also control the whole government. Since it was easier for the president of the National Government to secure a personal following among the presidents and vice-presidents of the Five Yuan than for the latter to act in unison against the former's personal domination, the president of the National Government was able to control the council from the very beginning.

From the start Chiang Kai-shek was President of the National Government; an older man of wise and accommodating nature, T'an Yen-k'ai, was President of the Executive Yuan; and Hu Han-min was merely President of the Legislative Yuan. Therefore, if Hu Han-min had really intended to use the Five-Yuan system to check the domination of any one leader, his aims were doomed to failure from the first.

The Five Yuan never had a chance to function properly. In the beginning the council of the National Government was too powerful. Then, in November 1930, after Chiang Kai-shek became concurrently President of the Executive Yuan upon the death of T'an Yen-k'ai, the Executive Yuan was too powerful for the other Yuan. When Lin Sen became President of the National Government and Wang Ching-wei head of the Executive Yuan, the Political Council of the party, either in full council or through its subcommittee on National Defense, became too powerful. Throughout the war, the dominant position of overlordship was assumed by the Supreme National Defense Council, headed first by the President of the Military Commission, then by the Leader of the Party, in both cases Chiang Kai-shek. In April 1947, the Council of the National Government again recovered some of its original importance, but Chiang Kai-shek as President of the National Government remained in firm control of the council. It was always difficult for the Yuan to exercise their powers independent of the all-powerful domination of a leader. When that leader happened also to be identified with the Executive Yuan, the latter had too free an exercise of power upon which the other four Yuan could not bring any restraint to bear.

President and Council

In the National Government itself the relation between the president and the council is all-important. If the council has too little power or the president assumes the powers given to the council, it will be the president rather than the council who actually governs. If, on the other hand, the council both possesses and exercises important powers of government, and, whatever influence the president may wield he wields in his capacity of presiding officer of the council, the council and not the presidency will be the seat of power.

The Kuomintang at the time of its reorganization in 1924 inherited a strong dislike for the presidential type of executive, although it made an exception in the case of Sun Yat-sen, who was always ready to enjoy the powers of a chief executive of the presidential type. Upon his death, the inherited dislike of the party for a powerful one-man executive strongly reasserted itself. There were to be for the nation no president and for the provinces no governors. For both there was to be a council or collegiate form of government, with a presiding officer in each case given the courtesy title of chairman or president.[7] This was the guiding principle of the original Organic Law of the Nationalist Government promulgated by the Kuomintang on July 1, 1925. The same principle persisted in all the subsequent revisions of that Law, although during the two brief periods of November 1930 to December 1931, and September 1943 to April 1947, the revised Law did confer on the president the powers of a presidential type of executive.

According to the Organic Law of July 1, 1925, the president was a mere presiding officer elected from among the members of the council. He was merely a titular head. The powers of the council were concentrated in the standing committee of the council rather than in the president. The Law of March 10, 1927, while retaining the mechanism of a standing committee, even dispensed with the president. The president-less council continued until February 1928, when the revised Law of February 13 reverted to the earlier system of having both a president and a standing committee. There cannot be any question, however, that under all these Laws the presidency, whenever that office existed, was not substantial and the government was really collegiate in nature.

The law of October 8, 1928 setting up the Five Yuan was more ambiguous.

It provided that the members of the National Government should exercise the powers of the government in a council of state. This suggested that the president was still only a presiding member of the council. But the law had dropped an old provision that the president should be elected by and from the members of the council. In fact, Chiang Kai-shek, like T'an Yen-k'ai before him, was elected president by the party. Furthermore, the law made conflicting provisions regarding the command of the armed forces. In one provision, it said the National Government commanded the armed forces. In another, it bade the president be the commander-in-chief of the armed forces. Chiang Kai-shek naturally interpreted the latter provision in his favor and assumed the command personally. Thus, whatever be the correct interpretation of the law, the fact was that the president in the person of Chiang Kai-shek became a powerful chief of state in a position completely different from all his predecessors.

From October 1928 to November 1930 the presidential powers, except those exercised in the name of the commander-in-chief, were, in theory at least, inseparable from those of the council. The president, in controlling the deliberations of the council, in fact made the decisions for the council. The powers given to the council were also powers which the president enjoyed.

In September 1930 T'an Yen-k'ai, the wise and amiable President of the Executive Yuan, died. Forthwith Chiang Kai-shek had himself nominated the successor. He also caused the Organic Law of the National Government to be so changed [8] as to transfer the important matters of state from the jurisdiction of the council of the National Government to that of the Executive Yuan.[9] Chiang Kai-shek now presided over both the council and the Executive Yuan. Why he should have chosen to favor the lower organ at the expense of the upper has never been adequately explained. But one fact was clear. The presidents of the Yuan other than the Executive, including Hu Han-min, being members of the upper council only, were excluded from the important lower council, that of the Executive Yuan, which decided on important matters of state. If one remembers that the controversy as to whether a provisional constitution should or should not be adopted was beginning and that Hu Han-min was to be deprived of freedom a few months hence,[10] the transfer may well be assumed to have been made on grounds of personalities.

The Organic Law of December 30, 1931 so changed the system of government as to vest the executive power almost exclusively in the hands of the Executive Yuan. The Law provided that the President of the National Government was not to have political responsibility of a practical kind, not to appoint or to direct the presidents of the Five Yuan, and not to hold any concurrent office. The council of the National Government was to remain an honored but powerless body. Under the new provisions Lin Sen was elected president and thirty-two persons with honored names but holding at the time no offices of any real power were elected members of the council. This regime lasted from the end of 1931 to September 1943 when, upon the death of Lin Sen, the Organic Law was again radically revised to suit Chiang Kai-shek, the new president.

During the presidency of Lin Sen, the National Government was of such slight importance that a discussion whether the president or the council was the more important of the two would be meaningless. The real government of China was elsewhere. But, powers aside, Lin Sen succeeded to an amazing degree in winning both prestige and affection, not only for himself, but for the presidency as well.

Lin Sen was politically insignificant, but it is no exaggeration to say that seldom has a head of state in Republican China been so honored and loved by his countrymen. Physically he was of a dignified and stately demeanor. Politically he had been a veteran of the Kuomintang and active in parliamentary life. He had simple tastes, no personal ambitions, and practiced no nepotism, a thing from which Chinese politicians in power are seldom immune. He observed not only the letter of the law but its spirit as well. He understood his position well. He never tried to assert the powers that were denied to him by the Organic Law of December 1931. But he was not passive. He had truly national interests at heart, and he was never hesitant to argue for them at the party's Political Council of which he was a member. Above all, he worked for national unity before the war began and for victory after it had come. He was a truly good president. If his benign influence was not more widely and deeply felt, it was only because his wise counsel was not as extensively and seriously sought as it should have been.

The death of Lin Sen led to the election of Chiang Kai-shek as president and the prerequisite revision of the Organic Law of the National Government.[11] The disabilities imposed on the president in the earlier Law were removed and the president was restored to his former position of power and command as under the Law of October 8, 1928. But the new Law did nothing to the council of the National Government. If the council nominally enjoyed the high powers of government, the new president did not choose to let it function. There cannot, therefore, be any doubt that upon Chiang Kai-shek's resumption of the presidency it was again the president, and not the council, in whose hands the powers of the National Government were vested.

In April 1947, in order to admit the representatives of the minor parties, the Organic Law was further revised.[12] The council was again to be constituted as a "Council of State" in order to be cognizant of matters of state. It was again to have weekly meetings. In theory at least, a collegiate form of government with the president functioning only as the president of the council might have returned. But if actualities rather than untenable theories are to be emphasized, no one can gainsay the fact that it was the president alone and not the members of the council collectively who controlled the decisions and therefore wielded the power of the government. In other words, the National Government, in its closing year, was the government of the president, contrary to what the National Government was meant to be when it was first formulated at Canton.

The President

The President of the National Government was elected by the Central Executive Committee of the Kuomintang, as stipulated by the Organic Law. In the case of Chiang Kai-shek, he was actually elected by acclamation as there was no other contender and no other visible alternative. The term was to be three years. But when Chiang Kai-shek was elected, on September 13, 1943, the Kuomintang was pledging itself to the early adoption of a constitution. He was therefore expected to hold office until the constitutional government had been organized. A resolution of the Standing Committee of the Central Executive Committee in September 1946 did indeed so extend his term.

The powers of the President were derived from his position in the National Government. Being the head of the state, he represented the National Government both at home and abroad. Whatever orders and other actions the National Government might adopt, they were to be done with the President's signature. Therefore, if members of the council did not contest the exercise of the powers of the National Government by the President personally, one cannot well say that he was illegally exercising those powers. Only if the members of the council had contested that exercise, could the question have arisen whether the powers could be exercised by the President alone or must be exercised by the council collectively.

From his election in September 1943 to the reorganization of the National Government in April 1947, Chiang Kai-shek personally exercised the powers of the National Government. After the reorganization and the admission into the council of representatives of two minority parties, the powers of the National Government were in form, at least, exercised by the council collectively. But here the stark fact was again at variance with the form. Out of a total membership of thirty, the Kuomintang had eighteen. It was natural that the minor parties had no possibility of opposing a measure decided upon by the Kuomintang. As for the Kuomintang membership, the voice of its Leader naturally was the controlling one. In other words, through the domination of the Kuomintang members, Chiang Kai-shek, the President, dominated the whole council. The President might indeed consult the council, but the council had no effective power of forcing its opinion on the President.

Although the President was able to dominate the council, he did not perform all his acts through the council. Frequently he chose to by-pass it. He often issued orders directly to the civil and military officials of the government, both central and local. As these orders were invariably complied with, no question has arisen as to whether such orders constituted an illegal exercise of governmental powers, whether all such orders should be based on prior decisions of the council and issued through the proper Yuan, or whether the President as head of the National Government could indeed issue them directly and on his own initiative. Herein is an illustration of the general principle that when the government is too personal, it transcends so much of the law that the question of legality becomes utterly meaningless.

Under the Organic Law of April 17, 1947, there was also a vice-president of the National Government. His powers were not specified. In actuality, his function was confined to that of presiding officer at the council meetings when the President was absent. But this did not mean that when the President was absent, the Vice-President had the powers of the President. The powers of the President were exercised by Chiang Kai-shek alone.

The Council

Before 1947 the members of the Council of the National Government [13] were all elected by the Central Executive Committee of the party or its Standing Committee. They were usually the top leaders of the party, except when, during Lin Sen's presidency, men holding offices of power were deliberately excluded from the council by a resolution of the party. When representatives of the minor parties were admitted to the council in April 1947, customary party election procedure underwent a slight modification. The minor party representatives objected to being nominated by the Central Executive Committee of the Kuomintang. So the party, after agreeing to take into the council of the National Government certain members of other parties, simply let them be appointed to the council by the president.

As it stood in 1947–1948, the membership of the council comprised the five presidents and the vice-presidents of the Five Yuan, a number of other Kuomintang leaders known abroad to be liberal, the leaders of the Chinese Youth Party and of the Democratic Socialist Party,[14] and four non-party people, also claiming to be liberals. Since the last enjoyed no political following and the followings of the two minor parties were very meager, the non-Kuomintang members were in the council only on sufferance. The effectiveness or noneffectiveness of the council depended solely on the effectiveness or noneffectiveness of the Kuomintang members. But since the

Kuomintang members had to follow the President implicitly as the Leader of their party, they too had little independence in their roles.

In theory the council was the highest government organ of the nation. It decided on all important policies of legislation and administration. It made all important appointments. In theory, it controlled finances, the armed forces, and foreign relations. In practice, however, only those acts which needed legislation went through the council. Acts that were primarily executive in nature, such as a reorientation of foreign policy, were not generally presented to the council. Even in those items of business which were presented, the council members might not have a real voice, since, as has been said, the President enjoyed an enormous influence over the Kuomintang members, if not, indeed, over all members.

A brief sketch of the fortunes of the council may be useful here. In the more than three years between the inception of the National Government and the organization of the Five-Yuan Government under Chiang Kai-shek, the council never acquired real importance. For during this period of military campaigns important decisions were usually made in the councils of the party rather than in the council of the National Government. From October 1928 to November 1930, when Chiang Kai-shek, the President, met weekly with his small council of the National Government, the council was a working body and acquired an importance not possessed before or since. From November 1930, when Chiang Kai-shek's Executive Yuan became the dominant body of the government, until April 1947, when the council of the National Government became a functioning body again, the council of the National Government was a council in name only, and membership in the council was frankly considered a sinecure. It met seldom, whether under the presidency of Chiang Kai-shek or Lin Sen. In peacetime it met on the average of four times a year and during the war years there were all together only five meetings.

The meetings of the council during the years from 1930 to 1947 were poorly attended. Though the total membership was generally well over thirty, the average attendance was below ten. Such a body obviously could not perform real functions of government. During the prewar years, the council in its meetings therefore largely concerned itself with giving formal sanctions to certain modifications of the budget as provided by law. And when, by an empowering resolution passed at the beginning of the war, the Supreme Council of National Defense was enabled to modify the budgets at will, the council of the National Government lost almost all its statutory business.

When the council of the National Government was made a multiparty organization in April 1947, it recovered some of the importance it enjoyed in 1928–1930. As in those years, it again became a Council of State and had regular weekly meetings.

Staff Organization

Directly under the President of the National Government, there are three high officials, the Chief Civil Officer, the Chief Military Officer, and the Chief Budgetary Officer.[15] The first two officers need little comment as they did not differ materially from the principal aides one usually finds attached to the head of state. They correspond closely to the Minister of the Imperial Household and the Chief Aide who serve the Japanese emperor, or the officers in charge of the Civil and Military Establishments who serve the President of the French Republic. If there was anything special in the Chinese setup, it was that when Chiang Kai-shek was the President he did not rely solely on the Chief Civil Officer and his establishment for the kind of work such an office was meant to perform. Chiang Kai-shek was President of the Military Commission prior to succeeding Lin Sen in September 1943. As such, he had a great retinue of personal aides divided into three sections, the Military, the Civil, and the Personnel Sections. These were no petty bureaus. They were all headed by top men of either the army or the party. When Chiang Kai-shek reassumed the presidency, he continued to rely on his Military Commission aides. When the commission was finally abolished in 1946, the aides on whom Chiang Kai-shek continued to rely for assistance were incorporated into the Chief Civil Officer's and Chief Military Officer's establishments, and became their core.

The Chief Budgetary Officer was unique, and was not to be considered merely an aide with a high-sounding title. He occupied a substantial position in the Five-Yuan system of government.

In the early years of the Five Yuan government, there was a tendency to make absolute equals of the Five Yuan, though their functions and responsibilities might be of varying importance. There was a tendency to guard against preponderance of the Executive Yuan which occupied necessarily a favored position. It was this tendency which led to the creation of the post of Chief Budgetary Officer attached directly to the National Government and therefore removed from control by any of the Five Yuan. The argument for the creation of an independent budgetary establishment was that if the Minister of Finance, a member of the Executive Yuan, was given the power of preparing the Budget, the Executive Yuan would dominate the other Yuan and put an end to their independence.

The Chief Budgetary Officer had in Chinese a very obscure title,[16] but his principal function was to supervise the making and execution of the annual budgets.[17] When it is remembered that the Kuomintang Government was a complicated and overorganized structure and that for twenty years the National Government had been generally without substantial powers, the entrusting of budget-making to the Chief Budgetary Officer naturally added only to the cumbersomeness and irresponsibility of the budget-making. The office was retained not because of a lack of realization that it was superfluous and conducive to inefficiency, but because a group of Kuomintang members had become entrenched there, supported by the numerous budget personnel in the various branches of government, central and local, who were under its control.

XI

THE EXECUTIVE YUAN[1]

The Position of the Executive Yuan

According to the law, the Executive Yuan had always been the highest executive organ of the National Government. Whether it was in fact the highest, or how high it was, depended naturally on its relation, first, to the Kuomintang, second, to the President and Council of the National Government, and third, to any independent military authority that might be in existence.

Theoretically, the domination of the Kuomintang over the National Government should not have rendered inoperative the statutory provisions which make the Executive Yuan the highest executive organ of the National Government, providing the party had restricted its direction and supervision to the very top level of the government. But the Kuomintang had decided to do otherwise. The party councils and departments interfered with the government at all levels, at the level of the National Government which was superior to the Executive Yuan, and at the lower levels which were subordinate to the Executive Yuan, not to mention interference with the Yuan itself.

Such interference was in fact taking place constantly during prewar days. An administrative service or a local administration might be given orders or subjected to inquiries by certain party departments. During the war, the practice was even legalized. The Supreme National Defense Council could correspond directly with the Executive Yuan or with the subordinate ministries of that Yuan in connection with any administrative matter. In the presence of the Kuomintang organization, the Executive Yuan certainly did not enjoy anything like supreme executive power.

The relation of the Executive Yuan to the National Government also bears examination in order to determine the nature of the former's executive authority. In this case, the Council of the National Government was of less import. It was generally the position of the president that affected the position of the Executive Yuan.

As a rule, the cabinet that is under a strong type of president can never be powerful; a powerful cabinet can arise only when the head of state is stripped of actual powers of government, like the British king or the French president. This general rule is applicable even to the Kuomintang Government.

There have been alternating emphases on the relative dominance of the President of the National Government and the Executive Yuan, not only in the Organic Laws but also in the various constitutional drafts which finally led to the Constitution of 1946. At one time the President of the National Government was made all-powerful, and the Executive Yuan merely his secretariat. At another, truly independent executive powers were conferred on the Executive Yuan, and the President was to be a mere figurehead. Such *volte-faces* took place whenever there was the political necessity and practical possibility of checking a powerful personage from having too much power, without consideration of what would in the long run be better suited to Chinese conditions.

Under the terms of the Organic Law of the National Government of April 17, 1947, the position of the Executive Yuan was low and secondary. The President of the National Government alone was responsible to the Central Executive Committee of the Kuomintang. The President of the Executive Yuan, in common with the Presidents of other Yuan, was responsible not to the Central Executive Committee, but to the President of the National Government. Furthermore, all the Yuan presidents were appointed on the recommendation of the President of the National Government. Under these limitations, the President of the Executive Yuan could hardly thwart the will of the President of the National Government, unless he wielded enough influence in the councils of the party to overpower the President of the National Government. This he obviously could not do, since the President of the National Government was also the Leader of the Party.

Lastly, the position of the Executive Yuan also depended on whether it was able to exercise the military power of the government. If the military power stayed outside its grasp, the Executive Yuan was badly crippled. Even if it stayed within it, the Executive Yuan's control might still be ineffectual if the President of the National Government in his capacity as Commander-in-Chief exercised any direct control over the armed forces.

It has been unfortunate for the Executive Yuan that during the twenty years of its existence military power has invariably remained independent of it. During all these years, Chiang Kai-shek has either been at the head of the Military Commission or of the Government itself. In either case, he has had both nominal and actual control of the military administration and command of the field forces. Even when he himself was at the head of the Executive Yuan he preferred to exercise military power in his other capacities.

An opinion can be ventured here that unless the executive organ recovers the military power in full, it will never be able to effect an orderly administration of the nation.

The President of the Executive Yuan

The Executive Yuan had at its head a President and a Vice-President, the former often termed in Western writings "Premier." They were, up to 1947, always selected from among the members of the Central Executive or Supervisory Committees by either the Central Executive Committee in plenary session or its Standing Committee, or the Political Council. The Organic Law of the National Government of 1947 further provided that they should be nominated by the President of the National Government.

Aside from interim incumbents, there were for the period 1928–1948 only seven or eight regular incumbents of the presidency of the Yuan. Chiang Kai-shek himself was President a number of times. The other incumbents, with the exception of T'an Yen-k'ai before Chiang Kai-shek's first term and Sun Fo and Wang Ching-wei after, were either his relatives or close followers. Some of them were astute politicians. But, astute or otherwise, most of them had to play a role prescribed for them by Chiang Kai-shek. Sun Fo tried to be independent, but he lasted barely a month. Wang Ching-wei enjoyed greater prestige than any other except Chiang Kai-shek himself, but he yielded to Chiang Kai-shek in all matters of importance, in finance and in foreign policy, as well as in military affairs. Perhaps T'an Yen-k'ai was the most honored President of the Executive Yuan, but then the old soldier-scholar consistently chose not to be obstructive in matters on which Chiang Kai-shek's opinion happened to be pronounced.

The power of the President of the Executive Yuan varied always inversely with that of the President of the National Government. When the latter was the active head of government, the former naturally sank to the position of a highly placed bureaucrat. Vice versa, if the President of the National Government was only a nominal head, executive powers fell into the hands of the President of the Executive Yuan.

The President of the Executive Yuan had the right to act for the President of the National Government if the latter was unable to function. This did not, however, add very much to the prestige of the Yuan President. The occasion seldom occurred. When Lin Sen died, in August 1943, Chiang Kai-shek as the head of the Executive Yuan acted for a while as President of the National Government. But earlier, in 1930–1931, when Chiang Kai-shek took active military command at the front, he designated the President of the Legislative Yuan, instead of that of the Executive Yuan, to act for him as President of the National Government. After 1947, when the vice-presidency of the National Government was created, the President of the Executive Yuan was further removed from the succession.

The Vice-President of the Executive Yuan used to have a sinecure. He knew his position to be such and never cared to assert his position in the Yuan. It was during the war years when Chiang Kai-shek had to be much of the time away from the post of President that his deputy, H. H. Kung, who happened to be a very accommodating relative of Chiang's, assumed actual control of the executive routine and became virtually the head of the Yuan. In those days there was no material difference whether H. H. Kung was Vice-President, acting as President for Chiang Kai-shek, or was President himself—taking orders from Chiang Kai-shek. After the end of the war, the Vice-President consistently attempted to map out some sort of work for himself. The post remained nevertheless unimportant. No ambitious man had ever cared to serve as vice-president unless he served under Chiang Kai-shek. In that case, he usually had the satisfaction of considering himself the man second in importance in the Chinese political world, little realizing perhaps that the second in importance is of no importance.

The Members of the Executive Yuan

The heads of the ministries and commissions under the Executive Yuan were all voting members of the Executive Yuan Council, but the heads of the smaller establishments were not. The secretary-general and the chief of the Political Department of the Yuan were also usually considered members; there were special laws giving them that status. But in 1946 the Political Department was amalgamated into the secretary-general's establishment, and under the reorganization of April 1947 the secretary-general himself no longer enjoyed the status of a member.

Also, under the reorganization of April 1947 there were a number of what were known as ministers without portfolio, necessitated by the participation of the minor parties. Like the ministers of ministries and chairmen of commissions, they were full-fledged members of the Executive Yuan. All were collectively known as ministers. There were then twenty-two such members, fourteen with ministerial portfolios, four with commission portfolios, and four without. Whether the President and Vice-President of the Yuan were or were not "ministers" in this sense, we shall presently discuss.

The ministers, or the members of the Executive Yuan, were appointed by the President of the National Government with the consent of the council of the National Government on the instance of the President of the Executive Yuan. Herein lies the uncertainty as to who really controlled their appointment. According to the letter of the Organic Law of the National Government of 1947, it would seem that the President of the Executive Yuan had the greatest power. He had the initiative. As long as he could secure a slate of ministers to which neither the President nor the council of the National Government would impose objection, his hands were fairly free. But he himself was nothing but a faithful servant of the President of the National Government. As has been explained in the last chapter, he could not be otherwise. Therefore, he seldom chose to exercise any initiative. He took orders from the President. Or, to be more realistic, he took orders from the Leader of the Kuomintang. When Chiang Kai-shek was not President of the National Government, he nevertheless controlled the appointments, for he controlled the Political Council whose consent was necessary to these appointments.

The caliber of the ministers defies generalization. In the course of twenty years there were some able men, and, in some cases, the ability was even accompanied by devotion to high ideals. There were men whose only claims to a ministerial post were what is known as "revolutionary deeds" before the establishment of the regime. There were also men who were put there because either they themselves or their patrons had thrown in their lot with the Kuomintang Government or with the Leader of the Party. The two categories last described were usually, if not invariably, poor timber. In later years the accent on personal loyalty or dependability in the choice of ministers seems to have been more pronounced than ever. That emphasis naturally led to the nomination as ministers of a large number of men of bureaucratic or courtier type. The non-Kuomintang ministers with the exception of one or two were of even poorer repute. This was natural since the minor parties, enjoying even less following than the Kuomintang among the younger intelligentsia, had little good material to choose from.

The age of the ministers, both their natural age and their political age, is also revealing. The ministers in the early years of the Kuomintang regime were mostly young people. But, as the regime grew older, the age of the ministers increased. Most of the ministers of the later years, with the exception of the representatives of the minor parties, had been either ministers or high officials of the government for many years. If they had had any ideals or courage at the beginning of their political careers, they had largely lost them. New and younger men seldom found their way into the Executive Yuan. Whether the young and progressive men abstained because the regime had become too conservative, or the regime became conservative because the young and progressive men had abstained, is perhaps immaterial. The mischief was done, when a conservative or reactionary government had no young progressives among its personnel.

THE POWERS OF THE EXECUTIVE YUAN

According to the Organic Law of the National Government of April 17, 1947, the Executive Yuan, meeting as a council, was to be cognizant of the following matters:

1. Bills to be submitted in the Legislative Yuan;
2. Budgets to be submitted to the Legislative Yuan;
3. Amnesties to be submitted to the Legislative Yuan;
4. Declarations of war and negotiations for peace to be submitted to the Legislative Yuan;
5. The appointment or dismissal of administrative and judicial officials of or above the selected rank and of magistrates of *hsien* and mayors of municipalities;
6. All matters which could not be settled between the various ministries and commissions of the Executive Yuan;
7. Other matters which, according to law or in the opinion of the president of the Executive Yuan, should be decided in the Council.

These powers appear to be extensive and impressive. But there were great limitations, some obvious, some implied, and still others arising from the nature of party tutelage. There was no mention of the policy of the government, either foreign or domestic. The Executive Yuan enjoyed no automatic rights over foreign policy unless one could infer that the budgetary and war and peace powers necessarily covered the whole of it. But they did not. The same was true of the military policy. These were obvious limitations on the powers of the Executive Yuan.

The implied limitations arise from the dominant status of the President of the Yuan. Not only could he withhold from the ministers powers unenumerated by the law, but he frequently withheld the enumerated powers as well from being discussed and decided by the ministers in council. He interpreted the law. The ministers, being his subordinates, were hardly in a position to dispute his interpretation.

That party tutelage made the powers above enumerated unreal needs no elaboration. The Executive Yuan might discuss and decide, but the resolutions and decisions of the party councils, especially of the Party Political Council, were binding on the Yuan.

There were still other limitations. The other Yuan sometimes encroached upon the executive power. Judicial administration often rested in the hands of the Judicial Yuan; personnel administration, which affected the Executive Yuan more than any other, always remained under the Examination Yuan. There was also the Chief Budgetary Officer, who was directly responsible to the National Government and over whom the Executive Yuan had no jurisdiction. Then there was also the Military Commission which often dwarfed the Executive Yuan. These various agencies which disrupted the executive organ and encroached on the executive powers will be further discussed as we come to them. But we can best discuss here the way in which the independent economic agencies affected the Executive Yuan in the exercise of its powers.

For about fifteen years there always was an economic administration with varying names and functions, but on a high level and independent of the Executive Yuan. At first it was the National Economic Commission. This was a planning board, but it also undertook to administer a number of definite projects. During the war there was first the so-called Economic Committee and then the National General Mobilization Committee. Both committees had as members the heads of those ministries and commissions which had economic functions, and both had as their chairman and vice-chairman, respectively, the President and Vice-President of the Executive Yuan. But a great number of other members were drawn from outside the Executive Yuan. The large staff maintained by the two, and especially by the latter, was independent of the Yuan. Whatever might be their legal status, their existence tended to mutilate the economic functions of the Executive Yuan.[2]

In 1947 a new National Economic Council was set up. It was a large body; the ministers of the Executive Yuan participating in it were only a few among the many. Although the President of the Executive Yuan was chairman of the council, its moving spirit was supplied by a group of party workers whose leader was actually the vice-chairman. The council deliberated on the economic policies of the government and its decisions were binding on the economic agencies of the Executive Yuan. Whenever the Yuan and the council differed, either confusion or paralysis resulted.

These heavily organized economic councils were not the only agencies which encroached on the powers of the Executive Yuan. There was yet another agency less known but even more powerful. It was the Joint Office of the Banks and Credit Agencies of the Government. During most of its existence Chiang Kai-shek acted as its chairman, and the President or Vice-President of the Executive Yuan as vice-chairman. In a period of mounting inflation and gold transactions, banks occupied peculiar importance, and the Joint Office was one of the really important agencies of the government. With Chiang Kai-shek as its titular head, it dominated the economic scene. The inability of the Ministry of Finance to effectively control the banks and the ability of the Joint Office to fix the financial and economic policies for the government set into bold relief the economic impotence of the Executive Yuan.

The Executive Yuan Council

Meetings of the Executive Yuan as a council were held regularly once a week. For most of its existence, this institution was just called the "Meeting of the Executive Yuan"; only during 1930–1931, when Chiang Kai-shek as President of the Yuan discontinued the meetings of the National Government as a Council of State, did the Executive Yuan meet as "Council of State."

The President and the members of the Executive Yuan were the people legally authorized to attend the meetings of the Executive Yuan. But, like all other councils of the Kuomintang and the Kuomintang Government, the Executive Yuan Council also had so-called "attending members." The chief of the Political Department, when not a member, was always entitled to be an attending member. The heads of smaller establishments directly under the Executive Yuan, when they existed, were also attending members. In some years, the President of the Yuan even invited hosts of vice-ministers and vice-chairmen of commissions, representatives of the Military Commission, and the metropolitan mayor to attend the council meetings, thus swelling the council to an absolutely unmanageable size. When it is remembered that the attending members talked as much, or as little, as the regular members, the latter could hardly claim to be exclusive members of an exclusive body, as are the members of the British Cabinet.

The agenda were usually heavy and crowded. Seldom had the members time and opportunity to go through it all at the meeting. Most of the items printed in the agenda were considered accepted if nobody raised a question. The more important items were not always deliberated upon. The President mentioned them, made a brief comment on them, and announced that the proposals or reports were accepted. According to the "Procedure of the Meetings of the Executive Yuan," a decision was to be carried by the majority of the members present, and the President had to put the motions to a vote in the usual way. But in practice the position of the President was so dominant that his own judgments were generally accepted or acquiesced in by the body. It was only when he had no pronounced opinions on a subject that he allowed it to be freely discussed at the meeting. Even then he prevented the voting from taking place. He preferred to have the decision left in his hands. He might suggest that the majority opinion be the consensus of the council; but for reasons of his own he might also suggest that a less prevalent opinion be accepted. It was the absence of formal voting that lessened the actual difference between the members of the Yuan fully entitled to participate in the council and the so-called attending members, who were without right to vote.

Seldom were there general discussions of important matters at the council meeting. The time was exhausted by reports and explanations of the ministers concerning the matters falling into their respective spheres. The remarks of the President, especially, consumed a large portion of the time. Unless asked by the President to make comments, a minister usually remained reticent over matters not of concern to his own department. At these Executive Yuan meetings, instead of a general meeting of minds there were only a number of bilateral conferences between the President and specific ministers, with other participants constituting a kind of general audience. This situation resulted from the superior status of the President. If, therefore, a meeting of equals or a genuine meeting had been desired, the presiding officer would have had to be reduced to the status of a *primus inter pares*, which the President was not.

The Executive Yuan resorted very frequently to the use of committees. If the President wished to bring a proposal to the meeting, he might first appoint a committee for its preparation. When a thorny question came up before the meeting, instead of arriving at a decision, the council itself might appoint a committee for a more thorough preliminary study. The committees might be composed solely of ministers, or solely of staff members, or of both. The most general were committees composed of some secretaries of the Yuan and of the higher officials of the ministries and commissions concerned with the business in question. These expert committees often did a creditable piece of work and were a factor which kept the council meeting from falling into pitfalls.

Staff Organization of the Executive Yuan

The Executive Yuan maintained an immense secretarial staff, headed by a secretary-general and a deputy secretary-general. In earlier years there were two establishments, the Secretariat and the Political Department. The Secretariat was made up of secretaries and was to supervise the several administrations under the Executive Yuan. The Political Department consisted of councilors and was to draft laws and ordinances and to formulate plans and policies. Very soon the two were amalgamated in practice and the chief of the Political Department acted as the deputy-chief of the amalgamated establishments. In 1946 the amalgamation was legalized.

The Secretariat of the Executive Yuan was not as high in status as the Chief Civil Officer's establishment under the National Government, but it was far more influential. And this, in spite of the fact that the President of the National Government was the superior, in fact as well as in law, of the President of the Executive Yuan. An explanation is to be found in the traditions of Chinese bureaucracy.

In China of the old days, those bureaucrats who checked the reports and memoranda of the officials of a lower level always enjoyed an influence and authority over the government of that level. The bureaucrats in the Secretariat of the Executive Yuan similarly acquired a hold on the ministries and commissions of the Yuan and the provincial and municipal governments of the country. The reports from these ministries, commissions, and governments went through their hands and so did the instructions from the Executive Yuan. They were able to maintain intimate contact with them. They could do favors for them; they could also cavil at them. If they chose to be good civil servants, they could be efficient links. If they chose to be otherwise, their opportunities for manipulation were unlimited. But the secretaries of the National Government did not have these opportunities. The President of the National Government might be very powerful, but the Presidents of the Five Yuan, because of their status as elders, could take scanty notice of the secretaries of the National Government. The Five Yuan were much less dependent on the Secretariat of the National Government than the ministries, commissions, and local governments were on the Secretariat of the Executive Yuan.

The secretary-general of the Executive Yuan was an officer of special importance. If he was capable and had the confidence of the President of the Yuan, he could well emerge to dominate both the central and local administration of China, though he might have to remain more or less in the background. He was the key man of the administration. He wielded enormous influence. During the last years of the war, when Chiang Kai-shek was simultaneously the head of almost all civil and military establishments of importance, the chief secretary in each establishment became what was then known as "staff chief," and the system of government was known as "the staff chief system." Of all these staff chiefs, the secretary-general of the Executive Yuan was one of the most influential.

The Executive Yuan and the Other Yuan

From outside the government, the Executive Yuan had to subject itself to the orders and guidance of the councils of the party. Within the framework of government, it had dealings with the National Government above, the provincial and municipal governments below, and the four other Yuan and other great establishments by its side. While the establishments like the Military Commission and the National Economic Council were organs not conceived of by Sun Yat-sen in his Five-Yuan system, and their relations with the Executive Yuan had necessarily to remain on the basis of expediency and personalities, the relationship to be maintained between the Executive and the other Yuan might have been expected to follow the prescription of Sun Yat-sen.

But Sun Yat-sen, while insisting on a clear-cut division of the five governing powers and believing in their ability to work together to provide for a strong government, had almost nothing to say about their mutual relations. The Provisional Constitution for the Period of Tutelage or the organic laws had to regulate those relations. If they did not, possible conflicts could only be resolved either by superior authorities in law or by powerful leaders in fact.

The weaker Legislative Yuan tried in two ways to balance the stronger Executive Yuan. It demanded again and again, in accordance with the Organic Law of the Legislative Yuan, the attendance of the President and the members of the Executive Yuan at its meetings or at the meetings of its committees for questioning, presumably in connection with legislative business. A questioning of that kind was bound to acquire the proportions of a parliamentary interpellation.[3] The Executive Yuan members were always reluctant to present themselves on the Legislative floor. Whether the Legislative Yuan should have power to compel their presence and what responsibility they had before the Legislative Yuan were not precisely regulated anywhere.

There was also controversy regarding the competence of the Legislative Yuan in the international field. Did all international agreements fall within the terms of the law which gives the Legislative Yuan the right to pass on international matters of importance? On any given agreement, the Executive and the Legislative Yuan might have different interpretations. Naturally the former would claim that a certain act was either not international or not important, whereas the latter would claim that it was both.

These conflicts between the two Yuan were not contemplated by the propounder of the Five-Power Constitution. If they occurred, it was only because a legislative organ, in order to safeguard its existence and maintain its dignity of position, was apt to struggle for a share in general policies of a political nature, which led inevitably to some sort of conflict with the executive branch of the government. The conflicts in the past never led to very serious results. In the first place, the Legislative Yuan was too weak to be strongly assertive. In the second place, the party leaders, and especially the Leader in later years, were always able to apply strong pressure for the solution of conflicts. But the fact remains that the Executive Yuan has to expect checks and balances to be applied by the Legislative Yuan.

There were conflicts of a similar nature between the Executive Yuan and the Control Yuan. The members of the latter had a right to bring impeachment against all officials, high and low, not even excepting the president of the National Government, for acts either in contravention of law or in dereliction of duty. Impeachments on the latter account against high officials with political duties could not generally be dissociated from considerations of policy. A president of the Executive Yuan might think that he is doing very well, but a member of the Control Yuan, holding a different view as regards his policy, might claim that he has committed dereliction of duty. In fact, impeachments or attempts at impeachment had arisen out of such differences. If its members were to have their way, the Control Yuan could be a more effective killer of governments than the Parliament of the Third French Republic. Though by some expedient improvisations of one kind or another by the party leaders, the conflicts were generally resolved in favor of the Executive Yuan, the problem was by no means solved.

The Executive Yuan was also hampered by the Examination Yuan's controlling the personnel administration and by the Control Yuan's auditing function. The Ministry of Personnel, under the Examination Yuan, had the sole charge of personnel administration, with a body of very strict rules. The Ministry of Audit under the Control Yuan had a body of even stricter rules concerning disbursements and other accounts. Both ministries were in a position to interfere in the conduct of administration, though they might not possess a sympathetic understanding of the administrative process.

The Executive Yuan's Control of the Provincial Governors

The provincial governments of China were not like the French prefectures, placed under a Ministry of the Interior. Together with the governments of certain large cities, they were directly under the control of the Executive Yuan. This difference was made necessary by the size and the stature of men in control of the provinces. The task of their general supervision was so stupendous that even the Executive Yuan was not equal to it.

Theoretically, the Executive Yuan supervised provincial governments as a whole, and the individual ministries and commissions supervised the different administrative services of the provinces. On the surface, there should be no difficulty in the Yuan's exercising an effective general control, but there were factors which did interfere with that control. During the two decades of the Kuomintang regime, a great majority of the heads of provincial governments were military commanders. In fact, at the close of the Tutelage regime in 1948, they were almost all military men. These military men were either obedient or not obedient to Chiang Kai-shek. If they were not, the provinces under their control naturally remained semi-independent and had little necessity to take orders from the Executive Yuan. If they were, they gladly took orders from Chiang Kai-shek. Were the Yuan not headed by him, its orders would be little heeded.

But when Chiang Kai-shek himself was at the head of the Executive Yuan, he often chose not to control too tightly the military type of provincial governors. There were at any one time a number of notoriously incompetent governors who were military men. They may have been shuffled about a little, but seldom were they removed outright. Unless they showed signs of disloyalty to Chiang Kai-shek personally, they were tolerated rather than disturbed, for disturbing them might have meant also disturbing the kind of balance among the rival military factions on which Chiang Kai-shek depended for his personal supremacy.

Chiang Kai-shek's military politics have produced grievous effects on local administration. They prevented the Executive Yuan as such from having a wise, free, and effective exercise of its power. It can be imagined that removing a provincial head backed by a powerful military faction might be the occasion of some disaffection. But the Executive Yuan could certainly bring the pressure of public opinion to bear on the incumbent, especially if it could name a good man as his successor. In trying to substitute a good man for a bad, advantages would be on its side, rather than on the side of the faction supporting the bad man. It was unfortunate that the Executive Yuan was never given an adequate opportunity to try to round up the bad and the notoriously incompetent governors of provinces. If the Executive Yuan had had such an opportunity, it is possible that the provincial administrations would not have been so indifferent to the public interest.

XII

THE MILITARY POWER[1]

The Chinese Tradition of Civilian Government

One of the significant differences that distinguish good government from bad is the subordination of military power to political power and military personnel to political personnel. The military mind tends to be narrow and irresponsible. The militarists may be experts, but their *expertise* often prevents them from giving due weight to interests other than military. Military power, unless put in its proper place, usually runs amuck and takes the whole country with it.

The English-speaking democracies of the Western world have had more blessings from the disappearance of a standing army and the subordination of the military to the political than even the historians of those democracies realize. Up to very recent times China was also signally free from military domination. It was invariably during the worst lapses of good government that the military gained the upper hand. In normal times the governing authority was singularly civilian in nature. A conquering horde, inseparable from military leadership, after founding a new dynasty, generally lost its military character and settled down as a civilian regime. Unless it did so it never really succeeded in founding a dynasty and was soon replaced by a conquering regime of a more promising type, which knew how to transform itself from a military to a civilian organization.

The strength of the civilian tradition in Chinese government may be illustrated by some of the great military upheavals of the last seven centuries. The Mongol conquerors who founded the Yüan Dynasty never rid themselves of the military nature of their organization. The Yüan Emperors suffered from that. They were never quite able to develop a strong and well-balanced administration throughout their Empire. Weakness soon followed their initial successes and persisted throughout the dynasty — a short dynasty of barely three generations. Benefiting by the experiences of the Yüan, the Ming and the Manchu founding emperors, although all of them were primarily military-minded, installed civilian regimes as soon as their conquests had ended. It was due to the strength of the tradition of civilian rule that some of the greatest military commanders of the Ming and Ch'ing Dynasties who were in origin scholars, at once resumed civilian status when their campaigns were over.[2]

Emergence of a Military Tradition

The misfortune of modern China is that at the time of the multitude of paper reforms which enshrouded the country in the first decade of this century, she should have entertained a serious liking for the military institutions of Prussia and Japan. The Prussian tradition had been adopted wholeheartedly by the receptive Japanese *Samurai* when the Japanese looked to the West for instruction. When the time came for China to look abroad for instruction, she adopted the military institutions of Japan and Prussia.

In 1907, in imitation of the Japanese staff organization, the Manchu Government established the Council of Military Consultation,[3] which was placed directly under the throne and made independent of the cabinet. It was presided over by a prince of the blood, who had received his military training in Japan. The Ministry of War and the newly created Ministry of the Navy were also headed by military men. As in Japan, the Presiding Minister of this new Council, corresponding to the Chief of Staff, was directly responsible to the emporor. As in Japan, again, the War and Navy Ministers, though members of the cabinet, also enjoyed direct access to the emperor.

Selection of military men for Ministers of War and of the Navy represented a departure from past practice. In the old days the regular scholar-officials had usually held the high posts of military administration; supreme command had been given to civilians more often than to military men; only the actual command of garrisons and of army units had invariably been reserved for the professionals. The departure was undoubtedly inspired by the successes of the Japanese and Prussian military machines under this form of organization and by the anxiety of the Court to maintain firm and direct control over the New Army which was just being created. Henceforth the military administration was to become independent of, and eventually to dominate, the civilian administration.

When Yuan Shih-k'ai became President in 1912, he retained the Manchu innovations. He maintained direct control over the armed forces through the General Staff Board (the successor of the Council of Military Consultation) and the War and Navy Ministries, which were headed by military men. He even went further. He created an Office of the Supreme Command[4] in his palace and required the daily attendance there of the chiefs or deputies of the three military establishments. In other words, though these establishments continued to function, Yuan Shih-k'ai by this stroke of evil genius became his own Minister of War and of the Navy and Chief of the General Staff.

This new military tradition was carried on after Yuan Shih-k'ai's death, though the effectiveness of the control by the head of government naturally varied with his position vis-à-vis the Northern militarists.

Militarism and the Revolutionists

The fondness of Sun Yat-sen and his party for the institution of Military Government and their repeated resort to that institution[5] were certainly no deterrents to this new military tradition. Not only in the Military Government itself would the military men dominate and the military spirit prevail, but the civilian government that followed in the wake of the military could scarcely escape military domination.

As has been explained in a previous chapter, the Revolution of 1911 was an uprising in the army. For years the revolutionists had been inciting the army to revolt, and uprisings in the garrisons and other army posts had been frequent before 1911. After other reactionary regimes succeeded the Manchus, the revolutionists pursued their old tactics, trying to persuade the army commanders to sever their relations with the Northern regime and to join with the revolutionists. Sun Yat-sen's party, in order to obtain quick successes, did not hesitate to make use of the militarists, thus creating a dependence which must have left an indelible impression on the Kuomintang.

The way in which Sun Yat-sen established his revolutionary base at Canton had a more direct impact. The last five or six years of his life were devoted to alternately coöperating with and fighting the vacillating and undependable Kwangtung militarists. Sun Yat-sen probably had a perfectly clear conscience in these military maneuvers. He wished to make his revolution succeed, and to make the base secure he was justified in resorting to any means at his disposal, which naturally included enlisting aid from the militarists. But, in consequence, his denunciations of the Northern warlords lost much of their moral fervor, and it became difficult to inculcate in his followers an acute awareness of the dangers which the domination by military men could bring to them and their cause.

Military Basis of the Kuomintang Regime

Although the military tradition of the previous two decades had been strong and dangerous, the reorganized Kuomintang of 1924 seemed to be only partly aware of it. To the extent that the party vehemently denounced the Northern militarists and sought to eradicate them, there was full awareness. On the other hand, the party's emphasis on the military Academy at

Whampoa and its readiness to incorporate into the Revolutionary Army whatever militarist remnants sought to climb aboard the Revolutionary band wagon hardly indicated lively awareness.

At the time of its founding in 1924, the Whampoa Academy was to have been strictly subordinated to the party. It was modeled on the academy for Red Army officers in the Soviet Union. The party's commissar in the Academy was to have sole charge of the political training of the cadets, and to share the general administration with the president of the Academy. But when the original commissar of the Academy, Liao Chung-k'ai, a radical and very capable leader of the party, was assassinated in August 1925, Chiang Kai-shek became supreme in the Academy in his capacity as its president. No doubt the Academy contributed notably to the successful consolidation of the Canton regime and to the Northern Expedition. But it is equally certain that the Academy cadets became more personal followers of Chiang Kai-shek than stanch supporters of the Kuomintang, unless one regards Chiang Kai-shek as indistinguishable from the Kuomintang.

During the Northern Expedition, the Revolutionary Army became unduly swollen through the absorption of the militarist remnants. There were four army groups in the Revolutionary Army. Leaving aside the question of the complexion of the three army groups not directly commanded by Chiang Kai-shek, his own First Army Group certainly did comprise a great many militarist remnants. Since their absorption was effected either by or on orders from Chiang Kai-shek, the more such remnants joined, the greater became the need for skillful management. By the end of the Northern Expedition, the skilled managerial services of Chiang Kai-shek had become well-nigh indispensable.

At the beginning, Chiang Kai-shek's indispensability to the Kuomintang was of a purely military nature. In his later years Chiang Kai-shek became much more than a military personality. His interest and his activities covered the whole field of politics. He became leader of his party and also leader of the government his party had established. Administration, diplomacy, finance, economics, and the morals of the people — all took his attention. But he owed his rise to the fact that he was a military man. As such he was made head of the military academy and later appointed commander-in-chief of the Revolutionary Army. After the conclusion of the Northern Expedition, he was regarded by many as the man who would be able to so reorganize the Army as to rid the nation of the curse of militarism and warlordism. Had he done so, he might have become a more effective political leader. But he either would not, or could not, do it.

Chiang Kai-shek is essentially a military man. All military men tend to idealize the military virtue of obedience and consider military support as the most dependable prop a government could have. If therefore there is in the state an organized political force as powerful as or more powerful than the armed forces, the military may not be able to dominate the scene except in time of war. But if there is not, the military will have no difficulty in maintaining themselves in a position of dominance in peace as well as in war. In China, after the Revolution of 1911, the nearest approach to a powerful check on military power then was the reorganized Kuomintang in its early years. But when Chiang Kai-shek acquired a position of leadership in the Kuomintang without at the same time outgrowing his military mentality, the party ceased to be such a restraining influence. Even had the anti-military members and factions of the Kuomintang wished to impose a continued check on the military, the latter, headed by Chiang Kai-shek, had become too powerful to suffer effective restraint.

The Military Stage was to have ended with the Northern Expedition. But the Period of Political Tutelage could not really begin as long as the country was infested with armed forces and the military remained dominant. It was with the aim both of reducing the size of the Army and putting it in its proper place that the Army Reorganization and Disbandment Conference was called early in 1929.[6] There were undoubtedly many reasons for the failure of the conference, but most important was the reluctance of high army leaders to see their own divisions eliminated. Chiang Kai-shek, though he had by this time acquired the status of political leadership and responsibilities, shared their reluctance.

The wars between the rival military factions followed immediately after the failure of the conference. The leadership of Chiang Kai-shek was assured. Then ensued the campaigns against the Communists. These campaigns made military domination necessary; but military domination also made the military campaigns inevitable. Whatever be the cause-effect relationship, Chiang Kai-shek's military leadership had to be acknowledged. The country might suffer from civil war, but his military leadership was more firmly established than ever.

Thus the Whampoa Academy and the swollen Revolutionary Army were the original military foundations of the Kuomintang regime, and the incessant civil wars pursuant to the founding of the regime were the operations which kept both the Academy and the Army flourishing.

Military Organization: 1925–1937

Up to 1946 the Military Commission of the National Government[7] almost uninterruptedly had charge of the nation's military affairs. When the commission was first set up in July 1925, a few days after the establishment of the National Government itself, it was put directly under the guidance and supervision of the party and was entrusted with the administration and command of all the armed forces and military organizations. It was conceived strictly as a committee in form as well as in spirit. Its chairman was coöpted from among the members. Decisions were to be made by a two-thirds majority of the members present. The several important establishments of the commission were to be separately placed under the supervision of individual members. At that time, the commission was really one of the three great governing organs established by the Central Executive Committee of the Kuomintang, the other two being the Political Council and the Council of the National Government. The relation between the Government Council and the Military Commission was facilitated at the beginning by a very close interlocking of the personnel.

When the Northern Expedition began, the Military Commission was reorganized. Although still possessing the highest powers of military organization and administration, it was placed under the government. The members were to elect a standing committee which was in turn to elect a chairman. The committee spirit was retained.

But the beginning of the Northern Expedition also saw the creation, on July 7, 1926, of the post of Commander-in-Chief of the Nationalist Revolutionary Army, outside of the Military Commission. Chiang Kai-shek was appointed to this post and was authorized to act concurrently as chairman of the commission. He very naturally argued that the expedition necessitated the concentration of power solely in his hands, since military operations would not permit lengthy consultations or divided counsels. But the leaders of the party were unwilling to yield all control. There was a compromise, which was embodied in the law providing for the reorganization of the General Headquarters of the Commander-in-Chief.

Three restrictions were imposed on the Commander-in-Chief. First, the General Headquarters of the Commander-in-Chief, before the expedition was actually started, was required to be physically housed with the Military Commission, and, whenever the Commander moved to the front, a security committee was to act for him and to remain responsible to the Political Council of the Central Executive Committee of the Party. In this way, the party tried to retain some control over the acts of the Commander-in-Chief. Second, the Commander's authority was restricted to command over those armed forces which had been activated for the expedition. Those at the rear for garrison purposes remained under the jurisdiction of the Military Commission, which was also to continue to have sole jurisdiction over the general policies of military administration as distinguished from the strictly strategic and tactical policies. Third, when demobilization was completed following the successful conclusion of the expedition, the General Headquarters was to be forthwith abolished.

The compromise signified that the party was willing to give the Commander-in-Chief of the Nationalist Revolutionary Army full powers of command and at the same time was anxious to maintain its control over the military. It was a sensible compromise.

Two years of the Northern Expedition culminated in Chiang Kai-shek's military supremacy. Whether, at the end of the expedition, he enjoyed that supremacy in his capacity as Chairman of the Military Commission or as the Commander-in-Chief of the Revolutionary Army was immaterial. Merely to abolish the General Headquarters would have been of no significance; had the civilians wished to regain control over the military, something more fundamental would have had to be attempted. But all attempts have hitherto failed.

At the close of the Northern Expedition it was agreed by all sides that the Revolutionary Army should be reduced and reorganized and that a Ministry of War, to be subordinated to the government like all other ministries, should be established to replace both the Military Commissions and the General Headquarters. But, as previously noted, the Reorganization and Disbandment Conference ended abortively. Although the Ministry of War was established, it soon took orders not from the Executive Yuan, but from the President of the National Government in his capacity as Commander-in-Chief of the armed forces.

It is to be remembered that with the establishment of the Five Yuan Government in October 1928, Chiang Kai-shek became the President of the National Government. Of course all heads of government have the power of high command and even the title of commander-in-chief. But in Chiang Kai-shek's case he chose to assume actual command and in March 1929 he even established a General Headquarters of the Commander-in-Chief of the Army, Navy, and Air Force, distinct from the offices of the National Government. The General Staff Board, the Inspectorate-General, and the War Council, which were set up either simultaneously with, or a little later than, the Ministry of War, were placed directly under the General Headquarters. But the Ministry of War assumed, as did the Ministry of the Navy subsequently, an ambivalent character. Both were constituent ministries on the newly established Executive Yuan; as such, their ministers had to take orders from the Executive Yuan. Both were also brought under the direct command of the President-Commander, exactly like the other three military establishments. Thus the military power became attached closely and almost exclusively to the President-Commander. The ability of the party to control the Executive Yuan did not give it control of the military. Such control could be exerted only if the party were able to control the president who was also commander-in-chief.

Chiang Kai-shek was forced out of the presidency in December 1931. Under the new Organic Law of the National Government, his successor,

Lin Sen, was prevented from actual exercise of the governing powers. This opportunity for the Executive Yuan to gain control over the military through the Ministries of War and of the Navy soon slipped out of its hands. The war in Shanghai in the early months of 1932 brought Chiang Kai-shek back and the Military Commission with him.

The Military Commission of the National Government was reëstablished in March 1932. In theory it was to be a collective body. As regards the organization and the training of the forces and other general military policies, the commission was to act as a committee and the powers of the chairman were to be restricted to those of a presiding officer. Only when in command of actual military operations was the chairman to receive the powers usually delegated to a commander. In other words, a continuance of the distinction which had existed at the beginning of the Northern Expedition was specifically provided for in the Law which had created the new Military Commission. In the earlier period Chiang Kai-shek as Chairman of the Commission had had two personalities corresponding to the Chairman of the Commission and the Commander-in-Chief of the Revolutionary Army. As it had in the earlier experiment, the distinction in law again failed to prevent Chiang Kai-shek from gaining complete control of the military power.

Although Chiang Kai-shek was now only Chairman of the Military Commission and not the President-Commander, he acted very much the same as when he was not. He kept the powers of the commission in his own hands. Meetings of the commission were seldom held, and at the meetings, when held, the Chairman acted as a superior and the other members never strove to be his peers. The commission of course had the authority, like the President-Commander, to exercise direct control over the Staff Board, the Inspectorate-General, and the War Council, and to share with the Executive Yuan the control of the Ministries of War and the Navy. This authority became virtually the Chairman's.

Even though the Chairman personally was able to exercise all the powers of the Military Commission, control of civil affairs was supposed to remain outside of his competence. But Chiang Kai-shek, the Chairman, came to have such civil powers when in 1932 the General Headquarters for Bandit-Suppression were established for the Communist-infested provinces and he was made Commander-in-Chief. Within these provinces the Commander-in-Chief was either by law or by party resolutions given complete power over administrative and even party authorities as well as military authorities. Since the communists were widely spread, this General Headquarters covered one area after another. The wider the area covered, the more extensive geographically became the sway of the Chairman of the Military Commission, who invariably took on the high command of the anti-communist campaign.

Military Organization During the War: 1937–1946

The outbreak of the war in July 1937 was the occasion for advocating the substitution of a purely military government for the National Government of the Five Yuan. For a time there did exist a military government of full powers, but the Five-Yuan skeleton was also allowed to continue. It was not until a half-year later that the civilian government was again acknowledged to be the Government — in theory at least.

At the beginning of the war there was a demand that the existing Military Commission be transformed into a "Grand Headquarters" to act as the Government for the duration, and that Chiang Kai-shek, the Chairman of the Commission, be given the title and the powers of "Generalissimo." Though the Political Council of the Central Executive Committee of the Kuomintang did pass a resolution to that effect on August 10, 1937, neither the commission nor Chiang Kai-shek accepted the title. The National Government continued. Pursuant to a law of a later date, the chairman, Chiang Kai-shek, assumed the top command of the armed forces and the responsibility for national defense. But he never officially appropriated the title "Generalissimo."[8]

There were both external and internal explanations for the hesitation to resort to a purely military form of government. The system of government through a "grand headquarters" was peculiarly Japanese. The Japanese emperor had created a "grand headquarters" during the Russo-Japanese War and had supplanted the civilian government. To imitate the Japanese system of military government seemed to be utterly inappropriate for a government dedicated to resisting Japanese militarism. Then, too, the difficulty involved in equating the position of an all-powerful generalissimo with that of the President of the National Government and in disposing of the Yuan presidents caused those who advocated the creation of a generalissimo and a grand headquarters to modify their opinions.

Though the idea of supplanting the National Government by a military government was abandoned, the organization of the Military Commission was for almost half a year in a state of continuous expansion, commotion, and confusion. Numerous departments in charge not only of military, political, and economic functions of the government but also of publicity and training functions which had hitherto belonged to the party were organized and reorganized. Most of the departments of the Central Executive Committee of the party were placed under the control of the Military Commission. Many of the ministries and commissions under the Executive Yuan were either duplicated or depleted of actual business. The other four Yuan were not abolished but they were placed in abeyance on their own volition. To all intents and purposes, the Military Commission was the government of China during the first six months of the war.

The organization and powers of the Military Commission were more clearly defined by the Organic Law of the Military Commission of January 17, 1938. The most fundamental was the following article:

> Article One. The National Government, for the purpose of securing national defense and marshalling soldiers and civilians in the conduct of the war, establishes directly under the National Government the Military Commission and authorizes the Chairman of the Commission to exercise the powers provided for under Article Three of the Organic Law of the National Government.

Since Article Three, referred to, gives the National Government command of the armed forces, the chairman naturally becomes the commander-in-chief of the armed forces. By another article, he is also empowered "to direct the people of the whole nation for the purpose of national defense." Still another article stipulates that the members of the commission are to assist the chairman, thus doing away with the originally collegiate character of the commission and making the chairman the superior of the whole body. With this law of 1938, Chiang Kai-shek acquired the high powers necessary for conducting the war against Japan.

But beginning from 1938 it was arranged that the Military Commission should no longer undertake the functions that appertained in normal times to either the ministries and commissions of the Executive Yuan or the departments of the party. The commission thereafter set up a great number of subordinate administrations, but, generally speaking, they were all military in nature.

The Military Commission consisted of from seven to nine members, most of whom concurrently headed the more important establishments of the commission. The chief and deputy-chiefs of the General Staff were the three principal assistants of the chairman. The Staff Board, the Inspectorate-General, the War Council, the Aeronautics Commission, the Supply Services, and a host of other agencies concerned with military administration together constituted a great over-all military establishment. In addition, the commission had under it the numerous headquarters organizations, both at the capital and throughout the country, charged with the command of the forces, such as the High Naval Command and the headquarters of the various war areas. The Ministry of War continued to be under the joint jurisdiction of both the Executive Yuan and the Military Commission.

But the functions of the Military Commission were not confined to military matters alone. There was at one time a Commission for War-Zone Party and Government Affairs, which had, theoretically at least, most extensive powers of a political nature. At another time, its Bureau of Transport Control was empowered to fix transport priorities and even to administer some means of transportation directly. At all times the Political Department, charged with the indoctrination of the armed forces, civilians, and enemy prisoners, ostensibly to prosecute the war, embarked upon all kinds of cultural work and duplicated many of the undertakings of the Publicity Department of the party and the Ministry of Education of the Executive Yuan.

More than this, there was an Office of Councilors and an Office of Aides to the Chairman. Both might sound innocuous, but their activities, especially the latter's, indicated that the Chairman of the Commission was no mere military head of the government. The Councilors delved into economics, finance, general administration, and foreign affairs. In the determination of foreign policy, they frequently overshadowed the Foreign Minister.

The Aides were even more confidential assistants and advisers, and therefore also more influential. They were divided into three sections, the first on military affairs, the second on civil affairs, and the third on personnel. The head of the first section was concurrently in charge of military intelligence and espionage. The third section kept personal records of the people prominent in all walks of life, presumably in order to be able to advise the chairman whenever he might want to enlist their services. Actually this section, headed by a leader of the Organization Group of the party, was in a position to censor and recommend all appointments to Chiang Kai-shek in his multitudinous capacities of leadership. Its influence was immeasurable, though it might have little to do with the military personnel. Still greater influence was enjoyed by the Aides of the second section. They were the eyes and ears of the chairman. They were in a position to screen the individuals and the information which were to reach him.

It must be remembered that of the various high party and government posts held by Chiang Kai-shek during the war, he and the public alike considered the Chairmanship of the Military Commission to be the most responsible. It was in that capacity that he was both addressed and spoken of, as "Chairman Chiang," and material reaching him or appointments made with him in any of his various capacities were generally channeled through the second section. By taking on the multifarious political, military, and other activities, the "Office of Aides to the Chairman of the Military Commission," innocuous as it might sound, clearly demonstrated that the Chairman occupied the seat of power in the state. Legally, the Chairman was the head of the military establishment and was charged with the responsibility of conducting the war. But extralegally, if not illegally, the Chairman had all other powers conferrable by the party or the government. He could have exercised his nonmilitary powers in his other capacities. To the extent that he chose, as he often did, to act through the Military Commission, he sacrificed the observance of the law to expediency.

Nationalization of the Armed Forces

It is obvious that the inability to put the military in its proper place has plagued China for the last generation. That the Chinese Army has been ill disciplined and badly organized is equally obvious. A measure of neutralization, which would release the armed forces from personal and partisan loyalties and other political biases, is recognized as constituting the first prerequisite for the improvement not only of the forces themselves, but also of the general administration.

In the past the Kuomintang Government has naturally refused to admit that the armed forces which it maintains were anything but national. It was not until the last years of the war when, in order to facilitate the conduct of the war against Japan, American military advisers pressed for a truly united national Chinese army, consisting of both Kuomintang and communist forces and free of party affiliations, that both the Kuomintang and the Communist Party alike had to concede that such a genuine nationalization was desirable. Nothing resulted, however.

When, after the war, General George C. Marshall of the United States came to mediate between the Kuomintang and the Chinese Communists, he considered the amalgamation and consolidation of the two opposing armies to be of paramount importance to his mission. By mutual agreement,[9] the two sides pledged gradually to reduce and to amalgamate their armies, so that within eighteen months there would remain only sixty divisions, under a single united command. There was also to be a new Ministry of National Defense, firmly established within the Executive Yuan, in lieu of divided and irresponsible control in the days of the Military Commission.

If it had been carried out, the Marshall proposal would have made possible not only a vast reduction in the number of divisions, but also an effective control of the military by the civil branch of the government. Unfortunately, the whole undertaking collapsed and the army reorganization did not materialize as planned.

The Ministry of National Defense was, however, established on July 1, 1946, superseding the Ministry of War. The various departments and establishments of the Military Commission were either dissolved or absorbed by the new ministry. The Army, the Navy, the Air Force, and the Supply Force were organized as parallel services, and were brought under the command of the Chief of the General Staff who is responsible to the Minister for the orders he issues. Each of the four forces has a commander-in-chief, but the Chief of the General Staff, assisted by the deputy chiefs for each force, has power over all of them in matters of strategy and tactics.

This streamlined ministry, which anticipated by a year a similar reorganization in the United States, was based solely on American advice and was created as a gesture of willingness to heed American advice. In itself, it is not a bad device, provided the Minister of National Defense is both a capable and a powerful political leader, and provided also that the Chief of the General Staff limits his authority to purely staff matters and does not encroach on the political sphere of the Minister. With these provisos, the device should have succeeded in subordinating the military to the civil authority.

But such has not been the result. To date, the incumbent of the ministry has always been a military man, and the Chief of the General Staff has often been politically meddlesome. The head of state, whether as President of the National Government or as President of the Republic, under the Constitution of 1946 has been, since the reorganization, as eager to exercise personally the powers of command as he was when Chairman of the Military Commission. In other words, the military organization has been somewhat simplified by the substitution of a Ministry of National Defense for the complex mechanism of the previous decades, but the irresponsible use of the military power has remained unchanged. No civilian authority has recovered an effective check on military power.

Problems Created by the Supremacy of the Military

The supremacy of the military creates problems in all spheres: political, constitutional, and administrative, not to mention the effect of a large army on the national economy.

Aside from the fact that it has an all-powerful leader in Chiang Kai-shek, the Kuomintang is disrupted by its inclusion of a number of factions. The military group centered on the graduates of the Whampoa Academy is not the only faction and has in fact not been the most powerful; but because the Whampoa Group controls the armies of the Kuomintang Government, it has been an important factor in the disunity of the party. It has also prevented the party from engaging in purely political activities which might have enabled the latter to become more deeply rooted in the nation.

Constitutionally, the domination by the military is always a danger. It negates the true spirit of constitutionalism. In a constitutional government political parties must have untrammeled freedom to oppose one another without resorting to war, the people must have their rights adequately protected by the courts against all violators, and the assembly elected by the people must be all-powerful in the expression of the wishes of the people. But when the military becomes dominant, the parties cannot oppose each other without fighting real wars, nor can the courts do anything against the military, nor can the wishes of the representatives prevail. These general observations were equally valid in the days of Yuan Shih-k'ai and the warlords. Any new attempt at constitutionalism, if it is intended to be a genuine and serious attempt, will therefore have to be preceded by the disappearance of military domination.

Administratively, military domination enfeebles the civilian authorities. The secondary role of the Executive Yuan in relation to the Military Commission needs no further emphasis. As a matter of fact, the military interference in civilian administration is not nearly as bad in the central government as in the local, where the domination of the military has prevented the development of decent and orderly administration. It is noteworthy, though entirely understandable, that the few good provincial administrations that the Chinese have experienced during the last two decades have been, without exception, under civilian leaders who happened to be strong enough to withstand military interference.

The economic consequences of military domination are equally disastrous. One result has been disproportionate military expenditures. Ever since the establishment of the Kuomintang regime, when expenditures could be roughly known, half or more of the total annual budget has always been spent on military items, to the detriment of services of a more constructive nature. Defenders of the military expenditures would of course plead the fact that wars, both civil and foreign, which the government has had to undertake made such expenditures necessary. But the sad thing is that in China the military men, restrained neither by law nor by a sense of responsibility for the popular welfare, have always found wars to be necessary and these "necessary wars" have constantly depleted the coffers of the state and wrought desolation on the countryside. Has there been since the establishment of the Republic any war except the war against Japan which has been popular and for which money has been willingly spent by the people?

There can be no salvation for China until the military is brought under proper control. The armed forces must be so reduced in size as to be compatible with the economic capacity of the nation. They have to be nationalized. As a first condition of securing their loyalty to the nation and removing them from politics, they must be neutralized and freed from allegiance to individual leaders or political groups. This must be done. If it is necessary to have a powerful political group to check the military, such a group must be developed. Or, if a mass force is necessary for the purpose, such a force must be organized. For, unless the military is confined to its proper place, orderly government is impossible. The proper control of the military may not mean the instant realization of orderly government, but orderly government is dependent on proper control of the military. China has suffered at the hands of the militarists in the recent past and still suffers today. She will cease to suffer only when a future regime is able to dominate instead of be dominated by the militarists.

XIII

LEGISLATION AND THE LEGISLATIVE PROCESS

The Legislative Yuan in the Five-Power Government

Parliaments are the products either of long evolution or of conscious imitation. Since most modern parliaments are more or less modeled after the British Parliament, directly or indirectly, and since the Mother of Parliaments is no logical creation and has a multitude of functions and capacities, scarcely any modern parliament can be said to be an organ of legislation and that alone.

But Sun Yat-sen tried in his Five-Power Constitution to make the Legislative Yuan an organ of legislation only. He did not want the Legislative Yuan endowed with functions that could not be considered strictly legislative. He wanted the control of the executive by censure, impeachments, and other actions lifted from the hands of the legislators. His Legislative Yuan was therefore necessarily a less powerful body than a modern parliament of the usual type.

That is not all. The Legislative Yuan is not even to enjoy exclusive power of legislation; it has to share it with the all-powerful National Assembly. Sun Yat-sen considers the initiative and referendum to be what he calls "political powers" of the people, while legislation itself is considered a "governing power." If, therefore, the National Assembly, acting in the place of the people themselves, enjoys the initiative and the referendum, the legislative power of the Legislative Yuan is automatically diminished. The initiative and referendum in the hands of the people cannot be frequently exercised and cannot effectively diminish the legislative power of the Legislative Yuan. But the National Assembly is a constituted body. Not only can it frequently and constantly exercise the powers of the initiative and referendum, but the nature of that exercise can be totally different from the people's. The Assembly can sit and deliberate, formulate a legislative program, and still be within its rights. Such a program, if insisted upon by the Assembly, would have to prevail over the Legislative Yuan, and the latter would consequently be no more than a rubber stamp to the Assembly's wishes or a drafting bureau for the Assembly.

The division of powers in regard to legislation was never carefully worked out by Sun Yat-sen. One thing is clear. Unless the National Assembly becomes a mere façade, which evidently was not Sun Yat-sen's intention, the Legislative Yuan will not have the complete powers of legislation, not to mention the other powers that are usually enjoyed by modern parliaments.

Sun Yat-sen's failure to define clearly the relationship between the National Assembly and the Legislative Yuan has given rise to incessant controversies whenever the question of the status of the Legislative Yuan has come up. The controversies have always centered on the choice between two alternatives: whether to restrict the meetings and functions of the National Assembly in order to make the Legislative Yuan a powerful legislature, or to reduce the Legislative Yuan to the status of a drafting bureau, in order to enable the Assembly to assume the powers of an all-powerful parliament.

In 1928 Hu Han-min and Sun Fo proposed that the Legislative Yuan be neither the one nor the other. It was to be a large-sized legislative committee of the all-powerful Council of the National Government, of which the Executive Yuan would be the executive committee. The Legislative Yuan, had the original proposal been carried out, would have been neither important nor unimportant. Its fortunes would have had to depend on the ability of its president and vice-president to influence the discussions of the Council of the National Government and of the Executive Yuan as members of both bodies.

The proposal was not adopted. As established by the Organic Law of the National Government of October 8, 1928, the Legislative Yuan of forty-nine to ninety-nine members was, generally speaking, nothing more than an exalted drafting bureau. This became especially true when the Council of the National Government began to be actively occupied in all matters of state. Hu Han-min was the President of the Legislative Yuan and an important personality, and therefore lent prestige to it, but, aside from this, the Legislative Yuan was hardly more than a continuation of the Law Bureau which had been in existence for over a year before the birth of the Legislative Yuan.

The Legislative Yuan had at times asserted a position of political prominence, not envisaged by the Organic Law of the National Government of 1928. If it had succeeded, the success was usually the result of default by some other organs of the government. It had on several occasions publicly censured the Executive Yuan or its president and thus seemed to have acquired some political prestige. But on these occasions the Executive Yuan was in retreat. Had the Executive Yuan resisted, it is inconceivable that the impotent Legislative Yuan could have successfully maintained its case against the executive.

The President of the Legislative Yuan

The President of the Legislative Yuan, like the Presidents of all the other Yuan, was appointed by the Central Executive Committee on the nomination of the President of the National Government from among the members of the Council of the National Government. In actual practice, the persons to be nominated as heads of the Yuan were appointed first to the National Government in order to give them the necessary qualifications. The most important step was the selection of the candidate by the Leader of the Party. Once that selection was made, the candidate would first find himself elected or appointed to the Council of the National Government, then nominated by the President, and at last appointed to the presidency of the Legislative Yuan by the Central Executive Committee. After the inauguration of the multiparty government in April 1947, formal appointment by the Council of the National Government was also required.

The President and members of the National Government and the Presidents of the five Yuan were each, after 1943, appointed for a three-year term. Before 1943 the terms of all of them were two years only. Be it long or short, the length of the term had no real significance. All these prominent officials actually held office at the pleasure of the Leader of the Kuomintang. If it was necessary to appoint a new man to the post, the incumbent could always be persuaded if not commanded to resign. If there was no such necessity, he was either reappointed at the end of his term, or the term could be indefinitely prolonged by a party resolution. Thus, Sun Fo was first appointed President of the Legislative Yuan by the Central Executive Committee in plenary session in March 1932 but continued to hold the office up to the very end of the National Government in 1948.

There were, from 1928 to 1948, only three presidents of the Legislative Yuan, Hu Han-min, Lin Sen, and Sun Fo. Lin Sen held the post only for a brief interval in 1931 after the detention of Hu Han-min. Hu Han-min and Sun Fo between them have molded the Legislative Yuan into something reflecting their own personalities. Hu Han-min was an honored leader. Though he was stubborn and conservative, he was also tenacious, hard-working, public-minded, and, withal, loyal to what he considered to be the teachings of Sun Yat-sen and the mission of the Kuomintang. Among his coworkers in the Yuan, there were perhaps a score who shared his political outlook and were blessed with the same virtues. Though the Legislative Yuan enjoyed no political prominence even in his days, it did, under his leadership, work hard and produce the legislation necessary for the new regime. If the laws were not well carried out, it was not to be blamed.

Sun Fo is a different personality. Like Hu Han-min, he has political ambitions of a high order. But while Hu Han-min was full of tenacity, this does not seem to have impressed Sun Fo as a virtue. Hu Han-min's heart was in politics. But, failing to get the top political post, he nevertheless tried to do a good job in the Legislative Yuan. Sun Fo, on the other hand, failing to get a political post of greater importance, seemed always to belittle the legislative work. He never tried to improve the *esprit de corps* in the Yuan. He never interested himself in raising the standards of legislation. He allowed the Legislative Yuan to drift.

The Vice-President of the Legislative Yuan was appointed in the same manner as the President. The post was of course a sinecure. Only if the President was incapacitated for a considerable length of time could the Vice-President acquire importance.[1]

The President of the Legislative Yuan was unique. Unlike the presidents of other parliaments, he was not one of the members of the legislature, but was their master. Although the Rules of the Legislative Yuan assigned to him only the role of a presiding officer as far as the proceedings of the Yuan were concerned, he was to all intents and purposes the veritable ruler of the Yuan, as will be seen later.

The Members of the Legislative Yuan

Before the 1947 reorganization of the government when minor party representatives were admitted into the various branches, the Legislative Yuan could have from 49 to 99 members. The maximum was never reached, and the membership was usually a little over 80. It rose to 99–149 in 1947.[2]

The members were appointed by the President of the National Government on the nomination of the President of the Yuan. Before 1947, prior consent always had to be given to these appointments by the Political Council, and, as far as Kuomintang members were concerned, such consent was not waived in 1947. The form of consent of the Council of the National Government was also required by the Organic Law of the National Government of April 1947.

Generally, the President of the Yuan had the greatest say in these appointments. Custom demanded that all geographic sections, if not all provinces, be amply represented. Expediency, usually carefully observed, required that none of the important factions of the Kuomintang be ignored or left out. Furthermore, there must be a number of lawyers to attend to the drafting of new codes and the revision of old ones. The quotas agreed to be accorded to the minor parties in 1947 had, of course, to be filled up by the candidates of those parties. Aside from these considerations, the President of the Legislative Yuan had a fairly free hand in the choice of the members. Once a man was permitted to be the President of the Yuan, he was usually not begrudged the opportunity to appoint a few of his own following as members of the Yuan.

The term of office of the members was, according to the law, only two years. But the members were usually continued from term to term, and in 1934 a party resolution prolonged their terms to last until the inauguration of the constitutional government. The virtually continuous incumbency of most of the members had the effect of restricting their President's freedom of appointment. Only Sun Fo's long years in office enabled him to fill with his own followers the numerous vacancies that occurred from time to time.

The caliber of the members was both mediocre and unpolitical. There were at the beginning many veterans of the Kuomintang, who, though conservatives like Hu Han-min, were at least politically minded. But they passed away or grew too old. Lawyers and economists who were appointed when they were comparatively young also grew too advanced in age to be able to grapple with the problems of the day. As for Sun Fo's own men, few were both interested in and qualified for the work of the Legislative Yuan. The members who represented the parties other than the Kuomintang were if they differed at all from the rest, not only less experienced in public affairs, but also even less public-spirited.

The *esprit de corps* of the members was low after the forcible removal of Hu Han-min as their chief. They felt that theirs was not an important role. By remaining members, they could have neither the satisfaction of doing a useful and constructive piece of work nor the prospect of achieving greater political eminence. They stalled for time. The more ambitious left rather than be stalemated. Altogether, the members were neither a contented nor an ambitious group. The soaring inflation of the last years which reduced their income to a ridiculous sum further dampened their spirits. For the members of the Legislative Yuan, high officials though they undoubtedly were, were compensated with a fixed salary alone and did not enjoy the privileges of many bureaucrats, who could usually draw on many kinds of official allowances, legal or not quite legal.

When the Constitution of 1946 was adopted and a new government was being mooted, there was apprehension among the members of the Legislative Yuan as to their future employment. They were, with very few exceptions, not politicians, and were not good at hobnobbing with party workers. They were also out of contact with the professions from which they had been drawn and could not with profit return to them. Fortunately for them, their claim to be seated first in the Constitutional Assembly of 1946 and then to be officially welcomed into the new Legislative Yuan of 1948 was graciously acceded to by the Kuomintang. Their jobs are now again secure, though that security makes one wonder whether the new Legislative Yuan is to continue to be a home for the distinguished unemployed.

The Sittings of the Legislative Yuan

The Legislative Yuan of 1928–1948 usually held a weekly sitting. Occasionally it had extra sittings, and it might also declare long vacations. The sitting itself lasted for only three or four hours. The Legislative Yuan was not a body known for its hard work. Whether its disinclination for work was the result or the cause of its sinking importance is open to discussion, but there can be no doubt that that disinclination was somehow connected with its lack of importance.

The sittings were regulated by the Rules of the Legislative Yuan of January 13, 1929, subsequently revised. The Rules in general resembled those of other legislative assemblies both as regards the subject matter treated and the method of transacting legislative business. The significant difference was to be found in the position of the presiding officer. The President of the Legislative Yuan, according to the Rules, enjoyed more power than the most powerful presiding officer of a representative assembly.

For a sitting, one-third of the total membership constituted a quorum. The actual attendance was varied. At times it was hardly many more than a quorum. Members often considered attendance more an obligatory gesture than an exercise of power. In order to procure a larger attendance, the expedient of salary reduction in case of unauthorized leave of absence was sometimes resorted to.

A member who wished to speak on the floor of the Legislative Yuan had to be recognized by the President. But debates or spirited discussions were rare. As will be explained later in the chapter, the Legislative Yuan enjoyed no real powers of either legislation or budget. When real power was lacking, the incentive for debate could hardly exist. In the years before the war the Legislative Yuan made several attempts to criticize the Executive Yuan's handling of foreign affairs and, in recent years, its handling of economic and financial affairs. In these criticisms, the discussions became more enthusiastic. But in all debates eloquence seldom rose to a high order. The members had very little actual experience in debate. Their speaking consisted generally of either brief questions or equally brief explanations about a certain proposal or certain points in a proposal. Eloquence was seldom called for.

Voting was also regulated by the Rules. It might be by a show of hands or by rising. Originally it required a majority of the members present to pass any motion; after 1935 plurality was considered sufficient. These regulations, however, need not be taken seriously. Voting seldom took place. Most of the bills, resolutions, and motions adopted by the Legislative Yuan were by unanimous consent on suggestion from the Chair. Some such pronouncement as the following was made by the Chair: "The Chair takes such and such to be the consensus of the Yuan. If no contrary opinion is expressed, the bill (or resolution or motion) shall pass." And of course the bill (or resolution or motion) was then passed.

Even within the Rules of the Legislative Yuan there was confirmation of the dominant position of its president. He must recognize the members before they were able to speak. He fixed the agenda for the sitting and in the midst of the sitting he was free to rearrange the order of business. It was of course possible for a group of members, if large enough, to thwart his wishes. By resorting to parliamentary fights, by taking advantage of the Rules to insist on speaking and on taking votes, they might be able to force a majority decision against the personal views of the president. But such fights were clearly inconceivable, considering that the members were appointed on his recommendation and could be discontinued at the end of their terms. The Rules therefore rather secured than weakened his position of superiority over the members.

The Committees of the Legislative Yuan

To facilitate its work, the Legislative Yuan maintained a number of committees. The four standing committees on Law, Foreign Affairs, Finance, and Economics were continuous from the first. The fifth standing committee, on Military Affairs, was suspended for a number of years, but was revived early in the war. Also there were occasional committees charged with more specific functions. The best known was the committee on the constitutional draft. These committees were, however, resorted to rather infrequently.

The membership of the committees was neither elected nor appointed, but haphazardly made up. Members of the Legislative Yuan could freely choose to attach themselves to any of the committees. Consequently the committees were of very uneven size. Sometimes the President tried to reduce that unevenness by persuading members of a large committee to transfer themselves to a small one. Still the unevenness persisted. It is unnecessary to add that there is no coherence in any committee.

Each committee had a chairman appointed by the President of the Legislative Yuan with the prior consent of the Political Council of the party. There were times when these chairmen achieved a political prominence comparable to that held by the ministers of the Executive Yuan. If the latter were admitted as ex officio members of the Political Council, the former frequently also claimed the right to be so admitted. But generally these chairmen, who were usually as unpolitically minded as the rank and file of the Yuan members, were contented with an inferior position.

The five committees were all concerned with preparation for legislation. That the work of the Committee on Law should be legislative is self-evident, but the other committees were occupied with the same kind of work. The

Committee on Foreign Affairs considered a treaty which was to be ratified in very much the same manner as the Committee on Law considered a proposal to be enacted. In a similar manner, the Committee on Military Affairs made a preliminary study of bills on military matters. But the Committee on Foreign Affairs had no authority to discuss foreign policy nor had the Committee on Military Affairs the right to review military policy. Since all were concerned with legislation, the Committee on Law, being cognizant of all legislation except that on economic and military affairs, the budget, and treaties, was naturally the most important and the most busily occupied of all.

But the committees could not be any more important than the Yuan itself. Even the busiest of all, the Committee on Law, seldom met more than once a week. The other committees met much less frequently. The committee meetings considered the bills or the budget or the treaties and agreements which had been referred to them. Since, however, most, if not all, of these proposals had been discussed by the Political Council or its committees, of which the chairmen of the Legislative Yuan committees were not infrequently members, the consideration was likely to be cursory and brief. The chairmen might report to the members the discussions in the Political Council and suggest either complete compliance or certain modifications, to be presented to the Political Council if the Yuan should agree. In all events, heated argument or minute study seemed to be out of place. The members were, in a way, all defeatists. They were conscious that they had no authority to challenge the Political Council. If so, why not submit? If submission was necessary, why labor to discuss the proposals at great length or with minute care? A political personage without power generally tends to be irresponsible. This is nowhere better illustrated than in the business of the committees of the Legislative Yuan.

The defeatism perhaps also came from the fact that the members of the Legislative Yuan were more technical than political. Few of them had had experience in politics or had engaged in political activity. In the committees, the service required of them was certainly more of a technical than of a political nature. They were not supposed to know or be interested in the political effects of the measures before them. The higher authorities in the party and in the Executive Yuan were the ones to know and to be interested in such matters. The committees of the Legislative Yuan therefore confined themselves to scrutinizing measures in the light of existing legislation. They might try to remove some of the discrepancies and loopholes not intended by the prime movers of the measure. When they had done so, they considered their work well accomplished. Most of them were frankly not interested in politics or in the political effects of measures.

In conclusion, it may therefore be said that the committee stage, though necessary, was not important. But the reports of the committees were usually accepted by the Legislative Yuan. That is just one more indication of the frustrated role of the Legislative Yuan.

The Powers of the Legislative Yuan

As stipulated by the Organic Law of the National Government, the Legislative Yuan had power to deliberate and pass on (1) bills, (2) budgets, (3) amnesty, (4) declarations of war, (5) treaties of peace, and (6) other important matters in international relations. These actions not only were within the competence of the Legislative Yuan, but they devolved on it as duties. In addition, the Organic Law of the Legislative Yuan itself entitled the Yuan by resolution to bring into question the action of other Yuan and their ministries and commissions regarding the execution of laws and resolutions it had passed. For that purpose the Legislative Yuan and its committees were further entitled to request the heads of those bodies or their representatives to be present at the Yuan or its committee meetings.

The enumerated powers of the Legislative Yuan were all self-explanatory except the last one concerning "other important matters in international relations." When in 1932 and 1933 the Executive Yuan concluded two agreements for the cessation of hostilities with the Japanese commanders, one negotiated by the representatives of the Ministry of Foreign Affairs and the other by the military commanders on the spot, it failed to send them to the Legislative Yuan for ratification. The Legislative Yuan alleged that this violated the law. But the Executive Yuan countered that the agreements touched only on field activities of the Army and were therefore completely within the discretion of the executive branch. The controversy was finally settled by the Political Council, which ruled in favor of the Executive Yuan. The party being the sovereign, that decision had to be accepted as final, although a more reasonable interpretation would have supported the contentions of the Legislative Yuan.

The power of the Legislative Yuan to question the other branches of government also caused controversy between the Legislative and the Executive Yuan. It was true that the Legislative Yuan had no means, for instance, to compel the President of the Executive Yuan or a minister to answer its questions orally or to be present in person for questioning. Nevertheless the Legislative Yuan could keep on asking the questions and requesting his presence. Repeated refusal not only would impair the good relationship between the Legislative and Executive Yuan, but would also betray a lack of self-confidence on the part of the latter. This would be very much to its disadvantage.

There were only a few occasions on which the President of the Executive Yuan appeared before the Legislative Yuan, but those appearances were all trying to him, for he was questioned and severely criticized. In fact, they usually denoted the decline and fall of the particular president involved. The Legislative Yuan never desired to embarrass a president who was himself a strong man or who was being heartily supported by a strong man. This tendency to attack only a weak incumbent of the presidency of the Executive Yuan perhaps explains why the Legislative Yuan was not able to develop its questioning power so as to give itself a new importance. Needless to say, such questioning power on the part of the Legislative Yuan was never contemplated by Sun Yat-sen.

Legislative Procedure

Legislative procedure under the Kuomintang regime was a very complicated matter. It was not to be found alone in the Rules of the Legislative Yuan. Earlier, it was governed as well by two resolutions of the Central Executive Committee of the party: the Law on Legislative Procedure of March 1, 1928, and the Principles Regulating the Exercise of Governing Powers of June 10, 1928. Later, the Law Providing for the Standards of Law- and Ordinance-Making of May 14, 1929, revised on June 4, 1943, and the resolution of the Standing Committee of the Central Executive Committee on the Essentials of Legislative Procedure of June 23, 1932, revised April 20, 1943, came to govern the procedure of legislation.[3]

A distinction between what was and what was not considered law must first be attempted. Since law-making bodies were numerous, there was great necessity for making this distinction, on the part of the government, lest the courts be thrown into hopeless confusion. But the distinction was not always easy to make. Roughly speaking, a law was something which had passed through the Legislative Yuan in conformity with its three leading procedures. In other words, a decree which had not gone through this legislative mill was technically not a law. The Law Providing for Standards of Law- and Ordinance-Making further provided that the following matters must be regulated by law: (1) the rights and duties of the people; (2) the organization of the organs and agencies of the state; (3) the amendment or repeal of a law in force, and (4) the regulation of matters which according to the law in force should be regulated by law. To recapitulate, all important matters were to be regulated by law, and a law had to be passed by the Legislative Yuan in due form.

But the laws governing legislative procedure were not scrupulously adhered to. Several amendments of the Organic Law of the National Government itself never received the enactment of the Legislative Yuan. And the orders and decrees made either by the National Government itself or by the

Yuan and their subordinate ministries and commissions often touched on matters requiring legislative enactment.

As for the legislative procedure proper, it is profitable to distinguish between the principles of law and the provisions of the law. Before its enactment by the Legislative Yuan, the Political Council's consent to the principles must first be secured. But no law governing the legislative procedure was altogether exact and explicit on this point. Just what was meant by principle? The lack of a precise definition was the cause of the Political Council's undue interference with the legislative power of the Legislative Yuan.

A law could be proposed by (1) the Political Council, (2) the National Government, (3) the four Yuan other than the Legislative, and (4) members of the Legislative Yuan if countersigned by not less than five of them. As a matter of fact, with the exception of the several codes of law which the Legislative Yuan considered to fall peculiarly within its competence, the members seldom made proposals. The several ministries and commissions of the Yuan, especially those under the Executive Yuan, were the bodies responsible for most of the legislative bills. When something within the jurisdiction of a ministry needed legislation, that ministry would draft a bill and submit it to the consideration of the Yuan in control of the ministry. If the Yuan accepted it, it would then send the bill to the Legislative Yuan, either by way of the Political Council or directly. Similarly, a bill that was drafted by the Chief Budgetary Officer was forwarded to the Legislative Yuan in the name of the National Government. So, although the National Government and the four Yuan were the only government organs having the right of proposal, the actual proposing was generally done by the organs at a lower level.

The proposals were first considered by the Political Council in order to have the principles of legislation approved. Procedures on different categories of proposals differed slightly. The proposals made by the Political Council itself were naturally presumed to embody only acceptable principles. The proposals from other government quarters were either first approved by the Political Council, or, by order of the Political Council, might be referred to the Legislative Yuan for preliminary consideration. In the latter case, the enacted bill had to go to the Political Council for approval. To save time, the Council usually passed on the proposal before it was sent to the Legislative Yuan. As for the proposals made by the members of the Legislative Yuan, the Legislative Yuan might either formulate principles and petition the Political Council for approval, or simply petition the Political Council for a set of principles. In every case, consideration by the Political Council as to the principles of the bill was necessary.

The Legislative Yuan might make its own comments regarding the principles which had obtained the approval of the Political Council. It seldom did so, being consistently inclined to be passive.

The procedure with which the Political Council took up the consideration of legislative proposals was generally as follows. The full Council might or might not have a preliminary discussion. Whether it did or did not, the proposals were, with rare exceptions, always referred to one of its committees for more detailed study. Upon receiving the report, the full Political Council made a decision and the proposal was then ready for discussion by the Legislative Yuan.

Theoretically, the Political Council only decided on the general principles of the proposed legislation. But there was nothing to prevent the Council from adopting a fully formulated bill with detailed provisions. There could not be a valid distinction between a principle and a provision. The Council, if it regarded a certain piece of legislation as so important that it could not afford to let any of its decisions be modified, might, of course, write out the provisions with great exactness. When the law was written out by the Political Council, the Legislative Yuan's enactment became of course purely perfunctory.

The committees of the Political Council varied in number. At one time the number and nomenclature of these committees were nearly identical with those of the committees of the Legislative Yuan. As a rule, the Political Council tended to maintain more committees. Such matters as education and communication were generally taken care of by committees set up for those subjects.[4]

Since there was a tendency for the Political Council to consider all legislation as involving important principles of policy and since the amount of legislative business was large, the committee stage grew in importance. Aside from the few highly controversial or purely declaratory items of business which Chiang Kai-shek, as President of the Political Council, or of the Supreme National Defense Council during the war, chose to handle himself at the full Council meetings, the committees were really the fixers. The reports of the committees were generally accepted by the full Council.

It thus came about that the few men who happened to head these committees were, in the legislative sphere, masters of the National Government. They were more influential than the chairmen of the committees of the Legislative Yuan. The latter, if also members of the committees of the Political Council, might have had some voice in the decisions. But as members, their voice was hardly comparable to that of the chairmen. When it is remembered that the chairmen of the committees of the Political Council might also have held concurrently responsible positions in the government, their influence can be further appreciated.

When legislative proposals finally got to the Legislative Yuan for enactment, a long and elaborate procedure awaited them. They were placed on the agenda in an order in which proposals from the Political Council preceded those from the government organs. Among the proposals from the latter, those from the National Government preceded those from the various Yuan. The proposals of the members of the Legislative Yuan were placed at the bottom. This order, though stipulated in the Rules of the Legislative Yuan, might be changed at the discretion of its president.

The Rules also provided for three readings of the proposals. The first reading was by title only. At this stage the government organ proposing the legislation might send representatives to make explanation and the Legislative Yuan might also demand such explanations from them. Next came the committee stage. When the committee had made its report on the bill, the Yuan was to decide whether to proceed with the second reading. The second reading was by articles. Amendments were in order. If there were too many amendments, the bill might be recommitted for the purpose of redrafting.

The second reading, insofar as discussion by the Legislative Yuan was concerned, was the most important and substantial. In earlier years the debates at this stage were sometimes quite animated. But in late years the usual procedure was to adopt the bill as reported by the committee.

The third reading was generally confined to textual corrections and was of no importance.

Any or all of the readings might be omitted either by the demand of one-third of the members present or at the discretion of the president. As the Political Council went more and more into legislation and as the Legislative Yuan had less and less freedom of action, such omissions became in fact only too common.

The enactments of the Legislative Yuan were still subject to review by the Political Council. This might be done by action of the Political Council. Also, in the case of a proposed bill voted down by the Legislative Yuan, the president of the Yuan could request the Political Council to have it reconsidered. This latter arrangement proceeded from the theory that the president, being necessarily a leading and responsible member of the Political Council, must seek to protect the interests and preserve the freedom of the Council, and must therefore consider the Yuan no more than the instrument of the Council. These safeguards were of no significance, since the Legislative Yuan was both too weak and too apathetic to assert its will in possible contradiction to that of the Political Council.

The quality of legislation depended first on the quality of the legislators and second on the legislative procedure. The members of the Legislative Yuan were really secondary legislators, since the members of the Political Council enjoyed a far more important role in legislation. Therefore, in the personal elements that went into their making, the quality of the laws was naturally circumscribed by the quality of leadership in the Political Council. If the members of the Political Council had either no interest in or no knowledge of the realities of the state and society, the laws were naturally apt to be either unprogressive or unworkable or both.

As for the legislative procedure, the action of the Political Council and the Legislative Yuan together had at least enabled most proposals to be rather carefully considered. Chaos and negligence there might still be, but, as compared with the previous years of the Republic, legislation under the Kuomintang regime was characterized by better draftsmanship and was far more competent.

In conclusion, one gets the impression that in legislation the failure was not so much in the technique as in the spirit. It was the lack of realistic and enlightened political leadership among the legislators that was chiefly responsible for the kind of legislation that has failed to cope with the changing needs of the nation.[5]

XIV

FINANCE AND THE BUDGET

History of the Budget System in China

If budgeting is something which no wise government can afford to neglect, only in a modern or a democratic government does it become a necessity. For, when public revenue and expenditures are closely geared to the national economy, or when the people, through their representatives, seek to control the government by supervising its expenditures, the government has no alternative but to establish a budget and to live within it as well as it can.

In monarchical China complete financial data for any period was lacking. The wiser among her rulers never allowed the treasury to become empty nor resorted to unusual or extraordinary levies. But there was no pretense of making out an annual or a periodic budget. If actual expenditures were not allowed to be in excess of the revenue, it was only the fortunate result of wise governing.

With the coming of constitutional trends in the last years of the Manchu Dynasty, budgeting also came into vogue. In 1910 a budgetary law of a provisional nature was promulgated, and budgetary estimates for 1911 were made and sent to the Legislative Council for adoption. This marked the beginning of a modern budget in the history of China.

After the Republican revolution, the Peking regime continued to grapple with the problem of establishing a budget. That was, however, just a façade. Budgeting, being a sign of democracy, the government of Peking was anxious to be adorned by that sign. The more removed it was from democracy, the more eagerly did it want to give the appearance of governing according to a budget. But it was inevitable that in the midst of civil wars and in the absence of a real parliament no genuine budgeting was possible, and no budget was passed or executed.

The revolutionary regime of the Kuomintang at Canton began in great financial difficulties. Prior to the Northern Expedition, the area under its control was small, and financial resources were slender. Furthermore, the administration of the customs and salt revenue, two of the principal revenues of the Chinese state at that time, was in foreign hands hostile to the revolutionary regime. Financial difficulties thus compelled the regime to appreciate the advantages of strict budgeting in addition to discovering new sources of taxation and modernizing the methods of collection.

This early emphasis on modern financial administration was followed by the continuous endeavors of the National Government at budget-making. Prior to the final enactment of a budget law on September 24, 1932, there were numerous preliminary trials. The Budget Committees and Finance Committees, composed of representatives from the Central Executive Committee and high dignitaries of the government having to do with finance or financial legislation, were set up one after another as special organs of the National Government to frame the budget and supervise its execution. Pending the enactment of a definitive budget law, annual budgetary procedures were promulgated. In April 1932, for the first time in Chinese history, a more or less carefully prepared budget for the year 1931–1932 was carried through both the Political Council and the Legislative Yuan. Had not first the anti-communist campaigns and then the war against Japan called for immense expenditures for war purposes, workable annual budgets might have been set up soon afterward.

The Budget Law of 1937

The Budget Law now in force is that of April 27, 1937, accompanied by the Decree of September 23, 1938, providing for its execution. The Law came into force on the first day of 1939. But this does not mean that subsequent budgets were necessarily formulated in accordance with the terms of the Law. In fact no budget has ever been so formulated, as we shall see. With the establishment of the so-called constitutional government in May 1948, certain provisions of the Law, such as those connected with the Political Council, have also been rendered inoperative. Nevertheless the Law of 1937 offers an illuminating study of the complex machinery of the tutelage government.

The Law of 1937 was the culmination of a number of provisional budget laws. In the five or six years previous to the adoption of the Law, the National Government had been making annual budgets in accordance with the provisional laws mentioned above. With this previous experience as a guide, the Law of 1937 should have been made workable. But it erred on the side of overelaboration. The Chinese administrative mechanism was not sufficiently organized to be equal to its execution.

According to the Law, the fiscal year coincides with the calendar year.[1] The preparation of the budget begins about fifteen months prior to the opening of the fiscal year. There are five stages in the process. The first involves the making of estimates prepared by the several spending departments and then compiled by the Chief Budgetary Officer. The second is the consideration and approval of these estimates by the Political Council, presumably on the fundamental points of policy involved. The third is the revision and final compilation of the estimates by the Chief Budgetary Officer in accordance with the decisions of the Political Council. The fourth is the discussion by the Executive Yuan and the enactment by the Legislative. The final stage is the promulgation by the National Government.

The first preliminary estimates have of course to be made out by the spending departments directly. These estimates are scrutinized by the ministries, the Yuan above them, and the National Government itself on the part of the central authorities, and by the provincial government on the part of the local authorities. In making out these preliminary estimates of expenditures, the spending departments and the revising authorities have to adhere to the policy directives which the Political Council issues through the government to governmental organizations throughout the country. In issuing the policy directives the Political Council in turn is supposed to have considered the recommendations of the Chief Budgetary Officer and of the Ministries of Audit and Finance concerning the means of improvement in financial administration. Meanwhile, these latter authorities concerned with finance are to keep the Political Council well advised. The Political Council is to make out its policy well in advance of the fiscal year and to acquaint the government with it. Then the hierarchy of government departments are to produce their preliminary estimates of expenditures again well in advance of the fiscal year, for the five Yuan and the National Government must send in their respective estimates to the Chief Budgetary Officer not later than the end of March.

The estimates of revenue are to be made out by the Ministry of Finance as soon as the Five Yuan and the National Government have completed their estimates of expenditure. They must be sent to the Chief Budgetary Officer not later than the middle of April. The Chief Budgetary Officer is to complete the compilation of the estimates both of expenditure and of revenue not later than the middle of May.

The consideration and approval of the final budgetary estimates by the Political Council is of the same nature as the approval of principles in the case of legislation. Usually it is rather on its Expert Finance Committee than on the full Council itself that the burden of consideration falls. The matter of finance can, however, become so controversial that the Political Council often resorts to appointing a special committee consisting of the presidents of the Five Yuan and the Ministers of War and Finance to resolve the controversies that may arise.

The figures approved by the Political Council are sent back to the Chief Budgetary Officer who must turn them over within fifteen days to the ministries and provincial governments and other departments of government of a similar rank. These authorities have to make out revised estimates according to the approved figures and send them back to the Chief Budgetary Officer before September 20. He in turn completes the budget and sends it to the Executive Yuan for discussion.

The discussion by the Executive Yuan has to be speedy and brief because the Law of the Budget provides that this Yuan must complete its consideration of the budget by October 10.

Finally comes the consideration of the budget by the Legislative Yuan. Roughly speaking, the budget is treated similarly to a proposal of law. There is, however, this difference. The budget, when received, is at once referred to the Finance Committee. The Legislative Yuan is forbidden to add to the expenditures. It is also required to enact the budget not later than December 1, thus leaving one full month for the governmental departments to prepare themselves for its execution. If, however, the Legislative Yuan is unable to approve the budget in due time, it must then pass on the undisputed items and make out a provisional budget by December 5, in order to enable the government to lay its hands on some funds when the fiscal year begins. Within a month of the promulgation of the provisional budget the Executive Yuan is to iron out the differences that it may have with the Legislative Yuan. When the latter finally enacts the definitive budget of the year, the provisional one is considered superseded.

The Law of the Budget, as far as its provisions go, is indeed impressive. But its impracticability is obvious. Its very elaborateness makes it inoperative. Too many are given a hand in the making of the budget. The authority is too divided. The timetable can never be kept. The starting date is too far in advance of the fiscal year to make accurate estimates possible. Yet, these defects all proceed from the one essential defect: the Five-Yuan structure is too complicated a scheme for either efficient or intelligent government.

The Budget-Making Power Under the Law of 1937

As a rule, in a democratic government of modern times, the budget-making is shared by the Legislature and a Ministry of Finance of the executive branch. The latter is in control of the collection and expending of revenues. With it must rest the preparation of the budget, naturally with the approval of the highest executive authority. The former represents the will of the people, and since the budget is the one single piece of legislation which reflects the general program of the government, naturally the power of final approval is reserved to the Legislature. The institution of a budget bureau in the United States departs somewhat from the general pattern, but is in no way a contradiction of the principle. The President of the United States is the highest executive authority. The Budget Bureau as well as the Treasury Department is directly responsible to him. As long as he can secure concerted action by both of them, the authority for the preparation of the budget is by no means divided.

Compared with the general pattern of budget-making in democratic governments, the most outstanding peculiarity of the handling of the budget in China under the Law of 1937 is the multiple division of power. The drawing-up of the estimates of expenditures is a function scattered throughout the whole government, not even centralized in the hands of the Chief Budgetary Officer. The estimates of revenue remain in the hands of the Ministry of Finance. The approval of the budget is divided between the Political Council and the Legislative Yuan.

The Chief Budgetary Office was a very curious innovation. It was ill conceived and it added confusion to an already confounded system of government. It was originally proposed by Hu Han-min after the establishment of the Five Yuan and after he had failed to gain the presidency of the Executive Yuan. His purpose was to give effective equality and independence to the Five Yuan and to protect the weaker ones from domination by the Executive Yuan. To transfer the function of preparing the budget from a ministry of the Executive Yuan, the Ministry of Finance, to a Chief Budgetary Officer outside of the Five Yuan and directly under the control of the National Government was his means to that end.

The Budgetary Office was set up in 1931, charged, among other things, with the final and centralized preparation of the budget. The institution later received strong support from the Organization Group of the party because it had enabled that faction to penetrate into all branches of government by manning the branch budgetary offices with their faithful adherents.

But the existence of the Budgetary Office has not contributed either to economy or to efficiency. It has not had enough power to work for economy. When it was first established, the National Government, at least the presidency of it, had great powers. But soon, after the revision of the Organic Law of the National Government in December 1931, the presidency was reduced to a position of impotence and the Council functioned even less. The Chief Budgetary Officer ceased to have strong political support from above. He was in no position to exact the compliance of the Yuan to whatever recommendations of economy and efficiency he might have proposed. In the process of preparing the budget, his Office, thenceforward, has existed more in form than in substance and has served only to delay the procedure.

The budget-approving power is also nowhere centralized. The budget is, after all, a much more complicated affair than any other single piece of legislation and is a measure of great importance. The Political Council may be confident enough to tackle a legislative measure, but to tackle the budget requires ability, effort, and power, all three. Ordinary members of the Political Council have too little power to make their influence felt on the budget. The important members of the Executive Yuan, if they happen to be members of the Political Council, are always reluctant to discuss the budget with the more plebeian members of the Political Council. Unless a special committee composed of the powerful men in the government is set up, as has been frequently done in the past, the Political Council is unsuitable for the purpose of discussing the budget.

The Legislative Yuan is also not to be entirely ignored. In theory at least, it does enjoy some real power. Though it cannot augment the items of expenditure, it does have the right otherwise to modify the figures, as provided for by the Law of the Budget. The budget is made up of figures and the figures can be subjected to indefinite numbers of modifications. The Legislative Yuan can therefore always propose changes and alterations and yet at the same time claim not to have affected the essentials which may have been decided upon by the Political Council. In fact, when it does do such things, there is no way out for the government except to request the Leader of the Party to apply pressure on the recalcitrant members of the Legislative Yuan through its president.

These considerations suffice to explain why under the National Government, a government of great complexities, the elaborate Budget Law of 1937 could never work. Consequently, some much less elaborate procedure was necessary.

Budget-Making During the War Years

During the war years the government was in a dilemma with regard to the budget. On the one hand, it hesitated to proclaim the desuetude of the Budgetary Law which it had taken great pains to establish. On the other, that law was clearly unworkable, especially since the war called for quick granting of money, and measures of expedition were needed.

For the first few years of the war, the budgets were simply adapted from those of the preceding years, when the Budgetary Law had not yet come into force. Beginning from the Budget of 1940, the government promulgated what may be called "transitional provisions for the making of the budget." Meant for a certain specific year, these provisions lapsed as soon as the budget was duly promulgated. They were, however, continued by fresh promulgation from year to year with only minor modifications.

The transitional provisions have tended first to shorten the length of the period for the preparation of the budget, and second, to omit some of the steps a budget had to go through according to the Budget Law. Instead of some fifteen months ahead, the initial stages were to begin in July of the year preceding the fiscal year concerned. The initial step was for the Supreme National Defense Council, which was the wartime equivalent of the Political Council, to arrive at a general policy and apportion the annual expenditure, on the proposal of the Executive Yuan in collaboration with the Chief Budgetary Officer. The second step was the preparation by the spending departments of the estimates of expenditure, and by the Ministry of Finance of those of revenue, both in conformity with the general figures decided upon by the Council. In the process of this preparation the Executive Yuan would pass on the estimates. The estimates thus prepared were then to be forwarded to the Chief Budgetary Officer for compilation. This constituted the third step. The fourth step was the final approval by the Council. The Expert Finance Committee of the Council would usually make the preliminary study, and the Committee on General Budget, with the presidents of the Five Yuan, the Chief of the General Staff, and the Minister of Finance always as members, would meet to thrash out the more weighty controversies that might have arisen between the different branches of the government. The consideration by the Council itself would usually be perfunctory, as would the last step, the final enactment by the Legislative Yuan.[2]

Even this presumably simplified procedure was too complicated for smooth running. Though discussion under the transitional provisions was centered in the Supreme National Defense Council, the other government authorities entitled to have a say in the budget under the provisions of the Budget Law still had at least the power to glance at the budget. Furthermore, the Central Planning Board, a new creation during the war, was by the transitional provisions also given a share in all the first three steps of the preparation.

Greater simplification was thus needed. It was to be found in the person of the Leader of the Party who was the Chairman of the Supreme National Defense Council and also the President of the National Government. He determined the general policy and did the apportioning. When the estimates were finally drawn up and expenditures happened to exceed revenues, he was the man who in the name of the Council cut down the expenditures. He did these things often in bold strokes and sometimes in too arbitrary a manner. But since the machinery of the party and the government was so complicated, it was perhaps to be considered fortunate that there was such a Chairman-President to do the arbitrating. The more he arbitrated, the less were the other authorities able to acquire competence and a sense of responsibility. The more these latter authorities sank into incompetence and irresponsibility, the more would the Chairman-President have to be called upon to arbitrate. The great motif of the Kuomintang Government was in fact nowhere better demonstrated than in the budget-making. It is thus not incorrect to say that the budget power resided in the Leader of the Party, both in theory and in practice.

The Finances of China

The demands of the National Treasury during the days of the Manchus were light, except when there were rebellions to crush. In ordinary times, the Court was able to balance its revenues and its expenditures fairly well. Its revenues consisted largely of land and salt taxes, and special contributions were meager. But its expenditures were also small.

In the last decade and a half of their dynasty, the Manchus were burdened with the indemnities they had to pay to the victors in the Sino-Japanese War of 1894–1895 and in the Boxer Rebellion of 1900. They also had incurred foreign and domestic loans for new undertakings such as railways and manufactures, which had to be repaid. The foreign powers now controlled both the customs and the salt gabelle, which had developed into the principal sources of revenue. The powers helped to increase the yields in order to enable the government to discharge its increasing obligations. This process continued until, in the first years of its existence, the Kuomintang Government was able to put an end to it.

The finances of the Peking regime were a continuation of those of the Manchus. For meeting deficits it usually had to rely on foreign loans, and their price was generally the tightened control of China's revenues by the loaning powers. Natural resources such as iron and coal mines were also mortgaged to them. The principal source of revenue which the government could count on without foreign control was the land tax, but the civil wars between the rival warlords and the resultant complete control by the warlords of geographical areas of varying size cut away that revenue. The warlords usually levied the land tax far into the future. In the last years of the Peking regime, the Central Government became a virtual mendicant.

Against this picture of helplessness, the Kuomintang Government, when it was established in Nanking in 1927, was first of all resolved to establish solvency and a modern system of financial administration. Not only had it buoyant confidence in itself, but it also had the experience gained when in control of the smaller areas of the South. The first thing it did was to regain the administration of the customs and salt gabelle from the foreign powers and the sovereign right to fix the rate of customs duties. With that achieved by 1931, the revenue from the customs and the salt leaped high and constituted a strong financial prop for the government. The second thing the government did was to increase the rate of excise duties and to consolidate their collection. Other less important, though equally profitable, sources of revenue were also explored and made use of. And, finally, for the first time in Chinese history, centralized collection of the more important revenues was attempted, and with considerable success. With all these reforms accomplished, the finances of the National Government rested on a workable basis. Had it not been for the anti-communist campaigns in the few years before the Japanese War began in 1937, the finances could have been put on an even firmer basis.

The budget prepared for the fiscal year 1937–1938, that is, the budget prepared before the war began, was balanced in round numbers at C.N.C. $1,000,000,000.[3] In the revenue, the customs duties, the salt and the excise taxes occupied respectively 37 per cent, 23 per cent, and 18 per cent of the total. The other taxes were therefore comparatively insignificant.[4] As for expenditures, the military items amounted to 39 per cent and the loan servicing, 32 per cent. In other words, the services for economic and cultural betterment of the people and other civil services made only minor claims on the state. But that was not all; around $400,000,000 of expenditures were not listed in the budget. Some of this large sum was announced as a "special fund for constructive purposes," but a larger portion was kept secret. Mainly it was spent for military purposes such as the purchase of arms, munitions, and airplanes, and the construction of forts and military roads. The balanced budget of one billion dollars was after all not balanced, and the military expenditure was actually far above 39 per cent, perhaps twice that much. How this sum was covered by income was a secret. It might be assumed that it came either from the government banks or from resorting to the printing press. Fiscally, the exemption of such a large sum from the workings of the budget had a very bad influence. In a way, the government's irresponsible spending during the war was encouraged by the free use it had made of this sum before the coming of the war. It was a dangerous expedient altogether.

The war plunged the government into a whirlwind of inflation. To carry on the war successfully, new income was of course needed, in the form either of loans or of taxes. As port after port and province after province fell into the hands of the enemy, stable taxes on customs and salt and the excise tax dwindled. Contributions from the richer classes of people in some equitable form of taxation would have constituted a most desirable and suitable source of revenue. But the government failed to tap that source. It hoped for loans. But for a time foreign loans were unavailable and domestic loans, unless made collectible from the richer classes, were bound to fizzle out as most of them did. The only resort which was left was that of the printing press. For years the government denied that there was inflation, but inflation had already become malignant by the fourth year of the war.

With almost all taxable sources gone, the government finally in 1941 decided to make use of a tax which had lapsed in importance. The land tax which had become a source of local finance was now declared a central government revenue and also made a tax in kind. During the subsequent years, this tax often ran as high as 70 per cent of the government's total revenue, which covered generally from 35 per cent to 60 per cent of its total expenditure. The administration of the tax might have been badly managed; still, under the conditions of the war accompanied by disorganization and deterioration of the administrative machinery, that percentage amply demonstrated the possibilities of the tax. Had there been no inflation, or had the inflation been a less malignant one, a more efficiently administered land tax in kind might have saved the government from much of its difficulties. If, in addition, equitable and substantial contributions had also been levied from the richer merchants and people other than the landowners, there might have been even a viable war finance. Such things were, unfortunately, not done, and the government is still suffering from its omissions.

A comparison of the percentages of one kind of revenue with those of another, and an estimate of the ratio of total revenues to total expenditures for the present are meaningless, since the inflation has so spiraled as to become unpredictable.[5]

Financial Administration

The government departments which are concerned with financial administration at one stage or another are the Ministry of Finance of the Executive Yuan, the Budgetary Office, formerly of the National Government but transferred to the Executive Yuan in 1948, and the Ministry of Audit of the Control Yuan.

The collection of revenue and the defraying of government expenses are the duties of the Ministry of Finance. The Central Bank of China which serves as the repository of governmental funds, insofar as the administration of those funds is concerned, is strictly under the supervision of the Ministry. Revenues go into the Bank and expenses are drawn on it.

For the collection of revenue, the Ministry of Finance has under it a number of administrations. Those handling customs, salt, and general excise are the most important. The administration of income tax collection is only gaining in importance. The administration of land tax in kind is shared by the Ministries of Finance and Food. The collection and the transportation are the duties of the Ministry of Food, but there is also a smaller service in the Ministry of Finance charged with the accounting of that tax.

In the days of the Peking regime, revenue collection was as divided as the country itself. The warlords were apt to gain control of the revenues collected in their areas. The Central Government lacked the physical power to get them properly delivered. This was not only true of land tax and the transit taxes levied in those days. Even the customs and the salt tax, parts of which were earmarked for the amortization of foreign loans, were frequently appropriated by the local chiefs for their own use. When the Kuomintang Government was finally established in Nanking, it first sought to regain these revenues by reasserting an effective control over the collectors throughout the country. It then consolidated the tax administration and appointed men of modern training to the collectors' posts. Modern bookkeeping and accounting also received increased emphasis. Taxes collected were ordered to be deposited in the government banks. The Central Bank is now the only depository.

As far as the machinery for the collection of revenues is concerned, the accomplishment of the Kuomintang Government in the first five years of its existence in Nanking constituted a remarkable contrast to what had existed before. Corruption there still was. The cost of collecting was still too high. Nevertheless, the improvement over the past was marked.

The function of the Budgetary Office is not confined to the preparation of the annual budget. The Chief Budgetary Officer is also a comptroller-general. He controls the government expenditures by the hierarchy of accounting officers he appoints to every unit in the hierarchy of government. For instance, large organizations like the Executive Yuan have a large staff of accounting officers, and a small government university has only a few or just one officer. All of them are either directly or indirectly responsible to the Chief Budgetary Officer. Before expenses are defrayed, the spending authority must get a permit from the accounting officer attached to the organization, and, legally, no permit can be issued unless it is within the provisions of the enacted budget. In this way the Chief Budgetary Officer through his subordinates retains a prior control over every item spent. In addition, the accounting officers of course record every item spent and check every item with either the vouchers or the receipts if any.

The Ministry of Audit examines and verifies the accounts. It does more. The Ministry of Finance, to draw on the Central Bank, must first receive an authorization from the Ministry of Audit in order to enable the latter to prevent unauthorized spending, that is, spending not within the enacted budget. For instance, the Ministry of Communications may want to turn a certain sum over to one of its railway administrations for the construction of a certain bridge and it approaches the Ministry of Finance for that amount. The latter ministry cannot, however, allocate the funds unless the amount was so provided in the budget. In any case, it has to get an authorization from the Ministry of Audit before it can turn over the money to the Ministry of Communications.

The budgetary provisions can be ambiguous. It is here that the Ministry of Audit can greatly restrict the freedom of the spending departments. The latter may claim that a certain expenditure, for instance, the one for the construction of a bridge, is authorized by the budget, but the former may adopt a stricter and different interpretation of the budgetary provision concerned, which results in the denial of that claim. When either budgetary provisions are clearly definable or the Ministry of Finance is powerful enough to be both the faithful guardian of funds and the sympathetic advocate of proper expenditures, such a delay or impasse may not arise. But when provisions are ambiguous and the Ministry of Finance is weak, such a delay or impasse results and the authority and personal intervention of the Leader of the Party may again be necessary.

The auditing of the Ministry of Audit has over the years tended more and more to be a formality. It has little reality. The auditors are not as profusely strewn over the country as are the accounting officers. Yet they must audit all the accounts rendered by the accounting officers. Obviously they are physically unequal to the task. As a result, while they still cling to the forms, they entirely fail to inquire into what lies behind. For instance, a certain expenditure requires a receipt. The auditors can be very strict that the receipt is produced, but they little care as to its validity, even when the receipt is obviously fraudulent.

In theory the laws of China prescribe that when the fiscal year is closed, and all accounts are audited, the Ministry of Audit is to render an actual account for the settlement of that year to be passed by the Legislative Yuan.[6] That, however, has never yet been done. The military expenditures still lie beyond the purview of the Ministry of Audit. As long as this is so, the auditing is really of little significance.

A survey of the financial administration would call for the following general observations. The collection of revenues and the custody of public funds were greatly improved during the first years of the Nationalist regime. Accounting and auditing have perhaps yielded more red tape than real assistance to either economy or honesty in fiscal administration. With inflation mounting, accurate budgetary estimates impossible, and corruption rampant, a retrogression has set in. An honest and efficient fiscal administration can only go hand in hand with a more or less balanced budget. China will not again see such an administration until the restoration of peace makes the restoration of a balanced budget again possible.

XV

ADMINISTRATION AND ADMINISTRATIVE PROCESS [1]

The delineation of the administrative power is rather peculiar in modern China. Since the modern laws of China are closer to the laws of the continental nations than to the English and the American, the sphere of administrative discretion is great. Administrative activities often emanate from the implied power of the government and are in no need of legislative authorization. But whereas the broad interpretation of administrative power on the continent of Europe also entitles the government to organize itself freely for the purpose of administration, the Chinese government has always relied on legislation to create or abolish or even modify an administrative organization. The creation of a new ministry requires legislation; so does even the creation of a minor bureau. This was so in the period of the Peking regime; it has been so also with the Kuomintang regime. The anomaly cannot be easily explained although the existence of a similar anomaly in Japan may have influenced the Chinese.

Central Departments of Administration

The administrative establishments are naturally placed under the Executive Yuan. Occasionally, there have been establishments having both advisory and administrative functions located outside that Yuan. When that happens, confusion and conflict usually result. For instance, the functions and activities of the Reconstruction Commission, which existed in the early years of the Nationalist regime, so duplicated the activities of the Ministry of Communications that it had to be amalgamated with the Ministry. At present no such independent administrative agencies of importance are in existence.

Since 1947 there have been fourteen ministries and three commissions.[2] They are:

1. The Ministry of the Interior
2. The Ministry of Foreign Affairs

3. The Ministry of National Defense
4. The Ministry of Finance
5. The Ministry of Economic Affairs
6. The Ministry of Education
7. The Ministry of Communications
8. The Ministry of Agriculture and Forestry
9. The Ministry of Social Affairs
10. The Ministry of Food
11. The Ministry of Water Conservancy
12. The Ministry of Justice
13. The Ministry of Health
14. The Ministry of Land
15. The National Resources Commission
16. The Mongolian and Tibetan Affairs Commission
17. The Overseas Chinese Affairs Commission

In addition, there are many committees and commissions created by the Executive Yuan, responsible to it for the administration of some specific items of business nominally belonging to one or more of the regular ministries and commissions. Such committees and commissions, consisting of ministers and commission chairmen or their subordinates, should not be considered independent establishments. They are arrangements by which the specific items of business can be facilitated. They receive no extra authority and require no extra officials.

The functions of most of the ministries and commissions are self-evident. But some need explanation. The Ministry of Social Affairs has mainly two functions, one to administer what is generally known as social legislation, and the other to exercise a control over the organized groups of the country, whether professional, political, eleemosynary, or even academic. Since a poor country like China is in no position to have much social legislation, the first function is bound to be nominal. The Ministry is, therefore, chiefly maintained to give the state an added exercise of police authority. It used to be a department under the Central Executive Committee of the Kuomintang. Its character has not undergone much change since the transfer to the Executive Yuan.

The Ministry of Food arose out of the necessity to collect and transport the grains which were the tax in kind on the land. Grains of course do not constitute the only foodstuff available in China or used by the Chinese. But the Ministry has not had either the ability or the resources to tackle the other forms of food. In other words, the Ministry of Food is really the Ministry of Grain.

The Ministry of Land was elevated from a smaller administration headed by an administrator of an inferior rank. Land administration according to the Kuomintang ideology has to concern itself with some kind of egalitarian redistribution. But since order has never been quite established throughout the country, land surveys have never been thoroughly made and the financial means needed for the redistribution are also not available, the activities of the Ministry can be little more than drawing up paper plans.

The National Resources Commission serves as a general directorate for the various mines and manufactures it has organized. It is interested in heavy industries and in the exploitation of minerals. It seeks to establish a state monopoly of the mines, heavy industries, and power plants.

The Mongolian and Tibetan Affairs Commission is the lineal but emaciated descendant of the once-powerful superintendency of Inner Asian tributary states (Li-fan Yuan) in the Ch'ing Dynasty. It is maintained to supervise the governments in Mongolia and Tibet and to secure their proper adherence to the Central Government. But in doing little, it has done badly. Of course, the close adherence to China of Tibet and Mongolia is a political desideratum; the prerequisite must be a strong and orderly government in the center. If the Commission is competent at all, it can at least make a study of the multifarious and complex problems of Tibet and Mongolia, upon the solution of which will depend the future of Tibet and Mongolia. But the Commission does not seem to be gifted with that foresight.

Finally, the Overseas Chinese Affairs Commission also deserves an explanation. The Kuomintang was heavily indebted to the Chinese overseas for both financial contributions and personal support for the Revolution of 1911. It is to the credit of the party that it has always been interested in their welfare. But it has not been able to accomplish much. In the first place, China has never been able to solve the problem of dual citizenship of its nationals who are domiciled in other countries. As long as that problem remains, China's conflict of interest with the countries involved is well-nigh insoluble. In the second place, for those of her nationals who reside abroad but who are not claiming the citizenship of the countries in which they reside, China has been too poor and too weak to be of material help. Consequently, the Overseas Chinese Affairs Commission has also been largely an idle agency.

Administrative Organization

With necessary variations, which are especially true of the Ministry of National Defense and the National Resources Commission, the central departments of administration are organized in an almost uniform fashion. There is a minister or a chairman at the head of each. There are two vice-ministers or vice-chairmen under him, though in some commissions there is only one. Then in each there are a number of services, the one for general administration, comprising such diverse functions as archives, purchase, pay roll, and clerical work. Other administrative services are organized under various names. Some of the more important ones have for their organization high-sounding names. But their chiefs have the same rank and in the administrative hierarchy they occupy the same kind of position. They all may be called directors of services.

Each service is subdivided into a number of sections, headed by a section chief. Frequently there are assistant directors and assistant section chiefs. The assistant director is often a senior section chief of the service and the assistant section chief is the ranking official in the section. They seldom have statutory duties. They are given the titles either in recognition of their seniority or because the director or the chief desires to secure assistance in a more general way.

The sections are sometimes further subdivided into subsections with a senior member designated as a subsection chief. These subsections are not statutory creations and are only for the purpose of facilitating transaction of business in an internal way. Generally, it is to the section that the bulk of administrative officials are assigned.

The above represents the pyramid of bureaucratic organization of the Chinese administration. It is the normal thing. The Chinese have a great weakness for uniformity or stereotyped organization. No matter whether the stereotype pattern of organization is conducive to the transaction of a certain business, it is almost invariably followed. One would think that the administration of public health and of foreign relations must be very dissimilar and should call for different systems of organization. Yet the organization into services and sections is nearly identical in the two ministries concerned. Even in the Ministry of National Defense, with the exception of the organization for the command of the armed forces, the same skeleton of organization is also to be observed. The same is roughly true of the National Resources Commission.

The commissions differ from the ministries in that besides the chairman and the vice-chairman, they have a number of other commissioners. However, this fact does not materially affect the similarity of the organizational principle in both the ministries and commissions. The commission as such meets very infrequently. The commissioners who are not chairmen or vice-chairmen generally consider themselves outsiders and seldom seek to inquire into or to interfere with the affairs of the commission.

In every ministry or commission, the minister or chairman, being head of the agency, is naturally the most important figure. His position, however, can be better appreciated when the positions of his subordinates are first understood.

The creation of two vice-ministers was originally meant to secure for

China the advantage of representation of both political and expert elements at the top of the ministerial organization. It was taken from the British model. The first vice-minister, the so-called political vice-minister, was to assist the minister in correlating the work of the ministry with the party councils and with other political factors in the government and in the party. He was to be a political figure and his tenure of office was to be subject to political vicissitudes. The second vice-minister, the so-called administrative vice-minister, was to be like the British permanent under-secretary, a permanent official in charge of the real administration. The idea was well conceived. But in actual experience the original intention has been completely forgotten. The two are indistinguishable and may be neither political enough to be of political help to the minister nor expert enough to be competent administrators. Their position depends entirely on whether they have the confidence of the minister or are so strongly backed by forces or high personages outside of the ministry that they can even overshadow the minister himself. If they have either confidence or backing, they can be powerful at the ministry. If they have neither, they are liable to be uncomfortable figureheads.

The directors of services and the chiefs of sections constitute perhaps the mainspring of the administration. The directorates of services and their subordinate sections are easily comparable to the internal organization of a ministry of the French Republic. But it is difficult to compare them with the bureaucratic organization of American departments. The directorates are, relatively speaking, higher in order than the American bureaus. They are fewer in number and have a wider scope of functions than the American bureaus or divisions. But the Chinese section is inferior to the bureau or division in America, for the former is generally not an integral administration in itself, while the latter often is.

As between the director of service and the chief of section, the former is thus of greater importance. Directors are usually permanent officials, though they have as yet no legal protection against dismissal. Of the directors in a ministry or a commission, the one in charge of the general administrative service since he is always a trusted lieutenant of the minister or chairman, holding office at his pleasure, is always a pivotal figure. The other directors are often men of long administrative experience and are usually, if the service is a professional one, professional men. They function rather independently of the minister's political views. Among them there are a great number of able and competent men. It is this class of public servants that does credit to the Kuomintang regime in contrast to the incompetent administration under the Peking regime. Unfortunately, the economic deterioration which has severely affected both their own living and the resources of the services they administer has been so disheartening that they have lost much of their former zest for work.

The section chiefs not being in sole charge of anything like an integral administration are less able to demonstrate their ability even when they have it. They are seldom equal to acting on their own initiative, even when permitted. They serve primarily as assistants to their directors. They have a tendency rather to stick to the red tape than to promote the substantive part of their business.

The bureaucrats working in the sections under their chiefs have even less initiative and are even fonder of red tape. Their invigoration may have to depend on some kind of administrative reform which would give the lower echelon of officials a more direct contact with the actual business in which they are engaged. For instance, the officials of the section in charge of primary schools in the Ministry of Education should not be mere desk bureaucrats relying for their knowledge of the schools on statutes and reports alone, but should have more personal acquaintance with school conditions.

Besides the regular hierarchical setup in the ministries and commissions, there are also, in each, groups of secretaries, councilors, and technicians or experts. The secretaries, who usually number around half a dozen, are on the level either of the directors or of the section chiefs. They are usually the minister's own choices, and their tenure can be terminated at his will, though they are also treated as civil servants. Being his confidants, their importance in the administration depends of course on the kind of assignment given to them.

The councilors' duties are generally concerned with the preparation of laws to be proposed to the Legislative Yuan and orders to be promulgated by the ministry or the commission itself. They are all on the same level as the directors of services. In fact, they are the senior staff of the organization. But since they are necessarily either lawyers or experts on legislation, they usually have very little to do with anything. The councilorship has, more often than not, become a sinecure.

The technicians or experts are of great variety. Some ministries and commissions, for example the Ministries of Health or of Communications or the National Resources Commission, are in need of real technicians to serve as planners or inspectors. In such organizations their number is apt to be large and many of them do perform real services. In some other ministries where technical service is either out of place or not yet organized, the technicians are presumably also out of place. Nevertheless, almost all ministries and commissions maintain a number, sometimes quite large, of experts, and their heads are able to evade most of the civil service requirements in making appointments. The appointment of an expert in these organizations is thus generally a means of placement for some unemployed office-seeker or one who is hardly suited for any real job.

The regular hierarchy of services and sections manned by directors and chiefs and a host of bureaucrats is the backbone of each agency and the groups of secretaries, councilors, and experts are its staff officers. On the other hand, the budgetary, statistical, and personnel officers attached to each agency are extraneous to the internal administration. Over them the minister or chairman has no control.

There is now in every ministry or commission a chief accountant and a chief statistician with varying numbers of assistants, the former in charge of budget preparaton and accounts and the latter in charge of statistics. The chief in a bigger establishment is on the level of a director of service and in a smaller one on that of a section chief, but in both cases he is appointed on the recommendation of the Chief Budgetary Officer and takes orders from him. He is under the control of the head of the administration only in regard to the scope and content of his work, but so far as the manner of his work is concerned he is under the control of the Chief Budgetary Officer.

The personnel officials of a ministry or a commission are organized like the accountants and the statisticians, except that they are appointed through and are responsible to the Ministry of Personnel of the Examination Yuan. Their establishment can also be a big or a small one. In actual operation, the Organization Group of the Kuomintang has always retained a firm control over them, the control by the Ministry of Personnel being purely of a formal kind.

Independent Agencies and Advisory Bodies Attached to the Administrative Departments

There are four kinds of agencies attached to yet not quite forming an integral part of the departmental organization. In some cases they have reduced administrative efficiency and in others they seem to have opened up new vistas for wisdom and thoroughness in administration.

First, there are the semi-independent commissions or agencies nominally under a ministry or a commission, but enjoying practically full independence. Their only effective link with their parental organization, the ministry or the commission, is through the person of the minister or chairman, who either serves as head himself or directs the head of the commission or agency concerned. Such commissions and agencies are created usually because the functions they are entrusted with are either of great magnitude or of such a nature as to call for a more or less independent administration. Not infrequently such commissions or agencies are subsequently converted into full-fledged ministries or commissions. The Ministry of Land was so separated from the Ministry of the Interior. So was also the National Resources Commission from the Ministry of Economics.

Second, there are government corporations attached to a ministry or a commission. The two government-operated airlines are so attached to the Ministry of Communications. The China Textile Company is similarly a subsidiary corporation under the Ministry of Economics. Such corporations are perhaps a necessary form of organization if the government is to go into business. The question is how the directorate of the corporation should be composed and what supervision the ministry or commission should exercise. A detailed examination of those two aspects of organizational relations between an administrative department and a government corporation is out of place here. It must suffice to say that the powers given to a corporation are seldom strictly defined and, in the absence of a strict definition, departmental interference has been too great to allow the corporation to be managed with the efficiency expected of a business concern. Also the department generally puts too many officials into the directorate who have no special claim to competence in the business.

Third, all administrative departments resort to the use of a large number of advisory commissions. Theoretically speaking, these commissions should only give advice and should in no way undermine the responsibility of the departmental officials concerned. But in practice such advisory bodies, while by no means able to enforce the adoption of their decisions, do enable the departmental officials to be evasive. They are apt to render conflicting advice and when such advice is given, the departmental officials feel absolved of sins of both commission and omission.

Finally, nearly all departments are in the habit of convening national conferences once every few years. Senior officials of the department, heads of the provincial administration, representatives from other departments, and scores of experts are ordered or invited to take part. The minister or the chairman always appoints himself as the presiding officer. The total membership may be anywhere from one to three hundred and the conference meetings may last for several days. A conference of this kind may prove to be quite beneficial to the administration concerned, if the membership is well chosen, matters to be discussed are well selected, and meetings both in full session and in committees well-conducted. Unfortunately the tendency for the minister or chairman to increase his own personal prestige in these conferences has been marked. He likes to invite great numbers of people to be present. The proposals are usually too ill conceived and too numerous to be put into execution. The only meaningful use of these conferences seems to be confined to acclaiming some difficult or unpopular measures the department has already decided upon. The most notable example of this was the adoption of the land tax in kind by the Third National Financial Conference convened by the Ministry of Finance in 1942.

The Role of the Departmental Head

The position of a minister or a chairman depends on his powers over subordinates in the department as well as on his share of power in the Executive Yuan. In an earlier chapter, it has been said that though in theory, by his membership in the Yuan, he shares the powers of the Yuan, in practice he is entirely subordinate to the President of the Yuan. As such, he can have no real power unless the President grants it to him. What is worse, the President may even interfere with his exercise of the departmental powers. It may well happen that he is appointed or maintained in his position on sufferance for some political reason. One or more of his assistants, a vice-minister or even a director of services, for instance, may be closer to the President than himself. When such a situation occurs, it is not unusual to find that instead of the department head occupying the post of command, one or another of his assistants gives the commands for him.

Except when a superior authority, such as the President of the Executive Yuan just mentioned or the still higher authorities of the party, is interfering with the exercise of his departmental powers, the departmental head holds those powers both in theory and in practice. By law, he is always given the authority to manage the business and supervise the officials and establishments of the department. Then, the regulations for the transaction of departmental business, a set of rules adopted by each department but more or less identical with all departments, are so drawn up as to give the head full and direct control over all the business and personnel. It is true that the regulations invariably provide for a weekly departmental conference to be attended by all the senior officials, councilors, directors, senior secretaries, and the chiefs of accounting, statistical, and personal establishments. The policies and the other important items of departmental business are to be considered by it, but, like all the meetings under the Kuomintang regime, the chairman always has the power of a leader, and the department head who presides over the departmental conference always reserves to himself powers of decision regardless of the wishes of the majority.

That the department head is all-powerful in the department is, however, not a serious drawback in itself. What is serious is his unmethodical and arbitrary exercise of his powers. As Chinese civil servants have not elevated themselves to a conscientious neutrality, the department head is often reluctant to rely on them indiscriminately. Instead, he singles out a few for his trust and confidence. When this is done, the departmental hierarchy loses its usefulness. Matters of importance are transacted somewhat irregularly and haphazardly. Even the director in whose realm the matter falls may be entirely by-passed. Deprived of the more important and hence also more interesting business, the hierarchy buries itself in routine. Red tape mounts, bureaucratism is nurtured, and the department head ignores these developments, for he is satisfied if the things in which he takes a personal interest are accomplished without delays at the lower levels. In other words, the way he exercises his powers in the department is often not conducive to evoking the best administrative capacities of the department officials. His authority is often the deterrent to their taking initiative and working in harmony.

Local Administration [3]

The provincial and the *hsien* administrations generally take orders from the central administration and perform whatever duties are delegated to them by the central authorities. The province is not a self-governing unit by any means. The *hsien* theoretically is, but in the past its government has been more an agent of the central administration than of itself.

There are in China at present thirty-five provinces and twelve municipalities of provincial status.[4] With a slight deviation in Sinkiang,[5] all provinces are uniformly organized under one law.[6] Like the National Government, there is a government council consisting generally of seven to eleven members with one of them appointed chairman of the provincial government and some others concurrently heads of the provincial administrative departments. In theory, it is a committee form of government, but in practice the chairman is the virtual governor, able to control the members of the government, both as individuals and collectively as the government council.

Below the governing council, headed by the chairman, there are usually four provincial departments of administration, in charge of civil affairs, finance, public works, and education. The Peace Preservation Corps is generally also in existence. Sometimes the chairman himself acts as the commander; sometimes a member of the government does so. But it is not stipulated that the commander must be a member of the government. Then there is always a secretary-general. Theoretically, the regular administrative departments constitute the main bodies of provincial administration. But because of the dominance of the chairman and also because of the ascendancy of the military personnel in the last decade, it is quite common for the secretary-general, always a trusted subordinate of the chairman, and the commander of the Peace Preservation Corps to outrank the commissioners of the departments in importance.

The commissioners of the departments are under the dual control of the chairman of the provincial government and the ministers or chairmen of the kindred central government departments. As for the nature of the relation between the provincial chairman and the heads of the central departments, there is much ambiguity. The law governing the organization of a central department always carries a provision that its minister or chairman, in the administration of the services falling within his competence, shall exercise general supervision over the provincial government. But the chairman of the provincial government being usually of a political stature comparable to the central government minister himself, it is difficult for the latter to issue direct orders to the former. The general practice has been for a central government minister to issue direct orders to the provincial commissioners and hold them in strict control. If differences between him and the chairman of the provincial government should develop, they are usually solved by the decisions of the Executive Yuan which can order both with an undisputed authority.

Unlike the province, which was, up to the adoption of the new Constitution of 1946, not meant to be a self-governing area, the *hsien* has always been considered or intended to be self-governing. From the last years of the Manchus when China began to remodel her government after the West, numerous laws purporting to grant local self-government to the *hsien* have found their way into the statute books. But, in general, there has been no real self-government for the *hsien*. The *hsien* authorities have been as much the agents of the provincial government as the provincial ones are those of the central government.[7]

There are now a little over two thousand *hsien* in the thirty-five provinces.[8] For the uniform organization of the *hsien* government, there was at first the Organic Law of June 5, 1929, enforced on October 10 of the same year. It was later superseded by the *Outline for the Organization of the Several Levels of Hsien Government* of September 19, 1939,[9] which introduced the so-called "new *hsien* system." Under both laws, there is an appointed *hsien* magistrate and a number of administrative bureaus headed by chiefs also appointed by the central government. Under neither law is there a committee form of government, the magistrate being the superior officer, in law as well as in fact. The differences between the two laws are mainly as follows. First, the "new *hsien*" is supposed to be able to develop its own material resources and to undertake a great number of economic and welfare functions for the locality, whereas the services rendered by the *hsien* under the law of 1929 were less economic in nature. Second, the 1929 law purported to give the people of the *hsien* sufficient political training to enable them to exercise the four political rights by the end of a six-year period; the *Outline* fully reëstablished the so-called *pao-chia* system which favors the heads of the family, in total disregard of the principle of equality, and which sets up a chain system of guarantees in order to insure the elimination of bandits and dangerous elements in the countryside.[10]

The new *hsien* system was said to be in general operation throughout the government areas in the last years of the war. According to the reports of the Ministry of the Interior, modern functions such as public health, roads, reforestation, and education, as well as the more traditional functions of relief and police have all made considerable progress. Functions that are necessary to peace and order within the *hsien* and to the security of the state in general, such as the training of militia, the promotion of civic organizations, and, above all, the in-training of the various cadres of local administrative personnel, were said to have all been successfully tackled. But, considering the limited funds and personnel (an average *hsien* government has a staff of about eighty), at the disposal of the *hsien*, and the general complaint against the low quality of the *hsien* administration, the reports were apparently compiled more to please Chiang Kai-shek, once the personal sponsor of the new *hsien* system, than to depict the true state of *hsien* government.

While it would be incorrect to say that all the functions actually undertaken by the *hsien* governments are functions of the state, the more important ones certainly are. The *hsien* officials from the magistrate down are judged not by their success or failure to maintain schools or health stations, but by their ability to collect conscripts and land tax, and during recent years also to manipulate the elections in conformity with the directives of the central authorities. The *hsien* of 1948 is no closer to being a government by and for the people of the *hsien* than it was in the last years of the Manchu Dynasty. The same is in a large measure true of the governments of the subdivisions of the *hsien*,[11] and that in spite of the organization of the representative or direct assemblies on the various levels.[12]

Administrative Action

Administrative action in China is a mixture of traditional and Western ways. The adoption of the administrative procedure of the West does not exclude the free play of the bureaucratic spirit of the old days. Paper work is still much emphasized and actual conditions which should have been the basis of administrative action are often neglected.

Central departments and provincial governments alike are fond of formulating administrative legislation with or without the advice of extra-departmental elements. Administrative orders are, generally speaking, badly drafted and are apt to be vague and not rigorously enforced.

Both central departments and provincial governments issue general directives and special instructions. The central administration has a tendency to centralize administration. The general directives therefore tend to be all-inclusive, making little allowance for local variations. When they are found to be inapplicable in some localities, they are often allowed to lapse instead of being replaced by a set of revised or readjusted directives applicable to those localities. A sounder administration would allow in the general directives a greater latitude to the local authorities, or resort more to special instructions.

The departments keep a strict surveillance over their subordinate authorities, whether their own agencies or the corresponding departments of the provincial governments. On a multitude of occasions, the subordinate authorities are required to petition for approval before they can act. The latter, in order not to be held responsible for too many things, have also acquired the habit of seeking prior approval or instructions. The relation between the provincial and the *hsien* authorities is the same.

The administrative action referred to in all that has been said above consists essentially of paper work, which has indeed become a curse. Initiative is shunned and responsibility is evaded. But since orders are orders, the bureaucrats on a lower level are in the habit of performing on paper, and on paper alone, most of the administrative acts required of them. This is even true with regard to the impetuous orders given to them through their department heads by the Leader of the Kuomintang. For instance, when the Leader wanted to modernize the district administration throughout the country, it was shortly so modernized, on paper, though in reality very little improvement ever took place.

Both the provincial and central departments of administration, the latter especially, have thus far made very little use of inspection by means of which many countries of the West have been enabled to administer their services of state more effectively and efficiently. An administrative order which involves work of a positive nature cannot be considered carried out unless the agent issuing the order is able to review the work according to some ascertainable standards by means of inspection. Not only are such technical administrations as telegraphic communication and malaria control in need of constant inspection, but even administrations of a more general nature such as schools or consular offices would reach a greater state of efficiency if they were subject to more searching inspection than they have received.

In theory, one of the duties of the departmental technicians and experts is inspection and some departments maintain a number of inspectors in addition. But owing partly to the lack of suitable criteria for measuring the standards of performance and partly to a tendency of the inspecting officials to protect their fellow bureaucrats, inspection has only infrequently been taken seriously. The lack of effective inspection is one of the causes of the failure of the Chinese administration to modernize itself.

Administrative Reforms [13]

There was much agitation for administrative reform during the years preceding the war. Even during the war and the recent years of civil war, such agitation has never entirely ceased. The aim of all proposed reforms is the promotion of administrative efficiency, of the need for which almost every Chinese has been conscious.

One popular demand has been that the administrative organization must be simplified and made more consistent. But for a period of fifteen years no sooner have superfluous or duplicating or conflicting agencies been suppressed than new agencies, useless or even harmful, have been created. This is partly accounted for by the love for new organizations, a peculiarity common to all administrations the world over. It is also partly due to the weakness of the Leader of the Kuomintang for resorting to new agencies whenever he is dissatisfied with the older agencies, or when he considers it politically expedient to reward some people with jobs in new agencies of his government that would not otherwise be available.

The second group of proposed reforms are technical in nature. They are concerned with the improvement of the administrative personnel and materiel. The problem of personnel will be discussed in a later chapter.[14] As for the problem of materiel, there are two aspects, the management of documents and archives, and the matter of purchase. Some sort of centralized purchasing has often been advocated as an effective means of getting rid of corruption. But unless the officials are better paid and there is a real accounting system, it is hard to see how centralized purchasing can necessarily be a cleaner transaction than a number of piecemeal purchases. The management of documents and archives has been the subject of a great deal of discussion, mainly perhaps because Chinese administration for long centuries has been a victim of paper work. Numerous devices have been advanced as giving promise of reducing paper work or simplifying the recording of documents. But the inertia of the Chinese bureaucrats has been too great to be easily receptive to the proposed changes. And, what is more, unless they acquire greater initiative and responsibility, the reduction of the amount of paper work and the simplified recording, even if achieved, would not add much to real administrative efficiency.

A third proposed reform, now forsaken, was the so-called "triple-linked system of administration" which was preached by the Leader of the Kuomintang for a few years after 1940.[15] This system, which was indirectly derived from the Soviet system of planning, was to have three parts, the planning, the execution, and the appraisal. In order that the departments should be fully enabled to execute the plan, the Leader propounded another principle of his, the so-called "responsibility by levels," that is, that officials at each level of the hierarchy were to bear a certain amount of responsibility. The intent was not only praiseworthy but also accorded with common sense. The remarkable thing was that this idea of giving a little responsibility to the officials should be treated both as a dogma and a movement and so much forensic ado should have been devoted to it. Yet all this time the Leader himself was doing things very much in his usual arbitrary and unmethodical fashion, leaving none of his subordinates either able or willing to take the initiative and be responsible for it.

There was still another reform proposal advocated by the Leader and supported with undiscriminating zeal by his followers. This was the so-called "staff system." Each high administrative chief was to equip himself with a chief staff officer or a chief aide to handle for him his general administrative responsibilities so as to leave him time and leisure for the consideration of the more important problems concerned with his administration. The idea was a combination of the military commander's reliance on his chief of staff and of the Chinese viceroys' and governors' traditional reliance on their aides. Chiang Kai-shek himself has, in holding simultaneously a multitude of important posts, relied heavily on his secretaries-general for the transaction of routine business. But he has never quite succeeded in leaving the routine entirely in their hands. He interceded often. Regardless of the worth or worthlessness of the proposal, it has not produced the type of administrator desired by him.

The reforms or proposed reforms above-mentioned apply to the central and local administration alike. In the sphere of local administration, three suggested reforms are worthy of note, not for their intrinsic merit which may be negligible, but for the way the measures were considered and carried out.

The first had to do with the redivision of the provinces. In recent decades there has been much sentiment in favor of carving out a large number of provinces, ranging from sixty-seven to one hundred, from the existing ones. But with the exception of the division of the original three Northeastern Provinces into nine, no other redivision has been effected, for the central government is apprehensive lest the cutting up of the old and historical provinces cause unnecessary turmoil of a particularist nature.

The second reform measure was related to the first. In lieu of creating small provinces, the existing provinces were divided shortly before the war into a number of inspectorates with an administrative inspector in charge of each area. In the days of the anti-communist campaigns before the war, this new institution was held as the key to the improvement of the *hsien* administration. Chiang Kai-shek advocated the reform and for many years personally appointed most of the inspectors. But enthusiasm for the institution was later superseded by the panacea of the new *hsien* system.

The third was the so-called "consolidated offices system." When the prewar campaigns against the communists were going on, Chiang Kai-shek considered the system of "consolidated offices" to be a vital reform in provincial administration. Prior to the reform, the provincial administrative departments and the secretariat of the provincial government itself had transacted their business separately, each on its own premises. Chiang Kai-shek ordered that as far as possible they be centered on one premise and their instructions and directives be issued in the name of the chairman of the provincial government rather than in their own names. In some provinces the obedient officials took Chiang Kai-shek's orders so literally as to build a new office large enough to accommodate the secretariat and the departments under one roof. Speeches and pamphlets in praise of the system were commonplace. As was to be expected, this reform led to no appreciable results of beneficent nature and was soon forgotten.

All these failures in administrative reform do not for a moment suggest that reforms are not needed. On the contrary, they are very much needed. But first things must come first if real reforms are to result.

Administrative efficiency depends on a number of factors. An adequate but not overlarge or overcomplicated organization, a body of well-trained and energetic civil servants, well paid and well taken care of, and a wise and trusting political leadership are all needed to enable the administrative machinery to operate smoothly and efficiently. But there is more. The most fundamental requirement is that the men engaged in administration must have a belief in the objective of the administration. They must believe that there is a good purpose in view and that the government is serious about that purpose. When they cannot honestly entertain such a belief, there is no possibility of securing a good and efficient administration. In this sense, the failure of all the past attempts at administrative reform may well be attributed either to the lack of a good purpose or to nobody's believing in the seriousness of that purpose.

XVI

THE EXAMINATION YUAN AND THE CIVIL SERVICE

The Examination Power

The inflation of examination into a separate power on a par with the other powers of the state arose out of the sense of national pride which abounded in Sun Yat-sen's treatment of the moral, social, and political problems of China. In his view the examination power of old China, together with the censorial power, had been exercised independently by the monarch, who was in control of the other three powers of legislation, administration, and justice, and the Chinese examination system was excellent and had enabled the country to select its most talented citizens for public service.

But Sun Yat-sen's novel suggestion that, in addition to the appointed officials, candidates for elective offices should also go through an examination was perhaps belaboring the point. In raising the civil service examinations to a high plane of state power, he had to broaden their application. Evidently he did not quite realize the difficulties involved in examining candidates. If the examination were technical, none but technically trained persons would be eligible for elective offices. That would certainly be the undoing of all popular elections. If, on the other hand, the examination were a kind of qualifying test, very loosely applied, it would be superfluous. It would be better to prescribe a few qualifications for an elective office than to subject the candidates for that office to a loose kind of examination. In neither case could the examination be both sensible and practicable.

Therefore, whether the examining power should or should not be one of the mutually independent powers of the government depends largely on whether the civil service examinations and the administration of the civil service can or cannot be entrusted to a subordinate agency of the executive branch of the government. In the West, they have indeed been so entrusted. If in China they can also be so entrusted, the advocacy of a separate and independent examination power would lose much of its cogency. In fact, during the two decades of the existence of the Examination Yuan, and presumably of its unhampered exercise of the examining power, the emphasis has always been on making the Yuan fully an equal in the brotherhood of Yuan rather than on arriving at a system of examination better than that obtaining in the West.

The Examination Yuan

The Examination Yuan was as highly organized as the other Yuan. In common with the other Yuan, it had a President, a Vice-President, and hosts of councilors and secretaries, the latter headed by a secretary-general. Then there was an Examination Commission and a Ministry of Personnel.[1]

The President and Vice-President were appointed in the same manner as those of other Yuan. There was one incumbent of the presidency [2] during the twenty-year period of the National Government. This was for two reasons. He was a man who, though not necessarily trained as a Confucian scholar, had come to be a fanatic Confucianist and traditionalist, and who saw in the post opportunities for reëstablishing a Confucian culture for China. But the other high leaders of the Kuomintang did not see the same light and considered the post somewhat unattractive. This difference of views had enabled the original appointee to remain entrenched in his office for twenty years.

The President exercised complete control not only over officials of the Yuan, his direct subordinates, but over the Commission and the Ministry as well. He was not much interested in the routine which went on in the Ministry of Personnel, but the pattern of the examinations which the Examination Commission conducted was very much his personal choice.

The vice-presidency was always a sinecure given to whomsoever the Leader of the Kuomintang thought convenient to bestow favors upon. He accepted the office in an understanding spirit and usually took no interest in the affairs of the Yuan.

The Examination Commission consisted of a chairman, a vice-chairman, and from seven to eleven members. Its bureaucratic hierarchy was not unlike that of an administrative department. For administrative purposes the chairman had the position and powers of a departmental head, but in the conduct of examinations the Commission functioned like a board with other members fully participating. When examinations were held, persons from the academic and professional fields as well as from officialdom were appointed examiners. In this, the Commission were merely imitating the traditional method of appointing scholar-officials as imperial examiners as practiced by the Board of Civil Office in the old days.

The Ministry of Personnel was organized exactly like a ministry of the Executive Yuan and needs no description.

The Examinations

For six centuries before the establishment of the Republic the examinations were held very regularly. Both the provincial and the imperial examinations took place once every three years, the latter half a year after the former. It was the successful candidates in these examinations who provided recruits for the administration of the empire. The abolition of the examinations in 1905 not only cut off the steady supply of recruits but also dimmed the scholar's prospects of getting placed in the civil service. Off and on after 1905 some special examinations were held, although not based on literary excellence. But they were not adequate as a substitute for the old system.

When the Republic was established, the civil service examinations system of the West was introduced. Laws to that effect were enacted and various civil service examination boards were instituted. It was, however, not until 1916 that the first examination took place.

The examinations of more recent years have been influenced directly by those undertaken by the Peking government. This is an interesting point to observe, for the examinations held by the Peking regime were under the over-all supervision of the cabinet and were, therefore, not independent of the executive branch of government. Imitation of that system seems to imply a view on the part of the imitators that the excellence of examinations has nothing to do with whether the supervisory authority of the examinations is or is not a part of the executive branch.

In accordance with Sun Yat-sen's views, there have been three kinds of examinations: those for candidates for elective offices, those for candidates for appointive offices, and those for professional and technical men.[3] In addition, the Examination Commission undertakes when requested, or on its own initiative, to give examinations, on behalf of the ministries concerned, for those who go abroad for study.

The examinations for professional and technical men[4] have generally been designed to scrutinize the formal qualifications of the candidates concerned rather than to examine their actual knowledge or fitness. Only in rare cases have real examinations been held. In a period of about five years, from the time these were first held late in 1942, to June 30, 1947, a total of 20,931 professional and technical men comprising accountants, agricultural experts, engineers, and medical men were accepted as competent.

The holding of these above-mentioned examinations betrays a tendency towards extreme authoritarianism. In a non-authoritarian state, the qualifications of a professional man to practice his profession rest with the professional association either completely or as regulated by the state. But in China it is for the state both to fix the qualifications and to conduct the examinations on that basis. Although both the fixing and the examining which have so far been undertaken are of a very loose kind, so loose and so lightly and haphazardly conducted that they cannot be compared with the more rigorous attention to high standards of proficiency observed by Western professional associations, the monopoly of the examination power by the government deserves to be emphasized. Is it merely due to the Examination Yuan's ambition to achieve respectable membership in the brotherhood of Five by increasing its powers? Or does the Yuan think seriously that it can do a better job of setting up professional standards than the professional associations themselves? If it is the former, we can only hope that some day the Examination Yuan will outlive its inferiority complex. If it is the latter, the presumption is dangerous.

Examinations for candidates for elective offices were, as mentioned above, advocated by Sun Yat-sen and stipulated in the *Fundamentals of National Reconstruction*. As long as there were no elections to be held there was no necessity for such examinations. But when the *hsien* and provinces were ordered, in June 1938, to organize local assemblies at various levels, the examinations became necessary. After a few provisional statutes were tried, a definite law [5] was promulgated in 1943. However, since written examinations, as provided for in the law, were impossible to enforce, the examination process was only verification of qualifications. It was not difficult for any man free of criminal record or political offense to be duly qualified. The verification was done almost exclusively by the provincial and local authorities, and the Examination Commission did no more than approve perfunctorily the lists of persons submitted by the local authorities, and issue certificates to the qualified persons. In this way, the number of persons duly qualified to stand for provincial and other local elective offices reached the high total of 1,890,875 by the end of June 1947. It is not for a moment to be presumed that the mass verification represented by this total could be anything but superficial or that the candidates thus qualified for election could at all meet the sanguine expectations of Sun Yat-sen.

But the success or failure of the examination system of the Kuomintang government will be judged neither by the examinations for professional and technical men nor by those for candidates for elective offices, but rather on the examinations for appointive offices, for the last is still by far the most important.

There are three kinds of examinations for appointive offices (civil service examinations): the higher examination, the ordinary examination, and the special examination.[6] The higher examination is theoretically for the top cadre of administrators. Successful candidates are appointed to a rank which should enable them to reach in time the top of the service. Only university graduates or candidates who can claim a comparable education are qualified to take the examination. The ordinary examination is for average civil service appointments, and graduates of senior middle schools or those with a comparable education are eligible for the examination. The special examinations can be for either a position of higher or ordinary grade. They are special in the sense that the successful candidates are usually appointed to a specific service or even to a specific job.

In a way, the classification into these three kinds of examinations is not altogether logical. Both the higher and the ordinary examinations, especially the former, have been divided into a number of subjects. Since, in late years, there have been no less than seventeen subjects in the higher examination[7] and candidates in different subjects must take different examinations, special examinations of the higher standard could conceivably be integrated into the higher examinations. And since the ordinary examinations are also divisible into different subjects, special examinations of the ordinary standard could be similarly integrated.

All the civil service examinations are conducted by the Examination Commission or under its direct supervision. Since the ordinary examinations are held in different provinces, and the higher examinations are generally held at important centers throughout the country, a great many boards of examiners have to be set up. The examiners are usually selected on the spot from persons in official, academic, and professional life. They have to make out the questions and read the answers. Associated with each board of examiners is an administrative staff whose duty is to take charge of the business side of the examination.

Both the board and the staff are solemnly appointed. There is a conscious effort to enshroud both sets of officials with the kind of solemnity mystically associated with Imperial Examination Commissioners in older days. Much of the traditional terminology once closely associated with the imperial examinations is still in use. Imitation of the tradition so enchanted the president of the Examination Yuan that at times he even ordered the examiners to be put strictly *incommunicado* for the duration of the examination period and up to the moment when the results of the examination were announced.

If there has been a conscious effort to carry on the old form, there has also been a continuation of the old spirit. In the old days the essential meaning of the examination was to direct Confucian scholars, indoctrinated with a profound sense of loyalty to the monarch, into the channels of official life. Once the service of the best educated had been enlisted, the country was considered safe for the monarchy. The men in charge of the examinations today seem to have been thoroughly imbued with the wisdom of that arrangement. They want to secure for the service of the state the most promising graduates of the schools and universities. But in the process of selection great emphasis seems to have been put on the candidates' conformity to the current political beliefs of the regime. This is especially true in the case of the higher examinations. If the designs of the Examination Yuan had fully succeeded, there would certainly have been a continuation of the old tradition, the complete identification of education with statecraft and the sterilization of education in the interest of maintaining the status quo. They have not fully succeeded partly due to the maladministration of the civil service in the sense that successful candidates have not always been given desirable positions, and partly due to the shunning of public service by the graduates themselves. This failure is perhaps a blessing in disguise, for the deadening imperial tradition of yoking education with officialdom has not been successfully revived.

The examinations, both higher and ordinary ones, being primarily meant for the graduates of universities and schools, are naturally academic, and are apt to repeat the graduation examinations of the universities and schools. On the whole, the subjects in which the candidates are examined are not suited to test either general intellectual excellence in the way British candidates for the administrative class are tested, nor professional competence in the way candidates for the higher civil service positions in other countries are tested. Few successful candidates have shown either brilliance or professional competence or can be favorably compared with the more capable of those officials who have entered the civil service by some other qualification, such as academic or professional experience.

Whatever be their quality, the officials recruited from the examinations have not played a very important part in the Chinese bureaucracy. In a period of sixteen years, up to the end of June 1947, there were only 3409 successful candidates of the higher examinations, and 4267 of the ordinary examinations. Put together, they represent only a small fraction of the Chinese bureaucracy.

Post-Examination Training

The question whether a successful candidate should be forthwith appointed to a post and considered a permanent member of the civil service, or given a prior period of training or probation has been of concern to the Examination Yuan.

Under the Peking regime, successful candidates of the high civil service examination had to go through a period of probation. For the officials of the judiciary, whether recruited by civil service examination or by some special arrangement, a year of in-training was required before they were appointed. The relative excellence of the judicial service as compared with other services was in a large measure due to that more or less thorough in-training.

The Kuomintang regime at Nanking continued the practice of its predecessor in regard to in-training for the judicial service. Whenever the number of successful candidates who have passed the high examination is not large enough to make up a training group, law graduates intending to enter the judicial service are also often admitted. There are, however, differences between the in-training of recent years and that of the Peking days. At Peking, the training was nonpartisan and more thorough. At Nanking it has been generally a half-year program and partisan control has been marked.

For the successful candidates of high and ordinary examinations in general, the Kuomintang in 1939 also ordered a period of in-training. Theoretically, two examinations began to be required, the preliminary and the final. Theoretically again, the in-trainees were required to undergo a final examination before they were considered successful candidates and fit for appointment. The alleged reason for requiring the in-training was that due to the conditions of the war, the education of the candidates had been inadequate and the examinations had become somewhat confused, so much so that only a program of in-training could make up for their deficiencies.

In reality, the in-training of those years was of little or no value to the successful candidates insofar as their professional competence was concerned. During the war years, the successful candidates of the high examination generally received their training at the Central Political Institute (now called National Political University) which used to be under the direct supervision of the Central Executive Committee of the Kuomintang and has always been a training center for young party members intending to serve the party or the government. It has been known not only for its partisan nature, but for its strong tinge of the Organization Group of the party as well. Thus, when successful candidates of the preliminary examination were put into training there, indoctrination and partisan alignment of a special nature became the order of the day, while training of a professional or general administrative nature was sorely neglected. The trainees generally became either opportunists or cynics. No wonder that the more ambitious and uncompromising of the university graduates tended to shun the civil service.

In this connection, it may be recalled that the training programs of the Kuomintang, especially the Central Training Corps at Chungking during the war years, tried on a much greater scale to indoctrinate, group after group, the officials in all the key posts of the civil service, the armed forces, the party services, and education. Officials from all over the country were ordered to live on the grounds of the Corps for a period of two or three weeks, ostensibly to receive training in party doctrines and government policies, but actually to be molded personally and directly by the Leader of the Kuomintang, concurrently also the Chief of the Corps. While there, they also had to listen to the so-called lectures of high officials and thereby supposedly to familiarize themselves with the actual administration. But there was little or nothing they could learn during those weeks. If they wished, they could of course make desirable contacts which might be of profit to their careers, but that was all they could do.

What was true of the Central Training Corps in Chungking was also true of the provincial training corps in the provinces. There of course the trainers were the officials of the provincial governments and party organizations, and the trainees were drawn from the provincial and local officialdom and party workers.

During the war years, candidates successful in the high examination were usually, after a period of in-training in the Central Political Institute (averaging six months), sent to the Central Training Corps for a finishing course; and candidates successful in the ordinary examinations usually received their in-training in the provincial training corps. When thus thrown together with other officials and party workers called up for a brief period of training, they naturally shared the experience of those officials and party workers. In other words, they had little additional administrative or professional training per se; they were merely indoctrinated and enabled to make desirable personal contacts.

The candidates, after going through the in-training, were persuaded to join the party if they had not yet become party members. All this having been done, the final examination, the post-training examination, was either considered to have already taken place or in some other way dispensed with. The candidates were deemed fully qualified to be admitted into the civil service.

The Ministry of Personnel and the Administration of the Civil Service

The Ministry of Personnel is, according to the law, in complete charge of the administration of the civil service. The Examination Commission is only to examine or otherwise to qualify the candidate for appointive offices. Where the Commission's responsibilities end, the Ministry's begin.

China being a centralized state, the jurisdiction of the Ministry extends throughout the country. In the past the Ministry has had, apart from the personnel establishments attached to each tier of local government, a number of regional offices for the purpose of administering the civil service more effectively. These regional offices are now in a fluid state, for the Examination Yuan is considering setting up branch offices of the Yuan as a whole which would have charge of the examination functions *inter alia.*

The first duty of the Ministry of Personnel is to arrange the appointment of those who have been successful at the examinations. In consultation with the various central departments and local governments, which are naturally the employers, the candidates are assigned to posts. Once assigned, the departments and local governments cannot refuse to take them in, though they are not always properly integrated. In the case of successful candidates for the high examination who carry a high rank, the departments and governments are especially apt to be wary. They generally have a low view of the capabilities of fresh graduates of the universities. Since they cannot openly defy the law, they frequently appoint the men to positions which carry no active duties. A favorite practice is to make them members of a study commission or of a commission to edit certain bulletins. The new appointees, if they are to get any substantive position, or to be able to climb the official ladder, must do a great deal to cultivate the good opinions of their superiors.

The recruits from the high examinations have not generally succeeded in becoming an important segment of the civil service. Those who have acquired a greater or lesser prominence have done so because they happened either to be exceptionally able or, more frequently, to be the graduates of the party institute, referred to above. As for the recruits from the ordinary examinations, they are submerged in the vast body of civil servants and have still less opportunity to demonstrate their superior qualifications.

Since theoretically only successful candidates of the examinations are to be appointed to office, those who were already officials had to be given special consideration. From 1930 to 1934 the Ministry of Personnel devoted most of its energy to looking into the qualifications of official incumbents and to conferring on them, if found duly qualified according to the laws specially enacted for that purpose, appropriate official ranks so that they might be treated as civil servants. This improvised arrangement had the effect of nullifying the advantages of those who later entered the civil service via the regular examinations. As a matter of fact, at all times men have been entering the civil service without passing the examinations. During the war, the number of such men was especially large. In the end, the Ministry of Personnel was obliged to give them appropriate rank, too, exactly as it had done for those who were appointed before any examinations took place. In other words, the Ministry has not been successful in insisting on examination as the only or even the principal method of recruitment.

When a civil servant is appointed for the first time, or an incumbent is recognized by the Ministry of Personnel as a qualified civil servant, he is given a rank. The ranking is thus a second function of the Ministry. To rank an appointee who has passed an examination is relatively simple. But to rank an official who for years has been in the service or an official who has been exempted from examination is often the occasion for dispute between the

Ministry and the official himself or the department which employs him. He may claim to be in possession of certain qualifications which entitle him to a certain rank, but the Ministry of Personnel may dispute such qualifications. There have been numerous cases in which an official of the rank of a director of service, failing to qualify himself on other accounts, presented some indifferent writing of his own and claimed it to be a work of originality which, according to the Law of the Appointment of Public Officials of March 22, 1933, entitles the author to be appointed to a high rank. In the matter of giving proper ranks to the civil servants, the Ministry is apt to lay emphasis on the form rather than the merits of the case. When the form is correct, it hesitates to probe further for fear that its authority might be flouted.

The third important function of the Ministry is the rating of the efficiency of the civil servants. Proper efficiency-rating of so many persons in the civil service obviously cannot be directly done by a centralized ministry. The preliminary work has to be undertaken by the departments themselves. In every department there is usually a committee on efficiency-rating, composed of the ranking officials of that department. They give each official a rating according to his faithfulness to the work as well as his professional knowledge and competence. This preliminary rating is submitted to the head of the department, or, in the case of a local government, to the head of that government, for approval or modification. Finally, the approved ratings of all departments are submitted to the Ministry of Personnel for final scrutiny. The Ministry possesses the authority to make revisions or call on the departments concerned to submit ratings anew.

The rating system cannot be taken very seriously, owing partly to the failure to work out criteria with which to judge the work of civil servants, and partly to the reluctance of the average department head to enforce a strict rating on his subordinates. It has probably done no good to the civil service. It has merely added so much more paper work to the administrative departments.

The grading in each rank, increase or reduction in emolument, and other rewards or minor penalties follow the rating. There is a body of minute regulations which governs these matters. Civil servants are seldom dismissed on account of a poor rating. As a rule, they are not seriously concerned with rewards or penalties except that they do care for a good grade, for salary scale is based on it and failure to make a certain grade also means failure to get regular increments. In this they are, however, blessed by the generous ratings given them by the departments, which are equally solicitous that their employees should not lose the opportunities for salary increases.

The Ministry of Personnel also has charge of the retirements and pensions of civil servants. There are laws governing such matters. But owing to the inability of the government to provide for a general pension system, retirement has never been enforced. Only those who are injured or the dependents of those who are killed in the performance of their duties actually receive pensions, and even these pensions are usually very meager.

The Ministry of Personnel is thus theoretically a powerful authority. If the Chinese Government were not insolvent, and were able to pay its civil servants well, and if the functions of the Ministry were strictly and conscientiously administered, the Chinese civil service might indeed be one of the very best in the world. Unfortunately the discrepancy between the theory and the practice is so great that there is little reality attached to the theory.

The Personnel Establishment

In every branch of the government, central and local, the Ministry of Personnel has been endeavoring to establish a unit in charge of the personnel of the branch concerned. In the discharge of its duties, the unit is under the dual direction of the chief of the branch and the Ministry of Personnel. In the ministries and commissions of the central government it is often a fairly big establishment on a par with a directorate of service. Enormous numbers of men are required to fill these establishments the country over. The Kuomintang has in the past offered intensive programs of training for those who intended to be personnel officers. The Central Political Institute of the party has also had many of its graduates employed in the personnel establishments.

The personnel establishments attached to the various branches of government should be considered not only as a means of direct control of the personnel by the Ministry of Personnel, but also as a manifestation of the power of the party. Insofar as the Organization Group of the party has always been careful to secure the appointment of their men to be the chiefs of the personnel establishments, the personnel of the various departments of the government, and consequently of the whole government, may be said to be under the control of that group.

The Civil Service

In spite of the great emphasis the Kuomintang government professes to place on it, the Chinese civil service is imperfectly organized in many ways. There is not even a strict definition as to who are civil servants and who are not.[8] The difficulty in this regard arises from the nature of the following categories of public servants: the high officials concerned with policy-making; teachers in government institutions, and advisers and consultants "invited" to serve in an advisory capacity; men in the armed services; police, customs, and postal officials, and employees in government corporations; and diplomatic and consular officials.

In other countries a minister or a department head is always considered outside the range of civil service. In a similar way, the chiefs of the Five Yuan and the heads of ministries and commissions should also be exempted from the restrictions of the civil service. They are indeed so exempted for most purposes, but for some purposes they and the ordinary officials are both designated by the term "public official." For instance, in the matter of emolument, the high officials and rank and file are spoken of together. Furthermore, not every so-called "political official" can claim to be much different from a higher "administrative official," terms created by the party without clear definition. In general, it may be safely said that the officials of the ministerial rank and their superiors are not considered civil servants.

The status of the professors in government universities and also of the numerous officials who are "invited"[9] to serve in consultative or advisory capacities is also hard to define. Most of these persons deliberately prefer to stay outside of the civil service and not be considered civil servants. They are certainly not subject to most of the disciplinary measures applicable to ordinary officials. But, in the matter of emolument, they are being more and more classified as civil servants. Also, if they should later be appointed into the civil service, their previous record as "invited" professors or officials counts in the making of a rank which they might not otherwise attain.

The man in the armed services should naturally be considered outside of the civil service. There should not be any mingling of the two. But in the matter of rank, the civil and military appointments, especially on the higher levels, often enter into the same system of classification. For instance, the commander-in-chief of each of the three armed forces carries the same rank as a minister, and they are thus often grouped together in some aspects of the civil service legislation.

Police officials are considered civil servants. So are the customs and postal officials. But the former in some respects approach the military officials in status. The latter, owing to the fact that the customs and postal service were, for a long time before the Kuomintang came into power, foreign-controlled and better paid, are still being paid on a preferred scale. Thus both are not quite identical with the bulk of the civil servants. As for the employees of government corporations, like the government banks, the differences between them and ordinary civil servants are still greater. Some would like to see them integrated into the regular civil service. The wisdom of so doing can well be questioned.

There are few tenable arguments for the differentiation of diplomatic and consular officials and also judicial officials from the general civil service and, in fact, there is not much differentiation. What distinctions there are usually concern either emolument or promotions.

The emolument of Chinese officials follows their ranks and grades. The

Japanese three-rank system was adopted at the beginning of the Republic and has since been adhered to. The "special" rank is reserved for ministers and chairmen of commissions and ambassadors and their superiors. The so-called "selected" rank is one to which the higher officials such as the vice-ministers and the directors of services are appointed. It is subdivided into eight grades. The third one is the "recommended" rank, and includes such officials as the section chiefs. It is subdivided into twelve grades. The lowest is the "delegated rank," so-called because the appointment is delegated to the heads of the agencies without requiring a presidential commission. It is subdivided into as many as sixteen grades. The rank is more important than the grade. The difference in ranks means not only that the posts differ but also that the qualifications of the appointees are different. The grades on the other hand are only a scale for salary raises.

After the establishment of the Five-Power Government, a pseudo-rank, the "elected" rank, was added to the original ranks to denote a small number of high officials — the President of the National Government and the presidents of the Yuan, who were chosen or "elected" by the Central Executive Committee of the party before being appointed by the President of the National Government. It is, however, not really a distinctive rank. It only denotes the mode of their original selection. The presidents of the Yuan, too, carry the "special" rank, as far as the laws governing public officials are concerned.[10]

The classification of all public officials into three ranks is neither logical nor convenient. In fact, if the officials of the special rank whose duties are political in nature and who are, therefore, outside the pale of the civil service, are excepted, the Chinese civil service in the last resort is divisible into only two categories. The descriptives "selected," "recommended," and "delegated" really describe nothing. The oversimplified classification makes it difficult to assign to the numerous categories of civil servant a proper rank. Promotions from one rank to another become too rigid. No wonder that some proponents of civil service reform have been demanding that instead of the three-rank system a modern job system should be adopted.

The salary scale according to which public officials are paid is also defective. The highest officials, those of the special rank, receive $800 a month as salary and a greater amount for allowances. But the officials of the lowest grade of the delegated rank receive only $55 without any allowance. The discrepancy is too great to be healthy. A university graduate with professional training, unless he is successful at the high examination, could probably be appointed only to a lower grade of the delegated rank. He would be receiving not more than $100 a month. But if he is professionally employed in a private capacity, he would be drawing a considerably higher salary. Low government salary in this case has a tendency to discourage a professional man from going into the government. Also, the extremely low salary for the lowest grades of the delegated rank is conducive neither to efficiency nor to a spirit of self-reliance on the part of those officials concerned. Both the looseness of the Chinese administrative organization and the tyrannical attitude of Chinese high officials may indeed be attributed to the great discrepancy in the emolument of the high and low officials.

This salary scale has not been enforced since the beginning of the malignant inflation during the war. But the law concerning the emolument of the officials has not been amended or repealed. In fact, the relative scale is still being more or less maintained even to this day.

A very strict code of conduct consisting of a great number of injunctions is prescribed for public officials. In general it may be said that legally they are by no means privileged persons. They can neither unionize nor demonstrate. Redress against the disciplinary measures of their superiors, though not entirely unavailable, is circumscribed. In short, if Chinese officials live strictly within the law, they can hardly be of any danger to the rights and securities of the people over whom they rule. But in practice it is, of course, a different story. Officials, by grouping together, have always been powerful enough either to thwart zealous reforms from above or to terrorize the people below, or to do both. Only when the higher-ranking political leaders are honest, clean, able, and persistent, and all officials are well paid, can the former impose, if they want to, on the latter a policy of solicitous care for the interests of the people.

XVII

LAW AND THE ADMINISTRATION OF JUSTICE[1]

The Westernization of Chinese Law

Western criticism of Chinese law and judicial process has been more than theoretical. It took concrete form in the system of extraterritoriality, by which foreign nationals in China were subject to the jurisdiction, not of Chinese courts, but of judicial authorities maintained there by their own governments. The Manchu Court was not aware, when the British first wrung extraterritorial jurisdiction from China, in 1842, of the serious impairment involved of its sovereign rights. But as time went on and the Court became more familiar with the rules and usages of the international community, it was afflicted with a sense of loss and inferiority, and longed for the abolition of extraterritoriality.

Earlier European visitors to China had been of course cognizant of the differences between Chinese and Western law. But they were impressed by other differences as well. Dazzled by the grandeur and the brilliance of the Court at Peking, they were in no position to be critical. But by the time the mercantile classes of Western Europe came to China to trade, two significant changes had taken place. The industrial revolution had occurred in Europe with the consequence that the absence in Chinese law of adequate provisions to protect the rights of the trading community began to be keenly felt. Then, too, the Manchu Empire had been weakened and it was easier to find fault with a weak polity. During this period Western traders and missionaries as well made a concerted attack on Chinese law and Chinese administration of justice. They felt justified in demanding extraterritorial jurisdiction for themselves.

Thus, one of the very first results of the Western impact on China was the growing sentiment on the part of the Chinese that Western law was superior to Chinese law. When, following the introduction of Western codes and the inauguration of modern courts of justice, Japan was able to abolish extraterritoriality after 1894, the pressure for China to pursue the same course of modernization was persistent. That the law should be Westernized and modern courts should be organized was a tenet accepted by all. The promise of Great Britain, as stipulated in the renewed treaty of commerce in 1902 [2] "to relinquish her extraterritorial rights" when China had westernized her judicial system prompted the Manchu Government to inaugurate a program of legal reform.

In 1902 a Law Compilation Bureau was first set up to translate and edit Western law codes and to prepare new codes for China. It underwent many reorganizations and frequent changes of name, but it was in almost continuous existence at Peking for well over two decades, scarcely interrupted even by the Revolution of 1911. Its accomplishments were quite remarkable. While it was conscious that Western or westernized Japanese codes must form the basis of the new law of China, it was not oblivious of the Chinese legal tradition. The legal rules in the Great Ch'ing Code which are directly traceable to the celebrated T'ang Code of 653 were preserved, insofar as they were not in conflict with modern concepts of the individual and his proprietary rights. The Great Ch'ing Criminal Code of 1909 was the first of the endeavors. Since the civil and penal provisions were still together in one document, a new penal code, the so-called Provisional New Criminal Code,[3] was promulgated in 1911. The penal provisions in the earlier code were to be superseded, but the civil ones were to continue to be in force.

The Republican regime of Peking adopted no substantive new codes. Provisional procedural codes were added, but the two imperial codes of the previous years were accepted, with appropriate changes in name and some other slight modifications, as the civil and criminal codes of the Republic. The apparent inertia was not due to the fact that the Law Codification Bureau was idle. On the contrary, it was aiming at some definitive codes which should satisfy both the demands of the foreign powers which were reluctant to agree to the abolition of extraterritoriality and of the Chinese for whom an industrialized and modernized society was envisaged. The Bureau was both hesitant and cautious. It did not look with favor upon giving up the traditional rules of the old Chinese codes which had enjoyed great stability in the preceding centuries. Although no definitive codes were completed before the fall of the Peking regime, the work of the Bureau was nevertheless invaluable to the lawmakers of the Nationalist regime at Nanking.[4]

The Kuomintang government adopted a much bolder attitude towards code-making. From 1929 to 1931, all the necessary codes were promulgated, one after another. In 1935, the procedural codes, civil and criminal, as well as the Criminal Code, were revised.[5] In them there are undoubtedly legal rules without precedent in either the codes promulgated in the last years of the Ch'ing or the drafts of the Law Codification Bureau. For instance, the legal equality of women in respect of inheritance is one such new rule. But, on the whole, the new codes of the Ch'ing and the elaborately worked-out drafts of the Bureau formed the main bases of these codes. Incidentally, even the completion of these codes did not immediately terminate the Powers' extraterritorial jurisdiction. Some powers were forced to give up their extraterritorial rights through defeat in the two world wars. Others gave up the rights only after Pearl Harbor had made them allies of China. Only Soviet Russia of her own accord renounced her extraterritorial jurisdiction together with other treaties.[6]

An appraisal of the codes of the National Government can be approached from several angles. In draftsmanship the codes are, on the whole, well done. In concept, the Civil and the Criminal Codes are modern, but they do no violence to the ethico-legal traditions of the Chinese. If they have not been duly enforced, it is not because they are unenforceable, but because of the inaccessibility of the courts, the incompetence of the judges, and, especially, the interference of authorities other than the judicial in the administration of justice. However, the procedural codes, mainly based on those promulgated by the Peking regime, are not realistic. During the years of the Peking regime, the procedures, both civil and criminal, had proved to be too complicated to suit Chinese conditions. In the codes of the National Government there is none of the needed simplification.[7]

The Judicial Yuan [8]

The Judicial Yuan was organized like the other Yuan. Like them, it was headed by a President and a Vice-President, who were assisted by the usual secretaries and councilors. There is no need to inquire into the manner in which they were appointed or the powers which they enjoyed. Like the Presidents of the other minor Yuan, the Legislative, the Examination, and the Control Yuan, the President of the Judicial Yuan enjoyed a semipermanent tenure. The party or its leadership has considered it wise to interfere as little as possible with the incumbents of these presidencies. They were usually elder statesmen of the party. As elder statesmen, they were to be honored, and it would be impolitic for the party to incur their animosity. But since as presidents they wielded little political power, the party could afford to let them enjoy undisturbed the honors and emoluments of the office.

The powers of the Judicial Yuan should depend on a definition of the scope of judicial power set forth in the constitution or the organic law. But there was no definition or delineation of judicial power either in Sun Yat-sen's writings or in the fundamental laws of the Kuomintang regime. In the absence of such a definition or delineation, the powers of the Judicial Yuan naturally comprised the sum total of functions entrusted to it by the laws of the time.

At one time, the Judicial Yuan had the following agencies under it: the Ministry of Justice, the Supreme Court, the Administrative Court, and the Disciplinary Commission. Since these agencies were in charge respectively of judicial administration and the adjudication of civil and criminal suits, of administrative suits, and of impeachment cases, the powers of the Judicial Yuan which controlled and supervised them all must be considered to have been extended to judicial administration as well as to the whole field of ordinary and administrative justice. This gave rise to various controversies as to whether the judicial power should, in theory or in fact, be so extensive.

The Administrative Court is the highest organ for administrative justice, a function which can be considered as falling within either the administrative or the judicial power. In countries like France, it used to be considered to pertain to the former. In some other countries, the administrative courts are both independent of the executive and separated from the hierarchy of the ordinary courts. Under the Five-Yuan system, the administrative court has to be attached either to the Executive or to the Judicial Yuan. From the point of view of the Judicial Yuan, it has been fortunate that the Executive Yuan has never sought to dispute its jurisdiction over the Administrative Court.

The jurisdiction over the Disciplinary Commission was once disputed by the Control Yuan. The Control Yuan, which is in charge of impeachment, claimed that unless it controlled the authority which passed judgment on the guilt or innocence of an official impeached by the Control Yuan, the impeachment might be lightly disposed of. It therefore demanded that the Disciplinary Commission be made a constituent part of the Control Yuan. From the point of view of the Judicial Yuan, it was again fortunate that once the founders of the Five-Yuan Government had, in 1928, decided the controversy in its favor, the Control Yuan never renewed the dispute.

The most heated controversy has been concerned with the control of the Ministry of Justice. The Ministry is charged with organizing and providing for the courts and prisons and appointing the judges and other officials connected with judicial administration. It also directs the procurators and supervises their work in general. The question is: Are these functions administrative or judicial? They are undoubtedly concerned with justice. On that premise the Judicial Yuan demands that the Ministry be placed under its control. But they are in nature administrative, and in all countries of the world the ministry of justice is invariably a part of the administration. The Executive Yuan therefore has argued that for the sake of protecting the integrity of the executive it cannot relinquish the power of judicial administration. The controversy has never been entirely settled.[9] The Ministry of Justice has in the past two decades been shuffled about several times between the Judicial and the Executive Yuan. Since 1943, it has been placed under the Executive Yuan. But the Judicial Yuan has not ceased applying pressure on the Ministry, though necessarily subtly and indirectly.

Stripped of its jurisdiction over the Ministry of Justice, the Judicial Yuan's authority is now confined to supervising the Supreme and Administrative Courts and the Disciplinary Commission. But these are all courts and, as such, they function more or less independently. They are not subject to the interference of the Judicial Yuan. What functions remain which still can be performed by the Yuan itself? If there are few or none, what is the justification for its continued existence? The Judicial Yuan is in a difficult position, and it has not been able to give satisfactory answers to these questions.

Two solutions were attempted. One was to substantiate the functions entrusted by law to the Judicial Yuan, and the other was to assign to the President and Vice-President of the Yuan some really judicial (as distinguished from administrative or supervisory) duties.

Of the functions which belonged to the Judicial Yuan by law, the first was that of standardizing interpretations of laws and modifications of judicial precedents. This first function was in the first instance entrusted to a chamber president of the Supreme Court. If objection to his ruling was raised, either by the President of the Court or by a majority of the chamber presidents, or by the President of the Judicial Yuan, a new ruling had to be arrived at by all of them in conference. Thus it was really a function of the Supreme Court, rather than of the Judicial Yuan.

The second function of the Judicial Yuan was that its President had the power to submit to the President of the National Government recommendations concerning amnesty, reprieve, and the restitution of rights. But the initiative for amnesty, reprieve, and restitution had always rested with the Ministry of Justice, since the Ministry, in full knowledge of the conduct of the convicts, was the only agency in a position to advise on these matters. Though the Ministry was no longer a part of the Judicial Yuan, most recommendations were still being initiated by it.

Finally, the Judicial Yuan had the power to propose to the Legislative Yuan laws relating to the matters within its jurisdiction. But this last function was one of even less substance. If the Judicial Yuan had not been in existence, the need of the laws which it proposed would not have arisen, for those laws were usually concerned with the organization and procedure of the Yuan itself.

Since all the above-described functions of the Judicial Yuan had little reality, a further attempt was at one time made to justify its existence. By the Organic Law of the National Government of December 30, 1931, the

President and Vice-President of the Judicial Yuan were made the President of the Supreme Court and of the Disciplinary Commission respectively. It was thought that by charging the heads of the Yuan with active duties, the Yuan itself could be justified. But this was in itself a debatable expedient. The President of the Yuan functioning at the head of the Supreme Court, however active he might be, could not conceivably add any importance to the Yuan. He would be performing a purely judicial function in strict accordance with whatever rules of procedure the Court might have. The same would be true of the Vice-President of the Yuan functioning at the head of the Disciplinary Commission. The only valid argument for that arrangement was that the Presidents, being thus kept occupied, might not feel it necessary to busy themselves with finding means of substantiating the functions of an otherwise functionless body.

Even this debatable expedient was not tried for long. By a revision of the Organic Law of the National Government on March 15, 1932, the relevant article was so amended that the Presidents were permitted but no longer required to head the Court and the Commission. This revision was made necessary by the disinclination of the incumbents of the presidencies of the Yuan to sit as judges of the courts, being either unqualified or having little interest. Since then, the President of the Yuan has never assumed the presidency of the Court, though the Vice-President did for some time continue to act concurrently as the President of the Commission.

A provision of the Organic Law of the National Government which empowered the President of the Judicial Yuan, whenever he should deem it necessary, to sit with the Supreme Court, Administrative Court, and the Disciplinary Commission in their trials, was also meant to give substance to the functions of the President. It, too, was never used. In fact, this was only wise. His participation in those courts would be meaningless, if he only functioned as one of the judges, and would be a subversion of justice if he were to assert anything like a superior position over the judges of the court.

In short, no valid argument has been advanced and no effective means devised to justify the separate existence of the Judicial Yuan. Its only justification is that the Five Powers must be taken care of by five equally organized Yuan.

It is against this background of lack of function that the Constitution of 1946 stipulates that the Judicial Yuan shall have a number of Grand Justices to interpret the Constitution as well as to exercise the power of standardizing interpretations of laws and modifications of judicial precedents. These justices together with the President and Vice-President are, according to the Constitution, to be appointed by the President of the Republic with the consent of the Control Yuan. According to the new Constitution, therefore, the Judicial Yuan would be a collegiate body with functions of importance, but it would hardly be the organ envisaged by the early advocates of a powerful Judicial Yuan.

The Organization of the Courts[10]

There are today three tiers of ordinary courts: the district courts, the high courts, and the Supreme Court, corresponding to the *hsien*, the provinces, and the nation, respectively. At the beginning of the Republic, there was a fourth tier, the primary courts placed below the district courts. The judicial procedure, both civil and criminal, in the early years of the Republic generally required three trials. Therefore, a hierarchy of four was deemed necessary. The primary courts were, however, not extensively oganized. After a year or so, they were in fact abolished and the district court was ordered to take care of cases which would nominally have gone to the primary court in the first instance.

When the Kuomintang government was firmly established in Nanking, it sought to simplify both the judicial procedure and the hierarchy of courts necessary to carry out that procedure. The principle of three trials continued to be accepted, but cases which involved only minor advantages or punishments, were allowed only two trials. Three instead of four tiers of courts were considered adequate.

The Supreme Court is the highest court of the land. It has a president and about three score of judges, divided into civil and criminal chambers. Each chamber is headed by a president who is himself a judge. The Court President has the duties of assigning cases in the docket, according to a fixed rule, to the judges of the chamber.[11]

The judges of the Supreme Court have of course none of the distinction and prestige of the justices of its American counterpart. They are more numerous and they have not the authority to interpret the constitution which gives the American justices a unique position in the government. On the whole, they are, however, competent. If their decisions are lightly spoken of and not seriously regarded by the public in general, it is because of the general lack of respect for the courts rather than because of any lapse in justice. Any lapse of justice in the decisions of the Supreme Court that may occur is perhaps due more often to the pressure of business with which the judges are burdened[12] than to the quality of the judges.

But the Supreme Court has not been fortunate in its presidents. For most of the two decades of its existence, it has been presided over by men who have been neither jurists nor experienced judges nor even honest politicians. Although in law and in theory the president has no authority to interfere with the decisions of the judges and although the judges do develop a technique for resisting any undue interference of the president, not every judge is proof against such interference. A bad president is always capable of doing a great deal of harm, as has undoubtedly been done by some incumbents of the presidency.

The high courts are courts of second instance. Each province has one, as do some municipalities which do not come within the jurisdiction of any provincial government. For the more populous provinces branch high courts are established in order to be more easily accessible. At the end of 1946, there were 26 high courts with 102 branch courts.

The high court is organized similarly to the Supreme Court. It has a president and a number of chambers. The branch high court is administratively under the high court, and in most cases has no more than two chambers, one civil and one criminal. But its judicial capacity is identical with that of the high court itself.

The district court is the court of first instance. Theoretically, there should be one for each *hsien*. But at the end of 1946 there were only 479 such courts. Most of the *hsien* did not have fully organized courts. Instead, for each of them there was only a judicial section attached to the *hsien* government. There were 992 such judicial sections in 1946. The reason for the existence of so large a number of judicial sections is that whereas a fully organized district court has to have at least two chambers and a number of judges, the judicial section is a simple organization. It used to be in personal charge of the *hsien* magistrate, assisted by an assessor. In many places, this is still the case today, though there is an effort to appoint one or more judges with legal training to take charge of the trials.

The courts, though more numerous today than in previous years, are still insufficient. Both the district courts and the judicial sections are heavily burdened. For the large and small *hsien* alike, there is only one court or judicial section. It is not always easily accessible. For appeal, the litigant must go to a high court or one of its branches. It is likely to be even less accessible. Taking into consideration the vastness of the population and the absence of adequate means of communication, the insufficiency of the courts can be well appreciated.

The quality of the judges of the high and district courts is an even more serious problem than the insufficiency of courts. The judges are very uneven in quality. While the better ones, to be found usually in urban centers where the educational and economic standards of the population are comparatively high and the bar is in actual existence, are competent, the worst of them may be ignorant and disreputable. The assessors and judges who are attached to the judicial sections of the *hsien* governments are almost invariably poorly qualified.

There are several explanations for the generally poor quality of the judges of the high and district courts. First, the judges of these courts number probably around 5000 or more. There are not sufficient law schools in China to turn out qualified law graduates adequate in numbers to fill the posts that become vacant and thus gradually to improve the personnel. Second, the salaries of the judges are low and transfer from a remote place to a more accessible one is difficult. A judicial career for these reasons is comparatively unattractive. Finally, party and bureaucratic influence, which was much less felt prior to the coming of the Kuomintang regime, has interfered with the routine of judicial service. A judge who is faithful to his work may not be as rapidly promoted or as favorably transferred as one who has the proper connections. This naturally adversely affects the morale of the service.

Compared with the administrative civil service, however, the judicial service still enjoys a greater degree of stability and independence. Given better pay and a greater infusion of trained law graduates, it may still be expected to function satisfactorily.

Judicial Procedure

There is great similarity between civil and criminal procedure in China.[13] Since there are three levels of courts, the general principle is to allow the litigants three trials, following one after another from the lowest to the highest court. There are, however, many exceptions to this general rule. First, for civil cases involving only very small value or for minor criminal cases involving very light penalties, a summary procedure takes the place of the regular one at the court of first instance. This practice was carried over from the trials before the primary court, the lowest court in existence in the first years of the Republic. Second, both civil and criminal cases which are not of too serious a nature, are permitted only one appeal. That is to say, the decision of the high court will be final for them. And finally, in criminal procedure the court of first instance in cases of sedition and treason is the high court and not the district court. These exceptions notwithstanding, for perhaps the majority of cases the three trials are still available.

The trials at the court of first instance and on first appeal are concerned with both facts and law. But at the third trial, which invariably takes place before the Supreme Court, only questions of law and the question whether the lower courts in conducting the trial or trials have strictly followed the proper procedure are debated and decided. In other words, the Supreme Court does not itself inquire into the facts of a case.

In the trials at the court of first instance and at the intermediate appellate court, that is, the district and high courts, oral arguments are in order. At the Supreme Court generally only written arguments are admitted, though the court may, if it sees fit, also admit oral ones.

Advocates are allowed at all trials. For criminal cases, involving five years of imprisonment or more, the court must assign an advocate for the defendant if he has not engaged one himself. The members of the bar in the locality concerned are obliged to accept such an assignment and give gratuitous service, if necessary.

Criminal suits are initiated either by the complaint of the injured person as plaintiff or by information of those persons, private or official, who have knowledge of the crime, or by the surrender of the criminal himself. Generally speaking, complaint by the plaintiff has been accepted as the normal course for starting a criminal investigation by the procurator. This is in theory at variance with the system used in the early years of the Republic.

The controversy as to whether the state or the injured person should be responsible for the prosecution of the criminal was resolved in favor of the former during the Peking regime. The Kuomintang government has tended to favor the latter alternative. Thus, during the Peking days the procurators were almost as numerous as the judges and were organized exactly like the judges. For every court there was a procurator's office, and the judges and the procurators were equal in rank. Theoretically, it was for the procurators to detect and to prosecute crimes, the plaintiff occupying only the position of a witness. The Kuomintang government has modified that system. The procurators are not so numerous as the judges in court and are provided to assist the plaintiffs in conducting the criminal investigation rather than primarily to assume the responsibility for the detection of crime.

In actual practice, however, the difference has not been marked. The procurators of the present day tend to consider themselves full equals of the judges. The senior procurator attached to a court enjoys a position completely equal to that of the president of the court. Furthermore, in important cases the procurators are frequently ordered by the Ministry of Justice to initiate investigation. They function very much like the procurators of the Peking days or the police magistrates of continental Europe.

The indictment is normally in the name of the procurator in charge. After due investigation he decides either to let the case lapse or to bring an indictment before the court. From this stage on, the plaintiff or the injured party assumes more the position of a witness while the procurator becomes the official accuser in the interest of the state. At the trial he figures as actively as the defendant and his advocates. When the sentence is given, he too may appeal to a higher court. In criminal procedure, the procurator's role is still nearly as important as that of the judge.

At trial, whether at the court of first instance or on appeal, there is always a bench of judges. There is no jury in attendance. The requirement of a number of judges is meant to prevent the possible bias of a single judge. In the case of a summary procedure, mentioned above, a single judge suffices.

The few hundred courts of China are naturally overcrowded with litigations, civil and criminal. But in proportion to the population the litigations are not numerous. This is due to a number of causes. Traditionally, the

Chinese people are not litigious. They used to consider going to court, that is, bringing law suits before the *hsien* magistrate, as lacking in respectability. That sentiment still lingers to some degree. The lack of easy accessibility of the courts and the high cost of modern lawsuits also discourage an essentially poor people from resorting to litigation to solve their disputes. Many disputes are settled out of court, sometimes to the advantage of both parties, but more often to the advantage of the local gentry.

Administrative Adjudication

The justiciable disputes arising out of administrative acts are either settled by the administrative official or by a court employing a more or less judicial procedure. Roughly speaking, the English-speaking countries have adhered to the former practice; France and most other countries of continental Europe to the latter. But the difference between the two tends to be less and less marked as the English-speaking countries require their administrative commissions, when handling such disputes, to adopt a semijudicial procedure.

In the last days of the Manchu Dynasty, when political and legal reforms were being considered, the continental pattern was decided upon. Under the Peking regime of the Republic a high administrative court was organized and justiciable administrative disputes were settled in the last instance by it. A body of procedure was developed both by legislation and by judicial decisions, and the court was doing rather creditably until the increasing political chaos around 1920 put a stop to its effective functioning.[14] The Kuomintang government followed the same course. It too set up an administrative court to review the cases of persons who were dissatisfied with the decisions rendered by the highest administrative organs.

But whereas the administrative court of the Peking regime was placed under the President, the new Administrative Court is, like the Supreme Court, under the supervision of the Judicial Yuan. Again like the Supreme Court, the Administrative Court has a president and a number of judges divided into several chambers, each with a president chosen from the judges. But unlike the Supreme Court, the President of the Administrative Court serves also as a judge and president of one of the chambers. The judges are required to have had at least two years of previous service in subordinate positions of due rank. Among the five judges of each chamber, two must have had judicial service. These requirements are meant to insure that the judges will be familiar with the subject matter of the disputes which come up before the court for adjudication. In position the Administrative Court may therefore very well be compared to the French Council of State or the judicial sections thereof. Indeed, its freedom from administrative interference is in theory even greater than its French counterpart. But in actual authority and in prestige it is inferior. The obscurity of the judges, few of whom could claim to be either successful administrators or eminent jurists, is in itself an important cause of the low prestige of the court.[15]

The settling of judiciable administrative disputes is either by a simple administrative appeal or by an administrative appeal followed by adjudication by the Administrative Court. Both processes are regulated by appropriate laws.[16] No suits can be brought to the Administrative Court until the proper administrative authorities have failed to satisfy the petitioners.

Any man who is of the opinion that his property rights or other interests have been damaged or injured by either illegal or improper acts of any administrative authority, central or local, may bring an action against that authority to the authority next higher. Actions brought against an officer of a *hsien* government begin in a department of the provincial government. Actions brought against an officer of the Five Yuan and their ministries and commissions and also other organs directly under the National Government are taken to the original authority. If the ruling is unsatisfactory, the petitioner may make an appeal to an authority one step higher than the one which renders the ruling. No appeal is allowed over or above the Yuan. The rulings of the Yuan are final, as far as recourse to administrative appeal is concerned.

With the exception of the Executive Yuan, the administrative authorities, whether making a ruling in the first instance or on appeal, are, generally speaking, not judicially minded. They have a tendency to side with the agents who originally took the action out of which the dispute arose. This is only natural for administrative authorities everywhere tend to protect themselves against outside complaints. Nevertheless, this is bad, since it detracts from the good effects of the process of administrative appeal.

The Executive Yuan maintains a fairly good committee for deciding on appeals, and therefore appeals presented to this Yuan are more carefully and judicially considered. Those who raise complaints against inferior administrative agents have a final recourse, therefore, in case of unjust treatment, which is not at all unsatisfactory. Unfortunately, ordinary individuals who have inadequate legal knowledge and are afraid of the authorities generally do not dare to bring an administrative appeal to the Executive Yuan. It is usually done only by important persons who know that they can resort to an appeal to protect themselves against maltreatment by administrative agents. The Administrative Court is the last and final authority on justiciable administrative disputes. The petitioner, if he feels that full justice has not been done after going through a series of administrative appeals, may finally bring his complaint to the Administrative Court. The court considers the arguments of both sides, the complainant and the administrative agent, examines the administrative rulings which have been given during the course of administrative appeal, and renders accordingly a decision against which there is no further appeal. The decisions of the Administrative Court are reached with due deliberation since its docket is rather small [17] and the judges are ample in number.

But this does not necessarily mean that the court functions effectively. Its decisions over the past years betray weakness. They have too often gone no deeper than the letter of the law. They avoided both the intent of the law and the problem of administrative discretion. As long as the discretion taken in a particular case apparently has something to do with the purpose of the law governing that case, even though it be either unnecessary or not strictly aimed at achieving the purpose of the law, it is apt to be honored. The court may decide against administrative officials, when necessary, but it dislikes to make decisions adverse to the administration. This explains why the petitioner generally fails to get an award for damages, though the law entitles him to sue the administration for damages done to him when the case has finally reached the Administrative Court. To sum up, the Administrative Court has proved to be an institution of indifferent value. It has not misconducted itself. But to say that it, representing the judicial power, has been able to protect the rights of the people against the executive power would involve some exaggeration.

Disciplinary Adjudication

The Commission of Disciplinary Action against Central Government Officials, or simply the Disciplinary Commission, is not the only disciplinary court. Only actions against the general body of civil servants of the central government are brought before the commission. The officers of the armed forces are disciplined by military tribunals. Provincial and other local civil servants answer to provincial disciplinary commissions for actions brought against them. The high elective dignitaries and members of the Control Yuan, and the so-called political officials, namely, ministers, political vice-ministers, and the others, are disciplined by the Central Executive Committee of the Kuomintang or the Disciplinary Committee of the National Government respectively. These last two are more political than judicial in nature. The provincial disciplinary commission is largely composed of the judges of the high court of each province and could therefore be considered as the high court sitting in another capacity.

The Disciplinary Commission is on a par with the Supreme Court and the Administrative Court and is similarly organized. It has a chairman. In the past, the vice-president of the Judicial Yuan often held the post concurrently, so as to give the commission added prestige. The members, numbering from nine to eleven, enjoy a life tenure. A portion of them are required to be drawn from the judicial service.

Those nonpolitical civil officials of the central government against whom impeachment is preferred [18] are disciplined by the commission.[19] Generally, no argument takes place. The commission arrives at its judgment on the evidence of papers presented by the Control Yuan, the employing department, and the official concerned. Since the matter of criminal action connected with the case is within the competence of an ordinary court, the action of the commission is apt to be slowed down by the tardy criminal procedure of the court. Furthermore, as the heaviest discipline which can be given by the commission is dismissal and deprivation of the right to hold public office, it is often overshadowed by the pending criminal action. Considering the number of public officials in the central government and the recent statements of high government authorities that official corruption is widespread, the yearly average of about one hundred [20] handled by the commission is hardly indicative that the commission is exercising an effective check on the conduct of the central government's officialdom.

The Bench and the Bar

The quality of justice depends on a multitude of factors. The form and substance of the law, the organization of the courts, the litigants' general knowledge, and, in particular, his grasp of the law all have an important bearing on the administration of justice. The ordinary litigants, being mostly illiterate and ignorant of the law, especially the modern civil law, are at a disadvantage. The codes, both civil and criminal, substantive and procedural, may not be bad in themselves, but to the common man they are incomprehensible. As for the courts, their fewness and inaccessibility have already been commented upon. The paternalistic attitude adopted by the *hsien* magistrates of monarchical times toward the litigants was thus by no means an unqualified evil. An honest and sympathetic magistrate always tried to protect the interests of the humble by interpreting the laws and simplifying the procedures on their behalf, and by making himself more easily available and accessible than modern courts usually are.

The other factor on which the quality of modern justice depends is the quality of the bench and the bar. Modern court procedure makes the service of the bar almost indispensable. The greater the number of advocates available and the greater their appreciation of social and legal justice, the better will justice be administered. Unfortunately, in China the legal profession has developed slowly, few properly qualified persons have been admitted to the bar, and not all who have been admitted are well qualified by training and by standards of legal ethics. In the larger cities, there are a few score or even a few hundred practicing lawyers. There, corporations and other commercial concerns are able to provide for the legal profession a sufficient amount of remunerative activities, either as legal counsels or as advocates in litigation. For the countryside or for the smaller cities, the legal profession has no way of making a living and is practically nonexistent.

To some extent the quality of the judges depends on the vitality of the bar. When there is either no bar or the bar is unethical or ignorant, no standards of acumen in legal thinking and meticulousness in the observance of procedures are set or maintained. Though the bar is very restricted in China, it deserves note that better judges are usually to be found in places where the bar exists, and this in spite of the none too high repute the bar enjoys in the eyes of both the general public and the bench.

The low esteem in which the bar is held is due to a number of reasons. The more successful and prosperous lawyers of the big cities, with some exceptions, are engrossed in money-making. In their quest for fortunes, they may ignore ethics and stoop to many devious practices. They seldom feel a desire to work for the interest of wronged parties who happen to be poor. They incur not only the distrust of the general public but also the hostility of the honest and impecunious section of the bench.

The problem of the bar remains to be faced. The bar should be enlarged, popularized, and otherwise improved so that its services can be made available to the general public, judges can be more conscientious in the trials, and a fruitful source for the recruitment of judges can be made available. Or, if it is deemed that for the time being Chinese society is too poor to afford a good and widespread bar, some radical changes in Chinese judicial administration are called for. It may be that the judicial procedure has to be greatly simplified. Or it may be that a new and adequate program for the training of judges should be considered with more seriousness than it has hitherto received. To leave the bench and the bar as they now are would unduly retard the improvement of the quality of justice.

XVIII

THE CONTROL POWER

The Nature of the Control Power

Like his adulation of the old system of examination, Sun Yat-sen's concept of the institution of censors [1] also led him to overemphasize it and to see in it the foundations of an additional power. He considered the impeachment power of Western parliaments and the censorial power of old China to be essentially similar in nature. He assumed that Western writers' criticisms of the manner in which Western parliaments make use of their impeachment power implied sympathy with the Chinese censorial institution.[2] His own instinctive reverence for the Chinese tradition and the Western dissatisfaction with the Western system together emboldened him to advocate making the control power a fifth power of government.

But whether the control power remains within the limits of legislative competence or stands outside of the legislature and constitutes a separate power, the content of that power obviously cannot be the same as it was when the censorial system was in full force. In harmony with the old regime in which the emperor reigned supreme and ethical conduct and political activities were inseparable, the censors of old had a wide range of functions. The acts of private as well as public life formed the subjects of censorial review. Alleged intentions to commit certain deeds, and rumors of certain deeds as well as actual deeds themselves could justify a censor in preferring an impeachment. Furthermore, anybody who had anything to do with public life was liable to impeachment: the emperor and his household were not too high and the small gentry not too low.

An accurate analysis of the actual content of the old censorial power is not easy. But in addition to what is known in the West as the impeachment power, namely, the power to impeach an official for his illegal official conduct, the Chinese censors were certainly in the habit of doing a multitude of other things. They might voice their opinions on the imperial succession, on policies of a general nature, whether political, economic, or social, and on desirable institutional and administrative reforms. They might denounce or raise objection to imperial edicts. They might criticize the deportment and demeanor of all public persons including the emperor, especially at public ceremonies. They might investigate the administration for misconduct and search public accounts to detect corruption. They might propose the reopening of cases in which grave injustice was alleged, and on orders from the throne they might sit as cojudges at the retrial. It is plain that such a conglomeration of functions was possible only because there was no separation of powers and no distinction between things ethical and things political, and because it was to the interest of the emperor to give such a free sway to the censors. It is equally plain that such a conglomeration of functions is untenable in a republic with a Five-Yuan government.

But for a variety of reasons the new control power of today has a tendency to approach the old censorial power in magnitude. Sun Yat-sen's own extolling of the old system, the natural desire of the authorities of the Control Yuan to secure the widest possible power for the Yuan, the attachment of these same authorities to traditionalism, and the lack of a clear demarcation of the Five Powers have all contributed to the broad interpretation of the control power. Aside from the impeaching power, the Control Yuan has also the power to conduct inspections of a general nature and investigations into specific phases of administration. The audit also belongs to the Control Yuan. Out of this multitude of functions, the Control Yuan can even propose to government departments measures for the improvement of their administration. The Control Yuan's sphere of activity thus approaches pretty nearly that of the censors of old. But is this tenable? If the Control Yuan exercises its powers fully and effectively, the other Yuan will not be able to function properly. If the other Yuan are to remain powerful, the Control Yuan has to do much winking at their sins of omission and commission. Either alternative is unsalutary.

Organization of the Control Yuan [3]

The Control Yuan's over-all organization was in no way dissimilar to that of the other Yuan. There were the usual president, vice-president, secretaries, and councilors. Like the presidency of the Examination Yuan, the presidency of the Control Yuan was allowed to be occupied by one and the same man during the two decades of its existence, and for practically the same reason. Being a veteran Kuomintang leader, he must have a high post of honor. But the presidency being of no practical importance, he was allowed to retain it indefinitely. At some periods, as a protest against his Yuan not being permitted to function freely, he left his post for varying lengths of time. But he invariably returned without having gained a promise which would give the Yuan the freedom he desired.

The President of the Control Yuan, besides being the head of the Yuan administration, enjoyed a considerable share of the control power. At the beginning he interfered freely in impeachment cases. Later he was not allowed to do so, in theory. But since the appointment of the members of the Control Yuan was by his recommendation, he could not fail to have his influence felt in whatever acts the members might perform. Furthermore, his sole approval could authorize drastic action against officials and embarrassing recommendations to other branches of government as we shall later see.

The Vice-President of the Yuan deserved little notice. Like his counterpart in every other Yuan except the Executive Yuan, he occupied only a sinecure post.

The members of the Control Yuan, who used to number from 29 to 49 but were increased to a number between 54 and 74 at the time of the admission of the minor parties into the government in April 1947, were appointed in the same manner as the members of the Legislative Yuan. They were appointed by the President of the National Government on recommendation of the President of the Yuan. They had to be approved by the Political Council of the party before 1947, and, in the case of Kuomintang Party members, even after 1947. According to the revised Organic Law of the National Government of April 17, 1947, all of them had of course to receive their formal approval by the Council of State.

The members enjoyed certain privileges and immunities.[4] They were free from arrest or detention without consent of the Control Yuan, except when apprehended in *flagrante delicto*. They were not subject to dismissal, suspension, or reduction of salary except when expelled from the Kuomintang or convicted of criminal offenses or interdicted to hold property. They could not be charged with dereliction of duty except when proved to have received bribes or to have failed to impeach officials within their territorial jurisdiction[5] against whom definite charges based on generally known facts had been preferred by a citizen, or to have proposed impeachment on the basis of fabricated facts and at the instigation of some individual. These privileges and immunities of an extensive nature were meant to facilitate the unhampered exercise of their function and to protect them from intimidation from the outside.

The quality of the members of the Control Yuan was also not dissimilar to that of the members of the Legislative Yuan. Veterans and hangers-on of the Kuomintang and younger and better-trained students of law or of social sciences, also of the Kuomintang, were all to be found among the membership. They were of uneven quality and the majority of them were inclined to be resigned, to do little to unravel the uglier threads of the government, well knowing that they would not be allowed to go very far in that direction. After the admission of the minor parties, the influx of new members of even less competence and moral intrepidity caused further deterioration of the membership.

The members of the Control Yuan functioned for the whole nation collectively. But a number of them were also assigned to head regional organizations set up for the business of control in designated regions. They carried the title of Control Commissioner. The whole country was divided into seventeen regions. Usually two or more provinces constituted a region. Up to June 1947, for thirteen of these regions the Commissioner's offices were organized with a member of the Control Yuan as the Commissioner for each.

The division of the country into several regions for the purpose of insuring the good conduct of officials was a practice of the Ming and Ch'ing Dynasties. The new system might be said to be a continuation of the old. But there was a difference: during the monarchy, the viceroys and the governors were given both the titles and the duties of high censors. Being powerful personages in the provinces, they were in a position to perform their censorial duties effectively. Nobody was too high for them. Even the viceroy could be censored by the governor. But the control commissioner of recent years could hardly claim to be the equal, not to say the superior, of the high civil and military officials of the provinces. In rare cases when the commissioner, by age, seniority, public service, and exemplary personal conduct, earned great respect in the local communities, his authority perhaps stood unchallenged. But even there he felt hardly equal to bringing actions against the highest officials of the area. There the distinction between the one-power government of the emperor and the Five-Power government of the present day must be borne in mind. While the censors, deriving their power from the emperor, might prevail over all officials, their recent counterparts were only as powerful as the Control Yuan could make them.

The Control Yuan was made up of the President, the Vice-President, and the scores of members, and included the Ministry of Audit, the organization of which will be treated later in this chapter.[6]

Inspections and Investigations

Inspections and investigations as such do not necessarily become a part of the control power. Some power of investigation is evidently indispensable if the Control Yuan is to attend to its impeaching business properly, erring neither in the direction of indulgence nor of frivolous accusations. But for the Control Yuan to engage in systematic and periodic inquiries into the workings of the government or in country-wide inspection tours, independent of any pending case of impeachment, is tantamount to claiming for itself essentially political powers. Free and unhampered exercise of these powers could easily make the Control Yuan the most powerful organ of the government. The Legislative Yuan might legislate and the Executive Yuan might administer, but the Control Yuan would be in a position to tell them both whether or not they were doing things well. And if it gave unfavorable judgments, presumably it could and would bring about impeachments to get rid of the officials responsible. Had this happened, the government would be impotent indeed.

The inspection and investigation powers have never been clearly defined and the procedure of conducting the inspections and investigations has never rested on legislative acts.[7] Over the years of its existence, the Control Yuan, or, more exactly, its members have occasionally engaged in inspection tours and *ad hoc* investigations. To classify all these activities in terms of law would be difficult. Roughly, there is a distinction between inspection and investigation. The latter rests on law and is more specific in nature. The former is more grandiose in conception, but essentially vague in its meaning. It is doubtful whether an inspection by a member of the Control Yuan is any different from that undertaken by a private citizen capable of wielding some influence over public opinion.

The inspections which have thus far been undertaken may be divided into the regular ones by the Control Commissioners and the special ones by specially appointed commissions. The Control Commissioners among themselves were supposed to cover the whole country with regular and periodic inspections. Every year a Commissioner was required to spend between six and eight months in inspection tours in his own region, and was expected to visit no less than one-third of the districts therein. For those regions where the Control Commissioner's office was not organized, members of the Control Yuan might be temporarily dispatched to make a similar inspection. In 1947 the Control Yuan even proposed to extend its inspection overseas, treating Chinese citizens and Chinese officials alike at home and abroad. It was not done, because foreign exchange was not available.

These regular inspections were, theoretically at least, very extensive in nature. Nothing that touches on the activities of the government and on the living conditions of the people was beyond the purview of the inspector. There was no special emphasis beyond what the personal idiosyncrasies of the inspector or the peculiar conditions of the region might dictate. It was obvious that the usual inspecting personnel, consisting of the Control Commissioner and a few assistants, could not be in any way adequate to the task, considering the enormous area and the wide range of things covered. It was inevitable that with rare exceptions a tour of inspection degenerated into a tour of a visiting dignitary.

The special inspections thus far have all been concerned with the war and the subsequent demobilization. During the war there were two large-sized corps of inspectors, composed of members of the Central Supervisory Committee of the Kuomintang, of the national and provincial People's Political Councils, and of the Control Yuan itself. They covered an extensive ground, performed functions of a rather undefined nature, and were able to cause the removal of some abuses in the army and civilian ranks. At the time of the demobilization, the Control Yuan organized two inspection corps of its own to go into and inspect the areas recovered from the enemy. It also assigned other members to look into the various central administrations after they had been fully reëstablished in Nanking. None of these demobilization inspections was carried out with any thoroughness.

The apparent fruitlessness of the inspections is only partly due to the political impotence of the Control Yuan. The very idea that the Control Yuan should undertake large-scale inspections is perhaps preposterous. The Control Yuan neither legislates nor executes. It is not in a position to know how well the administration, including that of justice and of the civil service, is being conducted. Even if it were, the personnel required for the task would be enormous. But if it were given adequate personnel, it would then be far too powerful for the other branches of government to withstand. For them to survive, the inspection tours of the members of the Control Yuan have to be limited mainly to the business of impeachment.

The investigations are happily of a more limited scope. They are concerned with one or more particular officials or agencies against whom there have been complaints. But here again some features of the old censorial system reappear. The Control Yuan acts on news reports or even on hearsay as well as on a written complaint by an individual citizen. Hearsay is of course oftentimes unfounded. News reports can also be highly unreliable, since the law of libel is negligently administered in China and newspapers are practically immune from libel suits. Even the specific written complaints of private individuals are not too trustworthy.

Written complaints preferred by private persons are regulated by a decree of the Control Yuan.[8] Any individual may bring complaints in writing against any official. He is required to give his name and address, but is protected against possible reprisal by the injured party since the Control Yuan and the regional Control Commissioners are forbidden to divulge his identity. When a complaint is received, it is studied by a member of the Control Yuan or, if it is received at a regional office, by the Control Commissioner. And if it is found substantial enough to merit an investigation, action is started. The total number of petitions of complaint is great. Every year some three or four thousand are received, and about half of them are followed up with some kind of investigation.[9]

The investigations, whether occasioned by a written complaint or through other channels of information, may be undertaken directly by the officials of the Control Yuan or by the appropriate authorities on request of the Control Yuan. When a case is serious and likely to involve many people, the Control Yuan presumably would designate its own officials to conduct the investigation. In other cases, in which some irregularity or misunderstanding may have been the cause of complaint, the Control Yuan simply asks the responsible authority to make an explanation or the superior authority to conduct a preliminary investigation. Of the investigations occasioned by the written complaints of the people, only about one-tenth have been made by the Control Yuan officials directly.

Generally speaking, the investigations are concerned with a particular official or officials alleged to be delinquent. But in recent years the Control Yuan has on its own initiative plunged into some of the hottest political and administrative controversies of the day, for example, the Shanghai gold scandal and the Formosa riots, both in early 1947.[10] The gold scandal involved not only the fiscal policy of the government but also highly technical matters of the Shanghai business world. If the Control Yuan investigators had been assisted by technical counsel, they might have been able to get to the bottom of things. The employment of counsel not being a part of Chinese governmental practice, the investigators were clearly helpless and unequal to the task. Consequently, the reports on both cases were incompetent and generally unsatisfactory. All this means that the Control Yuan's meddling with cases such as these of great magnitude or intricacy is warranted neither by its constitutional position nor by its competence. Constitutionally, the whole government's position would be untenable if the Control Yuan meddled in matters of policy. Mechanically the Control Yuan has to be better and more extensively organized before it will have the *expertise* to do such investigating effectively.

Impeachment[11]

The Control Yuan has extensive powers of impeachment. It can impeach anybody in the public service, from the highest to the lowest, either for illegal acts or for dereliction of duty.

Any single member of the Control Yuan can propose an impeachment. The written complaint of a private individual or the information the member gets as a result of an inspection or investigation ordered on the initiative of the Control Yuan or from any other source can lead to impeachment proceedings. The proposal is considered by a committee of three members and the agreement of two is sufficient to establish the impeachment. If the committee by a majority vote decide against the impeachment, the case may be reconsidered by a second committee of five members. The majority decision of the second committee is final. Either the impeachment is dropped or it goes to one of the disciplinary organs for a decision of a more judicial nature.

Originally the impeachment committees were made up by the President of the Control Yuan. In order to prevent any personal element from entering into the impeachment action, the members of the Control Yuan are now assigned to these committees in an automatic order. Those who have a particular interest in the welfare of the person or persons impeached, such as relatives or friends, are ineligible to sit on the committees. But it is not to be supposed that the committees are careful and judicious bodies. They are too easily swayed by political considerations.

The Control Yuan may send inquiries to the disciplinary organs concerned, demanding to know the status of the cases there pending. But that is all. It has no way of forcing the actions of the latter, which are bound to proceed according to fixed rules highly judicial in nature. But in some cases urgent action is necessary in order to stop the official in question from persevering in whatever misconduct he may be accused of. In such a case the Control Yuan at the time of transmitting the impeachment to the disciplinary organ may simultaneously notify the superior of the accused to take immediate action on checking his misdeeds. That means that either the accused is suspended from office or an order is issued to him to desist from continuing the practice complained of. If the superior fails to do so, he is liable to disciplinary action when the accused, his subordinate, is found by the disciplinary organ to be guilty of the impeachment charges. Urgent measures of this kind are sometimes dutifully taken on request from the Control Yuan. But much depends on how the impeached official stands with his superior. If the superior sides with him, and also happens to feel politically strong enough to disregard the request of the Control Yuan, he will often refuse to take any action either to suspend the impeached subordinate from his post or to order him to suspend the measure in dispute. When that happens, the Control Yuan is powerless. It can only wait. The disciplinary organ is the only authority which is capable of removing the impeached official from office.

During the war the Control Yuan by a temporary decree [12] of the Supreme National Defense Council secured added authority to insist on urgent action being taken by the superior officials in such cases.

From February 1931 to the end of August 1946, 2175 officials in all were impeached and their cases referred to disciplinary organs for action. The majority of them were in general administration and almost nine-tenths were civilian officials. As for rank, it is natural that most of them should have belonged to the selected or recommended rank. But it is hard to believe that the figures adequately reflect the actual conditions of the Chinese bureaucracy. Take corruption, for instance. No one will believe that a significant portion of guilty officials has been impeached. Nor can one believe that military officials have been behaving much better than civilian, as the figures would lead one to think. The truth is that the Control Yuan has been able to perform its impeaching function only very haphazardly, and it has not felt equal to attacking the more firmly entrenched officials, especially those with the armed forces.

Since impeachment by the Control Yuan has only political but no legal effect on the official impeached, and since a considerable time is usually required by the disciplinary organ in passing a judgment on him, the Control Yuan likes to resort to publicity to make its impeachments effective. As soon as an impeachment is decided upon, and the documents in the case are transmitted to a disciplinary organ, the Control Yuan gives them out to the press. As the Chinese newspapers are fond of publicizing the bad acts of officialdom, if they can do so with impunity, the Control Yuan can naturally expect that these documents, incriminating as they must be, will be given prominence in the papers. Having done this, the Control Yuan will have already achieved the aim of its impeachment. The peculiar attitude of the Chinese people toward their officials, an attitude of instinctive fear and hostility toward incumbents of office, compounded with envy and admiration for their position, makes them especially prone to acclaim and believe any accusation that may be hurled against the officials. If, therefore, the impeachment is to condemn the person impeached, the mere publication of the impeachment documents is sufficient for the purpose. Whether the disciplinary organ finally resolves to punish or to absolve the impeached official becomes a matter of secondary importance.

Obviously, this practice of early and premature publication of documents related to an impeachment is open to grave objections. An innocent official against whom the Control Yuan has preferred charges either of illegal acts or of dereliction of duty stands hopelessly condemned in the eyes of the public once the charges are published. Even though he may later be cleared by the decision of a disciplinary organ, the unfavorable popular impression usually stands uncorrected. The danger of unfair accusation is all the greater, for the terms "illegal acts" and "dereliction of duty" are vague and ill defined and the members of the Control Yuan, like the old censors, easily abandon themselves to rhetorical flourishes and other exaggerations in writing out the act of impeachment. Under these conditions, the Control Yuan's contention that publicity is an effective weapon against the misconduct of the officials and should accompany an impeachment is not altogether justifiable.

There has been a protracted controversy between the Control Yuan and other branches of the government over the propriety or impropriety of the publication of impeachment proceedings by the Yuan. Publication hit the lowly and the high official alike. But it was not until the high ones were hit that a corrective measure was adopted. In 1934 a minister was impeached. It was a political impeachment, but studded with charges admissible under the Law of Impeachment. When the act of impeachment was published, there was a political upheaval. The Political Council of the party was obliged to adopt a general resolution forbidding the publication of either the act of impeachment or the defense of the impeached or any other news about the impeachment until the disciplinary organ in charge had rendered a decision on the case.[13] This prohibition incensed the Control Yuan and also discouraged it from readily bringing about impeachments, as it had hitherto done. It was never reconciled, and strove to have freedom of publication restored to it. Victory came when the Central Executive Committee in December 1941 again granted the Control Yuan the discretionary power to publish the relevant documents as soon as impeachment was established. Since May 1945, the Control Yuan has been again making public its impeachments. But this time it has made a more judicious use of publicity than it did before 1934, and no serious objection has been raised against the resurrected practice.

The basic factor affecting the proper functioning of impeachment is, however, neither the procedure of impeachment nor the matter of publication. Impeachments will not be effective or salutary unless the grounds for impeachment are well chosen. In a way, however indefinite and multifarious the grounds on which the censors of old could impeach officials, they were suited to the regime. The emperor then was above all officials. Impeachments were to enable him to exercise an effective control over all of them, prevent them from misconduct, and prod them to render better service. But there is no longer an all-mighty ruler like the emperor. Whatever be the theoretical and practical powers enjoyed by the party, by its Leader, or by its Political Council, the Yuan other than the Control Yuan do have certain independent powers. If these powers have been well used, obviously it would be bad for the Control Yuan to meddle with them. If it is contended that some of them could be better exercised by the Control Yuan, a clear delineation would still be necessary. Yet it is a fact that the impeaching powers of the Control Yuan oftentimes encroach upon the powers of the other Yuan without any clear delimitation being made.

Officials are impeached for either "illegal acts" or "dereliction of duty." All illegal acts, whether committed by a private individual or by an official, are punishable by the ordinary courts. In other words, the ordinary courts have jurisdiction over illegal acts of the officials as well as of private individuals. Having jurisdiction means also having the duty to prosecute the offenders. The question becomes: Who, the members of the Control Yuan or the procurators of the courts, are in a better position to detect the illegal acts of the officials? Who are better able to know whether an act is legal or not legal? Who are in a better position to effect detection? Granted that these questions cannot be answered always in favor of the procurators, the very smallness of the number of the Control Yuan members is a sufficient argument against the

Control Yuan's unlimited power of impeachment on the ground of "illegal acts." To be effective, the application of the law concerning "illegal acts" must be limited either to a small number of high officials or to some specific categories of official acts, so as to enable the Control Yuan members to concentrate on somebody and something of a special nature. The procurators of the ordinary courts might take care of the bulk of cases and the Control Yuan members might devote themselves to cases of a higher range where men of some political prominence and knowledge, which the Control Yuan members are supposed to possess, can be turned to best use. This might be a sensible division of work. But it is not done.

If impeachment for illegal acts has been the cause of confusion and has been ineffective, that for "dereliction of duty" is even more open to question. "Dereliction of duty" in countries with an established administrative jurisprudence may have definable meanings. But in the traditional Chinese sense it was only clear in the mind of the emperor. It varied with his whims or good sense. Having no responsibility for a sensible interpretation of the term, the censors had great latitude in accusing an official of dereliction of duty. Lamentably enough, the members of the Control Yuan of today behave as if they were censors serving an absolute monarch. Like the censors, they often charge an official with dereliction of duty, whenever they are of the opinion that the official concerned is not doing his duty well. This at once gives rise to immense political and legal difficulties. If the disciplinary organ absolves the impeached official, the Control Yuan feels slighted and cheated. But in order to sustain a case against the impeached official, the disciplinary organ is naturally constrained to establish some willful acts of commission or omission. To it, personal opinions or evaluations of an official act cannot form a basis of action against the person committing the act.

Dereliction of duty, strictly and legally interpreted, can be taken care of by an administrative tribunal. Interpreted broadly, it can be taken care of only by a superior in the administrative hierarchy, or, if committed by a political official, by a political body like the legislature. The superior knows best whether a subordinate official is or is not doing his job well. He can instruct and correct him and, if need be, initiate the proper process to have him removed. In the case of an official on the political level whose duty is to carry out policies of the government, only the legislator who enacts laws or other representatives of the people who have a right to pass on policies will be in a position to say whether a given policy is well carried out. In the former case, the Control Yuan lacks the intimate knowledge necessary to exercise control. In the latter case, it lacks the political power. The Control Yuan should not meddle in either type of case. The complaint which the Control Yuan has often raised against other branches of government for preventing it from impeaching high officials for dereliction of duty is really a reflection of its own failure to understand the modern system of government and to circumscribe its powers in harmony with the spirit of the system.

The Rectification Power

The power of rectification was considered by the Control Yuan a necessary complement to its impeachment power in time of emergency. As discussed above, the impeachment procedure is a long and complicated one and remedial actions cannot be easily and speedily realized. When the war began, the Control Yuan demanded a special kind of impeachment power which could produce more immediate results, and by the temporary decree of December 17, 1937, above referred to, it was given the so-called power of rectification.

According to this wartime decree, a member of the Control Yuan could bring a censure against an official whenever he deemed that the culpable act or acts of that official called for an immediate redress. Once this censure had been approved by the President of the Control Yuan, it was forwarded by the Yuan to the superior of the culpable official for action. In the case of a local official of the delegated rank, the Control Commissioner or a member of the Control Yuan on duty in the area concerned could submit the censure directly to the superior official simultaneously with its submission to the President of the Control Yuan. In either case, as soon as the superior official received the censure, he must at once discipline the official censured and effect other necessary remedies. If he was of the opinion that the censured official had done nothing wrong, he must report his reasons at once. Failure to act or to report without adequate reason justified the Control Yuan in immediately sending the documents of censure to a disciplinary organ as if the official concerned had been duly impeached. If the disciplinary organ adjudged the official guilty, his superior official who had failed to discipline him or had otherwise defended him was also subject to disciplinary action.

It can thus be seen that the effect of rectification was the same as impeachment. The only difference was that the procedure of rectification was much simpler and more direct.

For the period from January 1938 through August 1946, there were, in all, 884 cases of rectification, involving 1539 censured officials. These figures are considerably higher than those concerned with impeachment. The Control Yuan valued rectification as such an effective instrument of control that the wartime measure was explicitly adopted in the Constitution of 1946.[14]

The Warning Power

According to law, the Control Yuan has the power of impeachment and audit. Its powers of inspection and investigation are scarcely provided for by law. If they are lawful, they must be considered as implied in the impeaching power. The power of rectification may also be so construed. But the power of warning neither exists in the letter of the law nor is it implied by law.

However, during the war, following the temporary decree of the Supreme National Defense Council governing the exercise of the control power in wartime, the Control Yuan members gained the right to suggest improvements or reforms in the administration. Whenever an ordinary member or a Control Commissioner in the course of his inspection or investigation or reading over the petitions of private individuals sees something wrong or otherwise unsatisfactory in a government agency, he can, on approval by the President of the Control Yuan, propose to a superior agency either general reforms or specific corrections. The superior agency is, according to the above-mentioned ordinance, bound to effect the reforms or corrections suggested. No sanctions were provided by the ordinance in case of its refusal. Presumably the Control Yuan could bring an impeachment if the suggestions of its members were not heeded. In this sense, the proposals or suggestions might amount to a real warning. From 1938 through August 1946, 981 such proposals were forwarded to the various agencies of government. As many as 127 were concerned with military affairs. On paper this warning power seems to be an all-pervasive one. Since the decree in question has not been repealed, the Control Yuan evidently still enjoys the power of warning.

The possession of the power of warning which the Control Yuan prefers to term "the power of suggestion" is an unwarranted expansion of the control power. It may be in harmony with the old concept of the censorial power, but it is hardly permissible in the Five Yuan frame of government. If the Control Yuan is not representative of the people, it cannot exercise that power effectively, as past experiences have shown. If it becomes representative, the Legislative Yuan will presumably also have become representative. For the Control Yuan to continue wielding that power would put an undue burden on the Executive Yuan which has necessarily to be responsible also to the criticisms of the Legislative Yuan. The problem for the Control Yuan therefore is how to exercise effectively the powers it should have rather than to have too many powers which it cannot effectively exercise.

Audit [15]

Government auditing is the function of the Ministry of Audit. As in the countries of continental Europe and Japan, there used to be under the Peking regime a Court of Audit placed directly under the President of the Republic and independent of the administrative departments. It accomplished very little as there were then neither budgets to speak of nor a well-ordered financial administration. When the National Government began to function in Nanking, a similar Court of Audit was ordered to be reëstablished. Before it was organized, the Five Yuan Government had come into being and the Control

Yuan claimed audit as falling within its jurisdiction. So, instead, the Ministry of Audit was set up.

The Ministry of Audit is organized [16] like any other ministry headed by a minister, two vice-ministers, and the usual staff of secretaries and councilors. But unlike them, its principal staff consists of the auditors, assistant auditors, and inspectors, and not of the ordinary run of service directors, section chiefs, and other minor officials.

The auditors and assistant auditors are grouped together into three corps, one for pre-auditing, another for post-auditing, and the third for inspection. They all have to be trained experts and their tenure is protected by law. In fact, most of the auditors have been competent and honorable persons. They can be favorably compared to any other part of the civil service, including the judicial officials. If they are oftentimes spoken of disparagingly in Chinese political circles, they are perhaps undeservedly shouldering the blame for the unrealistic nature of their function.

In the performance of their function, the auditors naturally divide the business among themselves and each is assisted by a number of assistant auditors and inspectors. Important questions, both of fact and of law, are discussed and resolved by the assembly of auditors, presided over by the Minister of Audit.

The accounts of the central government are audited by the Ministry directly. To facilitate auditing on the spot, the Ministry has established branch offices in most of the provincial governments. In some of the corporations and special administrations of the central government, such as the railways and the state-owned China Merchants' Steam Navigation Company, branch offices of varying size have also been established. These branch auditing establishments correspond very closely to the budgetary and personnel establishments attached to the central departments and local governments. All of them serve as instruments of intensified central control.

The functions of the Ministry of Audit can be divided into three categories, pre-auditing, post-auditing, and inspection. Pre-auditing is meaningless unless there is a fixed budget and the auditors are given the authority to supervise the general execution of the budget, including the supplementary grants. The Ministry of Audit has this power of supervision. But since in the past there have rarely been budgets enacted according to a fixed procedure and in due time, the supervision cannot be effectively executed. The Ministry has had to abide by the specific grants which the highest organ of the government (for the duration of the war generally the Supreme National Defense Council) might make from time to time. The Ministry of Audit does claim that insofar as there are budgetary allocations to be observed, it strives to see to it that the spending departments do not overrun the limits of the sums allocated or reserve funds allowed.

The warrants for both receipts and disbursements, in order to be valid, must have prior endorsement by the Ministry of Audit. This is also a requirement in pre-auditing, as it serves to deter the collecting and disbursing agencies, generally the Ministry of Finance and its subordinate officials, from loosely administering the funds. The necessary previous endorsement of an independent authority reminds them of their duty to abide by the principles embodied in the budget-planning and the specific budgetary provisions concerning revenue and expenditure. Not only are they not allowed to collect or disburse outside of the budget, but they are also obliged to conform to whatever considerations of economy may have been circularized by the government. Because of the inflation and the consequent dislocation of Chinese finance, the Ministry of Audit has in late years been less and less able to insist on all warrants being previously endorsed. For the last two years or so, the warrants it has endorsed have amounted to only a small part of the total revenue and an even smaller part of the total expenditure.

Post-auditing by the Ministry of Audit consists of the audit of the government accounts and of the profit and loss accounts of the government concerns. The work has not been satisfactorily performed, largely because of the inability of the Ministry to lay its hands on the records of military expenditures and also its tendency to emphasize the form more than the substance of the vouchers and bills and the like that may be attached to the accounts, as has been discussed earlier.

Another post-auditing operation is to approve the actual accounts submitted in settlement of the fiscal year.[17]

The third category of functions are those of inspection. The auditing authorities may at any time demand to inspect any operating department to see the cash funds, bonds, and other financial documents that may be in its possession. The material owned by a government agency is also open to inspection. The auditing authorities make a note of depreciation and in case of neglect on the part of the officials responsible for custody they may propose remedies. The government agencies, when inviting bids for contracts or having auctions, must also invite representatives of the auditing authorities to be present. Besides, the auditing authorities, whenever they like, may question any government agency in connnection with fiscal matters. This last is a general authorization purported to facilitate the work of the auditors.

From the above, the conclusion can be readily drawn that the Ministry of Audit is more than a purely auditing organ. In many ways, it is conceived as a part of the control power or as an effective instrument to add substance to that power. Since no government activities and departments can be dissociated from finance, an effective anterior and posterior control of the fiscal operations is in itself an exercise of the control power. But there is another aspect. Auditing and inspection presumably would lead to the unearthing of various kinds of corruption, abuses, and inefficiency. These findings are presumably to furnish material for impeachment actions. The theory is as convincing as the system is elaborate. But when no real budget is in existence, and the Ministry of Audit is not allowed to touch on the most vital part of the expenditure, and the members of the Control Yuan do their impeaching loosely but not fearlessly, the theory is lost and the system does not work.

XIX

THE PEOPLE'S POLITICAL COUNCIL

The National Government of the Kuomintang was a government of tutelage. The Kuomintang never considered it necessary to have the representatives of the people participate in it. During the war and immediately afterwards an institution called the People's Political Council was maintained, but the essential nature of the tutelage was by no means affected by its existence. There was no function which the government could not perform without its intercession; nor could it compel the government to heed its voice. In fact, the Council was never incorporated into the government. The Organic Law of the National Government might undergo revisions, but the People's Political Council was not once mentioned in the successive texts of that Law.

The Question of a People's Assembly for the Period of Tutelage

Soon after the Kuomintang had gained control of the whole country in 1928, the dispute arose as to whether there should be a representative body for the Period of Tutelage. Those who favored the establishment of such a body based their argument on Sun Yat-sen's *Fundamentals of National Reconstruction*, in which he had advocated the election by those *hsien* which had attained self-government of one representative each to form a people's assembly. Sun Yat-sen did not explicitly say whether such an assembly was to be only for the particular province or for the nation as a whole, whether there should be such assemblies for both the individual provinces and the nation. A reasonable interpretation would be for both the nation and each province to have an assembly. The majority of the leaders of the Kuomintang, however, decided that the government of tutelage should not have such a body and the Tutelage Constitution of 1931 made no provision for it.

The demand for a representative body was not thereby silenced. Every time there was a crisis, domestic or external, a clamor arose for some form of popular participation in government. The Japanese seizure of Mukden and the surrounding country in 1931 was the occasion for an especially loud and insistent clamor. The party yielded to public opinion by agreeing to call an Emergency Conference [1] and also to have half of the members of the Legislative and Control Yuan elected by the people.[2]

The Emergency Conference was convened in April 1932 at the then emergency capital of Loyang. As its members were all appointed by the government, it could hardly be considered a representative body. The concession to the general public was a meager one. The non-party members appointed to the Conference were independents friendly to the party; the other parties then still underground or outlawed were hardly represented. But even the exclusion of opposition parties did not prevent the Conference from calling on the government to establish a people's assembly before October 10 of the same year.

To this demand for a representative assembly the party's reaction was both unrealistic and unwise. Instead of complying with the demand and relying on national support for a general resistance against the invader, the party adopted an extravagant program which it had perhaps little intention and still less determination of fulfilling. At a plenary session in December 1932, the Central Executive Committee of the party resolved to call the Constituent National Assembly in March 1935, and also a People's Political Council before the end of 1933 to prepare the country for a democratic government. Having passed these generous resolutions the party ordered repealed those provisions in the Organic Law of the National Government relating to the election of a half of the Legislative and Control Yuan members.

The Resolutions of December 1932 were never carried out. In March 1933, only four months after the full body of the Central Executive Committee had made its solemn decisions, the Standing Committee of the same body made a new and contrary decision. Arguing that the National Assembly as provided for in the *Fundamentals of National Reconstruction* could not be readied by 1935 since local self-government could not be expected to be completed that year, it decided to call an extraordinary Congress of the Party in July 1933 to consider the question whether, in view of the popular demand, the National Assembly should not be convened earlier without regard to the completion of local self-government. It further decided that the People's Political Council should be left to the Congress to pass upon. If the Congress of the Party should favor an early convening of the National Assembly, it would then be possible to dispense with the Council.

Thus there was no People's Political Council in 1933. The Party Congress was postponed and postponed again. It did not meet until November of 1935. When it did meet, it resolved to call the National Assembly the following year, and to omit the transitional organ of the Council. The repeated demands for, and the equally repeated promises of, a representative body all came to naught. Those who made the demand were disillusioned, for they well knew that theirs was not an excessive demand; they only wanted a consultative body to lead the country gradually to a democratic form of government. Those who made the promises were too interested in the monopoly of political power to realize the effect of unredeemed promises on their own prestige. The disillusionment on the one hand and the loss of prestige on the other indeed plagued the nation until it was cast into a different mood by the war in 1937.

Establishment and Evolution of the Council

The year 1937 witnessed the outbreak of the war and the emergence of a kind of united front. The Kuomintang, through its Central Political Council, ordered the setting up of a National Defense Advisory Council to advise the government and to hear reports from the government.[3] Leaders of the erstwhile opposition parties as well as independent leaders, all together twenty-four in number, were invited by the government to serve on the council. The chairman and vice-chairman of the Supreme National Defense Council acted as the chairman and vice-chairman of the Advisory Council, and provided a close link between the leaders of the Kuomintang on the one hand and those of the non-Kuomintang elements on the other.

Although the Advisory Council was a purely advisory body and had no authority to compel the Kuomintang government to do anything against its will, its service and influence were considerable. It served as the symbol of national unity. It was able to rally all elements of the country for the task of the war. It was also able to alleviate the rigors of one-party government. Its success was due to several factors. The onslaught of a foreign invasion had the effect of striking a patriotic chord in the heart of every man, whatever his political bias might have been. The body was small, the members all had a high sense of responsibility and sacred trust. The government of the Kuomintang, assured of national support, was willing to admit the council into its confidence. The responsible ministers of the government went before the council to air their woes and to seek counsel and encouragement. Altogether, the government and the council collaborated closely and with mutual understanding.

The smallness of the Advisory Council, while in itself conducive to quick action and confident exchange of views and opinions, was open to one serious objection. Those Kuomintang aspirants as well as important members of other parties and non-party leaders, who had been left outside, demanded to be admitted. At first the Supreme National Defense Council decided to expand the Advisory Council and to increase its membership to seventy-five. This plan had it been realized would have given an overwhelming majority to the Kuomintang.[4] The other parties which had been enjoying some real influence in the restricted council were naturally averse to seeing themselves reduced to a minority. They demanded instead an assembly, with a larger membership. Their idea was that an assembly would have more real powers and would give them more adequate representation.

Finally, the Extraordinary Congress of the Kuomintang, meeting in March 1938, resolved that for the purpose of facilitating the conduct of the war, a representative body should be instituted. Subsequently, the Central Executive Committee decided that that representative body should be none other than the People's Political Council, an institution the name of which had been tossed about in the previous years, and the nature of which was understood to be only advisory. If it can be said that nomenclature is something important in Chinese political life, the resort to the name the "People's Political Council" was destined forever to settle the fortunes of the organ about to be established.

The first People's Political Council was convened on July 7, 1938, and the last terminated on March 28, 1948, on the eve of the convening of the National Assembly under the Constitution of 1946. During the decade of its existence, there were four Councils in all.

As time went on, increasing efforts were made by the Kuomintang to control the council, and there was also a mounting desire on the part of its members to have seats in the council. As the Kuomintang control increased, the proportionate strength of the other parties decreased. Beginning in March 1941, at the first session of the Second Council, the bulk of the communist members abstained, leaving only one or two in attendance. Even this sort of symbolic attendance was discontinued after 1945.

The increase of membership was accompanied by the extension of the elective principle and the increase of the powers of the council. Changes, however, were nominal. Election generally meant tighter control by the party machine in the provinces. Whatever new powers were granted, they were seldom visualized as means of compelling the government to be more responsive to the desires of the general public. The members might indulge in personal attacks on the leading officials of the government, both central and local, but those attacks produced little effect on the conduct of the government. In its role as a kind of check and balance of the Kuomintang Government, the council grew steadily weaker even as its powers became more numerous and its membership larger. Altogether, from the First to the Fourth, the People's Political Council grew progressively impotent and disappointing.

The Membership of the Council

There were 200 members in the First and 240 in the Second and Third Councils. In the Fourth Council the number was at first 290 but was increased to 362 in 1947.[5] The increase of the Second over the First was dictated by the necessity of giving more adequate representation to notable individuals outside the government, including both critics and supporters of the regime. The three increases at the outset of and during the term of the Fourth Council were necessitated in succession by the demand for increased representation of the provinces, by the restoration to China of Formosa and the provinces of the Northeast after the Japanese surrender, and by the participation of the minor parties in the government.

From the very beginning of the council's life, the members were divided into four categories, representing (1) the provinces (and municipalities), (2) Mongolia and Tibet, (3) the Chinese overseas, and (4) individuals noted for their leadership in educational and business activities or noted for their political endeavors.

The second and third categories were of little importance. There were only six for each category in the first two councils, and eight in the other two councils. Twice as many candidates as the number of members allotted were nominated respectively by the Mongolian and Tibetan Affairs Commission, and Overseas Chinese Affairs Commission; the members were selected and finally approved by the Central Executive Committee of the Kuomintang or a committee which it might designate for the purpose. The members naturally were Mongolians and Tibetans or overseas Chinese, but they did not necessarily enjoy a great influence among their own peoples. Many Mongolian members of the council had resided elsewhere and lost contact with the Mongols of Mongolia.

The first and fourth categories formed the bulk of the council membership. The number of the first category was raised from the original 88 to 90, to 164 and finally to 199 at the beginning of the Fourth Council. With the restoration of the lost provinces in 1946 and with increased representation given to the minor parties in 1947, the number was further raised to 229. At the First Council, the members of the first category were selected under an intricate procedure. For every member, the government and party organization of the province concerned nominated two candidates, and the Supreme National Defense Council also nominated two. The Central Executive Committee or a committee designated by it did the final choosing.

Beginning from the Second Council, the members of the first category were elected by the Provincial Political Council. But the election was by no means a free one. The interplay of the factional politics of the Kuomintang was at its worst in the process of the election. The Provincial Councils were of course Kuomintang dominated. The Central Executive Committee of the party generally required these councils to elect only from a list of candidates previously approved by it, which usually tried to give fairer or less unfair representation to the desirable non-Kuomintang elements of the country.

But the provincial party organization was often in the hands of a party faction and was only interested in getting its own men elected. Whatever be the merits or demerits of an indirect election, the results of the elections by these Provincial Councils, judged by the caliber of the men who secured election, were unsatisfactory. The men were usually strongly partisan or factional in attitude and devoid of a sense of responsibility to the interests of the nation as distinguished from those of their own localities.

Not a small portion of the members of the first category were, however, appointed and continued to be appointed up to the very last. Some provinces were held by the invader or by the communists. Others, although under the control of the government, never had a Provincial Political Council in existence. For these provinces, appointment of representatives by the central party organization continued to take the place of election by the Provincial Political Council. This gave the party a somewhat greater freedom of selection, though the candidates had to be men from the provinces concerned.

Members of the fourth category were always appointed. They numbered 100 out of a total of 200 in the First Council, and 138 out of a total of 240 in the Second. But the number dropped to 60 in the Third and increased to only 75 in the Fourth. By May 1947 it was still only 119 out of a total of 362. The reduction was the direct result of the increase of the elected members.

For every member of the fourth category, the Supreme National Defense Council nominated two candidates, from whom the Central Executive Committee made the final choice. In practice, the choice was made from a large list of claimants, first by an all-powerful committee of the Supreme National Defense Council, and finally by the Leader of the Party, who was also the Chairman of the Defense Council. During the first years there was a conscientious effort by the party to name well-known leaders of the country, regardless of their political proclivities. Unlike the members of the other categories, their choice was not contingent upon considerations of locality. The party leaders, when or if they cared to enlist the support of a man of caliber, could make him a member of the People's Political Council without fear of being thwarted by the objections or manipulations of the local party machine. In fact, this was done at the beginning. But, as time went on, there was increasing reluctance to have such persons represented on the council.

As has been described, the domination of the Kuomintang increased with the successive councils. But that domination was an irresponsible one. By law and party resolutions respectively, the officials of the government and the members of the Central Executive and Supervisory Committees were barred from standing for election or nomination as members of the People's Political Council. Thus, the higher leaders of the Kuomintang did not sit in the council. Those minor leaders who were there often acted with little sense of responsibility for the real interest of the party and still less for that of the nation.[6]

As for the non-Kuomintang members of the council, a distinction should be drawn between the independents and the adherents of a party. The communists frequently abstained. When they were present, they often remained silent except on matters which they considered to be of vital importance. The representatives of the other parties were on the whole timid and incoherent. They seemed to be more interested in getting the status of their parties established than in compelling the Kuomintang government to adopt their policies, if any. In matters of political liberty, their voice was feeble and faintly raised. The independents, who adhered to no political party or group, were usually either supporters of the regime or interested in the promotion of their own interests, be they cultural, economic, or particularist. Few of them were actually interested in politics.

As to the occupational distribution of the members, there was a predominance of those who had for years done nothing but live on government or party jobs. These people were often unable to think in terms of public interest. They were generally more concerned with the advancement of their own personal political interest. This was true of the partisan adherents of all parties, the minor ones as well as the Kuomintang.

Education was the second dominant profession. Some 15 per cent of all the members were teachers or educational administrators. At one time there was hope that this group might become politically influential and throw their influence on the side of enlightenment and progress. Unfortunately, cohesion was not a marked virtue among them and interest in personal advancement was rarely forgotten. As a rule they manifested little genuine independence, especially if such independence might cause them some personal inconvenience.

The liberal professions were not well represented. Most of the professionals who became members of the council usually had party affiliations and their attitude was seldom distinguishable from the partisan adherents of the parties.

In general, the members were not effective as representatives of the people at large, though most of them were assiduous in working for the narrower interests of the parties to which they belonged. To do them justice, that weakness was no reflection on them as persons. It was perhaps more a reflection on the political leadership of the Kuomintang tutelage, for that leadership had given rise to the kind of political standard which limited the social and political horizons of the members of the council.

The term of the members was, according to the law, always one year, subject to indefinite extension, whenever deemed necessary by the National Government. It was extended almost without exception. It was the custom to prolong the term if, at the time of the expiration, the government had not yet been able to order the election or otherwise complete the selection of the succeeding council. Furthermore, the government was always reluctant to remove an incumbent from office. Of the 200 members of the First Council, some 110 were thus continued up to the very last council. Only those who made themselves ineligible by holding appointive offices were discontinued. However, a few severe critics of the regime were also dropped either by the government or by their resigning as a protest against the government.

THE ORGANIZATION AND PROCEDURE OF THE COUNCIL

A Speaker and a Vice-Speaker presided over the meetings of the council during the First Council. Later a Presidium, first of five members, subsequently expanded to seven, was substituted. Wang Ching-wei, Vice-Chairman of the Supreme National Defense Council, was the first Speaker. When he left the government on his way to puppetdom, Chiang Kai-shek, the Chairman of the Defense Council, took up the Speakership. That a responsible leader of the Defense Council should concurrently be the Speaker of the People's Political Council was a continuation of the previous practice of having the Kuomintang's Supreme National Defense Council and the other parties' National Defense Advisory Council linked together in the person of one and the same presiding officer. The Vice-Speaker of the People's Political Council was, however, designated by the Central Executive Committee from among the members of the council.

The Presidium, whether of five or of seven, was elected by members of the council. Non-members were also eligible. This was the only way to secure the election of some responsible leaders of the party and government, since by law such leaders were disqualified to be members. Chiang Kai-shek continued to be elected to the Presidium until his assumption of the presidency of the National Government in September 1943.

The Speaker and the Vice-Speaker and later the members of the Presidium took turns presiding over the meetings of the council. The presiding officer naturally enjoyed the power of recognition. But the other two important powers, the power of fixing the agenda and that of appointing the chairmen of the committees, were in the beginning exercised solely by the Speaker and later in fact by the leaders of the government.

The Speaker or the Presidium was assisted by a large secretarial staff headed by a secretary-general who was invariably a party member of high rank. In theory the secretariat of an assembly should have no political significance whatsoever. Its function is merely to provide an administrative machinery for the assembly to which it is attached. The principal secretary may have the duty of advising the presiding officer on matters of parliamentary law, and that is all. But the practice of having powerful secretaries-general was so common with the Kuomintang regime that the secretary-general of the People's Political Council was also a powerful political figure in his own right. Next to the Speaker or the Kuomintang chiefs on the Presidium, he was easily the most powerful personage of the council. He shared much of the power that belonged to the Speaker or the Presidium.

The procedure of the People's Political Council was partly provided for in the Organic Articles and partly by the Rules of the Procedure of the People's Political Council and Sun Yat-sen's *Parliamentary Law*. In the beginning the council was to have quarterly sessions of ten days each. After April 28, 1939, the stipulated sessions became semiannual. On April 5, 1944 the length of the session was extended to fourteen days. The government had the right to extend the session or to convene an extraordinary session. Neither of these rights were of course utilized. The main concern of the government, during the decade of the council's existence, was to avoid its convening. Thus the stipulated sessions were never as promptly called as the law provided.[7]

During the sessions the council usually sat both mornings and afternoons, except when its committees were having meetings. The plenary meetings were used either to hear reports from the ministers or to discuss measures. These meetings were, however, necessarily few in number, too few indeed to be adequate for the purposes for which the council was established. Even in a fourteen-day session there might not be more than twenty half-day sittings. The other half days were spent in committee meetings, ceremonies, or holiday recesses. No matter how crowded the agenda might be, the government consistently refused to have the stipulated duration of the session prolonged.

The standing committees of the council were few in number. There were, during the first three councils, only five such committees, in charge of military affairs, foreign affairs, interior, finance and economics, and education and culture, respectively. Besides these standing committees, special committees might be and were set up, from time to time. In fact, two special committees, one on prices and the other on judicial administration and relief, usually appointed by the earlier councils, became practically standing committees during the Third and Fourth Councils. However, the government majority was always reluctant to allow other special committees to set up, as it was apprehensive lest such committees be likely to create more hostility than otherwise toward the government.

The committees, both standing and special, were not well organized. Members of the council were free to make their own choice of committee assignments. It often happened that some committees were overcrowded while others were disproportionately small. Generally a member might belong to only one of the standing committees. The membership of a special committee naturally included those who moved for its creation, but the Speaker or the Presidium might ask some other members to serve on it. For each committee there were usually three cochairmen, all designated by the Speaker or the Presidium. The Kuomintang always had a faithful member as one of the chairmen, and this Kuomintang chairman was invariably able to have the committee proceedings well in hand. To preserve the appearance of multiparty coöperation a member of the other parties was usually designated to be one of the three.

The Resident Committee, a recess committee, was in a class by itself. It was a delegation of the council. At first it was composed of twenty-five and later of thirty-one members, elected by ballot by the members of the council at the last sitting of each session. The government majority was usually careful in securing representatives of the other parties elected to the committee. The Speaker and Vice-Speaker or later the members of the Presidium were ex officio and additional members.

The Resident Committee usually met once every two weeks throughout the recess of the council and enjoyed practically all the powers granted the council itself.[8] In addition, it was to promote the carrying out of the resolutions passed by the council. At the beginning of the ensuing session, the committee made a report of its work and its life was at an end.

The Resident Committee was thus the People's Political Council in miniature and somewhat made up for the latter's ineffectiveness resulting from its brief and infrequent sessions. But obviously the committee could not be expected to gain for the council a political stature which the council itself failed to gain.

The daily sittings of the council, except when engaged in hearing the reports of the ministers and other government leaders and the questions put to them, ran on a fixed pattern. Proposals and other substantive motions having usually been first referred to the committees, the plenary sitting was to hear the committee reports and to act upon them. On these reports as well as on other incidental business, the tendency of the members was to do more talking than the shortness of the session would permit, while that of the Speaker or the Presidium, representing the government, was to allow as little debate as it could. Most of the wranglings taking place on the floor were between the members, especially non-Kuomintang ones, on the one hand, and the presiding officer on the other. It was therefore interesting to observe Chiang Kai-shek, when he was presiding, sweep aside all technicalities of parliamentary procedure and cut short all kinds of parliamentary wranglings in a military fashion.

The debates of the council on matters other than procedural were as a rule not attractive. There were instances of eloquence and more of declamation. But sustained debates on the merits of a question were rare, partly due to the lack of time allowed and partly due to the absence of a strong minority. Generally the presiding officer also lacked the skill to recognize the speakers in a proper order and so to guide the debates as to rule out the irrelevant talks.

The voting could be by show of hands, by rising, or by ballot. The first method was the most commonly used, the second only very rarely, and the third never. The absence of any kind of a recorded vote was easily explained by the fact that the decisions of the council had little binding force on the government, as will be discussed a little later in this chapter.

The Powers of the Council

When it began in 1938, the People's Political Council had the following powers: (1) "For the duration of the War, the Government shall submit to the People's Political Council for approval all important policy plans, domestic and foreign, before they are put into execution." (2) "The People's Political Council may make proposals to the Government." (3) "The People's Political Council shall have the power to hear the reports from the Government on its several administrations and to put interpellations to the Government." Towards its end, it had received two more powers: (4) "In preparing the budget the Government shall before it becomes final, submit it to the People's Political Council or its Resident Committee for preliminary examination." (5) In addition, the council had some powers of investigation.[9]

The power to pass on the government's important domestic and external measures was on the face of it a sweeping one. But there were two jokers, one arising out of the vagueness of the language of the law, the other being an explicit proviso. The term "important policy plans" could be differently interpreted. It might include any concrete measure of importance or it might only signify what the government consented to style "policy plans," such as the Kuomintang government was in the habit of adopting at the beginning of every year. The government seldom failed to submit its annual "policy plans" to the council, it is true, but the "policy plans" were no more than policy planks. The numerous items, running generally to about a hundred, were generally vague and often meaningless. For instance, there might be an item proclaiming the government's determination to work for the closest harmony with the Allied Powers or an item emphasizing the desirability of removing illiteracy. To approve these items meant no more than approving a man's professed intention to do good. To be sure, some items were more concrete and approval of an item, or a proposal suggesting an alternative would compel the government to take a definite action or one even at variance with its original intention. That, however, was obviated by the fact that the government enjoyed the sole power of legislation.

The policy plans, approved by the council with or without amendments, were not automatically in force. They had to be finally passed by the Supreme National Defense Council and then referred by it to the proper departments of government which in turn wrote the necessary statutes or decrees providing for their execution. The government was therefore the ultimate authority to give definite shape to the vague plans. In so doing, it could alter the plans freely.

There was finally a sweeping proviso embodied in the same provision which empowered the council to pass on the important policy plans of the government. In case of emergency, the Chairman of the Supreme National Defense Council could, according to the Organic Articles of the Defense Council, resort to appropriate actions by means of decrees, and he was not bound to submit the policy plans to the People's Political Council, nor if and when they had been approved by it, to order the departments concerned to execute them. This proviso left the Supreme National Defense Council with complete liberty to ignore the People's Political Council as far as the so-called "policy plans" were concerned.

The second power of the People's Political Council, namely, to make proposals to the government, was equally empty. The People's Political Council might propose, but the Supreme National Defense Council was not obliged to accept. The proposals turned out by each session were indeed numerous. In the earlier sessions when the total membership was around 200 and the length of the session was ten days, usually around 100 proposals were submitted and adopted. In the later sessions when the membership rose to 300 or over and the sessions lasted a fortnight, the number of proposals became as high as 400 and more. The members proposed lightly and the council acted indulgently. Seldom were proposals flatly negatived by the council. For the Supreme National Defense Council to have accepted and honestly carried out many of these proposals would indeed have been both unwise and impracticable.

Any member of the People's Political Council had the right to submit a proposal if he could secure twenty, later reduced to five, other members to countersign it. The reduction in the number of countersignatures required was not meant to encourage the submission of proposals, but was a concession to the minor parties who had often had difficulties in securing the required number of countersignatures to some of the more controversial proposals they submitted. But the reduction did result in the submission of many more proposals in the last years of the council, so many that there was less and less adequate discussion even in the committees.

The proposals were not in the nature or form of a bill. Usually there were long-winded explanations but the suggested remedies or recommendations were often brief and loosely worded. Some of the proposals were subjected to much criticism in the committees and were amended. The committees sometimes even went so far as to recommend the tabling of some of the most objectionable proposals, either from the point of view of merit, or from that of politics as seen by the majority. But such drastic steps were taken infrequently. What the committees recommended were with rare exceptions accepted by the council in plenary session. This explains why nine-tenths of all proposals went through the council and were later forwarded to the Supreme National Defense Council.

The proposals covered practically every field of government action. They were not infrequently in conflict with each other. The provincial representatives who were in the great majority during the last two councils were especially prone to submit proposals of a local nature, the granting of special relief, for example, or the opening up of highways in a certain area. The signs of logrolling were discernible in the last councils. If all proposals had been carried out, the total expenditure would have run to fantastic figures. The members of the council did not care. They know that their proposals would very likely not be acted upon by the government. What they cared about was a little publicity for themselves and a talking point for their constituents. The government did not care either, for, if it could ignore the proposals after the council had adjourned, why should it bother to argue with the members of the council and thereby incur their displeasure? It was only those proposals which implied a personal condemnation that the government leaders concerned had to make an effort to defeat or tone down.

But this does not mean, however, that the Supreme National Defense Council would turn down outright the proposals it did not like. On the contrary, it preferred to appear to be accepting all the proposals sent to it by the council. Most of the proposals were innocuous. The Defense Council could conveniently instruct the appropriate government departments to have them acted upon. For instance, a proposal to have an agricultural college established somewhere would thus be referred to the Ministry of Education for action. If the college was organized, well and good. If the ministry raised difficulties, it could present such difficulties to the Defense Council and the latter could report back to the People's Political Council that it had faithfully tried to carry out the original proposal.

On measures of a more general nature the Defense Council could usually claim that they were either being acted upon already or were under consideration. For instance, the People's Political Council might propose that there should be a greater effort to make full use of Lend-Lease. The Defense Council in this case could say that it had been making the effort and would continue to do so. Even with regard to very strongly worded criticisms, the Defense Council might still laud the intentions of the proposal, only to contend that the time was not yet opportune, or plead other obvious difficulties for reform. In a word, the Supreme National Defense Council could omit doing anything which it was not inclined to do without appearing to have said a single "no" to the proposals of the People's Political Council.

The third power, that of the council to hear the reports from and to put interpellations to the government, was not intended to be of a serious nature, but, as it developed, it became the most significant of all the powers. The reports were both written and oral. The former came from all the Five Yuan, and, in the case of the Executive Yuan, from each of its ministries and commissions. Few of these reports could be said to have contained all the truth and nothing but the truth. In fact, truths were often not in the report; instead a great deal of apologia, exaggeration, or irrelevant figures were to be found there.

Only the ministers and the commission chairmen of the Executive Yuan made supplementary oral reports. Some of these officials did creditably but the majority of them gave sorry performances. It was generally after and against the oral reports that questions were raised.

The questions or interpellations were also of two kinds, oral and written. On receiving these questions, the ministers and other responsible officials of the government could have the choice of replying in writing or in person or not replying at all. To not reply at all was considered discourteous and could serve to inflame the temper of the council. The written reply was considered as a sign of diffidence and, as time went on, few ministers could afford to insist on giving only written replies and not to venture oral ones.

It was the oral altercations between a member of the council and a minister that created some of the most spirited scenes during the otherwise dry and sterile proceedings of the council. Those ministers who were unpopular or considered incompetent were especially open to attack and castigation. When an oral questioning was on, it was not unusual to see the minister concerned present on the floor of the council in a jittery mood although he might be flanked with hosts of his subordinates in anticipation of questions from the floor. Those were ugly scenes indeed, with the interpellators sparing no effort to embarrass the ministers and the ministers having little confidence to help them maintain a desirable serenity.

Did these questions or interpellations produce a salutary effect on the government? To the extent that the ministers were invariably more susceptible to public opinion during or immediately before a council session, the questions seem to have been a healthy check on the government. But, however badly a particular minister might have acquitted himself during the question-and-answer encounter, he was never dismissed nor did he even lose prestige. Furthermore, the members of the council seldom manifested a uniform courage in cornering the ministers with devastating questions. Some of the most strongly entrenched ministers, either because of their control of the armed forces or of equally powerful and brutal elements, were seldom subjected to embarrassing questions. The members usually chose as their victims those officials who lacked such forces behind them. In so discriminating, the kind of moral force which could have been behind their crusade against delinquent ministers was to a considerable extent lacking. Thus the actual effect of the interpellating power of the People's Political Council was more like that which was produced by the well-meaning but ill-considered impeachments of the censors of old rather than that which generally results from the interpellations of modern parliaments.

The fourth power of the council or its Resident Committee, namely, to examine the budget, was not a substantial power either. It could only examine; its comments had no binding force on the government. In fact, the full council never had the opportunity to exercise the examination. The budgetary estimates were always referred to the council during its adjournment. They were examined by the Resident Committee instead. When it is remembered that the Chinese budgetary procedure is highly complicated and that ultimately it was always the Supreme National Defense Council or, to be more exact, its chairman, who fixed the budget, one more discussion by the People's Political Council or its Resident Committee could mean very little indeed.

The fifth or investigating power of the council was a matter of slow growth. At the beginning there were no statutory provisions for the exercise of that power. Nevertheless, the council through committees appointed by it did do some investigation, either on its own volition, or at the request of the government. On December 24, 1940, the Organic Articles of the council explicitly authorized the council to appoint investigating committees to conduct investigations requested from it by the government. Still later, in September 1944, there was a further authorization, by which the council or its Resident Committee, when in its view the actual operation of certain measures needed investigation, could request the government to conduct the necessary investigation. The results of the investigation, whether conducted by the government or by the council, could be the occasion for the council or its resident committee to submit remedial proposals to the government.

The investigation power was never quite real. The authorization of 1944 amounted to no more than giving the council and especially its resident committee the power to warn the government about certain weak phases of the administration. The council might request the investigation, but the government was not obliged to comply. Even if it did, it could do so perfunctorily or give itself a whitewashing. As for the investigations undertaken by the council on behalf of the government, they seldom led to remedial legislation or other concrete reforms. Some investigation commissions of the council, notably the Szechwan-Sikang Inspection Commission of 1939, produced excellent reports. But those reports had no greater authority than those produced by privately sponsored commissions of inquiry. Time and again the council demanded the power to institute the usual kind of parliamentary investigation committee of its own. But the government never saw fit to grant that power.

Summing up, it can be seen that of the five powers enjoyed by the People's Poltiical Council only the power to submit proposals was constructive in nature; the rest were all negative and critical. Since on the one hand there was no sanction in the event of the government's refusal to heed the criticisms of the council and, on the other hand, the proposals of the council were usually a mixture of ill-advised and often impracticable exhortations, ambitious schemes, and projects of local and personal interest, it was natural that the council had not been enabled by the possession of these powers to help push the Kuomintang Government a step nearer to a democratic form of government.

An Evaluation of the People's Political Council

Whether an institution like the People's Political Council was a success or a failure largely depended on whether it had promoted national unity, whipped up the war efforts of the government, and, finally, led the country towards democracy. These were not idle objectives or utopian hopes. However difficult their full achievement might be, some achievement was expected of the council by the more progressive elements of the Kuomintang as well as by the people at large. The resolutions of the Congress and Central Executive Committee of the Kuomintang in 1938 for the creation of the council explicitly stated these objectives. Expressions of public opinion at the time of the inauguration of the council bore witness to the same intent.

The council in the first years of its existence certainly satisfied that common urge felt by all parts of the country in or out of the government for unity. The arrival at the capital in the summer of 1937 of leaders and representatives from the parties and groups which previously had been proscribed was the occasion for rejoicing. This rejoicing continued when the creation of the People's Political Council a year later seemed to insure the continuation of unity. Consequently, the renewed rift between the Kuomintang government and the communist forces early in 1941 was a cause for anxiety and uneasiness. The harmony that had previously obtained in the council began to evaporate. From that time on, the discord became more and more pronounced and the communist members of the council generally abstained from the sessions of the council. There were elements in the council which continuously worked for unity and the avoidance of internal conflicts in the face of the common enemy. The successive secretaries-general also remained loyal to the idea that the council must be relied upon as the one instrument of unity. Unfortunately, from 1941 on, the council became more and more ineffective in the fulfillment of its mission, as more and more of its members lost sight of that mission.

As an instrument for whipping up the war efforts of the government the council was successful in the sense that it unwaveringly insisted upon carrying the war to a final victory and that it did provide frequent opportunities for exchange of different outlooks from the various regions of the country, thereby doing away with some of the most depressing attitudes prevailing in the war-torn regions. But inasmuch as the council had no power over the government, it failed to prompt or compel the government to a better conduct of the war.

As a training ground for democracy the council failed lamentably. The failure was less due to inadequacy in the educational qualifications or professional competence of the members than to the kind of leadership that affected the workings of the council. The members as individuals were not necessarily inferior to those generally found in the assemblies of other countries. But too many of them had too little or no sense of responsibility. In order to curry favor with the authorities they were both too obedient to the government and too intolerant of opposition opinions and nonpartisan views of major policies. The representatives of the small parties also were to blame. They lacked not only political courage but were also generally incapable of forgetting the smaller interests of party, even when faced with greater issues at stake. More than all these, the attitude of the Kuomintang or, to be more exact, Chiang Kai-shek's leadership of the Kuomintang, was to blame. The Kuomintang was not willing to see an assembly of independent political stature develop, capable of differing as well as agreeing with the government in the best interests of the country. The way in which the party fixed the personnel and controlled the proceedings of the council definitely relegated the council to a position of no importance from which it could not emerge to become a democratic assembly with commensurate powers.

During its existence, the council, sometimes because of the demand of the opposition parties and sometimes on orders from the government, passed several resolutions for the convening of a constitutional assembly to give the country a new constitution.[10] But these efforts were usually political maneuvers. That explains why these few members of the council who were genuinely interested in the council's steady, even though slow, groping for democracy felt that their own efforts were always being thwarted by these maneuvers.

The People's Political Council undoubtedly served some useful purposes during the war. But it definitely failed to grow into a democratic assembly, to act like one, or to give the country a solid foundation for unity. These were perhaps interrelated objectives; the failure of one inevitably carried with it the failure of all. And the worst was that these failures produced profound effects on the future. Failure to achieve unity during the war years has led to greater disunity. Failure to make an honest effort to become a democratic assembly has led to the rise of flagrantly undemocratic assemblies.

XX

WARTIME DEMANDS FOR CONSTITUTIONALISM[1]

Sun Yat-sen's Ideas of Transition from Tutelage to Constitutionalism

Sun Yat-sen was very explicit that the final political aim of the Revolution was constitutional government. It was unequivocably stipulated in the *Fundamentals of National Reconstruction* that as soon as the majority of provinces should have completed the establishment of local self-government, the National Government was to convene a National Assembly to pass on the draft constitution prepared by the Legislative Yuan. Once the Constitution was promulgated, the nation would have entered into the Constitutional Stage.

There were no provisions of a positive nature in the *Fundamentals* as to when the Legislative Yuan should commence preparing the draft. By implication it could not be earlier than the Initial Stage of Constitutionalism, for the Five Yuan were not to be established until then and the draft would have to be based on the experiences of the Tutelage Period and the Period of the Initial Stage of Constitutionalism. To make an intelligent interpretation of the *Fundamentals*, the Legislative Yuan, together with other Yuan, was to be organized as soon as one of the provinces had established local self-government in all *hsien* and it might then begin the preparation of the draft constitution upon the basis of the *Fundamentals*. It was also to use the experience gained during the whole period from the beginning of tutelage to the time when the majority of the provinces might have established local self-government in their areas, at which time a National Assembly was to be convened.

The provisions of the *Fundamentals* may be too sanguine, but they make sense. If the Legislative Yuan had not been established at the very beginning of the Tutelage Period and had not begun drafting the constitution until after one or more provinces had reached the stage of local self-government, the question of promulgating a constitution might have been conveniently deferred. And if the Kuomintang government had set its heart earnestly on the work of tutelage, and had been able to complete it within a short period, the Legislative Yuan, the draft constitution, the National Assembly, and, finally, the constitution, might have come into orderly being one after another, closely adhering to the *Fundamentals*.

But unfortunately the Kuomintang Government ran into endless difficulties. First, there was the premature organization of the Legislative Yuan. Then followed the promise of the Central Executive Committee of the Kuomintang, on June 10, 1929, to complete the work of tutelage (the establishment of local self-government in all the provinces), within six years or by 1935. Finally, the Legislative Yuan started to prepare the draft as early as 1933, when not a single province had had local self-government. Obviously this draft could not have the benefit of adequate experience of tutelage and local self-government to use as guides. Moreover, if the Kuomintang did not complete the tutelage by 1935 (as it indeed failed to do), it would either have to give a constitution to a people who were not yet prepared for constitutional government or go back on its promises and thereby discredit itself in their eyes. For nearly twenty years, the Kuomintang was never able to overcome the difficulties which it chose to impose upon itself until it finally decided to disregard the *Fundamentals* of Sun Yat-sen, convene the National Assembly, adopt the constitution, and tell the world that the China it had mistutored for so long was ready for a constitutional government. This took place in 1946.

The demands for the drafting and enactment of a constitution earlier than was contemplated by Sun Yat-sen arose from a conglomerate of elements. Genuine believers in Western democracy demanded it as a principle. Those who were dissatisfied with the Kuomintang regime demanded it as an alternative. While both these groups had few ulterior motives in demanding a constitution, there were others whose interest in the constitution was manifestly of a different kind. They urged constitutionalism on the government in order that their own political fortunes might benefit by the resultant governmental reorganization. During the last few years when American influence has been strong and American desire for democratic reforms vociferous, those elements, foreseeing the benefits of possible American support, struck ever more boldly for a constitutional, democratic form of government.

That all these elements were to be found inside as well as outside the Kuomintang further complicated the situation. That some of these elements frequently changed their position in regard to the need, the wisdom, or the urgency of having a constitution made the situation even more complex. If one were to examine carefully the various demands for constitutionalism in the last two decades one would be bewildered by the changeful moods of Chinese political leaders and the absence of a genuine, not to say powerful, movement for constitutionalism.

THE PREPARATION OF A DRAFT CONSTITUTION

The first serious demand for a constitution came from within the Kuomintang itself. The earlier demands were only for a provisional constitution for the Tutelage Period. But in April 1932, a few months after the Mukden Incident and the Shanghai War, while the Emergency Conference was meeting at Loyang and making demands for popular participation in the government, Sun Fo started a publicity campaign of his own to the effect that constitutionalism should be inaugurated as soon as possible and that the Legislative Yuan should commence at once with the work of drafting a constitution. At first the party as a whole was opposed to such a radical deviation from Sun Yat-sen's *Fundamentals*. But soon it was clear that, in terms of actual politics, to oppose constitutionalism was to lose political advantage to those who championed it. Furthermore, Sun Fo had virtually made his acceptance of the presidency of the Legislative Yuan conditional on the Yuan's being authorized to draft a constitution at once, and it was at that time considered dangerous to leave Sun Fo outside the government.

Thus came the solemn resolution of December 19, 1932 of the Central Executive Committee approving Sun Fo's proposal to convene a constituent National Assembly in March 1935 to promulgate a constitution, and to order the Legislative Yuan to prepare a constitutional draft beforehand. This resolution was the starting-point of the Legislative Yuan's Draft Constitution of May 5, 1936.

Sun Fo assumed the presidency of the Legislative Yuan in January 1933. Almost at once he appointed a Drafting Committee of thirty-seven with himself acting as the chairman. The main principles of the draft were deliberated and decided upon by the committee; the drafting was at first left in the hands of the vice-chairman. When his preliminary draft of 214 articles was published in the newspapers it was met by severe criticism. In form it savored too much of a commentary on the *Three People's Principles*.[2] The committee had to do a complete recast, and the committee's draft, the Preliminary Draft, as it was published by the Legislative Yuan on March 1, 1934, was not only shorter (160 articles) but was couched in more intelligible language. It was, however, the beginning of a long series of easy and drastic turnabouts in the texts of the Draft Constitution, turnabouts which reflected either the absence of seriousness or the lack of conviction on the part of the framers of the draft.

When its draft was completed and published, the Drafting Committee was dissolved. A second committee of thirty-six, the Revision Committee, was appointed on March 22, 1934 to examine and revise that draft. It was headed by a new chairman and was quite different in personnel from the Drafting Committee. The draft was subjected to a thorough overhauling and the revised version, known as the "Revised Preliminary Draft," was published on July 9, 1934.

Then came the consideration of the revised draft by the Legislative Yuan itself. From September 14 to October 16, 1934, the Legislative Yuan met eight times and finished three readings. More changes were effected. The Draft Constitution of October 16, 1934, as passed by the Legislative Yuan, was different from both the Preliminary Draft of the Drafting Committee and the Revised Preliminary Draft of the Revision Committee. In length the Preliminary Draft was the shortest of all and in draftsmanship perhaps the best. In substance, the most important changes were concerned with the powers of the National Assembly and the position of the executive vis-à-vis the elected body.

As has been said earlier in this work, the problem of presidential versus cabinet form of government has always been a controversial issue among the politicians and publicists of China.[3] This was so in the time of the Peking regime, and the controversy has continued. In the Preliminary Draft, the high powers of the National Assembly, which would meet only once every three years, were to be continuously exercised by a small recess committee, the National Committee. The President was to have no actual powers while the Executive Yuan was to be the real executive, responsible to the Legislative Yuan which, with the National Committee approving, could vote no confidence in the President of the Executive Yuan. The impeachment by the Control Yuan of the highest officials of the government was also to be passed upon by the committee. Thus under the provisions of the Preliminary Draft, the principle of a responsible cabinet was fully established, with the National Committee, more than the Legislative and Control Yuan, serving as the virtual repository of political power.

In the Revised Preliminary Draft, the recess committee of the National Assembly was renamed "Committee of the National Assembly." The powers of the committee were substantially reduced. While it still retained some powers of direct control over the Legislative Yuan, the latter was principally responsible to the President alone. On the whole, the form of government visualized by the Revised Preliminary Draft was more a presidential than a cabinet government.

The Draft of the Legislative Yuan abolished the recess committee entirely. The National Assembly became a sovereign body in name only. Real power now went to the President and the Legislative Yuan, but the latter was not to hold the former responsible for the exercise of his powers. As far as the relation between the executive and the legislative branches of the government was concerned, the new arrangement was not too different from the American system of presidential government.

The changes that occurred in the three drafts within the short period of half a year are worth examining and should not be dismissed as mere quibbles, for they were to recur again and again. The Legislative Yuan was obviously inclined to favor a strong legislature, but it had to yield to pressure from quarters that were enjoying actual supremacy at the time and were therefore insisting upon a strong executive. Nevertheless, it reflected badly on the courage and conviction of the Legislative Yuan that it allowed itself to be jockeyed into abject submission. It was particularly vulnerable in the role it assigned to the National Assembly. In the first two drafts the assembly was kept alive and active during its long hibernations by the institution of a recess committee. But the recess committee was finally done away with on the pretext that it would confuse the otherwise clear-cut division between the political powers of the people and the governing powers of the government. But in abolishing the recess committee, the Legislative Yuan rendered the National Assembly a nonfunctioning body of empty powers, and also elevated itself to something approaching a Western parliament in power. In Kuomintang ideology, such a structure has always been considered a bad confusion of political and governing powers. Altogether, the frequent changes in the text of the drafts countenanced or actively sought by the Legislative Yuan did the Yuan little credit and did not inspire the respect or confidence of the public in the whole series of drafts.

From October 1934 to May 1935, when the National Government solemnly promulgated the Draft Constitution, the draft, as passed by the Legislative Yuan, ran the gauntlet of the scrutiny of the party councils. It was before the Central Executive Committee for consideration, but that committee, instead of carefully going into it itself, merely laid down a general principle on December 14, 1934, and instructed its own standing committee to make a further study of the draft. The latter evidently had difficulties in arriving at a formula which would be consistent with the principle thus laid down. It was not until October 17, 1935 that it was able to write down five points for the guidance of the Legislative Yuan. They were as follows:

1. The principles of the *Three People's Principles*, the *Fundamentals of National Reconstruction* and the *Provisional Constitution for the Period of Tutelage* should form the basis of the Draft.

2. In providing for the organization of the government, realistic political experiences should be taken into consideration so as to establish a system which can function with ease and also keep the national energy concentrated.

3. The organization of the central and local governments should be regulated by law; only their respective powers need be stipulated in the draft, and that only in a general way.

4. The date and manner of coming into force of those necessary provisions of the Draft which could not be enforced at once or throughout the country should be provided for by law.

5. The provisions of the Draft should not be too numerous and the language of it should aim at simplicity and clarity.

Based on these instructions, the Legislative Yuan made a quick work of revision. On October 24, 1935, a revised draft again passed out of the legislative mill.

Compared with its draft of a year earlier, this second draft was much shorter and still further inclined to concentrate power in the hands of the President. Two full chapters, those on military affairs and on finance, were deleted. The three separate chapters on "province," "*hsien*," and "municipality" were shortened and amalgamated into a single chapter. Many of the powers granted to the Legislative Yuan under the earlier draft were now taken away, mostly in favor of the President, whose position in the government rose to an unprecedented height and whose power could be checked only by a practically nonfunctioning National Assembly. This was fully in accordance with the standing committee's desire to meet the realistic political requirements of the day and to confer on the government of Chiang Kai-shek, who was destined to be the President, adequate powers which would enable him to "function with ease" and to "keep the national energy concentrated" in the government. The self-denial of the Legislative Yuan in willingly curtailing its own substantial powers was of course a purely compulsory act. These changes, satisfactory as they might have seemed to the high officials of the Kuomintang, were by no means acceptable to those who were still considering the adoption of a constitution as a step away from personal dictatorship.

But the Central Executive Committee of the Kuomintang was not yet satisfied. On November 1, 1935, it passed a resolution suggesting that the forthcoming Congress of the Party should make a further examination of the draft and formulate directives for further revisions. The Congress on November 21, 1935 in turn passed the travail of the examination on to the Central Executive Committee created by it. On December 4, the new Central Executive Committee appointed a committee of nineteen to examine the draft. After a few meetings, the committee produced a twenty-three-point commentary. The gist of this commentary was further to increase the extent and the invulnerability of the presidential power and to make it possible for the government to postpone coming into force or even to modify certain constitutional provisions by mere legislative enactment. The Standing Committee of the Central Executive Committee on April 23, 1936 accepted this commentary and referred it to the Legislative Yuan for incorporation in the draft.

So the Legislative Yuan had to make further revisions of the draft. This it did on the 1st and 2nd of May 1936 and the revised version was promulgated by the National Government on May 5, 1936, and was known as the "Draft Constitution of May 5, 1936."

There were three main differences between the final draft and the revised draft of October 24, 1935. First, the term of the National Assembly was increased from four to six years, the ordinary session was to be every third instead of every other year, and the convening of an extraordinary session on the demand of the members required the agreement of two-fifths instead of one-fourth of the members. In other words, the people would have less frequent exercise of their elective power and their elected representatives also less chance to meet as a body and to exercise the granted power. In the final draft, the "political power" of the people became even less real than it had been in the earlier draft.

The second difference was in the further enhancement of the president's position. His term was increased from four to six years. He now had the power to convene extraordinary sessions of the National Assembly. He could summon a meeting of the presidents of the Five Yuan for consultation. Furthermore, the president had the power to issue emergency decrees and to make emergency financial dispositions. These decrees and dispositions had to be subsequently approved by the Legislative Yuan, to be sure, but the period within which he was required to submit these emergency measures to the Yuan was as long as three months.

The last important difference was the incorporation in the final draft of a series of temporary provisions which rendered practically meaningless the coming into force of the Constitution. The date for the coming into force of the Constitution was to be fixed by a law and therefore not necessarily identical with the date of the promulgation, and different dates could be fixed for the different provisions of the Constitution. Though the magistrates of the *hsien* and the mayors of the municipalities were to be elected, the temporary provisions provided that in those areas where local self-government had not been completed they should continue to be appointed by the central government. Finally, there were also provisions providing for the appointment by the president of half of the members of both the Legislative and the Control Yuan before a majority of the provinces had completed local self-government, though again the permanent constitutional arrangement was for the election of all members by the National Assembly.

The whole process in which the Draft Constitution of May 5, 1936 reached its final form was extremely illuminating. It reflected both the reluctance and the hesitation of the Kuomintang to enter into a constitutional regime. Reluctance, because it realized that deviation from Sun Yat-sen's *Fundamentals of National Reconstruction* would cause and was causing the party endless difficulties. When it allowed the Legislative Yuan to go prematurely into constitutional drafting, it had already deviated from the *Fundamentals*.

From the point of view of political strategy, it had now little choice but to go through with the adoption of a constitution. But in so doing, it was deviating more and more from the *Fundamentals*. It was losing all its ground as the party of political tutelage. On the other hand, it was extremely reluctant to descend from the height of the party of tutelage to the level of an ordinary political party because, quite naturally, it was unwilling to part with power. All this was just too bad for the Kuomintang.

The Kuomintang should have made an honest and serious attempt at tutelage with the strong conviction that, in the end, true democracy would materialize. Failing that, it should have made an equally honest and serious attempt to abandon its position of tutelage and transform the regime into a Western kind of parliamentary government, even though such might not be to the taste of Sun Yat-sen. But it did neither, and it had to face all kinds of political woes.

The Draft Constitution of May 5, 1936 [4]

The Draft Constitution of May 5, 1936 was a document of eight chapters and 148 articles.[5] The chapters dealt with (1) General Provisions; (2) National Assembly; (3) Rights and Duties of the Citizens; (4) Central Government; (5) Local Government; (6) National Economy; (7) Education; and (8) the Enforcement and Amendment of the Constitution. There was also a preamble.

In draftsmanship this definitive draft was much superior to all the earlier drafts. But when it came to those parts which bore a close textual resemblance to the *Three People's Principles*, the phraseology became vague and ambiguous. The chapters on the rights and duties of the citizens and on national economy were full of terms and phrases which did not read well and were open to conflicting interpretations, especially the provisions related to the Principle of the People's Livelihood, the most ill-explained of the Three Principles.

Take, for instance, Article 121, "the state may, in accordance with law, regulate private wealth and enterprises when such wealth and enterprises are considered detrimental to the balanced development of national economic life." To carry out this article would obviously mean encountering countless insurmountable difficulties of constitutional interpretation, unless the state chose to identify its arbitrary power with constitutional righteousness. There was little prior legislation covering such matters as private wealth, private enterprise, and a balanced national economic life. Legislation on these matters subsequent to the adoption of the constitution would be in substance more important than the constitutional provision, and different legislatures would be bound to give different meanings to the provision. Steady and consistent growth of a constitution would not be helped by having such matters carelessly put into the text.

In substance the following subjects merit discussion.

1. *The Form of the State.* Article 1 says that "The Republic of China is the *San-min chu-i* Republic." This was in imitation of Article One of the Constitution of July 10, 1918 of the Russian Soviet Federated Socialist Republic. Substitute *San-min chu-i* for "Socialist Soviet" and the terminology was identical. The advocates of the novel phraseology usually argued that "San-min chu-i Republic" would emphasize the unique character of the Chinese Republic, distinct both from the Soviet and the representative governments of the West. But insofar as the distinction from the Soviet state was concerned, no emphasis was necessary. The Kuomintang in 1936 was well known for its antipathy toward Soviet Russia; and insofar as it was meant to be different from the Western democracies, the phraseology created opposition, not only from the other parties, but also from people who looked to the West for political and constitutional models. The term "San-min chu-i Republic" was for long years to stand as a bone of contention among those who were obsessed with the terminology of political expression.

2. *The Rights and Duties of the Citizens.* On this question the controversy centered around the possibility of curtailing by statute the liberties of the citizens. In the draft, each grant of liberty was in the following form: "all citizens shall have freedom of ———, such freedom shall not be restricted except in accordance with law." In form, the second clause was protective, but in effect it was really a proviso, that is, the freedom could be limited by statute. The proponents of the draft could easily argue that every freedom had to be defined by law and its guarantee also provided by law. If the law-making body could always be on the side of the people and favor their full enjoyment of the liberties, indeed no valid objection could be taken. But the opponents of the Kuomintang regime knew very well that in China legislatures had usually been submissive and the Legislative Yuan had not been known to be able or desirous of resisting proposed legislation purported to restrict the liberties of the people. They demanded that the grants of liberties should not carry with them the possibility of statutory limitations. The protagonists and the antagonists could reach no agreement and the controversy went on and on.

3. *The Division of Power between the Central and Local Government.* There were in the *Fundamentals of National Reconstruction* these provisions: "Affairs of national interest shall be entrusted to the central government and those of local interest shall be entrusted to the local governments. There shall be neither undue centralization nor undue decentralization." The provision was merely platitudinous and could not at all serve as any

guide to the proper division of power between the central and local governments. But the framers of the draft always harked back to the platitude. Whatever division they might propose, they always claimed to have followed the dictate of Sun Yat-sen. The actual provisions of Chapter Five of the draft dealing with these problems were very much weighted on the side of centralization, or even overcentralization, and were thus the object of severe criticism by those who held that China was not suitable for a high degree of centralization.

The three problems mentioned above, while controversial enough, had little immediate effect on the political situation of the day. But the following two were of a different connotation.

4. *The Demarcation between "Political Powers" and "Governing Powers."* Sun Yat-sen had claimed the demarcation of political and governing powers as his distinct contribution to political science. Since his death, the less critical of his followers have tried to implement that theory and have more or less come to the conclusion that in the *hsien* the people should exercise the powers of election, recall, initiative, and referendum, the four political powers of the people; and for the country as a whole, the National Assembly elected by the people should exercise these powers for them. According to these followers, the five governing powers should be strictly reserved to the government. It was this kind of reasoning that led to the denial to the National Assembly of all effective powers, except the powers of electing and recalling the government heads, of initiating and holding referenda on laws, and of amending the constitution, to be exercised during the one-month session of each three-year period. Under this arrangement neither the people themselves nor their directly elected representatives, the members of the National Assembly, would have any effective voice in the affairs of the government. Nor could the Legislative Yuan claim to have much power of control over the strong executive. It certainly did not have the power to overthrow the executive, for that power was exclusively vested in the National Assembly. No wonder that the critics of the draft preferred the obliteration of the distinction between the political and governing powers and the creation of a more powerful assembly, either in the form of the Legislative Yuan or in the form of a continuing committee of the National Assembly. Those leaders of the Kuomintang who were likely to hold the executive power were on one side of the controversy and those who were likely to be members of such an assembly were on the other.

5. *Presidential versus Cabinet Form of Government.* The problem of presidential versus cabinet government hinged even more patently on personalities involved. The apologists for the provisions tried to give an impression that the powers of the president, sweeping as they undeniably were, arose from the necessity of balancing the Five Powers. They maintained

that the Executive Yuan was not a feeble body, presidential government was not contemplated, and the National Assembly stood above all of them, like a towering giant. But the critics were not convinced by such spurious arguments as these. They saw in the draft only a powerful president, compared with whom the other organs of government were all dwarfs. To them the dangers of a constitutionalized personal dictatorship were too apparent to be ignored. They objected.[6]

All these problems and the controversies arising therefrom are not to be dismissed as of only theoretical importance. The failure of the Legislative Yuan and the councils of the Kuomintang to think and act wisely and in conformity with the interests and demands of the public, and thus to provide for adequate answers to these problems, led to a number of disastrous results. It shook the general confidence of the public and created suspicion and apprehension on the part of its opponents and rivals. It barred the door to a possible softening of the authoritarian regime which the party had established and to the advent of a more libertarian regime which the more conservative nonpartisan leaders of the country could support with a clear conscience. It led to one controversy after another. The promulgation of the Constitution of December 25, 1946 and the establishment of a new government under that constitution naturally leave these problems unresolved and the controversies unsettled.

Wartime Demands for Constitutional Government

Before the Kuomintang government had time to call the National Assembly to adopt the Draft Constitution of 1936, the war had broken out. During the war, there were a series of demands for more democratic government. In the beginning these were mild in nature. As time went on, unqualified constitutional government was demanded.

At the outset of the war when there was, in spirit at least, a genuine national front, nobody sought to demand from the government the promulgation of a constitution and still less the immediate transition to a constitutional regime. All the demands of a democratic nature were quite in accordance with the Kuomintang's doctrines of tutelage. The non-Kuomintang leaders asked for two things only, consultative assemblies for all levels of government and an accelerated program of self-government at and below the *hsien* level. To these demands the Kuomintang could of course pose no objection. Thus, in the so-called *Program of Armed Resistance and National Reconstruction,*[7] formulated by the Party Congress in March 1938 and voted unanimously by the First People's Political Council in July of that same year, both these objectives were emphasized.

Following the convening of the People's Political Council for the nation in 1937, the political councils for the provinces were also inaugurated during the following year. By 1944, all the provinces which were still free and under the control of the government at Chungking had had these councils set up.

In 1929 the government promulgated the so-called *Outline for the Organization of the Several Levels of Hsien Government*,[8] a kind of general charter of local government. It was in fact a statute. By its enforcement, the *hsien*, and the several levels of local units below it, all came to have either an elected representative assembly or a direct assembly of the citizens of the unit. The official figures on this matter were most encouraging. For instance, in May 1945, 880 out of a total of 1385 *hsien* and municipalities under the control of the National Government had elected Provisional Political Councils, and the majority of the lower units had also elected a direct assembly.[9]

On paper, the creation of these local assemblies could not but be heartening to those who were craving for a greater degree of popular government. In fact, if these assemblies had been genuinely representative and strong enough to serve as a forum of public opinion and a check on the usually arbitrary and oftentimes abusive exercise of power by the appointed local officials, army commanders, and other central officials who happened to be stationed in their respective areas, a sound foundation for democratic government would have been laid and Sun Yat-sen's *Fundamentals of National Reconstruction* with respect to local self-government would have been substantially fulfilled. But these hopes were not realized. Almost all the local assemblies were hand-picked and tightly controlled by either the *hsien* magistrate or the *hsien* organization of the Kuomintang or by the two acting in unison. They were utilized to give certain outcries or expressions of opinion cherished by the authority, but they were not encouraged and very often not allowed to remonstrate against or otherwise differ from the authorities.

In 1939 the constitutional movement was renewed for the first time since the beginning of the war. Some members of the People's Political Council had been voicing their aspirations for the modification of the tutelage. At the fourth session of the First Council held in September of that year the smaller parties formally demanded by way of proposals the early though not immediate termination of the tutelage. The first reaction of the Kuomintang was hostile. But in the end instead of resisting or complying with the demand, it proposed in the same session that the government convene the National Assembly for the adoption of the Constitution. This sudden turnabout was a surprise to the council. Apparently it was conceived as a brilliant tactical move by the Leader of the party himself. The party majority was instructed to make the proposal and then vote for it. The smaller parties, realizing that they had nothing to lose, naturally had no objection to the new proposal. But those members in the Kuomintang as well as those outside it who were anxious to see the regime make steady, even though slow, progress towards real constitutional government were not happy, well knowing that the tactical move would result in the further discrediting of constitutionalism.

Pursuant to the above-mentioned proposal, the People's Political Council appointed a committee of twenty-five known as the "Association for the Promotion of Constitutionalism."[10] The Central Executive Committee of the party also decided in November 1939 to convene the National Assembly on November 12, 1940. Thus the smaller parties and the Kuomintang alike again plunged themselves into the futilities of constitution-making.

The association's principal function was to examine and suggest modifications in the Draft Constitution of 1936 in the light of the changed conditions of the time. On March 30, 1940, it finished its work and a revised draft was submitted. It differed from the Draft of 1936 in several important aspects. It was shorter, the entire chapter on education having been deleted. It provided for a large recess committee of 150 to 200, elected by and to act for the National Assembly during its long recesses, and, in addition, to enjoy the parliamentary powers of expressing nonconfidence in the ministers and of approving the declaration of martial law, amnesty, declaration of war, treaties of peace, and other treaties. The vote of nonconfidence by this committee would entail the resignations of the ministers concerned. If the President and Vice-President of the Executive Yuan receiving such a vote were sustained by the President of the Republic, the latter could convene the National Assembly for an ultimate decision which would entail either the resignation of the heads of the Executive Yuan or a new election of the recess committee.

The Association for the Promotion of Constitutionalism in proposing the creation of this recess committee of the National Assembly was doing little more than restoring the framework as embodied in the original draft of March 1, 1934 drawn up by the Drafting Committee of the Legislative Yuan. But this restoration was intolerable to the Kuomintang, whose constitutional theories for years preceding the war had consistently tended toward making invulnerable the executive branch of the government under the President. When the revised draft was reported to the People's Political Council, it was severely attacked by the Kuomintang majority. Finally, on April 6, 1940, the council passed the strange resolution to submit to the government for consideration both the revised draft of the association and the members' adverse opinions on the recess committee. Shortly afterward, on September 18, 1940, the controversy was resolved by the decision of the Standing Committee of the Central Executive Committee to postpone indefinitely the convening of the National Assembly. By that postponement the government and the party had no further necessity to compose the differences between the association's draft and the contrary opinions. This ended another episode in that kaleidoscopic history of constitution-making.

For a number of years the matter of constitution-making was again in total eclipse. Then in 1943, mainly as the result of foreign criticisms of the dictatorship, the Kuomintang again decided to talk about a libertarian and constitutional regime. To meet the exigencies of the time, Chiang Kai-shek in his capacity of President of the National Government spoke to the People's Political Council in September 1943 of the desirability of setting up an organization to prepare for constitutional government. Acting on that suggestion, the Presidium and the government agreed to set up a joint committee of 39 to 49, known as the "Association to Assist in the Inauguration of Constitutionalism,"[11] to be composed of members of the Presidium of the People's Political Council as ex officio members and of members of the Central Executive and Supervisory Committees of the Kuomintang, members of the People's Political Council and other suitable persons, all to be designated by the Chairman of the National Supreme Defense Committee. The chairman also acted as the president of the association.

The stipulated functions of the association were as follows: (1) to submit to the government proposals related to the establishment of a constitutional regime; (2) to inquire into the state of the provincial and other local assemblies; (3) to investigate the enforcement of laws and decrees related to the promotion of a constitutional regime; (4) to provide for contact between the government and the civic bodies concerning discussions on constitutional and other political problems; and (5) to examine any matter concerned with the inauguration of a constitutional regime on the request of the government. These were functions which could mean either much or nothing. The policy of the government was to temporize. It was up to those who were demanding constitutionalism and who were now included in the association to make some reality of those functions.

The association lasted for over two years. Among other things, it made a study of the Draft of 1936. But the presence of the members of the Central Executive Committee and the lessons the new body had learned from its predecessor, the Association for the Promotion of Constitutionalism, prevented it from doing anything drastic. It first called for comments on the draft from all quarters, and then instructed a subcommittee to make a summary study both of the draft itself and the comments thereon. The final conclusions arrived at by the association consisted of thirty-two points. Most of these points were in defense of the draft. Whatever modifications were suggested were almost all unimportant. Indeed the association had taken too seriously to heart the lessons of the frustrated efforts of its predecessor.

The failure of the People's Political Council to make any headway to "promote constitutionalism," still less to "assist the inauguration of constitutionalism," convinced those members of the council, especially the representatives of the smaller parties, that the constitutional movement must be carried on outside the council. Consequently, they warmly welcomed the Political Consultative Conference, which was called mainly for the purpose of arranging a peaceful settlement between the two major contenders to power, the Kuomintang and the Communist Party.

Wartime Demands for Freedom

Side by side with the demands for constitutionalism there were also demands for the removal of various restrictions on freedoms of individuals and of political groups alike. The Kuomintang as the tutelary party, though it did not promise the inauguration of constitutional government, did pledge itself to guarantee adequately the freedoms of expression, press, assembly, and association within the limits of the Three People's Principles and of law.[12] Since the pledge was a part of the *Program of Armed Resistance and National Reconstruction*, and the *Program* was voted by both the Party Congress and the People's Political Council in 1938, it was easy for the members of the council and the people at large to demand the removal of harsh restrictions on the popular liberties and to persist in so demanding.

At the very first session of the People's Political Council in July 1938, there were proposals calling on the government to give full protection to the freedoms of the people and, in case there were laws which happened to contravene the spirit of the *Program*, to repeal or amend them. These proposals were sometimes moved separately and sometimes linked together with proposals for the creation of more local assemblies. They were numerous; at session after session they kept popping up. With the exception of the demands for according legal status to political parties, which the Kuomintang was reluctant either to comply with or flatly to reject, almost all proposals of this nature got through the council and were submitted to the Supreme National Defense Council for action.

But the Defense Council seldom acted in a straightforward manner. It was not in a position to reject these proposals, for rejection would mean going back on the word of the *Program*. It was even less willing to accept and implement them with the necessary legislation or administrative action, for acceptance and implementation would necessitate the removal of a great many obnoxious restrictions. Instead, dallying was its favorite answer to the proposals. Sometimes it defended the restrictions as being necessary to the conduct of the war. Sometimes it issued lukewarm orders to the officials, instructing them to pay more attention to the rights of the people, but not effectively threatening them with punishment in case of malfeasance. But all the time it claimed that it was giving the people the maximum freedom possible under wartime conditions.

As a matter of fact, the situation deteriorated rapidly as the war went on. Whereas at the beginning of the war there was a fair amount of political freedom and publications and speeches were fairly free from restraints, by 1943 public expressions disapproving the government's conduct of the war, attacking the leaders of the government, or otherwise critical of the government, could seldom find their way into print or onto the platform. It was a most unfortunate development. One could of course attribute to the rising tension between the Kuomintang and the communists the tightening of the press, but in large measure, the suppression of civil liberties was due to the government's mistaken intolerance of public criticism and the fear of losing political control of power. Had it been able to allow the public an increasingly greater amount of free speech and free press, its own deterioration might have been arrested. Public criticism might even have brought about the improvement of the administration; but the government chose to do otherwise. The choking of public criticism was the cause for more criticism. The evil process went on until some break became necessary. That came in 1943.

By 1943, the criticism of the government and the demands for greater freedom of press and of assembly and for more adequate protection of personal liberty, voiced unreservedly on the floors of the People's Political Council, had reached a stage where it became necessary for the government to make some concession. This the government did by agreeing to the appointment of the Association to Assist in the Inauguration of a Constitution, mentioned above.

During its existence the association sought to advance the cause of popular liberties along these lines: First, it succeeded in having the government issue, on July 15, 1944, a decree for the better protection of the freedom of person.[13] Second, it urged the government either to abolish or relax the censorship of the press and it was able to have the Standing Committee of the Central Executive Committee of the Kuomintang, on June 12, 1944, effect some relaxation in the restrictions of the press other than the dailies. Third, it also discussed the desirability and the ways and means of allowing the people to organize freely for political purposes.

The demand for better protection of the freedom of person was occasioned by the prevalence of illegal arrests by all kinds of authorities, civilian and military. Theoretically the Habeas Corpus Law of June 21, 1935 had never been abrogated, but no serious attempt had ever been made to have it enforced. By 1944, administrative and military authorities had in the name of the war arrested and imprisoned so many people and in such an outrageous fashion that there was a terror in the countryside and it was actually undermining the conscription program. The decree of July 18, 1944, which was to take effect on August 1, forbade the arrest, detention, punishment, and trial by any other than the legal authority invested by law with the right of arrest, detention, punishment, and trial. It also required that the lawful authorities making the arrest must not detain the person arrested longer than forty-eight hours if no suspicion existed against the person arrested. In case they found out that they had no jurisdiction over the person arrested, he must be handed over to those who did. The decree was entirely praiseworthy both in letter and in spirit, but the effect was negligible.[14]

The demand for the relaxation of censorship was the result of intolerable restrictions placed on the press. There were restrictions both on newspapers and on other publications, and the censorship for both was in the hands of the party. Censorship of newspapers was rigid in the extreme. The association suggested the advisability of relaxation, but the government, pleading the exigencies of war, refused to consider it. The censorship of newspapers was not abolished until January 1946, at the time of the Political Consultative Conference.

As for the censorship of publications other than newspapers, the "Regulations Governing Censorship of Wartime Publications and Standards of Censurable Information" as they stood after the final revision of June 20, 1944 were both rigid and arbitrary.[15] Further, it was badly administered. Not only was the publication of critical reviews difficult, but also the publication of books of a general or even learned nature. The delay was itself intolerable. The corrections required were frequently difficult to comply with. It was in the light of this deplorable state of things that the association asked the government to consider abolishing the censorship or at least to relax and rationalize the standards and improve the administration.

The government's answer was not satisfactory. It consented to a partial abolition of the censorship and a revision of the standards. Publications which did not touch on military affairs, politics, and foreign relations were exempt from the censorship, it was true. But authors or publishers still ran the risk of punishment if the publications violated those revised standards which, though more reasonable than the previous ones, were still severe and capable of arbitrary interpretations. The party censorship authorities, both at the capital and in the provinces, were made a part of the government, it was true; but there was little change in personnel. Altogether, there was not much improvement except that noncontroversial matters like a text on technology could now see print in a much shorter time. It was also not until January 1946 that censorship on publications other than newspapers was finally abolished.

If the demands for the protection of freedom of person and freedom of the press were in reality little satisfied, the demand for freedom of political association was not satisfied even on paper. The responsibility for the nonrealization of that freedom was, however, shared by the government and the smaller parties alike. In a session of its Central Executive Committee held in

May 1945, the Kuomintang had resolved that after the government had consulted the association, a law on political association should be enacted. But when the government asked for the views of the association, the latter hesitated to make any suggestions on the pretext that some of its leading members were away attending the San Francisco Conference on the organization of the United Nations and their return was being awaited. No stringent demand was ever advanced by the association as long as it lasted, in spite of the exhortations to that effect by a few independent spirits of the Kuomintang who happened to be members of the association.

In many ways, the failure of the Association to Assist in the Inauguration of Constitutionalism to make any effective headway toward the establishment of the few liberties indispensable to enlightened government was a great misfortune. Had there been some tangible progress in that direction instead of paper constitutionalism, which became the order of the day after December 1946, the Chinese people would have gained some real blessings of Western democracy.

The Question of the National Assembly

There were two separate though necessarily related controversies over the question of the National Assembly. One had regard to the make-up and position of the assembly as an institution under the new constitution; the other was concerned with the make-up, the manner, and the date of convening the constituent assembly. In this section, only the latter will be dealt with.

It was meaningless for the Legislative Yuan to prepare a draft constitution unless the convening of a constituent convention was also contemplated. Thus when the Central Executive Committee in December 1932 ordered the Legislative Yuan to prepare a draft, it also decided to convene the National Assembly in March 1935 for the adoption of the constitution. But owing to the fact that the tutelage had no prospect of completion before March 1935, the Kuomintang authorities subsequently decided to convene a Party Congress to make a final decision in regard to the date of the convening of the National Assembly. The congress was postponed and postponed again. When it finally met in November 1935, it again promised to convene the assembly within 1936 and in December the Central Executive Committee further fixed November 12, 1936 as the date.

Coming after these decisions, the Organic Law of the National Assembly and the Electoral Law were promulgated by the National Government on May 4, 1936, and amended on May 21, 1937. The assembly was to have 1200 elected delegates and 240 delegates appointed by the government, with the members and reserve members of the Central Executive and Supervisory Committees of the Kuomintang as ex officio members and the President and members of the National Government, Presidents and Vice-presidents of the Yuan, ministers (of ministries) and chairmen (of commissions) and such other persons as might be given permission by the Presidium of the Assembly, as attending members. Aside from the 1200 elected delegates, the other delegates, who at that time might be as many as 600, would of course belong to the highest cadres of the government and the party organization.

The elected delegates were divided into three categories: 665 by geographical areas, 384 by vocational bodies, and 155 by a special procedure. All citizens who had taken the Oath of Citizenship [16] were entitled to participate in the election. Generally a citizen was to join in the geographic constituency in which he resided. But if he happened to be a member of a vocational or professional association, such as a farmers' association, labor union, merchants' association, the professional associations of lawyers, accountants, doctors and pharmacologists, newspapermen and engineers, an educational association, or universities and colleges, he was to vote with that body. If he belonged to more than one body he must make a choice of one. Those who were citizens of the four northeastern provinces which were under Japanese occupation, and of Mongolia and Tibet, the Chinese overseas, and, finally, members of the armed forces and of the military academies were to vote under a special procedure.

The suffrage was direct and voting was by secret ballot. But the candidates were nominated not by the voters themselves, but by the authorities in the respective fields. Candidates standing for the geographic constituencies including those in Tibet and unoccupied Mongolia were nominated by the local officials below the *hsien* level. Those for the vocational bodies and for the overseas and army and military academies were nominated by the constituted authorities of those bodies, of the Overseas Affairs Commission and the commanding officers respectively. The candidates to be elected by the citizens of the northeastern provinces and of occupied parts of Mongolia who were residing in the unoccupied provinces and by Tibetans residing in other parts of China were nominated directly by the National Government. All nominees were to be many times more than the delegates. Out of these numerous nominees, the government selected two or three times as many candidates as there were delegates to be elected, depending on the nature of the constituency.

It will be seen that the control by the government was complete. The preliminary lists of candidates were made up by the constituted authorities who could be expected to be Kuomintang members. The final screening was performed by the National Government which was certainly in the hands of the leaders of the Kuomintang. The election was thus no more than an expression of preference for one of the nominees of the party. No wonder the other parties subsequently voiced the strongest objection to that election.

The election began soon after the Election Law went into force on July 1, 1936. But when the war broke out a year later, out of 1200 there were still 250 yet to be elected, largely because the northern provinces of Shantung, Hopei, and Chahar, together with the two municipalities of Peiping and Tientsin, were then under a semiautonomous regime and the authorities there refused to order the elections, both geographical and vocational. This accounted for 167 of the missing delegates. Also, the 45 delegates for the three northeastern provinces were not yet chosen.

While the election was going on, the Central Executive Committee of the party, meeting in February 1937, decided to have the National Assembly convened on November 12 of the same year. The outbreak of the war compelled the party to postpone the convening indefinitely. In November 1939, following the resolution of the People's Political Council urging the government to convene the National Assembly, the Central Executive Committee again fixed November 12, 1940 as the date of the convening. On September 18, 1940, the Standing Committee of the Central Executive Committee decided that, owing to the difficulties of communication, the date should be postponed but all preparations for the convening should not be suspended. While as late as April 1941 the Central Executive Committee was still professing that the National Assembly would be convened as soon as possible, its Standing Committee on October 19, 1942 decided to have the assembly indefinitely postponed, this time pleading the difficulties arising out of the war in the Pacific as the cause.

In September 1943 the Central Executive Committee again resolved that the National Assembly should be convened within one year after the end of the war. To this Chiang Kai-shek made a sudden change by announcing to the Association to Assist in the Inauguration of Constitutionalism, on March 1, 1945, that the National Assembly would be convened on November 12, 1945, in spite of the fact that there was no prospect of an early termination of the war. These decisions, resolutions, and announcements were unbelievably confusing and perplexing. They must have confused the leadership of the Kuomintang itself. But they were no less perplexing to the students of that phase of Chinese political development, for they betrayed neither seriousness of honest intentions nor a common-sense conception of practical politics. The persons responsible for them naturally suffered in being discredited. But the country had to suffer with those irresponsible persons.

The sudden decision of Chiang Kai-shek to call the National Assembly plunged the leaders of various parties into an angry mood. Aside from the Kuomintang hierarchy which had hand-picked the delegates to the National Assembly, none of those who had been demanding either an increased enjoyment of liberties or the termination of tutelage or a full constitutional regime were interested in the assembly elected in 1936–1937. In fact, they loathed it.

In the past, not only the opponents of the Kuomintang but the liberal members of the party as well had freely expressed the view that the old delegates, not being freely elected and having been elected a long while ago, should not be seated and that an entirely new constituent assembly should be created instead. But the party oligarchy had always been consistently opposed to unseating the delegates they themselves had had elected. The decision of Chiang Kai-shek to make a *fait accompli* of the managed assembly caused those opposed to the seating of the old delegates to protest against and to contest the decision of the governing party. They voiced their sentiment in the People's Political Council session of July 1945. But they were not in agreement among themselves. Only a few of them stood adamant for a new election based on free and universal suffrage. The majority seemed to be more interested in jockeying for seats. If the Kuomintang was willing to give them sufficient seats, they were not on principle opposed to tolerating the seating of the 1936–1937 delegates. On this question of the National Assembly, the People's Political Council's decision was merely to request the government to secure agreement of the several parties in regard to the composition of the assembly before it was convened. The problem was not resolved by the People's Political Council.

XXI

THE CONSTITUTION OF 1946

The opposition parties' demands for constitutional government and the government's promises to convene the National Assembly for the adoption of a constitution, however repeatedly made, might have continued on and on without leading to anything concrete. It was the convening of the Political Consultative Conference in January 1946 that gave the opposition and the government alike an impetus to hasten the coming of a constitution. The motives were different. The former desired it to break the monopoly of government by one party; the latter, as a means of defense. But both needed it as a weapon.

The Political Consultative Conference and Constitution-Making

The principal function of the Political Consultative Conference was to arrange for the peaceful solution of the conflict that was hovering over the nation. It had a series of problems to solve, as will be described in greater detail in a later chapter.[1] It discussed the problems of the revision of the Draft Constitution of 1936 and of the membership of the National Assembly because they were matters in dispute among the parties which had all professed constitutional government as their final political goal. When the conference adjourned on January 31, agreement had been secured on every one of the five items on its agenda, and a resolution was passed on each.

On the Draft Constitution, the conference proposed numerous radical revisions[2] and called for the establishment of a committee of review to put the revisions into proper form.

First, the National Assembly was to be no more than a general gathering of the representatives of the *hsien*, provincial and central assemblies, enjoying merely the rights of election and recall of the President of the Republic and of initiative and referendum. In other words, the Assembly as an organic body was abolished; the retention of its name was intended, though in vain, to save the feelings of the Kuomintang which had always considered the National Assembly essential in its system of government.

Second, there was to be a responsible government of the usual type, with the Executive Yuan corresponding to the cabinet and the Legislative Yuan to the parliament. Like the parliament, the Legislative Yuan was to be directly elected by universal suffrage.

Third, the names of the other three Yuan were retained. But the Control Yuan was transformed into an upper chamber, elected by the provincial assemblies and exercising the functions of consent, impeachment, and other control. The Judicial Yuan was made identical with the supreme court, composed of a number of justices nominated by the President with the consent of the Control Yuan. The Examination Yuan was to become collegiate, its members were to be appointed like the justices of the Judicial Yuan, and it was to be denied authority over the qualification of candidates for elective offices.

Fourth, the President was allowed to enjoy emergency powers, but only on the action of the Executive Yuan. Furthermore, the emergency decrees had to be voted upon by the Legislative Yuan within one month after their publication.

Fifth, concerning local government, the province was to enjoy local self-government and home rule. The governor of the province was to be elected directly by the people.

Sixth, the freedoms of the citizens were to be guaranteed by the constitution and restriction by statutes was barred. Election was to be regulated by a special chapter in the constitution. The right of home rule by the non-Chinese nationalities who inhabited a definite area was to be guaranteed by the constitution.

Seventh, fundamental national policies were to deal with, among other things, national defense, foreign policy, national economy, and cultural and educational policies. In all, the policies formulated gave voice to the high ideals of peace, good neighborliness, social reform, and a democratic, egalitarian, and scientific spirit.

Eighth, constitutional amendment was to be the responsibility of the joint assembly of the Legislative and the Control Yuan, thence to be ratified by the gathering who elected the president.

These were, indeed, radical departures from the Kuomintang's Draft Constitution of 1936, though in terminology almost all that was in the draft was scrupulously retained. The dominant chord of the revision was the distrust of government by one man, a system to which the Kuomintang was hopelessly tied and which its opponents were most determined to break. To be sure, both were thinking in terms of the starkest of realistic politics.

The Committee for the Reviewing of the Draft Constitution was to consist of twenty-five members, with each of the five groups of the Political Consultative Conference naming five, and ten experts nominated by the conference from outside. It was to finish within two months a revised Draft Constitution, to be based on the above-mentioned principles and with reference to the views of the two Associations above-mentioned and of others. But for reasons which will presently be discussed, the committee was not permitted to finish its work according to the terms of the reference.

The die-hards of the Kuomintang tried their very best to torpedo the conference while it was still sitting. When that failed, they succeeded in securing, at the plenary session of the Central Executive Committee held in the first days of March, the passage of a resolution calling for the modification of the revision agreed upon by the conference and for reverting to some of the original arrangements in the Draft of 1936. First, the restoration of the National Assembly as an organic body, second, the return from cabinet government to presidential government, and, third, the toning down of provincial home rule were their three demands.

Whether these points were or were not subsequently accepted by the delegates of other parties is not quite clear. The Kuomintang maintained that they were and therefore the changes were valid. The communists and their friends said that they did not accept them. Whatever be the case, the Reviewing Committee did propose the changes as desired by the Kuomintang. But the committee was not able to draft a complete text. By May 1946 new outbursts of armed conflicts, especially in the Northeast, and controversies concerning the application of other conference resolutions than that of the Draft Constitution had created such an impasse that the resumption of a session of the Reviewing Committee was impossible. The revised Draft Constitution as it was later presented to the National Assembly in November was the work of the delegates of the Kuomintang and of the parties allied to it, without the consent of the communists and their friends.

On the National Assembly, the Political Consultative Conference drew up a four-point resolution. First, due to the Kuomintang's insistence on accepting the delegates elected in 1936–1937, the 1200 delegates elected or to be elected under the Electoral Law of 1936 were accepted. In addition, 150 delegates were assigned to Formosa, the northeastern, and other provinces, under both the geographical and vocational categories. Further, 700 more delegates were to be apportioned among the several parties and the independents. In all, there were to be 2050 members. Subsequently, it was agreed that the 700 should be apportioned as follows: Kuomintang, 220; communists, 190; Democratic League, 120; Youth Party, 100; and independents, 70. Second, the National Assembly thus constituted should be convened on May 5, 1946 to adopt the constitution and to do that alone. Third, the adoption of the constitution was to require the consent of three-fourths of the delegates present.

Fourth, within six months after the promulgation of the constitution, officials of the new government organs should be elected and these organs should be convened in accordance with the provisions of the constitution.

The agreement on the National Assembly was arrived at with the greatest difficulty, greater than that on any of the other four controversial problems. The Kuomintang's insistence on making good the mandates of its hand-picked delegates was the main obstacle to any just settlement. The sacrifice of the principle of universal suffrage and the abandonment of a new general election consented to by the other parties brought forth many criticisms. The Kuomintang members were justly condemned for preferring to grasp the seats they coveted rather than be right. Their own defense was that this was the only way to reach an agreement. They claimed that the acceptance of the old delegates was a necessary evil, and that the evil was minimized by confining the function of the Assembly to the adoption of a constitution and by the tacit understanding that the Kuomintang would honor the agreed new version of the Draft Constitution and instruct their delegates to act accordingly. Since the opposition consisting of the communists and the Democratic League would be assured of one-fourth of the 2050 delegates, they would be in a position to prevent any deviation from the agreed version being railroaded through the Assembly.

To insure that both the guarantee of one-fourth of Assembly membership to the communists and the Democratic League and the pledge of the Kuomintang to instruct its delegates to accept the version of the Reviewing Committee would be honored, the conference resolved that the National Government should be forthwith reorganized, so that all parties might have an opportunity to supervise the execution of, among other things, the resolutions of the Draft Constitution and the National Assembly. But such a government never appeared. In the meantime, liberties had been taken with the principles governing the revision of the Draft Constitution, and armed conflicts between the government and the communists had increased. By September of 1946, the laudable efforts of the Political Consultative Conference had been completely frustrated and dissipated. The transitory phase marked by attempts at national conciliation and personified by the People's Political Council and the Political Consultative Conference came to a close. An entirely new period, one of immense physical destruction and thoroughgoing eradication began.

The National Assembly of 1946

Amidst a civil war which surpassed in extent and in intensity all wars, foreign and domestic, since the days of the Taiping Rebellion, the National Government of the Kuomintang adopted a new constitution in 1946.

The election and appointment of National Assembly delegates as agreed upon by the Political Consultative Conference were to have been completed under the auspices of a multipartisan transitional government. When that had been done, the Assembly was to enact a constitution on the basis of a draft prepared by a multipartisan committee, the Committee for the Reviewing of the Draft Constitution, according to the principles agreed upon by the parental conference. Neither of these conditions materialized. The National Government, after some successes over the communist forces in the fall of 1946, decided to convene the National Assembly.

In this move, the Kuomintang had the hearty support of the Youth Party and to some extent also the support of the Democratic Socialist Party and the independents who had figured in the Political Consultative Conference. The Communist Party and the Democratic League opposed the move since it violated both the letter and the spirit of the resolutions of the conference. They abstained.

There was little doubt that the convening of the Kuomintang-controlled Assembly and the adoption of a draft, the provisions of which had given far more power to the President of the Republic than had the resolutions of the conference, would lead to an irrevocable break between the Kuomintang and the communists and close all doors for conciliation. Accordingly, a number of groups, notably the Democratic League, urged the government not to convene the National Assembly on November 12, as proclaimed by the government on October 10, immediately after it had wrested Kalgan from the hands of the communists. There was a three-day postponement, but that was all. The communists and the Democratic League insisted on the observance of the procedure fixed by the Political Consultative Conference. The government insisted on calling the Assembly after the three-day postponement was up. The opposition parties protested by absenting themselves from the Assembly.

The National Assembly as convened on November 15, 1946 was a body of 1744 members, presumably consisting of 1200 for the categories stipulated under the Organic Law of the National Assembly of 1936, 150 for Formosa and other areas as agreed upon in the resolution of the Political Consultative Conference, and the rest new appointees of the government and the two participating parties. There were 118 and 54 delegates from the Youth Party and the Democratic Socialist Party, respectively. In the month before the convening, the government was making appointments to the Assembly almost constantly. On one day the government by mandate might be announcing the appointment of a person; the following day it might by another mandate be announcing the resignation of the same person. The appointments were made most haphazardly. The main concern was that there should be sufficient numbers appointed and, if possible, delegates who would be respectable enough to give the Assembly some prestige or, in any case, delegates pliable enough to give the government an easy majority. But aside from the total abstention of the communists and the adherents of the Democratic League, also conspicuous by their absence were those truly independent spirits who longed for a peaceful solution of the Kuomintang-Communist conflict and orderly progress of the nation but who were disgusted with the precipitating acts of the government.

The National Assembly was formally opened on November 15. On November 18–19, it spent four sessions on the business of electing a Presidium of forty-six members. Then, on November 25–26, it deliberated and adopted its Rules of Procedure. From November 28 to December 25, it held twenty sessions for the three readings of the Draft Constitution. On the final day, the Constitution was unanimously adopted.

Although there was a total of 1744 delegates, elected and appointed, the attendance at the sittings was always somewhere between 1300 and 1500. But an average attendance of 1400 was already too big for deliberative purposes. The sittings were usually noisy and disorderly.

The sole function of the Assembly was to consider the Draft Constitution as revised by the Kuomintang leaders in collaboration with their friends; the eight committees into which the Assembly was divided were all concerned with the various parts of the draft. The committee stage came between the first and the second readings. Proposals of amendments as well as the relevant parts of the draft were first considered by the committees. In addition, there was a joint committee composed of three members elected from each committee (one ordinary member and two from the nine-man presidium of the committee), nine from the Presidium of the Assembly, and three elected by each geographical, professional, or special group of delegates. This joint committee was the all-powerful committee.

The sessions of the Assembly were often tumultuous. Knowing that the draft, which was presented to it on November 28 by Chiang Kai-shek in person as the head of the National Government, had to be accepted in its broad outlines, the members entertained a feeling of resentment that they were to be nothing more than mere rubber stamps. Though the large majority of them had not the faintest mandate from the people and the elected delegates were not by any means freely elected, they nevertheless assumed that they were the voice and the sovereign assembly of the Chinese people. They pretended that they had both the authority and the power to ordain whatever constitution they liked. They proposed a great number of amendments to the draft. But the government had its own obligations. The draft had already departed substantially from the resolution of the Political Consultative Conference. Nevertheless, it represented a compromise between the views of the Kuomintang and the other two parties participating in the Assembly, the Youth Party and the Democratic Socialist Party. To alter the draft might easily cause the bolt of those two parties, an occurrence which the Kuomintang could not afford to let happen. Sovereign or not sovereign, it was to the interest of the Kuomintang that the Assembly, composed mainly of its followers, should do its bidding without fail.

On two points the Kuomintang die-hards did attempt to change the provisions of the draft. They desired the restoration of the term "San-min chu-i Republic" instead of the more ambiguous and redundant phraseology of Article I in the draft. They also wanted to further reduce the elements of cabinet government. Their ideal was of course presidential government as provided for in the Draft of 1936. On the first point, the Youth and Democratic Socialist parties insisted that the term "San-min chu-i Republic" be avoided. They were of course a small minority and could be easily outvoted. But they could bolt the Assembly as a last resort. On the second point, the leaders of the Kuomintang and the government were rather coy. They might at heart approve the views of the die-hards, but to do so would be to make a sorry spectacle of themselves, for they had repeatedly promised first the Political Consultative Conference and then the two parties participating in the Assembly that the Kuomintang would not prescribe an all-powerful presidency for the Republic. Neither "San-min chu-i Republic" nor a pure type of presidential government was substituted for the arrangements in the revised draft.

The Assembly became involved in two other controversies, both of which affected the personal position of a great number of the delegates. First, there was a move to transform the constituent Assembly into the First Assembly under the new constitution. If this were done, the delegates would automatically have continued to be delegates for a term of six years. They did not succeed in accomplishing this. The only concession made was that their mandate should not terminate until the convening of the First Assembly. Second, there was a proposal to disqualify the officials from standing for election as delegates to the National Assembly. This amendment, if passed, would have obliged the officials to resign from their posts before announcing their candidacy for the National Assembly. That would indeed have given the future Assemblies greater independence from the manipulations of the officials. Though popular with those members of the Kuomintang who had not often been in power, the proposal was a violent shock to Kuomintang officialdom. A compromise was reached. Officials were only disqualified to stand for the National Assembly in the constituency where they were officials.

But the greatest controversy which almost broke up the Assembly was concerned with neither the controversies between the Kuomintang and the other parties nor with the self-interest of the delegates. It was the proposal of the Northern delegates to move the capital back to Peiping that caused the greatest tumult. For years, the people in the Northern provinces have resented the numerical predominance of Southern leaders in the high posts of the government. As a protest, they demanded that the capital be moved back to the North. Chiang Kai-shek would not hear of this proposal. But in forcing his Northern followers to desist from making the demand, he caused a split among the Kuomintang delegates of the Assembly.

Nevertheless, no matter what the nature of the controversy, Chiang Kai-shek succeeded in having all his ideas and strategies accepted by the vast majority of the Assembly. The Constitution as passed by the National Assembly on December 25, 1946 was very much the same as the one handed to it by the government. The whole Assembly felt relieved; the Kuomintang leadership, because they could claim to have ended the tutelage and given the people a constitution; the other participating parties because they could expect the Kuomintang to give them a few posts in the government; the delegates, because at long last they had served in the National Assembly and had adopted a constitution. But beyond the precincts of the Assembly and the narrow interests represented there, gloom prevailed. To the vast majority of the Chinese people the adoption of a constitution and the organization of a government under it by one dominant party without the participation of the parties of opposition signified the final extinction of the vanishing hopes for a peaceful settlement.

The Constitution of December 25, 1946 [3]

The Constitution adopted by the National Assembly on December 25, 1946 is a document of fourteen chapters and 175 articles. In draftsmanship it is fairly satisfactory, more so than any of the series of drafts that preceded it. Allowing for the differences in terminology arising out of the differences in concept, it is probably as good as the equally belabored Constitution of October 10, 1923. The repeated revisions and redrafting had not failed to improve its wording and phrases. The least satisfactory parts, as far as draftsmanship is concerned, are the Preamble, Article I described above, and the whole of Chapter XIII dealing with national policies. They all have to do with Sun Yat-sen's bequeathed teachings. The faulty wordings and phrases in the teachings directly affect constitutional provisions which seek to translate those teachings into statutory form.

In substance the following topics deserve attention:

1. The Bill of Rights is a usual one and not very much different from that in the Draft Constitution of 1936 or earlier constitutional documents. But the phrase which qualifies the grant of freedom by saying that "such freedom shall not be restricted except in accordance with law" is deleted.

2. The sovereignty of the people is implemented in Chapter III (The National Assembly) and Chapter XII (Election, Recall, Initiative and Refer-

endum). Chapter XII is principally concerned with suffrage, eligibility, voting procedure, and the special rights of women. The age qualification for voters is fixed at twenty, and for those standing for election at twenty-three, unless otherwise stipulated. There is nothing unusual in the procedure. Equal, direct and secret voting is emphasized. So is open election campaigning. There are also stipulations that women and population groups with special modes of living, meaning, of course, such groups as the T'ai, the Lo-lo, and the Miao-yao, should have a quota of elected representatives of their own; the reference to women is intended to give them stimulus to seek elective offices.

The National Assembly is elected by the people under various categories, geographical and vocational. In addition, women's organizations form a category by themselves. For the provinces, each *hsien* (or municipality on the same level as the *hsien*) elects one delegate. But the number of delegates to be elected by areas not yet made into provinces and by the vocational and other special groups are to be determined by law. The total membership can therefore be easily swollen to thousands if the legislature succumbs to the pressure of the areas and groups demanding a larger representation.

The functions of the Assembly are generally those of an electorate and a constituent assembly. It elects and recalls the President and Vice-President, amends the constitution, and votes on amendments that may be proposed by the Legislative Yuan. The only function, which does not generally belong to an electorate or a constituent assembly and yet is enjoyed by the Assembly, is that of bringing impeachments against the President and Vice-President. Even this last can be considered a part of its function of recall. Because of the simplicity of functions, the National Assembly meets only once every three years, unless the discharge of its duties obliges it to have an extraordinary session. The term of the delegates is six years.

3. The governmental structure is provided in Chapters IV–IX, dealing with the Presidency, Administration, Legislation, Justice, Examination, and Control, respectively; in other words, the organization and functions of the Five Yuan plus those of the presidency.

The system of the executive, as far as the provisions go, is not clear-cut. It can be either a presidential or a cabinet system of government, depending on the development of the political situation in terms of both personalities and political parties. If the President is a man who covets power, there are provisions he can make use of to establish a presidential system of government, for it is he who selects the head of the Executive Yuan. If, on the other hand, the political parties are influential and the leadership is democratically selected, a cabinet government can well result, since the Legislative Yuan, through its majority, has the right to approve the President's choice of the head of the Executive Yuan and hold that Yuan responsible for all acts and policies of the executive. To go further, if the Legislative Yuan is supple and willingly submits to the President, the latter can become a dictator without violating any of the constitutional provisions. The minority in the Legislative Yuan has no effective check on the President, if he chooses to exercise his powers in a personal and dictatorial manner. But if the majority party in the Legislative Yuan prefers a responsible government of the Executive Yuan, there are ample provisions to have that form of government.

The Executive Yuan is headed by the President of the Yuan. He alone is appointed by the President of the Republic with the consent of the Legislative Yuan. The other members of the Yuan, including the Vice-President, are therefore selected by the President of the Yuan. But there is a large measure of joint responsibility, for every member of the Yuan is obliged to submit matters of importance to the Executive Yuan Council.[4]

The Legislative Yuan, under the new Constitution, is a full-fledged parliament, as in any Western country. Its special feature, like that of the National Assembly, lies in the composition of its membership, for there are representatives of both geographic and vocational constituencies.

The Judicial Yuan is both a constitution-interpreting organ and an over-all administrative office for the high courts of various jurisdictions, very much like the Judicial Yuan of the old days. According to the resolution of the Political Consultative Conference on Constitutional Draft, the Yuan was to be nothing more than the supreme court of the nation, enjoying also the power of interpreting the constitution. But according to the Constitution of 1946, it retains its old position, with this new power added to it.

There is little change in the Examination Yuan, except that it is now to be a collegiate organization and its President, Vice-President, and members are all appointed by the President of the Republic with the consent of the Control Yuan in exactly the same manner.

The Control Yuan retains its old organization and functions. The power of rectification which the Control Yuan exercised but which was not explicitly granted in the Organic Law of the National Government is now so granted. There are two other innovations both proposed by the Political Consultative Conference; first, that the members of the Yuan be elected by the provincial (and municipal) assemblies, and second, that the President's appointment of certain high officials charged with nonpolitical functions be approved by the Yuan. These innovations have the effect of making the Control Yuan resemble the American Senate, minus the latter's legislative function.

Clearly, the new structure is very much of an improvement over that of the National Government. If political parties of vitality and independence, in the sense that they do not depend on a military leader for their existence, exist, a democratic government of the Western type may indeed evolve. The great drawback is that a strong-man type of politico-military leader can build with equal ease, and is destined to build, a personal dictatorial government out of the seemingly democratic provisions of the constitution.

4. The division of powers between the central and local governments is regulated in Chapter X. The Constitution seems to have established a threefold division of the powers of government. Not only is there the juxtaposition of the central and provincial governments, but there is also that of the provincial and the *hsien* governments. Some matters are for the central government alone to legislate and execute. Others are for the central government to legislate, but the execution may be handled by the central government itself or delegated to the provincial or even *hsien* government. Still others are for the province to legislate, but the province may either execute the laws itself or delegate their execution to the *hsien*. Finally, there are matters which are legislated and executed by the *hsien* alone.

This complicated arrangement represented a reaction against the highly centripetal tendencies of the Kuomintang government, especially in the last years of the war. Whether the provisions can be faithfully observed depends very much on whether the provincial and *hsien* regimes can become both strong and popular governments. A weak local government can never resist a central government. A strong but unpopular government will turn readily into a particularist regime or even warlordism, but can never become a cog of a smooth-running machine of divided powers. Furthermore, the success of the constitutional arrangement will have also to await a clearer definition of the powers enumerated under various articles of the Constitution. For instance, "the educational system," "provincial education," and "*hsien* education" are listed as matters falling within the separate competence of the various governments. But they certainly have to be defined before a clear and reasonable distinction among them can be made.

5. The system of local governments of the provinces and their *hsien* is given in Chapter XI. Since the province and the *hsien* are each entitled to have a fundamental "Law of Self-Government" to be adopted by an assembly elected specifically for that purpose, the Constitution merely prescribes that both units should have a popular elected assembly and an elected executive, governor in the case of the province and magistrate in the case of the *hsien*. The proposed home rule, so to speak, is not very meaningful, however. The law of a lower unit is invalidated if it conflicts with that of a higher unit; and whether it is in conflict or not, the interpretation is in the hands of a government organ of the higher unit. Therefore, unless the powers divided among the central and local governments are clearly defined, which they are not, it is to be presumed that the advantage of dispute will always be on the side of the central government.

6. National policies form a separate chapter, Chapter XIII. There are sections dealing with national defense, foreign affairs, national economy, so-

cial security, education and culture, and the special welfare of border regions, respectively. Some of these sections were carried over from the Draft of 1936, but some others were new. The section on national defense is an emphasis on the neutrality of the armed forces desired by the non-Kuomintang parties of the Political Consultative Conference. The profession of faith in world peace and international coöperation is the expression of a noble sentiment, spun out at a time when the conference was in a rather exuberant mood. The special provisions for the groups of people living in the border regions testify to a new consciousness that internal harmony among the different racial groups of China and a balanced development of the nation are conditional on the rapid cultural and economic advancement of those groups. If it means anything at all to have the more fundamental national policies outlined in the fundamental document, Chapter XIII of the Constitution of 1946 is certainly an improvement over the corresponding parts in the Draft of 1936.

7. Amendment of the Constitution is made either by the National Assembly alone or by resolution of the Legislative Yuan combined with ratification by the Assembly. Amendment by the Assembly requires one-fifth of the total membership for the initiation of a resolution, the attendance of a two-thirds quorum to consider it, and finally, a majority of three-fourths of the members present to pass on it. If the action is taken first by the Legislative Yuan, one-fourth of its membership is required to initiate the resolution, a three-fourths quorum to consider it, and a majority of three-fourths of the members present for the passage. But the referendum vote of the National Assembly on the constitutional resolutions of the Legislative Yuan requires no special quorum and only a bare majority. On the surface, the amending process is not an easy one. But if the Assembly happens to be dominated by one party, and that party also happens to be dominated by one leader, the amending process is not as difficult as it would appear.

Two general conclusions on the Constitution of 1946 can now be attempted. The first is concerned with the question whether it is in agreement with the constitutional resolution of the Political Consultative Conference. If the Constituent National Assembly had been a genuine sovereign assembly, popularly elected and representing the will of the people, it would be of little import whether the resolutions of an inter-party conference, which the Political Consultative Conference certainly was, were or were not adhered to. But since the National Assembly which met in 1946 was not such a sovereign assembly, the agreement solemnly entered into by all parties was essential to the general observance of the Constitution by the nation as a whole. It was this factor that compelled both the Kuomintang and its allied parties which enacted the Constitution to claim that the Constitution was in essential agreement with the resolution of the conference, and the other parties, which opposed it, to claim to the contrary that the resolution had been violated. A fair appraisal would seem to indicate this: while most of the lesser changes suggested by the resolution were embodied in the Constitution, the all-important checks placed on the powers of the President of the Republic were not.

The second general conclusion is that aside from the point just mentioned, the Constitution is a fairly good document, better in draftsmanship, more democratic in spirit, and more satisfactory in the framework of government that it purports to build up than any other constitution, provisional constitution, or draft constitution, the Republic has had, with the possible exception of the ill-fated Ts'ao K'un Constitution of 1923. Indeed, the two constitutions are in more than one way comparable and kindred documents, similarly created and equally vulnerable.

Preparatory Work for the Enforcement of the Constitution

Acting on the last article of the Constitution that the preparatory procedure for the enforcement of the Constitution should be fixed by the Constituent National Assembly, the said Assembly on December 24, 1946 laid down the following points. First, the Constitution was to be promulgated by the National Government on January 1, 1947. Pursuant to the promulgation, all existing laws which happened to be in conflict with the Constitution were to be amended or repealed and the amending or repealing was to be completed before the convening of the First National Assembly. Second, within three months after the promulgation, the National Government was to complete the legislation of laws for the organization of the National Assembly and the Five Yuan and also laws for the election and the recall of the delegates to the Assembly, President and Vice-President of the Republic, and members of the Legislative and Control Yuan. Third, the election for the delegates of the Assembly and members of the Legislative and Control Yuan was to be completed within six months after the promulgation of the electoral laws. The members of the Control Yuan could be elected by the Provisional Provincial Assembly in case an elected provincial assembly had not come into being. Fourth, the First National Assembly was to be convened by the President of the National Government, the First Legislative Yuan to convene itself seven days after the adjournment of the Assembly, and the First Control Yuan to be convened by the President of the Republic after the adjournment of the Assembly. In order not to delay unduly the convening of these three elected assemblies, they could be convened as soon as two-thirds of the total membership had been duly elected and the six-month period allowed for the election had elapsed.

After enacting the Constitution and making these arrangements for its enforcement, the National Assembly, pretending that it had the sacred duty to supervise the enforcement, declared its term of office extended to the day when the First National Assembly would be convened. The real motive of the members in so doing was not as public-spirited as they professed. They foresaw that the First National Assembly would not come into being according to schedule, and they also wished to avail themselves of the possibility of serving as the First National Assembly.

Pursuant to these decisions of the Constituent National Assembly, the National Government first promulgated the Constitution on January 1, 1947, and started to amend or repeal the laws which were in conflict with the provisions of the Constitution. The required organic and electoral laws were enacted also in due time. But the elections themselves were not completed within the time prescribed by the Constituent National Assembly. For, whereas law-making, especially the making of nonrealistic laws, is easy, election is an act involving not only parties but also the factional and personal strife within the dominant party and cannot be done in a hurry.[5]

XXII

THE NEW GOVERNMENT OF 1948

The First National Assembly

Pursuant to Article 34 of the Constitution, the Law for the Election and Recall of the Delegates of the National Assembly of March 31, 1947, together with the more detailed regulations for the enforcement of that Law, was enacted and promulgated. The number of delegates for the geographic constituencies including the Mongolian Banners is fixed by the Constitution itself. Every *hsien* (or municipality) elects a minimum of one delegate and for each half million population in excess of the minimum of one half million, the *hsien* is entitled to elect an additional delegate. Every Banner elects four delegates. The Legislative Yuan also gave generous quotas of delegates to the other categories. This generosity found further expression when, in response to demands for increased representation, larger quotas were granted.[1]

The Law for the Election and Recall of the Delegates also prescribes that candidates standing for the election have to be either sponsored by five hundred voters in the constituency or proposed by a political party. In either case, their names must be registered with the election authorities. The former method was intended as a concession to independent candidates not members of any party. But as a party the Kuomintang was such a powerful organization that real independents rarely had the courage to run in competition with its men, and the pseudo-independents usually depended upon it to secure the signatures of the five hundred voters necessary for entering their names on the list of candidates. The candidates' qualification was the Kuomintang's desire for them. The nominations were quite tightly controlled by the machine of the Kuomintang.

But there were internal conflicts within the Kuomintang. The party organization was in the hands of the Organization Group, a powerful but unpopular faction. Its failure to do justice to all factions of the party and to appreciate the personal influence which some of the party members, not adherents of the group, enjoyed in their home *hsien* or their professions, caused these members to seek nomination by sponsorship of the voters in defiance of the party's instruction that all members had to clear with the constituted authorities of the party in order to become candidates. This open defiance of the decisions and authorities of the party complicated the Assembly elections to an extent unforeseen by the leaders of the Kuomintang.

The election contests were thus preceded by what one may consider nomination contests. A member of any party who wanted to stand for the election had to work for nomination by his party. Failing that, he had to secure no less than five hundred voters to sponsor his candidacy. The same was more or less true of a nonparty aspirant. He too had to rely on some party, or, to be more correct, the Kuomintang, to secure the required number of voters for the sponsorship of his candidacy. When such assistance was not forthcoming, he cast about to see what resources he himself possessed, either in the way of personal friends or finances, which would substitute for the assistance of the Kuomintang.

In the election of the National Assembly in 1947, those aspirants who were neither influential members of any party nor nonparty people who commanded high prestige and held political views acceptable to the Kuomintang had to spend much time and money first to secure the sponsorship of five hundred voters and then to win the election itself. Such private candidates, as distinguished from official candidates nominated by the parties, stood very little chance of election when they were pitted against strong official candidates. Fortunately for them, official candidates were not always strong. The candidates of the two small parties were usually unheard of persons gifted neither with professional competence nor with political ability, and those of the Kuomintang were not always its best men or best vote-getters. Many hundreds of Kuomintang irregulars, so to speak, won election over the official candidates of the Kuomintang, as well as over those of the small parties.

In rare cases where the candidates, official or unofficial, were men of acknowledged leadership and had popular prestige or political influence in the constituency, they encountered little difficulty of election. But in most cases the candidates had little chance of election unless they were backed by the Kuomintang or government machine which had the vote to deliver. The heads of local government areas in the *hsien* constituencies and the officers of the vocational unions and associations were all-powerful. In any analysis of the caliber and character of the three thousand delegates of the National Assembly, these considerations must be borne in mind. They explain the presence of a few big names and a good number of rather honest people, as well as the overwhelming predominance of Kuomintang regulars who could not and did not want to depart from the ways and means of the last twenty years.

But in spite of the heavy controlling hand of the Kuomintang Party machine, the election of 1947 was unsatisfactory both to the Kuomintang high leadership and to the party machine. It was unsatisfactory to the party machine not only because too many irregulars succeeded in getting themselves elected, but also because the factions in rivalry with the Organization Group were quite successful. The inability of the Organization Group to exercise an undisputed control of the Assembly was to cause difficulties in the vice-presidential election. It was unsatisfactory to the high leadership of the Kuomintang because it caused fresh discord between the Kuomintang and the two small parties.

It had originally been agreed between the Kuomintang, on the one hand, and the Youth Party and the Democratic Socialist Party, on the other, that the latter would be assured of 300 and 260 seats respectively. The Kuomintang had thought that by not naming a candidate of its own in constituencies where the other two had entered candidates, the required number of seats could be safely secured for them. But two miscalculations caused this arrangement to miscarry. First, the Kuomintang party machine underestimated the ability of some members, not followers of the machine, to secure the nomination and election without its blessings. Second, the Kuomintang also underestimated the hopelessness of the other two parties. In spite of their having been artificially fed and chivalrously supported by the Kuomintang, and in spite of the fact that many new members had joined them in order to secure easy election, either the repute of the parties was so low or their candidates were so unacceptable that only a few of their candidates succeeded in getting elected. The Youth Party elected 70 and the Democratic Socialists, 68. The disappointed parties made an outcry and threatened to boycott the Assembly, and the disappointed Kuomintang had to do some placating.

The Kuomintang first tried to persuade all their own members nominated and elected without the intercession of the party to yield their seats in favor of the official candidates of all parties, thereby expecting to seat both its own regulars and the nominees of the other two parties. There was not only the matter of seats promised to the other parties but the defeated official candidates of the Kuomintang themselves had also to be accommodated. But neither persuasion nor threat nor a combination of both produced the desired results. Preferring to incur expulsion from the party to giving up their seats, most of the successful unofficial candidates defied the orders and entreaties of the Kuomintang. The number of seats yielded and made available for the official candidates were not enough to satisfy the needs of the Kuomintang and still less those of the other parties. In the face of the unsolved tangle, the central election authorities withheld again and again the announcement of the final election results.[2] When on the eve of the convening of the Assembly on March 29, 1948, 2832 delegates were announced as definitively elected, the wrangles had not ended.

Two days before the convening, Chiang Kai-shek, as Leader of the Kuomintang, called a conference of the party's delegates to the Assembly, and announced a twofold principle for the solution of the difficulties; first, where the candidate of a friendly party, meaning the Youth and the Democratic Socialist Parties, was involved, the elected Kuomintang candidate must give up the seat; when only members of the Kuomintang were involved in the contest, the one who got the largest vote should be declared elected, whether he was an official nominee of the party or nominated by the voters. He instructed that certificates of election should go to those thus qualified. In the meantime, through various strategies, the Youth and Democratic Socialist Parties were given 230 and 202 seats respectively in the Assembly, partly from the seats which were or should be yielded by the Kuomintang candidates and partly from the quota of seats for those areas where election had not taken place, such as constituencies in the northeastern provinces.

But even the authority of the Leader was not quite sufficient to settle all contests. A number of those Kuomintang members who considered themselves duly elected and who were now ordered to yield their seats to the "friendly parties" refused to yield. Instead, they staged a sitdown strike inside the Assembly building when it was about to commence its session. At that, more expedients were suggested. Some proposed the addition of 300 to the Assembly, thereby seating all contestants. Others made the novel suggestion that the term of six years be shared by the contestants: the official candidates of the parties to hold the office during the first half, and the unofficial candidates who succeeded in the election to hold office for the other half. Both these proposals were seriously considered but finally abandoned. The wrangle went on for a few more days after the convening of the Assembly on March 29, but finally all the unofficial candidates of Kuomintang membership who claimed to have been elected were dealt with by being admitted to the Assembly or by promise of other considerations. On April 6, the Assembly was finally in a position to discuss its own organization.

The First National Assembly was formally opened on March 29, 1947 and adjourned on May 1. The first few days were spent in an attempt to settle the electoral contests. From March 31 to April 5 it engaged itself in the business of electing a presidium. At first, a presidium of twenty-five was elected. When it was expanded to eighty-five, a new election was made necessary. From April 7 to 9, the Assembly deliberated and adopted its Rules of Procedure. Then came a few days devoted to the discussion of domestic and external politics, with the ministers making reports and the delegates interpellating them. From April 15 to 18, a campaign to amend the Constitution was undertaken resulting in the adoption of so-called "Temporary Provisions." When that was done, the Assembly went into the business of electing the President and the Vice-President of the Republic.

The election and the passage of the "Temporary Provisions" will be discussed in a later section. Amending the Constitution was well within the competence of the Assembly, but demanding records from the government and interpellating its ministers was another question. If the purpose was merely to have an exchange of views between delegates of the Assembly and members of the government, it could have been better served elsewhere and in a more informal way than on the floor of the Assembly. If the purpose was to secure an account of the work of the government, the Assembly was duplicating the function and encroaching upon the authority of the Legislative Yuan. By being required to hold itself responsible before the Assembly as well as before the Legislative Yuan, the government was in an untenable position. In requiring the reports to be made on the floor of the National Assembly followed by interpellations, the Assembly was openly violating the Constitution; and in not resisting the unconstitutional demands of the Assembly, the government was equally guilty. The government of course had reasons for nonresistance. Its leaders wanted to be as inoffensive to the Assembly as possible, and in case too serious difficulties should arise, they knew that they could count on the Leader of the Kuomintang to hold the delegates in check. Still the deal further discredited both the Assembly and the government.

Although the Assembly had the right to amend the Constitution, the wisdom of doing so was obviously in doubt. The Constitution had been enacted only sixteen months earlier and some three-fourths of the delegates of the Constituent National Assembly were also delegates of the First National Assembly. For them to demand radical amendments to the Constitution so shortly after its enactment and promulgation was inconceivable. But that section of the Kuomintang which had originally opposed the reduction of the powers of the National Assembly and the establishment of a responsible cabinet government, as proposed by the Political Consultative Conference, was still craving the restoration of a powerful presidency and the establishment of an Assembly with more substantial powers. Consequently various amendments along these two lines were proposed by the delegates. It was only the fear of unfavorable reaction from the democratic West and of the two minor parties' threat to bolt the Assembly that led to Chiang Kai-shek's haranguing the Kuomintang delegates on April 24 not to attempt any formal amendment of the Constitution. Instead, "Temporary Provisions" for the increase of the presidential powers were adopted.

These provisions, besides satisfying Chiang Kai-shek's own demand for more power, were also gratifying to the National Assembly. By virtue of a provision that the National Assembly should be called not later than the end of 1950 to consider whether the Temporary Provisions should be continued or repealed, the Assembly was sure of an early meeting, earlier than the scheduled triennial date provided for in the Constitution. For it is a fact that the delegates of the National Assembly, though distinctly not legislators, like to have as frequent and long sessions as possible. They cannot reconcile themselves to the idea that their periodic and obligatory function is to elect the President and Vice-President, and that they are not to do anything else unless there is a constitutional necessity for so doing.

The Assembly proved to be the most boisterous and unorganized of all assemblies China has had so far. In the last few years there have been three very large Kuomintang or Kuomintang-dominated assemblies, the Sixth Congress of the Party in May 1945, the Constituent National Assembly of November–December 1946, and the present Assembly. In actual attendance, the first one was around 1000, the second around 1500, and the last around 2000. The larger the number, the less orderly and parliamentary it became. The present Assembly is unique in the sense that it resembles neither a Western parliament, for there is in fact only one party, nor the national assembly of a country with a party dictatorship, for the Kuomintang delegates in the Assembly are badly split into factions, incapable of harmonious action and unheedful of party decisions beyond taking the orders of a leader who is not above capriciousness. Even those who think that progress may result from the careful working of even a bad institution will have to stretch their optimism very far in order to justify their belief in the present Assembly. It is already a more perverse type than its predecessor of 1946. At any rate, it is fair to say that judging by the First National Assembly, China seems to be farther and farther away from the democratic type of government of the West.

The President of the Republic

The Constitution has no stipulation about the election of the President and Vice-President beyond saying that they are to be elected by the National Assembly. Their election and also their recall are provided by the Law for the Election and Recall of the President and Vice-President, of March 31, 1947. According to this Law, the President and the Vice-President are separately elected. Candidates have to be nominated by no less than one hundred members of the National Assembly. The candidate who receives the majority of the votes cast is elected. If no one is elected on the first ballot, the Assembly is to choose one from the three who receive the highest number of votes. If after the third ballot, still none is able to receive a majority of votes cast, the choice will on the fourth ballot be limited to the two receiving the highest votes. Thus by the fourth ballot, some one is sure to receive a majority of the votes cast, and he is declared elected.

As for the recall, the initiative is taken either by the National Assembly or by the Control Yuan. One-sixth of the total membership of the Assembly may in writing and with stated reasons propose to recall the President or the Vice-President. This recall proposal is published by the secretary-general of the National Assembly as soon as received. If within thirty days after publication nobody disowns the signatures or if the disowning by those whose names are in the list does not reduce the number of the valid countersignatures to less than the required one-sixth, the proposal is forwarded to the President of the Legislative Yuan, who in turn summons the National Assembly to meet within one month to act on the recall. Simultaneously with the summoning of the Assembly, the President or Vice-President to be recalled is notified of the recall proposal and is entitled to send to the National Assembly his defense, which is also forthwith published by the secretary-general. To recall the President or Vice-President on the initiative of the Assembly, a majority vote of all the members of the Assembly is necessary. If the recall action is initiated by the Control Yuan in the form of an impeachment, a vote of two-thirds of the members present in the National Assembly is necessary. When the National Assembly has voted against the recall, those members of the National Assembly proposing the recall cannot make a second proposal against the same incumbent. Also, the delegates of the National Assembly are not allowed to initiate a recall action within one year after the inauguration of the President or Vice-President.

The powers of the President are of course enumerated in the Constitution. Naturally, he has all the powers usually pertaining to a head of state. What needs to be considered here are his powers of issuing decrees, of appointment, of command, of settling the disputes among the Yuan, and finally, his emergency powers.

Decrees issued by the President of the Republic must, according to Article 37 of the Constitution, be countersigned by the President of the Executive Yuan or by him and the head of the ministry or commission concerned. In this, there is no change between the new Constitution and the superseded Organic Law of the National Government. Unless therefore the President of the Executive Yuan could develop a high degree of independence, accruing from his leadership of a majority in the Legislative Yuan to which he is responsible, the power of the President of the Republic under the new Constitution would remain as supreme as it was in the past.

Concerning the power of appointment, the Constitution provides that "the President shall in accordance with law, appoint and remove civil and military officials" (Article 41). Presumably, the civil servants in general would continue to be appointed according to civil service laws in force. The appointment or election of the Presidents and Vice-Presidents of the Yuan having been provided for by the Constitution, only the manner of appointment of those high officials who used to be appointed with the approval of the Political Council of the Central Executive Committee of the Kuomintang is in doubt. In the days of the National Government, the nomination of these officials, if they happened to be under the Executive Yuan, had to be considered also by the Executive Yuan. But that is dispensed with under the new Constitution. In theory, therefore, one of two alternatives may follow. Either the Legislative Yuan will authorize the different Yuan and their ministries and commissions to appoint all the officials not classified under the civil service; or, in the absence of such a law, the President of the Republic will presumably enjoy a freer power of appointment than the President of the National Government.

The power of command hinges on whether the President of the Republic is to take personal command or to remain merely a symbol of high command, leaving actual control of the armed forces in the hands of the Minister of National Defense, who is to consider himself an integral part of the Executive Yuan. In the past, the head of state has so liberally construed the relevant constitutional provision as to consider the power of command to belong to him personally, and to him alone. Unless there is a change of concept, a new practice is not likely to ensue. If the President of the Republic continues to be so interested in command of the armed forces, he is also likely to exercise personally the power of appointment of military officials. Shorn of the military power it is inconceivable that the Executive Yuan can ever be held responsible before the Legislative.

The power of settling disputes among the Yuan, though given to the President, should not be of much importance, since a conflict between the Legislative Yuan and the Executive Yuan is to be solved according to the provisions of the Constitution and the other three Yuan, each having a special function to discharge independently of the Legislative and Executive Yuan, should not come into any conflict with any Yuan at all. However, the grant of power to the President does in some ways give an opening wedge for presidential interference. In this sense, the article in question (Article 44) is worse than superfluous.

The emergency powers of the President are, according to the Constitution (Articles 39, 43), two in number. The first is that the President is legally authorized to declare martial law. The said declaration must be either previously approved or subsequently ratified by the Legislative Yuan which has the right to ask the President to lift the martial law. The second is that the president in case of natural calamity, epidemic, or a serious financial or economic crisis, may, when the Legislative Yuan is in recess, by resolution of the Executive Yuan Council and in accordance with the Emergency Decrees Law, issue emergency decrees necessary to cope with the situation. The said decrees are to be presented to the Legislative Yuan for ratification, failing which they are to lapse at once.

These are extensive powers. With the support of the Executive Yuan, the

President of the Republic can, during the recess of the Legislative Yuan, govern the country with decrees. With the support of the Legislative Yuan also, the President can so govern the country at all times. Analysis of these emergency provisions thus reinforces the remark made above [3] that unless the Legislative Yuan becomes an organ of vitality with the presence of more than one political party of strength and influence, a presidential government instead of a responsible cabinet government will result from the new constitutional arrangement.

But somehow the government that was about to be organized in May 1948 was not satisfied even with this extensive grant of emergency powers. Before electing Chiang Kai-shek as President of the Republic, the National Assembly on April 18 adopted the so-called "Temporary Provisions for the Duration of Mobilization to Suppress the Rebellion." [4] These provisions authorize the President, for the period in question, by resolution of the Executive Yuan Council, to take any emergency measure in order to prevent the state or the people from facing immediate dangers or to cope with financial or economic crises; and the said measures are not subject to the procedural limitations of Articles 39 and 43 of the Constitution. The only restraints which the representatives of the people could hope to place on the emergency measures of the President are, first, the Legislative Yuan might under Article 57 by resolution ask the Executive Yuan to modify or annul such measures, and second, the First National Assembly would have a chance to discuss, not later than December 25, 1950, the extension or repeal of the Temporary Provisions themselves. But both are ineffective restraints. Under Article 57, the President could veto such a resolution of the Legislative Yuan and the veto could be overruled only with a two-thirds majority. It is scarcely conceivable that the President would not even command a following of one-third of the Legislative Yuan. As for the reconsideration by the National Assembly, it is even less of a restraint. The Assembly which was willing to grant the President these Temporary Provisions in 1948 is not likely to begrudge him the same grant in 1949.

The enactment of the "Temporary Provisions" meant only that the president who was presently to be elected could not tolerate any interference of the Legislative Yuan in his exercise of the emergency powers, or any delay interposed by that Yuan in that exercise. Like many other things that have happened since the promulgation of the Constitution on January 1, 1947, this too is a sad commentary on the actual operation of the Constitution. The eagerness of the National Assembly to change the Constitution to suit the President-to-be and the latter's impatience to secure the willing coöperation of the Legislative Yuan are sure indications that, Constitution or no Constitution, the power of the President is not to be checked.

Analyzing the Constitution of 1948 and comparing it with the laws and practices preceding it, one may even say that the President of the Republic is a more powerful figure than the President of the National Government, unless, as has been repeatedly pointed out, a responsible Executive Yuan becomes a reality. For the new President has retained, except for the power of appointing the Presidents of the Five Yuan, almost all the powers of the old President. But whereas the old President had in theory to transact the presidential business in the State Council, no such council is now in existence. Thus it may be said that the new President combines the powers that formerly belonged to the President and to the State Council of the National Government. The President is the sole successor to the National Government of the last two decades.

The Organic Law of the President's Office of March 25, 1948 is also fully in harmony with the spirit of the times. The State Council is no more. But the President has the right to appoint an indefinite number of Grand Councilors, to act as his high advisers severally. The newly created Advisory Council may also be considered the continuing body of the State Council, for many members of the old body were appointed as members of the new. The War Council, formerly placed directly under the National Government, is now supplanted by the Advisory Council on Strategy, also an adjunct of the President's Office. The Chief Secretary, his Chinese title slightly changed, and the Chief Military Officer remain with their large-sized staffs. The elaborate establishment of aides, previously a unique and influential staff establishment of the Chairman of the Military Commission, is now placed under the supervision of the Chief Secretary. Indeed, very little remodeling was necessary to transform the old National Government into the new President's Office.

The incumbent too is the same Chiang Kai-shek. As the Leader of the Kuomintang which is the dominating party in the National Assembly, it was a foregone conclusion that Chiang Kai-shek and no one else would be elected President of the Republic under the new Constitution. But on April 4 Chiang Kai-shek declared to the Central Executive Committee of his party that he preferred a more active job and wished the party to elect someone else to the presidency. The committee said no and he was duly elected on April 19, though not before the enactment of the Temporary Provisions. Another Kuomintang veteran, Chü Cheng, formerly President of the Judicial Yuan, was persuaded to stand for the presidency to contest the election. Chü Cheng received 269 to Chiang Kai-shek's 2430 votes, and Chiang Kai-shek was elected.

The election of the vice-president lasted four ballots and took a full week to accomplish. It was more of a real contest, for it revealed how badly divided the factions of the Kuomintang were. Li Tsung-jen, commander of one of the four Army Groups of the Northern Expedition, had started early and was the hopeful candidate, but Chiang Kai-shek was lukewarm towards his candidacy and the Kuomintang machine was even hostile. Besides Li Tsung-jen, there were three other aspirants from the Kuomintang. The machine favored one of these three. In order to prevent Li Tsung-jen's election, it proposed that the party nominate a candidate for the vice-presidency. If this had been done, Li Tsung-jen and the two others who would not have received the Kuomintang nomination would of course have stood little chance of being elected. The three joined hands and demanded the so-called "open candidacy" and secured Chiang Kai-shek's approval of it. All four became candidates without official party sponsorship. When balloting started, Li Tsung-jen led all the other candidates in votes received, but did not have a majority. There was much maneuvering and countermaneuvering as the protracted balloting went on. Finally Li Tsung-jen was elected on the fourth ballot, in spite of the hostility of the party machine of the Kuomintang.

The Executive Yuan

The Organic Law for the new Executive Yuan [5] was also enacted by the old Legislative Yuan. Except that the Budgetary Office was made a part of the Executive Yuan instead of remaining directly under the President as it had been in the National Government, there was not much difference between the new and the old organization. The principal difference lay in the relationship between the Executive Yuan and the Legislative Yuan. Though the President of the Executive Yuan continued to be nominated by the President of the Republic, as he was by the President of the National Government, his appointment was now conditional on the approval of the Legislative Yuan. The original intention of such an arrangement was to have a man who could lead and secure the support of the majority of the Legislative Yuan named as President of the Executive Yuan, thereby holding the executive branch responsible to the legislative branch.

But in the organization of the new government in May 1948, reality departed widely from theory, and the practice of old was repeated. In the first place, though there was an overwhelming Kuomintang majority in the Legislative Yuan, the majority was so divided that there was no compact majority faction. No single faction or bloc of factions was in a position either to nominate or to insist on the nomination of a leader of its own. It was left for the President of the Republic, as the undisputed leader of the Kuomintang or of all Kuomintang factions in the Legislative Yuan, to nominate the President of the Executive Yuan. The President nominated a man who leads no faction at all. The majority of the Legislative Yuan agreed to vote him in because he was less objectionable than the leader of any powerful faction and also because as the personal nominee of the Leader of the Kuomintang, he had to be accepted.

Theoretically, again, the ministers of the Executive Yuan were to be named by the President of the Executive Yuan. He should have power to select his own ministers in very much the same fashion as the heads of the British and French cabinets: otherwise it would be meaningless to require the approval of the Legislative Yuan of his nomination. But the personal choices of the President of the Republic, as of old, prevailed.

In fact, the new Executive Yuan as announced on May 31, 1948 is very much a continuation of the old. The change in personnel is very slight. As far as the personnel is concerned, to call it a new reorganized cabinet would require no little stretch of the imagination, and to consider it a new cabinet constitutionalized and revitalized would indeed require much sophistry.

There are in the new Executive Yuan, not counting its President and Vice-President, twenty-two ministers; thirteen of them ministers of ministries, three, chairmen of commissions, one, the Chief Budgetary Officer of the Ministry of the Budget, and the rest ministers without portfolio. According to the official announcement, four of the ministers belong to the Youth Party and three are nonpartisan independents. While the first four are genuine members of that party allied to the Kuomintang, the three independents are hardly more independent of the Kuomintang than the President of the Yuan himself. The Democratic Socialist Party abstained. But there are, among the list of ministers without portfolio, two vacancies waiting to be filled. Presumably, when that party decides to join and is able to nominate its own candidates, it can readily join the Executive Yuan. Whatever that party may do, the essential nature of the new Executive Yuan is definite beyond any doubt. It is a Kuomintang government.

The most disheartening thing about the reorganized Executive Yuan is not that it is not a truly multiparty body, but that it is not even a revitalized Kuomintang body. Perhaps it is just as utopian, if not more so, to hope for a revitalized Kuomintang government as to hope for a truly multiparty government. The Leader of the Kuomintang has not changed. The dominating power and influence of the Leader has not changed. Changes in the government are naturally out of the question.

The Legislative Yuan

The Organic Law of the Legislative Yuan of December 25, 1947 and the Law for the Election of the Members of the Legislative Yuan of March 31, 1947 were both passed by the old Legislative Yuan. In pursuance of the electoral law, elections took place on January 21–23, 1948. There are 773 members of the Legislative Yuan to be elected. There is both geographical and professional representation, in the manner of the election of the delegates of the National Assembly.[6] Every province (or municipality of the provincial rank) with a population below three millions, elects five members. For every million in excess of three millions, an additional member is allotted. Women are not given a separate representation. The electoral law only requires that in every group of constituencies one member must be a woman if the quota is below ten, and there must be one additional woman for every ten in excess of the first ten.

The struggles for nomination and election were similar to those experienced in the election of the National Assembly. The same conflict raged between the Kuomintang-sponsored candidates and Kuomintang members sponsored by voters, in this case 3000 in geographical constituencies, 500 in vocational ones, and 200 in the case of a woman candidate. The same wrangle arising out of the demands of the small parties to be guaranteed certain quotas by the Kuomintang dismayed the Kuomintang leadership. Benefiting by the experience of the Assembly election held earlier, the Kuomintang required every candidate sponsored by it to deposit with it a written pledge to decline to serve as a member of the Legislative Yuan. With this instrument in hand, the party actually called on its successful candidates to yield the seats to the unsuccessful candidates of the other parties. But even by doing this, the guaranteed quotas still could not be filled, as the yielding could take place only in the same constituency in which the contestants were involved. When the Legislative Yuan finally met on May 10, 1948, the Youth and Democratic Socialist Parties were still protesting by abstaining and some makeshift means were necessary to satisfy them.

On the whole, the caliber of the members of the Legislative Yuan is superior to that of the delegates to the National Assembly. The more active politicians prefer membership of the Yuan to that of the Assembly, in spite of the shorter term of office, a term of only three years. Of the Kuomintang leaders, the elders are usually found in the Assembly, but the younger and more ambitious ones choose to be seated in the Legislative Yuan.

Unlike those of the old Legislative Yuan, the President and Vice-President of the new Yuan are elected from among the members, and the committees, increased to nineteen, also elect their own chairmen.[7] The First Legislative Yuan elected Sun Fo, President of the old Yuan, as President. Sun Fo, who has drawn himself closer and closer to the Kuomintang machine during the last years, had hoped to become the Vice-President of the Republic and at the same time retain the presidency of the Yuan. He failed to secure the vice-presidency of the Republic but was rewarded with the presidency of the Legislative Yuan. This does not mean, however, that he will be able to control its members, as he did in the old Yuan. Of the members of the present Yuan, the most compact as well as the largest bloc represents the Organization Group of the Kuomintang. Whether the Legislative Yuan will be a restrained or a tyrannical body or even a paralyzing influence will depend on how the members of that group behave.

Already the Legislative Yuan is proving itself difficult for the Executive Yuan. Although the Kuomintang-dominated Legislative Yuan had, in accordance with the expressed wish of Chiang Kai-shek, to accept his nominee as President of the Executive Yuan, it by no means acknowledged the accepted nominee as a leader. After his first appearance before the Legislative Yuan to announce the policy plans of the new government, he was subjected to endless devastating questions. Unless the Leader of the Kuomintang gives the politically weak President of the Executive Yuan full support by constantly applied strong pressure on the Legislative Yuan, the position of the President of the Executive Yuan may prove to be untenable.

The Leader can easily give such support to the President of the Executive Yuan, since there now exists a delicate system of checks and balances between the Executive and the Legislative Yuan. According to Article 53 of the Constitution, the Legislative Yuan can express its disapproval of the policies of the Executive Yuan by resolution and can demand a change of those policies, while the Executive Yuan, with the approval of the President of the Republic, can ask the Legislative Yuan to reconsider the latter's resolution. Only when the Legislative Yuan sustains that resolution by a two-thirds majority is the President of the Executive Yuan compelled either to comply or resign.

Under this arrangement, an Executive Yuan supported by the President of the Republic needs the support of only one-third of the Legislative Yuan members. In other words, with such support from the President of the Republic and one-third of the Legislative Yuan, the President of the Executive Yuan will be able to disregard the majority of the Legislative Yuan by vetoing all its resolutions unacceptable to him. The arrangement is superbly fitted to the existing conditions, in which the dominant personal leadership of the President of the Republic and Leader of the Kuomintang is not averse to using a weak President of the Executive Yuan to carry out his own wishes.

The Control Yuan

According to the new Constitution, the Control Yuan becomes a representative assembly, elected by provincial and other local assemblies of a similar rank and the overseas Chinese, but not by vocational groups as is the case with the National Assembly and the Legislative Yuan. Each province elects five and each municipality of the provincial rank, two. The Mongolian Banners elect eight in all, and Tibet and the Chinese overseas, eight each. The total membership is 219.

The election of the members of the Control Yuan in 1948, being by the provincial and other assemblies, was more orderly than those for the members of the National Assembly and the Legislative Yuan. Older men preferred the Control Yuan to the Legislative Yuan. Competition was less keen and the term of office is six years, twice as long as that of a member of the Legislative Yuan. But this does not mean that the Control Yuan was satisfactory. Since most of the provincial assemblies are in the hands of the Organization Group of the Kuomintang, many outstanding members of the Kuomintang and other independent nonpartisan leaders were not able to compete with the adherents of the group.

According to the Constitution, the President and Vice-President of the Control Yuan are also elected from among the members of the Yuan. The election took place on June 8, 1948. Both the President and the Vice-President of the old Yuan were continued in office. As has been said before, the new Control Yuan had the powers both of control and of giving consent to certain appointments of the President of the Republic. The function of control takes either the form of impeachment or of rectification, a form which was not provided in the Law of Impeachment of June 24, 1932, but was in actual use during the war.[8]

An Appraisal of the New Government of 1948

The new government of 1948 follows the new Constitution of 1946. There are in that constitution provisions which could be used either to perpetuate a dictatorship or to bring about a more democratic government of the Western type. But the ways and spirit of the new government of 1948 definitely lean on the side of the *status quo*. If there are two alternatives present, one to continue the old system and the other to explore the possibilities of a new one, it is always the former in which the men of power trust.

The key to the understanding of this phenomenal reliance on the *status quo* is of course the personality of Chiang Kai-shek. His unchanged personality dominates the new government as much as it dominated the old one. The new government could not be different from the old. If there should develop any difference, it is likely to come from the existence of too many assemblies which all can lay claim to being representatives of the sovereign people, whether directly or indirectly elected. A complicated mechanism like the present one, not accompanied by any respect for the law or any spirit of mutual toleration among the different organs of the state, is likely to lead to greater concentration of power in one strong man than to the prevention of the abuse of power, one of the most cardinal principles of constitutionalism.

XXIII

POLITICAL PARTIES[1]

Political parties come into existence either when there are elections to be contested and the control of assemblies to fight for, or else when there are revolutions to lead and the power gained by revolutions to guard. According to their differences of aims, parties will differ in nature. The parties which fight for elections and for the control of the majority of an assembly usually tolerate and even welcome the existence of other parties. Those which are revolutionary and are eager to keep the fruits of revolution to themselves tend to be monopolistic. China has witnessed both types.

Parties at the End of the Manchu Dynasty

China did not have any political party until the last years of the Manchu Dynasty. The T'ung Meng Hui of Sun Yat-sen was a revolutionary party.[2] Opposed to the T'ung Meng Hui and having as its purpose the support of the Manchu rulers was the Nation-Preservation Association of K'ang Yu-wei and Liang Ch'i-ch'ao, organized in 1898, and rechristened in 1900 the Emperor-Preservation Association.[3]

Prior to the short-lived Reform Movement of 1898 led by K'ang Yu-wei and Liang Ch'i-ch'ao, there had existed many associations for the propagation of Western ideas of government and administration. It was on the strength of these associations that the two reform leaders organized their Nation-Preservation Association. When the abortive Reform Movement failed and they fled to Japan, they organized the Emperor-Preservation Association, which was to have a continuing influence on the political parties of the next half century.

In the modern West, parliamentary parties have sprung up contemporaneously with a constitution, for that fundamental law is usually followed by the rise of elected assemblies. It happened likewise with China. In 1908, after the Manchu Court promised the promulgation of a constitution, an Association to Prepare for the Establishment of Constitutional Government, headed by certain leading scholars not in government service, was organized. In 1910, as the result of the convening of the provincial assemblies, an Association of Comrades to Petition for the Parliament[4] was organized by the leading politicians in the provincial assemblies. Some of the leading spirits in the second Association had also been active in the first Association, but the first was not thereby dissolved. Both these organizations were important because in a sense they were the precursors of the Progressive Party in the future Republic.

When the Central Legislative Council was convened, those members of the Council who were adherents of the Association to Prepare for the Establishment of Constitutional Government formed the Friends of the Constitution Association. They were generally members elected by the provincial assemblies who took a position in opposition to the government. To support the government, the appointed members of the Council formed the Association for the Realization of Constitutionalism and the "Club of 1911."[5] In many ways the party alignment in the Council vis-à-vis the government, was not dissimilar to that of the early days of the Japanese Parliament. This was natural, for at that time the Manchu political system was copied after the Japanese.

Political Parties in the First Years of the Republic

After the Revolution of 1911 had succeeded in overthrowing the Manchus, parliamentary life of a more active type could be expected. There was a short period of feverish formations and transformations of political parties. In the brief space of two years, three stages of development may be noted.

The first period, occurring in the first months of 1912, witnessed the coming into the open and the subsequent disintegration of the T'ung Meng Hui, the rise of successors to the Friends of the Constitution Association, and the formation of other new parties. Six main parties or groups came into existence. The first was the recently emerged T'ung Meng Hui. The second was the United Party,[6] an amalgamation of the original Kuang Fu Hui faction of the T'ung Meng Hui and a part of the Association to Prepare for the Establishment of Constitutional Government. The third, the United Republican Party,[7] was also an offshoot of the T'ung Meng Hui, of which its leaders had formerly been members. This party was particularly significant because the Political Study Association of 1916–1917 and the Political Study Group of the present Kuomintang may be said to have been its lineal descendants. The fourth party, the People's Society,[8] was new and grouped around the person of Li Yuan-hung. The fifth and sixth parties[9] sprang out of the Friends of the Constitution Association. In this period, the republican Legislative Assembly, a provisional parliament, was sitting in Nanking and was about to be moved to the North. While all these six parties had some adherents in the Senate, party alignment in the Senate was in a state of great fluidity.

The second period, coinciding with the meeting of the Legislative Assembly in Peking and the election of the parliament in the winter of 1912–1913, saw the gradual crystallization of government and opposition parties. In May 1912, under the promptings of Yuan Shih-k'ai, then President, the United Party and the People's Society together with other smaller groups amalgamated into the Republican Party. In August, the T'ung Meng Hui and its offshoot, the United Republican Party, strengthened also by a number of smaller parties, organized the Kuomintang or Nationalist Party. A little later, in October, the Democratic Party was formed by the amalgamation of the two parties which had succeeded the Friends of the Constitution Association and the old Emperor-Preservation Association of Liang Ch'i-ch'ao. The Republican Party was Yuan Shih-k'ai's own party. The Kuomintang was not yet in outspoken opposition but was instead interested in winning the parliamentary election. The Democratic Party, rich in scholarship and experience gained both in constitutional agitation and in the central and local assemblies prior to the Revolution of 1911, was as yet undecided just what line to pursue. All three parties represented influential elements. In addition, the United Party, though it participated in the formation of the Republican Party, continued to maintain a separate existence.

The third period, which coincided with the meeting of the Parliament of 1913, was in a way the heyday of parliamentary parties in China. Under the leadership of Sung Chiao-jên the Kuomintang had won the election and won it decisively. It was the party of the young. Although heterogeneous, it was nevertheless liberal, buoyant, and intent on establishing a parliamentary democracy for China. The other three parties, the Republican Party, the United Party, and the Democratic Party, all to the right of the Kuomintang and all apprehensive of its ascendancy, had amalgamated into the Chinputang, or Progressive Party, as a measure of self-defense and self-preservation. The Chinputang supported Yuan Shih-k'ai while the Kuomintang was critical of his government. The Kuomintang had the majority in the Parliament and hoped to organize a responsible government. Had Yuan Shih-k'ai been willing to forego the personal exercise of the powers of government and to tolerate a cabinet government responsible to the elected parliament, the two parties might actually have trodden the paths of a conservative and a liberal party. Certainly if there has in the past half century ever been any prospect of that development in China, there was never a more auspicious moment. But of course no dictator of Yuan Shih-k'ai's type would tolerate such a prospect.

As soon as the smaller parties had gravitated logically into two camps, the Kuomintang and the Chinputang, Yuan Shih-k'ai decided to destroy them both. His first blow fell naturally on the Kuomintang, the party of opposition. Opportunist and cowardly elements of that party were bribed by Yuan Shih-k'ai to bolt the party and form separatist groups. After the unsuccessful anti-Yuan Shih-k'ai uprising of 1913 led by the more radical elements of the Kuomintang, the more enlightened elements of the Chinputang and the more conservative elements of the Kuomintang who had remained aloof showed signs of mutual understanding and sympathy with the rebels. Yuan Shih-k'ai therefore chose to wreck the Chinputang too. With money and patronage, he organized his own parties. By the end of 1913 the Parliament had been compelled to adjourn as a result of Yuan Shih-k'ai's outlawing of the Kuomintang, and the Chinputang had also been wrecked. By wrecking the two great parties, Yuan Shih-k'ai may indeed have dealt a death blow to parliamentary parties in China for all time.

The Splinter Parties of 1916–1923

The Parliament of 1913 was revived in 1916–1917 and again in 1921–1923. During these intervals, parties were also somewhat revived. Between the second dissolution in 1917 and the second restoration in 1922, there was, in the North, Tuan Ch'i-jui's parliament, and, in the South, the continuation of the old Parliament of 1913. In both there were also parties and groups.

When the Parliament met in 1916–1917, the old cleavage between the Kuomintang and the Chinputang could still be seen, though neither of them was revived in name. The Kuomintang was badly split into several groups or associations. Some owed allegiance to Sun Yat-sen, but others were ready to be associated with the central and local provincial regimes that were in power.[10] The Chinputang was more fortunate in that it was in the beginning divided into only two such groups, the Constitution-Discussion Association, headed by the politician T'ang Hua-lung, and the Constitution-Research Comrades' Association, headed by the scholar Liang Ch'i-ch'ao. They were soon reunited into the Constitution-Research Association.[11] There were of course minor offshoots from the Chinputang. But for practical purposes the Constitution-Research Association was the sole inheritor and was at the time much more effective in politics than all the branches of the old Kuomintang combined.

While Tuan Ch'i-jui was in control of the Peking Government with his hand-picked parliament, from 1918 to 1920, a host of new parties all owed personal allegiance to Tuan Ch'i-jui. However, the group of Liang Ch'i-ch'ao, now known as the "Research Clique," was still actively in existence, naturally on the side of Tuan Ch'i-jui.

Those members of the Parliament of 1913 who assembled in the South at Canton after its second dissolution in 1917 were generally of Kuomintang origin. They were divided into more or less the same groups as those into which they had originally been divided in 1916–1917 at Peking, as has been described in a previous chapter.[12]

The old parliament was again summoned to meet in Peking in 1922. The multifarious groups of 1916–1917 underwent further disintegration. Only a minority of the Kuomintang members of 1913 were now in attendance. A part of them, faithful followers of Sun Yat-sen, who had by this time renamed his party the "Chinese Nationalist Party," or Chung-kuo Kuomintang, engaged in little activity other than long-range publicity for their party. The Political Study Group was more active and generally supported Li Yuan-hung, the restored President. The Research Clique above-mentioned was active without any fixed allegiance to anybody. At this time their acknowledged leader, Liang Ch'i-ch'ao, engrossed in academic research, was no longer much interested in realistic politics. A host of newly-created small groups were doing nothing but bargaining for personal advantages of the most sordid kind. It was these scores of so-called political groups that accepted the bribes of Ts'ao K'un and elected him President of the Republic under the Constitution of October 10, 1923.

Rise of the Contemporary Parties

The few years around 1920 were particularly significant in the development of political parties. The parties before this period had so degenerated and discredited themselves that a new order was necessary. The parties that existed during the last years of the Manchu Dynasty had not been too satisfactory, but they were no worse than the first parties in Japan in the Meiji era. The bipartisan system of 1913, before it was destroyed by Yuan Shih-k'ai, was more promising. But the disintegration of the two major parties into numerous and unstable splinter groups in 1916–1917 was a sign of decay, and by 1920–1923 the decay had become a disease of great malignity. It could hardly go any further. In the political morass created by that process of disintegration a new growth was inevitable and hence powerfully abetted.

There were other reasons for the rise of new parties and the thorough overhauling of old ones. The Bolshevik Revolution of 1917 and the German Revolution of 1918, followed immediately by the adoption of the Weimar Constitution, were great stimulants to Chinese thinking, both political and social. The disheartening decisions reached at the Paris Peace Conference and the interminable civil wars that divided the country not only into North and South, but also (in both North and South) into numerous hegemonies, created among the Chinese in general, and the younger generation in particular, a great desire for national strength and cohesion. This produced a degree of national consciousness unknown in the past. The new parties rose in the floodtide of this national consciousness. The Chinese Communist Party was one product of this period. The reorganized Kuomintang, a virtually new party, was another. Anarchist and socialist parties sprang up. Nationalistic societies were organized both at home and abroad. All owed their origin to the above influences.

Of the newly born parties of those years, the Kuomintang and the Chinese Communist Party prospered. Other socialist parties withered as soon as they were started, partly because of the lack of leadership or the disreputable deeds of the leaders, and partly because of the vitality and rapid growth of the Kuomintang and the Communist Party. The same diseases and disadvantages that caused the withering of the socialist parties also killed most of the nationalistic parties. These parties were usually begun by Chinese students studying abroad. Their organizers, upon their return to China, either lost interest in politics or were absorbed by the two established parties or, worse still, became renegades pure and simple. The only surviving party was the Young China Party, to be known later as the Chinese Youth Party.

But nationalism nurtured another crop of political parties and groups, when the Japanese conquest of China started. The National Socialist Party, the National Salvation Group, the Vocational Education Group, and the Rural Reconstruction Group, all of which were destined to have a role during the war, sprang up in the 1930's as the result of the Japanese menace to Chinese national existence and the hesitation of the government to resist the invader. They came to thrive on patriotic fervor and popular disaffection with the regime.

An earlier organization, the Third Party, which remained more or less inactive in its early existence, also began to be active about the same time. A dissident faction of the Kuomintang, which was to become in 1948 the Revolutionary Committee of the Kuomintang, was of later origin. Both are imbued with intense nationalism and economic radicalism. They too may be said to have been rooted in the new currents that swept China around 1920.

Not only were all the parties that grew up after the early 1920's the products of the new currents, but their fortunes have all been strongly molded by either the attitude of the Kuomintang towards them or their attitude towards the Kuomintang. The Kuomintang has been the dominant party for the last quarter of a century. Their relationship to the Kuomintang has meant everything to them. In giving a brief account of them in the following pages, the nature of that relation has to be stressed in each case.

The Chinese Youth Party

The Chinese Youth Party[13] had its origin in 1918, when some students in China and Japan organized the Young China Study Association. Five years later, the same group of people while in Paris transformed it into the Young China Party. It proclaimed itself for democracy and against warlordism. It emphasized patriotism to the extent of neglecting both the cultural rejuvenation and the economic betterment of the Chinese people. In other words, its aims were narrowly political. At the time when the Kuomintang and the Communist Party were coöperating to destroy the very same warlordism the Young China Party was organized to combat, it was favoring Wu P'ei-fu, the chief of a Northern militarist faction, as a patriot incarnate and the savior of the Chinese nation. It carried on a so-called anti-Red campaign and considered the Kuomintang no less red than the communists. Consequently, when the Nationalist Revolution of the Kuomintang succeeded, the Young China Party was virtually outlawed.

The decade 1927–1937 was one of lean and difficult years for the party. To give itself greater dignity or status, it changed its name into the "Chinese Youth Party," a name which is similar to the names of the Kuomintang and the Communist Party.[14] But its surreptitious activities were mainly confined to the province of Szechwan, for Szechwan was the home province of most of its leaders, and was then under a number of warlords, each the ruler of his own area and all semi-independent of the Kuomintang Government at Nanking. By keeping on good terms with the local warlords, the party was able to control some of the schools in that province and thus continued to enjoy some influence with the Szechwan student class. Outside of Szechwan, it was also able for a few years to maintain some connection with the remnant warlords of the Northeast. In fact, the four annual party congresses from 1928 through 1931 were all held in Mukden. But with the ousting of the civilian and military authorities of the Northeast by the Japanese, the Youth Party also had to seek safe quarters elsewhere.

Towards the close of the decade of the 1920's, however, the Kuomintang had very much mitigated its animosity toward the Youth Party and this improved feeling was reciprocated. Some of the leaders of the Youth Party developed amicable contact with the Kuomintang leaders at Nanking. When the war came, it was not difficult for the Kuomintang to invite the Youth Party to join the National Defense Advisory Council or for the latter to accept the invitation.

Nobody knows how many members the Youth Party has at present, or has had in the past. Up to the end of the war, the greater proportion of its membership was still to be found in the province of Szechwan. Since it is now a small party favored by the Kuomintang regime, it may conceivably have recruited many members elsewhere in the recent past. But it is extremely doubtful if it can have more than 30,000 members in all. The party has by now supposedly opened up various provincial (and municipal) branches. But in most places there exists only a junta, rather than an executive elected by its membership in the locality. The leaders of the Youth Party sometimes claim that intellectuals, professional men, and small businessmen are the dominant elements of the party. Undoubtedly, a great number of teachers and students of the schools of Szechwan are in the party, but, even there, many more are in the Kuomintang fold. It may not be incorrect to say that the Youth Party consists mainly of the landlords, schoolteachers, and students in Szechwan and a sprinkling of bureaucrats and businessmen elsewhere who have recently joined the party with the more or less explicit purpose of gaining ready-made seats in the numerous central and local assemblies established by the Constitution of 1946. The Youth Party may represent anything, but it can hardly be said to be the party of the youth.

The organization of the Youth Party is largely identical with that of the Kuomintang, with the whole apparatus of national congresses, central executive and examination committees, standing committee of the central executive committee, and provincial, *hsien*, and other subordinate local organizations. There is even a youth organization on the local level not unlike the defunct Youth Corps of the Kuomintang. The party has had, since its first congress at Paris in December 1923, nine subsequent congresses. The last one, the tenth, was held at Chungking in 1945, when the Political Consultative Conference was about to take place.

The leadership of the Youth Party has always been a small oligarchy of about half a dozen people. In 1945–1946, as the prospects of the party's getting into power or, to be more correct, of securing official posts for its members, became an immediate reality, there was an attempted revolt by the outs. It failed to check the oligarchy. Though there are one or two sensible and well-meaning men among the leaders of the party, the dominant mentality is thoroughly medieval. Compared with them, most of the Kuomintang leaders could certainly claim to be modern and progressive-minded.

The policies and platforms of the Youth Party are not too far removed from those of the Kuomintang. They are full of platitudes and vague aspirations. If anything, the Youth Party is more nationalistic than the Kuomintang, the Nationalist Party, and decidedly more conservative in its economic tenets. In practice, it has been known for its strong anti-communist attitude more than for anything else.

A party like the Youth Party, with its antediluvian leadership and with a program which is a bad mixture of plagiarism and bigoted self-righteousness, can find no place in a country where there is an established government with some amount of self-confidence. That is why when the Kuomintang had a more or less effective government, the Youth Party had to seek shelter under semi-autonomous warlords supported by private armies or thriving on foreign support. It finally got a share of power only as the government of the Kuomintang became conscious of its own weakness.

The Democratic Socialist Party

The Democratic Socialist Party[15] of Carsun Chang has had a most colorful history. The spiritual mentor of this party was Liang Ch'i-ch'ao, who, being no longer living, should not be held responsible for its activities. It was formed by the amalgamation of the National Socialist Party of Carsun Chang and the Chinese Democratic Constitutionalist Party formed by Chinese living in North America. The latter party was the lineal successor of the Emperor-Preservation Association of K'ang Yu-wei and Liang Ch'i-ch'ao, and the leaders of the former, including Carsun Chang, were, in greater and lesser degrees, associated with the Research Clique of Liang Ch'i-ch'ao in its various phases.

The National Socialist Party began in 1931 when a magazine called *Tsai-sheng* (The national renaissance) was published, and a society was founded for its sponsorship. Three years later, the group adopted the name "National Socialist Party" and its leaders, mostly professors, began to proselytize the students in earnest. When the war began, they were invited to join the National Defense Advisory Council, in common with the leaders of other small parties and groups.

But the National Socialist Party had great difficulty in recruiting new members. The party organization was extremely weak. Whatever adherents there were were either Carsun Chang's personal friends, mostly fellow followers of Liang Ch'i-ch'ao in earlier times, or former students.[16] Throughout the war, members of the party probably did not number over several hundred.

When the war ended, Carsun Chang searched for recruits and reinforcements in order to make his party a reality. First a group led by an ex-warlord, a brother of T'ang Hua-lung[17] and consisting mainly of the old adherents of T'ang Hua-lung, joined it. Then in 1946 the Democratic Constitutionalist Party also came in, and the amalgamated parties adopted the new name of Democratic Socialist Party. The sudden expansion presented, however, new difficulties for the party. Carsun Chang was personally more interested in giving China a constitutional document than in actually entering politics to make that document a reality. The newcomers, led by T'ang Hua-lung's brother, were on the contrary only interested in sharing the spoils, which the small parties were sure to get if they chose to enter the Kuomintang-dominated government. There was division, both among the members of the original National Socialists and the amalgamated Democratic Socialist Party, as to what attitude to adopt in regard to immediate participation in the government. The result was entirely unsatisfactory. The party was badly split as soon as it expanded.

When Carsun Chang consented to permit his followers of the National Socialist Party to join the Constitutent National Assembly of 1946, certain other leaders bolted. At the time the Democratic Socialist Party held its first party congress in Shanghai in August 1947, a secessionist congress also went into action. There are now two Democratic Socialist Parties, one led by Carsun Chang and the other by the head of the former Democratic Constitutionalist Party, each claiming to be the orthodox organization and denouncing the other as the bogus one. The secessionist organization is known as the Reformist Democratic Socialist Party.

The organizational principle of the Democratic Socialist Party is, like that of the Youth Party, similar to the Kuomintang's. There are as usual the congress and the central executive and supervisory committees. Carsun Chang himself was elected by the first party congress as chairman.

If the leadership of the Youth Party is an oligarchy, that of the Democratic Socialist Party can be said to be an anarchy under the titular leadership of Carsun Chang. Carsun Chang is neither an organizer himself nor a man able to pick capable men to organize for him. As a result, there is really no Democratic Socialist Party other than Carsun Chang, the leader. His decision to have the party join the government at Nanking practically stripped the party of other leaders commensurate in rank and prestige with himself.

The policies and programs of the Democratic Socialist Party are in general close to those of any social democratic party.[18] They are more liberal than those of the Youth Party, but, in theory at least, not quite as liberal as those of the Kuomintang. Needless to say, the people who are now representing the Democratic Socialists in the assemblies of the new government are not democrats and still less socialists. Most of them are just office-seekers.

The Third Party

The Third Party had its origin at the time of the Kuomintang-Communist split in 1927 at Wuhan (Wuchang and Hankow). When this split occurred, Teng Yen-ta, an able organizer who had served under Chiang Kai-shek as the political commissar of the Kuomintang in the General Headquarters of the Nationalist Revolutionary Army, proposed that after the communists' dissolution and declaration of secession from the Third International and the reorganization of the Kuomintang, the adherents of the two parties should be incorporated into one party. The proposal was naturally impracticable but he had made his attitude clear. He was for a radical revolution to be undertaken by a national but not an international party. The Kuomintang disowned him, but for a while he continued to consider himself a Kuomintang member. In 1929, at an assembled congress of his followers, he organized the so-called Provisional Action Committee of the Kuomintang and the beginnings of the Third Party were laid.

Subsequently, Teng Yen-ta was arrested and after a long imprisonment was murdered in Nanking in 1931. When the group had its second congress in 1935, the leadership had been assumed by Chang Pai-chün. At this congress, the name of the group was changed to the Liberation Action Committee of the Chinese People.[19] The name "Third Party," however, is better known and frequently employed by the group itself. At the outset of the war, Chang Pai-chün was invited to serve on the National Defense Advisory Council. In 1938 he was able to hold the third congress of his group at Hankow.

According to the literature issued by the group, the party maintained an elaborate organization modeled after the Kuomintang. But there has not apparently been a central organization, not to mention local ones. It is extremely doubtful whether it has ever had any great number of close adherents, though Chang Pai-chün himself may enjoy considerable influence with the labor unions in some areas.

In policies and program, the Third Party adheres to the Kuomintang program as it stood at the time of its First and Second Congresses, that is, previous to the split with the communists. The Third Party thus appropriates the Three Principles of Sun Yat-sen as its principles and the Kuomintang's early policies of catering to the interest of farmers and laborers as its policies.

The National Salvation Association

In addition to the three small parties just described, there are three other recognized political groups whose leaders were invited to serve on the National Defense Advisory Council when the war broke out. They are the National Salvation Association of the Chinese People, the Chinese Vocational Education Association, and the Chinese Rural Reconstruction Association.

The National Salvation Association had its beginnings in 1936 when some civic leaders of Shanghai, who were hostile to the Kuomintang Government and who stood for immediate resistance to the Japanese, formed a federated National Salvation Association of Shanghai. The leading organizers of this association were heterogeneous in terms of their antecedents. Some were young professors and editors; others had had considerable experience in the years of the old parliament. All of them were dissatisfied with the Kuomintang regime and all were able agitators. They agitated for an immediate resistance to the Japanese, and they also agitated for the cessation of the war on the communists, the release of political prisoners, and the formation of a national front of salvation so as to make resistance possible. Their most effective instruments of action were the students' strikes and demonstrations. When the effects of this agitation were felt in the North, the group changed its name into the National Salvation Association of the Chinese People,[20] by which it has since been known.

In November 1936, seven of the leaders of the group were arrested in Shanghai. Their arrest so boosted the number of adherents and sympathizers that they actually became the third most powerful party, next to the Kuomintang and the Communist Party. When the war began, the arrested leaders were released and they advocated a general mobilization, especially in the rural areas, as a means of offsetting the greater effectiveness and mobility of the Japanese armed forces. Because the Salvation people sounded like communists, and many of them happened to be men of conviction and to be able to move about in the rural areas with ease, they were looked upon with suspicion by respectable people, people who inherited the literati-official traditions of old. They were to the left of all parties except the communists, but lacked the armed forces of the communists. During and after the war they were more persecuted than anybody else.

The Vocational Education Group

The active elements of the Chinese Vocational Education Association[21] have been mixed up in politics ever since its foundation. This explains why there is a Vocational Education Group as a political party in China.

The Chinese Vocational Education Association was founded in 1917 with the leading spirits of the Provincial Educational Association of Kiangsu as the active leaders; Huang Yen-p'ei was the moving spirit in both. Both associations had performed meritorius services in the advancement of education, but in their eagerness to solicit the financial and political support of the authorities the leaders were frequently tied up even with reactionary warlords. Since the Nationalist Revolution of the Kuomintang was aimed at those warlords, among others, these leaders became *persona non grata* to the Nationalist regime of the Kuomintang. Mild persecution followed. But with the Japanese menace hovering over the heads of the Chinese people, this group also sought popularity by demanding an early war of resistance. The reward was the usual invitation to join the National Defense Advisory Council.

In the early years of the war, the Vocational Education Group was cooperative. Whatever criticisms of the government it offered were mild and well-intended. But its criticisms grew in intensity as the misconduct of the government increased. In the last years of the war, it often held round tables at Chungking and invited leaders of business and the professions to formulate programs of reform to be presented to the government. Immediately after the war it went so far as to organize the "Democratic National Reconstruction Association"[22] which was perhaps intended to serve as the cornerstone of a new party. Naturally, as activities of this kind multiplied, no love was lost between the Group and the Kuomintang.

The organization of the Vocational Education Association differs greatly from that of a political party. Its members are, as a rule, not interested in personal political careers and hence a detailed analysis of their leaders would be superfluous.

The Rural Reconstruction Group

Like that of the Vocational Education Group, the parent body of the Rural Reconstruction Group, the Chinese Rural Reconstruction Association,[23] was itself a nonpolitical organization. It was founded to promote and to put into practice the theory that the national reconstruction of China has to proceed from rural reconstruction as conceived by its founder, Liang Shu-min. A Chinese scholar of ascetic habits and mystic temperament, Liang Shu-min (Sou-ming) in his earlier years delved extensively into Buddhist philosophy and the philosophies that underlie Western civilization. In more recent years, he has found solace in his theory of national reconstruction, with an accent on agriculture and the organization of village life and a further accent on having the intelligentsia absorbed in village activities. In 1930 he founded the Shantung Research Institute of Rural Reconstruction. Subsequently, in collaboration with other rural reconstruction agencies, he founded the Chinese Rural Reconstruction Association and thereby became the more or less acknowledged leader of the whole movement for rural reconstruction.

Liang Shu-min had had some earlier experience in provincial government and had interested himself in the improvement of local administration at the lower levels. But his work in Shantung made him more and more profoundly interested in the character and the structure of Chinese society and created in him an interest in social and political reforms as well. After the war began, he worked with the guerrillas and came into intimate contact with the communist administrations behind the Japanese lines of occupation. He perhaps is still not interested in politics, as the term is commonly understood, but in his groping for a way out of the present social and political chaos he is not averse to advancing practical proposals of political settlement. Since it is difficult to spell out his politics with great precision, the political position of his group is equally difficult to determine.

The Democratic League

The position of the small parties was growing progressively worse by the end of 1939. They were rather well-treated by the Kuomintang at the beginning of the war and they had expected that their position would improve as their association with the Kuomintang endured. When no such improvement occurred, the leaders of all the secondary parties organized a liaison association[24] in the winter of 1939–1940, with the communists manifesting a friendly interest. After the government took action against the Communist New Fourth Army early in 1941, the small parties and groups effected a more formal organization in the Grand League of Democratic Political Groups of China.[25]

The Grand League was joined by a number of individuals who were not members of any of the constituent groups. These individual members of the League were more articulate than any constituent groups and incurred greater hostility on the part of the government. In October 1944, at one of the most critical moments of the nation and when the government was in a very vulnerable position, the Grand League was further reorganized, renamed the Chinese Democratic League,[26] and began to function like a new political party. Naturally, the hostility of the Kuomintang towards the League increased.

But the League was a conglomeration of groups, which were none too compatible. The Third Party and the National Salvation Association were as much to the left of center as the Youth Party was to the right. There were sharp personal conflicts among its leaders. The Kuomintang waited for an opportunity to hasten the League's disintegration, and that opportunity was not slow in coming.

There had always been some internal rivalry between the rightist and leftist groups in the League, not so much over matters of policy as over the control of the League machinery. At an extraordinary congress of the League in October 1945, the rivalry came to a breaking point. The Youth Party which had had the effective control of the secretariat was now divested of that control. Only in name was one of its leaders allowed to remain at the head of the League secretariat. Real control passed into the hands of the more radical groups and the individual members of the League.

By this time, the war had been terminated and the multiparty talks to arrange for a peaceful settlement of the Kuomintang-Communist conflict were being contemplated. The Political Consultative Conference was in the offing. The Kuomintang promised the Youth Party a number of Conference seats, out of all proportion to its relative strength, on condition that it dissociate itself from the League line. The Youth Party embraced the opportunity with relish and received five seats as against nine for all the parties and groups which remained in the League. To all intents and purposes, it had seceded from the League.

With the Youth Party separated, the Kuomintang began to try the same tactics on the National Socialist Party. It took a longer time for the National Socialist Party to make up its mind. At a meeting of the central executive committee of the League held in Shanghai in the summer of 1946, it was still wavering. In the end it chose to participate in the National Assembly of November–December, 1946. It too thus seceded from the League, though one section remained with the League and refused to have anything to do with the National Assembly. Those National Socialists who were led by Carsun Chang were later amalgamated with the Democratic Constitutionalists to form the Democratic Socialist Party. As has been pointed out above, the united party was split into two almost as soon as the union took place. Whether the Reform Democratic Socialist Party has continued to be a member of the League remains obscure.[27]

While this process of proselytizing and disintegration was going on, what was left of the League became more and more uncompromising in its attitude toward the Kuomintang Government and more and more adamant in its insistence on carrying out in full the several resolutions of the Political Consultative Conference. Increasingly it leaned on or was driven to the side of the communists. Half a year after the government had openly declared the communists rebels or "bandits," it also, on October 27, 1947, outlawed the Democratic League as accessories of the "bandits."

The outlawing was an occasion for political negotiations. It was insisted by the government that if the leaders of the League would formally issue an order for its dissolution, no arrests except in the case of overt acts would take place. The League leaders contended that they had no powers of dissolution unless a League congress would so declare. But a few days after the government decreed the outlawing, the League leaders capitulated. They issued a circular announcing the dissolution of the League.

While the outlawing and dissolution were taking place, a number of active League leaders secretly left for Hong Kong. They regarded the dissolution circular as being issued under duress and refused to be bound by it. The League branches in other places outside of China, such as those in Singapore, acted likewise. In January 1948, the League called a third congress at Hong Kong. By this act, the Democratic League considered itself as having been fully revived.

The membership of the Democratic League has always been an indeterminate affair. There have been from the very beginning the so-called individual members, that is, individuals who joined the League as individuals and not as members of other parties or groups. The Chairman of the League, Chang Lan, is such an individual, as are many of its other prominent leaders. But at the heyday of the League, as many as three small parties and three political groups were in it. The Youth Party, the National Socialist Party, and the Third Party were all participants. The National Salvation Group, the Vocational Education Group, and the Rural Reconstruction Group were also members. At some times the understanding was that these units formed the constituent parts of the League; at other times it was stated that the members

THE GOVERNMENT OF CHINA, 1948

(Detailed organization is generally the same as that under the National Government of 1947)

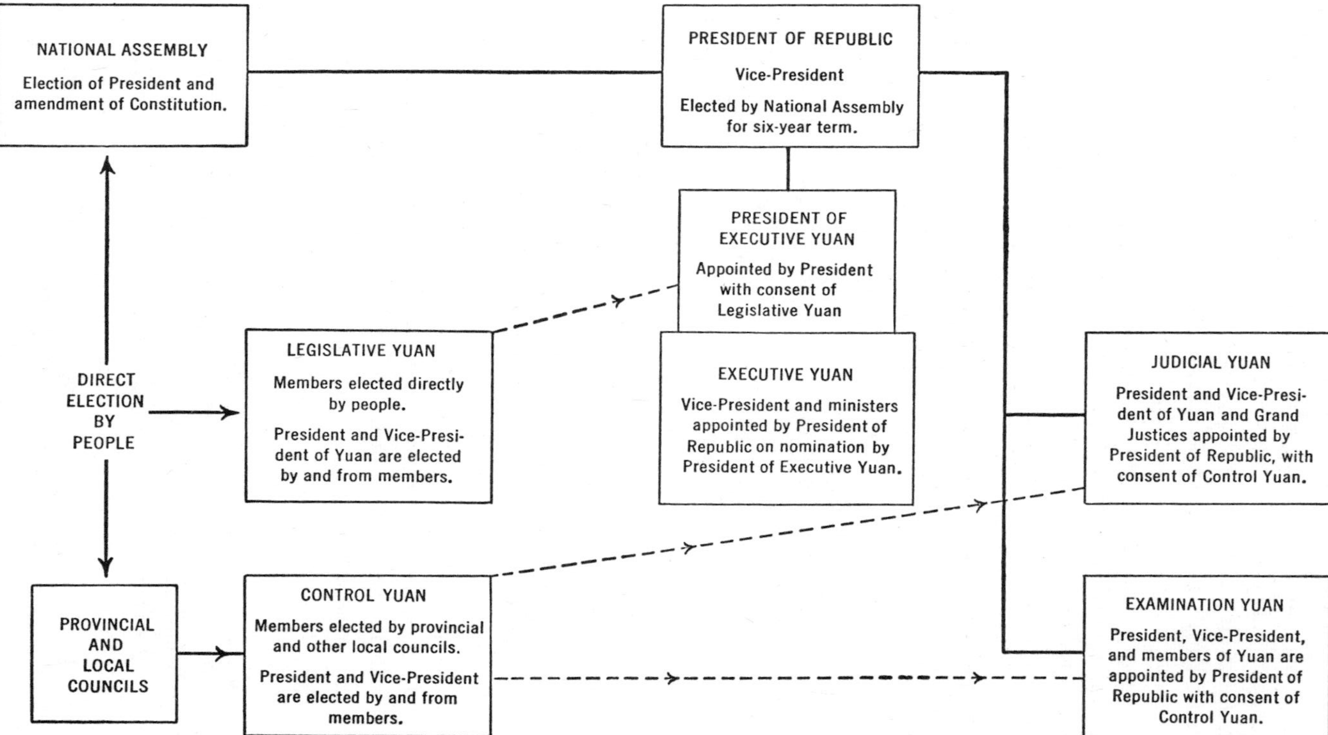

NOTE: Dotted line indicates constitutional check on the President's power of appointment.

of these units joined the League merely as individuals. The exact status has never been fully clear. The former appeared to be more in accord with common sense. However, since the secession of the Youth Party and Democratic Socialist Parties have made the League more homogeneous, and since it is now outlawed, there appears a likelihood that in time, the League may become a party composed only of individual members.

Aside from the membership resulting from the participation of the parties and groups mentioned above, no one knows for sure just how many and what sort of people have been or are adherents of the Democratic League. At the time of the Political Consultative Conference, a considerable number of university and middle school students seemed to be in the League, though the League itself disclaimed any recruitment among students. A number of politicians, both civil and military, who were disaffected with the Kuomintang Government, were also members of the League. The Kuomintang has always been under the apprehension that the League had a considerable following in the ranks of labor unions, but that apprehension may not have been well grounded in fact.

The organization of the Democratic League was largely similar to that of the other parties, including the Kuomintang. The Central Executive Committee, as elected by the Extraordinary Congress of October 1945, consisted of about sixty persons, half of whom were the leaders of the six constituent groups and the other half of whom represented a great variety of professions and political antecedents. The heterogeneity of the membership of the Committee reflected perhaps the heterogeneity of the membership of the League. Analyzing the list, one would gain the impression that such an organization could not easily acquire either political power or mass following in the country. Power it certainly did not gain. If it did gain some amount of mass following, it was perhaps due more to the unpopularity of the object of its attack than to the positive qualities of its own leadership. First to survive and then to play a more vigorous part in the future, the Democratic League needs further consolidation of its leadership and renewed consecration to a new democracy.

In policies and program, the Democratic League emphasizes democratic ideals as they are known in the West. In that, it is more outspokenly Western than the Kuomintang claims to be. In economics, it is to the left of the Youth Party and the Democratic Socialist Party but to the right of the Third Party. It is perhaps quite close to the economic principles of the Kuomintang. This is another proof that as far as the professed principles of parties are concerned there is little choice between the parties of China today. They are all democratic. They all tend to be socialistic. No believer in free enterprise could find any satisfaction in the economic planks of any party.

The Communist Party[28]

The Communist Party was even more a product of the new currents that permeated China in the years around 1920 than was the Reorganized Kuomintang of 1924. The miserable failures of the political leaders at Peking were suddenly brought into sharper relief by the successes of the Bolshevik Revolution, the disgraceful treatment meted out to China by the Powers at the Peace Conference, and the spread of Western intellectual and philosophic theories into China at the hands of capable leaders. All this galvanized the young Chinese intelligentsia into a reëxamination of the destiny of their country. The student movement of May 4, 1919 was the immediate result. The rise of a host of nationalist organizations stressing the one most prominent aspect of that general reaction, namely, nationalism, was another. Both the Kuomintang and the Communist Party were products of those times, though they were far more than merely nationalistic. They emphasized social, economic, and cultural changes as well as the winning of national independence.

As early as 1918, discussion of socialist theories and institutions became popular. Societies were founded and magazines were published. In 1919, the Socialist Youth, an organization frankly in sympathy with Bolshevism, was formed, with branches both in the northern capital and in cosmopolitan Shanghai. In France, Chinese students organized the Young China Communist Party in 1920. This was probably the first time that the name "Communist Party" was adopted by any group of Chinese. For a time the organization was dominated by a romantic spirit. Though some of its participants did become convinced communists, others later turned to lead the Young China Party, the predecessor of the Youth Party of today.

By 1921 the adherents of communism had become sufficiently numerous and widespread to make possible the formation of a regular party. On July 1 of that year, an organizing congress of the Chinese Communist Party was convened in Shanghai. In June 1922, at its second party congress held in Canton, the party formally joined the Third International and deliberated on the question of how to coöperate with the Kuomintang, the representatives of the Third International being then active in the ranks of both the Kuomintang and the Communist Party. However, no definitive decision was reached on the question of Kuomintang-Communist coöperation at that congress. It was not until after Li Ta-chao, one of the Communist Party leaders, had joined the Kuomintang in his own personal capacity in August 1922, that the third congress, meeting in Canton in June 1923, approved its members joining the Kuomintang as individuals.

Since that time, the Chinese Communist Party has had a most checkered history.[29] From 1923 to 1927 it was the active partner in the Nationalist Revolution. While in partnership with the Kuomintang, its service was alternately solicited and abhorred by the Kuomintang. In 1927 the famous split occurred, first in Nanking and then in Wuhan. Then there began a long period of persecutions and civil war, to be terminated only by the outbreak of the War of Resistance in 1937. The growth of the communist movement has of course put the party in a category different from that of the small groups mentioned above.

The decade of Kuomintang-Communist strife was one of great hardship for the communists. Not only were they hard pressed all the time by an organization of superior military and material resources, but they also suffered internal difficulties of leadership and policy. The party in China was a branch of the Third International; the internal dissensions and fluctuations of policy that affected the latter invariably caused repercussions in the former.

During the first two years after the split of 1927, the primary concern of the communists was to escape extermination. They did not quite know what to do, for the International was also bewildered by the changing Chinese scene. There were sporadic coups and *putsches* here and there, but there was no correlated or sustained policy. The years 1930 and 1931 constituted the period of domination by Li Li-san, who believed that insurrection in urban centers was the only road to the seizure of power by the proletariat. The Li Li-san line, after its complete failure, was finally discarded. From 1931 to 1934, the communists established the Chinese Soviet Republic at Juichin in Kiangsi province and concentrated their energy on making that area the nucleus of an ever-expanding soviet state. A proletarian dictatorship of the city workers was relegated to the background, but revolutions in both land tenure and social structure were attempted with vigor.

The National Government of the Kuomintang at Nanking never relaxed its military pressure on the Soviet Republic. In the winter of 1934–1935, the communists finally broke away from the ever-tightening cordon of government forces and made the now-famous Long March into the northwestern corner of Shensi Province, there to establish a new soviet government, that of the Shensi-Kansu-Ninghsia Border Region. The communists had previously been agitating for the cessation of civil war, and now they demanded the formation of a united front. The Sian Incident of December 1936 facilitated a working arrangement with the Kuomintang. Early in 1937 the Central Executive Committees of the Kuomintang and the Communist Party each deliberated on measures of coöperation, and a tentative agreement was reached. After the war broke out, the Communist Party issued on September 22, 1937 a solemn declaration, pledging itself to support the leadership of the Kuomintang in the common war against the Japanese. Thus the decade of Kuomintang-Communist strife ended and a new period of collaboration began.

Full collaboration, however, did not last very long. By 1939, armed conflicts by which the government sought to gain some advantage had already begun to reappear. In January 1941, the Communist New Fourth Army was ordered disbanded and clashes ensued, becoming more and more frequent as the war became more and more stalemated. Immediately after the Japanese surrender, serious attempts were made to secure a peaceful settlement and the eventual reunification of the country. But by the fall of 1946 a full-scale civil war had ensued, and is still raging. These events will be treated in greater detail in the next chapter.

The present organization of the Chinese Communist Party is very obscure to the outside world. The party membership is said to be around two and one-half millions. If so, the common people of the countryside must have formed the bulk of the party. But, considering that the communists during and since the war have been productive in the arts and literature, it is plain that a considerable number of the intelligentsia have also found their way into the communist ranks. The party is bidding them welcome. Whether the participation of large numbers of the intelligentsia is likely to change the vista of the party in some significant directions and, if so, in what directions, remains to be seen.

As for the leaders of the Communist Party, some old ones left the party early in the period of the Kuomintang-Communist split. The Trotskyite purges rid the party of some of its other early leaders. But many veterans continued to guide its destiny. The proportion of high commanders of the communist forces who are on the central committee is notably high.

The structure of the communist organization is similar to that of the Kuomintang, both being copied after the Russian Communist Party. There is a central committee of forty-four members and thirty-three alternates, with Mao Tse-tung as chairman. In its actual working, however, the communist central political bureau is far more effective than the Political Council of the Kuomintang and the secretariat of the Communist Party is far more powerful than the secretariat of the Kuomintang. "Democratic centralism" is supposedly the organizational principle for both parties. But if there is in either little democracy of the Western type, there is certainly more effective centralism in the Communist Party.

Owing to the exigencies of the civil war, the local organization of the Communist Party is adapted to the needs of the place and the time, not handicapped by a uniform hierarchy suited only to normal times. There is usually a communist party bureau for every area under communist control. The local bureaus are naturally obliged to abide by the general principles of the party and directives issued from the center. But they seem to enjoy a fair amount of independence and to be capable of taking action necessary at the time or on the spot without strict reference to the central organization. In this way the communists may have succeeded in escaping many of the abuses of a centralized party bureaucracy.

The policies of the Communist Party have undergone changes as its position vis-à-vis the other parties of the nation has changed. The vicissitudes of world politics have also produced profound effects on the policies of the party. The basic doctrines to which the Communist Party has adhered are consistently Marxist. But like all philosophic doctrines, or doctrines of social philosophy, Marxism too admits various and variable interpretations from time to time. It is therefore far more significant to know the policies which are actually being evolved and practiced than merely to make a perfunctory analysis of the Marxist ideology to which communist parties the world over are dedicated.

The three prewar phases of the Communist Party line were successively anti-imperialist revolution, proletarian revolution, and soviet revolution. When the communists were in partnership with the Kuomintang, their main concern was directed against the imperialist powers of the capitalist world who were also enemies of the Soviet Union. Immediately after the split, the party took the line that its mission was a proletarian revolution, which of course is in strict accordance with Marxist teachings. The last phase was akin to the Stalinist line of socialism within one state. While that phase lasted, the communists talked little about the industrial proletariat, but directed their attention to the achievement of a Chinese Soviet Republic which they thought would fit as well into the Chinese pattern of social structure as the Soviet Union fits into the Russian pattern.

While all the three prewar phases of the communist party line were either Marxian or closely correlated to the policies of the Third International, the war and postwar phases have been more realistic in the sense that the party has been motivated by the desire to achieve a successful revolution at home as speedily as possible.

The political and economic measures which the communists adopted on their arrival at the Shensi-Kansu-Ninghsia Border Region in 1935 were mild compared with those taken in the days of Juichin. They chose to resort to less drastic measures, for they were anxious to keep the countryside with them. They later advocated a national front against the Japanese and for a time actually submitted to the leadership of the Kuomintang in carrying on the war, for they were anxious to be the vanguard of a popular national cause. Then, on January 15, 1941, their leader Mao Tse-tung published his long essay, *New Democracy*,[30] in which, while paying homage to both Marxism and *San-min chu-i*, he advocated a joint dictatorship by all revolutionary classes[31] and the realization of the twin tenets of Sun Yat-sen's Principle of Livelihood—the limitation of capital and the equalization of land ownership. From the "new democracy" to "coalition government,"[32] which was the subject of Mao Tse-tung's report on April 24, 1945 to the seventh congress of the party, the transition was easy. The main trend in the war and postwar phases of communist policy has been to gather the maximum number of friends in order to fight the minimum number of enemies.

Since 1935, the Communist Party has alternately sought collaboration with and fought battles against the Kuomintang. But it has not changed from the idea of a united front or coalition, although the scope of that front or coalition has by no means remained unchanged. It is now engaged in a life and death struggle with the Kuomintang. If it could be crushed by the Kuomintang, no more would be heard of the coalition. But if it crushes the Kuomintang, the coalition idea may have to be worked out anew.[33] Whether it would countenance a real coalition in the sense that the non-communist elements would be allowed to organize and to voice different opinions on all practical issues, or would again resort to a party dictatorship, as once was contemplated by Sun Yat-sen for his party, of course only the future can tell. But if its solicitous care of the sentiments and opinions of the other parties in the past is any indication, a good prospect for a genuine coalition does seem to exist.

Since 1931, when it began to entrench itself in Juichin, the Chinese Communist Party has always had fixed areas to govern and it can therefore be judged by the administrative measures which it has adopted and carried out. There was a considerable difference between the Juichin phase and the Shensi-Kansu-Ninghsia Border Region phase of communist administration. In Juichin, there was almost as much damage done to the countryside as to the landlord class itself. But the administration in the Border Region was much more sensible and constructive. In other areas, violence seems to have appeared here and there. Accurate appraisal is difficult on account of lack of accurate information about the communist-held areas. But, judging by the stability of the currency, efficacy in rationing, and the apparently efficient system of supply for their armed forces, land reforms must have been effected and order seems to have been established in places where control of the communists has been firm. The communists also claim that in their areas people's representative councils have been created for all levels below the *hsien*. Eyewitnesses who have had opportunities to observe the working of these councils are of the opinion that they are genuinely representative.

The Revolutionary Committee of the Kuomintang

With the elimination of Hu Han-min and Wang Ching-wei, one by death and the other by degeneration into a puppet, Chiang Kai-shek became the undisputed leader of the Kuomintang and secessions seemed to be no longer likely or possible. But one did materialize.

For a long time the widow of Sun Yat-sen, a woman of great humility, devoted to her deceased husband and equally devoted to his principles as they were interpreted in the last days of his life, had stood aloof from the official Kuomintang and hopes were centered around her that she might lead a new movement in the party. But she has never interested herself in practical politics. In the last years of the war, Sun Fo, the son of Sun Yat-sen, also championed a more democratic and radical program of action than the party pursued.[34] Many Western observers considered him a hopeful leader of a radical wing of the party. That hope has also vanished.

In the absence of a more open reform movement, a semi-secret group which called itself the San-min chu-i Comrades' Association[35] sprang up in Chungking in the last years of the war. Its leaders were never publicly known, but probably a number of former leaders of the Kuomintang who had been stripped of power were active in the association. The political views of the association were usually close to those of the Democratic League. In economic views, it demanded a return to the policies of the Kuomintang as they stood in the middle 1920's. In both it was divergent from the practice of the official Kuomintang of the day. It is no wonder that it dared not come into the open.

Then, in January 1948, it was reported from Hong Kong that the Kuomintang leaders in exile there had organized a Revolutionary Committee[36] under the leadership of Li Chi-shen and Feng Yü-hsiang. This committee was not a continuation of the San-min chu-i Comrades' Association, but many members of that body seemed to have taken part in its organization. It is doubtful, however, whether the new group would be able to recruit and organize its adherents in territories under the control of Nanking. If not, its position would be not unlike that of the Democratic League, namely, a position in which the central headquarters existed alone and was not supported by a hierarchy of organizations operating in the open.

Its policies and programs, as described in its manifesto of January 3, 1948, bore a close resemblance to those of the Third Party, or of the Kuomintang before the split of 1927. Thus it could work harmoniously with the Democratic League and the Chinese Communist Party, both of which maintain an organization or personnel in Hong Kong.

XXIV

PARTY POLITICS AND STRUGGLES

The pattern of party activities in a country varies according to the pattern of government. During the period from about 1910 to about 1923, there was intermittently a central authority with varying degrees of power and influence, and the parties were comparatively alive. They struggled for power and the struggle was in theory concerned with the control of the central assembly. In practice, this was often not the case. The military leaders in control of the government either subverted the parties to become their personal instruments or openly disregarded the actions and resolutions of the assembly. Still, there was a resemblance between the activities of the Chinese parties in this period and those of the parliamentary groups on the continent of Europe.

Since the fall of the Peking regime and the establishment of the National Government of the Kuomintang, party life has departed radically from the old pattern. As dictatorship parties brook no rivals, a bitter strife between the Kuomintang and the Communist Party ensued. Though there was some mitigation of animosities between the two parties during the war years when a semi-united front existed, the Kuomintang continues to deny equal treatment to all parties and the Communist Party tolerated no hostile ones. With the end of the war and the renewal of the civil war there has come a still different phase of party life. Both the Kuomintang and the Communist Party have solicited the support of the small parties that are friendly or loyal to them, both have declared open war on the parties in the opposite camp, but both are complete masters in their own areas.

The pattern of party life as it stood in the pre-Nationalist period has been briefly touched upon in a previous chapter. The different phases of the more recent period remain to be examined.

The Suppression of Political Parties, 1927–1937

The Northern Expedition of the Nationalist Revolutionary Army was frankly a military measure and was considered to be the most important step in the Military Stage of Sun Yat-sen's program of national reconstruction. It swept away almost all parties. The Communist Party was an exception because it formed a part of the revolutionary force. The Youth Party was also an exception because it was able to seek protection in provinces to which for years the National Government was unable to extend its control. Excepting these two, for years no other parties were in existence. It was not until the Japanese had begun their invasion and the National Government had been weakened that the new groups and remnants of the old parties began to be active again.

With the Communist Party, the Kuomintang carried on a relentless war. Even at the time they were working together to plot the Nationalist Revolution, the coöperation between the two was never hearty and free from suspicion. With the death of Sun Yat-sen in 1925, collaboration became more and more difficult. Touched off by the open break in 1927, armed conflict became the order of the day. The strife was no longer merely political and the parties to the strife were more in the nature of armies than political parties.

Against the Youth Party and other suspected groups of similar nature, the Kuomintang was almost as ruthless. For some years after its split with the communists, the Kuomintang maintained that it was the party of revolution. It was therefore as intolerant of the groups to its right as it was of the communists to its left. It denounced all *étatist* sects,[1] such as the Youth Party undoubtedly was. It also denounced liberals who did not subscribe to all the Three People's Principles or who tried to interpret the second Principle as something akin to the democracy of the West. In the very first years of the Nationalist regime in Nanking, not only were political organizations holding a different faith suppressed, but even individuals daring to stress constitutional democracy were under attack. For years, no one dared to organize a party or group in opposition to the Kuomintang. The Youth Party which refused to disband either had to go underground or to escape to safer places.

After the Mukden Incident of 1931, there was a modification of this attitude toward parties and groups other than the Communist Party. Toward the latter, the relentless civil war continued. Toward the others, the legal and political restraints underwent some relaxation. The situation nevertheless remained most obscure. Individuals who were known to have been and conceivably were still adherents of other parties were tolerated and even given honors. But open activities on the part of these parties were not permitted, as the famous arrest of the seven leaders of the National Salvation Group in 1936 would indicate. At that time, a law, couched in broad and harsh terms and purporting to protect the state,[2] was still in force and almost any expression or activity critical or hostile to the government could expose the person responsible for it to prosecution. To say that no political parties or groups could have lawful existence before the outbreak of the war would seem to be quite correct in law as well as in fact.

Parties During the War Years

The outbreak of the war in 1937 was the occasion for the parties to come into a sort of semi-united front. In the sense that the other parties joined the government and shared the responsibility for the conduct of the war, there was no united front. In the sense that they supported the Kuomintang Government in the conduct of the war and sent their representatives to stand by the government and thus compose the differences among the parties in the interest of the war effort, there was a united front — at least in the first years of the war.

The gathering ground of the parties was at first the National Defense Advisory Council and, after 1938, the People's Political Council. In the Advisory Council, the parties worked together more or less harmoniously. No serious discord arose. The same may also be said of the first year of the People's Political Council.

But even in those years the non-Kuomintang parties failed to have their status as independent parties fully recognized by law. The Communist Party was, comparatively speaking, the most privileged. The Youth Party and the National Socialist Party come next. The Third Party and three other groups got the least recognition. The Communist Party of its own accord issued a declaration[3] pledging its adherence to the Three People's Principles of the Kuomintang, promising its support of the government in the carrying on of the war, and agreeing to place its army and government under the control of the National Government. Whether the Kuomintang was or was not willing to recognize the legal status of the Communist Party, its actual existence could not be ignored. The Youth Party and the National Socialist Party were in less advantageous positions. They had no well-organized party machinery in existence. Yet they did not wish to be considered inferior to the Communist Party. Half a year after the communist declaration of collaboration with the Kuomintang, the leaders of these two parties arranged an exchange of notes with the Kuomintang. The leader of each sent a letter to the Leader and Deputy Leader of the Kuomintang pledging the support of his party in the sacred war; and the Kuomintang leader replied.[4] But these letters did not give much help to the parties concerned. They were no longer persecuted but they could make little headway.

During these early years of the war, the position of the parties hinged not so much on the attitude of the Kuomintang as on their own popularity. Because of the war and its leadership in it, the Kuomintang had become popular again. The Communist Party which championed the cause of war was definitely popular. Squeezed between the two great coöperating parties, the smaller parties and groups had little chance to grow. Neither their programs nor their leadership was remarkable. They were looked upon by the public with toleration, perhaps, but without any enthusiasm. In these circumstances, they could hardly demand better or more completely equal status than they had already obtained.

The communists were never worried by the question of legal status. Both in a negative and a positive way they were in a far more advantageous situation than the smaller parties. Their party was strongly entrenched in the Shensi-Kansu-Ninghsia Border Region. There was little danger of their being ousted from that area. And now that the country was at war, they also hoped to increase their popularity and following by their war work, both in battles and in other directions. Their organ, the *New China Daily News*, was thriving, first at Hankow and then at Chungking. Their leaders were even able to make public appearances in cities other than the capital. The very fact that the communists were able to make their appeal for the war effort unquestionably enhanced both the prestige and the popularity of the Communist Party. The communists seemed to be well satisfied.

Thus, despite the inability of the small parties to secure a status fully equal to that of the Kuomintang, the situation of the parties during the first years of the war was not unsatisfactory. The Kuomintang, the largest party, controlled the government and was maintained by the state. The Communist Party, the second largest, was entrenched in a small area, effectively fighting the war shoulder to shoulder with the Kuomintang and also extending its influence. The small parties were disgruntled. But with the possible exception of the National Salvation Group, which was doing useful work in whipping up popular enthusiasm for the war, none of them could make much of an appeal to the public. They were doing little, and, on account of their lack of vitality and strength, could make little contribution to the war.

This more or less satisfactory situation took a turn for the worse in the winter of 1939–1940. The factors which caused this deterioration were numerous and complex. First, the successes of the guerrilla warfare of the communists had won them acclaim, especially from foreign quarters, and were producing two reactions, the tendency of the communists to make extensive claims concerning their war effort and a feeling of uneasiness on the part of the Kuomintang. Second, the flight of Wang Ching-wei and his subsequent treacherous utterances and acts had been disowned and denounced by the Kuomintang. But the communists took advantage of the sins and crimes of that Deputy Leader of the Kuomintang, and persisted in casting aspersions on the Kuomintang leadership in general, which had unfortunately often entered into surreptitious peace deals and was consequently most sensitive to communist accusations. Finally, the sense of false security, a very tangled psychological reflex arising out of the inability of the Japanese to make a quick finish of their conquest,[5] was creating in the government leaders a complacent attitude which was to afflict the Chungking Government for years to come. Complacency meant less enthusiasm, less single-mindedness in the war effort, and more calculation about internal political matters. Any one of these developments was enough to create mistrust between the Kuomintang and the communists. Together they could not fail to produce devastating effects on interparty relations. These relations deteriorated rapidly. The armed clash early in 1941 in the lower Yangtze (the New Fourth Army incident) doomed the Kuomintang-Communist collaboration.

As the Kuomintang and the Communist Party ceased to be friendly, the government revived the repression which it had seen fit to relax during the first years of the war. Also, a complacent government is always a bad government; to be complacent when the danger from the enemy had by no means disappeared could not but be demoralizing. Instead of doing its best to ward off these dangers with a single-mindedness which would have secured for it the sympathy and the support of the populace, as it did in the first years of the war, the Chungking Government got into the habit of blaming political and economic deterioration on the communists and on the war. It was incapable of self-criticism. It looked upon all criticism as being animated by political motives. It believed that as a means of self-defense it was justified in resorting to more and more repressive measures. As the administration became more corrupt, inefficient, and paralyzed, there was more articulate criticism. As more criticism was voiced, the government resorted to more repression. The vicious circle went on, and an entirely new relationship between the parties resulted.

As has been said, the small parties and groups were not happy in the very first years of the war. But they were then by no means anti-Kuomintang or pro-communist. As between the two, the Kuomintang and the communists, they were perhaps much nearer to the side of the former. The altered situation arising out of the government's increasing intolerance altered the alignment of parties.

About the time of the formation of the Association of the Comrades of United National Reconstruction[6] by the small parties and groups in the winter of 1939–1940, parallel action began to be customary between them and the communists. The communists, though they never joined the coalition organization of the small parties, lent a helping hand to it. In the demand for relaxation of the restraints on popular liberties, for the early termination of tutelage, and, in the last year of the war, for multiparty consultations to prepare for a coalition government of all parties, the communists and the other small parties and groups naturally took a similar or parallel, though not necessarily identical, stand.

For three years, beginning early in 1941, the Kuomintang had allowed spasmodic conflicts with the communists to continue without ever critically examining their consequences. The government, while not entirely forgetting the foreign enemy, took whatever advantage it could against the communists. Whenever and wherever possible, the government forces battled and disarmed the communist forces and the communist forces in retaliation ambushed and dislodged the government forces. Yet the government claimed to be innocent and to have acted only in self-defense. The general advantage in this conflict naturally lay with the government side which enjoyed far more financial and material resources, not to mention its position as the internationally recognized government of the nation. The government believed that the communist forces, whose pay and supply of arms had been discontinued, had no possibility of persevering and still less of success in such a long-drawn-out conflict. But partly due to the weakness of the government itself, and partly due to the rich experience the communists had gained in their guerrilla warfare, the calculations of the government turned out to be wrong.

While this disastrous fratricide was going on, the common enemy, Japan, had redoubled its war effort. Both the governments allied to China and thinking Chinese became convinced that in order to win the war the fratricide had to be terminated. It was this pressure from both within and without that finally led the government to consent to negotiations for the settlement of the outstanding differences between the two parties. The negotiations began in May 1944.[7] However, after repeated trials, they all came to naught. Aside from the less important questions of the status of the Communist Party and the extent of control by the government of the communist-held Shensi-Kansu-Ninghsia Border Region, the two sides could not agree on the major question of the size of the communist forces.[8]

The government's sudden announcement, on March 1, 1945, of its decision to summon the National Assembly elected about ten years previously to meet in November created consternation in the minds of the other parties. It was generally feared that both the constitution which would be adopted and the subsequent government which would be created under that constitution would so completely ignore the interests of the other parties that they had better offer some resistance at once. The resistance took the form of reinforcing the demand for a multiparty conference, a device which the communists had demanded as early as March 1941, to solve the common conflicts between the Kuomintang and the parties in opposition.

The small parties offered, in the summer of 1945, to send representatives to the communists at Yenan to bring about the resumption of negotiations. They succeeded in bringing the communist representatives back to Chungking to attend a forthcoming session of the People's Political Council. Negotiations were resumed. But there was again no settlement of the outstanding differences between the government and the communists. The government insisted on summoning the National Assembly; the communists countered with their demand, now made more unequivocal, for a multiparty conference. The small parties imperceptibly joined hands with the communists in also favoring such a conference.

Thus the political mismanagement of the Kuomintang had earned for it most unhappy results. Whereas in the first years of the war its position was secure and its leadership was not disputed, it had now to face the almost united opposition of all the other parties and groups.

Parties in the Political Consultative Conference

The negotiations between the Kuomintang and the communists in 1944 and 1945 had failed to achieve a settlement. The mediation efforts of the small parties and nonparty members of the People's Political Council in the summer of 1945 had also ended in vain. When the war ended in August 1945, civil war loomed large. To avoid it, a new approach was necessary. The demands of public opinion were at last heard and Chiang Kai-shek, the Leader of the Kuomintang, was obliged to arrange a conference with Mao Tse-tung, the Leader of the Communist Party and Chairman of its Central Committee.

But, when the Conference opened in Chungking, the government was in no hurry to seek a settlement. The joint communique,[9] published on October 10, 1945, was an agreement in principle only, leaving most of the controversial issues unsolved. Yet it was significant in the sense that the government acknowledged the necessity of reunion to be arrived at by peaceful means. It was also significant that it accepted the necessity of a multiparty conference for the discussion and solution of the outstanding political controversies that were facing the nation. This was the genesis of the Political Consultative Conference of 1946.

But the government was, however, reluctant to have the Conference organized. It was not until the Marshall mission was announced and the mediation policy of Washington was made explicit in Truman's policy statement of December 15, 1945 that it began in earnest to make arrangements for the Conference. After consultation with other parties, a few organizational and procedural rules governing the Conference were made public on January 7, 1946. In the meantime, arrangements as to the number of delegates each party should have and as to who should represent the nonparty sections of the nation had also been settled.

The Political Consultative Conference opened on January 11, 1946, under the chairmanship of Chiang Kai-shek, both in his capacity as President of the National Government and as leader of the largest party, and with the presence of the American mediator, George C. Marshall. There were eight delegates from the Kuomintang, seven from the Communist Party, nine from the Democratic League (minus the Youth Party), five from the Youth Party, and nine representing the nonparty people of the nation, all together, thirty-eight in number.

There was much maneuvering and bickering in the composition of the Conference. Each party naturally fought for as large a quota as it could get. The quotas given the four parties were certainly no indication of their relative strength. The Kuomintang's or the government's quota was relatively too small. The Kuomintang practiced self-abnegation, for it counted on the delegates of other parties and groups to be more friendly to it than to its opponent, the Communist Party. It was absolutely sure of the support of the delegates of the Youth Party which had been given a generous quota of five. It was also sure that the great majority of the Democratic League delegates would be more than benevolently neutral. It strove hard to knock out the nominees proposed by the communists for the nonparty delegates. It succeeded in insisting that the nominees proposed by it be accepted by the communists and the Democratic League. But there was one miscalculation. In giving large separate representation to the Youth Party which at that time was still a constituent part of the Democratic League, the government alarmed and irrevocably offended the League, and, in the Conference, the delegates of the League were less than neutral towards the government.

The most indefensible aspect of the composition was the small number and the personnel of the nonparty delegates. When the Political Consultative Conference was called, the People's Political Council was held in abeyance. The delegates of the parties might indeed represent their parties well, but they could scarcely represent the nation as a whole. Unless the nonparty delegates were both numerically strong and well chosen, the Conference could hardly claim to be anything more than an interparty device. But there were only nine such delegates, less than one-fourth of the total; and out of those nine hardly more than two could be said to be nonadherents of any of the four well-represented parties. In fact, most of them were adherents of the Kuomintang.

The Conference was in session from January 11 to January 31, 1946. Thanks to Marshall's astute and forceful mediation, the government and the communist leadership had, on the eve of the Conference, agreed to issue orders for the cessation of the armed conflict. The tripartite Executive Headquarters, consisting of commissioners representing the two sides of the conflict and the mediator, was immediately established and began to function. All this had to be arranged for at once, for the cessation of hostilities had been considered by all concerned to be the prerequisite for fruitful consultations in the Conference.

The Conference itself tackled five problems: (1) the reorganization of the National Government; (2) the formulation of a program of policies to be followed by the reorganized government; (3) the reorganization of the armed forces; (4) the revision of the Draft Constitution of 1936; and (5) the problem of a constituent national assembly. All five issues were controversial in the extreme, but they were well selected and formed one integral whole. The central theme was the realization of peaceful transition to a democratic government in which all parties and sections of China could participate and none should fear unlawful or military suppression by another.

It was thought that all the troubles arising out of party dictatorship and civil war could be cleaned up by the adoption of a constitution on which all parties had expressed agreement. To insure that such a constitution would be adopted, a constituent assembly was to be formed in accordance with an agreement especially made for that purpose. To insure that the constituent assembly would be adequate to its task, an interim government was to be set up. To insure that the interim government would not go wrong, a program of policy, the "Program of Peaceful National Reconstruction," was to be adopted. Armed conflict was considered to be the most disrupting influence. Therefore, there was also to be an agreement on the reorganization of the armed forces of the nation and the ways and means of bringing about the amalgamation of the communist and government forces into one really national instrument. The agenda of the Conference was sensible and the men who made it were remarkable for their insight and perspicacity.

There were incessant maneuvers and countermaneuvers in the Conference. The general tendency of the Kuomintang was to maintain as much of the *status quo ante* as possible. It was not willing to part with the power it had enjoyed for two decades. The Communist Party, being the party of opposition, spared no efforts to emphasize peace, unity, and democratic government. The Youth Party generally went along with the government. So did the majority of the delegates of the so-called "nonparty group." The Democratic League was in a very advantageous as well as embarrassing position. Its position was embarrassing because it found itself sandwiched between two strong antagonists, each with an armed following. But it was also advantageous, because peace and democracy, for which the League stood more vociferously than any others, were popular with the general public, and, at the same time, the League was not handicapped by the stigma of possessing an army. But in insisting on unconditional democratization of the government, the League incurred the wrath of the party in power. As it incurred the wrath of the Kuomintang, it was wooed by the Communist

Party. By the middle of the Conference it was definitely known to be on the side of the communists.

The whole Conference was thus split in two, with the Kuomintang, the Youth Party, and the six or seven nonparty delegates forming one side, and the communist and the Democratic League delegates, reinforced by one or two nonparty delegates, forming the other. The one side had about eighteen or nineteen delegates and the other about seventeen or eighteen. Only one or two persons remained neutral and outside either camp. This development was significant in that it has continued to be the pattern of party alignment up to the present.

In spite of the incessant strife among the rival camps in the Conference, agreement was reached on every one of the five topics under consideration.[10] The government was to be so reorganized as to vest the highest government power in a State Council of forty members, half to be Kuomintang members and the other half to be non-Kuomintang men with the proviso that the nonparty nominees to the State Council, when objected to by one-third of the accepted nominees, would be dropped, and the further proviso that a two-thirds majority would be required to effect any change in the Program of Peaceful National Reconstruction. This veto power to be enjoyed by one-third of the State Council was considered by the Communist-Democratic League minority to be essential to the faithful execution of all the resolutions of the Conference. The minority was promised enough seats in the State Council to avail itself of the veto. Unfortunately, this promise was only a verbal one. Subsequently, the Kuomintang consistently refused to give that minority fourteen councilorships, alleging that the Youth Party would accept no fewer seats than allotted to the League and, therefore, there were not as many as fourteen seats to be given to the communists and Democratic League as minority parties.

As for a program of policies to be followed by the reorganized interim government, agreement was reached without too much difficulty. The Program of Peaceful National Reconstruction was a well-balanced and well-considered document, though it was a bit too idealistic to be realizable.

On the reorganization of the armed forces, the agreement was on general principles only. But a military subcommittee composed of one delegate each from the government and the Communist Party with Marshall as mediator was able on February 25 to reach a full and detailed agreement on the reorganization of the armed forces and the amalgamation of the communist forces in a national army.[11]

The agreements on the Constitution and on the National Assembly were also secured, as has been described in an earlier chapter.[12] Thus when the Conference adjourned on the last day of January 1946, there was general jubilation throughout the country.

From a strictly partisan point of view, the resolutions of the Conference were completely satisfactory to neither the Kuomintang nor the Communist Party. But from the national point of view, they were as good as could have been obtained at the time. Any party which could think in terms of the future, rather than in those of immediate gains and losses, should have embraced the national rather than the partisan point of view. But this did not happen to be the case with the Kuomintang.

Trouble had been brewing even before the adjournment of the Conference. Meetings held in Chungking to publicize the work of the Conference were often disrupted by organized mobs, and the speakers, usually non-Kuomintang delegates of the Conference, were as often threatened with physical violence. When celebrations took place after the successful conclusion of the Conference, the reaction of the Kuomintang party machine was even more irate.

It was equally despairing that the situation which developed in the Northeast soon after the adjournment of the Conference rendered the chance of successful operation of its resolutions extremely slim, if not irrevocably lost.

The problem of the Northeast was complicated beyond description. According to an understanding reached by the two parties when the order of January 10 for the cessation of hostilities was issued, the government forces were not enjoined from moving into and about in the northeastern provinces and such movements were not to be affected by the general injunction against troop movements. At that time, Soviet troops were still in occupation in Manchuria. The government had hoped that upon the withdrawal of the Russians, it could move its troops in to take over control of the provinces. However, by early March 1946, when the government was ready to send its forces in, the Northeast had already been occupied by the communists. The government accused the communists of having broken the agreement by moving its troops ahead of the government. The communists claimed that the forces in question were their underground forces of the Northeast and were not transferred there from the outside. Acrimonious accusations and counteraccusations ensued, but no solution was found to be acceptable to both.

The failure of the Conference to foresee developments in the Northeast and make arrangements concerning them was a mistake which should have been rectified as soon as it became obvious. Unfortunately, neither side was in a conciliatory or compromising mood. The government, encouraged by American aid, felt sure that it could gain complete armed control of the area in a very short time. The communists were firmly convinced that they were entitled to be there and that they could retain what they had got without conceding anything to the government. Both sides were adamant. No negotiated settlement was feasible.

While the problem of the control of the Northeast was growing worse, other equally serious developments were endangering the whole framework set up by the Political Consultative Conference. The angry reactions of the Kuomintang councils toward the Conference resolutions and the hostile demonstrations of Kuomintang organizations in various places against opposition leaders of the Conference had created a general atmosphere of gloom as compared with the jubilant mood of the general public in the last days of January. By April, the more discerning observers of the situation had to come to the sad conclusion that the well-balanced design of the Conference had been wrecked.

George C. Marshall, the American mediator, continued to work for peace when he returned in April from a visit to his own country. In June, he was joined in his peace endeavors by a new American ambassador. Various alleviating measures and expedients were tried, some aiming at the reorganization of the government, some at the removal of hindrances to the lines of communication, and others at truces here and there. But in their inability to stand for a fair solution of the Northeast tangle and to insist on strict compliance with the five admirably integrated resolutions of the Political Consultative Conference, the mediators were getting farther and farther away from a successful consummation of their peace efforts.

The National Government was the government recognized by the foreign powers, and, as such, enjoyed immense advantages over its adversary. It had at the time of the Political Consultative Conference yielded to the pressure from the United States and had accepted compromises imposed upon it by the Conference. With the reorientation of the world situation and the polarization of the Washington and Moscow groups of powers, it was no longer subjected to external pressure for coalition with the communists as it had been in the winter of 1945–1946.

The civil war began in earnest in the summer of 1946. By October it was in full swing. In the middle of October the government took advantage of the recapture of Kalgan to summon the National Assembly. This it did without the consent of the parties to the Political Consultative Conference. When the opposition parties opposed the measure on the ground that it was contrary to the resolutions of the Conference, and the government persisted in summoning the Assembly, the whole episode of the Political Consultative Conference came to an end.

But the effect of the Conference on Chinese party life is destined to be profound. At the time of the Conference there was the possibility of forming a number of fairly strong middle-of-the-road parties or groups. If those parties and groups had risen and had been able to play their part well, neither the Kuomintang nor the Communist Party could have afforded to lose their support, and something like a multiparty system might have thus ensued.

But, instead, the Kuomintang was persistently bent on reducing such parties or groups to mere obsequious satellites. If a middle-of-the-road party or group refused to be abjectly compliant, the Kuomintang would rather have it go over to the communist side than tolerate it as an independent or neutral element. This strategy was obvious at the very beginning of the Political Consultative Conference. By the time the Conference ceased to exist, a pattern of party life had already been cut for the years to come. There were to be no major parties other than the Kuomintang itself and the Communist Party.

Kuomintang Policy Regarding Other Parties

Strictly speaking, the Kuomintang's attitude toward political parties has always been consistent. It has never chosen to tolerate other parties. This was so before the war. This has been so since the civil war between the Kuomintang and the communists was resumed in the early fall of 1946. There was some slight prospect of a change during the war years, but that prospect evaporated almost as soon as the Political Consultative Conference ended.

The present policy of the Kuomintang is to plant as many small parties as possible by its side. There have to be such parties, for it desires to have the government it controls no longer appear as a Kuomintang dictatorship. But such parties must be small and subservient, for a really free and independent party, enjoying freedom of organization and propaganda throughout the country, could easily become popular and grow to dangerous proportions. In other words, a party can either place itself at the disposal of the Kuomintang and receive assignments of office, whether elective or appointive, from it, or try to pursue a popular course and be suppressed by the Kuomintang.

The Youth Party and the Democratic Socialist Party are the two small parties accepted by the Kuomintang as trustworthy friends or allies. Both are pliable and reliable; and both are used by those weaker Kuomintang factions which need outside assistance in their intraparty maneuvers for power.

The corollary of the policy of maintaining satellities is to destroy those who refuse to be satellites. The destruction takes various forms. The communists are to be annihilated. The Kuomintang has no scruples in this regard, for all communists are considered to be engaged in rebellion, and rebellion has to be crushed by every means at the disposal of the state. The Democratic League, which has since the days of the Political Consultative Conference sided with the communists, is considered an accessory to the rebellion. Its fate must be the same as that meted out to the principals. The status of the Revolutionary Committee of the Kuomintang is less clear, since it has not operated, peacefully or otherwise, in the territory held by the government. Nonetheless, its leaders have also been outlawed.

Actual armed conflict between the government forces and the communists has continued since the winter of 1939–1940. At first such conflicts were intermittent and both sides claimed to have acted only in self-defense. In the North where the Japanese were in effective control of large cities and the principal arteries of communication, the communists had been able to entrench themselves in the countryside, largely because of their well-developed methods of guerrilla warfare. They benefited by their greater mobility and grass-roots connections with the populace. The government complained bitterly about the communists' continuous expansion, both during the latter part of the war and in the early days after the surrender.

When the surrender occurred, the communist forces in the North usually got swift control over places vacated or half-heartedly held by the Japanese, notwithstanding the order of Chiang Kai-shek, as Chairman of the Military Commission, forbidding the Japanese to surrender to the communists.

The surrender was thus the occasion for frequent conflicts between the two forces over a wide area. After the agreement on the cessation of hostilities was signed on January 10, 1946, and the American-assisted truce teams of the Executive Headquarters came fully into operation, for nearly half a year conflicts (aside from those in the Northeast) became much less frequent. But by July, they had again flared up and in some places on a formidable scale. By September and October, the civil war had become an all-out affair with the government spokesman predicting the complete annihilation of the communist forces within a period of three months. The communists were at that time on the defensive. Nevertheless, they accepted the challenge. Instead of surrendering to the government's political offensive and participating in the National Assembly called by the government, they chose to protest and stand aloof from it. They well knew that that meant war to the bitter end, but they considered it the only alternative to extermination.

On February 28, 1947, the government ordered the communist delegations to the central government as well as those attached to the Political Consultative Conference and the Executive Headquarters and all other communist personnel [13] to withdraw to their own areas. This was done very much in the fashion of issuing passports to the representatives of a country at war. War was indeed declared shortly thereafter.[14]

As far as the civil war itself was concerned, the communists continued to be on the defensive. They lost Yenan, their twelve-year central seat of government. They were worsted both in Shantung and the Northeast; but by the late summer of 1947 the government forces seemed to have spent themselves. For them a critical phase began.

The Democratic League was declared an illegal organization on October 27, 1947. There was no clarification as to the legal effect of this government declaration on the individual members. But the political effect was very soon made clear. The government spokesmen accused the League of having conspired with the communist "bandits" in the rebellion, especially in the Northeast. The accusation exposed the League people to the same punishment as the communists. Some League leaders escaped the country. Those who stayed were put under protective custody. Whatever the difference in treatment of the different leaders of the League, the League as an organization was effectively outlawed. It had no better legal status than the Communist Party.

The Revolutionary Committee of the Kuomintang was not organized until January 1948. Its predecessor, the San-min chu-i Comrades' Association, was never in the open and its utterances were also comparatively mild. The Kuomintang organization, not willing to force an open split, had preferred to take no action against it. But the Revolutionary Committee was another matter. Being centered in Hong Kong and in collaboration with the communist and the League elements in that British colony, it was both more dangerous and more difficult to reach. It had to be outlawed, though the outlawing has had little effect on the organization.

For the Kuomintang then, political parties by 1948 were either to be treated as satellites or as enemies to whom no quarter could be given.

Communist Policy on Political Parties

The Communist Party no less than the Kuomintang started as a monopolistic party, believing in the doctrine of one state, one party. About the same time that the Soviet Union in the face of the Nazi threat modified its anti-capitalist policy and sought allies in the West, the Chinese communists also began to advocate a united national front against the Japanese enemy. Since both the Russians and the Chinese communists were at that time members of the Third International, parallel policies were to be expected.

Up to the end of 1936, if not later, the Kuomintang always considered the advocates of a united front, such as the National Salvation Group, to be mouthpieces of the communists. After the Sian incident of December 1936, when Chiang Kai-shek was detained and then released by a strange combination of forces and events, the idea of a united front imposed itself even upon the Kuomintang leadership. Fighting between the government and the communist forces ceased. The nation was getting ready for a united front, in spirit at least. From that time on, the Communist Party championed the freedom of political parties. It cultivated the good opinion of the small parties and groups. It was even successful in maintaining a better than correct relation with the Kuomintang itself. It gained both in influence and in good repute. For it, the period was one of prosperous growth.

Beginning from about 1939, and certainly from 1941, the Kuomintang-Communist relationship worsened steadily and rapidly. But the Communist

Party continued to profess its willingness to consider the Kuomintang as the leading party of the country and to work with it, both for purposes of resistance and of subsequent reconstruction. In the meantime, it had also continued to cultivate good relationships with the other parties. The devastating effects of the war, together with the maladministration of the Kuomintang Government and the indefatigable efforts of the Communist Party to woo the poorer farmers of the countryside, especially in the North, brought about a further expansion of the Communist Party and a proportionate decline in the influence and prestige of the Kuomintang. This process continued until, by the time of the Japanese surrender, the Communist Party had reached such a strong position that it could demand a genuine coalition government, to be arranged by a multiparty conference in which it would like to consider itself the equal of the Kuomintang.

At the time of the Political Consultative Conference, the position of the Communist Party was as follows: it wanted a coalition government; it still acknowledged Kuomintang leadership, but would like to have a substantial say in the coalition; it assiduously championed the interests of the other parties in the hope that they would be on its side rather than on the side of the Kuomintang in case a division should occur in the coalition. If this analysis of Communist Party strategy as seeking merely freedom of competition is correct, no objection could be raised. And if the Kuomintang had been willing to pursue a similar competitive strategy, the winner, whichever it might be, would have fully deserved the victory. But the Kuomintang could not be persuaded to adopt the same strategy, being afraid both of open competition and of communist infiltration tactics.

There was the problem of the communist armed forces to be solved. The Kuomintang insisted that the Communist Party, on account of its having an armed following, could not be treated as a mere political party. The Communist Party retorted by saying that unless the government forces, which were no less than party forces, were also neutralized and brought under nonparty control, it could not suffer its forces to be disbanded or neutralized. But the Kuomintang left this problem of the party armed forces unsolved and refused to consider itself a mere political party. Instead, it took on the role of a state in securing to itself advantages denied to the Communist Party, in spite of the latter's astute strategy. It succeeded in refusing to budge from its established position in the government and disregarded the resolutions voted by a multiparty body.

When the Political Consultative Conference phase of recent Chinese history came to a close toward the end of 1946 and the civil war was resumed on a full scale, the Communist Party continued to harp on a multiparty coalition of all parties. It did not give up the idea of working with parties which were willing to enter into coalition with it, but insisted on admitting only what it considered the progressive and democratic elements of the Kuomintang into the coalition. In other words, it considered the Kuomintang of Nanking its sworn enemy, no less than the Kuomintang so considered it. The cutthroat civil war, not only in actual armed conflict, but also in theory, was thus fully and squarely joined.

The Communist Party may continue for years to advocate coalition or a national front, minus its sworn enemy, of course. But a coalition from which the Kuomintang is excluded will be dominated by the communists. No other parties with comparable strength and following are in existence or in sight. The pattern of party life in the past has prevented the emergence of independent middle-of-the-road parties. A coalition under the leadership of the Communist Party, if and when it becomes a reality, cannot in substance be different from government under the strong leadership of one party.

The Prospect of Political Parties

In party as well as in governmental structure, China has been heavily under the influence of the outside world. Forty years ago, it was the Japanese system which was conscientiously imitated. Later, the parties degenerated into splinter groups, to some extent resembling the parliamentary groups of those countries of the continent of Europe where democracy did not do well. It was this degeneration that caused a shudder in the minds of many Chinese and paved the way for Sun Yat-sen's gravitation toward a monopolistic party after the fashion of the Communist Party of Russia.

In Sun Yat-sen's mind, a monopolistic party must take up the work of training the people to the ways of a modern nation, in both political and economic matters. But Sun Yat-sen did not specify whether ordinary parties, as distinguished from a monopolistic party which the Kuomintang certainly was destined to be, should eventually reappear in China after the people had been trained in the exercise of the rights of election, recall, initiative, and referendum. That the Kuomintang failed to realize the Three Principles and to train the Chinese people in the use of its political rights does not necessarily prove that Sun Yat-sen was wrong or that the theory of one-party dictatorship was unsound. It shows that the Kuomintang, as it has been led by its leaders of the last twenty years, has failed; but it proves nothing else, neither the feasibility nor the infeasibility of party tutelage. The Chinese in the future still have to make the choice between the party system of the Western democracies and that which was advocated by Sun Yat-sen. Past experiences are of little value. Experiments with both have failed. If the Kuomintang tutelage is a failure, the multiparty system was certainly no less a failure. The choice has to be made less in the light of past experiences than against the background of the social structure of the Chinese people.

The multiparty system has succeeded best in those countries where political issues do not go so deep as to rend the society into irreconcilable camps and where the middle class is powerful or at least more powerful than any other force or combination of forces. The middle class does have one great virtue. It may abhor violent change, but it is usually in sympathy with gradual improvements, the cumulative result of which over the generations may produce a stabilizing effect. In China such a class is not in existence. The poor are very poor, but very numerous. The rich are very rich, but very few in number. The people who stand in the middle form but a small number and in spite of some beginnings of modern industries during the last half century their number is not growing.

Because of the absence of a middle class, Chinese political parties before the rise of the Reorganized Kuomintang were based on the official-literati class. Their numbers were so small that they could not effect a mild program of improvement. They were also too weak to resist either warlordism or a popular revolution. Two decades of Kuomintang tutelage has not substantially changed the structure of Chinese society. No middle class has arisen. It is difficult to see how a multiparty system which failed in the past could be made to work now.

On the other hand, the reaction against a possible repetition of the system of party dictatorship is strong. The failure of Kuomintang tutelage has discredited the theory of party tutelage. There is an instinctive hostility toward any continuation of the system because of fear of the recurrence of this sad experience.

Anyone who tries to theorize on a party system that would fit China must be in a quandary. He can be blind neither to the sheer impossibility of the one alternative, nor to the strong reaction against the other. Those who still believe in a monopolistic party as the better alternative, whether it be the Kuomintang or the Communist Party, must learn that faith alone is not sufficient, and military successes are delusive. Such a party must be able to find support from the great mass of the people, by helping them to improve their lot.

XXV

THE OUTLOOK FOR A GOVERNMENT FOR THE PEOPLE AND BY THE PEOPLE

In a country like China, where a century-old clash between the old and the new is gaining momentum as the result of eight years of war of resistance and the polarization of the rival ideologies of the outside world, the social changes that are taking place will have a profound effect on the forms and methods of government. To speculate on the future of the Chinese government, or to consider what reforms are desirable and feasible, is extremely difficult. Contemplated reforms are meaningless unless they can be projected against the background of the social evolution that is fast taking place.

The problems of government we have come across in the previous chapters of this book are various. While there are fundamental ones, the solution of which has to await the solution of the social problem, there are also relatively simple problems, capable of simple solutions.

. . . .

All thinking Chinese, not excepting the men in the government themselves, have been struck with the defects and inefficiency of the administration.

If one were to measure the importance of China's problems by the volume of public discussion they have created, one would conclude that the defects in the administrative organization and the inefficiency of the administrative method outranked all other problems in importance. But this is not true. In themselves they are relatively simple problems. Gaps, overlappings, and illogical arrangements in the administrative organization can be easily rectified whenever the high leaders of the government are endowed with a certain amount of business sense and have no necessity for resorting to the manipulation of governmental agencies as a means of maintaining personal power.

The same is true of the methods of administration. For most of the last generation they have been distorted by certain officials mainly because distortion has been a contrivance for concentrating power in a few hands. Such evils as the capricious issuance of personal orders by an all-powerful leader to any official, high or low, and the lack of a sense of responsibility even on the part of high officials of the government, are liked and defended by no one and are condemned by everyone. They exist because the leader is erroneously of the opinion that they make his control secure. Whenever the top level leader or leaders have more business sense and are desirous of having a well-ordered administration, as distinguished from complete personal control of the administration, these evils can and will be readily removed.

In stating that the problems of administrative mechanism and efficiency are of minor importance and are capable of easy solution, it is not suggested that the solution can be of a perfectionist kind. No perfection is possible in these matters. Even the best of all administrations, such as existed in the earlier part of the T'ang or of the Ch'ing Dynasty in China or the administration of the Prussian state before the first World War, were not perfect. An administration which succeeds in executing the policies of the government should be considered a good one. To that extent there can be little doubt that, given a businesslike leadership, which does not identify meddling and interference with cleverness, there can be established in China a fairly good administration. The Chinese civil servants of today are immensely better and abler people than their predecessors in the last generation. The available younger men who can be drafted into the civil service are equally good, if not even better. Simplify their machinery, let them be convinced that they are performing a function for the good of the state and the people, and give them adequate power and responsibility, and they will not fail to acquit themselves creditably, no less creditably than the civil servants of some of the best-governed contemporary countries.

. . . .

The problem of centralization versus decentralization is more difficult of solution. It cannot be solved by the mere substitution of good leadership for bad. It entails first a careful and realistic consideration of the activities that the Chinese state hopes to undertake in the near future, and second, a careful study of the sentiments and resources of the different areas of the country. Division of functions between the central and local governments is meaningless when those functions have no likelihood of being undertaken. To assign a certain function to a province which has no resources for its discharge is to kill the function. To assign a function of which the province is jealous to the central government would be equally unwise.

Moreover, the centrifugal tendencies of the peripheral areas and populations must be well balanced with a strong central government. To deny to those areas and populations any degree of home rule would arouse the resentment of the populations concerned. To accede indiscriminately to their demands for home rule would be tantamount to ceding them to any strong neighbor who may lie across the borders. Special care therefore must be taken to give them sufficient home rule to satisfy their longings without losing their adherence.

The Chinese people are, generally speaking, not federal-minded, and the Chinese state has always been a unitary one. But the problem of centralization versus decentralization does exist today. Overcentralization makes many of the uniform laws unworkable and inoperative, and creates discontent in places where social and economic conditions are markedly different. Overdecentralization means the negation of a nation-state and in some places actual disintegration. The solution of the problem will necessitate a system by which the provinces and the special groups in the population will be enabled to exercise a varying amount of home rule on the one hand, while on the other hand there will be a central government with sufficient powers to maintain national unity and to promote the broader interests of the nation. But the solution will not lie in a federalist constitution. It has to be something more flexible, to admit easy adaptations made necessary from time to time by trial and error.

. . . .

The recurrent personal dictatorships, often of a military man, ever since the days of Yuan Shih-k'ai, have also been the antithesis of good government of any kind. The experience of the last forty years has been that when such a dictatorship was in existence civil war, heavy taxation, and dependence on foreign aid were the usual accompaniments, and law and order no longer remained the care of government. This is not to say that the absence of a military dictatorship will necessarily mean peace and prosperity and law and order, but it does demonstrate that there will be no such blessing unless military dictatorship disappears.

In a country like China where there have been no powerful political parties unconnected with military power, nor other influential bodies like the Christian Church or trade unions, no one is in a position to offer an effective resistance to a dictator who is backed by military power. Aside from the dictator himself, the next most powerful group is often the instrument of the dictator, whether that instrument be the army or the bureaucracy or a political party. Unless there should be created a powerful organization which could command a following as powerful as the military power itself, there is no possibility of eliminating military dictatorship. In the past, most of the attempts to combat such a dictatorship have taken the form of creating a new military force. They failed, for a military force which succeeds in ousting a dictatorship almost invariably sets up a new military dictatorship.

The problem of dictatorship by military men thus poses a very fundamental issue: how to create a non-military force which can overthrow military dictatorship and yet at the same time prevent its recurrence. Such a force must necessarily be identical with the mass of the people who have acquired the material and moral means necessary for its organization.

. . . .

Whether there should be democracy in China and, if so, what kind of democracy would be best suited to China, is a far more complex problem than it appears. Since the early days of the T'ung Meng Hui, democracy has been accepted by most disinterested thinking Chinese as the final goal of modernization, and it should be. But there has been little agreement as to what form democracy should take. Is it to be modeled after the Swiss cantons or after the English-speaking countries? Or is it to be a democracy as envisaged in the 1936 Constitution of the Union of Soviet Socialist Republics? Or is it to be still another form? Even if it were agreed that Chinese democracy should follow that of the English-speaking countries, the alternative choices of a cabinet government of the British type and a presidential government of the American type could still remain a baffling problem.

The problem of democratic reforms is broad enough to embrace most of the constitutional problems that have faced China during the last forty years. Such familiar controversies as the one-party versus the multiparty system, cabinet government versus presidential government, bicameralism versus unicameralism, direct versus indirect election of the president, the question of the distinction of political and governing powers, and a score of other problems are all concerned with the meaning of democracy and the application of democratic ideals.

To resolve any of these controversies requires an inquiry into the capabilities of the Chinese people. If the people are poor, illiterate, disorganized, and impotent, then party systems, whether one-party or multiparty, make little difference as far as the welfare of the people is concerned. The same is true of all the other controversies. Whatever alternatives were chosen could make no difference to the people.

In all these controversies, the matter of form as distinct from reality has plagued the Chinese political thinkers and constitution-makers of the last forty years and more. Almost every writer and constitution-maker accepts and professes the democratic ideal and desires for China whatever democratic pattern may have impressed him or caught his fancy. But the capabilities of the people seldom bother him. He lets his wishful thinking have full sway. He thinks that once there is a democratic institution, both the people and the government will behave democratically, the former expressing their will in the proper channels and the latter abiding by the people's will. Sun Yat-sen, who believed in tutelage, was perhaps the only exception to this overemphasis on the form, to the neglect of the reality. Had he succeeded in making his party, the Kuomintang, a true political elite, imbued with a sense of power not for power's sake but for the sake of giving the people the capacities for democratic organization and control, he might indeed have succeeded in making the reality agree with the form. Unfortunately, he failed; or, to do him full justice, the Kuomintang failed him.

The problem of form versus reality remains. The Chinese government will continue to be either weak and unstable or strong but bad for the people, or even both, until form conforms to reality.

On this question of form and reality, the empire of old was more fortunate in that it did possess the virtue of having the form and the reality in full agreement. Ability to wield power was in the hands of the few. That was the reality. Power was confined to the few. So the form did no violence to the reality. The advantages of strength and stability resulting from such a system of government were quite obvious. But even if it were possible to ignore the demoralizing influence it had on the character of the people, the impact of the West has put a definite end to it. No return is possible.

The most disturbing influence which has come from the West is the emphasis Western philosophy places on the dignity and worth of each individual. Traditional Chinese thinking was not averse to the concept of individual dignity, but reserved it for men of high status alone. The common man might be patronized and even treated with consideration, but he had no claim to inalienable moral and legal rights or personal dignity. Western philosophy, on the other hand, whether it be the rationalism of the eighteenth century or the utilitarianism of the nineteenth, or the Marxism of today, tends to idolize either the individual as such or the mass of individuals. In either case, it differs from the Chinese idolization of the few who were or could aspire to be of high estate and in power. The partiality of the West for the individual man has had such influence on the Chinese people that in their minds power can no longer be confined to the few and equality must be attained.

This refusal to accept government by a few has let loose a great surge of democratic revolution in China. At times, when the revolution seems to have succeeded, general contentment follows and government is easily maintained. But when it dawns on the people that the success is illusory or the revolution is frustrated, the revolutionary movement begins anew. The process continues and has not been and cannot be arrested.

Since the people are not able to fight for democracy, and yet definitely want it, a contradiction exists. That contradiction cannot be removed except by the people's acquiring the ability to fight for democracy.

. . . .

But how are the people to acquire that ability? Obviously, it will not be gratuitously given to them by the men who have monopolized power. They will acquire it only as the result of phenomenal improvement in their economic and educational status. Radical economic reforms and changes in the entire social outlook of the people are called for. When the masses have attained the opportunity to live and work in peace, to be removed from both fear and want, to have the rudiments of education and be conscious of their own dignity, they will have both the interest and the ability to make a reality of any form of government that may be considered democratic.

Economic reforms which would enable the masses to work and enjoy the benefits of work must be primarily directed at removing the shackles which have reduced the vast mass of the people to the present state of poverty and insecurity, and at giving them the opportunities and the assistance for acquiring improved means of livelihood. To be more concrete, there must be a revolutionary change in the system of landholding whereby the motto "the tiller must own his own land," accepted by the Kuomintang and the Chinese communists alike, will be given an honest realization. Usury which has wrought unspeakable misery to the farmers must be eradicated. Side by side with the land reform and the elimination of usury, handicrafts and industry must be encouraged and when necessary even promoted by the state itself. For it is clear that with the Chinese social structure as it is, improvement of the lot of the farmers, who constitute three-fourths of the population, means improvement of the nation as a whole. But the Chinese population being unusually large in proportion to the arable land available, agriculture alone would never help the Chinese people to acquire a decent standard of living. To encourage handicrafts and industries simultaneously with land reform is the only way to give them the kind of economic uplift necessary to their acquiring an interest in politics.

In addition to freedom from want, they must also have freedom from fear. They are not going to have this freedom from fear until they have more education and are able to feel that they are as good as any in the community and have as much right to express their views on affairs of common interest. There have been in the past, and are even now, farmers who are relatively free from want and yet either feel no interest in government or are afraid to express themselves. The reason is that they have not had the necessary education to realize that they are inferior to no one. Therefore, education of a certain kind is as important as the improvement of material well-being. Education may or may not consist of schooling. The essential thing is that the people be taught that politics is not the exclusive concern of the men in power or of those who have the privileges of birth and high education.

Only when the people have thus obtained the means of livelihood and an interest in political affairs can a democracy be sustained. Then the people will have both the ability and the enlightened self-interest to prevent a regime from becoming the government by and of the few. They will have the ability to do it because they will not be economically dependent on the ruling class.

Their self-interest will direct them to do it because their newly acquired economic status will be protected only by a regime in which they maintain an interest.

. . . .

When such reforms in the national economy and such changes in the social outlook of the Chinese have taken place, real democracy in all its essentials will be achieved. When democracy has both form and reality, the small variations in the form become unessential. If the people prefer to invest substantial executive powers in the president, a presidential form of government may conceivably ensue. The president cannot become a personal dictator, for nobody can ever dictate to a self-reliant and politically educated people. The people may also prefer an elected directorate enjoying both executive and legislative powers by mandate from the people. For the same reason, the directorate too cannot degenerate into an oligarchy. Military dictatorship or warlordism will be out of the question. Nobody would dare to make the attempt. If he dared, he would be overthrown in no time. Even the more difficult problem of centralization versus decentralization can be satisfactorily solved. With a politically conscious people as the masters of the nation, powerful but dedicated to their own mass interests, there should be no fear of separatism or disintegration of the Chinese nation. When no such fear exists, it will be only natural to grant a full share of local self-government to the provinces, especially to population groups which are distinctly dissimilar in culture to the bulk of the Chinese people.

If these major problems of Chinese government (the appropriate form of government, the prevention of warlordism and personal dictatorship, and the problem of centralization versus decentralization) can be solved as soon as there is a democratic reality, then the less fundamental problems can be handled with much greater ease. Administrative organization can be easily attained. Statutes can bear a closer correspondence with the conditions of society. Bad organization, bad administration, and bad legislation in the past have been mainly attributable to dictatorial leadership. Since dictators cannot survive the emergence of self-reliance and public interest among a people, these comparatively minor abuses can be easily reduced to a point where the new government can be favorably compared with the better governments in other countries.

. . . .

Nobody will claim that the herculean task of economic reform and political education of the masses will be easy. But it is not impossible. Nay, there are forces which are working for such reforms and such education. Nationalism is one, and that urge which for lack of a better term may be described as an urge for equality is another.

Nationalism has become a factor in Chinese life ever since the turn of the century. But it has never been so all-permeating as it now is. In the past, the Chinese have felt that they were being oppressed or otherwise discriminated against by the more powerful nations of the world. While this negative side of nationalism may still to some extent operate on the Chinese mind, there is now also a positive side. The Chinese desire to see their nation strong and prosperous, not so much to claim a position of eminence over others as to satisfy their own longing for a more developed and better ordered national life. The ever-widening scale of great wars and the ever-present danger of such wars, not to mention the uncomfortable situations arising out of the rivalry of the great powers, have given them a conviction that they must develop their national strength. It is necessary first to enable the Chinese people to live unmenaced by others and second to let them throw their weight in support of peace.

Present-day China is so distraught and so apparently chaotic that superficial observers, especially unsympathetic ones, are unable to detect how deeply nationalistic the Chinese people really are. They cannot believe that the poor people of China could be conscious of their own nation. Whatever expressions of such consciousness there are among the more educated classes are generally considered negative in nature, or, to be exact, anti-foreign. But it is a fact that the bulk of the Chinese, the poor as well as the rich, the uneducated as well as the educated, are immensely nationalistic in the positive sense. For example, they are convinced that only the rise of their own nation will prevent the recurrence of catastrophic wars, not by domination over other nations, but by the redoubling of the strength of peace.

Nationalism will be a powerful factor on the side of radical economic and social changes. Every Chinese with any sensitivity of mind who is not bound to vested interests realizes that there is no future for the Chinese nation unless it is speedily renovated by the economic and social uplifting of the entire people. The true and noble nationalism of today is inseparably linked with the determination to effect that general uplift.

Side by side with nationalism, egalitarianism is also a powerful factor. There is as yet no equality. But the political and social agitators for the last quarter of a century have done their work. The common man's stoic attitude of contentment and resignation has given way to a desire for the betterment of his economic lot. He feels that he is entitled to it. The more he suffers from the devastations of war and the exploitations of the high and the rich, the more indelible the effect of that agitation on him. Equality appeals to the common man as a means of self-preservation.

As an ideal, equality has become a thing of general acceptance. It is less challenged than in some of the outwardly more advanced and progressive nations of the West. That in the past many agitators for that ideal have not practiced it is not a deterrent to its remaining the commonly acknowledged ideal. On the other hand, that the more faithful agitators have done much to make equality a reality adds to the strength of the people's conviction that equality should come and must come.

The idea of equality is irresistible. It has never been successfully resisted anywhere. Once it had a chance to break loose, it could be held in check only when the bulk of the people were deceived into thinking that they were actually enjoying the benefits of equality. That was possible only in countries where the conditions of inequality among the different social strata were graded and not polarized. But polarization has always been the case in China. It is now an accelerating process. With the bulk of the people very poor and with a few very rich enjoying the material benefits of wealth or political power, the irresistibility of the egalitarian ideal can be easily appreciated.

The egalitarian ideal will be a great impetus and a great force for the radical economic and social changes necessary to the realization of democracy. It also accelerates the momentum of these changes, once they have started. The more real equality there is, the more will the people who are likely to benefit by equality make further demands for it. This tendency is indeed noticeable in all countries which have egalitarian legislation, whether it takes the form of mild alleviating measures, or of social democracy, or of communism.

No doubt there are at the present moment also great obstacles in the path of radical economic and social reforms. Some of them come from within. The vested classes are always opposed to such reforms. Wherever they are entrenched, thence comes the opposition. Some of the obstacles come from without. A radical transformation of the Chinese, though ultimately it should be to the advantage of all nations, is yet unwelcome to people who think that their own class interests will be damaged by that transformation. Yet precisely because the moving factors for that transformation are nationalism and egalitarianism, the opposition of the reactionary groups, especially foreign ones, only serve to strengthen those factors within China and thereby give further impetus to the economic and social changes desired.

. . . .

If it is a correct observation that because of the impact of the West the Chinese cannot stop at anything short of some form of real democracy, and if it is a correct postulation that the Chinese will not have any real democracy unless there are prior economic and social changes on a major scale, and, further, if it is also correct reasoning that a strong desire for national independence and economic equality will lead to those major changes, then we are led, in effect, to a restatement of Sun Yat-sen's Three Principles of the People. This is not a strange coincidence. Sun Yat-sen's final aims were surprisingly far sighted and his motives were none other than patriotism in its noblest form. He desired a democratic, socialistic, and prosperous nation to take the place of a medieval and degenerate empire or the remnants of that empire. The same aims and motives are uppermost with most Chinese thinkers of today; the same conditions which he proposed to abolish still exist; and the same forces which he in his last years sought to employ are at work. The coincidence is natural.

There is nothing wrong with the Three People's Principles. There may be found inept illustrations, misstatements of facts, overexaggerated tirades, and even bits of faulty reasoning here and there if Sun Yat-sen's lectures on the Principles are carefully examined. In the expositions of a host of self-styled theorists of the *San-min chu-i* major blunders and mistakes may be seen. But why make the *San-min chu-i* responsible for those blunders and mistakes? The Three Principles are not to be construed outside of the context of Sun Yat-sen's whole outlook as it stood about 1924.

More than that, even Sun Yat-sen's Three Stages of the Revolution may be found to be the true path to the successful achievement of the reality above referred to. That a Military Stage to sweep away the militarist obstacles to revolution is necessary is only too plain to need comment. Tutelage, if it means anything at all, is to gain for the people an interest in public affairs and a sense of equality, a sense that anyone has as much right and ability as any other person to express his views on public affairs. It would not be surprising if a successful revolution when considered in retrospect should be found to have gone through both the Military and Tutelage Stages before it finally reached a real constitutional government of democratic forms. It would not be surprising if all the expedients, compromises, and substitutes which are at variance with the general procedure of the Three Stages should be found to have retarded the successful accomplishment of Sun Yat-sen's final aims.

But one thing is certain, that whoever attempts to achieve Sun Yat-sen's Three Principles, or, confining ourselves to matters of government, to achieve democratic reality as the basis of democratic form, must, in order to be successful, excel in several ways the past Kuomintang which has failed. Success requires more understanding of the problems of the people with which the Principles are concerned. A successful regime must identify itself more with the people and must not consider itself to be above the people. It must be more truly nationalistic, more truly socialistic, and more truly democratic than a regime which makes mere professions or bad distortions of the Principles.

. . . .

It may be suggested that a revolution like that herein suggested would call for a radical change in the conception of human values. It does, indeed, and it is a good thing that change is already going on.

In a revolution like this, the mentality of the elite, who are the organizers of revolution and the conservators of good government alike, is of signal importance. It is not enough that they be capable and devoted to the aims of revolution. Even having an attitude of *noblesse oblige* is not enough. What is most needed of them is to identify themselves with the mass of the people and to claim no distinctions. Theirs must be an utterly selfless work. They must do everything possible to stimulate the people to develop an interest in public affairs. But they must not expect to assume perpetual leadership or to perpetuate the elite. To do either would always mean the existence of a ruling class and the continuation of the old Chinese tradition that the people must be ruled over by the few.

The elite of the past were not without brilliant leaders. They overthrew tyrants, they rectified abuses, they effected reforms. But never for once were they so selfless as not to think that they were the natural leaders of men. Nor could they reconcile themselves to the idea that all men could be equal and that no elite should be in perpetual existence. Hence they never forsook the positions of eminence and the roles of leadership. For the old regime, they were indeed fitting leaders of men. If the leaders of the present day maintain this superior view of their own importance, real democracy is plainly out of the question. Fortunately, such a superior view is now confined to the older and more antiquated part of the elite. The new and young ones, the ones who have both numbers and youth in their favor, have a different point of view. They are convinced that their mission is to help the people acquire an active interest in political affairs and then sink themselves into the masses. They have a different set of human values. They desire the people rather than the elite to become the true masters of the nation's destiny.

The new and young people who are well educated and active in public affairs, in other words, the real elite, have a further virtue. They are impatient for the achievement of economic reform, political equality, and the reality of democracy. They fully realize that in a world of active changes a China which does not quickly develop into a strong and prosperous nation is a nation lost. They are determined to achieve in their lifetime those great political, economic, and social reforms, since they know them to be the prerequisite of a strong and prosperous nation.

Their ranks were at first small. The majority of the educated could not forget that they were, and were destined to continue as, the leaders of men. As leaders of men, they could not countenance their own submergence in the multitude of aroused people. Fortunately for the future of China, the new elite are gaining in numbers.[1] And as they gain in numbers, they cannot fail to give a new direction to the leadership, which may finally achieve economic changes and changes in the social outlook of the Chinese in a reasonably short period.

. . . .

A heartening note should therefore serve as a concluding remark. The government as it has existed is faulty in form as well as poor in its output. Amidst the wanton destruction wrought by the civil war and the accompanying miseries suffered by the people, the day seems to be dark indeed. But in contrast with the darkness of the present, there is also a confidence and determination that the people must be and can be aroused to erect a government which will work for their own economic and social uplift, and which they will be able to control. Since that confidence and that determination will brook no delay in the arrival of a real government for the people and by the people, there can be genuine optimism for the future of the nation.

NOTES

NOTES

CHAPTER I

1. For general histories of China, see Bibliography A, section 4. For geography, George B. Cressey, *China's Geographic Foundations* (1934), is the best reference. Albert Herrmann, *Historical and Commercial Atlas of China* (1935), is very useful. L. H. D. Buxton, *China, the Land and the People* (1929), and Cressey, *Asia's Lands and Peoples* (1944), are also recommended.

2. Cressey, *Asia's Lands and Peoples*, p. 42, gives 4,380,535 square miles as the area of China in 1944. Subtracting 580,150 for Outer Mongolia and 64,000 for Tannu Tuva, also Cressey's figures, one gets 3,736,385 square miles for the area of China today.

3. According to the statistics of the Bureau of Population of the Ministry of the Interior, the population as of June 30, 1947 was 461,006,285. This figure may be far from accurate. Since statistics about China, whether Chinese or foreign, official or private, are generally inaccurate, no attempt at exactness in figures will be made in this book. Generally, only rough figures which the author considers reasonable will be given.

4. As generally accepted by Chinese of the present day, the several regions comprise the following provinces:

   1. Northeastern: Liaoning, Liaopei, Antung, Kirin, Sungkiang, Nunkiang, Heilungkiang, Hokiang, Hsingan, Jehol.
   2. Northern: Shantung, Hopei, Honan, Shansi, Shensi, Chahar, Suiyan.
   3. Northwestern: Kansu, Ninghsia, Chinghai.
   4. Southeastern: Kiangsu, Anhwei, Chekiang.
   5. Central: Kiangsi, Hupei, Hunan.
   6. Southern: Fukien, Taiwan, Kwangtung, Kwangsi.
   7. Southwestern: Yunnan, Kweichow, Szechwan, Sikang.

   The Provinces of Sinkiang and Tibet form regions of their own.

5. See John L. Buck, *Land Utilization in China* (1937), and Karl J. Pelzer, *Population and Land Utilization* (1941). On the recurrence of famine, see Walter H. Mallory, *China; Land of Famine* (1926).

6. On soil, see James Thorp, *The Geography of the Soils of China* (1936). On the inhabitability of Sinkiang, see R. F. C. Schomberg, "Habilitability of Chinese Turkestan," *Geographical Journal* (1932), pp. 505–511.

7. Besides Cressey's works above referred to, see H. Foster Bain, *Ores and Industry in the Far East* (1933). An old study by Wilfred Smith, *A Geographical Study of Coal and Iron in China* (1926), and Juan Vei Chow, "Mineral Resources of China," *Economic Geology*, vol. XVI (1946), no. 4, are also of value.

8. For an interesting hypothesis, see Li Chi, *The Formation of the Chinese People* (1928). See also Carl W. Bishop, *Origin of Far Eastern Civilizations* (1942).

9. See E. H. Parker, *A Thousand Years of the Tartars* (1924).

10. *The Shu-ching* (Book of history) and *Shih-ching* (Book of odes) have been translated by James Legge, *Chinese Classics*, vols. III, IV (1893–1895).

11. For some of the Han and T'ang exploits, see the following two interesting articles: Friedrich Hirth, "The Story of Chang K'ien: China's Pioneer in Western Asia," *Journal of the American Oriental Society*, XXXVII (1919), 89–152; and Aurel Stein, "A Chinese Expedition across the Pamirs and Hindukush, A.D. 747," *New China Review*, IV, 161–183.

12. See L. H. D. Buxton, *The Peoples of Asia* (1925). See also Sergei M. Shirokogoroff, *Anthropology of Northern China* (1923), and *Anthropology of Eastern China and Kwangtung Province* for a discussion of some of the races of China.

13. There are a few other groups, all very small. But the Hakka of Kwangtung and Kwangsi are definitely Chinese.

14. See Chen Ta, *Population in Modern China* (1946).

15. These comprise principally the shopkeepers other than those in modern business, but should also include owner-operators of old-style boats and carts engaged in the transportation business.

16. In the apportionment above given, the dependents in a family who have no distinct occupation of their own and are not entered in another group are considered as having the same occupation as the head of the family and are so counted. Those who have a number of occupations at one and the same time are counted only once, their principal means of livelihood being used as the criterion. Arbitrariness is inevitable in both these considerations.

For instance, the wife of a carpenter or an artisan may well be a farm hand. As such, she herself should naturally be classified as being occupied in agriculture. But their unproductive minor children have also to be arbitrarily divided, partly under the father's, and partly under the mother's, occupation. Roughly, the whole family of a married man in public service has been classified as being in public service. The same is true of the family of those in modern business and in liberal professions. Only three out of four of the dependents of a farmer or of an entrepreneur or of his employees, two out of four of the dependents of a modern laborer, and one out of four of those of an artisan, a peddler or a household or office laborer have been classified as having the same occupation. No dependents of the common soldiers are classified under soldiery. These differentiations have been adopted for obvious reasons. Taking the average size of the Chinese family to consist of five members (or 5.4 on June 30, 1947, according to the statistics of the Ministry of the Interior), one or more family members of those less profitable occupations is usually obliged to have an occupation of his own.

As to what constitutes one's principal means of livelihood, it is again possible to entertain different notions. An official may be a landlord; a carpenter may at the same time be a farmer. To classify so many landlord-officials as landlords and so many others as officials, or so many carpenter-farmers as carpenters and so many others as farmers is purely arbitrary. But unless some venture along these lines is dared, however arbitrary it may be, it is impossible to gain any idea of the occupational structure of Chinese society.

17. The 12 per cent for farmer-owners may appear to be underestimated, but it may not be. The members of an average-sized farming family, owning, let us say, one acre of land, have to be either tenants or farm hands in order to earn enough for the family to live on. A part of them, therefore, should be entered in the class of tenants and farm-laborers.

18. Some old-style shopkeepers are rich, but their number is small, certainly smaller than .5 per cent of the total population. Therefore, no entrepreneur is counted as well to do in the percentage apportionment.

19. See John L. Buck, *Chinese Farm Economy, a Study of 2866 Farms in Seventeen Localities and Seven Provinces in China* (1930), and Fei Hsiao-tung, *Peasant Life in China: A Field Study of Country Life in the Yangtze Valley* (1939).

20. See Paul Monroe, *A Report on Education in China* (1922). For a special aspect of education, see Cyrus H. Peake, *Nationalism and Education in Modern China* (1932).

21. The official statistics may sometimes put the literacy figure as high as 35 per cent. The official figures are extremely dubious. It is safe to say that few men over 40 or women over 30, belonging to the group of the poor, have had the benefits of modern school education. Of the men below 40 and women below 30, it is doubtful whether half of them have ever gone to school. It is also to be remembered here that unless one attends school for at least two years, more or less consecutively, one cannot be expected to be able to read in future years. Bearing all this in mind, the illiteracy figure of 75 per cent is perhaps a conservative estimate.

22. See Olga Lang, *Chinese Family and Society* (1946). No definitive account exists of either the family system or the family life.

23. On the religious beliefs of the Chinese, see León Wieger, *Histoire des Croyances Réligieuses et des Philosophiques en Chine, depuis l'origine jusqu'à nos jours* (1917). Confucianism cannot be considered a religion. It is more a state cult. See John Knight Shryock, *The Origin and Development of the State Cult of Confucius* (1932).

24. Zoroastrianism was in existence in China from about 550 to 845.

25. The best account in Chinese is the recent work of T'ang Yung-t'ung, *Han Wei Liang-Chin Nan-pei-ch'ao fo-chiao shih* (A history of Buddhism in the Han, Wei, the two Chin, and the Southern and Northern Dynasties).

26. The fullest account in English on Christianity in China is Kenneth Scott Latourette, *A History of Christian Missions in China* (1929).

Christianity came to China in the Middle Ages. Nestorianism existed in China from about 600 to 845. Nestorianism, Zoroastrianism, and Manicheism, a heretic Christian sect heavily colored by Zoroastrianism and Buddhism, were all effectively suppressed in 845 at the time of the "destruction of Buddhism." The temples of the three non-Buddhist religions were spoken of by the Chinese Buddhists of the T'ang Dynasty (618–907) as "The Three Barbarian Temples."

During the Mongol Dynasty (1279–1368) Christianity was in evidence both at the capital and at other cities. But with the overthrow of the Dynasty, it was extinguished.

It is more correct to take the sixteenth century as the beginning of Christianity in China, for it has been in continuous existence since then.

27. At the time of the "destruction of Buddhism" in 845, there were 40,000 monasteries and 700,000 monks and nuns.

28. *Hsing.*

29. *Sheng-yün hsüeh.*

30. See Adolf Reichwein, *China and Europe: Intellectual and Artistic Contacts in the Eighteenth Century* (1925).

31. The term "feudalism" as employed in the following pages denotes the form of state rather than the class structure of society.

CHAPTER II

1. On the development of Chinese political thought, the following recent Chinese works are outstanding: (1) T'ao Hsi-sheng, *Chung-kuo cheng-chih ssu-hsiang shih* (A history of Chinese political thought); (2) Hsiao Kung-ch'üan, *Chung-kuo cheng-chih ssu-hsiang shih*; and (3) Lü Chen-yü, *Chung-kuo cheng-chih ssu-hsiang shih.* Of these, Hsiao Kung-ch'üan's is the most careful. A good introductory work is Lin

Mousheng's *Men and Ideas, an Informal History of Chinese Political Thought* (1942). Fung Yu-lan's *Chung-kuo che-hsüeh shih* (A history of Chinese philosophy) and Alfred Forke's *Geschichte der alten Chinesischen Philosophie* (1927) also deal extensively with political thought. Vol. I of Fung Yu-lan's book has been translated by Derk Bodde under the title *A History of Chinese Philosophy* (1937), and chapters of Vol. II, also translated by Bodde, have appeared in the *Harvard Journal of Asiatic Studies.*

2. Concerning this period, Liang Ch'i-ch'ao's pathfinding treatise, *Hsien-Ch'in cheng-chih ssu-hsiang shih* (A history of pre-Ch'in political thought), is still the best. It has been translated into English by Chen as *A History of Chinese Political Thought during the Early Tsin Period* (1930).

3. *Shih chi* (Historical records) was started by Ssu-ma T'an and after his death completed by his son, Ssu-ma Ch'ien (born *c.* 145, died between 86–74 B.C.). A large portion of the *Shih chi* has been translated by Chavannes as *Les Mémoires Historiques de Se-ma Ts'ien* (1895–1905). For a discussion on Ssu-ma T'an, see I, xiii-xxi.

4. The historian Pan Ku (died A.D. 92), in his *Han shu* (Han history), listed the Tsung-heng (Vertical-Horizontal) School, the Tsa (Mélange) School, the Agriculturalists, and the Novelists, in addition to Ssu-ma T'an's six schools, making a total of ten schools, all of which were supposed to have flourished in the pre-Ch'in centuries. Of the Mélangists and the Novelists little need be said. The former generally represented a rehash of the other schools, and the latter touched only on the trivial. The Agriculturalists were supposed to have emphasized land-tilling as the foundation of good government; but it is possible that none of the school lived at all, to say nothing of their alleged writings. The "Vertical-Horizontal" men were great practitioners of statecraft peculiar to the Warring States Period, when the politically ambitious were eager to form either vertical or horizontal (north to south or east to west) alliances to advance the fortunes of the states they happened to serve. Their writings are no longer in existence. Judging from their sayings as recorded in *Kuo-t'sê* (Statecraft), they seem to have been solely interested in arriving at power to the exclusion of anything concerned with either the nature of the state or that of political power.

Part of the Annals in the *Han shu* have been translated by Homer H. Dubs as *The History of the Former Han Dynasty* (1938 and 1944).

5. The best known of the *Yin-yang* School was perhaps Tsou Yen (*c.* 305–249 B.C.), of whose theories we can only indirectly gain some knowledge. He seems to have imagined both the infinity of the universe and of time. Concerning time, he advanced the theory of five cycles, one inevitably succeeding the other, when the previous one has outlived its blooming period. This theory obviously justified the supplanting of the decaying Chou Dynasty by the Ch'in Dynasty.

Hui Shih and Kung-sun Lung were the best-known Logicians. Hui Shih is known to us only through the *Chuang-tzu*, but Kung-sun Lung left us the *Kung-sun Lung-tzu.* According to modern terminology, they would perhaps be regarded rather as epistemologists than logicians.

6. Lao-tzu was perhaps the most legendary of all the figures we are prepared to treat in these pages. However, it may be on good ground to say that one Li Er lived about the time of Confucius, and this Li Er was later spoken of by his disciples and followers as Lao-tzu and his teachings were reduced to writing in the time of the Warring States as the *Lao-tzu.*

The *Lao-tzu, or Tao-te ching*, is a work of about five thousand words, but very difficult to read. Among the many versions in Western languages, Arthur Waley's *The Way and Its Power* (1934) is perhaps the best.

7. The work attributed to Chuang-tzu is known as the *Chuang-tzu*, which is a

collection of essays of rather unidentifiable authorship. For translations from the *Chuang-tzu*, see Fung Yu-lan, *Chuang-tzu* (1932), and Herbert A. Giles, *Chuang Tzu, Mystic, Moralist, and Social Reformer* (1926).

8. Shang Yang's work, the *Shang-tzu*, has been translated by J. J. L. Duyvendak as *The Book of Lord Shang* (1928).

9. Han Fei's work, the *Han Fei-tzu*, has been translated by Liao Wen Kuei as *The Complete Works of Han Fei Tzu, A Classic of Chinese Legalism* (1939). In Chinese, Wang Hsien-shen's *Han Fei-tzu chi-chieh* (Collected annotations of Han Fei-tzu) is still the outstanding commentary.

10. In spite of much controversy concerning the genuineness of the *Mo-tzu*, it is perhaps safe to say that it represents Mo Ti very much as the *Analects* does Confucius. For translations of Mo Ti's work, the *Mo-tzu*, see Alfred Forke, *Mê Ti des Sozialethikers, und seiner Schüler philosophische Werke* (1922), and Mei Yi-pao, *The Ethical and Philosophical Works of Motse*. See also Mei Yi-pao, *Motse . . . the Neglected Rival of Confucious* (1934). In Chinese, Liang Ch'i-ch'ao's *Mo-tzu hsüeh-an* (A study of Mo-tzu's writings) is a very valuable commentary.

11. The chapter on the eight schools of *Ju*, *Hsien-hsüeh*, in the *Han Fei-tzu* is not in Liao's translation above referred to.

12. Chapters from the *Hsün-tzu* have been translated by Dubs as *The Works of Hsüntze* (1928). See also Dubs, *Hsüntze, the Moulder of Ancient Confucianism* (1927).

13. The *Meng-tzu* of Mencius has been translated by Legge as *The Works of Mencius*, in *The Chinese Classics*, Vol. II. See also Leonard A. Lyall, *Mencius* (1932), and Ivor A. Richards, *Mencius on the Mind: Experiments in Multiple Definition* (1932).

14. See Waley, *The Way and Its Power: A Study of the Tao Te King and its Place in Chinese Thought*, a good introduction to the Confucianists, Legalists, and Taoists. See also K. T. Spalding, *Three Chinese Thinkers* (1947), discussing Mo-tzu, Chuang-tzu, and Hsün-tzu in turn.

15. *Lun-yü*, the *Analects of Confucius*, was most probably compiled by the indirect disciples of Confucius during the Period of Warring States, and somewhat retouched by the Confucian scholars of the Former Han Dynasty. There are many translations in Western languages. Waley's *The Analects of Confucius* is probably the best.

16. On Tung Chung-shu, see Lin Mousheng, *Men and Ideas*, chap. ix.

17. The *Ch'un-ch'iu* (Spring and autumn annals), together with its most important commentary, *Tso-chuan*, are to be found in James Legge's translation, *The Chinese Classics*, Vol. V.

18. It should be added here that the hitherto vague consciousness that the barbarians must not be allowed to disturb the rule of the Chinese had also become mature and outspoken. So in his reading of the *Ch'un-ch'iu*, Tung Chung-shu also made the idea of supporting the King (*wang*) and outlawing the Barbarians (*i*), a part of the Confucian doctrine of the Great Unified Empire.

19. Translations from the *Huai-nan-tzu* may be found in Evan Morgan, *Tao, the Great Luminant* (1933).

20. The *I-ching* (Book of Changes) has been translated by Legge as *The Yi King* (Sacred Books of the East), vol. XVI (1882).

21. *Hsin* and *hsing*.

22. *Tao T'ung*. Here *tao* means the "way" in general, not the *tao* of the Taoist in particular. According to Han Yü, the *tao* in Confucianism was passed on from Emperors Yao and Shun to Confucius, through the founding kings of the Three Dynasties (Hsia, Shang, and Chou). The long lineage was supposed to have made the "way" infallible and immutable, admissible only of elaboration and development.

23. As early as the Chin Dynasty, during the reign of Chen Ti (326–342), the theory that Buddhist monks owed no allegiance to the temporal ruler had already come into existence. The monk Hui T'ung (fifth century) elaborated this theory and it became a political force. This was a contributing factor in the conflict between Buddhism and the state and led to the "destruction of Buddhism" in 845, during the reign of Wu Tsung (841–846) of the T'ang Dynasty. Hence the Ch'an school of Buddhism which later prospered always evaded this theoretical controversy and chose to accept the temporal rule as it was.

24. *Chih li.*

25. Summarily stated, Chou Lien-hsi, the author of *T'ai-chi t'u* (Design of the supreme ultimate or totality), was obviously under heavy influence of the Taoists. His emphasis on *ch'eng* (sincerity) as the origin of all perfect relationships and good behavior and as the thing which makes up what is known as *sheng* led his followers to the pursuit of *li.* The theorizings of the Ch'eng brothers are generally undistinguishable. But the Elder Ch'eng took *li* to be the same as nature and consequently incapable of an existence apart from matter, whereas the Younger Ch'eng emphasized knowing, knowing the what of every matter. This difference led to the differentiation of the two branches known as the Mind and *Li* Schools, championed respectively by Lu Chiu-yüan and Chu Hsi.

Chu Hsi insisted on the probing of *li* in every bit of matter, taking *li* to be a kind of abstract concept extractable from all matter.

Lu Chiu-yüan took issue with Chu Hsi, saying that knowing one's own mind leads to the knowledge of matter.

Wang Shou-jên was, however, the clearer exponent of the mind theory. He denied the existence of *li* apart from mind. He preached practicing what one does know as the way to pursue *li.*

Yet, however great may have been the controversy within the *Li* School about epistemology, they all deviated very little from the traditional Confucianist acceptance of the post-Ch'in political regime.

Important works in Western languages on Sung and Ming Confucianists include: J. P. Bruce, *Chu Hsi and his Masters* (1923); Bruce, *The Philosophy of Human Nature by Chu Hsi* (1922); Huang Siu-chi, *Lu Hsiang-shan, a Twelfth Century Chinese Idealist Philosopher* (1944); Frederick G. Henke, trans., *The Philosophy of Wang Yang-ming* (1916); and Wang Tchang-tche, *La Philosophie Morale de Wang Ying-ming* (1936). Lu Hsiang-shan is another name of Lu Chiu-yüan.

26. See H. R. Williamson, *Wang An-shih* (1937).

27. *Chou li* (The rites of the Chou) purports to give a picture of the orderly life that prevailed at the beginning of the Chou Dynasty, the kind of life that Confucius cherished. See Edouard Biot, *Le Tcheou-li ou Rites des Tcheou* (1851, reprinted, 1939).

28. Above, p. 22.

29. The Classicists were those who specialized in the so-called Han learning, also known as *p'u-hsüeh.* Ku Yen-wu, Ch'ien Ta-hsin, Wang Ming-sheng, Tai Chen, Tuan Yü-ts'ai, were some of the more famous Classicists. See Arthur W. Hummel, ed., *Eminent Chinese of the Ch'ing Period* (1943–1944).

30. See William J. Hail, *Tseng Kuo-fan and the Taiping Rebellion* (1927). See also W. L. Bales, *Tso Tsung-t'ang, soldier and statesman of old China* (1937).

31. Below, p. 51.

32. Ku Yen-wu also happened to be an eminent Classicist. *Jih-chih lu* (Day to day reflections) was his principal work, but his *Chün-hsien lun* (On prefectures and *hsien*) was more exclusively concerned with political institutions. He condemned the

"*li* learning" and his comments on the so-called *sheng-hsüeh* (studies on the writings of the sages) were openly derogatory. "Prolific studies without any insight"; "to practice those studies would be a shame": these were some of his strictures. On both Ku Yen-wu and Huang Tsung-hsi, see Hummel, ed., *Eminent Chinese*.

33. Mention has already been made of K'ang Yu-wei's political thought, which was traditionally Confucian. K'ang Yu-wei and Liang Ch'i-ch'ao (1873–1929), teacher and pupil, were the leaders of the Reform Movement of 1898. Though Liang Ch'i-ch'ao had a much more flexible mind than his teacher and though, after the Revolution of 1911, he accepted republicanism in good faith, he supported the Manchu Regime in 1898, and the reforms he advocated were in no way prejudicial either to the monarchical order or to any of the Confucian studies.

CHAPTER III

1. Most of the subjects treated in this chapter are covered by various recent treatises on the history of Chinese law and institutions. None of these treatises is quite satisfactory, but Ch'eng Shu-te, *Chung-kuo fa-chih shih* (A history of Chinese law and institutions), and Ch'en Ku-yüan, *Chung-kuo fa-chih shih* are recommended. Primary sources are the *Chiu-t'ung* (Nine complete works) and the *Chih-kuan chih* (Treatise on offices) in the Dynastic Histories. Chi Yün's *Li-tai chih-kuan piao* (Tables on offices of the dynasties) and Sun Jung's *Ku-chin fa-chih piao* (Tables on law and institutions of ancient and modern times) are more serviceable. For the Ch'ing Dynasty, William Frederick Mayers's *The Chinese Government, a Manual of Chinese Titles, categorically arranged and explained* (1897), and Hsieh's *The Government of China, 1644–1911* (1925) may be referred to.

2. Besides Chi Yün's work cited, Kao I-han's *Chung-kuo nei-ko chih-tu ti yen-ko* (The evolution of the Chinese cabinet system) is useful. See also T. H. Koo, "Constitutional Development of the Western Han Dynasty," *Journal of the American Oriental Society*, XL, 170–193.

3. Some Chinese histories, mostly based on forged classics, are full of idyllic accounts of the administrative institutions of the early Chou. Since there is no authentic material to substantiate those accounts, they will be omitted here.

4. These three great dignitaries were coming into existence during the Ch'in Dynasty, but were not formally styled the Three *Kung* (Three Lords) until Ching Ti's time. Their individual titles varied from time to time. At the beginning of the Han they were known as *Hsiang-kuo, T'ai-wei, and Yü-shih ta-fu*, herein rendered, respectively, as chancellor, marshal, and recorder. Dubs, in his translation of *The History of the Former Han Dynasty*, above referred to, adopted the terms chancellor of state, grand commandant, and grand secretary which are clumsy and less exact. At the time of Ching Ti, they were called *Ssu-t'u*, in charge of men, *Ssu-ma*, in charge of affairs pertaining to Heaven, and *Ssu-k'ung*, in charge of affairs pertaining to the Earth. It was also claimed that these were the titles in vogue early in Chou times.

5. *Men-hsia* literally means "under the threshold." The word *sheng*, which was eventually to designate what is now known as province, had a curious origin. All the three secretariats were placed inside the palace; in Chinese, they were *chin-chung*. "Chin-chung" was changed to *sheng-chung* in Han Yuan Ti's time (48–39 B.C.) in order to avoid the use of the word *chin* which happened to be the name of the father of the empress. *Sheng* for province was taken from the word *sheng* in *sheng-chung*.

6. A variation of the *Chung-shu* Secretariat.

7. *Chiu Ch'ing*. The Three *Kung* and Nine *Ch'ing* were the highest dignitaries in ancient times.

8. The material on this topic can be gathered from the *Hsüan-chü chih* (Treatise on examination) which usually forms a part of the Dynastic Histories. The term "civil service" in this section denotes practically all public officials of the empire.

9. According to the so-called system of "Nine Graded Recommendees," the recommendees were entered in nine separate grades, theoretically according to their caliber, but in fact according to their status by birth. The result was that the high graded recommendees always came from the aristocratic clans and families.

10. Before the Sui, the so-called *chien-chü* (recommendation) was real. From the Sui to the Ch'ing inclusive, the so-called *chih-chü* (instituted recommendation) was really a kind of special examination. During the Ming and the Ch'ing there was the so-called *pao-chü* (guaranteed recommendation) with which the high dignitaries recommended successful candidates of the examination for appointment, or incumbent officials for promotion. Though in the Dynastic Histories these three are all known as "recommendation," they are in reality quite different one from the other.

11. See Robert des Rotours, *Le Traité des Examens Traduit de la Nouvelle Histoire des T'ang.* For the Liao Dynasty, see an interesting article by Karl A. Wittfogel, "Public Office in the Liao Dynasty and the Chinese Examination System," *Harvard Journal of Asiatic Studies*, X (1917), 13–40.

12. So-called because the style of the essay propounding classical truism must be in eight paragraphs of varied but definite lengths with prescribed beginnings and endings.

13. Chinese writings abound in tales and descriptions of the famous examinations, showing that rigidity was carried to absurd limits.

14. See Edouard Biot, *Essai sur l'Histoire de l'Instruction Publique en Chine* (1847).

15. See a discussion of family influence on the examinations in E. A. Kracke, Jr., "Family vs. Merit in Chinese Civil Service Examinations under the Empire," *Harvard Journal of Asiatic Studies*, X (1947), 103-123.

16. See Kao I-han, *Chung-kuo yü-shih chih-tu ti yen-ko* (The evolution of the Chinese censorial system), and *Chien-ch'a chi-tu shih-liao* (A sketch history of the control institution), ed. by a compilation bureau of the Control Yuan. See also, Richard L. Walker, "The Control System of the Chinese Government," *Far Eastern Quarterly*, VII (1947), 2–21.

17. Called *Yü-shih yuan*, or members of the Office of the *Yü-shih*.

18. Again like the *Yü-shih*, both the name and the function of these *Chi-shih-chung* went through many vicissitudes from the Han to the T'ang. During the T'ang, the function was greatly emphasized and two new dignitaries, called the *Chien-i ta-fu*, Left and Right, coequal in rank with the *Yü-shih ta-fu*, were created. They ranked above a host of officials, including the *Chi-shih-chung*. They and the *Chi-shih-chung* were all empowered to remonstrate.

19. For a general introduction, see Jean Escarra, *Le droit chinois* (1936). For sources, see the *Hsing-fa chih* (Penal treatise or Treatise on punishments) in the Dynastic Histories.

20. There is as usual the difficulty of rendering the Chinese terms into English. *Tien*, which means a body of fundamental law, is here rendered as "Law." *Lü*, which means a body of statutes, is here rendered as "Code." The best treatise on the *lü* of the early dynasties is Ch'eng Shu-te, *Chiu-ch'ao lü k'ao* (A study of the *lü* of nine dynasties). There is a translation of *Ta-Ch'ing lü-li* by Sir Thomas Staunton, under the title of *Ta Tsing Leu Lee. . . the fundamental laws and a selection from the supplementary statutes of the Penal Code of China* (1810). See also a fuller French translation by Le P. Guy Boulais, entitled *Manuel du Code Chinois* (1924).

21. The terms in Chinese are *sheng* for province, and *fu* for prefecture. The *hsien* is sometimes rendered in English as district, but the original is more commonly used. In the latter part of the Ch'ing, the *tao* (circuit) was interposed between the *fu* and the *hsien*.

22. Similar titles were given to the highest local dignitaries during the Ming Dynasty.

23. The diplomatic function was virtually unknown. This was due to the fact that the empire, following upon the close of feudalism, was a universal state, juxtaposed neither with an all-powerful church like Rome, nor with states like herself.

24. The magistrate of the *hsien* was very frequently judged by his competence to adjudicate litigation with dispatch and justice. Chinese literature, especially in the form of biographies and popular story books, abounds in this aspect of the magistrate's life.

25. See Liang Fang-chung, "I-t'iao-pien fa" (The single whip system) in *Chung-kuo chin-tai ching-chi shih chi-k'an* (Chinese modern economic history journal), IV, 1.

26. See *Discourses on Salt and Iron: a debate on State Control of Commerce and Industry in Ancient China*, translated by Esson M. Gale from Huan K'uan's *Yen-t'ieh lun* with introduction and notes (1931).

27. A *han-lin* was a scholar who had passed the highest examination with honors.

CHAPTER IV

1. The best reference for this chapter and for chaps. v and vi is Li Chien-nung, *Chung-kuo chin-pai-nien cheng-chih shih* (A political history of China in the last century). This is an augmented edition of his earlier work, *Tsui-chin san-shih-nien Chung-kuo cheng-chih shih* (A political history of China in the last thirty years). See also Paul H. Clyde, *The Far East, a History of the Impact of the West on Eastern Asia* (1948) and Arthur H. Smith, *China in Convulsion* (1901).

2. Arnold H. Rowbotham, *Missionary and Mandarin. The Jesuits at the Court of China* (1942).

3. The best account in English of this period is Meribeth E. Cameron, *The Reform Movement in China, 1898–1912* (1931); see also Hawkling L. Yen, *A Survey of Constitutional Development in China* (1911).

4. In his unsent letter to Li Hung-chang about 1893, Sun Yat-sen urged on him more thorough-going reforms than the minister had hitherto advocated. This letter, probably genuine, can be found in any complete works of Sun Yat-sen.

5. George Nye Steiger, *China and the Occident: The Origin and Development of the Boxer Movement* (1927).

6. Li Chien-nung, *Chung-kuo chin-pai-nien cheng-chih shih*, I, 229.

7. Most of the important constitutional texts cited in this book are conveniently given as appendices in Wang Shih-chieh and Ch'ien Tuan-sheng, *Pi-chiao hsien-fa* (Comparative constitutional law). The English translations are mostly to be found in Pan Wei-tung, *The Chinese Constitution: A Study of Forty Years of Constitution-Making in China* (1946). For the Constitutional Principles of 1908, see *U. S. Foreign Relations, 1908*, pp. 191–196.

8. For the English text, see *China Year Book, 1912*, pp. xxiii–xxiv.

9. Tzu-cheng yuan is sometimes rendered as "Parliament." Since half of its membership as well as its President were appointed and it had no full legislative powers, "Legislative Council" seems to be a better translation.

10. See chap. vi, below.

11. Men like Ch'en T'ien-hua, Sung Chiao-jen, Chang Ping-lin, and Huang Hsing were all original members and important officers of the T'ung Meng Hui. In other words, the student class, literary scholars, and generally respectable people were amply represented.

12. Besides Li Chien-nung and Cameron, cited above, see also P. H. B. Kent, *The Passing of the Manchus* (1912).

13. The Chinese name Ts'an-i yuan is generally rendered as "senate." This is perhaps a correct rendering when Ts'an-i yuan is the upper chamber of a legislative assembly. Under the Organic Law of the Provisional Government of December 2, 1911, the Provisional Ts'an-i yuan was the sole chamber. "Legislative Assembly" seems to be a better rendering.

14. For English text, see *U. S. Foreign Relations, 1914*, pp. 38–41.

CHAPTER V

1. For a detailed account of the governmental structure and functions, both central and local, in so far as they are provided by the written laws and constitutions, see Ch'ien Tuan-sheng *et al.*, *Min-kuo cheng-chih shih* (A history of the political institutions under the Republic). The organization and functions of every department of the government are there analyzed according to the letter of the law. The footnotes in the work give references to the primary sources. In Western languages, see Wu Chih-fang, *Chinese Government and Politics* (1934), Harold M. Vinacke, *Modern Constitutional Development in China* (1920), T. T. Ouang, *Le Gouvernement de la Chine Moderne* (1923), and W. W. Willoughby, *Constitutional Government in China* (1922), all on the Peking Government.

On the political history of this period, Li Chien-nung's work above cited is the best. In English, chapters in H. F. MacNair, *China in Revolution* (1931), Harold A. Van Dorn, *Twenty Years of the Chinese Republic*, and Stanley K. Hornbeck, *Contemporary Politics in the Far East* (1916) may be consulted.

2. The erstwhile reformists formed the backbone of the Chinputang (Progressive Party) which supported Yuan Shih-k'ai. See below, p. 71.

3. For English text, see *China Year Book 1914*, pp. 490–499.

4. *U. S. Foreign Relations, 1914*, pp. 56–60.

5. It is to be remembered that Yuan Shih-k'ai was elected on October 6, 1913 for a term of five years, to begin on October 10, 1913.

6. For English text, see Pan, *The Chinese Constitution*, Appendix F.

7. In the last months of World War I, Japan had by agreement with the Peking Government, of which Tuan Ch'i-jui was Premier, secured rights to train Chinese troops for participation in the war against Germany. In February 1919, there was another agreement which provided for the training arrangement to continue until the conclusion of a peace treaty with Germany.

8. See below, Appendix C.

9. For English text, see *The China Year Book, 1926–1927*, pp. 1234–1238.

10. The confusions and the rapid change of events that affected the Southern regime which had continued to exist since 1917 will be treated in greater detail in the following chapter.

11. For a list, see below, Appendix B.

12. The membership of the Canton Parliament was not entirely the same as the one at the time of 1916–1917, but it claimed to be the same body. See below, pp. 86–87.

13. See below, chap. xxiii.

14. See below, chap. xii.

15. The Northern militarists were collectively known as the Peiyang militarists because when Yuan Shih-k'ai had charge of the training and organization of the New Army he was the Imperial Peiyang Commissioner. There were in the last decades of the Manchu Dynasty two super-viceroys, the Imperial Nanyang and Peiyang Commissioners. *Nan-yang* and *Pei-yang* mean respectively Southern and Northern Seas.

16. Sie Ying-chou, *Le Fédéralisme en Chine: Etude sur quelques constitutions provinciales* (1924).

17. After the overthrow of Ts'ao K'un, in November 1924 and the assumption of power by Tuan Ch'i-jui, Sun Yat-sen went north to confer with Tuan Ch'i-jui. When he was passing through Tientsin, the French went so far as to refuse him passage through their concession. This was just one of such hostile acts against him.

18. For some of the social and political problems of the day, see Bertrand Russell, *The Problem of China* (1922).

CHAPTER VI

1. For this as well as the following chapter the best introduction is Li Chien-nung, *Chung-kuo chin-pai-nien cheng-chih shih* (A political history of China in the last century). Chapters in Wang Shih-chieh and Ch'ien Tuan-sheng, *Pi-chiao hsien-fa* (Comparative constitutional law), and Ch'en Ju-hsuan, *Hsin-ting chung-kuo hsien-fa shih* (A history of the Chinese constitution, new revised edition), are useful. In English, MacNair, *China in Revolution*, Nathaniel Peffer, *China, the Collapse of a Civilization* (1930), Harold M. Vinacke, *A History of the Far East in Modern Times* (1941), and H. A. Van Dorn, *Twenty Years of the Chinese Republic* (1932), are also recommended.

There is no good history of the Kuomintang. Tsou Lu's *Chung-kuo kuo-min-tang shih-kao* (Draft history of the Kuomintang) is a source book on the early history (up to 1924) of the party. Hua Lin-i's *Chung-kuo kuo-min-tang shih* (A history of the Chinese Kuomintang) is too brief. There is also Hsieh Pin's *Min-kuo cheng-tang shih* (A history of political parties under the Republic), which touches on the Kuomintang before the Reorganization. In Western languages, Thomas Tze Chung Woo, *The Kuomintang and the Future of the Chinese Revolution* (1928); T'ang Leang-li, *The Inner History of the Chinese Revolution* (1930); Harold R. Isaacs, *The Tragedy of the Chinese Revolution* (1938); and M. N. Roy, *Revolution and Counterrevolution in China* (1946) represent the several points of view. Woo is inclined to the left. T'ang follows Wang Ching-wei. Isaacs was a Trotskyite. Roy is an orthodox communist. There is no book on Kuomintang history in Western languages by a rightist; Gustav Amann, *Sun Yatsens Vermachtnis: Geschichte der Chinesischen Revolution* (1928) is unsatisfactory.

On Sun Yat-sen, *Tsung-li ch'üan-chi* (Complete works of the Tsung-li), edited by Hu Han-min, gives the fullest information. In Western languages there are many biographies, of which Lyon Sharman's *Sun Yat-sen, His Life and its Meaning* is the most careful and critical.

2. *Tang* means party. The term *kuomin* which was to be intimately associated with the government and politics of China for years to come needs some explanation. *Kuo* means country and *min* means people. The nearest rendering of *kuomin* is therefore nation, and the adjective should be nationalist. In a circular to all the branches of the Kuomintang the world over, on November 10, 1920, Sun Yat-sen ordered that the party was to be known as "The Kuo Min Tang" and the translation to be "Chinese Nationalist Party."

3. *Hsing Chung Hui* means Revive China Society. *Hua Hsing Hui* means Chinese Revival Society. *T'ung Meng Hui* means Together Sworn Society.

4. See the article Sun Yat-sen contributed to the first issue of the *Min Pao* (The people's herald) in 1905. The article appears in his complete works.

5. See the Manifesto of the "Military Government," a document prepared by the T'ung Meng Hui either in 1905 or a little later. It is included in the complete works of Sun Yat-sen.

6. Chung-hua ko-ming tang.

7. Political Study Society (Cheng-hsüeh hui); Good Friends Society (I-yu she); Political Club (Cheng-yü Club); The Friends of the People Society (Ming-yu she). The Political Study group was, roughly speaking, the forebear of what is known as the Political Science Clique of today. The more current translation "Political Science" is not apt. It should be "Political Study," a term which we shall adopt throughout this book. The most famous leader of the Friends of the People was Lin Sen, who was destined to be the president of the National Government for over a decade.

8. See above, p. 72.

9. See below, p. 363.

10. The English translation of the joint statement is to be found in *The China Year Book, 1923*, p. 863.

11. Borodin was a veteran Russian communist and had had rich experiences in international activities. Galens later turned out to be Marshal Blücher who was at the head of the Soviet Far Eastern Army in the early years of the Sino-Japanese War. He was a first class military organizer and strategist.

12. For an explanation see p. 411, chap. vi, note 2.

13. The meeting place was chosen for the reason that there in the Western Hills was the embalmed body of Sun Yat-sen awaiting burial in Nanking. In doing so, the rightists were of course claiming that they were the faithful followers of the deceased and were also invoking his spirit for their guidance, a typically Chinese gesture.

CHAPTER VII

1. There is no good biography of Chiang Kai-shek either in Chinese or in a Western language. Hollington K. Tong's authorized biography, *Chiang Kai-shek: Soldier and Statesman* (1937), is of course nothing but laudatory. On Wang Ching-wei, T'ang Leang-li's *Wang Ching-wei, a Political Biography* (1931), and Wang Ching-wei's own *The Chinese National Revolution, Essays and Documents* (1931) may throw some light on the man. T'ang Leang-li was a follower of Wang Ching-wei and became a Japanese puppet with his hero.

2. From now on, "President" instead of "Chairman" was to be employed by official Chinese translations for the office of the chairmanship of the Government Council, though that office was always known in Chinese as "Chu-hsi," from 1925 to 1948.

3. It was called the Taiyuan Draft, because the last stage of the drafting was done at Taiyuan, the capital of Shansi, Yen Hsi-shan's own province, when Peiping was being threatened. It bears the date of December 27, 1930.

CHAPTER VIII

1. Of Sun Yat-sen's ideas, the *San Min Chu I* is the most important part. It is rendered in English by Chen as *San Min Chu I: The Three Principles of the People*, and in French by P. M. d'Elia as *Le Triple Démisme de Suen Wen* (1930). But more can be found in *Tsung-li ch'üan-chi* (Complete works of Tsung-li) and Tsou Lu's *Chung-kuo kuo-min-tang shih-kao* (Draft history of the Kuomintang), cited above. The best Chinese

commentary is still Chou Fo-hai, *San-min chu-i li-lun ti t'i-hsi* (The theoretical system of San min chu i). In Western languages, Paul M. A. Linebarger, *The Political Doctrines of Sun Yat-sen, an Exposition of the San Min Chu I* (1937) is the only work of some size. But Sharman, *Sun Yat-sen, His Life and Its Meaning*, is far more valuable. Concerning Kuomintang organization, see below, Appendix F.

2. See above, p. 90.

3. Maurice William, *The Social Interpretation of History* (1921). See also his *Sun Yat-sen versus Communism* (1932).

4. *San Min Chu I* (Chen's translation), p. 383.

5. See Tsui Shu-chin, "The Influence of the Canton-Moscow Entente upon Sun Yat-sen's Political Philosophy and Revolutionary Tactics" (MS, 1933).

6. The program of the Kuomintang as adopted by the Sixth Congress on May 18, 1945 consists all together of thirty planks, ten under each Principle. Under the second Principle, there are such planks as the securing of the various freedoms including academic freedom, the inauguration of local assemblies, and the election of chief administrators of the areas up to the level of the *hsien*, conscription of labor service, and the achievement of compulsory education. Under the third Principle, there are planks for the levying of a progressive income tax and the fixing of a minimum on the inheritance allowed, the socialization of all urban lands, the taking over and distribution of all lands not tilled by the owner himself who is to be compensated by land bonds, the establishment of collective farms, the institution of social insurance, the registration of property of officials of government and of employees of government-owned enterprises, and also the fixing of a maximum on such property. The land policy herein adopted was in theory more radical than what the Congress of the Chinese Communist Party had provided for in April of the same year. For resolutions of the Sixth Congress on party program, see *China Handbook 1937–1945*, pp. 40–59.

7. The party is not unaware of the degeneration of its members. In the "Present-Day Organizational Outline of the Chinese Kuomintang" passed by the joint session of the Central Executive Committees of the party and the corps on September 12, 1947, there is among other things the following item: "There shall be special emphasis on absorbing into the Party excellent farmers, workers, and young intelligentsia to form the main body of the revolutionary force."

8. See below, Appendix G.

9. Wang Ching-wei was elected Deputy-Leader at the same time. Since his expulsion from the party in 1939 as the result of his treason, the office of Deputy-Leader has remained unfilled.

10. See Chiang Kai-shek's *China's Destiny* (1947) for an insight into the character of the man and the policies he professed.

11. "The Present-Day Organizational Outline of the Chinese Kuomintang," adopted by the Central Executive Committee in September 1947, has the following to say on "democratic centralism": "Pursuant to the principle of democratic centralism of our Party, the authorities on all levels shall be elected by democratic methods, the minority shall respect the majority, the Leader shall lead the whole Party, the lower-level authorities shall obey the upper-level authorities, the organizations of all levels shall regularly submit work reports to the members, and the members shall carefully scrutinize the work and resort to frank mutual criticism."

12. The groups of the Kuomintang have figured prominently in the news of Western countries. The three groups herein treated are known in the West as the C. C. Clique, the Whampoa Clique, and the Political Science Clique.

13. In the Sixth Congress, in May 1945, the two groups coalesced to pass a very radical economic platform.

14. Like the formal amalgamation of the party and the youth corps, the two services were also ordered to amalgamate, in 1946. But there has been no more real amalgamation than there has been suppression of sectarian organizations. Considering them useful and even necessary instruments of their survival, the groups in control of those services simply would not give them up. In June 1948, after the so-called constitutional government was set up, the Executive Yuan sent a bill to the Legislative Yuan for the creation of a bureau of investigation to be placed under the Ministry of Justice. If this bureau had come into being, the two older secret services would have had to merge. But in the face of a strong undercurrent of opposition from the Legislative Yuan, the bill was withdrawn.

CHAPTER IX

1. For text of the *Fundamentals*, see Appendix E. Earlier, in 1920, Sun Yat-sen had written on the "Strategy of Revolution" in his *Chung-kuo ko-ming shih* (History of the Chinese revolution). The "strategy" was also concerned with the steps in the three periods of Military Government, Tutelage, and Constitutionalism. There were in the two writings discrepancies which were a source of difficulty when the party came to the detailed elaboration of a program. The *Fundamentals* being of a later date (1924) should be accepted as Sun Yat-sen's considered opinions.

2. *China Handbook, 1937–1943*, p. 116.

3. For English text, see *The Chinese Year Book, 1935*, pp. 63–66.

4. "Committee," "commission," "council," "conference," and some other words are not always distinguishable from each other. Translated into Chinese, they are even more confusing. "*Wei-yüan-hui*" is the term most frequently employed to denote a committee form of organization. But it would be incorrect to render "*wei-yüan-hui*" in every case as "committee." The standard of uniformity has to be surrendered in favor of a more differentiated rendering of the term. "*Wei-yüan-hui*" will be rendered as: (1) "committee" when it is a body of several members deliberating on matters referred to it by a larger body without itself exercising administrative powers or maintaining subordinate administrative organizations; (2) "commission," in the case of a similar body with administrative powers or subordinate administrative organizations; (3) "council," if it is a commission of the most exalted kind deliberating on matters of state; or (4) "conference," if the body is of a more temporary nature.

Different names have been used at different times by the Kuomintang to denote essentially the same organ. They are: *Cheng-chih wei-yüan-hui*, *Cheng-chih hui-i*, *Kuo-fang tsui-kao hui-i*, and *Kuo-fang tsui-kao wei-yüan-hui*. For the last two, the common rendering is "Supreme National Defense Council," which has been followed in this book. For the first two, the common rendering is "Central Political Council." The adjective "central" comes from the "central" in the full name of the organ, namely, the Political Council of the Central Executive Committee, and is rather out of place. Therefore the first two have both been simply rendered as "Political Council" throughout this book. See Appendix H.

5. The attending members are ones who are not members of the body and have no right to vote. They can only participate in the debate, but since in most of the meetings of the Kuomintang and the Kuomintang Government no vote is taken, the attending members are hardly distinguishable from the ordinary members.

6. Since 1935, the committees have been known as "expert committees." The chairman and vice-chairman and some of the members are members of the Political Council, or, during the war years, of the Supreme National Defense Council, but the majority of

the committee members are often drawn from government and party departments, and sometimes even non-Kuomintang people are invited to serve as members of these "expert committees."

7. See below, p. 202.

8. In Chinese, *Tang-cheng kung-tso k'ao-ho wei-yüan-hui*. It has been variously rendered as "Party and Political Work Perscrutation [*sic*] Committee," "Party and Government Work Evaluation Committee," etc. But it was more a commission than a committee.

CHAPTER X

1. On this chapter and chaps. xi–xix, the best references are Ch'en Chih-mai, *Chung-kuo cheng-fu* (The government of China), Ch'ien Tuan-sheng *et al.*, *Min-kuo cheng-chih shih* (A history of the political institutions under the Republic), and Wang Shih-chieh and Ch'ien Tuan-sheng, *Pi-chiao hsien-fa* (Comparative constitutional law). In addition, Hsü Ch'ung-hao, *Chung-kuo cheng-chih kai-yao* (An outline of Chinese political institutions) is also of some value. In English, Tsao Wen-yen, *The Constitutional Structure of Modern China* (1947), is comparatively the most satisfactory. There are also Wu Chih-fang's *Chinese Government and Politics* and Paul M. A. Linebarger's *Government in Republican China* (1938); both cover only the early years of the Kuomintang Government. Two year books, *China Handbook* and *The Chinese Year Book*, are in many ways much more valuable than any other works in English for an understanding of the Kuomintang Government.

2. In Chinese, the term "Kuo-min cheng-fu" is employed; "cheng-fu" is "government." In both "Kuo-min cheng-fu" and "Kuomintang," "Kuo-min" is a derivative of "nation." If Sun Yat-sen was correct in ordering, on November 10, 1920, his party organizations overseas to translate "Kuomintang" as "Nationalist Party," "Kuo-min cheng-fu" should also be correctly rendered as "Nationalist Government." But in May 1928 the translation was officially changed to "National Government," the change being occasioned by the government's desire to lessen the hostility of the Powers towards Chinese nationalism at that time.

3. For the English texts of the Organic Law of the National Government of October 8, 1928, and of December 30, 1931, see Pan, *The Chinese Constitution*, Appendices K, M. The English text of the latter law can also be found in *The China Year Book, 1935*, pp. 66–68.

4. The Organic Law of the National Government of December 30, 1931 was in open variance with Chapter VII of the Tutelage Constitution of 1930. The resolution of the Central Executive Committee in December 1935, prolonging indefinitely Lin Sen's term of presidency, was also in open variance with Article XIII of the Organic Law of December 30, 1931.

5. Sun Yat-sen has a uniform name for all the Five Organs. He calls them *yuan*. Hence Executive Yuan, Legislative Yuan, Judicial Yuan, Examination Yuan, and Control Yuan. In Chinese, *yuan* is either council or a great office. To avoid confusion and inexactness, "Yuan" is employed throughout this book.

6. The proposal was sent from Paris, signed jointly by Hu Han-min and Sun Fo.

7. The Chinese word for "presiding officer" is *chu-hsi*, meaning literally one holding the host's seat, whereas the President of the Republic has always been known as *tsung-t'ung*, meaning one having a general control of things. The head of the National Government was always styled *chu-hsi*. The *chu-hsi* of the National Government should be rendered as "chairman" instead of "president." It is only for the sake of conformity with the general usage that the term "president" is here employed.

8. The Revised Organic Law of the National Government of November 24, 1930.

9. The meeting of the Council of the National Government was originally styled *kuo-wu hui-i* (Meeting on state matters) and that of the Executive Yuan, *hsing-cheng-yüan hui-i* (Executive Yuan meeting). According to the revised Law, the Executive Yuan meeting now acquired the name of *kuo-wu hui-i* (Meeting on state matters) and the meeting of the Council of the National Government was given the name of *kuo-min cheng-fu hui-i* (Meeting of the National Government).

10. See above, p. 98.

11. The Organic Law of the National Government of September 15, 1943.

12. The Organic Law of the National Government of April 17, 1947.

13. The members of the National Government always carried the title *kuo-min cheng-fu wei-yüan* (Committee members of the National Government). The names for the collective body and for the meetings of that body were not uniform. The "Council of the National Government" is employed to denote all of them unless otherwise specified.

14. See below, chap. xxiii.

15. The translations of these officers and their offices are not by any means uniform. In the official Chinese translations they are apt to be: Director of the Department of Civil Affairs, Director of the Department of Military Affairs, and Comptroller General and Comptroller General's Office.

16. He is called *chu-chi-chang*, meaning "head in charge of accounting." In order to make "accounting" sound logical, statistics and accounts, in addition to budget-making, were also assigned to him as his functions, resulting in much duplication and confusion with other departments of government.

17. See below, chap. xiv.

CHAPTER XI

1. On the Executive Yuan and on the other four Yuan as well, the reports, *Kung-tso pao-kao* (Work reports) presented to every session of the Central Executive Committee and the People's Political Council are valuable sources of information.

2. As a matter of fact, the National General Mobilization Committee confined itself to the functions of rationing and price control. It had a very big staff. It often sent out strident orders in the name of Chiang Kai-shek. But the job was mangled.

3. For instance, the appearance of T. V. Soong, just before he resigned from the presidency of the Executive Yuan on March 1, 1947, turned out to be a rout.

CHAPTER XII

1. Parts of this chapter appeared in *Pacific Affairs*, September 1948. There is no standard work on the military forces of China. Evans Carlson's *The Chinese Army: Its Organization and Military Efficiency* (1940) is in fact the only book on the subject.

2. The eminent Confucian scholar of the Ming Dynasty, Wang Shou-jen (above, p. 406, chap. ii, note 25), led a successful campaign against a great rebellion. So did Tseng Kuo-fan, Tso Tsung-t'ang, and Li Hung-chang against the Taiping Rebellion for the Manchu emperors. None of them, all great and powerful, ever thought of taking the throne himself or having a continued hold of the military power.

3. *Chün-tzu yuan.*

4. *T'ung-shuai pan-shih-ch'u.*

5. The T'ung Meng Hui in 1906, the Chinese Revolutionary Party in 1914, and the Kuomintang in 1924 all envisioned a *chün-cheng-fu* or "military government." The Revolution of 1911 started with a military government. Sun Yat-sen's own Canton Government in 1918 also was one. In 1922 his military government was called *Ta-yuan-shuai ta-pen-ying* or the Grand Headquarters of the Generalissimo.

6. See above, p. 103.

7. In Chinese the full title is *Kuo-min cheng-fu chün-shih wei-yüan-hui*, *kuo-min cheng-fu* meaning National Government, *chün-shih* meaning military affairs, and *wei-yüan-hui* meaning committee. The whole term has generally been rendered as National Military Council. But accepting the criteria adopted in the translation of the term "committee" (see above, p. 414, chap. ix, note 4), it is here rendered as Military Commission, for the organ met only infrequently while its administrative functions were many.

8. Chiang Kai-shek never assumed the title of *Ta-yüan-shuai*, the equivalent of "Generalissimo."

9. The Agreement of February 25, 1946, for Military Reorganization and for the Integration of the Communist Forces into the National Army. For English text, see *China Handbook, 1937–1945*, (rev. ed. with 1946 Supplement), pp. 755–758.

CHAPTER XIII

1. The vice-president functioned from the time of Hu Han-min's detention early in 1931 to Sun Fo's assumption of office early in 1933.

2. The Revised Organic Law of the Legislative Yuan of April 22, 1947 added fifty to the original membership. By agreement, they were apportioned as follows: Kuomintang, 17; Youth Party, 13; Democratic Socialists, 12; Independents, 8.

3. Chinese names for these laws are: *Li-fa ch'eng-hsü fa* (Law on legislative procedure); *Chih-ch'üan hsing-shih chih kuei-lü* (Principles regulating the exercise of governing powers); *Fa-kuei chih-ting piao-chun-fa* (Law providing for the standards of law- and ordinance-making); *Li-fa ch'eng-hsü kang-ling* (Essential of legislative procedure).

4. See above, p. 143.

5. For legislation in recent times, see Yang Yu-ch'iung, *Chin-tai Chung-kuo li-fa shih* (A history of modern Chinese legislation), and Hsieh Chen-min, *Chung-hua-min-kuo li-fa shih* (A history of legislation of the Chinese Republic).

CHAPTER XIV

1. In 1938 and before, the Chinese fiscal year was from July to June of the next year.

2. After September 1944, the People's Political Council also acquired the right to a preliminary consideration of the budget. But that consideration had no binding effect on the government. See below, p. 292.

3. This is in Chinese dollars. The U. S. $1 was convertible at $3.35 in Chinese currency, a fixed rate at the time.

4. See Alfred C. Tao, "A Study of the Tax Structure in China; with some recommendations for the post-war period" (typewritten thesis).

5. The original estimated expenditures for the first half-year of 1948 amount to C.N.C. $960,000,000,000,000. In July, the Legislative Yuan of the new constitutional government voted the revised figure of C.N.C. $2,400,000,000,000 for that half-year.

6. The Law of Actual Settlement, August 8, 1938.

CHAPTER XV

1. *Ch'üan-kuo hsing-cheng hui-i chi-lu* (Proceedings of the National Administrative Conference, June 1944) throws a great deal of light on the matters treated in this paper.

2. According to the Organic Law of the Executive Yuan of April 22, 1948, there was to be a Ministry of Postal- and Tele-communications. It was never organized. The Organic Law of December 25, 1947, under which the new Yuan of June 1948 was organized,

lists seventeen ministries and commissions and omits the Ministry of Postal- and Telecommunications.

3. Professor Wang Kan-yu of National Nankai University at Tientsin has undertaken a study of local government in China which will be published as a companion project to this volume. A good book on Chinese local government and administration is Ch'en Pai-hsin, *Chung-kuo ti-fang chih-tu chi ch'i kai-tsao* (Chinese local government and its reconstruction).

4. These municipalities would correspond to the county boroughs of England if we consider the province as corresponding to an English county. Tibet is outside the scope of the provinces and municipalities. It is a territory with an administration of its own, unlike the provincial one and only very loosely tied to the central government.

5. In order to enable participation by leaders of the many races of the province, Sinkiang has a larger government council. For a short while after the restoration in 1945, Formosa too had a different form of government, but it has since taken up the standard form.

6. The Organic Law of Provincial Government of March 23, 1931. For provincial administration in general, see Shih Yang-cheng, *Chung-kuo sheng-hsing-cheng chih-tu* (the Chinese provincial administrative system).

7. See Wang Kan-yu, "The Hsien (County) Government in China" (1947), typewritten thesis, and Ch'eng Fang, *Chung-kuo hsien-cheng kai-lun* (a general course on Chinese *hsien* government).

8. According to the semiannual census of the Ministry of the Interior, issued on July 14, 1947, there were all together 2122 *hsien* (including about 100 municipalities of the *hsien* rank and administrative districts not yet raised to the full status of a *hsien*). There are within these *hsien* 53,969 *hsiang* and *chen*, 657,882 *pao*, 6,688,436 *chia*, and 86,262,337 families. Of these 2122 *hsien*, no less than 550 are at this time (Aug. 31, 1948) in the hands of the communists.

9. For English text of the *Outline*, see *China Handbook, 1937–1945*, pp. 122–126. The title is translated differently in the *Handbook*.

10. The *pao-chia* system which groups the families into *chia* and *chia* into *pao* for the purpose of mutual guarantee of good conduct is really a kind of police system, prevailing during the various periods of old China. It was based on the family, and it still is. It was revived during the years of anti-communist campaigns before the war, and was greatly relied upon for the purposes of conscription and the collection of land tax during the war. See Wen Chün-t'ien, *Chung-kuo pao-chia chih-tu* (Chinese *pao-chia* system).

11. The new *hsien* is divided into *hsiang* (rural districts or townships), and *chen* (urban districts or townships), which are in turn subdivided into *pao*. A group of six to fifteen families makes up a *chia*, and a group of six to fifteen *chia* makes up a *pao*. The intermediate area, *ch'ü*, which stands between the *hsien* and the *hsiang* and *chen*, was made optional by the *Outline* of 1939, though in most places it is still preserved. The *chia* has a chief elected by the heads of the families. The chiefs of these lower units, though they are elected by representative assemblies or directly by the heads of the families, are nevertheless controlled by the chiefs of the higher unit. Within the *pao* and *chia*, the *pao* and *chia* chiefs are quite influential and can be a terror to the people under their control.

12. For the *chia*, the heads of the families act directly as the assembly. The *pao* assembly is elected by the heads of the families. The *hsiang* or *chen* people's representative assemblies are elected by the *pao* assembly. Finally, the *hsien* political council is elected by the *hsiang* and *chen* people's representative assemblies.

13. See Ray Chang, "Trends in Chinese Public Administration," *Information Bulletin*, vol. III, no. 5 (Feb. 21, 1937), pp. 99–121.

14. See below, ch. xvi.

15. See above, p. 145.

CHAPTER XVI

1. Under the Constitution of 1946, the Examination Yuan is to be composed of the Examination Members headed by a president and a vice-president. The Examination Commission as a separate organ no longer exists.

2. Tai Ch'uan-hsien (Tai Chi-t'ao).

3. Article 86 of the Constitution of 1946 omits the first and lists only the latter two. Presumably candidates for elective offices are no longer subject to examination.

4. Law for the Examination of Professional and Technical Personnel, December 27, 1944.

5. Law for the Examination of Candidates for Elective Offices in the Provinces and Districts, May 17, 1943. See Pao Cheng-ch'iu, *Kung-chih hou-hsüan-jen k'ao-shih chih li-lun yü shih-shih* (the theory and practice of the examination of the candidates for elective offices).

6. The revised Law of Examination, July 31, 1935, and the Law of Conducting the Examinations, July 31, 1935.

7. They are: general administration; educational administration; fiscal administration; finance and credit administration; economic administration; social administration; land administration; coöperative administration; police administration; health administration; domicile- and population-registration administration; judicial officials; diplomatic and consular officials; accountants and auditors; statisticians; public works officials; and coroners.

8. In law a civil servant is known as *kung-wu yüan* (public official). It has never been possible to find out the exact figures of the total number of civil servants. According to the statement made before the Resident Committee of the People's Political Council by the president of the Executive Yuan on May 8, 1947, there were at that time some 620,000 all told. This evidently included everyone in the public services except the armed forces and the police and the employees of the government corporations engaged in business, but it is doubtful whether it also included the teachers in government schools other than those directly maintained by the Central Government.

9. The Chinese word *p'in* (to invite) cannot be exactly rendered in English. The person who is "invited" to serve is expected to be treated with more respect by his superior than a person who is merely appointed to an office, however high. The employer-employee relation borders on that between a host and a guest, so to speak.

10. In Chinese the several ranks are as follows: *hsüan-jen* (elected rank); *t'e-jen* (special rank); *chien-jen* (selected rank); *chien-jen* (recommended rank); *wei-jen* (delegated rank); and *p'in-jen* (invited rank).

CHAPTER XVII

1. The most complete bibliography on the subject is the mimeographed *Bibliography of Modern Chinese Law in the Library of Congress*, compiled and edited by China Legal Section, Far Eastern Unit, Bureau of Foreign and Domestic Commerce, U. S. Department of Commerce.

2. Article XII reads: "China having expressed a strong desire to reform her judicial system and to bring it into accord with that of Western nations, Great Britain agrees to give every assistance to such reforms, and she will also be prepared to relinquish her extra-territorial rights when she is satisfied that the state of the Chinese laws, the

arrangement for their administration, and other considerations warrant her doing so."

3. The Code of 1909 was known in Chinese as *Ta-Ch'ing hsien-hsing hsing-lü*, a modernized version of the old *Ta-Ch'ing lü-li*. Naturally it comprised administrative and civil, as well as criminal, provisions. The Code of 1911, *Chan-hsing hsing-lü*, was a criminal code in the Western sense of the term.

4. For some aspects of the work of the Law Codification Bureau, see Wang Chung Hui, *Law Reform in China* (1919).

5. General Principles of Civil Code, May 23, 1929 and the various Books of Civil Law, promulgated separately in 1929 and 1930; Code of Civil Procedure, December 26, 1930 and February 13, 1931; New Code of Civil Procedure, February 1, 1935; Criminal Code, March 10, 1928; New Criminal Code, January 1, 1935; Code of Criminal Procedure, July 28, 1928; New Code of Criminal Procedure, January 1, 1935. The Civil Code has been translated into English as *The Civil Code of the Republic of China* by Hsia, Chow, Liu, and Cheng, and into French as *Code Civil de la République de Chine* by Ho; the New Code of Civil Procedure of 1935 into French as *Code de Procédure Civile (révisé) de la République de Chine, (1er juillet 1935)*, by Ricard; the Criminal Code of 1928 into English as *The Criminal Code of the Republic of China* by Burdett in collaboration with Liang, and into French as *Code Pénal de la République de Chine* by Escarra; the New Criminal Code of 1935 into English as *The Criminal Code of the Republic of China* by Chang and into French as *Code Pénal de la République Chinoise* by Ricard, Kou, Leblanc, and Wang; and the New Code of Criminal Procedure into English as *The Code of Criminal Procedure of the Republic of China and the Court Agreement relating to the Chinese Courts in the International Settlement of Shanghai* by the Legal Department of the Shanghai Municipal Council, and into French as *Code de Procédure Pénale de la République Chinoise* by Leblanc. Treatises in Chinese on these codes are very numerous. Escarra's *Le droit chinois* is still the best general commentary in Western languages on the codes. On the Civil Code, see also V. A. Riâzanovskiĭ, *Chinese Civil Law* (1938).

6. There are many monographs on extraterritoriality in China. See George W. Keeton, *The Development of Extraterritoriality in China* (1928), and Georges S. de Morant, *Extraterritorialité et Intérêts Etrangers en Chine* (1925).

7. For a brief survey of the judicial reform, see Edgar C. Tang, "Judicial Reforms in China," *Information Bulletin*, vol. III, no. 1, pp. 1–27. For a balance of Westernism and traditionalism, see an article by Roscoe Pound, "Comparative Law and History as Bases for Chinese Law," *Harvard Law Review*, LXI, 749–762.

8. The Organic Law of the Judicial Yuan of February 13, 1943. See an article by the president of the Yuan on the wartime judicial administration, Chü Cheng, "War-time Judicial Administration," *China Quarterly*, IV, 11–16.

9. The Constitution of 1946 continued to place the Ministry of Justice under the Executive Yuan.

10. Law for the Organization of the Courts, October 28, 1932. It has been translated by Théry as *Loi d'Organisation des Tribunaux*.

11. Organic Law of the Supreme Court, August 14, 1928.

12. Take the fourteen-month period from February 1946 to March 1947, for example. The Supreme Court had altogether 32,947 cases, of which 4077 were pending at the beginning of the period. During the period, the court was able to settle 16,297 cases, leaving 16,650 cases unsettled. Even if 11,055 puppet-treason cases are subtracted from the total, the docket was still much too large to be properly adjudicated by the court. Figures are from a work report of the Judicial Yuan to the People's Political Council in May 1947.

13. The Civil Procedural Code of January 1, 1935, and the Criminal Procedural Code of January 1, 1935, as revised on December 26, 1945.

14. See Liang J'en Kié, *Étude sur la Jurisdiction Administrative en Chine* (1920).

15. Organic Law of the Administrative Court, November 17, 1932. It has been treated by Théry as *Loi d'Organisation de la Cour Administrative.*

16. Law of Administrative Appeal, January 8, 1937, and the Administrative Procedural Law, July 27, 1942. These in their unamended forms have been translated by Théry as *Loi sur les Recours en Matière Administrative (24 mars 1930)* and *Loi sur les Procès Administratifs (17 novembre 1932)* respectively.

17. From February 1946 to March 1947 inclusive, there were altogether 131 cases in the docket with 81 decided and 50 still pending at the end of the period.

18. See below, chap. xviii.

19. The Law for the Discipline of Public Officials, June 1931. See also a monograph by Wu Fu-cheng, a member of the commission, *Kung-wu-yüan ch'eng-chieh chih-tu* (the system of discipline of public officials).

20. The data available for the period from February 1946 through March 1947 were: total in the docket, 280; settled, 177. The figures were smaller for the previous years.

CHAPTER XVIII

1. See above, pp. 38–40.

2. In Sun Yat-sen's lecture on the "Five-Power Constitution," he attributed to Burgess favorable comments on the Chinese censorial system as compared with the Western system of parliamentary impeachment. But such an attribution was not warranted. See John W. Burgess, *The Reconciliation of Government with Liberty* (New York, Charles Scribner's Sons, 1915), pp. 5–7.

3. The Revised Organic Law of the Control Yuan of January 19, 1937. For a general survey of the organization and work of the Yuan, see Edgar C. Tang, "Five Years of the Control Yuan," *Information Bulletin*, vol. II, no. 7, pp. 117–131.

4. Law for the Protection of the Members of the Control Yuan, June 24, 1932.

5. This of course referred to those members only who were in charge of a definite region.

6. Under the Constitution of 1946, the members of the Control Yuan are to be elected and the president and vice-president of the Yuan are to be elected by and among the members. The title of Control Commissioner is abolished, but regional offices of the members are maintained. Instead of a Minister of Audit, the official is called Auditor-General. Presumably his office will not be very different from the Ministry of Audit. In other words, the organization and operation of the Control Yuan of 1928–1948 will not be much affected by the new Constitution.

7. The Regulations Governing Investigations by the Control Yuan, January 21, 1934, is a Control Yuan decree. So also is the Regulations Governing the Circuit Inspections by the Control Commissioners, January 27, 1934. The Organic Law of the Control Yuan only authorized the Control Yuan to demand explanations from, or to conduct investigations in, the various departments of the government.

8. Regulations Governing the Acceptance of Written Complaints of Private Persons, June 27, 1933.

9. For the four-year period ending June 1937, 16,555 petitions were received and 6302 investigations were started. The figures for the period from July 1937 through August 1946 were respectively 29,944 and 17,972. Data in this chapter is drawn principally from a pamphlet entitled "Chien-ch'a chih-tu ti yün-yung" (The operation of the control institution), issued by the Information Office of the Executive Yuan in July 1947.

10. The government at that time was selling gold on the market. When the gold price, as compared with the commodity price, became too low, there was a rush of buyers and the government was compelled to declare a ban on gold transactions. In Formosa, due to unwise and, at places, corrupt administration, the Formosans rioted against government by the Chinese from the homeland.

11. Law of Impeachment, June 24, 1932. See Ch'en Chih-mai, "Impeachments of the Control Yuan," *Chinese Social and Political Science Review*, vol. XIX, pp. 331–366; 513–542.

12. The Temporary Provisions for the Exercise of Control Power for the Emergency, December 17, 1937.

13. The Resolution of the Political Council, July 11, 1934.

14. Article 20. "Rectification" is not a happy translation of the Chinese term *chiu-chü*, but to render *chiu-chü* as "censure" would be too general.

15. See above, pp. 215–216.

16. See above, p. 421, chap. xviii, note 6.

17. The Law of Actual Settlement, August 8, 1938.

CHAPTER XIX

1. Resolution of the Fourth Congress, November 1931.

2. The Organic Law of the National Government of December 30, 1931.

3. Organic Articles, August 10, 1937, passed by the Supreme National Defense Council which by that date had already supplanted the Political Council as the directing organ of the government.

4. In addition to the original twenty-four, the proposed council was to include thirty-two representatives of the provinces, chosen jointly by the government and the Kuomintang organization of the province, plus six representing Mongolia, Tibet, and the Chinese overseas, the five secretaries-general of the Five Yuan, and eight to be appointed by the Kuomintang. It was taken for granted that, with the exception of the last eight, the other new members would all be Kuomintang-controlled and very likely Kuomintang members.

5. The original Organic Articles of the People's Political Council were promulgated on April 12, 1936. They were never considered or passed by the Legislative Yuan. They were frequently amended, nine times in all. The last amended articles were of March 1, 1947. For English text of the Organic Articles of March 16, 1942, see *China Handbook, 1937–1943*, pp. 110–112.

6. At the Sixth Party Congress of the Kuomintang in 1945, many Kuomintang members of the People's Political Council were elected to the Central Executive or Supervisory Committees of the party. From that time on the party injunction against members of the Central Executive and Supervisory Committees having seats in the People's Political Council lapsed. But the more powerful members of the two party committees never became council members.

7. The sessions of the Council were as follows:
First Council, first session, July 6–15, 1938
second session, October 28 — November 6, 1938
third session, February 12–21, 1939
Second Council, first sessions, March 1–10, 1941
second session, November 17–30, 1941
Third Council, first session, October 22–31, 1942
second session, September 18–27, 1943
third session, September 5–18, 1944

Fourth Council, first session, July 7–20, 1945
second session, March 20 — April 2, 1946
third session, May 20 — June 2, 1947.

8. It did not have the power to examine and approve the policy plans which could be referred only to the council in full session.

9. For these five items, see Articles VI, VII, VIII, IX, X, respectively, of the Organic Articles of September 16, 1944.

10. See below, pp. 307–310.

CHAPTER XX

1. No book in Chinese gives an account of the political development between 1928 and 1948 which is nearly as good as Li Chien-nung's *Chung-kuo chin-pai-nien cheng-chih shih* (A political history of China in the last century), an account of the century before. All accounts are strongly partisan. In Western languages, the accounts are mostly journalistic. Paul M. A. Linebarger, *The China of Chiang Kai-shek: A Political Study* (1941), and Lawrence K. Rosinger, *China's Crisis* (1945) cover the greater part of the period. Linebarger supports the Kuomintang regime and Rosinger stands on the opposite side. For a discussion of some problems of this period, see Sun Fo, *China Looks Forward* (1944).

On the constitutional development of this period, see Ch'en Ju-hsuan, *Hsin-ting Chung-kuo hsien-fa shih* (A history of the Chinese constitution, new and revised edition), Wang Shih-chieh and Ch'ien Tuan-sheng, *Pi-chiao hsien-fa* (Comparative constitutional law), Ch'ien Tuan-sheng *et al.*, *Min-kuo cheng-chih shih* (A history of the political institutions under the Republic), and Wu Ching-hsiung and Huang Kung-chiao, *Chung-kuo chih-hsien shih* (A history of constitution-making in China).

2. The articles were grouped into five chapters, namely, General Principles, People's Nationhood, People's Rights, People's Livelihood, and the Protection of the Constitution.

3. See above, p. 73.

4. Translations in various Western languages of the Draft Constitution were published by the Legislative Yuan in book form in 1936. The English text can be found in Pan, *The Chinese Constitution: A Study of Forty Years of Constitution-Making in China*, Appendix O. For commentaries, see C. L. Hsia, "A Comparative Study of China's Draft Constitution with those of Other Modern States," *China Quarterly*, vol. 2, no. 1, pp. 89–101, and John Chin Hsiung Wu, "Notes on the Final Draft Constitution," *T'ien Hsia Monthly*, vol. 10, no. 1, pp. 73–88. Both authors were members of the drafting committees; John C. H. Wu was also the vice-chairman of the original Drafting Committee.

5. Article 146, stipulating that the Constituent National Assembly should also continue as the First National Assembly under the Constitution, was deleted on April 22, 1937 by the Standing Committee of the Central Executive Committee. The document was thereby reduced to one of 147 articles.

6. See an interesting article by Sun Fo, entitled "Chung-kuo hsien-fa ti chi-ke wen-t'i" (Some problems of the Chinese constitution), published in the Chinese dailies on October 10, 1934, discussing these same problems and defending the draft, as it stood then. The arguments therein advanced were equally valid for the definitive draft.

7. For English text, see *China Handbook, 1937–1945*, pp. 79–81.

8. See above, p. 227.

9. The Report of the Minister of the Interior to the People's Political Council in June 1945. At that time, only 31 of the 880 were elected, the rest were provisional councils consisting of appointed members. According to a later report, that rendered to

the People's Political Council in May 1947, the number of *hsien* councils had risen to 1356; *ch'ü* councils to 28,633; and *pao* direct assemblies to 381,658. See also, *Wang*, "The Hsien (County) Government in China," ch. vii. (typewritten thesis).

10. *Hsien-cheng ch'i-ch'eng hui.*

11. *Hsien-cheng shih-shih hsieh-chin hui.* For English text of the Regulations for the organization of this Association, see *China at War*, II, 69–70.

12. Item XXV of the *Program of Armed Resistance and National Reconstruction.*

13. For English text of the decree, see *China Handbook, 1937–1945*, pp. 265–267.

14. In a report of the association, published in July 1944, there were some summary observations on the enforcement of the decree by the members of the Association who were assigned to different areas for purposes of inspection. From all areas, the conclusion was the same. For example, the report of the members from one area said in part: "The Provincial and *Hsien* Governments, the Administrative Inspectorate, the Garrison Commandant, the Police and the Gendarmerie, the Secret Service, the revenue bureaus, the Consolidated Inspection Service, the Allocation Board for Motor Vehicles and finally the local officials below the *hsien* level, all were making arbitrary arrests and after effecting the arrest, further failed to surrender the arrested to the duly constituted judicial authorities."

15. For English text of the Regulations, see *China Handbook, 1937–1945*, pp. 517–520.

16. The Law of Citizens' Oath had obliged an individual to take an oath of loyalty to the *San Min Chu I* in order to enjoy the rights of citizenship.

CHAPTER XXI

1. For the organization and party alignment and party conflicts in the conference, see below, p. 376.

2. See *China Handbook, 1937–1945*, pp. 746–747.

3. See below, Appendix D.

4. On the day of the promulgation the government proclaimed that the chapter on the Bill of Rights had come into force as of that date. But civil liberties continued to be ignored by the authorities and in the case of adverse criticism and demonstrations the government itself was most oblivious to the fact that it too was obliged by the terms of the Constitution to tolerate such criticism and demonstrations as were not in violation of any law.

5. The electoral laws and their actual operation will be discussed in chap. xxii in connection with the election of the organs concerned.

CHAPTER XXII

1. The quotas were as follows:

	Original Apportionment	*Final Apportionment*
Hsien (or municipalities)	2,177	2,177
Mongolian Banners	57	57
Tibet	40	40
Border Racial Groups	17	34
Chinese Overseas	65	65
Vocational Groups	450	487
Agriculture		(134)
Labor		(126)
Fishing		(10)

	Original Apportionment	*Final Apportionment*
Business		(44)
Industry and Mining		(24)
Education		(90)
Liberal Professions		(59)
Women's Organizations	168	168
Population Groups with Special Habits	10	17
	2,984	3,045

2. The election was held on November 21–23, and if it had been according to schedule the results should have been announced on or before February 23.

3. Above, p. 326.

4. *Tung-yüan k'an-luan lin-shih t'iao-k'uan.*

5. The Organic Law of the Executive Yuan of December 25, 1947.

6. The quotas were as follows:

	Original Apportionment	*Final Apportionment*
Provinces (or municipalities)	660	622
Mongolian Banners	22	22
Tibet	10	15
Border Racial Groups	6	6
Chinese Overseas	19	19
Vocational Groups	56	89
Agriculture		(18)
Labor		(18)
Fishing		(3)
Business		(10)
Industry and Mining		(10)
Education		(15)
Liberal Professions		(15)
	773	773

7. There are for each committee from three to five so-called "convening members," elected from among the members of the committee (Article 5 of the Organic Law of the Legislative Yuan). This system of multi-chairmanship is a departure from the old Legislative Yuan, but follows closely the practice of the Kuomintang Congress, the People's Political Council, and the National Assembly.

8. Above, p. 273.

CHAPTER XXIII

1. There are no good books on the Chinese parties. Hsieh Pin, *Min-kuo cheng-tang shih* (a history of the political parties under the Republic) and Yang Yu-ch'iung, *Chung-kuo cheng-tang shih* (a history of Chinese political parties) are the better ones. Neither covers fully the period after 1924.

2. See above, pp. 81–83.

3. Pao-kuo hui and Pao-huang hui, respectively.

4. Yü-pei li-hsien kung-hui and Kuo-hui ch'ing-yüan t'ung-chih hui, respectively.

5. These three parties or groups were respectively called in Chinese, Hsien-yu hui, Hsien-cheng shih-chin hui, and Hsin-hai Club.

6. T'ung-i tang.

7. T'ung-i kung-ho tang.

8. Min she.

9. Kung-ho chien-she t'ao-lun hui (association for the discussion of republicanism and reconstruction) and Kung-ho t'ung-i tang (Republican united party).

10. See above, p. 72.

11. In Chinese they were Hsien-fa t'ao-lun hui, Hsien-fa yen-chiu t'ung-chih hui, and Hsien-fa yen-chiu hui, respectively.

12. See above, p. 86.

13. Chung-kuo ch'ing-nien tang.

14. It should be remembered that the Kuomintang and the Communist Party are known in Chinese as Chung-kuo kuo-min tang and Chung-kuo kung-ch'an tang, respectively. The new name of the Shao-nien Chung-kuo tang (Young China Party) became Chung-kuo ch'ing-nien tang.

15. Chung-kuo min-chu she-hui tang. This party has been known in the West as the "Social Democratic Party," but its leader, Carsun Chang, prefers to render it as "Democratic Socialist Party." See the *New York Times*, March 21, 1948.

16. Carsun Chang is a great admirer of special institutes like the London School of Economics and German High Institutes of Politics. In the past, he has organized three such institutions in succession under the patronage of men of power, but none of them has proved to be successful. All of them have been short-lived. Thus his student following has also been extremely small.

17. See above, p. 349. Among the leaders of the Chin-putang and Constitution-Research Association, Liang Ch'i-ch'ao was the theoretician and T'ang Hua-lung was the organizer and practical politician.

18. See Chang Chün-mai (Carsun Chang), *Li-kuo chih tao* (the way to establish a nation).

19. Chung-hua min-tsu chieh-fang hsing-tung wei-yüan-hui.

20. Chung-kuo jen-min chiu-kuo hui.

21. Chung-hua chih-yeh chiao-yü she.

22. Min-chu chien-kuo hui.

23. Chung-kuo hsiang-ts'un chien-she hsieh-hui.

24. Called T'ung-i chien-kuo t'ung-chih hui. For names of parties and groups which took part, see below, p. 360.

25. Chung-kuo min-chu cheng-t'uan ta-t'ung-meng.

26. Chung-kuo min-chu t'ung-meng.

27. Judging by its announcement in July 1948 of its support of the new Political Consultative Conference sponsored by the Communist Party, the Reform Democratic Socialist Party may have remained in the League.

28. Chung-kuo kung-ch'an tang. The literature in Chinese is enormous, but mostly partisan. For works in Western languages, see Roy, *Revolution and Counterrevolution in China*, for a Marxist analysis of the role of the party in Chinese revolution, Victor A. Yakhontoff, *The Chinese Soviets* (1934), T'ang, Leang-li, ed., *Suppressing Communist Banditry in China* (1934), and *Räte-China, Dokumente der chinesischen Revolution* (1934) for the Juichin soviet phase; Edgar Snow, *Red Star over China* (1944), Gunther Stein, *The Challenge of Red China* (1945), Stuart Gelder, ed., *The Chinese Communists* (1946), and Claire and William Band, *Two Years with the Chinese Communists* (1948), for the Border Region phase. With the exception of T'ang, who was at the time of writing a government spokesman, these accounts are all favorable to the

communists. Unfavorable comments by foreign authors in book form are few. One is Freda Utley, *Last Chance in China* (1947).

29. The dates of the party congresses of the Communist Party are as follows:

First	July 1921	Shanghai
Second	June 1922	Canton
Third	June 1923	Canton
Fourth	January 1925	Shanghai
Fifth	May 1927	Hankow
Sixth	August 1928	Moscow
Seventh	April 1945	Yenan

30. Mao Tse-tung, *China's New Democracy* (1946). There is also a version issued by the Chinese News Agency entitled *"Democracy," A Digest of the Bible of Chinese Communism* (1947). The two versions are different; the first one being communist and the second anti-communist.

31. Earlier, on December 15, 1939, in a brochure, *Chung-kuo ko-ming yü Chung-kuo kung-ch'an-tang* (The Chinese revolution and the Chinese Communist Party), Mao Tse-tung had already listed the revolutionary and the counterrevolutionary classes in China. The revolutionary classes, according to him, consist of almost all classes except the big landlords and big capitalists (as distinguished from "nationalist capitalists").

32. Mao Tse-tung, *On Coalition Government* (1945).

33. One of the communist slogans for the Labor Day calls for a Political Consultative Conference. The plan seems to have gained the support of the Democratic League, the Revolutionary Committee of the Kuomintang, and the Reform Democratic Socialist Party, all having their headquarters in Hong Kong at the present (August 31, 1948).

34. See Sun Fo, *China Looks Forward.*

35. San-min chu-i t'ung-chih hui. By 1945 it was known as Min-chu chien-she tso-t'an hui (Round table association for democratic reconstruction), a semi-open body.

36. Ko-ming wei-yüan-hui.

CHAPTER XXIV

1. There is great confusion in the use of the term "nationalism" and "étatism" and "nationalist" and "étatist." After Sun Yat-sen translated "nation" into *min-tsu*, there were separate words for "nation" and "state," previously used interchangeably by the Chinese. Since it was impossible to denounce a nationalist party, which the Youth Party eminently was, the Kuomintang denounced the Youth Party as *étatist.*

2. Law for the Speedy Punishment of Crimes Endangering the Republic, January 31, 1931. This law was superseded by the Law of September 4, 1937, which was finally repealed on January 28, 1946.

3. The declaration of September 22, 1937. For the principal points of the declaration, see *China Handbook, 1937–1945*, p. 67.

4. Letter of Carsun Chang, representing the National Socialist Party, dated April 13, 1938, and reply of Chiang Kai-shek and Wang Ching-wei, representing the Kuomintang, dated April 15, 1938; letter of Tso Shun-sheng, representing the Youth Party, dated April 21, 1938, and the reply of Chiang Kai-shek and Wang Ching-wei, representing the Kuomintang, dated April 24, 1938. These letters are to be found in full in *The Chinese Year Book, 1938–1939*, pp. 341–345.

5. The government had feared that the Japanese might win quickly. The failure of the Japanese to put an end to Chinese resistance after the capture of Nanking in December 1937 gave the Chinese leaders a new confidence in themselves. When, after

the loss of Canton and Hankow in October 1938, the Japanese again failed to push the war to a conclusion, the Chinese leaders felt that they could hold on indefinitely.

6. See above, pp. 359–360 and note 24 (p. 426).

7. In the period between the trouble over the disbandment of the New Fourth Army early in 1941 and the opening of the negotiations, suggestions for the resolution of the conflict were not wanting. For instance, in 1943 the communists had proposed a formula for the reorganization of the communist forces, the settlement of the status of the Communist Party and the administration of the communist-controlled Border Region. But no negotiations took place until 1944.

8. See reports to the People's Political Council by Chang Chih-chung and Lin Tsu-han representing respectively the government and the Communist Party, on September 15, 1944, *China Handbook, 1937–1945*, pp. 81–94.

9. *China Handbook, 1937–1945*, pp. 738–740.

10. The five resolutions of the Political Consultative Conference are given in full in *China Handbook, 1937–1945*, pp. 744–751.

11. For text of the agreement, see *China Handbook, 1937–1945*, pp. 755–758. See also above, p. 188.

12. See above, pp. 317–320.

13. Except for a few communists attached to the Chinese National Relief and Rehabilitation Administration.

14. There was a series of decrees culminating in the "Decree for the Mobilization to Suppress the Rebellion" (*Tung-yüan k'an-luan t'iao-k'uan*), July 1948. Most of the repressive measures of the government are now "legalized" on the basis of this decree of dubious legality.

CHAPTER XXV

1. It is interesting in this connection to note an account of Sun Yat-sen, relating how the intellectual classes gradually came to be accustomed to his views. In *Chung-kuo ke-ming shih* (History of the Chinese Revolution, published January 29, 1923), he wrote, "When I founded the Hsing Chung Hui — I had only a few score comrades. When the secret societies of the Yangtze provinces, Kwangtung, Kwangsi, and Fukien joined the Hsing Chung Hui, members began to increase. But there were still few members from the intelligentsia. The degenerated state of the Manchu regime and the ever-increasing danger from without, following the Boxer Rebellion of 1900, caused an exodus of the literati-gentry class to go abroad for study and created an impetus for reform movements within China. Then and not until then, the men of education who had considered revolution as high treason and had loathed me, began to have a change of heart. When the T'ung Meng Hui was founded, the students studying abroad all flocked to me." *Chung-kuo ke-ming shih* is in *Tsung-li ch'uan-chi* (Complete works of Sun Yat-sen, the President).

APPENDICES

APPENDIX A

CHRONOLOGY, 1912–1928

	North	*North-South Relations*	*South*
January 1, 1912			Sun Yat-sen inaugurated Provisional President at Nanking.
Feb. 12, 1912	Abdication of Manchu Emperor.		
Feb. 14, 1912		Yuan Shih-k'ai elected Provisional President.	
March 12, 1912		Provisional Constitution promulgated.	
April 2, 1912		Nanking Government moved to Peking.	
March 20, 1913		Sung Ch'ao-jen assassinated.	
April 8, 1913		Parliament convened.	
July–Sept., 1913		Revolution of 1913.	
Oct. 10, 1913	Yuan Shih-k'ai inaugurated President.		
January 10, 1914	Parliament dissolved.		
May 1, 1914	Yuan Shih-k'ai promulgated new Provisional Constitution.		
Dec. 12, 1915	Yuan Shih-k'ai proclaimed monarchy.		
Dec. 25, 1915			Anti-monarchical campaign launched in Yunnan.
March 22, 1916	Yuan Shih-k'ai rescinded monarchy.		
May 1, 1916			Military government organized at Chaoching, Kwangtung.
June 6, 1916	Death of Yuan Shih-k'ai.		
June 7, 1916		Li Yuan-hung assumed Presidency.	

	North	North-South Relations	South
June 29, 1916		Provisional Constitution revived.	
July 14, 1916			Military government dissolved.
August 1, 1916		Parliament reconvened.	
June 12, 1917	Parliament dissolved.		
July 1, 1917	Chang Hsün restored Manchu monarchy.		
July 2, 1917	Li Yuan-hung declared Feng Kuo-chang President and made Tuan Ch'i-jui premier.		
Aug. 25, 1917			Parliament met in extraordinary session at Canton.
Sept. 3, 1917			Military government organized and Sun Yat-sen elected Generalissimo.
May 4, 1918			Sun Yat-sen resigned from Generalissimoship.
May 21, 1918			Military Government reorganized with a Directorate under Kwangsi domination.
July 12, 1918			Regular session of Parliament announced.
Aug. 12, 1918	Anfu Parliament convened.		
Aug. 21, 1918		Wu P'ei-fu declared against civil war.	
Sept. 1, 1918	Hsü Shih-ch'ang elected President.		
Feb. 20, 1919		Peace Conference at Shanghai.	
August 7, 1919			Sun Yat-sen resigned from Directorate.
Aug. 12, 1919	Draft Constitution of Anfu Parliament.		
July, 1920	Chihli-Anhwei war.[1]		
October, 1920			Ch'en Ch'iung-min cleared Kwangtung of Kwangsi militarists.[2]
Oct. 30, 1920	Anfu Parliament dissolved.		
April 7, 1921			Sun Yat-sen elected President.

[1] Chihli was the faction led by Ts'ao K'un and Wu P'ei-fu; Anhwei, that led by Tuan Ch'i-jui.
[2] Not to be confused with the Kwangsi faction after 1928.

	North	North-South Relations	South
July–Sept., 1921		Hupei-Hunan war.	
April–May, 1922	Fengtien-Chihli war.[3]		
June 2–11, 1922	Hsü Shih-ch'ang forced out from and Li Yuan-hung restored to Presidency.		
June 16, 1922			Ch'en Ch'iung-min attacked Sun Yat-sen.
August 1, 1922	Old Parliament reconvened.		
1922		Sun Yat-sen and Fengtien and Anhwei factions vs. Chihli and Ch'en Ch'iung-min factions.	
March 2, 1923			Sun Yat-sen organized G.H.Q. and assumed Generalissimoship.
June 13, 1923	Li Yuan-hung forced out from Presidency.		
October 6, 1923	Ts'ao K'un elected President.		
Oct. 10, 1923	Constitution promulgated.		
Oct. 11, 1923		Sun Yat-sen launched Northern Expedition.	
Jan. 20–30, 1924			First Kuomintang Congress.
May–June, 1924			G.H.Q. cleared Kwangtung of Kwangsi faction.
Sept.–Oct., 1924	Kiangsu-Chekiang war.[4]		
Sept. 18, 1924	Ts'ao K'un ordered punitive campaign against Fengtien.		
Oct. 23, 1924	Feng Yü-hsiang turned out Ts'ao K'un.		
Nov. 24, 1924	Tuan Ch'i-jui became Chief Executive.		
Dec. 31, 1924		Sun Yat-sen arrived at Peking.	
Feb., 1925			Complete elimination of militarist remnants in Kwangtung and Kwangsi.
March 12, 1925		Death of Sun Yat-sen.	
July 1, 1925			Nationalist Government organized.

[3] Fengtien was the faction led by Chang Tso-lin.

[4] The Kiangsu side was under warlords of the Chihli faction and Chekiang's warlord, Lu Yung-hsiang, was formerly close to the Anhwei faction and was also in alliance with Chang Tso-lin. The Chekiang warlord was ousted.

	North	*North-South Relations*	*South*
Oct.–Nov., 1925	Fengtien-Chekiang war.[5]		
Nov.–Dec., 1925	Fengtien-Kuo-min-chün war.		
Jan.–March, 1926	War of Fengtien and Chihli factions against Kuo-min-chün.		
April 20, 1926	Tuan Ch'i-jui forced out.		
July 6, 1926			Chiang Kai-shek appointed C.-in-C. of Nationalist Revolutionary Army.
July 9, 1926		Northern Expedition started.	
Nov. 28, 1926			Nationalist Government moved to Wuhan.
April 18, 1927			Nationalist Government set up at Nanking.
June 18, 1927	Chang Tso-lin organized military government and assumed Generalissimoship.		
June 3, 1928	Chang Tso-lin left Peking.		
June 8, 1928		National Revolutionary Forces reached Peking.	

[5] In the Kiangsu-Chekiang war of September–October 1924, the Chekiang warlord, Lu Yung-hsiang, was ousted and Chekiang fell to Sun Ch'uan-fang, a Chihli warlord. Later by the help of Fengtien, Lu Yung-hsiang came to control Kiangsu. Still later the Fengtien warlords were in control of Kiangsu. Thus came about the war between Fengtien and Sun Ch'uan-fang, the new Chekiang warlord.

APPENDIX B

A LIST OF CONSTITUTIONS, PROVISIONAL CONSTITUTIONS, AND CONSTITUTIONAL DRAFTS, 1908–1946

1. *Hsien-fa ta-kang* (Principles of constitution), promulgated by the Manchu Government, August 27, 1908.
2. *Shih-chiu hsin-t'iao* (The nineteen articles), promulgated by the Manchu Government, November 2, 1911.
3. *Chung-hua-min-kuo lin-shih yüeh-fa* (Provisional constitution of the Republic of China), promulgated by the Provisional Government, March 11, 1912.
4. *Chung-hua-min-kuo hsien-fa ts'ao-an* (Draft constitution of the Republic of China), prepared by the Constitutional Commission of the Parliament, October 13, 1913, and known as the "Temple of Heaven Draft."
5. *Chung-hua-min-kuo yüeh-fa* (Provisional constitution of the Republic of China), promulgated by Yuan Shih-k'ai, May 1, 1914.
6. *Chung-hua-min-kuo hsien-fa ts'ao-an* (Draft constitution of the Republic of China), prepared by the Constitutional Commission of the Anfu Parliament, August 12, 1919, and known as the "Anfu Draft."
7. *Chung-hua-min-kuo hsien-fa* (Constitution of the Republic of China), promulgated by Ts'ao K'un, October 10, 1923.
8. *Chung-hua-min-kuo hsien-fa ts'ao-an* (Draft constitution of the Republic of China), prepared by the National Constitution Drafting Commission of the Tuan Ch'i-jui Government, December 12, 1925.
9. *Chung-hua-min-kuo yüeh-fa ts'ao-an* (Draft provisional constitution of the Republic of China), prepared by the Provisional Constitution Drafting Commission of the Yen Hsi-shan — Wang Ching-wei Government, October 27, 1930, and known as the "Taiyuan Draft".
10. *Chung-hua-min-kuo hsün-cheng shih-ch'i yüeh-fa* (Provisional constitution of the Republic of China for the period of tutelage), promulgated by the National Government, June 30, 1931.
11. *Chung-hua-min-kuo hsien-fa ts'ao-an* (Draft Constitution of the Republic of China), prepared by the Legislative Yuan and promulgated by the National Government, May 5, 1936, and known as the "Fifth of May Draft".
12. *Chung-hua-min-kuo hsien-fa* (Constitution of the Republic of China), promulgated by the National Government, December 25, 1946.

APPENDIX C

THE CONSTITUTION OF THE REPUBLIC OF CHINA, OCTOBER 10, 1923 [1]

Preamble

The Constituent Assembly of the Republic of China, in order to foster national glory, secure the national boundaries, promote social welfare, and defend human dignity, do hereby adopt this constitution and cause it to be promulgated throughout the land for faithful and perpetual observance by all.

CHAPTER I. FORM OF GOVERNMENT

Art. 1. The Republic of China shall be a unified Republic forever.

CHAPTER II. SOVEREIGNTY

Art. 2. The sovereignty of the Republic of China is vested in the people as a whole.

CHAPTER III. TERRITORY

Art. 3. The territory which originally belonged to the Republic shall be the territory of the Republic of China.

The territory and the division of it into areas shall not be altered except by law.

CHAPTER IV. CITIZENS

Art. 4. All persons who according to law belong to the nationality of the Republic of China are citizens of the Republic of China.

Art. 5. Citizens of the Republic of China shall be equal before the law, without distinction of race, class, or religion.

Art. 6. A citizen of the Republic of China shall not be arrested, imprisoned, tried, or punished except in accordance with law.

Any citizen under arrest may, in accordance with law, apply to the court by a "Petition for Protection" to have his person delivered thereto and the cause tried thereat.

Art. 7. The residence of citizens of the Republic of China shall not be entered or searched except in accordance with law.

Art. 8. The secrecy of letters and correspondence of citizens of the Republic of China shall not be violated except in accordance with law.

Art. 9. A citizen of the Republic of China shall be free to choose his residence and occupation; such freedom shall not be restricted except in accordance with law.

Art. 10. Citizens of the Republic of China shall be free to assemble and to form societies; such freedom shall not be restricted except in accordance with law.

[1] Based largely on the official translation in *Constitution and Supplementary Laws and Documents of the Republic of China*, China Commission on Extraterritoriality (Peking, 1924), with modifications by the author.

Art. 11. A citizen of the Republic of China shall be entitled to freedom of speech, authorship, and publication; such freedom shall not be restricted except in accordance with law.

Art. 12. A citizen of the Republic of China shall be free to honor Confucius and to profess any religion; such freedom shall not be restricted except in accordance with law.

Art. 13. The right of ownership of a citizen of the Republic of China shall be inviolable; provided that any necessary disposition for the public benefit may be made in accordance with law.

Art. 14. Liberties of the citizens of the Republic of China other than those provided for in this Chapter are recognized; provided that such liberties are not contrary to the principles of Constitutional Government.

Art. 15. A citizen of the Republic of China shall have the right to institute and carry on legal proceedings in a court of law, in accordance with law.

Art. 16. A citizen of the Republic of China shall have the right to petition the Parliament or the Administration in accordance with law.

Art. 17. A citizen of the Republic of China shall have the right to vote and to be candidate for election in accordance with law.

Art. 18. A citizen of the Republic of China shall have the right to hold public office in accordance with law.

Art. 19. A citizen of the Republic of China shall have the duty to pay taxes in accordance with law.

Art. 20. A citizen of the Republic of China shall have the duty to undertake military service in accordance with law.

Art. 21. A citizen of the Republic of China shall have the duty to receive elementary education in accordance with law.

CHAPTER V. PUBLIC POWERS

Art. 22. Of the public powers of the Republic of China, those relating to national affairs shall be exercised in accordance with the provisions of this Constitution; and those relating to local affairs, in accordance with the provisions of this Constitution and the Self-Government Law of the Province.

Art. 23. The following matters shall be subjects of legislation and execution by the Republic:

1. Foreign relations.
2. National defense.
3. Nationality law.
4. Criminal, civil, and commercial laws.
5. Prison system.
6. Weights and measures.
7. Currency and national banks.
8. Customs duty, salt tax, stamp tax, tobacco and wine taxes, and other consumption taxes, and all other taxes the rate of which shall be uniform throughout the country.
9. Posts, telegraphs, and aviation.
10. National railways and roads.
11. National property.
12. National debts.
13. Monopolies and licenses.
14. Examination, appointments, investigation, and protection of the civil and military officials of the country.
15. Other matters which, according to the provisions of this Constitution, relate to the Republic.

Art. 24. The following matters shall be subjects of legislation and execution by the Republic, or, under its order, by the local areas:

1. Agriculture, industry, mining, and forestry.
2. The educational system.
3. The banking and exchange system.
4. Navigation and coast fisheries.
5. Irrigation and conservancy concerned with and waterways extending to two or more Provinces.
6. General regulations relating to municipalities.
7. Eminent domain.
8. The national census and statistics.
9. Immigration, emigration, reclamation, and colonization.
10. The police system.

11. Public sanitation.
12. Relief work and administration of unemployed persons.
13. Preservation of such ancient books, objects, and remains as are of historic, cultural, or scientific interest.

A Province may enact local laws relating to the above subdivisions; provided that they shall not be contrary to the national laws. A Province may, pending legislation by the Republic, legislate upon the matters specified in subdivisions 1, 4, 10, 12, and 13.

Art. 25. The following matters shall be subjects of legislation and execution by a Province, or under its order, by a *Hsien*:

1. Provincial education, industry, and communications.
2. Management and disposal of Provincial properties.
3. Municipal affairs of the Province.
4. Provincial irrigation, conservancy, and engineering works.
5. The land tax, title-deed tax, and other Provincial taxes.
6. Provincial debts.
7. Provincial banks.
8. Provincial police and matters relating to public safety.
9. Provincial philanthropic work and work for public benefit.
10. Self-government of the lower grade.
11. Other matters assigned by national laws.

Where any of the matters above referred to concerns two or more Provinces, it may be undertaken by them jointly, unless it is otherwise provided by law. When the funds are insufficient, the deficit may, with the approval of the Parliament, be made good from the national treasury.

Art. 26. When any matter not specified in Articles 23, 24, and 25 arises, it shall be a concern of the Republic if by its nature it concerns the Republic and of a Province if by its nature it concerns the Province. Any controversy arising in this connection shall be decided by the Supreme Court.

Art. 27. The Republic may, in order to obviate the following evils, or when necessary for the promotion of public welfare, restrict by law any Provincial tax and its method of collection:

1. Impairment of the national revenue or commerce.
2. Double taxes.
3. Excessive fees, or fees detrimental to communications, charged for the use of public roads or other means of communication.
4. Taxes imposed by the Provinces or other local areas, detrimental to goods imported therein, for the purpose of protecting their local products.
5. Duties imposed by the Provinces or other local areas for the transit of goods.

Art. 28. A Provincial law conflicting with a national law shall be null and void. When doubt arises as to whether a Provincial law conflicts with a national law, interpretation shall lie with the Supreme Court.

The foregoing provision in the matter of interpretation shall apply when a Provincial Self-Government Law conflicts with a national law.

Art. 29. In case of a deficit in the national budget or financial stringency, the Provinces may, with the approval of the Parliament, be required to share the burden at rates increasing progressively with their annual revenues.

Art. 30. In the event of financial or extraordinary calamity, the locality concerned may, with the approval of the Parliament, be subsidized by the national treasury.

Art. 31. Controversies between Provinces shall be decided by the Senate.

Art. 32. The organization of the national army shall be based upon a system of compulsory citizen service. The Provinces shall, in general, have no military duty other than that of the execution of matters provided by the law of military service.

Citizens liable for military service shall be recruited and trained for different periods in recruiting areas of the whole country; but the stationing of standing armies shall be restricted to the areas required for national defense.

The military expenses of the Republic shall not exceed one-quarter of the national annual expenditure; provided that this provision shall not apply in case of war with any foreign country.

The strength of the national army shall be decided by the Parliament.

Art. 33. No Province shall enter into any political alliance.

No Province shall take any action detrimental to the interests of another Province or any other local area.

Art. 34. No Province shall keep any standing army or establish any military academy or arsenal.

Art. 35. If any Province fails to perform its duty as provided by a national law and refuses to obey after a warning by the Government, the Government may, with the national power, compel performance.

The aforesaid measure shall be stopped when it is disapproved by the Parliament.

Art. 36. In the event of an invasion with military force by one Province of another, the Government may intervene in accordance with the provisions of the last preceding article.

Art. 37. In the event of a change in the form of government or the destruction of the fundamental organization under the Constitution, the Provinces shall, until the original condition is restored, adopt and carry out joint measures to maintain the organization provided by the Constitution.

Art. 38. The provisions of this Chapter relating to Provinces shall apply to localities where *Hsien*, but not Provinces, have been established.

CHAPTER VI. THE PARLIAMENT

Art. 39. The legislative power of the Republic of China shall be exercised by the Parliament.

Art. 40. The Parliament shall consist of a Senate and a House of Representatives.

Art. 41. The Senate shall be composed of members elected by the highest local assemblies and other legally constituted electoral bodies.

Art. 42. The House of Representatives shall be composed of members elected by the electoral districts, the number of members elected in a district being proportional to its population.

Art. 43. The election of members of both houses shall be regulated by law.

Art. 44. No person shall be a member of both houses simultaneously.

Art. 45. No member of either house shall concurrently hold office as a civil or military official.

Art. 46. Each house may examine the qualifications of its own members.

Art. 47. The term of office for a member of the Senate shall be six years. One-third of the members shall be elected every two years.

Art. 48. The term of office for a member of the House of Representatives shall be three years.

Art. 49. Members referred to in Articles 47 and 48 shall, after the completion of a new election, not be relieved of their duties until the day before the opening of the session in accordance with the law.

Art. 50. Each house shall have a Speaker and a Vice-Speaker who shall be elected from among its own members.

Art. 51. Each house shall itself convene, open, and close its session; provided that extraordinary sessions shall be called under any of the following circumstances:

1. Upon the joint notice of one-third or more of the members of each house.
2. At the summons of the President.

Art. 52. The ordinary session of the National Assembly shall be opened on the first day of August in each year.

Art. 53. The period of the ordinary session shall be four months; such period may be extended, provided that the extension shall not exceed the period of an ordinary session.

Art. 54. The opening and closing of sessions shall take place simultaneously in both houses.

When one house is suspended, the other house shall simultaneously adjourn.

When the House of Representatives is dissolved, the Senate shall simultaneously adjourn.

Art. 55. Deliberations shall take place in the two houses separately. No bill shall be introduced simultaneously in both houses.

Art. 56. No deliberation shall commence in either house unless more than half of its members are present.

Art. 57. Deliberations in either house shall be decided by the vote of more than half of the members present. In the event of a tie, the Speaker shall cast the deciding vote.

Art. 58. An identical decision of both houses shall be the decision of the Parliament.

Art. 59. The sittings of the two houses shall be open to the public; provided that they may, at the request of the Government or by decision of the house, be closed to the public.

Art. 60. When the House of Representatives considers that the President or Vice-President is guilty of any treasonable act, he may be impeached by the votes of two-thirds of the members present; provided that two-thirds of the members shall be present.

Art. 61. When the House of Representatives considers that a Cabinet Minister is guilty of any act contrary to law, he may be impeached by the votes of two-thirds of the members present.

Art. 62. The House of Representatives may pass a vote of no-confidence against a Cabinet Minister.

Art. 63. An impeached President, Vice-President, or Cabinet Minister shall be tried by the Senate.

The decision that the person tried under the provisions of the above paragraph is guilty of a crime or has violated the law shall not be pronounced without the concurrence of two-thirds of the members present.

When the President or Vice-President is adjudged guilty of a crime, he shall be removed from his office; but the punishment to be inflicted shall be determined by the Supreme Court.

When a Cabinet Minister is adjudged to have violated the law, he shall be removed from his office and may also be deprived of his public rights. If he is guilty of a crime, he shall be delivered to a court of justice to be tried.

Art. 64. Each house may request the Government to institute an investigation in the matter of the conduct of an official acting contrary to law or to duty.

Art. 65. Each house may make proposals to the Government.

Art. 66. Each house may receive petitions of citizens.

Art. 67. Members of either house may address an interpellation to a Cabinet Minister or ask him to appear in the house to answer an interpellation.

Art. 68. Members of either house shall not be held responsible outside of the house for opinions expressed or for votes cast in the house.

Art. 69. A member of either house shall, during the session, not be arrested or kept under surveillance without the permission of the house except where taken in *flagrante delicto.*

When a member of either house is arrested in *flagrante delicto*, the Government shall at once report the cause to the house; but the house may, by its decision, ask for a suspension of judicial proceedings during the session and the surrender of the arrested member to the house.

Art. 70. The annual allowances of the members of both houses and the expenses shall be determined by law.

CHAPTER VII. THE PRESIDENT

Art. 71. The executive power of the Republic of China shall be exercised by the President with the assistance of the Cabinet Ministers.

Art. 72. Any citizen of the Republic of China forty or more years old, in full enjoyment of civil rights, and resident in the country for ten years or more, shall be eligible as President.

Art. 73. The President shall be elected by a Presidential Electoral College composed of all the members of the Parliament.

The election above referred to shall be held by secret ballot; provided always that two-thirds of the electors shall be present. The person who obtains three-fourths of the total votes shall be elected; provided that in the event of no one being elected after a second vote, a further vote shall be taken upon the two persons obtaining the highest numbers of votes in the second vote, and the one who obtains a majority vote shall be elected.

Art. 74. The term of office of the President shall be five years. In case of reëlection, he may hold office for a second term.

Three months prior to the expiration of the term of office of the President, the members of the Parliament shall themselves convene and organize a Presidential Electoral College for the election of a President for the following term.

Art. 75. When the President assumes office, he shall take oath as follows:

"I hereby swear that I will most faithfully observe the Constitution and perform the duties of the President."

Art. 76. In the event of the office of the President becoming vacant, the Vice-President shall succeed until the expiration of the term of office of the President.

In the event of the President being unable for any reason to perform his duties, the Vice-President shall act in his place.

If the office of the Vice-President is also vacant, the Cabinet shall act for the President. In such event, the members of the Parliament shall themselves within three months convene and organize a Presidential Electoral College to elect the next President.

Art. 77. The President shall be relieved of his office at the expiration of his term of office. If at that time a new President has not yet been elected, or has been elected but has not assumed his office, and the new Vice-President is also unable to act as President, the Cabinet shall act for him.

Art. 78. The election of the Vice-President shall be held in accordance with the provisions relating to the election of the President and shall take place at the same time. In the event of the Vice-Presidency becoming vacant, a new Vice-President shall be elected.

Art. 79. The President shall promulgate laws and supervise and secure their execution.

Art. 80. The President may issue mandates for the execution of laws or in pursuance of the authority delegated to him by law.

Art. 81. The President shall appoint and dismiss civil and military officials; provided that this provision shall not apply where this constitution or the law provides otherwise.

Art. 82. The President shall be the Commander-in-Chief of the Army and Navy of the Republic and shall be in command thereof. The organization of the Army and Navy shall be prescribed by law.

Art. 83. The President shall be the representative of the Republic with regard to foreign powers.

Art. 84. The President may, with the approval of the Parliament, declare war; provided that in the matter of defense against foreign invasion, he requests the approval of the Parliament after the declaration of war.

Art. 85. The President may conclude treaties; provided that treaties of peace and those relating to legislative matters shall not be valid without the approval of the Parliament.

Art. 86. The President may proclaim martial law in accordance with law; provided that, if the Parliament considers that there is no such necessity, he shall forthwith proclaim the withdrawal of martial law.

Art. 87. The President may, with the approval of the Supreme Court, remit or reduce punishments and restitute civil rights; provided that with regard to a decision in an impeachment case, no restitution of civil rights shall be declared without the approval of the Senate.

Art. 88. The President may suspend the session of the House of Representatives or the Senate; provided that no session shall be suspended more than twice and no suspension shall exceed ten days.

Art. 89. When a vote of no confidence has been passed against a Cabinet Minister, the President shall either remove the Cabinet Minister from office or dissolve the House of Representatives; provided that the House of Representatives shall not be dissolved without the consent of the Senate.

During the tenure of office of the same Cabinet Minister or during the same session, no dissolution shall take place a second time.

When the President dissolves the House of Representatives, he shall forthwith order a new election and fix a date, within five months, for the convocation of the House to continue the session.

Art. 90. The President shall not, for any offense other than treason, be liable to criminal proceedings before he has vacated his office.

Art. 91. The annual salaries of the President and the Vice-President shall be fixed by law.

CHAPTER VIII. THE CABINET

Art. 92. The Cabinet shall be composed of Cabinet Ministers.

Art. 93. The Premier and the Ministers of the various Ministries shall be Cabinet Ministers.

Art. 94. The Premier shall be appointed with the approval of the House of Representatives.

In the event of the Premiership becoming vacant when the Parliament is not in session, the President may appoint an acting Premier; provided that the nomination of the next Premier shall, within seven days after the opening of the next session of the Parliament, be submitted to the House of Representatives for approval.

Art. 95. The Cabinet Ministers shall assist the President and are responsible to the House of Representatives.

The mandates of the President and other documents concerning state affairs shall not be valid without the countersignature of a Cabinet Minister; provided that this provision shall not apply to the appointment or dismissal of a Premier.

Art. 96. A Cabinet Minister may appear and speak in both houses; provided that he may, for the purpose of making explanations of bills introduced by the Government, depute delegates to act for him.

CHAPTER IX. THE JUDICIARY

Art. 97. The judicial power of the Republic of China shall be exercised by courts of law.

Art. 98. The organization of the judiciary and the qualifications for judicial officials shall be prescribed by law.

The President of the Supreme Court shall be appointed with the approval of the Senate.

Art. 99. Courts of law shall, in accordance with law, accept and deal with civil, criminal, administrative, and all other cases; provided that this provision shall not apply where this Constitution or any law provides otherwise.

Art. 100. Trials in a court of law shall be conducted in public; provided that they may be held *in camera* when it is considered necessary for public peace or public morals.

Art. 101. A judicial official shall try and decide cases independently; no person whatsoever shall interfere.

Art. 102. A judicial official shall not, during his tenure of office, be subjected to a reduction of salary, suspension from office, or transference to another office otherwise than in accordance with law.

A judicial official shall not, during his tenure of office, be removed from his office unless he has been convicted of a crime or subjected to disciplinary punishment, provided that these provisions shall not apply in the case of an alteration in the organization of the judiciary or of the qualifications for entry thereto.

The disciplinary punishment of judicial officials shall be prescribed by law.

CHAPTER X. LAW

Art. 103. Members of the two houses and the Government may introduce bills; provided that, if a bill is rejected by either house, it shall not be reintroduced during the same session.

Art. 104. A bill passed by the Parliament shall be promulgated by the President within fifteen days after its transmission to him.

Art. 105. If the President disapproves a bill passed by the Parliament, he may, within the period for promulgation, state the reasons and request the Parliament to reconsider. If the two houses adhere to their original decision, the bill shall be promulgated forthwith.

If a bill has not been submitted for reconsideration and the period for promulgation has expired, it shall forthwith become law; provided that this provision shall not apply when the session of the Parliament is closed or the House of Representatives is dissolved before the expiration of the period for promulgation.

Art. 106. Law shall not be altered or repealed otherwise than by law.

Art. 107. When a resolution passed by the Parliament is submitted for reconsideration, the provisions relating to bills shall apply.

Art. 108. A law in conflict with the Constitution shall be null and void.

CHAPTER XI. FINANCE

Art. 109. The imposition of new taxes and alterations in the rates shall be made by law.

Art. 110. The approval of the Parliament shall be obtained for the floating of national loans and the conclusion of agreements increasing the burdens of the national treasury.

Art. 111. The House of Representatives shall have the right to deliberate first on a financial bill directly affecting the burdens of the citizens.

Art. 112. A budget shall be made annually by the Government of the annual expenditures and revenues of the Republic. The budget shall be submitted first to the House of Representatives within fifteen days after the opening of the session of the Parliament.

If the Senate amends or rejects a budget passed by the House of Representatives, the concurrence of the House of Representatives shall be obtained; if no such concurrence is obtained, the bill as originally passed shall forthwith become the budget.

Art. 113. The Government may, for special undertakings, provide in the budget funds for continuing expenditures for a previously fixed number of years.

Art. 114. The Government may provide a reserve fund to supply deficiencies in the budget or requirements unprovided for in the same.

Any defrayment made out of the reserve fund shall be submitted during the next session to the House of Representatives for subsequent approbation.

Art. 115. The following items of expenditure shall not be stricken off or reduced by the Parliament without the concurrence of the Government:

1. Expenditures legally due from the Government as obligations.
2. Expenditures necessary to carry out treaties.
3. Expenditures made necessary by provisions of law.
4. Continuing expenditure funds.

Art. 116. The Parliament shall not increase the expenditures in the budget.

Art. 117. After the commencement of a fiscal year and before the passing of the budget, the monthly expenditures of the Government shall be one-twelfth of the amount allowed in the budget for the previous year.

Art. 118. The Government may adopt financial emergency measures on account of a war of defense against a foreign power, suppression of rebellion, or relief for an extraordinary calamity when the urgency of the situation makes it impossible to summon the Parliament; provided that such measures shall be submitted to the Parliament for subsequent approbation within seven days after the opening of the next session.

Art. 119. An order for payment of an annual expenditure of the Republic shall first be referred to the Board of Audit for approval.

Art. 120. The actual settlement of the annual expenditures and revenues of the Republic shall be verified and confirmed each year by the Board of Audit and reported by the Government to the Parliament.

If the House of Representatives rejects such actual settlement or a bill for subsequent approbation, the Cabinet Minister concerned shall be responsible.

Art. 121. The organization of the Board of Audit and the qualifications of auditors shall be determined by law.

An auditor shall not, during his tenure of office, be subjected to a reduction of salary, a suspension of his functions, or a transference of office except in accordance with law.

The disciplinary punishment of auditors shall be prescribed by law.

Art. 122. The President of the Board of Audit shall be elected by the Senate.

The President of the Board of Audit may, in any matter relating to the report of the account, appear and speak in the two houses.

Art. 123. A budget or a bill for subsequent approbation shall, when it has been passed by the Parliament, be promulgated by the President after its transmission to him.

CHAPTER XII. LOCAL SYSTEM

Art. 124. Local areas are of two grades, the Provinces and the *Hsien.*

Art. 125. A Province may, in accordance with the provisions of Article 22 of Chapter V of this Constitution, make a Provincial Self-Government Law; provided that such law shall not conflict with the Constitution and the national laws.

Art. 126. The Provincial Self-Government Law shall be made by the Provincial Self-Government Law Assembly, composed of delegates elected by the Provincial Assembly, *Hsien* Assemblies, and legally constituted professional associations of the Province.

Each *Hsien* shall elect one delegate. The number of delegates elected by the Provincial Assembly and those elected by the legally constituted professional associations shall not exceed one-half of the total number of delegates elected by *Hsien* Assemblies; provided that candidates for election by Provincial Assemblies and *Hsien* Assemblies shall not be limited to members of the respective Assemblies. The election shall be regulated by Provincial law.

Art. 127. The following provisions shall apply to all Provinces:

1. A Province shall have a Provincial Assembly which shall be a unicameral representative body. The members of said Assembly shall be elected by direct action.
2. A Province shall have a Provincial Administrative Council which shall administer all matters of Provincial self-government. Said Council shall be composed of from five to nine Councilmen directly elected by the citizens of the Province. Their term of office shall be four years. Before a direct election is possible, an electoral college may be organized in accordance with the provisions of the last preceding article to elect such members; provided that a person in military service shall not be eligible unless he has been relieved of office for at least one year.
3. A Provincial Administrative Council shall have a Chairman who shall be elected from among the Councilmen.
4. Citizens of the Republic of China who have resided in the Province for one year or more shall be equal before

the law of the Province and be in full enjoyment of civil rights.

Art. 128. The following provisions shall apply to all *Hsien*:

1. A *Hsien* shall have a *Hsien* Assembly which shall have legislative power over all matters of self-government in the *Hsien*.
2. A *Hsien* shall have a Magistrate who shall be directly elected by the citizens of the *Hsien*, and shall, with the assistance of the *Hsien* Council, administer all matters of *Hsien* self-government; provided that this provision shall not apply before the judiciary shall have become independent and the system of self-government of the lower grade shall have become complete.
3. A *Hsien* shall have the right to retain a portion of the Provincial taxes raised in the *Hsien*; provided that such portion shall not exceed 40 per cent of the whole amount.
4. The Provincial Government shall not dispose of the property of the *Hsien*, or their self-government funds.
5. A *Hsien* may, in case of a natural or any other calamity, or on account of shortage of funds for self-government, apply to the Provincial Administrative Council; and may, with the approval of the Provincial Assembly, receive subsidies from the Provincial treasury.
6. A *Hsien* shall have the duty to enforce the national and Provincial laws and ordinances.

Art. 129. The separation of the Provincial and *Hsien* taxes shall be determined by the Provincial Assembly.

Art. 130. A Province shall not enforce special laws against one or more *Hsien*; provided that this provision shall not apply to laws concerning the general interests of the whole Province.

Art. 131. A *Hsien* shall have full power to execute matters of self-government. The Province shall not interfere except in matters of disciplinary punishment prescribed by Provincial laws.

Art. 132. National administrative matters in a Province or a *Hsien* may, as well as being executed by officials appointed by the Republic, be entrusted to the self-government organs of the Province or *Hsien*.

Art. 133. If a self-government organ of a *Hsien* or Province in the execution of any administrative matter of the Republic violates the law or ordinance, the Republic may, in accordance with law, inflict a disciplinary punishment upon it.

Art. 134. The provisions of this Constitution shall apply to areas where *Hsien*, but not Provinces, have been established.

Art. 135. Inner and Outer Mongolia, Tibet, and Chinghai may, in compliance with the common wish of the people of the area, be divided into two grades, the Province and the *Hsien*, and be governed by the provisions of this Chapter; provided that, pending the establishment of the Province and *Hsien*, their administrative systems shall be prescribed by law.

CHAPTER XIII. THE AMENDMENT, INTERPRETATION, AND VALIDITY OF THE CONSTITUTION

Art. 136. The Parliament may make proposals for an amendment to the Constitution.

Such proposals shall not be made without the concurrence of two-thirds or more of the members present in each house.

The members of either house shall not make a motion for a proposal to amend the Constitution unless such motion is signed by one-fourth of all the members of the house.

Art. 137. An amendment to the Constitution shall be made by the Constituent Assembly.

Art. 138. The form of government shall not be the subject of amendment.

Art. 139. If there is any doubt about the meaning of the Constitution, interpretation shall be made by the Constituent Assembly.

Art. 140. The Constituent Assembly shall be composed of the members of the Parliament.

The aforesaid Assembly shall not commence to deliberate without the presence of two-thirds of all the members, and shall not make any decision without the concurrence of three-fourths of the members present; provided that in matters of interpretation, decisions may be made with the concurrence of two-thirds of the members present.

Art. 141. The Constitution shall, under no circumstances, lose its validity otherwise than in accordance with the procedure of amendment prescribed in this Chapter.

APPENDIX D

THE CONSTITUTION OF THE REPUBLIC OF CHINA, DECEMBER 25, 1946 [1]

Preamble

The National Assembly of the Republic of China, by virtue of the mandate received from the whole body of citizens, in accordance with the teachings bequeathed by Sun Yat-sen in founding the Republic of China, and in order to consolidate the sovereign power of the state, safeguard the rights of the people, ensure social security, and promote popular welfare, do hereby adopt this Constitution and cause it to be promulgated and enforced throughout the land for faithful observance by all.

CHAPTER I. GENERAL PRINCIPLES

Art. 1. The Republic of China, founded on the Three People's Principles, is a democratic republic of the people, for the people, and governed by the people.

Art. 2. The sovereignty of the R public of China resides in the whole body of citizens.

Art. 3. Persons possessing the nationality of the Republic of China are citizens of the Republic of China.

Art. 4. The territory of the Republic of China, as constituted within existing boundaries, shall not be altered except by resolution of the National Assembly.

Art. 5. All the nationalities of the Republic of China shall be equal.

Art. 6. The National Flag of the Republic of China shall have a red background and, in the upper left corner, a blue sky with a white sun.

CHAPTER II. RIGHTS AND DUTIES OF THE PEOPLE

Art. 7. The people of the Republic of China, without distinction of sex, religion, race, class, or party affiliation, shall be equal before the law.

Art. 8. The freedom of person shall be guaranteed to the people. With the exception of apprehension in *flagrante delicto* which shall otherwise be provided for by law, no person may be arrested or detained except by a judicial or a police organ in accordance with the procedure prescribed by law. No person may be arraigned or punished except by a court of law in accordance with the procedure prescribed by law. All arrests, detentions, arraignments, or punishments not in accordance with the procedure prescribed by law may be resisted.

When a person is arrested or detained

[1] Based largely on Hoh Chih-hsiang's translation, with extensive modifications by the author. The original translation was first published by the Commercial Press, Shanghai, 1947.

as a criminal suspect, the organ effecting the arrest and detention shall, in writing, inform the person concerned and any relatives or friends designated by him of the reason for his arrest and detention, and shall, within twenty-four hours at the latest, hand him over for a hearing to a court of law having jurisdiction over the case. The person concerned or other persons may also apply to the court having jurisdiction over the case to make a demand, within twenty-four hours, that the organ effecting the arrest hand the suspect over for trial.

The said court shall not reject the application referred to in the preceding paragraph, and likewise shall not order that the organ effecting the arrest and detention first make an investigation and report of the case. The organ effecting the arrest and detention shall not refuse to hand or delay in handing over the suspect for trial, when a demand to that effect has been made by the said court.

When a person is illegally arrested and detained by any organ, he himself or other persons may apply to a court of law for an investigation. The court may not reject such an application and shall, within twenty-four hours, investigate the action of the said organ in effecting the arrest and detention and deal with the matter in accordance with law.

Art. 9. No person, except those in active military service, shall be liable to trial by a military court.

Art. 10. All persons shall have freedom of domicile and of change of domicile.

Art. 11. All persons shall have freedom of speech, teaching, writing, and publication.

Art. 12. All persons shall have freedom of secrecy of correspondence.

Art. 13. All persons shall have freedom of religious belief.

Art. 14. All persons shall have freedom of assembly and of association.

Art. 15. The right to exist, the right to work, and the right to property of all persons shall be guaranteed.

Art. 16. All persons shall have the right to petition, to file administrative appeals, and to institute legal proceedings.

Art. 17. All persons shall have the right of election, recall, initiative, and referendum.

Art. 18. All persons shall have the right to take part in public examinations and to hold public office.

Art. 19. All persons shall have the duty of paying taxes in accordance with law.

Art. 20. All persons shall have the duty of performing military service in accordance with law.

Art. 21. All persons shall have the right and obligation of receiving a citizen's education.

Art. 22. All other freedoms and rights of the people, not detrimental to social order or the public interest, shall be guaranteed by the Constitution.

Art. 23. The freedoms and rights enumerated in the preceding articles shall not be restricted by law, except in cases where such a restriction is necessary for preventing an obstruction of the exercise of the freedoms of other persons, averting an imminent crisis, maintaining social order, or promoting the public interest.

Art. 24. Any public functionary who illegally infringes upon the freedoms or rights of the people shall, besides being subject to disciplinary punishment in accordance with law, be held responsible under criminal and civil laws. The injured person may also, in accordance with law, petition the state for compensation for damages sustained.

CHAPTER III. THE NATIONAL ASSEMBLY

Art. 25. The National Assembly shall, in accordance with provisions of this Constitution, exercise political power on behalf of the citizens of the whole country.

Art. 26. The National Assembly shall be composed of the following delegates:

(1) One delegate to be elected by every *hsien*, municipality, or area of an equivalent status. In case the population exceeds five hundred thousand, one additional delegate shall be elected for every addi-

tional five hundred thousand. What constitutes an area equivalent to a *hsien* or to a municipality shall be determined by law.

(2) Delegates to be elected by Mongolia, four from every League and one from every special Banner.

(3) The number of delegates to be elected from Tibet shall be prescribed by law.

(4) The number of delegates to be elected by various nationalities in the border regions shall be prescribed by law.

(5) The number of delegates to be elected by Chinese nationals residing abroad shall be prescribed by law.

(6) The number of delegates to be elected by occupational groups shall be prescribed by law.

(7) The number of delegates to be elected by women's organizations shall be prescribed by law.

Art. 27. The functions and powers of the National Assembly shall be as follows:

(1) To elect the President and the Vice-President of the Republic.

(2) To recall the President and the Vice-President.

(3) To amend the Constitution.

(4) To ratify amendments to the Constitution proposed by the Legislative Yuan.

With respect to the powers of initiative and referendum, except what is provided for in items 3 and 4 of the preceding paragraph, the National Assembly shall formulate pertinent procedures and shall enforce them as soon as half of the *hsien* and municipalities of the entire country have put into effect the two political powers of initiative and referendum.

Art. 28. Delegates to the National Assembly shall be elected once every six years.

The term of office of delegates to each National Assembly shall end on the day when the next National Assembly meets.

Incumbent government officials may not be elected delegates to the National Assembly in constituencies in which their offices are situated.

Art. 29. The National Assembly shall meet ninety days prior to the date of expiration of the term of office of each President, the meeting to be summoned by the President.

Art. 30. In any of the following circumstances, an extraordinary session of the National Assembly shall be convened:

(1) When, in accordance with the provisions of Article 49 of this Constitution, it is necessary to hold a supplementary election of the President and the Vice-President of the Republic.

(2) When, in accordance with a resolution of the Control Yuan, an impeachment of the President or the Vice-President is instituted.

(3) When, in accordance with a resolution of the Legislative Yuan, amendments to the Constitution are proposed.

(4) When two-fifths or more of the delegates to the National Assembly request that a meeting be called.

When an extraordinary session of the National Assembly shall be convened in accordance with items 1 or 2 of the preceding paragraph, the President of the Legislative Yuan shall issue the notice for convening it. When an extraordinary session shall be convened in accordance with items 3 or 4, it shall be summoned by the President of the Republic.

Art. 31. The place of meeting of the National Assembly shall be the seat of the Central Government.

Art. 32. Delegates to the National Assembly shall not be held responsible outside the Assembly for views they express or for votes they cast at the meetings of the Assembly.

Art. 33. Without the permission of the National Assembly, no delegate may be arrested or detained during the period the National Assembly is in session, except in cases of *flagrante delicto*.

Art. 34. The organization of the National Assembly, the election and recall of delegates to the National Assembly, and the procedure governing the exercise of the functions and powers of the National Assembly shall be prescribed by law.

CHAPTER IV. THE PRESIDENCY

Art. 35. The President is the head of the state and represents the Republic of China in foreign relations.

Art. 36. The President shall command the land, sea, and air forces of the whole country.

Art. 37. The President shall, in accordance with law, promulgate laws and issue mandates, which must be countersigned by the President of the Executive Yuan or by the President of the Executive Yuan and the head of the ministry or commission concerned.

Art. 38. The President shall, in accordance with provisions of this Constitution, exercise the powers of concluding treaties, and of declaring war and negotiating peace.

Art. 39. The President may, in accordance with law, declare martial law, but his act must be approved or confirmed by the Legislative Yuan. When the Legislative Yuan deems it necessary, it may pass a resolution requesting the President to terminate the existence of martial law.

Art. 40. The President shall, in accordance with law, exercise the powers of granting general amnesties, special pardons, remission of sentences, and restitution of civil rights.

Art. 41. The President shall, in accordance with law, appoint and remove civil and military officials.

Art. 42. The President shall, in accordance with law, confer honors and award decorations.

Art. 43. In case of a natural calamity, an epidemic, or a serious national financial and economic crisis which requires emergency measures to be taken, the President may, when the Legislative Yuan is in recess, by resolution of the Executive Yuan Council and in accordance with the Emergency Decrees Law, issue emergency decrees necessary to cope with the situation, but such emergency decrees must, within one month after issuance, be presented to the Legislative Yuan for ratification. If the Legislative Yuan refuses consent, the said emergency decrees shall immediately become null and void.

Art. 44. In case of an inter-Yuan dispute, except as provided for in this Constitution, the President shall summon the Presidents of the Yuan concerned for consultation and settlement.

Art. 45. Any citizen of the Republic of China having attained the age of forty years is eligible for the office of President or Vice-President.

Art. 46. The election of the President and of the Vice-President shall be prescribed by law.

Art. 47. The term of office of the President and of the Vice-President shall be six years and, upon reëlection, they may continue to hold office for one other term.

Art. 48. The President shall, at the time of his assumption of office, take an oath as follows:

"I do solemnly and most sincerely swear before the people of the whole country that I shall faithfully abide by the Constitution, loyally perform my duties, promote the welfare of the people, safeguard the security of the state, and shall not betray the trust of the people. Should I break this oath, I am willing to submit myself to severe punishment from the state."

Art. 49. When the President's office becomes vacant, the Vice-President shall succeed to that office and continue therein until the expiration of the presidential term. When the offices of both the President and Vice-President become vacant, the President of the Executive Yuan shall exercise the functions and powers of the offices in their place and shall, in accordance with the provisions of Article 30 of this Constitution, summon an extraordinary session of the National Assembly to hold a supplementary election of the President and of the Vice-President, whose terms of office shall end upon completion of the unfinished presidential term.

When the President is unable for any cause to attend to the duties of his office, the Vice-President shall exercise his functions and powers. When both the President and the Vice-President are unable to attend to the duties of their offices, the President of the Executive Yuan shall exercise their functions and powers.

Art. 50. The President shall retire from office on the day his term expires. If, at that time, a President for the succeeding term has not yet been elected, or, if after having been elected, neither the President nor the Vice-President has yet assumed office, the President of the Executive Yuan shall exercise the functions and powers of the President's office.

Art. 51. The period during which the President of the Executive Yuan may exercise the functions and powers of the President's office shall not exceed three months.

Art. 52. Except in the case of rebellion or treason, the President shall not be liable to criminal prosecution, unless he has been recalled or has retired from his office.

CHAPTER V. ADMINISTRATION

Art. 53. The Executive Yuan is the highest administrative organ of the state.

Art. 54. The Executive Yuan shall have a President and a Vice-President, heads of various ministries and commissions, and a number of ministers without portfolio.

Art. 55. The President of the Executive Yuan shall be appointed on the nomination of the President of the Republic and with the consent of the Legislative Yuan.

During a recess of the Legislative Yuan, if the President of the Executive Yuan resigns or if his office becomes vacant, the Vice-President of the Executive Yuan shall discharge his duties, but the President of the Republic shall within forty days make a request in writing to the Legislative Yuan to convene a meeting of the Yuan and he shall nominate a candidate for the presidency of the Executive Yuan with a request that the Legislative Yuan give its consent thereto.

Pending the consent of the Legislative Yuan to the choice of the candidate for the presidency of the Executive Yuan who has been nominated by the President of the Republic, the duties of the President of the Executive Yuan shall be discharged *pro tem* by the Vice-President of the Yuan.

Art. 56. The Vice-President of the Executive Yuan, heads of various ministries and commissions, and ministers without portfolio shall be appointed by the President of the Republic upon the recommendation of the President of the Executive Yuan.

Art. 57. The Executive Yuan shall be responsible to the Legislative Yuan in accordance with the following provisions:

(1) The Executive Yuan shall have the responsibility of presenting to the Legislative Yuan its administrative policies and administrative reports. Legislative Members during meetings of the Yuan shall have the right to interpellate the President of the Executive Yuan and the heads of the various ministries and commissions of the Executive Yuan.

(2) When the Legislative Yuan disapproves an important policy of the Executive Yuan, it may pass a resolution requesting the Executive Yuan to alter the policy. The Executive Yuan, with respect to the resolution of the Legislative Yuan, may, with the approval of the President of the Republic, request the Legislative Yuan to reconsider it. If, at the time of reconsideration, two-thirds of the Legislative Members present at the meeting uphold the original resolution, the President of the Executive Yuan shall either abide by the said resolution or resign.

(3) If the Executive Yuan, with respect to an enactment of law, a budget estimate, or a treaty passed by the Legislative Yuan, deems such measure difficult of execution due to obstacles, it may, with the approval of the President of the Republic, within ten days after the delivery of any of the said measures to the Executive Yuan, request the Legislative Yuan to reconsider it. If, at the time of reconsideration, two-thirds of the members of the Legislative Yuan present at the meeting uphold the original resolution, the President of the Executive Yuan shall either abide by the said resolution or resign.

Art. 58. The Executive Yuan shall have an Executive Yuan Council, to be composed of the President and the Vice-President of the Executive Yuan, heads of various ministries and commissions and ministers without portfolio, with the President of the Executive Yuan as chairman.

The President of the Executive Yuan and the heads of its various ministries and commissions shall bring before the meetings of the Executive Yuan Council for decision bills to be presented to the Legislative Yuan concerning laws, budget estimates, declarations of martial law, amnesties, declarations of war, negotiations for peace, treaties and other important matters, or matters of common concern to various ministries and commissions.

Art. 59. The Executive Yuan shall, three months prior to the beginning of a new fiscal year, present to the Legislative Yuan the budget estimate for the following fiscal year.

Art. 60. The Executive Yuan shall, within four months after the end of a fiscal year, present the actual settlement to the Control Yuan.

Art. 61. The organization of the Executive Yuan shall be prescribed by law.

CHAPTER VI. LEGISLATION

Art. 62. The Legislative Yuan is the highest Legislative organ of the state, and shall be composed of popularly elected Legislative Members, who shall exercise legislative powers on behalf of the people.

Art. 63. The Legislative Yuan shall have the power to decide on bills concerning laws, budget estimates, declarations of martial law, general amnesties, declarations of war, negotiations for peace, treaties, and other important matters of state.

Art. 64. Legislative Members shall be elected in accordance with the following provisions:

(1) In the case of provinces and of municipalities under the direct jurisdiction of the National Government, where the population is below 3,000,000, five members shall be elected; where the population exceeds 3,000,000, an additional member shall be elected for every additional 1,000,000 persons.

(2) Members to be elected by various Mongolian Leagues and Banners.

(3) Members to be elected by Tibet.

(4) Members to be elected by various racial groups in the border regions.

(5) Members to be elected by Chinese nationals residing abroad.

(6) Members to be elected by vocational groups.

The election of Legislative Members, and the allotment of the quotas of women members in the various items of the first paragraph shall be prescribed by law.

Art. 65. Legislative Members shall hold office for a term of three years and are re-eligible; their election shall be completed within three months prior to the expiration of the existing term of office.

Art. 66. The Legislative Yuan shall have a President and a Vice-President to be elected by and from among the Legislative Members.

Art. 67. The Legislative Yuan may organize various committees.

The various committees may invite officials of the Government as well as private persons concerned to appear at their meetings for consultation.

Art. 68. The Legislative Yuan shall hold two sessions each year and shall itself convene the sessions. The first session shall last from February to the end of May, and the second session from September to the end of December. When necessary, the length of a session may be extended.

Art. 69. In any of the following circumstances, the Legislative Yuan may hold an extraordinary session:

(1) Upon written request of the President of the Republic.

(2) Upon application of one-fourth or more of the Legislative Members.

Art. 70. The Legislative Yuan may not propose an increase in the expenditures as set forth in the budget estimate presented by the Executive Yuan.

Art. 71. The Presidents of the various Yuan and the heads of the various ministries and commissions concerned may be present at sessions of the Legislative Yuan to present their opinions.

Art. 72. Statutory bills passed by the Legislative Yuan shall be sent to the President of the Republic and to the Executive Yuan, and the President shall, within ten days after their receipt, promulgate them, but the President may deal with them in accordance with the provisions of Article 57 of this Constitution.

Art. 73. Legislative Members shall not be held responsible outside the Yuan for opinions they express or for votes they cast within the Yuan.

Art. 74. Without the permission of the Legislative Yuan, no Legislative Member may be arrested or detained, except in *flagrante delicto.*

Art. 75. Legislative Members may not concurrently hold official posts.

Art. 76. The organization of the Legislative Yuan shall be prescribed by law.

CHAPTER VII. JUSTICE

Art. 77. The Judicial Yuan is the highest judicial organ of the state and shall have jurisdiction over the conduct of civil, criminal, and administrative cases, and of disciplinary punishment of public functionaries.

Art. 78. The Judicial Yuan interprets the Constitution, and shall also have the power to standardize the interpretation of laws and ordinances.

Art. 79. The Judicial Yuan shall have a President and a Vice-President, who shall be appointed on the nomination of the President of the Republic and with the consent of the Control Yuan.

The Judicial Yuan shall have a number of Grand Justices to attend to matters stipulated in Article 78 of this Constitution, who shall be appointed on the nomination of the President of the Republic and with the consent of the Control Yuan.

Art. 80. Judges shall place themselves outside political parties or factions and shall, in accordance with law, conduct trials independently, without being subject to any interference.

Art. 81. Judges shall hold office for life and may not be removed from office, unless they have been subject to criminal or disciplinary punishment or have been declared to be under interdiction. They may not be suspended, transferred, or have their salaries reduced, except in accordance with law.

Art. 82. The organization of the Judicial Yuan and of the various grades of the courts of law shall be prescribed by law.

CHAPTER VIII. EXAMINATION

Art. 83. The Examination Yuan is the highest examination organ of the state and shall have jurisdiction over such matters as examination, appointment, rank, rating, scale of salaries, promotion and transfer, security of tenure, commendations and awards, pensions, retirements, old-age grants, et cetera.

Art. 84. The Examination Yuan shall have a President and a Vice-President and a number of Examination Members to be appointed on the nomination of the President of the Republic and with the consent of the Control Yuan.

Art. 85. In the selection of public functionaries, a system of open, competitive examinations shall be enforced, and examinations shall be held in different areas with a fixed quota for each province or area. No person may be appointed to public office unless he has passed such examination.

Art. 86. Qualifications for the following shall be determined by the Examination Yuan through examinations in accordance with law:

(1) Qualifications for appointment as public functionaries.

(2) Qualifications for practice in specialized professions and as technicians.

Art. 87. The Examination Yuan may present to the Legislative Yuan statutory bills relating to matters under its jurisdiction.

Art. 88. Examination Members shall place themselves outside political parties or factions and shall, in accordance with law, exercise their powers and functions independently.

Art. 89. The organization of the Examination Yuan shall be prescribed by law.

CHAPTER IX. CONTROL

Art. 90. The Control Yuan is the highest organ of control of the state and shall exercise the powers of consent, impeachment, rectification, and audit.

Art. 91. The Control Yuan shall be composed of Control Members, to be elected by various provincial and municipal councils, the local councils of Mongolia and Tibet, and overseas Chinese communities. The allotment of their quotas shall be as follows:

(1) Five members from each province.

(2) Two members from each municipality under the direct jurisdiction of the National Government.

(3) A total of eight members from Mongolian Leagues and Banners.

(4) Eight members from Tibet.

(5) Eight members from Chinese nationals residing abroad.

Art. 92. The Control Yuan shall have a President and a Vice-President, to be elected by and from among the Control Members.

Art. 93. Control Members shall hold office for a term of six years and are reëligible.

Art. 94. When the Control Yuan exercises the power of consent in accordance with this Constitution, it shall do so by resolution of a majority of the Members present at a meeting.

Art. 95. The Control Yuan in the exercise of its supervisory powers may request the Executive Yuan and its various ministries and commissions to submit to it for perusal orders and various pertinent documents issued by them.

Art. 96. The Control Yuan may, in accordance with the nature of the work of the Executive Yuan and its various ministries and commissions, organize a number of committees to investigate the activities of these organs of the Executive Yuan with a view to finding out whether or not they have been guilty of violation of law or of neglect of duty.

Art. 97. The Control Yuan may, on the basis of the investigations and decisions made by the said committees, propose measures of rectification to be sent to the Executive Yuan and to the ministries and commissions concerned, calling their attention thereto and requesting them to effect improvement.

If the Control Yuan deems that any public functionary in the Central or in a local government is guilty of neglect of duty or of violation of law, it may propose measures of censure or of impeachment. If the case involves criminal law, it shall be referred to a court of law to be dealt with.

Art. 98. Impeachments by the Control Yuan of public functionaries in the Central or in the local governments may be instituted upon the proposal of one or more Control Members and upon the endorsement, after due consideration, of nine or more members.

Art. 99. In the institution of impeachments by the Control Yuan or of the personnel of the Judicial Yuan or the Examination Yuan for neglect of duty or for violation of law, the provisions of Articles 95, 97, and 98 of this Constitution shall be applicable.

Art. 100. Impeachment of the President or of the Vice-President of the Republic by the Control Yuan may be instituted upon the proposal of one-fourth of the Control Members and upon the endorsement, after due consideration, of the majority of the Control Members; and the same shall be brought before the National Assembly.

Art. 101. Control Members shall not be held responsible outside the Yuan for opinions they express or for votes they cast within the Yuan.

Art. 102. No Control Member may, except in *flagrante delicto,* be arrested or detained without permission of the Control Yuan.

Art. 103. Control Members may not concurrently hold other public offices or be engaged in any profession.

Art. 104. The Control Yuan shall have an Auditor-General, to be appointed on the nomination of the President of the Republic and with the consent of the Legislative Yuan.

Art. 105. The Auditor-General shall, within three months after the presentation of the actual settlement by the Executive Yuan, complete the examination of the same in accordance with law, and shall submit a report of his examination to the Legislative Yuan.

Art. 106. The organization of the Control Yuan shall be prescribed by law.

CHAPTER X. POWERS OF THE CENTRAL AND LOCAL GOVERNMENTS

Art. 107. The following matters shall be subjects of legislation and execution by the Central Government:

(1) Foreign affairs.

(2) National defense and military matters pertaining to national defense.

(3) Nationality law, and Criminal, Civil, and Commercial Codes.

(4) The judicial system.

(5) Aviation, national highways, national railways, navigation administration, postal administration, and telegraph administration.

(6) Central Government finance and national revenues.

(7) Allocation of national, provincial, and *hsien* revenues.

(8) State-operated economic enterprises.

(9) Currency system and state banks.

(10) Weights and measures.

(11) Policies of international trade.

(12) Financial and economic matters of an international nature.

(13) Other matters relating to the Central Government as stipulated in this Constitution.

Art. 108. The following matters shall be subjects of legislation and execution by the Central Government. Their execution may be delegated to the provincial and *hsien* governments:

(1) General rules governing provincial and *hsien* self-government.

(2) Division of administrative areas.

(3) Forestry, mining, and commerce.

(4) The educational system.

(5) Systems of banking and exchange.

(6) Shipping and coastal fisheries.

(7) Public utilities.

(8) Coöperative enterprises.

(9) Water and land communication, and transportation involving two or more provinces.

(10) Water conservancy, waterways, agriculture, and animal husbandry involving two or more provinces.

(11) Official grading, appointments, supervision and protection of officials in the Central and local governments.

(12) Land law.

(13) Labor law and other social legislation.

(14) Expropriation.

(15) Census-taking and compilation of statistics of the national population.

(16) Immigration and land reclamation.

(17) The police system.

(18) Public health.

(19) Relief, pensions, and unemployment assistance.

(20) Protection and preservation of ancient books, historical relics, and historical landmarks of cultural value.

With respect to the various items enumerated in the preceding paragraph, the province may enact separate laws and regulations, provided they are not in conflict with the national laws.

Art. 109. The following matters shall be subjects of legislation and execution by the province. Their execution may be delegated to the *hsien*:

(1) Provincial education, public health, industries, and communications.

(2) The management and disposal of provincial properties.

(3) Provincial municipal administration.

(4) Provincially operated enterprises.

(5) Provincial coöperative enterprises.

(6) Provincial agriculture and forestry, water conservancy, fishery and animal husbandry, and public works.

(7) Provincial finance and provincial revenues.

(8) Provincial debts.

(9) Provincial banks.

(10) Enforcement of the provincial police administration.

(11) Provincial charitable and public welfare enterprises.

(12) Other matters delegated in accordance with the national laws.

In case any of the various items enumerated in the preceding paragraph involves two or more provinces, it may, unless otherwise provided for by law, be undertaken jointly by the provinces concerned.

When a province, in undertaking the handling of any of the items in the first paragraph, finds its funds insufficient, it may, by resolution of the Legislative Yuan, be aided by the National Treasury.

Art. 110. The following matters shall be subjects of legislation and execution by the *hsien*:

(1) *Hsien* education, public health, industries, and communications.

(2) The management and disposal of *hsien* properties.

(3) *Hsien*-operated enterprises.

(4) *Hsien* coöperative enterprises.

(5) *Hsien* agriculture and forestry, water conservancy, fishery and animal husbandry, and public works.

(6) *Hsien* finance and *hsien* revenues.

(7) *Hsien* debts.

(8) *Hsien* banks.

(9) Administration of *hsien* police and defense.

(10) *Hsien* charitable and public welfare enterprises.

(11) Other matters delegated in accordance with the national laws and the provincial self-government law.

In case any of the various items enumerated in the preceding paragraph involves two or more *hsien*, it may, unless otherwise provided for by law, be undertaken jointly by the *hsien* concerned.

Art. 111. Apart from the matters enumerated in Articles 107, 108, 109, and 110, when an unenumerated matter arises, it shall fall within the jurisdiction of the Central Government if it is of national nature, of the province if it is of provincial nature, and of the *hsien* if it is of *hsien* nature. In case of dispute, the matter shall be settled by the Legislative Yuan.

CHAPTER XI. LOCAL GOVERNMENT SYSTEM

Section 1. The Province

Art. 112. The province may convene a Provincial Assembly to adopt, in accordance with the General Rules Governing Provincial and *Hsien* Self-Government, a Provincial Self-Government Law, but it shall not be in conflict with the Constitution.

The organization of the Provincial Assembly and the election of the delegates thereto shall be prescribed by law.

Art. 113. The Provincial Self-Government Law shall contain the following provisions:

(1) The province shall have a Provincial Council. Members of the Provincial Council shall be elected by the citizens of the province.

(2) The province shall have a Provincial Government and a provincial governor. The provincial governor shall be elected by the citizens of the province.

(3) Relationship between the province and the *hsien*.

The powers of legislation which belong to the province shall be exercised by the Provincial Council.

Art. 114. Upon the adoption of the Provincial Self-Government Law, it shall be immediately submitted to the Judicial Yuan. If the Judicial Yuan deems any part of it unconstitutional, the article violating the Constitution shall be declared null and void.

Art. 115. If, in the course of enforcement of the Provincial Self-Government Law, a serious obstacle should arise on account of a certain article therein, the Judicial Yuan shall first summon the various parties concerned to present their views, and then the Presidents of the Executive Yuan, Legislative Yuan, Judicial Yuan, Examination Yuan, and Control Yuan shall constitute a committee, of which the President of the Judicial Yuan shall be chairman, to propose measures of settlement.

Art. 116. Provincial laws and regulations which are in conflict with the national laws shall be null and void.

Art. 117. When doubt arises as to whether there is a conflict between the provincial laws and regulations and the national laws, the matter shall be interpreted by the Judicial Yuan.

Art. 118. The self-government of municipalities under the direct jurisdiction of the National Government shall be prescribed by law.

Art. 119. The local self-government system of the various Mongolian Leagues and Banners shall be prescribed by law.

Art. 120. The self-government system of Tibet shall be guaranteed.

Section 2. The *Hsien*

Art. 121. The *hsien* shall enforce *hsien* self-government.

Art. 122. The *hsien* may convene a *Hsien* Assembly to adopt, in accordance with the General Rules Governing Provincial and *Hsien* Self-Government, a *Hsien* Self-Government Law, but it shall not be in conflict with the Constitution or with the Provincial Self-Government Law.

Art. 123. Citizens of the *hsien*, with respect to matters concerning *hsien* self-government, shall, in accordance with law, exercise the powers of initiative and referendum, and with respect to the magistrate and other *hsien* self-governing personnel, shall, in accordance with law, exercise the powers of election and recall.

Art. 124. The *hsien* shall have a *Hsien* Council. Members of the *Hsien* Council shall be elected by the citizens of the *hsien*.

The powers of legislation which belong to the *hsien* shall be exercised by the *Hsien* Council.

Art. 125. *Hsien* laws and regulations which are in conflict with the national laws or with the provincial laws and regulations shall be null and void.

Art. 126. The *hsien* shall have a *Hsien* Government and a *Hsien* Magistrate. The *Hsien* Magistrate shall be elected by the citizens of the *hsien*.

Art. 127. The *Hsien* Magistrate shall administer matters of *hsien* self-government and shall also execute matters delegated to it by the Central and Provincial Governments.

Art. 128. The provisions governing the *hsien* shall, *mutatis mutandis*, apply to the municipalities.

CHAPTER XII. ELECTION, RECALL, INITIATIVE, AND REFERENDUM

Art. 129. The various kinds of elections stipulated in this Constitution, except as otherwise provided for by this Constitution, shall be carried out by the method of universal, equal, and direct suffrage and by secret ballot.

Art. 130. Citizens of the Republic of China having attained the age of twenty years shall, in accordance with law, have the right of suffrage. Except as otherwise provided for by this Constitution and laws, all citizens having attained the age of twenty-three years shall, in accordance with law, have the right to be elected to office.

Art. 131. The candidates in all elections provided for in this Constitution shall openly campaign for the election.

Art. 132. Coercion or inducement shall be strictly forbidden in elections. Suits arising out of elections shall be tried by the courts.

Art. 133. A person elected may, in accordance with law, be recalled by his constituency.

Art. 134. In the elections, the minimum number of women to be elected shall be fixed, and measures pertaining thereto shall be prescribed by law.

Art. 135. Measures with respect to the number and election of delegates of citizens in interior areas whose conditions of living and habits are peculiar to their section shall be prescribed by law.

Art. 136. The exercise of the powers of initiative and referendum by the people shall be prescribed by law.

CHAPTER XIII. FUNDAMENTAL NATIONAL POLICIES

Section 1. National Defense

Art. 137. The aim of national defense of the Republic of China shall be the safeguarding of the security of the state and the preserving of world peace.

The organization of national defense shall be prescribed by law.

Art. 138. The land, sea, and air forces of the whole country shall place themselves above all personal, regional, or party affiliations, shall be loyal to the state, and shall protect the people.

Art. 139. No political party or faction and no individual may utilize armed strength as an instrument of political struggle.

Art. 140. No member of the armed forces shall, during the period of active service, concurrently hold civil offices.

Section 2. Foreign Affairs

Art. 141. The foreign policy of the Republic of China shall, in the spirit of independence and initiative and on the basis of the principles of equality and reciprocity, cultivate friendly foreign relations and shall respect treaties and the United Nations Charter, in order to protect the rights and interests of overseas Chinese nationals, promote international coöperation, advance international justice, and ensure world peace.

Section 3. National Economy

Art. 142. National economy shall be based on the Principle of the People's Livelihood for equitable distribution of landownership and control of capital in order to obtain a well-balanced development of public economy and the people's livelihood.

Art. 143. All land within the territory of the Republic of China shall belong to the whole body of citizens. Private ownership of land, acquired by all persons in accordance with law, shall be protected and restricted by law. Privately owned land shall be liable to taxation according to its value and shall be subject to purchase by the government according to its value.

Mines embedded in the land and natural power which may be utilized economically for public benefit shall belong to the state and shall in no way be affected by the people's acquisition of the right of ownership over such land.

If any land has an increase in its value not through exertion of labor and the employment of capital, the state shall levy thereon an increment tax, the proceeds of which shall be enjoyed by the people in common.

In the distribution and adjustment of land, the state shall, as a principle, assist self-farming landowners and persons who make use of the land by themselves, and shall regulate their appropriate areas of operation.

Art. 144. Public utilities and other enterprises of monopolistic nature shall, as a principle, be publicly operated, but when permitted by law, they may be operated by the citizens.

Art. 145. The state, with respect to the wealth of private individuals and with respect to privately operated enterprises, shall restrict them by law, if they are deemed detrimental to the balanced development of the public economy and the people's livelihood.

Coöperative enterprises shall receive encouragement and assistance from the state.

The people's production enterprises and foreign trade shall receive encouragement, guidance, and protection from the state.

Art. 146. The state shall, through the employment of scientific technique, develop water conservancy, increase the productivity of land, improve agricultural conditions, plan for the utilization of land, and exploit agricultural resources, in order to bring about the industrialization of agriculture.

Art. 147. The Central Government, with a view to attaining a balanced economic development among the provinces, shall extend appropriate aid to poor and unproductive provinces. The province, with a view to attaining a balanced economic development among the *hsien*, shall extend appropriate aid to poor and unproductive *hsien*.

Art. 148. Within the territorial boundaries of the Republic of China, all goods shall be permitted to flow freely.

Art. 149. Private credit institutions shall be subject to state control in accordance with law.

Art. 150. The state shall establish extensive credit institutions for the people in order to relieve unemployment.

Art. 151. The state, with respect to Chinese nationals residing abroad, shall assist and protect the development of their economic enterprises.

Section 4. Social Security

Art. 152. The state shall provide appropriate opportunity for work to all persons who are capable of work.

Art. 153. The state, in order to improve the livelihood of laborers and farmers and to improve their production skill, shall enact laws and carry out policies for the protection of laborers and farmers.

Women and children engaged in labor shall, according to their age and physical condition, be accorded special protection.

Art. 154. Both capital and labor shall, in accordance with the principles of harmony and coöperation, develop production enterprises. Mediation and arbitration of disputes between capital and labor shall be regulated by law.

Art. 155. The state, in order to promote social welfare, shall enforce a social insurance system. To the aged, the infirm, and the crippled who are unable to earn a living, and to victims of unusual calamities, the state shall extend appropriate aid and relief.

Art. 156. The state, in order to strengthen the foundation of national existence and development, shall protect motherhood and carry out the policy of promoting the welfare of women and children.

Art. 157. The state, in order to improve national health, shall extensively establish sanitation and health protection enterprises and a system of public medical service.

Section 5. Education and Culture

Art. 158. Education and culture shall aim at the development among the citizens of a national spirit, a democratic spirit, a national morality, sound and healthy physique, sciences, and the knowledge and ability to earn a livelihood.

Art. 159. All citizens shall have equal opportunity of receiving an education.

Art. 160. All children of school age from six to twelve shall receive primary education without payment of tuition fees. Those who are poor shall be supplied with books by the Government.

Citizens who have passed school age but have not received primary education shall receive all supplementary education without payment of tuition fees, and shall also be supplied with books by the Government.

Art. 161. The several levels of government shall extensively establish scholarships to aid students who possess a good record in scholarship and in conduct but who are financially unable to pursue advanced education.

Art. 162. All public and private educational and cultural institutions in the country shall, in accordance with law, be subject to the supervision of the state.

Art. 163. The state shall lay emphasis on a balanced development of education in various areas, and shall promote social education in order to raise the cultural standard of the citizens in general; educational and cultural expenses for distant border regions and poor and unproductive regions shall be subsidized by the National Treasury. Important educational and cultural enterprises of these regions may be undertaken or subsidized by the Central Government.

Art. 164. Expenses for education, science, and culture shall not be less than 15 per cent of the total amount of the budget estimate in the case of the Central Government, not less than 25 per cent of the total amount of the budget estimate in the case of the province, and not less than 35 per cent of the total amount of the budget estimate in the case of the municipality or the *hsien*. Educational and cultural foundations established in accordance with law and their property shall be protected.

Art. 165. The state shall safeguard the livelihood of persons engaged in education, sciences, or arts and shall, in accordance with the development of the national economy, increase their remuneration from time to time.

Art. 166. The state shall encourage scientific discoveries and inventions, and shall protect old landmarks and relics of historical, cultural, or artistic value.

Art. 167. The state shall extend encouragement or subsidies to the following enterprises or individuals:

(1) Educational enterprises in the country which have been operated with a good record by private individuals.

(2) Educational enterprises of Chinese nationals residing abroad which have been operated with a good record.

(3) Persons who have made discoveries in learning or in techniques.

(4) Persons who have long been engaged in education and with a good record.

Section 6. Border Regions

Art. 168. The state shall accord legal protection to the status of the nationalities in the border regions, and shall render special assistance to their undertakings of local self-government.

Art. 169. The state shall positively undertake and assist the development of education, culture, communications, water conservancy, health, and other economic and social enterprises of various nationalities in the border regions; with respect to the utilization of land, the state shall, according to the climate and the nature of the soil and in the light of what is deemed suitable to the life and habits of the people, give the land protection and help in its development.

CHAPTER XIV. ENFORCEMENT OF AND AMENDMENTS TO THE CONSTITUTION

Art. 170. The term "law" as used in this Constitution, denotes a law that shall have been passed by the Legislative Yuan and promulgated by the President of the Republic.

Art. 171. Laws in conflict with the Constitution shall be null and void.

When doubt arises as to whether or not a law is in conflict with the Constitution, the matter shall be interpreted by the Judicial Yuan.

Art. 172. Ordinances in conflict with the Constitution or with laws shall be null and void.

Art. 173. The power to interpret the Constitution shall reside in the Judicial Yuan.

Art. 174. Amendments to the Constitution shall be made in accordance with one of the following procedures:

(1) Upon the proposal of one-fifth of the total number of the delegates to the National Assembly and by a resolution of three-fourths of the delegates present at a meeting having a quorum of two-thirds of the entire Assembly, an amendment may be made.

(2) Upon the proposal of one-fourth of the members of the Legislative Yuan and by a resolution of three-fourths of the mem-

bers present at a meeting having a quorum of three-fourths of the members of the Yuan, an amendment may be drawn up and submitted to the National Assembly for referendum. Such a proposed amendment to the Constitution shall be publicly announced six months prior to the opening of the National Assembly.

Art. 175. Matters provided for in this Constitution which require separate enforcement measures shall be prescribed by law.

The preparatory procedure for the enforcement of this Constitution shall be decided upon by the Constitution-making National Assembly.

APPENDIX E

SUN YAT-SEN'S FUNDAMENTALS OF NATIONAL RECONSTRUCTION, APRIL 12, 1924[1]

I. The National Government shall reconstruct the Republic of China upon the basis of the revolutionary principles known as the "Three Principles of the People" and the Five-Power Constitution.

II. The first principle of reconstruction is that of popular livelihood or the promotion of the general welfare. In order to meet the most urgent needs of the people for food, clothing, shelter, and communication with one another, the Government shall coöperate with the people in the improvement of agriculture so that all may have sufficient food, in the development of the textile industry so that all may have sufficient clothing, in the building of houses on a large scale so that all may have comfortable homes, and in the building and improvement of roads and waterways so that all may conveniently travel and transport their goods.

III. The next principle of reconstruction is democracy. In order that the people may be fitted for participation in government, the Government shall instruct them in the exercise of their rights of voting for public officers, and of initiative, referendum, and recall.

IV. The third principle of reconstruction is nationalism. The Government shall protect the racial minorities within the country and assist them so that they may become able to exercise their rights of self-determination and self-government. It shall also resist oppression from foreign Powers and at the same time shall revise the treaties with the Powers so as to secure national independence and equality with all nations.

V. The process of reconstruction shall be divided into three periods: the period of military operations, the period of political tutelage, and the period of constitutional government.

VI. During the period of military operations the area of operations shall be subject to martial law. The military authorities shall use their power to suppress reactionary and counterrevolutionary forces and to propagate the principles of reconstruction so that the people may be enlightened and the country unified.

VII. Military government shall cease in any province and the period of political tutelage shall begin as soon as order within the province is restored.

VIII. During the period of political tutelage the Government shall appoint trained men, who have passed the civil service examinations, to assist the people in the several *hsien* in preparing for local self-government. When a census of any

[1] In Chinese, *Kuo-min cheng-fu chien-kuo ta-kang.* This translation is largely based on one by Frank W. Price and S. S. Chow and Edward Bing-shuey Lee, as used by Arthur N. Holcombe in his *The Chinese Revolution: a Phase in the Regeneration of a World Power* (1931), Appendix B.

hsien shall have been taken, the land therein surveyed, an efficient police force organized, roads built throughout the *hsien*, the people trained in the exercise of their political rights and accustomed to the performance of their civic duties according to the principles of the Revolution, and when officers shall have been elected to serve as *hsien* magistrates and councilors, then the *hsien* shall be deemed fit for full self-government.

IX. The people of a fully self-governing *hsien* shall have the rights of voting directly for public officers, of recall, initiative, and referendum.

X. At the beginning of self-government in each *hsien* the value of all land in private ownership shall be assessed in the following manner. The landowners shall first declare the value of their lands to the *hsien* government, which shall impose taxes upon the declared valuations, and may purchase the lands at any time at the declared valuations. If thereafter the lands rise in value in consequence of public improvements or social progress, the unearned increment shall accrue to the community and shall not be appropriated by the landowners.

XI. The annual revenue from land, the increase in land values, the products of public lands, forests and streams, and profits from mines and the development of water power, shall be paid to the local government and shall be used for the development of local industries, the care of the young and the aged, the relief of the poor and the distressed, the care of the sick, and for other public needs.

XII. If a *hsien* shall not possess sufficient capital to develop its natural resources or its industries and commerce on a sufficiently large scale and additional capital from outside the *hsien* shall be required, the central government shall give the necessary financial assistance and the profits shall be divided equally between the central and local governments.

XIII. Each *hsien* shall contribute a certain portion of its revenues and other income to the central government, the exact proportion to be determined annually by the representatives of the people and not to be less than 10 per cent nor more than 50 per cent.

XIV. After self-government shall have been established, each *hsien* shall be entitled to elect one representative to the national assembly and to participate in the government of the nation.

XV. All candidates for public offices, either elective or appointive, shall be required to qualify for office by passing examinations which shall be held by the central government.

XVI. When all the *hsien* within any province shall become fully self-governing, the period of constitutional government shall begin in that province. The provincial assembly shall elect a provincial governor to supervise the operation of self-government within the province. In all matters of national concern the provincial governor shall be subject to the authority of the central government.

XVII. During the period of constitutional government political authority shall be duly distributed between the central government and the local governments. Affairs of national interest shall be entrusted to the central government and those of local interest shall be entrusted to the local governments. There shall be neither undue centralization nor undue decentralization.

XVIII. The *hsien* shall be the unit of self-government. The provincial government shall be the intermediary between the central and the *hsien* governments and provide for effective coöperation between them.

XIX. At the beginning of the period of constitutional government the central government shall complete the organization of the five departments (Yuan), which shall exercise the five constitutional powers, as follows: the Executive Yuan, the Legislative Yuan, the Judicial Yuan, the Examination Yuan, and the Control Yuan.

XX. The Executive Yuan shall provisionally consist of the following ministries: (1) the Ministry of the Interior, (2) the Ministry of Foreign Affairs, (3) the Ministry of War, (4) the Ministry of Finance, (5) the Ministry of Agriculture and Mining, (6) the Ministry of Labor and Commerce, (7) the Ministry of Education, and (8) the Ministry of Communications.

XXI. Prior to the promulgation of the Constitution, the heads of the Yuan shall be appointed by and responsible to the President and shall be removable by him.

XXII. The Constitution shall be drafted by the Legislative Yuan upon the basis of the *Fundamentals of National Reconstruction*, in the light of experience gained during the period of political tutelage and from constitutional government in the provinces, and shall be published for the information of the people and for their consideration prior to its final adoption and promulgation.

XXIII. When a majority of the provinces shall have reached the period of constitutional government, that is, when they have well-established local self-government in all *hsien*, there shall be a National Assembly with power to adopt and promulgate the Constitution.

XXIV. When the Constitution shall have been promulgated, the central political power shall be vested in a National Assembly. The Congress shall have power to elect and to recall the officers of the central government and to initiate laws and disapprove laws adopted by the central government.

XXV. On the day of the promulgation of the Constitution constitutional government shall be deemed to have been established, and the people shall hold a national election in accordance with the Constitution. Three months thereafter the provisional government shall be dissolved and the government elected by the people shall succeed to its authority. This will complete the program of national reconstruction.

APPENDIX F

THE STATUTE OF THE CHUNG-KUO KUOMINTANG AS REVISED BY THE SIXTH NATIONAL CONGRESS, MAY 16, 1945[1]

CHAPTER I. PRINCIPLES OF THE PARTY

Art. 1. The Three People's Principles and the Five-Power Constitution shall be the principles of the Chung-kuo Kuomintang.

CHAPTER II. PARTY MEMBERSHIP

Art. 2. Any person who willingly accepts the Principles, carries out the resolutions, and observes the discipline of the Party, and fulfills the duties and obligations imposed by the Party, may apply for Party membership and, upon his application being accepted, shall become a member of the Party.

Art. 3. A member on being admitted shall take an oath. The regulations governing the oath shall be separately prescribed.

Art. 4. A member shall have the rights of discussion, voting, election, and of being elected.

Art. 5. A member shall receive a certificate of Party membership from the Party Organ to which he belongs. The regulations governing the certificate shall be separately prescribed.

Art. 6. A member on changing his residence shall immediately report same to the Sub-*ch'ü* Party Organ at his original domicile and register at the Sub-*Ch'ü* Party Organ at his new domicile and become a member thereof. Failure to report or register within two months after his change of residence shall be treated as violation of Party discipline.

CHAPTER III. ORGANIZATION OF THE PARTY ORGANS

Art. 7. The Organizational Principle of the Party shall be democratic centralism.

The important decisions of a Party Organ of any level shall be passed by the organ of power at that level. Free discussion shall be permitted before a decision is reached. Obedience shall be obligatory on the part of every member, once the decision is made.

Art. 8. The hierarchy of the Party Organs shall be as follows:

A. Nation: National Congress; Central Executive Committee.

B. Province: Provincial Congress; Provincial Executive Committee.

C. *Hsien*: *Hsien* Congress; *Hsien* Executive Committee.

D. *Ch'ü*: *Ch'ü* Members' Assembly or Congress; *Ch'ü* Executive Committee.

E. Sub-*Ch'ü*: Sub-*Ch'ü* Members' Assembly; Sub-*Ch'ü* Executive Committee.

Art. 9. The Organs of Power of the Party shall be as follows:

[1] Translation by the author.

A. National Congress, or, after its adjournment, the Central Executive Committee.

B. Provincial Congress, or, after its adjournment, the Provincial Executive Committee.

C. *Hsien* Congress, or, after its adjournment, the *Hsien* Executive Committee.

D. *Ch'ü* Members' Assembly or Congress, or, after its adjournment, the *Ch'ü* Executive Committee.

E. Sub-*Ch'ü* Members' Assembly or, after its adjournment, the Sub-*Ch'ü* Executive Committee.

Art. 10. The Party may, according to the occupations and vocations of its membership, organize appropriate Party Organs. The regulations governing such Party Organs shall be prescribed by the Central Executive Committee.

Art. 11. The *Hsien* Party Organ and the Party Organs at higher levels shall each have a Supervisory Committee, consisting of Supervisory Members elected by the respective congresses.

Art. 12. A Party Organ shall carry out the orders of a higher Party Organ. If the lower organ experiences difficulties in their execution, it may submit its views in writing to the higher organ. If the higher organ persists in demanding their execution, it must be obeyed.

Art. 13. When necessary, the Party may organize Party Corps. The regulations governing such Corps shall be prescribed by the Central Executive Committee.

CHAPTER IV. THE ORGANIZATION OF PARTY ORGANS IN SPECIAL AREAS

Art. 14. The Party Organs in special administrative areas, such as Mongolia and Tibet, shall be of the same rank as the Provincial Party Organs.

Art. 15. The Central Party Organ shall determine whether a locality should be considered a special area for the administration of Party affairs.

Art. 16. The Party Organ of a special municipality shall be of the same rank as that of a province, and shall be under the immediate direction and supervision of the Central Party Organ.

Art. 17. The Party Organs of important municipalities and towns shall be of the same rank as those of the *hsien* and shall be under the immediate direction and supervision of the Provincial Party Organ.

Art. 18. Party Organs for important municipalities and towns shall be established, when locations for their establishment, submitted by the Provincial Party Organ, shall have received the approval of the Central Executive Committee.

Art. 19. The Overseas Head Organ shall have the same rank as that of the Provincial Party Organ; the Divisional Organ, that of the *Hsien* Party Organ; and the Branch Organ, that of the *Ch'ü* Party Organ.

CHAPTER V. TSUNG-LI (PRESIDENT)

Art. 20. The Party acknowledges the creator of the Three People's Principles and the Five-Power Constitution, Mr. Sun, as its *Tsung-li.*

Art. 21. Members shall accept the *Tsung-li*'s guidance and strive to promote the Principles of the Party.

Art. 22. The *Tsung-li* shall be the Chairman of the National Congress.

Art. 23. The *Tsung-li* shall be the Chairman of the Central Executive Committee.

Art. 24. The *Tsung-li* shall have the right to ask the National Congress to reconsider its resolutions.

Art. 25. The *Tsung-li* shall have the final power of decision with regard to the resolutions of the Central Executive Committee.

Addendum — When the *Tsung-li* died on March 12, 1925, the Second National Congress in January, 1926, accepted his Will and undertook to carry it out. This chapter is maintained as the Party's permanent memorial to him.

CHAPTER VI. TSUNG-TS'AI (LEADER)

Art. 26. The Party shall have a *Tsung-ts'ai*, to be elected by the National Congress. He shall exercise the powers appertaining to the *Tsung-li,* as provided in Chapter V.

CHAPTER VII. THE CENTRAL PARTY ORGANS

Art. 27. The National Congress of the Party shall be held every other year. The Central Executive Committee may convene an extraordinary congress when it considers it necessary or when requested by a majority of the provincial Party Organs and Party Organs of the same rank.

The Central Executive Committee may, in case of unavoidable contingencies, postpone the convening of the National Congress for a period not longer than one year.

Art. 28. The whole body of Party members shall be notified of the convening date and of the important items on the agenda of the National Congress three months before the convening.

Art. 29. Laws for the organization and election of the delegates to the National Congress shall be adopted by the Central Executive Committee.

Art. 30. The principal functions and powers of the National Congress shall be as follows:

A. To amend the Statute of the Party.

B. To examine the Work Reports of the Central Executive and Supervisory Committees.

C. To make decisions on the political programs and policies of the Party, and to discuss Party affairs and political problems.

D. To elect Central Executive and Supervisory members and reserve Executive and Supervisory members.

Art. 31. The number of Central Executive and Supervisory members shall be determined by the National Congress.

Art. 32. When vacancies occur among the Central Executive and Supervisory members, they shall be filled by the reserve Executive and Supervisory members, respectively and according to the proper order.

Art. 33. The functions and powers of the Central Executive Committee shall be as follows:

A. To represent the Party.

B. To carry out the resolutions of the National Congress.

C. To organize and direct the various Party Organs.

D. To control the finances of the Party.

Art. 34. The Central Executive Committee shall be obliged to carry out the resolutions of the Central Supervisory Committee. When necessary, the former may request the latter to reconsider its resolution once.

Art. 35. The Central Executive Committee shall meet in plenum every half year. The reserve Executive members may be present at such meetings. As many reserve Executive members present shall have the temporary right to vote as there are Executive members absent from the meeting, provided that the number of such reserve Executive members as have the right to vote does not exceed one-third of the Executive members present. All other reserve members present shall have only the right to discuss.

Art. 36. The Central Executive members shall elect from among themselves a number of Standing Members to constitute a Standing Committee. The Standing Committee shall perform the functions and powers of the Central Executive Committee during its adjournment, and shall be responsible to it.

Art. 37. The Central Executive Committee may, when necessary, appoint special committees.

Art. 38. The Central Executive Committee may designate its members or reserve members to visit the various Party Organs in order to guide them in their administration of party affairs.

Art. 39. The functions and powers of the Central Supervisory Committee shall be as follows:

A. To decide on disciplinary actions against Party Organs at the several levels and against individual members of the Party.

B. To audit the finances of the Party.

C. To examine the state of Party affairs in the whole nation.

D. To review whether the political activities of the members of the Party are based on the political programs and policies of the Party.

Art. 40. The Central Supervisory Committee shall meet in plenum every half year. The reserve Supervisory members shall be present at such meetings. As many reserve Supervisory members present shall have the temporary right to vote as there are Supervisory members absent from the meeting, provided that the number of such reserve Supervisory members as have the right to vote does not exceed one-third of the Supervisory members present. All other reserve Supervisory members shall have only the right to discuss.

Art. 41. The Central Supervisory members shall elect from among themselves a number of Standing Members to constitute a Standing Committee. The Standing Committee shall perform the functions of the Central Supervisory Committee during its adjournment.

Art. 42. The Central Supervisory Committee may designate members and reserve members to visit the various Party Organs in order to guide them in their administration of Party affairs.

Art. 43. The articles of organization for the Central Executive and Supervisory Committees shall be separately prescribed.

Art. 44. The National Congress and the plenary sessions of the Central Executive and Supervisory Committees shall be held at the place where the Central Party Organ is situated.

CHAPTER VIII. PROVINCIAL PARTY ORGANS

Art. 45. The Provincial Congress shall be held every year. An extraordinary congress may be held on the instance of one of the following:

A. On the instruction of the Central Executive Committee.

B. When considered necessary by the Provincial Executive Committee.

C. When considered necessary by the majority of the *Hsien* Executive Committees.

Art. 46. The laws for the organization and election of the delegates to the Provincial Congress shall be prepared by the Provincial Executive Committee and approved by the Central Executive Committee.

Art. 47. The functions and powers of the Provincial Congress shall be as follows:

A. To examine the Works Reports of the Provincial Executive and Supervisory Committees.

B. To plan the conduct of Party affairs in the province.

C. To discuss how the political programs and policies of the Party have been applied.

D. To elect the Provincial Executive and Supervisory members and reserve Executive and Supervisory members, whose numbers shall be determined by the Central Executive Committee.

Art. 48. The functions and powers of the Provincial Executive Committee shall be as follows:

A. To carry out the orders of the Central Party Organ and the resolutions of the Provincial Congress.

B. To organize and direct the Party Organs throughout the province.

C. To control the Party finances of the province.

Art. 49. The functions and powers of the Provincial Supervisory Committee shall be as follows:

A. To decide on disciplinary actions against the Party Organs and individual Party members under its juridiction.

B. To audit the Party finances of the province.

C. To examine the state of Party affairs in the province.

D. To review whether the political activities of the Party members of the province are based on the political programs and policies of the Party.

Art. 50. The Provincial Executive Committee shall meet once a week. The reserve Executive members shall be present at such meetings. As many reserve Executive members shall have the temporary right to vote as there are Executive members absent from the meeting, provided that the number of such reserve Executive members as have the right to vote does not exceed one-third of the members present. All other reserve Executive members shall have only the right to discuss.

The same provisions apply to the Provincial Supervisory Committee.

Art. 51. The Provincial Executive and Supervisory Committees shall each elect a number of Standing Members to perform the routine duties.

Art. 52. When vacancies occur among the Provincial Executive and Supervisory members, they shall be filled by the reserve Executive and Supervisory members respectively and according to the proper order.

CHAPTER IX. HSIEN PARTY ORGANS

Art. 53. The *Hsien* Congress shall be held every six months. An extraordinary Congress may be held on the instance of one of the following:

A. On the instruction of the Provincial Executive Committee.

B. When considered necessary by the *Hsien* Executive Committee.

C. On the request of the majority of the *Ch'ü* Executive Committees.

D. On the request of the majority of the Party members of the *Hsien*.

Art. 54. The laws for the organization and election of the delegates to the *Hsien* Congress shall be prepared by the *Hsien* Executive Committee and approved by the Provincial Executive Committee.

Art. 55. The functions and powers of the *Hsien* Executive Committee shall be as follows:

A. To examine the Works Reports of the *Hsien* Executive and Supervisory Committees.

B. To plan the conduct of Party affairs in the *Hsien*.

C. To discuss how the political programs and policies of the Party have been applied.

D. To elect *Hsien* Executive and Supervisory members and reserve Executive and Supervisory members, whose numbers shall be determined by the Central Executive Committee.

Art. 56. The functions and powers of the *Hsien* Executive Committee shall be as follows:

A. To carry out the orders of the superior Party Organs and the resolutions of the *Hsien* Congress.

B. To organize and direct the Party Organs at various places in the *Hsien*.

C. To control the Party finances of the *Hsien*.

Art. 57. The *Hsien* Executive Committee shall meet once a week. The reserve Executive members shall be present at such meetings. As many reserve Executive members shall have the temporary right to vote as there are Executive members absent from the meeting, provided that the number of such reserve Executive members as have the right to vote does not exceed one-third of the Executive members present. All other reserve Executive members shall have only the right to discuss.

The same provisions shall apply to the *Hsien* Supervisory Committee.

Art. 58. The functions and powers of the *Hsien* Supervisory Committee shall be as follows:

A. To decide on disciplinary actions against the Party Organs and individual Party members under its jurisdiction.

B. To audit the Party finances of the *Hsien*.

C. To examine the state of Party affairs in the *Hsien*.

D. To review whether the political activities of the Party members of the *Hsien* are based on the political programs and policies of the Party.

Art. 59. The *Hsien* Executive and Supervisory Committees shall each elect a Standing Member to perform the routine duties.

Art. 60. When vacancies occur among the *Hsien* Executive and Supervisory members, they shall be filled by the reserve Executive and Supervisory members respectively and according to the proper order.

CHAPTER X. CH'Ü PARTY ORGANS

Art. 61. The *Ch'ü* Members' Assembly shall be held every other month. When the size of the area or the number of the Party members under its jurisdiction is too large for the convening of a Members' Assembly, a *Ch'ü* Congress may be held instead if approved by the *Hsien* Executive Committee.

Art. 62. The functions and powers of the *Ch'ü* Members' Assembly or Congress shall be as follows:

A. To examine the Works Reports of the *Ch'ü* Executive Committee.

B. To plan the conduct of Party affairs in the *Ch'ü*.

C. To discuss how the political programs and policies of the Party have been applied.

D. To elect the *Ch'ü* Executive Committee members and reserve Executive members.

Art. 63. The functions and powers of the *Ch'ü* Executive Committee shall be as follows:

A. To carry out the orders of the superior Party Organs and the resolutions of the *Ch'ü* Members' Assembly or Congress.

B. To organize and direct the Sub-*Ch'ü* Party Organs at various places in the *Ch'ü*.

C. To control the party finances of the *Ch'ü*.

Art. 64. The *Ch'ü* Executive Committee shall meet once every week. The reserve Executive members shall be present at such meetings. As many reserve Executive members shall have the temporary right to vote as there are Executive members absent from the meeting. All other reserve Executive members shall have only the right to discuss.

Art. 65. The *Ch'ü* Executive members shall elect one of themselves to be the Standing Member to perform the routine duties.

Art. 66. Whenever vacancies occur among the *Ch'ü* Executive members, they shall be filled by the reserve Executive members according to the proper order.

CHAPTER XI. SUB-CH'Ü PARTY ORGANS

Art. 67. The Sub-*Ch'ü* Party Organ shall be the basic organization of the Party and shall have as a rule ten to fifty Party members.

Art. 68. The Sub-*Ch'ü* Members' Assembly shall be held once every month, and shall have the following functions and powers:

A. To examine the Works Report of the Sub-*Ch'ü* Executive Committee.

B. To adopt means for the conduct of Party affairs of the Sub-*Ch'ü*.

C. To study the principles and political programs of the Party and discuss Party affairs and political problems.

D. To elect the Sub-*Ch'ü* Executive members and the reserve Executive members.

Art. 69. The Sub-*Ch'ü* Party Organ shall have three Executive members and two reserve Executive members. The same shall constitute the Sub-*Ch'ü* Executive Committee, of which the functions and powers shall be as follows:

A. To examine the Works Report of the Secretary.

B. To recruit and train Party members.

C. To assign work for the Party members and to appraise their work.

D. To propagate the principles and political programs and policies of the Party.

E. To recommend good and able people of the locality (for Party membership).

F. To collect membership dues and income and special contributions from Party members.

Art. 70. The Sub-*Ch'ü* Executive Committee shall meet once every two weeks. The reserve Executive members shall be present at such meetings. As many reserve Executive members shall have the temporary right to vote as there are Executive members absent from the meeting. All other reserve Executive members shall have only the right to discuss.

Art. 71. The Sub-*Ch'ü* Executive members

shall elect one of their number to be Secretary to perform the routine duties.

Art. 72. Whenever vacancies occur among the Sub-*Ch'ü* Executive members, they shall be filled by the reserve Executive members according to the proper order.

CHAPTER XII. TERMS OF OFFICE

Art. 73. A delegate to a congress shall cease to function as soon as the session of the congress is terminated. He shall, however, report on the proceedings and results of the congress to the Party Organ he has represented.

Art. 74. The terms of the Central Executive and Supervisory members shall be two years; those of the Provincial, *Hsien*, and *Ch'ü* Executive members and of the Provincial and *Hsien* Supervisory members shall be one year; and those of the Sub-*Ch'ü* Executive members, six months.

The terms of office of the reserve Executive and Supervisory members of the Party Organs at the several levels shall be the same as those of the Executive and Supervisory members.

CHAPTER XIII. DISCIPLINE

Art. 75. A member shall dutifully observe the following rules of discipline:

1. He shall observe the Statute of the Party and obey the orders and abide by the resolutions of the Party.
2. He shall rigorously keep the secrets of the Party.
3. He shall not leave the basic organization of the Party.
4. He shall not criticize individual Party members or Party Organs, in public.
5. He shall not join other political parties.
6. He shall not engage in factional organization (within the Party).

Addendum—The Party has a historical mission to strive for. The success of the Party depends on the stringency of the discipline. All members of the Party shall make the common endeavor.

Art. 76. Any Party member who violates any of the enumerated rules of discipline shall receive accordingly one of the following punishments:

1. Warning.
2. Suspension of his rights as a Party member for a definite period.
3. Expulsion from the Party for a period.
4. Permanent expulsion from the Party.

Expulsion shall be based on the accusation of a Party Organ at the lower level and the decision of the Provincial Party Organ, and, before it is carried out, it shall have the final approval of the Central Party Organ.

When the whole body of Party members of a locality violate any of the enumerated rules of discipline, one of the following actions shall be taken against them:

1. The whole body of Party members shall be required to register anew and a discriminatory action shall be in order.
2. The whole Party Organ shall be dissolved.

Art. 77. When an individual Party member or the whole body of Party members of a locality are accused or impeached, his or their acts shall be carefully investigated by the Supervisory Committee of the Party Organ having jurisdiction over him or them. The said Supervisory Committee may decide on the action against him or them, to be carried out by the Executive Committee of the same Party Organ. If the person or persons against whom action is pending demur at the said action, he or they may make appeal to the Executive Committee at the superior level and, if necessary, in time to the National Congress. Pending the decision of an Executive Committee at a superior level, or of the National Congress, the said action shall nevertheless be carried out.

The same procedure shall apply when a Party Organ is accused or impeached.

The National Congress may decide to restore Party membership to an individual Party member or to the whole body of Party members of a locality.

CHAPTER XIV. FINANCES

Art. 78. The finances of the Party shall consist of the dues, income contributions, and special contributions paid by the Party members and other incomes.

Art. 79. The amount of membership dues and income contributions to be assessed shall be determined by the Central Executive Committee.

When a Party member is unemployed and his unemployment has been registered with the Party Organ to which he belongs, he shall be exempt from paying membership dues, provided that the said Party Organ shall have made a report of the circumstances of the unemployment to the superior Party Organ.

Art. 80. A Party member who fails to pay dues or income contributions for three months without due approval shall be suspended from the enjoyment of the rights of a Party member.

CHAPTER XV. SUPPLEMENTARY PROVISIONS

Art. 81. The power of interpreting this Statute shall belong to the National Congress, or, during its adjournment, to the Central Executive Committee.

Art. 82. This Statute shall take effect on the day it is resolved and published by the National Congress.

APPENDIX G

NATIONAL CONGRESSES AND PLENARY SESSIONS OF THE CENTRAL EXECUTIVE COMMITTEE OF THE KUOMINTANG

	Date	*Place*
First Congress	January 20–30, 1924	Canton
First Session of C.E.C.	January 31–February 6, 1924	Canton
Second Session of C.E.C.	August 15, 1924	Canton
Third Session of C.E.C.	May 18–25, 1925	Canton
Second Congress	January 4–19, 1926	Canton
First Session of C.E.C.	January 22–25, 1926	Canton
Second Session of C.E.C.	May 15–22, 1926	Canton
Extraordinary Session of C.E.C.	July 2–7, 1926	Canton
Third Session of C.E.C.	March 10–17, 1927	Hankow
Fourth Session of C.E.C.	February 3–7, 1928	Nanking
Fifth Session of C.E.C.	August 7–15, 1928	Nanking
Third Congress	March 18–27, 1929	Nanking
First Session of C.E.C.	March 28–April 8, 1929	Nanking
Second Session of C.E.C.	June 10–18, 1929	Nanking
Third Session of C.E.C.	March 1–6, 1930	Nanking
Fourth Session of C.E.C.	November 13–18, 1930	Nanking
First Extraordinary Session of C.E.C.	May 1–2, 1931	Nanking
Fifth Session of C.E.C.	June 13–14, 1931	Nanking
Second Extraordinary Session of C.E.C.	November 9–11, 1931	Nanking
Fourth Congress	November 12–23, 1931	Nanking
First Session of C.E.C.	November 22–29, 1931	Nanking
Second Session of C.E.C.	March 1–6, 1932	Loyang
Third Session of C.E.C.	December 15–22, 1932	Nanking
Fourth Session of C.E.C.	January 20–25, 1934	Nanking
Fifth Session of C.E.C.	December 10–14, 1934	Nanking
Sixth Session of C.E.C.	November 1–6, 1935	Nanking
Fifth Congress	November 12–22, 1935	Nanking
First Session of C.E.C.	December 2–7, 1935	Nanking
Second Session of C.E.C.	July 10–14, 1936	Nanking
Third Session of C.E.C.	May 15–22, 1937	Nanking
Extraordinary Congress	March 29–April 1, 1938	Wuchang
Fourth Session of C.E.C.	April 6–8, 1938	Wuchang
Fifth Session of C.E.C.	January 21–29, 1939	Chungking
Sixth Session of C.E.C.	November 12–20, 1939	Chungking
Seventh Session of C.E.C.	July 1–8, 1940	Chungking
Eighth Session of C.E.C.	March 24–April 2, 1941	Chungking

Ninth Session of C.E.C.	December 17–23, 1941	Chungking
Tenth Session of C.E.C.	November 12–27, 1942	Chungking
Eleventh Session of C.E.C.	September 18–23, 1943	Chungking
Twelfth Session of C.E.C.	May 20–26, 1944	Chungking
Sixth Congress	May 5–21, 1945	Chungking
First Session of C.E.C.	May 28–31, 1945	Chungking
Second Session of C.E.C.	March 1–18, 1946	Chungking
Third Session of C.E.C.	March 15–24, 1947	Nanking
Fourth Session of C.E.C.	September 9–13, 1947	Nanking
Extraordinary Session of C.E.C.	April 4–6, 1948	Nanking

APPENDIX H

EVOLUTION OF THE POLITICAL COUNCIL

JULY 11, 1924. *Cheng-chih wei-yüan-hui* (Political council). 12 members appointed by the *Tsung-li* from Central Executive and Central Supervisory Committees. Advisory capacity. Responsible to C.E.C. for party affairs and to *Tsung-li* for political and foreign affairs.

APRIL 1925. *Cheng-chih wei-yüan-hui.* Earlier membership enlarged by coöption after death of *Tsung-li,* no longer confined to members of C.E.C. and C.S.C. General direction and supervision of Government. Responsible to C.E.C.

JANUARY 1926. *Cheng-chih wei-yüan-hui.* 9 members (subsequently increased) elected by C.E.C. from among members of C.E.C. and C.S.C. (subsequently also from outside). Authority and responsibility unchanged.

JULY 4, 1926. *Cheng-chih hui-i* (Political council). 21 members, composed of the earlier members plus members of the Standing Committee of C.E.C. Authority and responsibility same.

MARCH 3, 1927. *Cheng-chih hui-i* (Wuhan). 15 members, 6 elected by C.E.C., plus 9 members of Standing Committee of C.E.C. Authority and responsibility same.

APRIL 17, 1927. *Cheng-chih wei-yüan-hui* (Nanking). 34 members, 21 of original *Cheng-chih hui-i* plus 13 newly coöpted members. Authority and responsibility same.

SEPTEMBER 1927. *Chung-yang t'e-pieh wei-yüan-hui* (Central special committee). Committee of 29. Highest organ of Party. Had authority of general direction and supervision of Government.

MARCH 1, 1928. *Cheng-chih hui-i.* Indefinite size. Members not confined to members of C.E.C. and C.S.C. Appointed variously by C.E.C., by Standing Committee of C.E.C., and by coöption. Authority and responsibility same.

SEPTEMBER 29, 1928. *Cheng-chih hui-i.* All members of C.E.C. and C.S.C. as members. Authority same.

OCTOBER 8, 1928. *Cheng-chih hui-i.* All members of C.E.C. and C.S.C. and Council of National Government as members, plus other members elected by C.E.C., not exceeding half of total membership of C.E.C. and C.S.C. Authority and responsibility same.

APRIL 15, 1929. *Cheng-chih hui-i.* Membership reduced, not to exceed one half of total membership of C.E.C. and C.S.C., plus large number of reserve members and attending members, all elected by C.E.C. Authority and responsibility same.

NOVEMBER 24, 1930. *Cheng-chih hui-i.* Size indefinite. Persons not members of C.E.C. and C.S.C. were eligible, but were not to exceed one fourth of *Cheng-chih hui-i* members who belonged to C.E.C. and C.S.C. Subsequently this limit was exceeded. Authority and responsibility same.

DECEMBER 1931. *Cheng-chih hui-i.* All members of C.E.C. and C.S.C. made members, and reserve members of C.E.C. and C.S.C., and subsequently other persons, made attending members. Authority and responsibility same.

DECEMBER 6, 1935. *Cheng-chih wei-yüan-hui.* 19–25 members, elected by C.E.C. plus great numbers of attending members. Authority and responsibility same.

MARCH 9, 1936. *Cheng-chih wei-yüan-hui.* All members of the Standing Committee of C.E.C. and C.S.C. made members in addition to the original 19–25 members. Authority and responsibility same.

AUGUST 16, 1937. *Kuo-fang tsui-kao hui-i* (Supreme national defense counsel). Large and indefinite membership. Actual exercise of authority in hands of its Standing Commmittee, appointed by Standing Committee of C.E.C. Authority and responsibility same.

JANUARY 28, 1939. *Kuo-fang tsui-kao wei-yüan-hui* (Supreme national defense council). Large and indefinite membership. With a Standing Committee of 11 designated by the Chairman, who was concurrently *Tsung-ts'ai* of the Party. Actual exercise of authority vested in Standing Committee or Chairman. General direction and supervision of Party, Government, and military affairs.

APRIL 1, 1946. *Cheng-chih wei-yüan-hui.* 19–25 members appointed by C.E.C. on nomination of the *Tsung-ts'ai*, plus all members of the Standing Committee of C.E.C. and C.S.C. and Kuomintang members in high government offices, as ex officio members, plus also indefinite numbers of attending members. General direction and supervision of the Kuomintang members of the Government. Responsible to C.E.C.

APPENDIX I

ORGANIC LAW OF THE CENTRAL PEOPLE'S GOVERNMENT OF THE PEOPLE'S REPUBLIC OF CHINA PASSED BY THE FIRST SESSION OF THE CHINESE PEOPLE'S CONSULTATIVE CONFERENCE ON SEPTEMBER 27, 1949[1]

CHAPTER ONE. GENERAL PRINCIPLES

Art. 1. The People's Republic of China is a state of the People's democratic dictatorship, led by the working class, based on the alliance of workers and peasants, and rallying all democratic classes and various nationalities within the country.

Art. 2. The Government of the People's Republic of China is a government of the People's Congress system based on the principle of democratic centralism.

Art. 3. Prior to the convocation of the All-China People's Congress through universal suffrage, the plenary session of the Chinese People's Political Consultative Conference shall exercise the functions and powers of the All-China People's Congress, enact the organic law of the Central People's Government of the People's Republic of China, elect the Central People's Government Council of the People's Republic of China and vest this Council with the power of exercising state authority.

Art. 4. The Central People's Government Council represents the People's Republic of China in international relations and assumes leadership of the state authority at home.

Art. 5. The Central People's Government Council shall set up a State Administration Council as the highest executive organ for state administration; shall set up a People's Revolutionary Military Council as the supreme military command of the state; and shall set up a Supreme People's Court and a People's Procurator-General's Office as the highest judicial and supervisory organs of the country.

CHAPTER TWO. THE CENTRAL PEOPLE'S GOVERNMENT COUNCIL

Art. 6. The Central People's Government Council shall consist of a chairman and six vice-chairmen of the Central People's Government and 56 council members elected by the plenary session of the Chinese People's Political Consultative Conference and a secretary-general elected by and from the Central People's Government Council.

Art. 7. The Central People's Government Council exercises the following jurisdic-

[1] This Appendix, added to the original manuscript for reference, has been taken from *The China Weekly Review*, October 15, 1949, pp. 104–105, as released in English by the New China News Agency.

tion in accordance with the common program enacted by the plenary session of the Chinese People's Political Consultative Conference:

1. Enactment and interpretation of the laws of the state, promulgation of decrees and supervision of their execution.
2. Determination of the administrative policies of the state.
3. Annulment or amendment of the decisions and orders of State Administration Council, which do not conform to the laws and decrees of the state.
4. Ratification, abrogation or amendment of treaties and agreements concluded by the People's Republic of China with foreign countries.
5. Dealing with the question of war and peace.
6. Approval or revising of the state budget and final accounts.
7. Promulgation of the acts for general amnesty and pardon.
8. Instituting and awarding of orders and medals and conferring of titles of honor of the state.
9. Appointment or removal of the following government personnel:
   a. Appointment or removal of the premier, deputy premier, and members of the State Administration Council; secretary-general and assistant secretaries-general of the State Administration Council; chairman, vice-chairmen, and members of the various committees and commissions; ministers and vice-ministers of the various ministries; president and vice-presidents of the Academy of Sciences; directors and assistant-directors of the various administrations; and manager and assistant-managers of the bank.
   b. Appointment or removal or ratification of the appointment or removal on the recommendation of the State Administration Council, the chairmen, vice-chairmen and main administrative personnel of various administrative areas and various provincial, municipal people's governments.
   c. Appointment or removal of ambassadors, ministers, and plenipotentiary representatives to foreign states.
   d. Appointment or removal of the chairman, vice-chairmen, and members of the People's Revolutionary Military Council, the commander-in-chief, deputy commander-in-chief, chief of staff, and deputy chief of staff of the People's Liberation Army, and the director and vice-director of the General Political Department of the People's Liberation Army.
   e. Appointment or removal of the chief justice, vice-chief justice and committee members of the Supreme People's Court, the procurator-general, vice-procurators-general, and committee members of the People's Procurator-General's Office.
10. Preparation for and convocation of the All-China People's Congress.

Art. 8. The chairman of the Central People's Government shall preside over the meetings of the Central People's Government Council and direct the work of the Central People's Government Council.

Art. 9. The vice-chairmen and secretary-general of the Central People's Government shall assist the chairman in the discharge of his duties.

Art. 10. The Central People's Government Council shall hold bi-monthly meetings convened by the chairman. The chairman may convene the meeting earlier or postpone it when necessary or upon the request of more than a third of the members of the Central People's Government Council or upon the request of the State Administration Council. More than half of the Council members are required to form a quorum and all resolutions shall be passed with the concurrence of more than one-half of the members present at the meeting.

Art. 11. The Central People's Government Council shall have a general office and may set up other subordinate working organs when necessary.

Art. 12. The organization regulations of the Central People's Government Council shall be enacted by the Central People's Government Council.

CHAPTER THREE. THE STATE ADMINISTRATION COUNCIL

Art. 13. The State Administration Council shall consist of a premier, a certain number of deputy premiers, a secretary-general and a certain number of members appointed by the Central People's Government Council.

Members of the State Administration Council may concurrently hold posts as chairmen of the various committees or commissions or as the ministers of the ministries.

Art. 14. The State Administration Council is responsible and accountable to the Central People's Government Council. When the Central People's Government Council adjourns, the State Administration Council shall be responsible and accountable to the Chairman of the Central People's Government.

Art. 15. The State Administration Council shall exercise the following jurisdiction on the basis and in pursuance of the common program of the Chinese People's Political Consultative Conference, laws and decrees of the State and the administrative policies stipulated by the Central People's Government Council:

a. Issue decisions and orders and verify their execution.

b. Annul or amend the decisions and orders of committees, ministries, commissions, academy, administrations, and bank, and all levels of governments, which do not conform to the laws and decrees of the state and the decisions and orders of the State Administration Council.

c. Submit bills to the Central People's Government Council.

d. Coordinate, unify and direct the interrelations, the internal organization and the general work of committees, ministries, commissions, academy, administrations, and bank and other subordinate organs.

e. Direct the work of local people's governments throughout the country.

f. Appoint or remove, confirm the appointment or removal of the main administrative personnel of the county and municipal level and above, not included in Article 7 (section 9-*b*).

Art. 16. The premier of the State Administration Council shall direct the affairs of the Council. The deputy premiers and the secretary-general of the State Administration Council shall assist the premier in the discharge of his duties.

Art. 17. The State Administration Council shall hold weekly meetings convened by the premier. The premier may convene the meeting earlier or postpone it when necessary, or upon the request of more than one-third of its members. More than half of the members of the State Administration Council are required to form a quorum, and resolutions shall be passed with the concurrence of more than one-half of the members present at the meeting.

The decisions and orders of the State Administration Council shall come into force with the signature of the premier or with the counter-signatures of the heads of the committees, ministries, commissions, academy, administrations, and bank concerned.

Art. 18. The State Administration Council shall set up a Committee of Political and Legal Affairs, a Committee of Finance and Economics, a Committee of Culture and Education, a Committee of People's Supervision, and the following ministries, commissions, academy, administrations, and bank, which shall direct their respective departments of state administration:

Ministry of Interior, Ministry of Foreign Affairs, Information Administration, Ministry of Public Security, Ministry of Finance, People's Bank, Ministry of Trade, Maritime Customs Administration, Ministry of Heavy Industries, Ministry of Fuel Industry, Ministry of Textile Industry, Ministry of Food Industry, Ministry of

Light Industries (not belonging to the above mentioned four industries), Ministry of Railways, Ministry of Post and Telegraph, Ministry of Communications, Ministry of Agriculture, Ministry of Forestry and Land Reclamation, Ministry of Water Conservancy, Ministry of Labor, Ministry of Culture, Ministry of Education, Academy of Sciences, News Administration, Publication Administration, Ministry of Public Health, Ministry of Justice, Commission of Law, Commission of Affairs of Nationalities, Commission of Overseas Chinese Affairs.

The Committee of Political and Legal Affairs shall direct the work of the Ministry of Interior, the Ministry of Public Security, the Ministry of Justice, the Commission of Law, and the Commission of the Affairs of Nationalities.

The Committee of Finance and Economics shall direct the work of the Ministry of Finance, the Ministry of Trade, the Ministry of Heavy Industries, the Ministry of Fuel Industry, the Ministry of Textile Industry, the Ministry of Food Industry, the Ministry of Light Industries, the Ministry of Railways, the Ministry of Post and Telegraph, the Ministry of Communications, the Ministry of Agriculture, the Ministry of Forestry and Land Reclamation, the Ministry of Water Conservancy, the Ministry of Labor, the People's Bank, and the Maritime Customs Administration.

The Committee of Culture and Education shall direct the work of the Ministry of Culture, the Ministry of Education, the Ministry of Public Health, the Academy of Science, the News Administration, and the Publication Administration.

In order to carry out their work, the committees may issue decisions and orders to the ministries, the commissions, the academy, the administrations, and the bank under their direction and other subordinate organs, and verify their execution.

The Committee of People's Supervision is responsible for the supervision of the execution of duties by government institutions, and government functionaries.

Art. 19. The ministries, commissions, academy, administrations, and bank may issue decisions and orders within their jurisdiction and verify their execution.

Art. 20. The State Administration Council shall have a secretariat to deal with day to day work and take charge of the files, archives and seal of the State Administration Council, etc.

Art. 21. The organization regulations of the State Administration Council and the committees, the ministries, the commissions, the Academy of Science, the administrations, bank, and the secretariat shall be enacted or ratified by the Central People's Government Council.

Art. 22. The Central People's Government Council may, when necessary, decide on the increase or reduction of the number or merging of the committees, ministries, commissions, academy, administrations, people's bank and the secretariat.

CHAPTER FOUR. THE PEOPLE'S REVOLUTIONARY MILITARY COUNCIL

Art. 23. The People's Liberation Army and other people's armed forces throughout the country shall come under the unified control and command of the People's Revolutionary Military Council.

Art. 24. The People's Revolutionary Military Council shall have a chairman, a certain number of vice-chairmen, and a certain number of council members.

Art. 25. The organization of the People's Revolutionary Military Council, and its administration and command shall be determined by the Central People's Government Council.

CHAPTER FIVE. THE SUPREME PEOPLE'S COURT AND THE PEOPLE'S PROCURATOR-GENERAL'S OFFICE

Art. 26. The Supreme People's Court is the highest judicial organ of the country, and is responsible for the directing and supervising of the judicial work of all the judicial organs of the country.

Art. 27. The Supreme People's Court shall have a chief justice and a certain number of vice-chief justices and a certain number of committee members.

Art. 28. The People's Procurator-General's Office has the greatest responsibility for the strict observance of the laws by all government institutions and government functionaries as well as nationals of the country.

Art. 29. The People's Procurator-General's Office shall have a procurator-general, a certain number of vice-procurators-general, and a certain number of committee members.

Art. 30. The organization regulations of the Supreme People's Court and the Office of the People's Procurator-General shall be enacted by the Central People's Government Council.

CHAPTER SIX. RIGHTS OF AMENDMENT AND INTERPRETATION OF THIS ORGANIC LAW

Art. 31. The right of amendment of the Organic Law of the Central People's Government belongs to the plenary session of the Chinese People's Political Consultative Conference, or to the Central People's Government Council when the People's Political Consultative Conference is not in session. The right of interpretation of the Organic Law belongs to the Central People's Government Council.

BIBLIOGRAPHY A[1]

BOOKS IN WESTERN LANGUAGES

Publications on China are enormous in number. A great majority of the more scholarly ones are concerned with the China of the past, dealing with particular aspects of Chinese culture, ancient texts, or other restricted and specific problems in Chinese history. A considerable number of books do discuss Chinese institutions and political philosophy, but few give adequate treatment to the origins and evolution of those institutions or to the background and consequences of that political philosophy. This is natural, since the interest of Chinese scholars in the past has been along these lines. Consequently, careful studies of institutions or political philosophy such as we now value have been neglected. Western scholars have necessarily been influenced by this emphasis or lack of emphasis.

It is true that books on the contemporary political scene in China are beginning to be published in greater numbers than a generation or even a decade ago. For our purposes, however, most of the recent publications of political interest are too journalistic to be of more than temporary value. Books on the government of China or on some aspect of it are still almost as rare as in the past.

Such being the nature of the publications in Western languages, it is not possible to present a selected bibliography of useful and valuable references such as could form a background for the understanding of Chinese government and politics of today and of the recent past. The majority of the useful materials will be found in newspapers, and in official reports and state papers issued from time to time by the governments of countries such as the United States and the United Kingdom which have a deep interest in China. The only drawback is that the newspaper materials are unorganized and the government reports and state papers are oftentimes unavailable to the general public or to the student.

The following is not a selected bibliography. Still less is it aimed at comprehensiveness. Rather it is a checklist of useful references. Since the more important references have already been commented upon in the footnotes in connection with the various topics treated, no further comments are deemed necessary here.

[1] In the preparation of this bibliography, free use has been made of Fairbank, *Bibliographical Guide to Modern China: Works in Western Languages*, draft, 80 pp. mimeo, Cambridge 1948.

1. BIBLIOGRAPHIES

Fairbank, John K., ed., *Bibliographical Guide to Modern China: Works in Western Languages*, Harvard University (mimeographed for private distribution), Cambridge, 1948. A critical bibliography which gives a more adequate coverage of political and constitutional topics than any other bibliography.

Gardner, Charles S., compiler, *A Union List of Selected Western Books on China in American Libraries*, American Council of Learned Societies, Washington, D.C., 1938. A list of 350 books and 21 periodicals of importance.

Goodrich, L. C., and H. C. Fenn, *A Syllabus of the History of Chinese Civilization and Culture*, 4th ed., China Society of America, New York, 1946. A brief bibliography which is adequate on cultural subjects.

Latourette, Kenneth S., *The Chinese, Their History and Culture*, 3rd ed., Macmillan, New York, 1946. Full and useful bibliographies at end of each chapter.

Pritchard, Earl H., ed., *Bulletin of Far Eastern Bibliography*, American Council of Learned Societies, Washington, D.C., vols. I–V, 1936–1940. Covers modern publications.

Far Eastern Quarterly, vol. I, no. 1, November 1941, to date, Far Eastern Association, Cornell University Press, Ithaca, New York. Continuation of Pritchard's bibliography, with special bibliographies issued by the *Far Eastern Quarterly*.

2. YEAR BOOKS

The China Year Book, London, Tientsin, and Shanghai, 1912– . Edited by H. G. W. Woodhead, H. T. Montague Bell, co-editor to 1921. Issues have appeared as follows: 1912, 1913, 1914, 1916, 1919 in London; 1921–1922, 1923, 1924, 1925, 1926, 1928, 1929–1930 in Tientsin; 1931, 1932, 1934, 1935, 1936, 1938, 1939 in Shanghai. Representing the British point of view, but very useful.

The Chinese Year Book, Commercial Press, Shanghai, 1936– . Published under the auspices of the Council of International Affairs. Issued as follows: 1935–1936, 1936–1937, 1937, 1938–1939, 1940–1941, 1943, 1944–1945. Representing generally the official point of view, but also useful.

China Handbook, 1937–1945, a Comprehensive Survey of Major Developments in China. New York and India, 1943– . Issues have appeared as follows: Macmillan, New York, 1943; rev. ed., India (1944); rev. and enl. ed. with 1946 supplement, Macmillan, New York, 1947. More partisan than the foregoing, but very useful.

3. PERIODICALS

A full list of periodicals and newspapers is included in Fairbank, *Bibliographical Guide to Modern China*, above cited, pp. 3–12. The more useful ones are as follows:

Amerasia; a Review of America and the Far East, New York, monthly, March 1937–1947. Edited by Frederick V. Field, Philip Jaffe, and others. Pronouncedly leftist.

China at War, China Information Publishing Co., Chungking, April 1938–December 1945. Continued as *China Magazine*, Chinese News Service, New York, monthly, May 1946– . Official but useful.

China Law Review, Soochow University Law School, Shanghai, quarterly, 1922–1933? Dealt primarily with legal topics.

China Magazine, Chinese News Service, monthly, New York, May 1946– . Continuation of *China at War*, China Information Publishing Co., Chungking, 1938–1945. Official, but useful.

China Quarterly, Shanghai and Chungking, quarterly, 1935–1939. Published first by the Institute of International Relations, the Pan-Asiatic Association of China, and the Institute of Social and Economic Research, and later by the China Quarterly Co. Articles on political subjects.

China Weekly Review, Shanghai, weekly, 1917– . From 1917 to 1921 the title was *Millard's Review of the Far East*; from 1921 to 1923, *Weekly Review of the Far East*. The most valuable periodical in regard to the contemporary scene.

Chinese Social and Political Science Review, Peking, quarterly, 1916–1937. Published by the Chinese Social and Political Science Association. Comparatively speaking, the most useful periodical for our purpose. Unfortunately discontinued.

Far Eastern Quarterly, Far Eastern Association, Cornell University, Ithaca, New York, quarterly, 1941– . Mostly historical studies. But there are a few articles on the modern period.

Far Eastern Survey, American Council, Institute of Pacific Relations, New York, fortnightly, 1932– . Excellent articles in recent years.

Foreign Policy Bulletin, Foreign Policy Association, New York, weekly, 1931– . Continuation of *News Bulletin*, weekly, 1921–1931. Useful information on contemporary topics.

Foreign Policy Reports, Foreign Policy Association, New York, 1931– . Continuation of *Editorial Information Service*, New York, 1925–1926, continued as *Information Service*, New York, 1926–1931. Occasionally informative reports on China.

Information Bulletin, published three times a month by the Council of International Affairs, Nanking, 1935–1937. More articles of political interest than in the *Chinese Social and Political Science Review*.

Pacific Affairs, Institute of Pacific Relations, New York, quarterly, 1928– . Generally devoted to economic and sociological studies. But also has articles of political interest.

4. HISTORY AND INTRODUCTORY READING

The best introductory reading on China is Fairbank, *The United States and China*. Latourette, *The Chinese, Their History and Culture*, and Eckel, *The Far East since 1500*, together provide a fairly good historical background to the modern Chinese scene. MacNair, *China in Revolution*, is the only book which presents with some adequacy the political history of the second and third decades of the present century. These books should be read by those who have little or no previous knowledge of China.

5. GOVERNMENT AND POLITICS IN GENERAL

There is not a single book which adequately describes or discusses Chinese government of the present period. Recommended here are: Wu Chih-fang, *Chinese Government and Politics*, Linebarger, *Government in Republican China*, and Tsao, *The Constitutional Structure of Modern China*. The last named is the most satisfactory of the three. There are about a score or more of journalistic reports on the political situation of the last decade, but few are objective. Sun Fo, *China Looks Forward* is recommended for the breadth of view the author displayed in his treatment of the domestic and external problems facing China in the last years of the war.

6. ALPHABETICAL LIST OF BOOKS AND PERIODICAL ARTICLES

(All titles cited in this book are included.)

Amann, Gustav, *Chiang Kaishek und die Regierung der Kuomintang in China*, K. Vowinckel, Heidelberg, etc., 1936.

———, *Sun Yatsens Vermachtnis: Geschichte der Chinesischen Revolution*, Vowinckel, Berlin, 1928. Translated by Frederick Philip Grove as *The Legacy of Sun Yat-sen; a History of the Chinese Revolution*, L. Carrier & Co., New York and Montreal, 1929.

Bain, H. Foster, *Ores and Industry in the Far East*, rev. enl. ed., Council on Foreign Relations, New York, 1933.

Bales, W. L., *Tso Tsung-t'ang; Soldier and Statesman of Old China*, Kelly and Walsh, Shanghai, 1937.

Band, Claire and William, *Two Years with the Chinese Communists*, Yale University Press, New Haven, 1948.

Bate, Don, *Wang Ching-wei, Puppet or Patriot*, R. F. Seymour, Chicago, 1941.

Bibliography of Modern Chinese Law in Library of Congress, comp. and ed. July–December 1944 by China Legal Section, Far Eastern Unit, Bureau of Foreign and Domestic Commerce, U.S. Department of Commerce, mimeo., China American Council of Commerce and Industry, Washington, D.C., 1945.

Biot, Edouard, *Essai sur l'Histoire de l'Instruction Publique en Chine*, B. Duprat, Paris, 1847.

Biot, Edouard, trans., *Le Tcheou-li ou Rites des Tcheou*, 3 vols., Imprimerie Nationale, Paris, 1851 (reprinted in Peking, 1939, by Wen T'ien Ko).

Bishop, Carl W., *Origin of the Far Eastern Civilizations: a Brief Handbook*, Smithsonian publication No. 3681, Washington, D.C., 1942.

Bisson, T. A., *Japan in China*, Macmillan, New York, 1938.

Borg, Dorothy, *American Policy and the Chinese Revolution, 1925–1928*, American Institute of Pacific Relations and Macmillan, New York, 1947.

Boulais, Le P. Guy, trans., *Manuel du Code Chinois*, Variétés Sinologiques no. 55, Imprimerie de la Mission Catholique, Shanghai, 1924.

Britton, Roswell S., *The Chinese Periodical Press, 1800–1912*, Kelly and Walsh, Shanghai, 1933.

Bruce, J. Percy, *Chu Hsi and His Masters; an Introduction to Chu Hsi and the Sung School of Chinese Philosophy*, Probsthain & Co., London, 1923.

Bruce, J. Percy, trans., *The Philosophy of Human Nature by Chu Hsi*, Probsthain & Co., London, 1922.

Buck, John L., *Chinese Farm Economy, a Study of 2866 Farms in Seventeen Localities and Seven Provinces in China*, University of Chicago Press, Chicago and Shanghai, 1930.

———, *Land Utilization in China; a Study of 16,786 Farms in 168 Localities and 38,256 Farm Families in Twenty-two Provinces in China, 1929–33*, 3 vols., University of Chicago Press, Chicago, 1937. Also published in Shanghai, 1937, by Commercial Press.

Buxton, L. H. D., *China, The Land and the People; a Human Geography*, Clarendon Press, Oxford, 1929.

———, *The Peoples of Asia*, Knopf, New York, 1925.

Cameron, Meribeth E., *The Reform Movement in China, 1898–1912*, Stanford University Press, Stanford University, California, 1931.

Carlson, Evans Fordyce, *The Chinese Army: Its Organization and Military Efficiency*, International Secretariat, Institute of Pacific Relations, New York, 1940.

Chan, Loi-ming, *The Development of Inter-Governmental Relations in China with Special Reference to Canton (Kwangtung Province)*, thesis, Harvard University, Cambridge, 1944. Typewritten.

Chan, Raymond Loi-ming, *An Outline of Inter-Governmental Relations in China*, mimeo., Harvard Graduate School of Public Administration, Cambridge, August, 1943.

Chang, Ray, "Trends in Chinese Public Administration," *Information Bulletin*, Council of International Affairs, Nanking, vol. III, no. 5 (Feb. 21, 1937), pp. 99–121.

Chavannes, Edouard, *Documents sur les Tou-kiue (Turcs) Occidentaux*, Commissionaires de l'Académie Impériale des Sciences, St. Petersburg, 1903. Printed in China, 1940, and reprinted in Paris, 1942, by Adrien-Maisonneuve.

Chavannes, Edouard, trans., *Les Mémoires Historiques de Se-ma Ts'ien*, 5 vols., E. Leroux, Paris, 1895–1905.

Chen, C. M. (Ch'en Chih-mai), "Impeachments of the Control Yuan," *Chinese Social and Political Science Review*, XIX (Oct. 1935–Jan. 1936), 331–366; 513–542.

Chen, Ta, *Population in Modern China*, University of Chicago, Chicago, 1946.

Chiang, Hai-ch'ao, *Die Wandlungen im Chinesischen Verfassungsrecht seit dem Zusammenbruch der Mandschu-Dynastie, unter besonderer Berücksichtigung der rechtlichen stellung des Staatshauptes*, Carl Heymanns Verlag, Berlin, 1937.

Chiang Kai-shek, *China's Destiny*, authorized translation by Wang Chung-hui, Macmillan, New York, 1947.

Chu Cheng, "War-time Judicial Administration," *China Quarterly*, IV, 11–16.

Civil Code of the Republic of China, translated into English by Ching-Lin Hsia, James E. Chow, Chieh Lu, and Yukon Cheng, Kelly and Walsh, Shanghai, 1931.

Clyde, Paul H., *The Far East, A History of the Impact of the West on Eastern Asia*, Prentice-Hall, New York, 1948.

———, *A History of the Modern and Contemporary Far East, A Survey of Western Contacts with Eastern Asia during the Nineteenth and Twentieth Centuries*, Prentice-Hall, New York, 1937.

Code Civil de la République de Chine, traduit du chinois par Ho Tchong-chan, Recueil Sirey (Société Anonyme), Paris, 1930–31.

Code of Criminal Procedure of the Republic of China and the Court Agreement relating to the Chinese in the International Settlement of Shanghai, China, translated by the Legal Department, Shanghai Municipal Council, Commercial Press, Shanghai, 1936.

Code Pénal de la République de Chine, promulgué le 19 mars 1928, entré en vigueur le 1er septembre 1928, traduit du chinois, avec une introduction, des notes, et une suite de textes complementaires et de documents annexes, par Jean Escarra. Préface de P. Garraud, M. Girard, Paris, 1930.

Code Pénal de la République Chinoise, texte chinois accompagné d'une traduction française par C. M. Ricard, Me Ph. Kou Cheou-Hi, P. C. Leblanc, et Wang Tse-Sin, Hautes Etudes, Tientsin, 1935.

Code de Procédure Civile (26 décembre 1930 et 3 février 1931) et *Loi sur la Conciliation en Matière Civil (20 janvier 1930)*, texte chinois et traduction française par Françoise Théry, Hautes Etudes, Tientsin, 1932.

Code de Procédure Civile (révisé) de la République Chinoise (1er juillet 1935), texte chinois et traduction française rev. et mise à jour à la date de promulgation du nouveau code par C. M. Ricard, Hautes Etudes, Tientsin, 1936.

Code de Procédure Pénale de la République Chinoise, texte chinois accompagné d'une traduction française sous la direction de P. C. Leblanc, Hautes Etudes, Tientsin, 1935.

Cordier, Henri, *Histoire Générale de la Chine*, 4 vols., P. Geuthner, Paris, 1920–1921.

Cressey, George B., *Asia's Lands and Peoples: A Geography of One-Third the Earth and Two-Thirds Its People*, McGraw-Hill, New York and London, 1944.

———, *China's Geographic Foundations, a Survey of the Land and its People*, McGraw-Hill, New York, 1934.

Criminal Code of the Republic of China (promulgated on 10th March 1928, by the Nationalist Government), translated into English by S. L. Burdett . . . in collaboration with Judge Lone Liang. . . . Dispatch Printing Co., Shanghai?, 1929?

Criminal Code of the Republic of China, translated into English by Chao-yuen C. Chang . . . foreword by the Hon. Sun Fo, Kelly and Walsh, Shanghai, 1935.

Dewey, John, "The Student Revolt in China," *New Republic*, vol. 20, August 6, 1919; and "The Sequel of the Student Revolt," *New Republic*, vol. 21, February 25, 1920.

Dubs, Homer H., *Hsüntze, the Moulder of Ancient Confucianism*, A. Probsthain, London, 1927.

Dubs, Homer H., trans., *The History of the Former Han Dynasty by Pan Ku*, 2 vols., Waverly Press, Baltimore, 1938, 1944.

Dubs, Homer H., ed. and trans., *The Works of Hsüntze*, A. Probsthain, London, 1928.

Dulles, Foster Rhea, *China and America, the Story of Their Relations since 1784*, Princeton University Press, Princeton, 1946.

Duyvendak, J. J. L., trans., *The Book of Lord Shang. A Classic of the Chinese School of Law*, A. Probsthain, London, 1928.

Eckel, Paul E., *The Far East since 1500*, Harcourt, Brace, New York, 1947.

Eléments de Droit Civil Chinois, translation of first three books of the Civil Code by François Théry, Recueil Sirey, Paris, 1939.

d'Elia, P. M., ed. and trans., *Le Triple Démisme de Suen Wên*, Shanghai, 1930. Translated as *The Triple Demism of Sun Yat-sen*, Franciscan Press, Wuchang, 1931.

Escarra, Jean, *Le Droit Chinois*, H. Vetch, Peiping, 1936 and Recueil Sirey, Paris, 1936.

Fairbank, John King, *The United States and China*, American Foreign Policy Library, Harvard University Press, Cambridge, 1948.

Fei, Hsiao-tung, *Peasant Life in China. A Field Study of Country Life in the Yangtze Valley*, G. Routledge & Sons, London, 1939.

Ferguson, J. C., "Political Parties of the Northern Sung Dynasty," *Journal of the North China Branch of the Royal Asiatic Society*, 1927, pp. 36 *et seq*.

Forke, Alfred, *Geschichte der alten chinesischen Philosophie*, L. Friederichsen & Co., Hamburg, 1927.

———, *Geschichte der mittelalterlichen chinesischen Philosophie*, Friederichsen, de Gruyter & Co., Hamburg, 1934.

———, *Mê Ti, des Socialethikers und seiner Schüler philosophische Werke* . . ., Kommissionsverlag der Vereinigung wissenschaftlicher Verleger, Berlin, 1922.

Franke, Otto, *Geschichte des Chinesischen Reiches*, 3 vols., Berlin, 1930–1937.

———, "Staatssocialistische Versuche im alten und mittelalterlichen China," *Sitzungsberichte der Preussischen Akademie der Wissenschaften, Philosophische-historische Klasse* (1931), XIII, 218–242.

Freeman, M., "The Ch'ing Dynasty Criticism of the Sung Politico-Philosophy," *Journal of the North China Branch of the Royal Asiatic Society*, 1928, p. 79 *et seq.*

Friedman, Irving S., *British Relations with China, 1931–1939*, International Secretariat, Institute of Pacific Relations, New York, 1940.

Fung, Yu-lan (Feng Yu-lan), *A History of Chinese Philosophy*, translated by Derk Bodde, H. Vetch, Peiping, 1937.

———, "The Philosophy of Chu Hsi," translated with introduction by Derk Bodde, *Harvard Journal of Asiatic Studies*, vol. 6, no. 1, March 1941.

———, "The Rise of Neo-Confucianism and its Borrowings from Buddhism and Taoism," translated with notes by Derk Bodde, *Harvard Journal of Asiatic Studies*, VII, 1–51, 89–125.

Fung, Yu-lan (Feng Yu-lan), trans., *Chuang-tzu*, Shanghai, 1932.

Gale, Esson M., trans., *Discourses on Salt and Iron: a Debate on State Control of Commerce and Industry in Ancient China, Chapters I–XIX*. Translated from the Chinese of Huan K'uan with introduction and notes, E. J. Brill, Leyden, 1931.

Gelder, Stuart, ed., *The Chinese Communists*, Victor Gollancz, London, 1946.

Giles, Herbert A., *A Chinese Biographical Dictionary*, B. Quaritch, London, and Kelly and Walsh, Shanghai, 1898.

Giles, Herbert A., trans., *Chuang Tzu, Mystic, Moralist, and Social Reformer*, 2nd ed., B. Quaritch, London, 1926.

Goodrich, L. Carrington, *A Short History of the Chinese People*, Harper, New York and London, 1943.

Granet, Marcel, *La Civilisation Chinoise; La Vie Publique et la Vie Privée*, La Renaissance du Livre, Paris, 1929.

Griswold, A. Whitney, *The Far Eastern Policy of the United States*, Harcourt, New York, 1938.

Grousset, René, *Les Civilisations de l'Orient*, 4 vols., G. Cres et Cie, Paris, 1930. Translated by Catherine A. Phillips as *The Civilizations of the East*, 4 vols., New York, 1931–1934, and H. Hamilton, London, 1934.

———, *L'Empire des Steppes: Attila, Genghis-Khan, Tamerlan*, Payrot, Paris, 1939.

———, *Histoire de l'Extrème Orient*, 2 vols., P. Guethner, Paris, 1929.

Hail, William J., *Tsêng Kuo-fan and the Taiping Rebellion*, Yale University Press, New Haven, 1927.

Henke, Frederick Goodrich, trans., *The Philosophy of Wang Yang-ming*, The Open Court Publishing Co., London, Chicago, 1916.

Herrmann, Albert, *Historical and Commercial Atlas of China*, Harvard University Press, Cambridge, 1935.

Hirth, Friedrich, *China and the Roman Orient: Researches into their ancient and medieval relations as represented in old Chinese records*, G. Hirth, Leipsic and Munich; Kelly and Walsh, Shanghai and Hongkong, 1885.

Hirth, Friedrich, "The Story of Chang K'ien: China's Pioneer in Western Asia," *Journal of the American Oriental Society*, XXXVII, (1919), 89–152.

Holcombe, Arthur N., *The Chinese Revolution: a Phase in the Regeneration of a World Power*, Harvard University Press, Cambridge, 1931.

Hornbeck, Stanley K., *Contemporary Politics in the Far East*, D. Appleton & Co., New York, 1916.

Hsia, C. L., "A Comparative Study of China's Draft Constitution with those of Other Modern States," *China Quarterly*, vol. 2, 1936–1937, no. 1, pp. 89–101. pp. 89–101.

Hsieh, Pao-chao, *The Government of China, 1644–1911*, Johns Hopkins Press, Baltimore, 1925.

Hsü, Yung-ying, *A Survey of the Shensi-Kansu-Ninghsia Border Region*, 2 vols., International Secretariat, Institute of Pacific Relations, 1945. (Mimeo.)

Hu, Shih, *The Chinese Renaissance*, University of Chicago Press, Chicago, 1934.

Hu, Shih (Suh Hu), "The Logic of Moh Ti and His School," *Chinese Recorder* (1921), LII, 668–677, 751–758, 833–843.

Huang, Siu-chi, *Lu Hsiang-shan, a Twelfth Century Chinese Idealist Philosopher*, American Oriental Society, New Haven, 1944.

Hudson, Geoffrey Francis, *Europe and China: a Survey of Their Relations from Earliest Times to 1800*, E. Arnold & Co., London, 1931.

Hummel, Arthur W., ed., *Eminent Chinese of the Ch'ing Period, 1644–1912*, 2 vols., U.S. Government Printing Office, Washington, D.C., 1943–1944.

Isaacs, Harold R., *The Tragedy of the Chinese Revolution*, Secker & Warburg, London, 1938.

Joseph, Philip, *Foreign Diplomacy in China, 1894–1900*, Allen and Unwin, London, 1928.

Juan, Vei Chow, "Mineral Resources of China," *Economic Geology*, vol. XVI, no. 4, June–July 1946.

Keeton, George W., *The Development of Extraterritoriality in China*, 2 vols., Longmans, Green, & Co., London, 1928.

Kent, P. H. B., *The Passing of the Manchus*, E. Arnold, London, 1912.

Koo, T. H., "Constitutional Development of the Western Han Dynasty," *Journal of the American Oriental Society*, XL, 170–193.

Kracke, E. A., Jr., "Family vs. Merit in Chinese Civil Service Examinations under the Empire," *Harvard Journal of Asiatic Studies*, vol. 10, no. 2, Sept. 1947, pp. 103–123.

Krause, F. E. A., *Geschichte Ostasiens*, 3 vols., Vandenhoeck und Ruprecht, Göttingen, 1925.

Lamb, J. D. H. (Lin Tung-hai), *Development of the Agrarian Movement and Agrarian Legislation in China, 1912–1930*, Yenching University, Peiping, 1931.

Lang, Olga, *Chinese Family and Society*, Yale University Press, New Haven, 1946.

Latourette, Kenneth Scott, *The Chinese, Their History and Culture*, 3rd ed., rev., two vols. in one, Macmillan, New York, 1946.

———, *A History of Christian Missions in China*, Macmillan, New York, 1929.

———, *A Short History of the Far East*, Macmillan, New York, 1946.

Lattimore, Owen and Eleanor, *China: A Short History*, Norton, New York, 1947.

Lattimore, Owen, *Inner Asian Frontiers of China*, American Geographical Society Research Series, no. 21, London and New York, 1940.

———, *Manchuria, Cradle of Conflict*, Macmillan, New York, 1932.

———, *Solution in Asia*, Little, Brown, Boston, 1945.

Leang K'i-Tch'ao (Liang Ch'i-ch'ao), *La Conception de la Loi et les Théories des Légistes à la Veille des Ts'in*, translated by J. Escarra and R. Germain, China Booksellers, Ltd., Peking, 1926.

Legge, James, trans., *The Chinese Classics*, 2nd ed., rev., 7 vols., Clarendon Press, Oxford, 1893–1895.

———, *The Yi King*, in *Sacred Books of the East*, ed. by F. Max Müller, vol. 16, Clarendon Press, Oxford, 1882.

———, *The Li Chi*, in *Sacred Books of the East*, ed. by F. Max Müller, vols. 27–28, Clarendon Press, Oxford, 1885.

———, *The Texts of Taoism*, in *Sacred Books of the East*, ed. by F. Max Müller, vols. 39–40, Clarendon Press, Oxford, 1891.

Li Chi, *The Formation of the Chinese People, an Anthropological Enquiry*, Harvard University Press, Cambridge, 1928.

Liang Ch'i-ch'ao, *History of Chinese Political Thought during the Early Tsin Period*, translated by L. T. Chen, Harcourt, Brace, New York, 1930.

Liang, J'en Kié, *Etude sur la Juridiction Administrative en Chine*, Jouve et Cie, Paris, 1920.

Liao, Wen Kuei, trans., *The Complete Works of Han Fei Tzu; a Classic of Chinese Legalism*, vol. I, A. Probsthain, London, 1939.

Lieu, D. K. (Liu Ta-chün), *China's Industries and Finance*, Chinese Government Bureau of Economic Information, Peking and Shanghai (*ca.* 1927).

Lin Mousheng, *Men and Ideas: An Informal History of Chinese Political Thought*, John Day, New York, 1942.

Linebarger, Paul M. A., *The China of Chiang Kai-shek; a Political Study*, World Peace Foundation, Boston, 1941.

———, *Government in Republican China*, McGraw-Hill, New York and London, 1938.

——, *The Political Doctrines of Sun Yat-sen, an Exposition of the San Min Chu I; a Dissertation*, Johns Hopkins Press, Baltimore, 1937.

Loi d'Organisation des Tribunaux (28 octobre 1932); Loi d'Organisation de la Cour Administrative (17 novembre 1932); Loi sur les Procès Administratifs (17 novembre 1932); Loi sur les Recours (en matière Administrative) (24 mars 1930), translated by François Théry, Hautes Etudes, Tientsin, 1933.

Lyall, Leonard A., *Mencius*, Longmans, Green & Co., London and New York, 1932.

MacNair, Harley Farnsworth, *China in Revolution: An Analysis of Politics and Militarism under the Republic*, University of Chicago Press, Chicago, 1931.

——, *Modern Chinese History—Selected Readings*, Commercial Press, Shanghai, 1933.

MacNair, Harley Farnsworth, ed., *China*, University of California, Berkeley, 1946.

de Mailla, J. A. M. de Moyriac, *Histoire Générale de la Chine*, 13 vols., Paris, 1777–1785. Based on *T'ung Chien Kang Mu.*

Mallory, Walter H., *China: Land of Famine*, American Geographical Society, New York, 1926.

Mao Tse-tung, *China's New Democracy*, New Century Publishers, New York, 1945.

——, *On Coalition Government*, New China News Agency (Yenan?), 1945.

Maspero, Henri, *La Chine Antique*, E. de Boccard, Paris, 1927.

Mayers, William Frederick, *The Chinese Government, a Manual of Chinese Titles, categorically arranged and explained, with an appendix*, 3rd and rev. ed. by G. M. H. Playfair, Kelly and Walsh, Shanghai, 1897.

McGovern, William Montgomery, *The Early Empires of Central Asia: A Study of the Scythians and the Part they played in World History*, University of North Carolina Press, Chapel Hill, 1939.

Mei, Yi-Pao, trans., *The Ethical and Political Works of Motse, translated from the Original Chinese Text*, A. Probsthain, London, 1929.

Mei, Y. P., *Motse . . . the Neglected Rival of Confucius*, A. Probsthain, London, 1934.

Michael, Franz, *The Origin of Manchu Rule in China, Frontier and Bureaucracy as Interacting Forces in the Chinese Empire*, Johns Hopkins Press, Baltimore, 1942.

Monroe, Paul, *A Report on Education in China*, Institute of International Education, New York, 1922.

de Morant, Georges S., *Extraterritorialité et Interêts Etrangers en Chine*, P. Guethner, Paris and Shanghai, 1925.

Morgan, Evan, trans., *Tao, the Great Luminant; essays from Huai Nan Tzu, with introductory articles, notes, analyses*, Kelly and Walsh, Shanghai, 1933.

Morse, Hosea Ballou, *The International Relations of the Chinese Empire*, 3 vols., Shanghai, 1910–1918; Longmans, London, 1918.

Morse, Hosea Ballou, and Harley Farnsworth MacNair, *Far Eastern International Relations*, Houghton Mifflin, Boston, 1931.

Norins, Martin Richard, *Gateway to Asia: Sinkiang*, John Day, New York, 1944.

Ouang, T. T., *Le Gouvernement de la Chine Moderne: essai sur la réglementation des pouvoirs publics et sur les rapports entre le gouvernement central et le gouvernement des provinces*, Jouve, Paris, 1923.

Pan, Wei-tung, *The Chinese Constitution: A Study of Forty Years of Constitution-Making in China*, Institute of Chinese Culture, Washington, D.C., 1946.

Parker, E. H., "Hwai-nan Tsz, Philosopher and Prince," *New China Review*, I, 505–521.

———, "Some More about Hwai-nan Tsz's Ideas," *New China Review*, II, 551–562.

———, *A Thousand Years of the Tartars*, 2nd ed., Knopf, New York, 1924.

Peake, Cyrus H., *Nationalism and Education in Modern China*, Columbia University Press, New York, 1932.

———, "Recent Studies on Chinese Law," *Political Science Quarterly*, Vol. 52, no. 1 (March 1937), pp. 117–138.

Peffer, Nathaniel, *Basis for Peace in the Far East*, Harper, New York, 1942.

———, *China, the Collapse of a Civilization*, John Day, New York, 1930.

Pelzer, Karl J., *Population and Land Utilization*, Part I of *An Economic Survey of the Pacific Area*, Institute of Pacific Relations, New York, 1941.

Pott, William S. A., *Chinese Political Philosophy*, Knopf, New York, 1925.

Pound, Roscoe, "Comparative Law and History as Bases for Chinese Law," *Harvard Law Review*, LXI, 749–762 (May 1948).

Pritchard, Earl H., *The Crucial Years of Early Anglo-Chinese Relations*, Pullman, Washington, 1936.

Räte-China, Dokumente der chinesischen Revolution, Verlagsgenossenschaft ausländischer Arbeiter in der USSR, Moskau-Leningrad, 1934.

Reichwein, Adolf, *China and Europe: Intellectual and Artistic Contacts in the Eighteenth Century*, translated by J. C. Powell, Knopf, New York, 1925.

Report of the China–United States Agricultural Mission, Office of Foreign Agricultural Relations, U.S. Dept. of Agriculture, Washington, D.C., "Report no. 2," May 1947.

Riazânovskiĭ, V. A., *Chinese Civil Law*, Tientsin, 1938.

Richards, Ivor A., *Mencius on the Mind: Experiments in Multiple Definition*, K. Paul, Trench, Trubner & Co., London, 1932.

Rosinger, Lawrence K., *China's Crisis*, Knopf, New York, 1945.

———, *China's Wartime Politics, 1937–1944*, International Secretariat, Institute of Pacific Relations, Princeton University Press, Princeton, 1945.

des Rotours, Robert, "Les Grands Fonctionnaires des Provinces en Chine sous la Dynastie des T'ang," *T'oung Pao*, 1928, pp. 219–332.

———, *Le Traité des Examens (Siuan-kiu-tche), traduit de la Nouvelle Histoire des T'ang (Sin T'ang chou)*, Librairie E. Leroux, Hautes Etudes, Paris, 1932.

Rowbotham, Arnold H., *Missionary and Mandarin: the Jesuits at the Court of China*, University of California Press, Berkeley, 1942.

Rowe, David Nelson, *China Among the Powers*, Harcourt, Brace, New York, 1945.

Roy, Manabendra N., *Revolution and Counterrevolution in China*, translated from the German edition of 1931, Renaissance Publishers, Calcutta, 1946.

Russell, Bertrand, *The Problem of China*, Century, New York, 1922.

Schomberg, R. C. F., "Habitability of Chinese Turkestan," *Geographical Journal*, 1932,

Sharman, Lyon, *Sun Yat-sen, his Life and its Meaning, a Critical Biography*, John Day, New York, 1934.

Shirokogoroff, Sergei M., *Anthropology of Eastern China and Kwangtung Province*, Commercial Press, Shanghai, 1925.

———, *Anthropology of Northern China*, Royal Asiatic Society, North China Branch, Shanghai, 1923.

Shryock, John Knight, *The Origin and Développment of the State Cult of Confucius*, Century, New York, 1932.

Sie Ying-chou, *Le Fédéralisme en Chine: Etude sur quelques Constitutions Provinciales*, H. d'Arthez, Paris, 1924.

Skrine, Clarmont Percival, *Chinese Central Asia*, Houghton Mifflin, Boston and New York, 1926.

Smith, Arthur H., *China in Convulsion*, 2 vols., F. Revell & Co., New York, 1901.

———, *Village Life in China*, Revell Co., New York, 1899.

Smith, Wilfred, *A Geographical Study of Coal and Iron in China*, Hodder & Stoughton, London, 1926.

Snow, Edgar, *Red Star over China*, Modern Library, Random House, New York, 1944.

Soothill, William E., trans., *The Analects of Confucius*, Yokohama, 1910. Ed. by Lady Hosie, Oxford University Press, H. Milford, London, 1939.

Spalding, K. T., *Three Chinese Thinkers*, The National Central Library, Nanking, 1947.

Staunton, Sir Thomas, trans., *Ta Tsing Leu Lee . . . the fundamental laws and a selection from the supplementary statutes, of the Penal Code of China*, Cadell & Davies, 1810.

Steiger, George Nye, *China and the Occident: the Origin and Development of the Boxer Movement*, Yale University Press, New Haven, 1927.

Stein, Aurel, "A Chinese Expedition Across the Pamirs and Hindukush, A.D. 747," *New China Review*, IV, 161–183.

Stein, Gunther, *The Challenge of Red China*, McGraw-Hill, New York, London, 1945.

Strong, Anna Louise, *China's Millions, The Revolutionary Struggles from 1927 to 1935*, Knight, New York, 1935.

Sun Fo, *China Looks Forward*, George Allen & Unwin, London, 1944.

Sun Yat-sen, *The International Development of China*, G. P. Putnam's Sons, New York, 1922.

———, *San Min Chu I: The Three Principles of the People*, translated by Frank W. Price, ed. by L. T. Ch'en, Ministry of Information of the Republic of China, Chungking, 1943.

Tamagna, F., *Banking and Finance in China*, International Secretariat, Institute of Pacific Relations, New York, 1942.

Tang, Edgar C., "Five Years of the Control Yuan," *Information Bulletin*, Council of International Relations, vol. II, no. 7, Nov. 11, 1936, pp. 117–131.

———, "Judicial Reforms in China," *Information Bulletin*, Council of International Affairs, vol. III, no. 1, January 11, 1937, pp. 1–27.

T'ang, Leang-li, *The Inner History of the Chinese Revolution*, G. Routledge & Sons, London, 1930.

———, Leang-li, *Wang Ching-wei, a Political Biography*, China United Press, Peiping, 1931.

T'ang, Leang-li, ed., *Suppressing Communist Banditry in China*, China United Press, Shanghai, 1934.

Tao, Alfred C., "A Study of the Tax Structure in China; with some recommendations for the post-war period," Ph.D. thesis, Harvard University, Cambridge, 1946. Typewritten.

Tawney, R. H., *Land and Labor in China*, Harcourt, Brace, New York, 1932.

Tcheng Chao-yuen, *L'Evolution de la Vie Constitutionelle de la Chine sous l'Influence de Sun Yat-sen et de sa Doctrine*, Librairie Générale de Droit et de Jurisprudence, Paris, 1937.

Thomas, Elbert Duncan, *Chinese Political Theories; a study based upon the theories of the principal thinkers of the Chou period*, Prentice-Hall, New York, 1927.

Thompson, Warren S., *Population and Peace in the Pacific*, University of Chicago Press, Chicago, 1946.

Thorp, James, "Colonization Possibilities of Northwestern China and Inner Mongolia," *Pacific Affairs*, Dec. 1935, pp. 447–454.

———, *The Geography of the Soils of China*, National Geographical Survey, Nanking, 1936.

The Ting Hsien Experiment in 1934, Mass Education Movement, Peiping, 1934.

Tong, Hollington K., *Chiang Kai-shek: Soldier and Statesman*, 2 vols., China Publishing Co., Shanghai, 1937.

Tsao, Wen-yen, *The Constitutional Structure of Modern China*, Melbourne University Press, Victoria, Australia, 1947.

Tsui, Shu-Chin, "The Influence of the Canton-Moscow Entente upon Sun Yat-sen's Political Philosophy and Revolutionary Tactics," Ph.D. thesis, Harvard University, Cambridge, 1933. Typewritten.

Tyau, Min-ch'ien Tuk Zung, *Two Years of Nationalist China*, Kelly and Walsh, Shanghai, 1930.

———, "The Work of Organization of the Legislative Yuan," *China Quarterly*, II, 73–88.

Utley, Freda, *Last Chance in China*, Bobbs-Merrill, New York, 1947.

van der Valk, Marc, *An Outline of Modern Chinese Family Law* (*Monumenta Serica*, Monograph II), H. Vetch, Peiping, 1939.

Van Dorn, Harold A., *Twenty Years of the Chinese Republic*, Knopf, New York, 1932.

Vinacke, Harold M., *A History of the Far East in Modern Times*, 4th rev. ed., Crofts, New York, 1941.

———, *Modern Constitutional Development in China*, Princeton University Press, Princeton, 1920.

Waley, Arthur, *The Way and Its Power*, London, 1934.

Wang, Ching-wei (Wang Chao-ming), *The Chinese National Revolution, Essays and Documents*, China United Press, Peiping, 1931.

Wang, Chung Hui, *Law Reform in China*, G. Allen & Unwin, London, 1919.

Wang, Gung-hsing, *The Chinese Mind*, John Day, New York, 1946.

Wang, Kan-yu, "The Hsien (County) Government in China," Ph.D. thesis, Harvard University, Cambridge, 1947. Typewritten.

Wang Tchang-tche, *La Philosophie Morale de Wang Ying-ming*, Imprimerie et librairie de T'ou-Se-Wè, Shanghai, 1936.

Wieger, Léon, *Histoire des Croyances Réligieuses et des Philosophiques en Chine, depuis l'origine jusqu'à nos jours* (1917), Hsien-hsien, 1927. Translated into English by E. T. C. Werner, Hsien-Hsien Press, Hsien-hsien, 1927.

Wilhelm, Hellmut, *Gesellschaft und Staat in China, Acht Vortrage*, Henry Vetch, Peking, 1944.

William, Maurice, *The Social Interpretation of History*, New York, 1921.

———, *Sun Yat-sen versus Communism*, Williams & Wilkins, Baltimore, 1932.

Williams, Edward Thomas, *China Yesterday and Today*, Thomas Y. Crowell, New York, 1923.

Williams, S. Wells, *The Middle Kingdom, a Survey of the Geography, Government, Literature, Social Life, Arts, and History of the Chinese Empire*, 2 vols., Scribner's, New York, 1901.

Williamson, Henry R., *Wang An Shih, A Chinese Statesman and Educator of the Sung Dynasty*, 2 vols., A. Probsthain, London, 1937.

Willoughby, Westel Woodbury, *Constitutional Government in China; Present Conditions and Prospects*, Carnegie Endowment for International Peace, Washington, 1922.

———, *Foreign Rights and Interests in China*, rev. ed., 2 vols., Johns Hopkins Press, Baltimore, 1927.

Wittfogel, Karl A., "Public Office in the Liao Dynasty and the Chinese Examination System," *Harvard Journal of Asiatic Studies*, vol. 10, no. 1, June 1947, pp. 13–40.

———, "The Society of Prehistoric China," *Zeitschrift für Sozialforschung*, Felix Alcan, Paris, 1939.

———, *Wirtschaft und Gesellschaft Chinas. Erster Teil, Produktivkräfte, Produktions- und Zirkulationsprozess*, C. L. Hirschfeld, Leipzig, 1931.

Woo, Thomas Tze Chung, *The Kuomintang and the Future of the Chinese Revolution*, G. Allen & Unwin, London, 1928.

Wu, Chih-fang, *Chinesc Government and Politics*, Commercial Press, Shanghai, 1934.

Wu, John Chin Hsiung, "Notes on the Final Draft Constitution," *T'ien Hsia Monthly*, vol. 10, no. 1, pp. 73–88.

Wu, Kuo-cheng, *Ancient Chinese Political Theories*, Commercial Press, Shanghai, 1928.

Yakhontoff, Victor A., *The Chinese Soviets*, Coward-McCann, New York, 1934.

Yen, Hawklin L., *A Survey of Constitutional Development in China*, Longmans, Green & Co., New York, 1911.

Zi, Étienne, "Pratique des Examens Littéraires en Chine," translated from the Latin by Ch. de Bussy and Henri Havret, *Variétés Sinologiques*, no. 5, Imprimerie de la Mission Catholique, Shanghai, 1894.

BIBLIOGRAPHY B

Books in Chinese

1. BIBLIOGRAPHIES

There are no compiled bibliographies which cover the subject matter of this book. In the book, *Modern China: A Bibliographical Guide to Chinese Works, 1898–1937* (Harvard University Press, 1950), compiled by John K. Fairbank and Kwang-ching Liu, sections on law, government, and politics of modern China are helpful, but the publications listed therein are largely confined to those that are to be found in Harvard libraries.

There are a number of book catalogues and finding lists prepared by Chinese publishers and individuals. They are not exhaustive and are apt to be unsystematically arranged. Most of them are listed in Fairbank and Liu's *Bibliographical Guide*. The printed catalogues of some university libraries like those of National Tsing Hua University and National Central University are more serviceable than the publishers' catalogues, for the former are better classified, and in the relevant sections on government and politics, useful references can be located with greater ease.

The reference lists either at the end of chapters or in footnotes in Hsiao Kung-ch'üan, *Chung-kuo cheng-chih ssu-hsiang shih* (A history of Chinese political thought), Ch'en Chih-mai, *Chung-kuo cheng-fu* (The government of China), and Wang Shih-chieh and Ch'ien Tuan-sheng, *Pi-chiao hsien-fa* (Comparative constitutional law) are as good bibliographies as can be found anywhere concerning the subject matter treated by these respective books. There is also a full bibliography in Ch'ien Tuan-sheng *et al., Min-kuo cheng-chih shih* (History of political institutions under the Republic).

2. YEAR BOOKS

There are two kinds of year books, those published by the commercial publishers and those by the various offices of the central government and provincial governments. For our purposes, the government publications are naturally more useful. But the reader should be warned that their publication is often irregular, the arrangement of data unsystematic, and figures unreliable. The more useful ones are *Chung-kuo nien-chien* (Chinese yearbook), published by the Commercial Press, vol. I, 1924; *Shen-pao nien-chien* (The Shen-pao yearbook), published by the Shen Pao annually for the years 1934, 1936, 1937; and *Kuo-ming cheng-fu nien-chien*, since 1933 (irregular). See bibliography in Ch'ien Tuan-sheng *et al., Min-kuo cheng-chih shih* (History of political institutions under the Republic).

3. PERIODICALS

There are several kinds of periodicals which supply material on Chinese government and politics. Many government and party organs publish periodicals which carry both official documents and special articles. A partial list of the periodicals is included in the bibliography in Ch'ien Tuan-sheng *et al., Min-kuo cheng-chih shih*. Of the critical reviews, the best are *T'ai-p'ing-yang* (The Pacific Ocean), monthly, 1917–1925; *Hsien-tai p'ing-lun* (The contemporary review), weekly, 1924–1928; *Tu-li p'ing-lun* (The independent review), weekly, 1932–1937; *Kuan-ch'a* (The observer), weekly, 1946– . The *Tung-fang tsa-chih* (The Far Eastern miscellany), monthly, 1908– , and *Kuo-wen chou-pao* (National news weekly), weekly, 1924–1937, are in a class by themselves. They carry much informative material, though their articles are generally not of a critical nature. Most of these reviews are listed in Fairbank and Liu, *Bibliographical Guide.*

4. GAZETTES AND OTHER OFFICIAL PUBLICATIONS

The Central Government, the Five Yuan and their ministries and commissions, and the provincial governments all publish gazettes. The *Cheng-fu ḳung-pao* or *Kuo-min cheng-fu ḳung-pao* (Government gazette or National Government gazette) has been a daily most of the time since its first publication in 1912. *Hsing-cheng-yuan ḳung-pao* (The Executive Yuan gazette) is a weekly. Others are generally either weekly or semi-monthly. The two above-mentioned are the most important. In addition, the *Chung-yang tang-wu yüeh-ḳ'an* (Central Party affairs monthly), 1928–1938, and its continuation, the *Chung-yang tang-wu ḳung-pao* (Gazette of Central Party affairs), also monthly, since 1929, contains a wealth of material on the Kuomintang. For a detailed list of the gazettes, see bibliography in Ch'ien Tuan-sheng *et al.*, *Min-ḳuo cheng-chih shih.*

5. COLLECTIONS OF LAWS AND DECREES

There are a great number of collections of laws and decrees, edited privately or by the government, adopted since the last years of the Ch'ing Dynasty. There are also collections of the resolutions and regulations adopted by the Kuomintang or its departments. Generally speaking, the ones published by the Commercial Press of Shanghai are more reliable and better edited. For a complete list, see bibliography in Ch'ien Tuan-sheng *et al.*, *Min-ḳuo cheng-chih shih.*

6. GENERAL WORKS ON MODERN POLITICAL HISTORY

The best general introductory reading that would help a foreign student to understand modern Chinese political history is Li Chien-nung, *Chung-ḳuo chin-pai-nien cheng-chih shih* (A political history of China in the last century). Chiang T'ing-fu (T. F. Tsiang), *Chung-ḳuo chin-tai shih* (A history of modern China) and Ch'en Kung-lu, *Chung-ḳuo chin-tai shih* are also useful. The former is a short book, but easily understandable to a foreign student. The latter is a more ambitious undertaking but less original. There are three recent works on general history of China, all entitled *Chung-ḳuo t'ung-shih* (A general history of China), one by Chang Yin-lin, another by Lü Ssu-mien, and the third by Chou Ku-ch'eng. Of the three, the first is the most brilliant, but to the uninitiated the more matter-of-fact narrative of Lü Ssu-mien is perhaps more useful.

7. BOOKS AND PERIODICALS

(This list of books and periodicals is arranged alphabetically according to romanization. All references cited in this book are included.)

Chang Chün-mai (Carsun Chang), *Li-ḳuo chih tao*, or *Kuo-chia she-hui chu-i* (The way to establish a nation, or national socialism), 1938.

張君勱　立國之道（一名國家社會主義）

Chang Yin-lin, *Chung-ḳuo t'ung-shih* (A general history of China). Consulted in unpublished form.

張蔭麟　中國通史

Ch'en Chih-mai, *Chung-ḳuo cheng-fu* (The government of China), 3 vols., Shang-wu yin-shu-kuan, Chungking and Shanghai, 1944–1945.

陳之邁　中國政府

Ch'en Ju-hsüan, *Hsin-ting Chung-kuo hsien-fa shih* (A new revised history of the Chinese constitution), Shih-chieh shu-chü, Shanghai, 1947.

陳茹玄 新訂中國憲法史

Ch'en Ku-yuan, *Chung-kuo fa-chih shih* (A history of Chinese law and institutions), Shang-wu yin-shu-kuan, Shanghai, 1934.

陳顧遠 中國法制史

Ch'en Ku-yuan, *Li-fa yao-chih* (The principles of legislation), Central Training Commission, Chungking, 1942.

陳顧遠 立法要制

Ch'en Kung-lu, *Chung-kuo chin-tai shih* (A history of modern China), Shang-wu yin-shu-kuan, Shanghai, 1935.

陳恭祿 中國近代史

Ch'en Lieh, *Fa-chia cheng-chih che-hsüeh* (The political philosophy of the legalists).

陳 烈 法家政治哲學

Ch'en Pai-hsin, *Chung-kuo ti-fang chih-tu chi ch'i kai-tsao* (Chinese local government and its reconstruction), Shang-wu yin-shu-kuan, Shanghai, 1939.

陳柏心 中國地方制度及其改造

Ch'en Pai-hsin, *Chung-kuo hsien-cheng kai-tsao* (Chinese *hsien* government and its reconstruction), Shang-wu yin-shu-kuan, Chungking, 1942.

陳柏心 中國縣政改造

Ch'en Pai-hsin, *Ti-fang tzu-chih yü hsin-hsien-chih* (Local self-government and the new *hsien* system), Shang-wu yin-shu-kuan, Chungking, 1943.

陳柏心 地方自治與新縣制

Ch'en Te-chang, *Chung-hua min-kuo hsien-fa shih-liao* (Historical documents of the constitution of the Republic of China), Hsin-chung-kuo chien-she hsüeh-hui, Shanghai, 1933.

岑德彰 中華民國憲法史料

Ch'eng Fang, *Chung-kuo hsien-cheng kai-lun* (A general course on Chinese *hsien* government), 2 vols., Shang-wu yin-shu-kuan, Changsha, 1939.

程 方 中國縣政概論

Ch'eng Shu-te, *Chiu-ch'ao lü k'ao* (A study of the *lü* during nine dynasties), Shang-wu yin-shu-kuan, Shanghai, 1938.

程樹德　九朝律考

Ch'eng Shu-te, *Chung-kuo fa-chih shih* (A history of Chinese law and institutions), Hua-t'ung shu-chü, Shanghai, 1931.

程樹德　中國法制史

Chi Yün *et al*, *Li-tai chih-kuan piao* (Tables on offices of the dynasties), various editions.

紀　昀　歷代職官表

Chiang Huan-wen, *Chan-shih ts'ai-cheng chien-she* (Wartime financial reconstruction), Kuo-min t'u-shu ch'u-pan-she, Chungking, 1942.

蔣煥文　戰時財政建設

Chiang T'ing-fu (T. F. Tsiang), *Chung-kuo chin-tai shih* (A history of modern China), Chungking, 1938.

蔣廷黻　中國近代史

Chien-ch'a-yuan chien-ch'a chih-tu pien-tsuan ch'u: *Chien-ch'a chih-tu shih-liao* (A sketch history of the control institution), Nanking, 1936.

監察院監察制度編纂處　監察制度史略

Ch'ien Tuan-sheng, Sa Shih-chiung, *et al.*, *Min-kuo cheng-chih shih* (History of political institutions under the Republic), Shang-wu yin-shu-kuan, Chungking, 1945.

錢端升，薩師炯　民國政制史

Ch'iu Ch'ang-wei, *Kuang-hsi hsien-cheng* (*Hsien* government in Kwangsi), Kweilin wen-hua kung-yin she, Kweilin, 1941.

邱昌渭　廣西縣政

Chiu t'ung (Nine complete works).

九通

Chou Fu-hai, *San-min chu-i li-lun ti-t'i-hsi* (The theoretical system of San-min chu-i), Hsin sheng-ming yueh-k'an she, Shanghai, 1928.

周佛海　三民主義理論的體系

Chou Ku-ch'eng, *Chung-kuo t'ung-shih* (A general history of China), 2 vols., K'ai-ming shu-tien, Shanghai.

周谷城　中國通史

Chu Chien, *Chih-p'ing lei-tsuan* (Cyclopaedia of orderly rule), 30 vols.

朱健 治平類纂

Chu Fang, *Chung-kuo fa-chih shih* (A history of Chinese law and institutions), Shanghai, 1931.

朱方 中國法制史

Fang Hsuan-ling, annotator, *Kuan-tzu.*

房玄齡注 管子

Feng Yu-lan, *Chung-kuo che-hsüeh shih* (A history of Chinese philosophy). Vol. I translated by Derk Bodde as *A History of Chinese Philosophy*, H. Vetch, Peiping, 1937. Bodde is also translating the second volume and a few chapters have appeared in the *Harvard Journal of Asiatic Studies.*

馮友蘭 中國哲學史

Hsia Chung-tao, *Han-fei-tzu fa-i* (The spirit of law in Han-fei-tzu), Shanghai, 1927.

夏忠道 韓非子法意

Hsiao Kung-ch'üan, *Chung-kuo cheng-chih ssu-hsiang shih* (A history of Chinese political thought), 2 vols., Shang-wu yin-shu-kuan, Shanghai, 1945–1946.

蕭公權 中國政治思想史

Hsiao Wen-che, *Chung-kuo hsing-cheng tu-ch'a chuan-yuan chih-tu yen-chiu* (A study of the Chinese administrative inspectorate system), Chungking, 1943.

蕭文哲 中國行政督察專員制度研究

Hsiao Wen-che, *Hsing-cheng hsiao-lü yen-chiu* (A study on administrative efficiency), Shang-wu yin-shu-kuan, Chungking, 1932.

蕭文哲 行政效率研究

Hsieh Chen-min, *Chung-hua-min-kuo li-fa shih* (A history of legislation of the Chinese Republic), Cheng-chung shu-chü, Shanghai, 1938.

謝振民 中華民國立法史

Hsieh Pin, *Min-kuo cheng-tang shih* (A history of the political parties under the Republic), Hsüeh-shu yen-chiu-hui, Shanghai, 1926.

謝彬 民國政黨史

Hsieh Ying-chou, *Kuo-min cheng-fu tsu-chih-fa yen-chiu* (A study of the Organic Law of the National Government), Hua-tung shu-chü, Shanghai, 1933.

謝瀛洲 國民政府組織法研究

Hsieh Wu-liang, *Ku-tai cheng-chih ssu-hsiang yen-chiu* (A study of ancient political thought), Shang-wu yin-shu-kuan, Shanghai, 1923.

謝无量 古代政治思想研究

Hsing-cheng-yuan, *Ch'üan-kuo hsing-cheng hui-i chi-lu* (Proceedings of the National Administrative Conference), Chungking, 1944.

行政院 全國行政會議記錄

Hsü Ch'üng-hao, *Chung-kuo cheng-chih kai-yao* (An outline of Chinese political institutions), Shang-wu yin-shu-kuan, Chungking, 1943.

許崇灝 中國政制概要

Hsü I-sheng, *Kuang-hsi sheng-hsien hsing-cheng kuan-hsi* (Province-*hsien* relation in Kwangsi), Shang-wu yin-shu-kuan, Chungking, 1943.

徐義生 廣西省縣行政關係

Hu Han-min, *San-min chu-i ti lien-huan hsing* (The interdependent nature of the Three People's Principles), Hsin-sheng-ming shu-chü, Shanghai, 1928.

胡漢民 三民主義的連環性

Hu Han-min, *Tsung-li ch'üan-chi* (Complete works of the Tsung-li), 4 vols., Ming-chih shu-chü, Shanghai, 1930.

胡漢民 總理全集

Hu Tz'u-wei, *Hsiang-chen tzu-chih* (Self-government in *hsiang* and *chen*), Szechwan Training Corps, Chengtu, 1942.

胡次威 鄉鎮自治

Hua Lin-i, *Chung-kuo kuo-min-tang shih* (A history of the Chinese Kuomintang), Shang-wu yin-shu-kuan, Shanghai, 1928.

華林一 中國國民黨史

Huang Pen-chi, *Li-tai chih-kuan-piao* (Tables on offices of the dynasties), 6 vols., Shanghai, 1880.

黃本驥 歷代職官表

Jao Jung-ch'un, *Hsin-hsien-chih* (The new *hsien* system), T'u-li ch'u-pan-she, Chungking, 1942.

饒榮春 新縣制

Kan Nai-kuang, *Chung-kuo hsing-cheng hsin-lun* (New treatise on Chinese administration).

甘乃光 中國行政新論

Kao I-han, *Chung-kuo nei-ke chih-tu ti yen-ko* (The evolution of the Chinese cabinet system), Shang-wu yin-shu-kuan, Shanghai.

高一涵 中國內閣制度的沿革

Kao I-han, *Chung-kuo yü-shih chih-tu ti yen-ko* (The evolution of the Chinese censorial system), Shang-wu yin-shu-kuan, Shanghai, 1926.

高一涵 中國御史制度的沿革

Ku Chung-hsiu, *Chung-hua min-kuo k'ai-kuo shih* (A history of the founding of the Chinese Republic), T'ai-tung shu-chü, Shanghai, 1914.

谷鍾秀 中華民國開國史

Ku Tun-jou, *Chung-kuo i-hui shih* (A history of the Chinese Parliament), Soochow, 1933.

顧敦鍒 中國議會史

Kuo Hsiao-wei, *Chung-kuo ko-ming chi-shih pen-mo* (A chronicle of the Chinese Revolution), Shang-wu yin-shu-kuan, Shanghai, 1912.

郭孝成 中國革命紀事本末

Li Chien-nung, *Chung-kuo chin-pai-nien cheng-chih shih* (A political history of China in the last century), 2 vols. This is an augmented edition of an earlier work, *Tsui-chin san-shih-nien Chung-kuo cheng-chih shih* (A political history of China in the last thirty years), Shang-wu yin-shu-kuan, Shanghai, 1947.

李劍農 中國近百年政治史

Li Hsien-yün, *Hsin-hsien-chih ti li-lun* (The theory of the new *hsien* system), Kuo-min t'u-shu ch'u-pan-she, 1940.

栗顯運 新縣制的理論

Li Tsung-huang, *Hsien-tai pao-chia chih-tu* (The contemporary *pao-chia* institution), Chungking, 1943.

李宗黃 現代保甲制度

Li Tsung-huang, *Hsin hsien-chih chih li-lun yü shih-chi* (The theory and practice of the new *hsien* system), Chung-hua shu-chü, May, 1943.

李宗黄 新縣制之理論與實際

Liang Ch'i-ch'ao, *Hsien-Ch'in cheng-chih ssu-hsiang shih* (A history of pre-Ch'in political thought). Translated into English by L. T. Chen as *A History of Chinese Political Thought during the Early Tsin Period*, and into French by Escarra and Germain as *La Conception de la Loi et les Théories des Légistes à la Veille des Ts'in*, Chung-hua shu-chü, Shanghai, 1923.

梁啟超 先秦政治思想史

Liang Ch'i-ch'ao, *Mo-tze hsüeh-an* (A study of the Motze).

梁啟超 墨子學案

Lo Chih-yüan, *Chung-kuo ti-fang hsing-cheng chih-tu* (Local administrative system in China), Tu-li ch'u-pan-she, Chungking, 1942.

羅志淵 中國地方行政制度

Lü Chen-yü, *Chung-kuo cheng-chih ssu-hsiang shih* (A history of Chinese political thought), Sheng-hua shu-tien, Shanghai, 1947.

呂振羽 中國政治思想史

Lü Ssu-mien, *Chung-kuo t'ung-shih* (A general history of China), 2 vols., K'ai-ming shu-tien.

呂思勉 中國通史

Pao Chen-ch'iu, *Kung-chih hou-hsüan-jen k'ao-shih chih li-lun yü shih-shih* (The theory and practice of the examination of the candidates for elective offices), Kuo-min t'u-shu che-pan she, Chungking, 1944.

鮑震球 公職候選人考試之理論與實施

Sa Meng-wu, *Hsien-fa hsin-lun* (A new treatise on constitutions), Chungking, 1943.

薩孟武 憲法新論

Shen Nai-cheng, *Chung-kuo ti-fang cheng-fu chih t'e-chih yü Chung-yang k'ung-chih-ch'üan* (The unique nature of Chinese local government and the power of central control), in *She-hui ko-hsüeh* (Social Science), published by the National Tsing Hua University, Peiping, vol. 1, no. 2, 1935.

沈乃正 中國地方政府之特質與中央控制權

Shih Yang-ch'eng, *Chung-kuo sheng-hsing-cheng chih-tu* (The Chinese provincial administrative system), Shang-wu yin-shu-kuan, Shanghai, May, 1947.

施養成 中國省行政制度

Sun Jung, *Ku-chin fa-chih-piao* (Tables on laws and institutions of ancient and modern times), 16 vols., 1906.

孫榮 古今法制表

Tai Chi-t'ao, *Sun-wen chu-i chih che-hsueh chi-ch'u* (The philosophical foundation of Sun Yat-senism), Canton, 1925.

戴季陶 孫文主義之哲學基礎

T'ang Yung-t'ung, *Han Wei Liang-Chin Nan-pei-ch'ao fo-chiao shih* (A history of Buddhism in the Han, Wei, the two Chin and the Southern and Northern Dynasties), 3 vols., Shang-wu yin-shu-kuan, Chungking, 1944.

湯用彤 漢魏兩晉南北朝佛教史

T'ao Hsi-sheng, *Chung-kuo cheng-chih ssu-hsiang shih* (A history of Chinese political thought), 4 vols., Nan-fang shu-tien, Chungking, 1942.

陶希聖 中國政治思想史

Ting Yuan-p'u, *Chung-kuo fa-chih shih* (A history of Chinese law and institutions), Hui-wen-t'ang, Shanghai, 1920.

丁元普 中國法制史

Tseng Yu-hao, *Kai-ting chung-hua min-kuo cheng-fu ta-kang* (An outline of the government of the Republic of China, revised edition), Shang-wu yin-shu-kuan, 1926.

曾友豪 改訂中華民國政府大綱

Tsou Lu, *Chung-kuo-kuo-min-tang shih-kao* (Draft history of the Kuomintang), Shang-wu yin-shu-kuan, Chungking, 1944.

鄒魯 中國國民黨史稿

Wang Chen-hsien, *Chung-kuo ku-tai fa-li-hsüeh* (Jurisprudence in ancient China), Shang-wu yin-shu-kuan, Shanghai.

王振先 中國古代法理學

Wang Ch'ung-hui, *Wu-ch'üan hsien-fa* (The five-power constitution).

王寵惠 五權憲法

Wang Hsien-ch'ien, *Hsün-tzu chi-chieh* (Collected expositions of the *Hsün-tzu*).

王先謙 荀子集解

Wang Hsien-shen, *Han-fei-tzu chi-chieh* (Collected expositions of the *Han-fei-tzu*).

王先慎 韓非子集解

Wang Shih-chieh and Ch'ien Tuan-sheng, *Pi-chiao hsien-fa* (Comparative constitutional law), 2 vols., rev. ed., Shang-wu yin-shu-kuan, Chungking, 1942.

王世杰、錢端升 比較憲法

Wen Chün-t'ien, *Chung-kuo pao-chia chih-tu* (The Chinese *pao-chia* system), Shang-wu yin-shu-kuan, Shanghai, 1935.

聞鈞天 中國保甲制度

Wu Ching-hsiung and Huang Kung-chiao, *Chung-kuo chih-hsien shih* (A history of constitution-making in China), Shang-wu yin-shu-kuan, Shanghai, 1937.

吳經熊, 黃公覺 中國制憲史

Wu Fu-cheng, *Kung-wu-yüan ch'eng-chieh chih-tu* (The system of discipline of public officials).

吳紱徵 公務員懲戒制度

Wu Ting-ch'ang, *Hua-hsi hsien-pi* (Desultory notes at Hua-hsi), 2 vols., Kweichow, 1940–1943.

吳鼎昌 花溪閒筆

Wu Tsung-tz'u, *Chung-hua min-kuo hsien-fa shih* (A history of the Chinese constitution), 2 vols., Peking, 1924.

吳宗慈 中華民國憲法史

Yang Hung-lieh, *Chung-kuo fa-lü fa-ta shih* (A history of the development of Chinese law), 1930.

楊鴻烈 中國法律發達史

Yang Yu-ch'iung, *Chin-tai Chung-kuo li-fa shih* (A history of modern Chinese legislation), Shang-wu yin-shu-kuan, Shanghai, 1936.

楊幼炯 近代中國立法史

Yang Yu-ch'iung, *Chung-kuo cheng-tang shih* (A history of Chinese political parties).

楊幼炯 中國政黨史

Yen Wan-li, *Chiao Shang-chün shu* (Annotated edition of the Book of Shang-tzu).

嚴萬里 校商君書

Yü I, *Chung-kuo fa-chih shih* (A history of Chinese law and institutions), Peiping, 1931.

郁 嶷 中國法制史

8. NAMES OF CHINESE PUBLISHERS

Cheng-chung shu-chü

正中書局

Chung-hua shu-chü

中華書局

Hsin-Chung-kuo chien-she hsüeh-hui[1]

新中國建設學會

Hsin-sheng-ming shu-chü

新生命書局

Hsin-sheng-ming yüeh-k'an she

新生命月刊社

Hsueh-shu yen-chiu-hui[1]

學術研究會

Hua t'ung shu-chü

華通書局

Hui-wen-t'ang

會文堂

K'ai-ming shu-tien

開明書店

Kuo-min t'u-shu ch'u-pan she

國民圖書出版社

[1] These two are not publishers but organizations in whose name books are published.

Min-chih shu-chü
民智書局

Nan-fang shu-tien
南方書店

Shang-wu yin-shu-kuan
商務印書館

Sheng-huo shu-tien
生活書店

Shih-chieh shu-chü
世界書局

T'ai-tung shu-chü
泰東書局

Tu-li ch'u-pan she
獨立出版社

Wen-hua kung-ying she
文化供應社

TRANSLITERATIONS OF CHINESE WORDS

Anfu 安福
Chan-hsing hsing-lü 暫行刑律
Ch'an 禪
Chang, Carsun, see Chang Chün-mai 張嘉森
Chang Chih-tung 張之洞
Chang Chün-mai (Carsun Chang, Chang Chia-shen) 張君勱 (張嘉森)
Chang Hsüeh-liang 張學良
Chang Hsün 張勳
Chang Lan 張瀾
Chang Pai-chün 章伯鈞
Chang Ping-lin (Chang T'ai-yen) 章炳麟(章太炎)
Chang Tso-lin 張作霖
chen 鎮
Ch'en Ch'i-mei 陳其美
Ch'en Chi-t'ang 陳濟棠
Ch'en Ch'iung-ming 陳炯明
Ch'en Ming-shu 陳銘樞
Ch'en T'ien-hua 陳天華
ch'eng 誠
Cheng-chih hui-i 政治會議
Cheng-chih wei-yüan-hui 政治委員會
Ch'eng Hao 程顥
Cheng-hsüeh hui 政學會
Ch'eng I 程頤
Cheng-yü Club (Cheng-yü chü-le-pu) 政餘俱樂部
Chi-shih-chung 給事中
chia 甲
Chia I 賈誼
Ch'iang 羌
Chiang Chieh-shih, see Chiang Kai-shek 蔣介石
Chiang Chung-cheng, see Chiang Kai-shek 蔣中正
Chiang Kai-shek (Chiang Chieh-shih, Chiang Chung-cheng) 蔣介石
chien-chü 薦舉
chien-i ta-fu 諫議大夫
chien-jen 簡任
Chien-kuo ta-kang 建國大綱
Ch'ien Ta-hsin 錢大昕
chih-chü 制舉
Chih-ch'üan hsing-shih chih kuei-lü 治權行使之規律
Chih-kuan chih 職官志
chih-li 至理
Chin-chung 禁中
Chin-shih 進士
Ch'ing 卿
Chinputang 進步黨
Chiu ch'ing 九卿
chiu-chü 糾舉
Chou-li 周禮
Chou Lien-hsi 周濂溪
Chou Tun-i 周敦頤
Ch'ou-an hui 籌安會
Chü Cheng 居正
Chu-chi-chang 主計長
Chu Hsi 朱熹
ch'ü 區
Chuang Chou 莊周
Chuang-tzu 莊子
Ch'un-ch'iu 春秋
Chün-cheng-fu 軍政府
Chün-chi-ch'ü 軍機處
Chün-hsien lun 郡縣論
Chün-tzu yuan 軍諮院
Chung-hua Ko-ming tang 中華革命黨
Chung-hua min-tsu chieh-fang hsing-tung wei-yüan-hui 中華民族解放行動委員會
Chung-hua chih-yeh chiao-yü she 中華職業教育社
Chung-kuo 中國
Chung-kuo ch'ing-nien tang 中國青年黨
Chung-kuo hsiang-ts'un chien-she hsieh-hui 中國鄉村建設協會
Chung-kuo jen-min chiu-kuo hui 中國人民救國會
Chung-kuo Kuomintang 中國國民黨
Chung-kuo Kung-ch'an tang 中國共產黨
Chung-kuo min-chu cheng-t'uan ta-t'ung-meng 中國民主政團大同盟
Chung-kuo min-chu she-hui tang 中國民主社會黨
Chung-kuo min-chu t'ung-meng 中國民主同盟
Chung-shan 中山
Chung-shu 中書
Chung-yang t'e-pieh wei-yüan-hui 中央特別委員會
fa 法
fa-kuei chih-ting piao-chun-fa 法規制定標準法
Feng Kuo-chang 馮國璋
Feng Yü-hsiang 馮玉祥
Hakka (k'o-chia) 客家
Han Fei 韓非
Han Fei-tzu 韓非子
Han-shu 漢書
Han Yü 韓愈
Han-lin 翰林
hsiang 鄉
Hsiang-kuo 相國
hsien 縣
Hsien-cheng ch'i-ch'eng hui 憲政期成會
Hsien-cheng shih-chin hui 憲政實進會

Hsien-cheng shih-shih hsieh-chin hui 憲政實施協進會
Hsien-fa ta-kang 憲法大綱
Hsien-fa t'ao-lun hui 憲法討論會
Hsien-fa yen-chiu hui 憲法研究會
Hsien-fa yen-chiu t'ung-chih hui 憲法研究同志會
Hsien-hsüeh 顯學
Hsien-pei 鮮卑
Hsien-yu hui 憲友會
hsin 心
Hsing-cheng yuan hui-i 行政院會議
Hsin-hai Club (chü-le-pu) 辛亥俱樂部
hsing 性
Hsing-chung hui 興中會
Hsing-fa chih 刑法志
Hsing-fa chih 刑罰志
Hsiung-nu 匈奴
hsiu-ts'ai 秀才
Hsü Shih-ch'ang 徐世昌
Hsüan-chü chih 選舉志
hsüan-jen 選任
hsün-cheng shih-ch'i yüeh-fa 訓政時期約法
Hsün-tzu 荀子
Hu Han-min 胡漢民
Hua-hsing hui 華興會
Huai-nan-tzu 淮南子
Huang Hsing 黃興
Huang Tsung-hsi 黃宗羲
Huang Yen-p'ei 黃炎培
Hui Shih 惠施
Hui T'ung 慧通
i 夷
I-ching 易經
I-yu she 益友社
jen 仁
Jih-chih lu 日知錄
Ju 儒
Ju-chen 女真
K'ai-huang 開皇
K'ang Yu-wei 康有為
Khitan (Ch'i-tan) 契丹
Ko-ming wei-yüan-hui 國民委員會
Ku Yen-wu 顧炎武
Kuang-fu hui 光復會
Kuang Hsü 光緒
Kung 公
Kung, H. H. (Hsiang-hsi) 孔祥熙
Kung-ho chien-she t'ao-lun hui 共和建設討論會
Kung-ho t'ung-i tang 共和統一黨
Kung-sun Lung 公孫龍
Kung-sun Lung-tzu 公孫龍子
Kung-tso pao-kao 工作報告
kung-wu yüan 公務員
K'ung-fu-tzu 孔夫子
Kuo Sung-tao 郭嵩燾
Kuo-fang tsui-kao hui-i 國防最高會議
Kuo-fang tsui-kao wei-yüan-hui 國防最高委員會
Kuo-hui ch'ing-yüan t'ung-chih hui 國會請願同志會
Kuo-min 國民
Kuo-min cheng-fu 國民政府
Kuo-min cheng-fu chün-shih wei-yüan-hui 國民政府軍事委員會
Kuo-min cheng-fu hui-i 國民政府會議
Kuo-min cheng-fu wei-yüan 國民政府委員
Kuo-ts'e 國策
Kuo-wu hui-i 國務會議
Kuo-yü 國語
Kuo-min chün 國民軍
Kuomintang (Kuo-min tang) 國民黨
Lao-tzu 老子
li 理
Li Chi-shen 李濟琛
Li Er 李耳
Li-fa ch'eng-hsü fa 立法程序法
Li-fa ch'eng-hsü kang-ling 立法程序綱領
Li-fan yuan 理藩院
Li Hung-chang 李鴻章
Li Li 李悝
Li Li-san 李立三
Li Ta-chao 李大釗
Li Tsung-jen 李宗仁
Li Yuan-hung 黎元洪
Liang Ch'i-ch'ao 梁啟超
Liang Shu-ming (Sou-ming) 梁漱溟
Liao Chung-k'ai 廖仲愷
Lin Sen (Lin Shen) 林森
Lin-shih yüeh-fa 臨時約法
Lo-lo 儸儸
Lu Chiu-yüan 陸九淵
Lu Yung-hsiang 盧永祥
lü 律
Lun-yü 論語
Mao Tse-tung 毛澤東
Men-hsia 門下
Men-hsia sheng 門下省
Meng-tzu 孟子
Miao-yao 苗猺
Min-chu chien-kuo hui 民主建國會
Min-chu chien-she tso-t'an hui 民主建設座談會
Min-ch'üan 民權
Min Pao 民報
Min she 民社
Min-sheng 民生
Min-tsu 民族
Mo Ti 墨翟
Mo-tzu 墨子
Nan-yang 南洋
Nei-shih 內史
p'ai-lou 牌樓
Pan Ku 班固
pao 保
pao-chia 保甲

pao-chü 保舉
Pao-huang hui 保皇會
Pao-kuo hui 保國會
Pei-yang 北洋
p'in 聘
p'in-jen 聘任
Pu 部
p'u-hsüeh 樸學
San-min chu-i 三民主義
San-min chu-i t'ung chih hui 三民主義同志會
Shang-shu 尚書
Shang-tzu 商子
Shang Yang 商鞅
Shao-nien Chung-kuo tang 少年中國黨
sheng 省
sheng-chung 省中
sheng-hsüeh 聖學
sheng-yün hsüeh 聲韻學
Shih-chi 史記
Shih-ching 詩經
Shih-chiu hsin-t'iao 十九信條
Shu-ching 書經
Shu-yuan 書院
Soong, T. V. (Sung Tzu-wen) 宋子文
Ssu-k'ung 司空
Ssu-ma 司馬
Ssu-ma Ch'ien 司馬遷
Ssu-ma T'an 司馬談
Ssu-t'u 司徒
Sun Ch'uan-fang 孫傳芳
Sun Chung-shan, see Sun Yat-sen 孫中山
Sun Fo (Sun K'o) 孫科
Sun Yat-sen (Sun I-hsien) 孫逸仙
Sun Wen, see Sun Yat-sen 孫文
Sung Chiao-jen 宋教仁
Ta-Ch'ing hui-tien 大清會典
Ta-Ch'ing hsien-hsing hsing-lü 大清現行刑律
Ta-Ch'ing lü-li 大清律例
Ta-Ming hui-tien 大明會典
Ta-Ming lü-li 大明律例
Ta-yüan-shuai 大元帥
Ta-yuan-shuai ta-pen-ying 大元帥大本營
Tai Chen 戴震
Tai Chi-t'ao, see Tai Ch'uan-hsien 戴季陶
T'ai-chi t'u 太極圖
Tai Ch'uan-hsien (Tai Chi-t'ao) 戴傳賢(戴季陶)
T'ai-wei 太尉
T'an Yen-k'ai 譚延闓
Tang-cheng kung-tso k'ao-ho
wei-yüan-hui 黨政工作考核委員會
T'ang Chi-yao 唐繼堯
T'ang Hua-lung 湯化龍
T'ang lui-tien 唐六典
T'ang Sheng-chih 唐生智
T'ang Shao-yi 唐紹儀
Tao, tao 道
tao-li 道理
Tao-te-ching 道德經
tao-t'ung 道統
t'e-jen 特任
Teng Yen-ta 鄧演達
tien 典
Tsa 雜
Tsai-sheng 再生
Ts'an-i yüan 參議院
ts'ao-an 草案
Ts'ao K'un 曹錕
Tseng Kuo-fan 曾國藩
Tso-chuan 左傳
Tso Tsung-t'ang 左宗棠
Tsou Yen 鄒衍
Tsung-heng 縱橫
Tsung-li 總理
Tsung-ts'ai 總裁
tsung-t'ung 總統
Tuan Ch'i-jui 段祺瑞
Tuan Yü-ts'ai 段玉裁
Tung Chung-shu 董仲舒
Tung-yüan k'an-luan lin-shih
t'iao-k'uan 動員戡亂臨時條款
T'ung-i chien-kuo t'ung chih hui 統一建國同志會
T'ung-i kung-ho tang 統一共和黨
T'ung-i tang 統一黨
T'ung-meng hui 同盟會
T'ung-shuai pan-shih-ch'u 統率辦事處
Tzu Chang 子張
Tzu-cheng yüan 資政院
Tz'u-hsi 慈禧
Tzu Ssu 子思
Wang 王
Wang An-shih 王安石
Wang Ching-wei
(Wang Chao-ming) 汪精衛(汪兆銘)
Wang Ming-sheng 王鳴盛
Wang Shou-jen 王守仁
wei-jen 委任
Wei-yüan-hui 委員會
Wu P'ei-fu 吳佩孚
Yen Fu 嚴復
Yen Hsi-shan 閻錫山
Yen Hui 顏回
Yen-chiu hsi 研究系
Yen-t'ieh lun 鹽鐵論
Yin-yang 陰陽
Yü-pei li-hsien kung-hui 預備立憲公會
Yuan 院
Yuan Shih-k'ai 袁世凱
Yü-shih 御史
Yü-shih chung-ch'eng 御史中丞
Yü-shih ta-fu 御史大夫
Yü-shih yüan 御史員
yüeh-fa 約法

INDEX